PRINCIPLES OF ECONOMICS

AN IRISH TEXT

FOURTH EDITION

D1584520

THE AUTHORS

GERARD TURLEY BA, MA(Econ), PhD lectures in Economics at the J. E. Cairnes School of Business and Economics, NUI Galway. He has worked as an economic consultant in Ireland and abroad.

MAUREEN MALONEY BSW, MBA, MEconSc lectures in Management at the J. E. Cairnes School of Business and Economics, NUI Galway. She has also worked as an economic consultant to SIPTU.

FRANCIS O'TOOLE BA, MMangtSc, PhD lectures in Economics at Trinity College Dublin. He has also worked as an economic consultant in the area of competition policy and regulation.

BONUS MATERIAL FOR

Principles of Economics, fourth edition

To access additional online material for this book:

- Go to www.gillmacmillan.ie and search for *Principles of Economics*. Click on the link in the right-hand column.
- Lecturers, log on using your username and password. If you do not have a password, register online and we will e-mail one to you.

PRINCIPLES OF ECONOMICS

AN IRISH TEXT

FOURTH EDITION

GERARD TURLEY
(NUI GALWAY)

with

MAUREEN MALONEY
(NUI GALWAY)

and

FRANCIS O'TOOLE
(TRINITY COLLEGE DUBLIN)

with contributions from
Matthew Coffey and Eithne Murphy

GILL & MACMILLAN

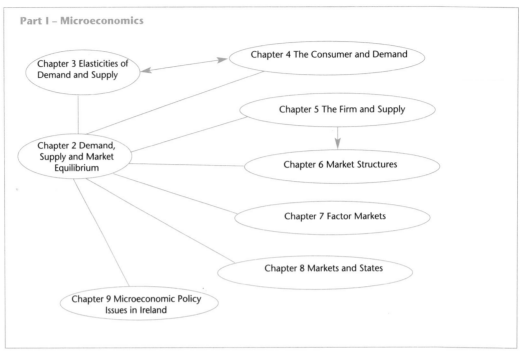

Part I – Microeconomics

Chapter 3 Elasticities of Demand and Supply

Chapter 4 The Consumer and Demand

Chapter 5 The Firm and Supply

Chapter 2 Demand, Supply and Market Equilibrium

Chapter 6 Market Structures

Chapter 7 Factor Markets

Chapter 8 Markets and States

Chapter 9 Microeconomic Policy Issues in Ireland

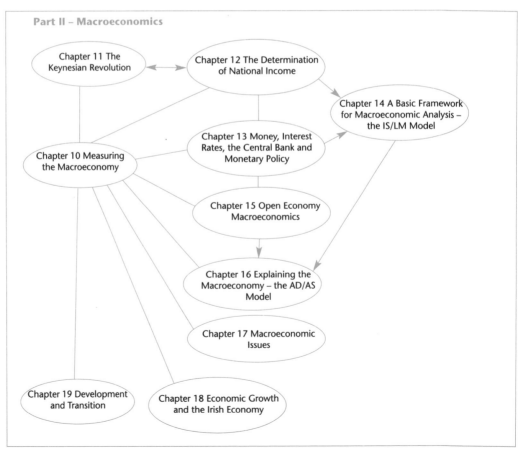

Part II – Macroeconomics

Chapter 11 The Keynesian Revolution

Chapter 12 The Determination of National Income

Chapter 14 A Basic Framework for Macroeconomic Analysis – the IS/LM Model

Chapter 13 Money, Interest Rates, the Central Bank and Monetary Policy

Chapter 10 Measuring the Macroeconomy

Chapter 15 Open Economy Macroeconomics

Chapter 16 Explaining the Macroeconomy – the AD/AS Model

Chapter 17 Macroeconomic Issues

Chapter 19 Development and Transition

Chapter 18 Economic Growth and the Irish Economy

Contents

Preface

'Normality is a fiction of economics textbooks.'

Joan Robinson (1903–83)

In 1948 the first mass-produced 'modern' textbook in economics was published. Since then, Paul Samuelson's *Economics* has sold millions of copies, being translated into over forty languages with nineteen editions. Many others, on both sides of the Atlantic, have tried to follow Samuelson's success. By the 1990s over fifty major introductory textbooks were available. American textbooks were soon adapted in order to meet the particular demands of the European market. European texts have also become popular.

An economics textbook for the Irish third-level market is not a new idea. In the 1920s the Educational Company of Ireland published *A Groundwork of Economics*, written by Joseph Johnston. Macmillan & Co. Ltd published an Irish edition of a well-established British textbook in 1963. It was called *Textbook of Economic Analysis* and was written by Edward Nevin. At a more advanced level, Desmond Norton wrote *Economic Analysis for an Open Economy: Ireland* which was published by the Irish Management Institute in 1980. A second textbook by Norton, entitled *Economics for an Open Economy: Ireland* was published in 1994. An intermediate macroeconomics textbook, *The Macroeconomy of Ireland* (and, more recently, *The Macroeconomy of the Eurozone*) by Brendan Walsh and Anthony Leddin has been updated regularly. Other introductory textbooks in economics by Irish authors include *Principles of Economics* by Moore McDowell and Rodney Thom (the European edition, with Robert Frank and Ben Bernanke) and *The Economic System* by Eleanor Doyle.

Notwithstanding these welcome developments on the publishing front, we believe that there is a need for an introductory third-level economics textbook. We hope that this book fills that gap. It covers the basic theory of both microeconomics and macroeconomics in a user-friendly way. Students are introduced to economic terminology and concepts. We attempt to reinforce these ideas by applying them in 'case studies' drawn from a number of sources including journals, newspapers, policy documents and CSO publications. An Irish section is included in most of the macroeconomic chapters. Wherever possible, we have used current national data.

Additional case studies and a wide range of questions conclude each chapter. It was our intention to provide a 'complete' text, not requiring supplements. We hope that readers will find this useful, challenging and a welcome addition to the existing stock of economics textbooks already on the market.

New material in the fourth edition

This edition includes new and up-to-date material on the Celtic Tiger and its aftermath, the financial crisis and global recession, the property crash and the banking crisis in Ireland, and the latest on the eurozone and sovereign debt crises. To reflect the changing economic conditions in Ireland – and elsewhere – since the publication of the third edition, there are new and/or updated sections in Chapters 9, 15, 17, 18 and 19, with new material specifically on Ireland's economic crisis. We also include a list of sources and readings for students of economics.

Many of the case studies are new and data have been updated, using the most recent information available (as at the end of 2010 in most cases), to reflect the enormous changes and significant developments in Ireland (within Europe) during the past five years. As before, answers to the end-of-chapter questions and the case studies can be found on the Gill & Macmillan website, www.gillmacmillan.ie.

CHAPTER 1

Introduction to Economics

'What is lacking [in economics] is any effective means of communication between abstract theory and concrete application.'[1]

BARBARA WOOTTON

'If all economists were laid end to end, they could not reach a conclusion.'[2]

GEORGE BERNARD SHAW

CHAPTER OBJECTIVES

Upon completing this chapter, the student should understand the:
- core principles of economics;
- differences between the neoclassical, institutional and Marxian schools of economics;
- approaches used to develop economic theory;
- features of the production possibility frontier;
- concept of opportunity cost.

OUTLINE

INTRODUCTION

This chapter is an introduction to some of the basic concepts that we will use throughout the book. As a starting point, the core principles of economics are outlined. We then present an overview of three different approaches to the study of economics. Next, we will consider two methods used by economists to develop economic theory. Finally, we will examine the production possibility frontier that is the most basic model of an economy.

1.1 TEN PRINCIPLES OF ECONOMICS

We define economics as the science of scarcity. It is a social science that studies aspects of human behaviour that relate to scarcity, choice and costs. As society's wants (and sometimes needs) exceed available resources, economics analyses what, how and for whom society produces. Although the scope of economics is very broad, its core principles are few and relatively straightforward. To quote Milton Friedman, one of the great economists of the twentieth century, 'What makes it [economics] most fascinating is that its fundamental principles are so simple that they can be written on one page, that anyone can understand them, and yet very few do.'[3]

It is true that economics as a discipline has a number of fundamental principles. It is also true that these principles are simple but that few of us fully appreciate them. It is a little more difficult to get agreement or consensus on what these principles are. As outlined in the next section of this chapter, there are a number of schools of economic thought, each emphasising different key principles. For example, whereas the neoclassical school will emphasise individualism and self-interest, institutionalists will highlight the core concept of institutions or mechanisms that structure economic behaviour and transacting, and the Marxist school will focus on social classes and conflicts. In addition, there is no scientific reason why the number of principles should be limited to ten. One could equally make the case for a different number of principles, either fewer or more than ten. In the end, we decided to confine the list to ten.

We now consider the selection of the ten principles. This is a difficult task as it requires the omission of some important ideas and concepts in economics. Many readers familiar with the discipline of economics may be surprised at the apparent omission of such key ideas as equilibrium processes, social relations and class struggles, institutions and property rights, the invisible hand, economic change and the role of the entrepreneur, sunk costs, the law of diminishing returns and so on. Omission of these and other ideas is not an admission of irrelevance. On the contrary, they are all important ideas in economics (and some of these are implicit in the list that follows). With ten principles to identify, however, we have to prioritise what we consider to be the most fundamental tenets of economics. Likewise, we reject the notion that economics can be reduced to one or two key ideas. We believe that such claims ignore some other essential concepts in economics.

In writing a principles textbook, our primary motivation when selecting ten principles of economics is to identify ideas and concepts that are fundamental to economic decision-making and to the behaviour of economic agents, whether consumers, firms or governments. These ten principles inform us in the ways that economists view, interpret and analyse the world. The purpose here is to help us understand what might be called the 'economic way of thinking'.

Students will find these ten principles recurring throughout the textbook. Some are identified early on in the book (for example, the principles of scarcity, of a co-ordination mechanism, of incentives), others throughout the text (the principles of trade and exchange, and of opportunity cost) and some appear closer to the end of the text (the principle of comparative advantage, the principle of an inflation–unemployment trade-off). Irrespective of placings and frequency, they all have one thing in common: they are, in our view, the 'core' principles of economics. We believe that if students understand these principles and their role and importance in economics, they will go a long way to understand the discipline of economics despite its complexities, viewpoints, perspectives and controversies.

1. The principle of scarcity

There are scarce resources in society. Wants or needs exceed means or the limited resources that are available. This is one of the most fundamental principles in economics. When faced with any economic problem or issue, this is the principle economists are most likely to apply. Since resources are scarce, it follows that the goods and services produced must also be limited. In these situations of scarcity, choices must be made. In turn, these choices involve costs – there is no 'free lunch'.

2. The principle of opportunity cost

The cost of anything is what you have to give up to get it. Economists call this 'opportunity cost'. It is the value of the next best alternative that must be forgone in order to engage in the action. We say that the cost of any action is measured in terms of forgone opportunities. When economists are considering costs, they are referring to opportunity costs and not simply money or explicit costs. These costs arise because choices are made, in the face of scarcity.

3. The principle of a co-ordination mechanism

As long as there is scarcity, there is a need for a co-ordination mechanism to allocate these limited resources and for a rationing device to decide who gets what of the available resources. The two co-ordination mechanisms are (decentralised) markets and (centralised) plans. The market and the plan are the two ways of organising economic activity. An economy where economic activity is predominately organised by means of the market is called a market economy. In the market economy, demand and supply will lead to an equilibrium traded price and quantity. Markets possess self-correcting mechanisms as any shortage or surplus will be eliminated through price adjustments. In the market economy, price is the rationing device and the instrument that guides economic activity. An economy where economic activity is primarily organised by means of collective action and a central plan is called a centrally planned or command economy. It is the planners who set prices and output targets. In the centrally planned economy, it is the plan that guides economic activities and outcomes. Queues sometimes formed part of the rationing device in the command economy.

The three fundamental questions in any economy, namely:

1. What to produce?
2. How to produce?
3. For whom to produce?

are resolved by markets, plans or some combination of markets and plans. Related to this is the observation that the central issue in economic policymaking is the degree of state involvement versus the role of market forces. Those in favour of more government rely on market failure to make their case. Those in favour of the market claim that government failure is the central problem. Most economies today are so-called mixed economies, whereby most goods and services are traded in markets but where the government plays a key role. Ireland is a good example of a mixed economy. Some economies, like North Korea, rely heavily on extensive government intervention. Other economies, like Hong Kong, rely extensively on the market. Most economies lie somewhere in between these two extremes.

4. The principle of rational self-interested behaviour

Rational self-interested behaviour is based on the assumption that decisions are made that best serve the objective of the decision-maker. Rational economic agents will pursue actions that will enable them to achieve their greatest satisfaction. For example, if firms wish to maximise profits, they take decisions that are consistent with this objective. Likewise, consumers may wish to maximise utility, and take decisions accordingly. In The Wealth of Nations (1776), Adam Smith wrote, 'The desire of bettering our condition comes with us from the womb and never leaves till we go into the grave.' We say that rationality is assumed to guide people's decisions.

5. The principle of incentives

Economic agents respond to incentives. The behaviour of households, firms, governments and other organisations changes in response to incentives that they face. These incentives can be material, moral or a mix of both.

6. The principle of marginal analysis *(cost -benefit principle)*

Economic decision-making is made at the margin. Economic actors make decisions by comparing marginal benefits with marginal costs. An action is taken only if the additional or extra benefits (marginal benefit) are at least as great as the additional or extra costs (marginal cost). This is known as the principle of marginal analysis, sometimes referred to as the cost-benefit principle.

7. The principle of trade and exchange

Trade, where exchange between both parties is voluntary, is mutually beneficial. Trade between individuals, firms or countries benefits both parties and increases national output. Trade and exchange increase society's well-being.

8. The principle of specialisation and the division of labour

Since Adam Smith's *The Wealth of Nations* in 1776 and his now classic pin-making factory example, economists have made the case for specialisation and the division of labour. Specialisation allows each person to do what he or she can do relatively well while leaving everything else to be done by others. Division of labour, on the basis of different talents, skills, knowledge and intelligence, results in greater output produced. Specialisation or the division of labour dictates trade and exchange.

9. The principle of comparative advantage

Nations can engage in mutually beneficial trade by specialising in what they do relatively best. Countries concentrate on activities for which the opportunity cost is lowest. According to this principle, countries engage in international trade in order to take advantage of their differences. This is an application of the opportunity cost principle to international trade.

10. The principle of trade-offs

Decision-makers face trade-offs or conflicts. A trade-off is simply an exchange – giving up one thing in favour of another. Trade-offs exist because of scarcity. Traditionally, the now-classic example used to portray the principle of trade-offs is the 'Guns or Butter' example. Some of the most common, important and controversial trade-offs in pursuit of economic goals include efficiency vs. equity, unemployment vs. inflation (in the short-run) and taxation vs. public spending.

We urge students to spend some time at this stage reading and understanding these ten principles of economics. Economic analysis, behaviour and decision-making is informed and governed by these fundamental ideas. Typically, economists think in terms of *scarcity, opportunity cost, trade-offs* and *rational self-interested behaviour*. They favour *trade, specialisation* and the law of *comparative advantage.* Decision-making is guided by *incentives* and actions are made *at the margin.* Economic activity is organised through *markets* and market outcomes can be improved by *government* action. An appreciation of these central ideas will, in our view, make economics more understandable and, in the words of Milton Friedman, 'most fascinating'. We leave it to the reader to decide.

1.2 ECONOMIC SCHOOLS OF THOUGHT

There are three principal economic schools of thought: neoclassical, institutional and Marxian. Each of these schools approaches the study of economics from very different perspectives. In future chapters we will see how the differences in outlook lead to disparate opinions about how to interpret economic events. Because they analyse problems differently, each school also advocates different types of policies to handle economic problems.

Neoclassical school

The neoclassical school emerged at the end of the nineteenth century and currently dominates economic thinking. Although economics is a social science, neoclassical economists use a method of study similar to that used in the natural sciences. The adoption of the deductive method (examined in greater detail in Section 1.3) separated neoclassical economists from the other social sciences and from other types of economist. This model begins with a theory that is either verified or refuted by data.

Neoclassical economists examine the choices made by individuals with limited resources and unlimited wants. They view consumers and producers, workers and employers as acting rationally and independently to promote their own self-interest. All participants in the market are able to calculate benefits and measure costs. Acting to promote their own self-interest, they promote the best interests of society. This is because society is viewed as a collection of individuals. Societal welfare is calculated by adding together the welfare gains made by individuals.

Exchange in markets is governed by contracts which are either formal (explicit) or informal (implicit). Parties enter into these contracts of their own free will. Milton Friedman (b. 1912) is an influential neoclassical economist who won a Nobel Prize for economics. He describes the market exchange in the following way, 'So long as effective freedom of exchange is maintained, the central feature of the market organization of economic activity is that it prevents one person from interfering with another in respect of most of his activities. The consumer is protected from coercion by the seller because of the presence of other sellers with whom he can deal . . . The employee is protected from coercion by the employer because of other employers for whom he can work, and so on. And the market does this impersonally and without centralised authority.'[4]

Friedman acknowledges the link between the economic system and the political system. He argues that market capitalism is the economic system that best supports libertarian democracy. Libertarians believe that individual liberty is the foundation of democracy. 'One person, one vote' demonstrates the right of any citizen to express their preferences through their vote. Friedman views what happens in the political process as mirroring the market process. The consumer expresses his or her preferences in the way that s/he spends money. An employee expresses his or her preferences in the trade or occupation that s/he chooses. In terms of the economy, consumers and firms should only be restrained in their consumption and production decisions if their actions have unintended negative side effects which harm people who are 'outside' of the market. (See Chapter 8 for a discussion of externalities.) Friedman believes that societies should rely on the market as much as possible because it is difficult to achieve consensus through the political process.[5]

As is typical of neoclassical economists, Friedman believes that government has an important, but limited, role. He states, 'The existence of a free market does not of course eliminate the need for government. On the contrary, government is essential both as a forum for determining the "rules of the game" and as an umpire to interpret and enforce the rules decided on. What the market does is to reduce greatly the range of issues that must be decided through political means, and thereby to minimize the extent to which government need participate directly in the game.'[6]

The goal of the neoclassical economic system is efficiency. Efficiency has three components:

i) *productive efficiency* means that all resources are employed using the best available technology;
ii) *economic efficiency* means that the economy is producing the quantity of goods and services preferred by its citizens; and
iii) *Pareto efficiency* means that there is no available alternative allocation that keeps all individuals at least as well off, but makes at least one person better off.

Pareto efficiency combines productive efficiency and economic efficiency.

Pareto efficiency does not imply equity. An economy can be 'Pareto efficient' even if income is very unevenly distributed. Neoclassical economists often argue against income redistribution in the form of taxation for the affluent and social welfare benefits for the poor. They believe that these policies diminish the market incentives that work best if people bear the fruits of their own efforts.

Institutional school

While the neoclassical school has a coherent political and economic ideology, the institutional school is a 'broad church'. Institutionalists view economics as the study of the ways in which institutions regulate the production of goods and services (see Information Box 1.1). They are united by the belief that the capitalist system requires periodic intervention to achieve social objectives. They are divided on the nature and frequency of that intervention.

The early institutionalists were also separated from the neoclassicals by the method that they used to study economic issues. While neoclassicals relied on the deductive model, institutionalists used the inductive model. They began with data and used them to build models to explain and predict economic phenomena. (See Section 1.3.)

A group of economists called the American Institutionalists emerged at the end of the nineteenth century as a reaction against the neoclassical school.[7] They attacked the neoclassical assumption that individuals in the market act rationally and independently.

Thorstein Veblen (1857–1929) is one of the most famous of the American institutional economists. He believed that human behaviour is not motivated primarily by self-interest, but by an individual's association with important institutions like family, church, school system and workplace. These institutions evolve slowly.

Veblen believed that the choices made by individuals of all classes are shaped by the 'conspicuous consumption' of the 'leisure class'. With tongue in cheek, Veblen observed that it is the 'duty' of a 'gentleman' of this class to '. . . change his life of leisure into a more or less arduous application to the business of learning how to live a life of ostensible leisure in a becoming way. Closely related to the requirement that the gentleman must consume freely and of the right kind of goods, there is the requirement that he must know how to consume them in a seemly manner.'[8]

Veblen states that, 'The leisure class stands at the head of the social structure.' They set the standards that the lower classes imitate. Each class imitates the one above it with the result that '. . . the members of each stratum accept as their ideal of decency the scheme of life in vogue in the next higher stratum, and bend their energies to live up to that ideal.'[9]

Veblen was very critical of patterns of consumption that wasted time, effort and goods. It was at variance with an 'instinct for workmanship' which inspired men to seek 'effective work' which was serviceable and efficient. Unfortunately, the work of the productive classes was not valued by a society seeking to imitate the unproductive leisure class.

The market in the circumstances that Veblen describes could never produce an outcome that maximises society's welfare, because production would be based on providing the goods and services needed for 'conspicuous consumption'. Veblen believed that government should intervene in the market by taxing the goods sought by the leisure class '. . . to compensate the persons who experience psychological losses in consequence of their display'.[10]

Unlike the neoclassical economists, some institutionalists were concerned about income distribution as well as efficiency. Uneven income distribution combined with technological improvements led to the production of surplus goods and services that the working class could not afford. Income redistribution could solve the chronic problem of over-production in the capitalist economy.

The criticism by the American institutionalists of the assumptions and methodology used by neoclassical economists may seem to be 'much ado about nothing'. It is an example of internal dissension that leads to change within academic disciplines. The Great Depression began at the end of the 1920s and continued into the next decade. This provided the external stimulus that led to the domination of economics by the institutionalists for the next few decades.

John Maynard Keynes (1883–1946) was the most important institutional economist. His attack on neoclassical economics is explained in detail in Chapter 11. For our purposes, he is important because he challenged the neoclassical belief that unregulated markets can be relied on to employ workers to produce the goods and services that maximise social welfare. Keynes explained how problems within the markets for goods and services led to unemployment which was involuntary. He argued that the neoclassical analysis of the labour market led to inappropriate policies which lengthened and deepened the depression.

Keynes saw government as an important and powerful institution that could intervene in the economy to resolve the problems inherent in the capitalist system. This central role for government, as a regulator of the economy, was far more powerful than that advocated by the neoclassical economists.

Neoclassical economists have challenged the models developed by Keynes and his followers. During the 1970s, these models were not useful in explaining the problems of inflation and unemployment which plagued western economies. However, a legacy of Keynes is the increased involvement of government in the economy. In the USA and the UK, neoclassical economists and their followers constantly challenge the involvement of government.

Other European countries, including Ireland, have followed a 'partnership model' where government is one of the 'social partners' along with other institutions including labour unions, business leaders, trade organisations and the voluntary sector (see Section 9.3). Advocates of this model recognise that problems in markets can have destabilising social effects. They discuss the ways in which government policy can be implemented to minimise the impact of market disruptions. Once a consensus emerges, government carries out the policies of the social partners.

Neoclassical economists are quick to point out that the interventions often blunt the incentives of the market. Institutional economists recognise the validity of this criticism. However, they argue that in small countries, labour and other factor inputs that become redundant may not be able to find employment, at least in the short run. Social welfare payments help to support them during their transition from one job to another.

To summarise, both neoclassical and institutional economists support the capitalist system. Neoclassical economists have greater confidence in the ability of the market to provide outcomes that are 'socially' beneficial. The need for government intervention is the exception, rather than the rule. Institutional economists believe that capitalist economies are prone to instability that can be minimised through government intervention.

INFORMATION BOX 1.1

Institutions

In any country, some set of rules, conventions and social norms for behaviour is essential for a stable society and economy. These are what we call 'institutions'. More formally, institutions are the humanly devised mechanisms or constraints that structure economic behaviour and interaction. They can be legal, financial, political, economic or social in nature. They can be formal or informal, slow or fast moving, evolving or designed, perfect best-practice or imperfect second-best.

Definition

Although there are different definitions of institutions, the most common one is taken from North (1990, 1991) where institutions are defined as formal rules, informal constraints and enforcement mechanisms. Examples of formal rules include constitutions, laws and regulations. Norms of behaviour, codes of conduct, conventions and customs are examples of informal rules or constraints. Enforcement mechanisms include the judicial system and third-party arbitration. Distinct from policies, institutions are the rules and social norms by which agents interact and exchange. Policies affect which institutions evolve but, in turn, institutions affect which policies are adopted. Institutional structure affects behaviour but, likewise, behaviour may also change existing institutional structures (World Bank 2002).

Institutions, including the organisations that implement the rules and codes of conduct, are important because these 'rules of the game' facilitate exchange and govern market transactions. Institutions are said to affect economic performance by determining the cost of transacting. As Olson (1992) remarks, 'A thriving market economy is not, contrary to what some say, simply the result of 'letting capitalism happen' – not something that emerges, spontaneously, out of thin air. It requires a special set of *institutional* arrangements that most countries in the world do not have.'

What are these institutions? Qian (2003), in describing institutional reforms in China, outlines a list of important best-practice institutions, to include '. . . secure private property rights protected by the rule of law; impartial enforcement of contracts through an independent judiciary; appropriate government regulations to foster market competition; effective corporate governance; transparent financial systems'. Likewise, Stiglitz and Ellerman (2001), in defending the so-called Stiglitz Perspective on reform, outline the institutional infrastructure, to include ' ... banking and financial systems, effective judicial systems to enforce contracts, competition, bankruptcy laws fairly and efficiently, and regulatory systems . . .'

Measurement

Measuring institutions empirically is a difficult task where despite recent research and some advances there is no consensus on a precise measure. Acknowledging the differences between measuring formal and informal institutions (using 'hard' measures for the former as opposed to 'soft' measures for the latter), a common criticism of the current measures or indicators of institutions is that they measure institutional outcomes (not inputs) rather than institutions per se. As of now, there is no universal measure – nor is it clear that there should be – that captures the different aspects (institutions/organisations, formal/informal, de jure/de facto, predatory/developmental, best-practice/transitional) of institutions and institutional change.

Since 1996, the World Bank has produced a set of institutional governance indicators known as the Worldwide Governance Indicators (WGI). The six indicators are political stability and absence of violence, voice and accountability (i.e. democracy), government effectiveness, regulatory quality, rule of law, and control of corruption, with each indicator based on a combination of various component indicators. The latest set of figures for the WGI can be found at www.govindicators.org.

Institutions and policies

Although the debate with respect to the speed, nature and sequencing of policy reforms has tended to dominate, second generation reforms including institutional reforms have proved more difficult, and, it is now believed by many, are more fundamental to achieving successful outcomes for countries embarking on reform and development. Success requires, at different stages, macroeconomic, structural and institutional reforms. Stabilisation, liberalisation and privatisation are necessary but not sufficient conditions to guarantee sustainable economic growth and an improvement in living standards. The institutional underpinnings of the capitalist system are needed for market reforms to work. Sound policies, to be effective, require a solid institutional setting. Likewise, poor institutions and weak governance will inhibit market reforms. Without these changes, the least-advanced economies of the world will continue to experience serious co-ordination problems. Market reforms without institutional reform will not improve economic prosperity: given the circumstances of each country, market reforms in the absence of institution building may undermine future economic development.

When examining the role and design of institutions, it is important to note that there is no one institutional setting that all countries need to adopt. This point is clearly made in Pickel and Wiesenthal (1997), with one of the authors writing that 'There are as many institutional configurations as there are actually existing market economies.' As in mature market economies, institutions differ, as between, for example, common and civil law, bank-based versus securities-based financial systems, centralised versus decentralised wage bargaining, and so forth. A good example of this is China which did not, at least initially, implement the best-practice institutions of the rule of law and secure private property rights, yet has still managed to perform very well with respect to growth and development. The key point is to recognise that there are alternative institutional arrangements and that the essential

→

reform is to find and follow the most appropriate institutional framework for each respective circumstance. Related to this debate is the question of what are the most important market-enhancing institutions and what constitutes their minimum critical core (in the same way as those who argue in favour of a minimum set of market reforms). Again the experience of many emerging markets, developing countries and transition economies would indicate a lack of consensus on this vexed topic. Of course, identifying these core institutions might be the relatively easy task. Acquiring them is probably the more difficult task.

Institutions and transition

In any setting, a stable society requires a set of rules and social norms for behaviour. The centrally planned system had its own institutional and organisational capital. Order in the socialist system was provided by the State and the Communist Party. All else, whether it was public ownership, the central plan, the soft budget constraint or shortages, followed from the one-party system. Although the fall of communism was greeted enthusiastically as a move towards freedom and prosperity, an unanticipated consequence of the collapse of the socialist state and the disintegration of the Communist Party was, at least in the early years of transition, an institutional vacuum filled by disorder, disorganisation and, in some cases, chaos (Djankov *et al.* 2003). As the state apparatus weakened, economic activity and production declined. Neither the market nor the market-supporting institutions emerged overnight. Although markets soon evolved, the institutions that facilitate and support market transactions were often slow to develop. With a weakened state capacity, many market-supporting institutions were either, at worst, absent or, at best, ineffective.

In the early years of the transition from plan to market, what was more apparent than institutional building was institutional destruction (of Soviet-type institutions). As capitalism and its institutions had taken centuries to evolve in the advanced market economies of the West, it was a misjudgement to think that they could be introduced to former socialist countries in a very short period of time. Moreover, existing institutions need to be (or made) suitable to available policy instruments. However, depending on a country's historical, cultural and social circumstances, the evidence from many countries indicates that the transplantation of best-practice institutions may be inferior to the adoption of transitional institutions. Qian (2003) argues that it is the adoption of so-called transitional – imperfect, unconventional but novel, sensible and complementary to initial conditions – institutions that explains why Chinese reforms worked, and ultimately explains China's recent impressive growth record.

Over time, with the support of a reconstructed state and international assistance, many of the formal institutions and organisations required for a stable society and a growing economy were developed. However, it was the more informal institutions and social norms – customs, traditions, codes of conduct – that, not surprisingly given the influence of culture and history, evolved more slowly (and often, as a result, undermined the new formal institutions). Aside from differences in how these institutions evolved, there was also significant cross-country or cross-regional variation with respect to institutional change. Whereas many of the Central and Eastern European countries managed to make good progress with respect to institutional reform (with EU enlargement and the adoption of the *acquis communautaire* playing an important role), institution building in former Soviet Union countries lagged behind. With the onset of the second decade in transition, more attention was paid to institutions and institutional reform. Over two decades on, although much progress has been made, there is still a long way to go in improving the institutional quality in many former socialist countries and, most especially, the former Soviet Union countries. Nevertheless, given an earlier view that institution building is inevitably a slow process, many countries did manage their institutional construction '. . . surprisingly quickly and successfully . . .', and furthermore, judging against countries of similar levels of economic development and per capita income, '. . . levels of measured institutional development are roughly as expected . . .', with some '. . . remarkable improvements in institutional measures over the 1990s . . .' (Murrell 2003, 2006).

Institutions and economics

Institutions, not an established part of the economic orthodoxy a couple of decades ago, are now an accepted element of the mainstream. This is a fundamental change in economics in less than two decades. The neoclassical slogan of 'getting the prices right' has been augmented (if not replaced, according to some) with the institutional mantra of 'getting the institutions right' but in some instances a particular focus (possibly too narrow) on 'getting the property rights right' or 'getting the contracting right'. It was Nobel Laureate Ronald Coase who wrote back in 1992 that 'The value of including . . . institutional factors in the corpus of mainstream economics is made clear by events in Eastern Europe. These ex-communist countries are advised to move to a market economy, and their leaders wish to do so, but without the appropriate institutions no market economy of any significance is possible. If we knew more about our own economy, we would be in a better position to advise them.' He went on to write in the same *American Economic Review* article, based on his lecture delivered on receipt of the Nobel Prize in Economic Sciences in 1991, that 'It makes little sense for economists to discuss the process of exchange without specifying the institutional setting within which the trading takes place, since this affects the incentives to produce and the costs of transacting.' The importance of institutions – both the institutional environment (rules of the game) and the institutional arrangement (mechanisms of governance) was recognised more recently (and before that, in 1991 and 1993 when Ronald Coase and Douglass North respectively were awarded the Nobel Prize) by the economics profession when the 2009 Nobel Prize in Economic Sciences was awarded (jointly) to Oliver Williamson (of University of California, Berkeley) for his work on institutions, governance and transaction cost economics.

Source: Turley and Luke, 2010.

Marxian school

The writings of Karl Marx (1818–83) and his colleague Friedrich Engels (1820–95) form the basis of the most radical approach to economics.[11] They viewed economics as the study of the relations that people enter into in the course of production and of how these relations change over time. Marx's research approach was called historical materialism. He observed the complex relationships between a society's method of production and other social institutions under economic systems that included slavery, feudalism and capitalism.

Marx believed that different economic systems were based on different classes. A class shared a common interest. Economic systems also differed in the way in which they controlled the production process. Under capitalism, Marx identified two classes. The bourgeoisie were the owners of capital (property, plant and machinery). Labour owned the 'muscle power' needed to produce the economy's goods and services. Capitalism was defined as an economic system which produced for profit using privately owned capital goods and wage labour.

Neoclassical economists and most institutional economists view profit as the payment made to the capitalist for his or her efforts and risk. The capitalist deserves or has a right to earn profit in the same way that a worker is entitled to his or her wage. Marx did not agree. He believed that labour was the source of all value. It produced the machinery used in the production process. Labour produced enough goods and services to pay their own wages. Any surplus that remained was the profit appropriated by the bourgeoisie. Profit was used to increase the stock of capital that was the capitalist's source of future profit.

Marx also did not agree with the neoclassicals that the relationship between employees and employers was based on mutually agreed contracts. The bourgeoisie/ labour relationship was characterised by conflict and exploitation. The way the surplus was split was a source of conflict among the classes. The bourgeoisie was concerned with not only the amount of profit, but also the rate of profit. Increasing the rate of profit required lowering costs, relative to sales. Since wages were an important component of cost, there was a constant struggle against labour to cut the wage bill in order to increase the surplus paid as profit.

Unemployment was a tool used by the bourgeoisie to control labour. The threat of unemployment silenced the voice of labour asking for higher wages and allowed the capitalist to increase their share of the surplus.

Like the institutional economists, Marx saw the capitalist system as unstable. Internal contradictions within the capitalist system caused the instability. Increasing capital accumulation meant that the output of the economy was constantly expanding. The low wages paid to labour meant that demand for the output was stagnant or falling. During periods of overproduction, profits fell. This led to cuts in production and increased unemployment. Marx believed that contractions of economic activity would deepen, leading to depressions of increasing length and severity.

Unlike the institutional economists, Marx did not see government as an institution that eased the increasingly violent swings in the production cycle. Like the neoclassical economists, Marx saw the government as protecting the rights of private property. However, the enforcement of these rights protected the profits and capital gained at labour's expense. Government, therefore, was an institution that colluded with the bourgeoisie to exploit labour.

From this brief discussion, it is obvious that Marx did not see the capitalist system as a fair distributor of society's output. He did not attempt to find policies to improve its faults. He predicted its ultimate collapse, caused by labour rising against the bourgeoisie. This would lead to a new political and economic system based on a classless society.

At the end of the twentieth century, we observed the collapse of the Communist economies that were supposedly based on the principles of Marx. Former economies associated with the Soviet Union are converting to capitalism with an almost religious fervour. Can we forget about the radical critique of Karl Marx?

Some argue that the threat of communism and socialism put 'manners' on capitalism. Concern about the spread of socialism prompted Pope Leo XIII to write an encyclical in 1891. In it, he affirmed the Church's belief that '. . . private property ought to be safeguarded by the sovereign power of the state . . .' In this statement, the Church supports the legislative framework for the capitalist system. However, Leo XIII also argued in favour of associations (trade unions) for labour and outlined the ways in which living and working conditions for workers should be improved either voluntarily or through legislation.[12]

Others argue that it was concern about social stability, rather than the grinding poverty of the unemployed, that led to the enactment of national social welfare legislation in the USA and western Europe during the Great Depression. According to this way of thinking, policies which moved the capitalist system towards socialism were not aimed at promoting social justice but at preserving the capitalist system.

Without the threat of socialism, the worst excesses of the capitalist system may resurface. Then the radical critique of Marx and Engels may gain new currency.

The characteristics of the different economic schools of thought are listed in Table 1.1.

TABLE 1.1: CHARACTERISTICS OF ECONOMIC SCHOOLS OF THOUGHT

	Neoclassical	**Institutional**	**Marxian**
Economics defined	Study of how individuals choose to allocate scarce resources among alternative uses	Study of how institutions regulate the production of goods and services	Study of the social relations that people enter into in the course of production and how these relationships change over time
Focus of analysis	Consumers and firms	Institutions	Classes or groups who share common interests, particularly the ownership of the factors of production
Behaviours analysed	Choices made by consumers and producers	Regulation of the boundaries of individual choice	Struggle between the classes in the pursuit of economic interests
Relationship between actors	Harmonious; based on implicit or explicit contracts	Based on existing or new institutional relationships	Conflictual; disagreements about the distribution of resources among classes
Technology	Assumes harmonious implementation of new technology as it is developed	Institutional arrangements facilitate the development and adoption of new technologies	Implementation of technology may lead to class struggles
Political system	Libertarian democracy	Interventionist democracy	Communist/socialist

Source: Based on the work of Terrence McDonough from the National University of Ireland, Galway.

1.3 ECONOMIC MODELS

A model is an abstraction of reality. It represents the real thing, but with less detail. A map is a model of the road system. The amount of detail that you need depends on how you are travelling. If you are driving from Galway City to Carndonagh, Co. Donegal, an ordinary road map of Ireland will do. If you are travelling on a bicycle, a series of Ordnance Survey maps, which show the byroads and elevations, is more appropriate.

Theories are developed using models that link the theory with the available empirical evidence. Like the road map, economic models attempt to simplify an issue, using only the necessary amount of detail. In this section, we will discuss two types of model that are commonly used by economists: the inductive model and the deductive model.

Both types of model are borrowed from the branch of philosophy known as logic and are based on inference. An inference 'is a proposition that is perceived to be true because of its connection with some known fact'.[13] There are two forms of inference: deduction and induction.

Deductive model

A deductive model is based on a set of premises, and conclusions follow directly from them. The model is tested using available data to determine if it can be disproved. Because of this process, deductive inferences are always conservative.[14] Testing can prove a theory to be false but it cannot verify or confirm that it is true.

To summarise, the deductive model moves from general (the theory) to specific (the data). Figure 1.1 shows the process of developing and testing a deductive model.

FIGURE 1.1: THE DEDUCTIVE MODEL

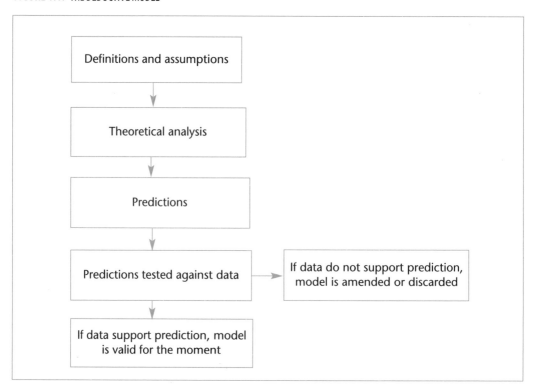

Definitions and assumptions

Theoretical analysis

Predictions

Predictions tested against data → If data do not support prediction, model is amended or discarded

If data support prediction, model is valid for the moment

Definitions and assumptions After the researcher identifies a problem of interest, s/he conducts a literature review to find any research that relates to the topic. Our knowledge about any subject increases incrementally. A researcher builds on the work of other people.

Suppose, for example, a researcher is interested in the relationship between income and education. She will search for any published or unpublished work on this topic.

Next she identifies and defines the variables that she intends to use to study the problem. For example, what is income? Does it include only the money received for paid employment, or does it also include transfer payments made by government? Does income include only wages and salaries or does it also include bonuses and stock options? We go through the same process for education. Is the researcher interested in the years spent in the educational system or the highest degree conferred? Will she include training? Does the training have to be certified by a governing body?

The researcher has to explain any assumptions that she is making. In this case, the researcher assumes that the years spent in the education system improve the knowledge, skills and ability of the individual.

Theoretical analysis In this step, the researcher develops the model that she intends to test. She explains the relationship between the variables.

For example, the researcher may decide on the following model:

$$Income = f(education)$$

This model states that income is a function of education or income depends on education. In this model, education is the independent variable and income is the dependent variable.

Also, the researcher has to identify the way in which these variables interact. This is based on the assumptions. If years in education improve the knowledge, skills and ability of an individual, education and income should move in the same direction. This is called a 'positive' relationship.

Predictions Based on the theoretical analysis, the researcher predicts the relationship that she will find when she tests her model with data. In this example, the researcher may predict that in Ireland, income increases with higher levels of educational attainment.

Predictions tested against data Next the researcher must locate the data to test her model. This can be quite difficult. If she cannot find information on the entire population of the country, or if that amount of information is simply too great, she must identify a sample that represents the population. Then she must find two pieces of information for each individual in her sample: their educational attainment and their income. Our researcher may find some information available from published sources, but not exactly in the form that she needs. Sending a questionnaire to the sample is expensive and people may not want to answer questions concerning their income.

However, let us assume that she does find the data and tests her model. There are two possible outcomes.

Data support prediction In this case the researcher finds a positive relationship between education and income. The data support the model's prediction. This means that although she or some other researcher may develop a better model in the future, in the meantime, this model is valid.

Data do not support prediction   In this case, the researcher makes the discovery that she has to amend or discard her model. There are two likely sources for this failure. First, she may have chosen the wrong independent variable. Perhaps experience is much more important than education as a predictor of income. In this case, she has to go 'back to the drawing board' to reconsider her variables, assumptions and relationships. Second, her data may not be sufficiently robust to test the model. In this case, she has to attempt to locate better data sources to retest the model. If she cannot amend the model, she has to discard it.

There are some benefits to the deductive model. First, the model is simple. It structures the research problem with a minimum of detail. Second, the model is transparent. This means that it is logical. Every step is clearly defined. Someone who follows the researcher using this method should be able to understand exactly what s/he did in order to criticise the results or to improve the model. Third, the model helps the researcher to think about cause and effect. This is useful, especially if policy can be used to change an independent variable. For example, in this situation, if the government wants to eliminate poverty, this model suggests that it should promote education. One policy could be to provide free third-level education.

There are also problems associated with the deductive model. Institutional economists argue that deductive models are too simple. A cause and effect relationship using a small number of independent variables is unlikely to adequately explain the complicated events that occur in developed economies. This simplicity can lead to incorrect policy decisions. For example, in the model that we used above we assumed that

$$Income = f(education)$$

However, an equally defensible model is that

$$Education = f(income)$$

In other words, children from families with high incomes are more likely to avail of opportunities that extend their years in the educational system than children from low-income families. Indeed, there is probably a virtuous circle between the two variables which cannot be explained using the deductive model.

If the model cannot identify 'cause and effect', the policy prescriptions based on the model will be incorrect. People with low incomes may not take up educational opportunities. Free education may end up being of greatest benefit to people on higher incomes.

A second problem with this type of model is the availability of data. In some cases, the data exist but are inaccessible, usually for reasons of confidentiality. In other cases, the data are of poor quality or not specific enough to test the particular model.

Inductive model

Both deductive and inductive models are based on their connection with data. The deductive model uses data to verify the theory. For the inductive model, the researcher 'seeks to use factual data to discover empirical correlations that can then serve in the construction of theories, which will, hopefully be useful in prediction.'[15] The inductive model moves from the specific to the general, from the data to the theory.

The steps for the inductive model are outlined in Figure 1.2.

FIGURE 1.2: THE INDUCTIVE MODEL

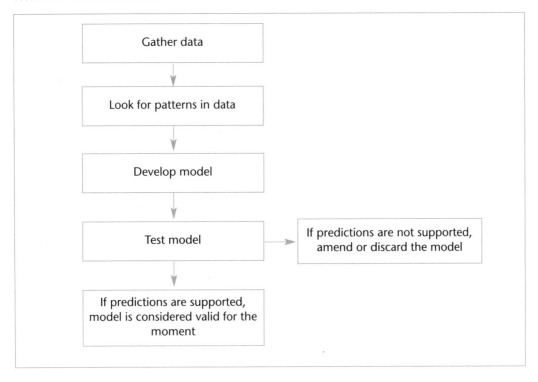

Gather data After identifying the problem that is of interest, the researcher looks for data. For example, suppose the same researcher is still interested in investigating the relationship between education and income. She might check all the available sources of information. The Census of Population, published by the Central Statistics Office (CSO) at five-year intervals, contains information about education and occupations for Irish households. Information concerning the hourly and weekly wage by industrial sector is published each month by the CSO. Information concerning unemployment and educational attainment is published annually by the OECD (Organisation for Economic Co-operation and Development). The Higher Education Authority (HEA) publishes information annually related to entry to third-level education and the principal economic status of the student's family.

Look for patterns in data Next the researcher looks for patterns in the data. For example, she might look to see if the children of farmers are more likely to attend third-level education than the children of factory workers. She might look to see if people with less education are more likely to be unemployed.

Develop model Based on patterns that she finds in the data, the researcher develops a model. The model may include a number of variables that the researcher found from various sources. It may involve observations about timing. Certain variables may lead changes in income while others may lag changes in income.

Test model The researcher may develop the model using data from all but the most recent years. She will then test the model using the most current data available. Depending on the results of the test, she will accept, amend or discard the model.

The inductive model also has admirers and critics. The benefits include increased realism. The researcher is not limited by beginning with fixed theoretical relationships that she attempts to verify with inappropriate data. This research approach is more pragmatic in the sense that it is 'data led'. The researcher begins with whatever data are available, with all of their faults and limitations. Connections between the variables are discovered by observation. The researcher lets the information 'speak for itself' rather than prejudging links between different variables.

However, this form of modelling is criticised because it does not isolate causation. The past association between two variables may be extended coincidence. Also, the availability of new information may substantially alter the theory. If the general form changes with new information, it undermines confidence in the validity of the process.

The deductive model continues to be the preferred method of developing economic theory, particularly for neoclassical economists.

CASE STUDY

Extract from *The Irish Times*
Males make the grade in university exams
by Emmett Oliver

Top degrees at university continue to be the preserve of male students with 521 of them having achieved that distinction in the latest Higher Education Authority figures.

While 110 fewer female students reached this level, it should be borne in mind that the number of first-class honours degrees awarded per annum is small – about 7 per cent of all degrees.

However, the recovery by men between school and college is surprising, as there are sometimes only three to four years between the Leaving Cert and final exams at university.

Even more surprising is that males get more top degrees even though there are 5,588 of them in university compared to 6,737 females.

Male students seem to increase their performance greatly during this time, according to Higher Education Authority (HEA) figures, which form part of its annual report, due to be published later this year. It covers degrees awarded in the State's seven universities in 1997/98.

Experts traditionally use the number of top degrees awarded as the primary measurement of how the sexes are performing at third level. So while women are getting to university in larger numbers, they are not taking their share of the top degrees.

So what lies behind the performance of men at university when so many of them fail to shine in school exams? One salient factor is that males tend to do courses where high marks are available.

In engineering there are large numbers of first-class honours degrees awarded, mostly to male students because there are more of them than women engineers . . .

So one of the central reasons female students lag behind their male counterparts is they are not doing such courses as engineering where first-class honours degrees tend to be awarded . . .

But even taking into account the dominance of men in engineering and information technology, there is no doubt there is an improvement in men's academic performance between school and university.

The explanations behind the 'catch-up' effect are varied. The Union of Students of Ireland has pointed to the large number of male lecturers as the reason females get 'marked down' in university exams.

It cited a report by Prof Catherine Belsey, an academic from University College, Cardiff, which showed that female students in its arts faculty were being under-marked before the introduction of anonymous marking . . .

Other possible explanations are that female performance is lowered in a co-educational environment like a university. Research has supported this trend at school level, where girls in single-sex schools often do better than those who share with boys. It may be factor in university for those girls who leave their single-sex school and find their performance dropping . . .

Source: The Irish Times, 18 September 2000

Questions

1. Suppose you read this article and decide to develop a model to explain which students receive first-class honours. Describe the deductive model. Begin with the deductive model using the following form:

$$\text{First-class honours} = f(X_1, X_2)$$

Choose two independent variables for X_1 and X_2 and explain why you chose them.

2. Describe the inductive model. What kind of data might help you to explain how first-class honours are awarded?

3. Which is the best type of model to study this issue?

Answers on website

1.4 PRODUCTION POSSIBILITY FRONTIER

We will finish this chapter by introducing a neoclassical model of the economy called the production possibility frontier. This model demonstrates the limits of an economy's production caused by resources that are finite. We begin by defining relevant terms and stating the assumption of the model.

Definitions and assumptions

> **Definition**
>
> *Factors of production are the resources of an economy. They include land, labour, capital and enterprise. They are sometimes referred to as the 'inputs'.*

Land represents all of the natural resources available to an economy. Labour is the muscle power and the brainpower of workers. Capital represents the durable assets used during the production process including plant and machinery. Enterprise represents the co-ordination of skills of people who organise the other factors of production.

One of the assumptions of the model is that all resources are 'productive'. A second assumption is that while resources can be transferred from one type of production to another, they may not be equally productive in alternative employment. This is because some factors of production are specialised. For example, a person trained to be a chef would be more productive at organising a kitchen than organising a factory.

Theoretical analysis

The production function expresses the relationship between the factors of production and the output of the economy (Q).

$$Q = f \text{ (land, labour, capital and enterprise)}$$

This equation states that the output of the economy is a function of its resources (see Section 5.2). Because resources are productive, there is a positive relationship between the factors of production and output. Any increase in the quantity or quality of inputs will increase the output of the economy.

The production possibility frontier shows the limits of production at a point in time. For this simple model of the economy, we concentrate on the production of only two goods. However, the predictions that we make can be applied to a more complex economy.

> **Definition**
>
> *The production possibility frontier (PPF) shows all possible combinations of two goods that can be produced using available technology and all available resources.*

As an example, we will consider an economy where capital goods (machines) and consumer goods are produced. Table 1.2 records some of the possible combinations of the two goods that can be produced with the available resources and technology.

TABLE 1.2: PRODUCTION POSSIBILITIES FOR CAPITAL AND CONSUMER GOODS

Combination	Consumer goods	Capital goods
a	20	0
b	19	1
c	16	2
d	11	3
e	0	4

Points a and e reflect the extreme cases where the economy produces only one type of good. At point a, the economy produces only consumer goods and at point e, the economy produces only capital goods. At all other points, some of each good is produced.

We can show the same information on a diagram. Figure 1.3 shows the PPF. Consumer goods are shown on the vertical axis and capital goods are on the horizontal axis. Both axes are measured in units.

The production possibility frontier shows all the combinations of consumer goods and capital goods which can be produced using the economy's limited resources. It is downward sloping. This means that there is a trade-off. Producing more of one good requires producing less of another good. This trade-off is an example of an opportunity cost.

FIGURE 1.3: THE PRODUCTION POSSIBILITY FRONTIER

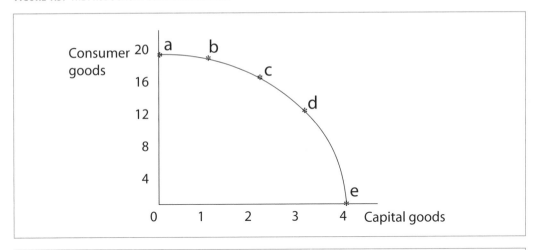

That is a rather laborious way of saying that if you spend €8 for a ticket to the cinema, you preferred that option to drinking a couple of pints at the pub or buying a book. These are alternative ways of spending €8. However, an opportunity cost is the 'best' opportunity forgone. Therefore, if on the day, the choice is between the cinema and the pub, the opportunity cost of your trip to the cinema is a visit to the pub.

In the case of the production possibility frontier, the opportunity cost of producing capital goods is consumer goods. Because the PPF is concave, we know that the opportunity cost is increasing. For example, the opportunity cost of producing the first unit of capital goods is one unit of consumer goods. To produce the second unit of capital goods, the opportunity cost is three units of consumer goods.

Why is the opportunity cost increasing? We stated in the assumptions that resources are not equally productive in alternative uses. Initially, the least productive resources are taken from the production of consumer goods and diverted to the production of capital goods. However, as more capital goods are produced, increasingly productive resources are taken from consumer good production. Therefore, the opportunity cost increases.

At every point along the PPF, all factors of production are employed. They are points of 'productive efficiency' as described in Section 1.2. Points inside the frontier are attainable but not efficient. This is because some of the factors of production are unemployed. Points outside the frontier represent combinations of goods that are unattainable. These combinations of goods cannot be produced because it is beyond the limits of the economy's resources and technology.

Predictions

Based on the definitions, assumptions and theoretical analysis, what predictions can we make using this model?

First, we can use the model to predict the reasons for economic growth. Output depends on the quantity and quality of the factors of production. Any of the following 'events' will cause the PPF to expand:

i) an improvement of human capital through education and training;
ii) the discovery of oil off the west coast of Ireland; and
iii) the implementation of new work practices which make labour more efficient.

Economic growth is shown in Figure 1.4.

FIGURE 1.4: ECONOMIC GROWTH

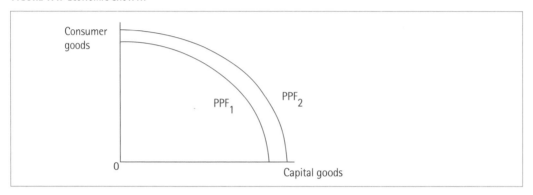

PPF_1 shows the original combinations of goods that the economy can produce. The improvement in the factors of production expands those combinations to the area bound by PPF_2.

Second, we can use the model to predict reasons for economic decline. Any of the following 'events' will cause the PPF to shrink:

i) emigration of Irish citizens;
ii) flooding which destroys the plant and machinery at an industrial estate; and
iii) deterioration of the national rail and road system.

Economic decline is shown in Figure 1.5.

FIGURE 1.5: ECONOMIC DECLINE

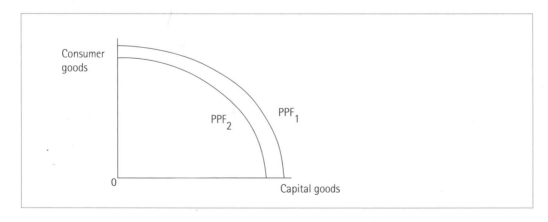

The original frontier, shown by PPF_1, covers a broader area than the new frontier, shown by PPF_2. The 'events' listed above mean that the productive capabilities of the country have decreased.

Can we predict where on the frontier a country's production will lie? The answer to this question is no. This model deals with the productive capabilities of the economy, not the preferences of its citizens. We need more information to predict the amount of consumer goods and capital goods that this economy will produce.

SUMMARY

1. The core principles of economics are: limited resources or scarcity; the need for a co-ordination mechanism to allocate resources and the role of market forces versus government; trade and voluntary exchange is mutually beneficial; the cost of something is measured in terms of the forgone opportunities; rational self-interested economic agents respond to incentives, face trade-offs and make decisions at the margin; specialisation and the case for the division of labour; and the law of comparative advantage.

2. The neoclassical school is the dominant school in economics in the western world. Neoclassical economists believe that individuals, acting in their own self-interest, also promote the best interests of society. Therefore, they argue against government involvement in the market. The correct role of government is to establish and enforce the 'rules of the game'.

3. Both institutional and Marxian economists agree that the capitalist economy is prone to instability. Institutional economists see government as playing a key role in stabilising the economy. Marx believed that governments protect the rights of the bourgeoisie at labour's expense.

4. Economists develop models to link theory with data. The deductive model is used most often to conduct economic research. It begins with definitions and assumptions. The next step is the theoretical analysis that identifies independent and dependent variables and explains how they relate to each other. Then, the researcher makes predictions and tests those predictions using data. If the data support the theory, the model is considered valid for the moment.

5. An inductive model begins with data. The researcher looks for any data that relate to the research topic. S/he then examines the data to see if there are any relationships between variables. These relationships are used to develop a theory. While inductive models are considered more realistic than deductive models, they are criticised because the relationship between variables derived from data may be coincidental.

6. The production possibility frontier (PPF) is a model of an economy. It begins with the production function. The output of an economy is a function of the factors of production, which include land, labour, capital and enterprise. The PPF shows the maximum amount of two goods that can be produced, employing all of the factors of production and using the best available technology. In relation to the PPF, the opportunity cost of producing more of one good is the decrease in production of the alternate good.

KEY TERMS

Scarcity	Economic efficiency
Co-ordination mechanism	Pareto efficiency
Opportunity cost	Institutional school
Market	Thorstein Veblen
Government	Conspicuous consumption
Division of labour	Leisure class
Trade	John Maynard Keynes
Voluntary exchange	Marxian school
Comparative advantage	Karl Marx
Marginal analysis	Bourgeoisie
Incentives	Deductive model
Trade-offs	Inductive model
Neoclassical school	Production possibility frontier
Milton Friedman	Factors of production
Productive efficiency	Production function

REVIEW QUESTIONS

1. What are the key ideas in economics?
2. How do the noeclassical economists define efficiency?
3. How do the neoclassical, institutional and Marxian views of government differ?
4. What is the connection between theories and models?
5. How does the deductive model differ from the inductive model?
6. Why do economies grow? Illustrate economic growth using the PPF.

WORKING PROBLEMS

1. Using the information in Table 1.3, answer the following questions:

TABLE 1.3: PRODUCTION POSSIBILITY FRONTIER

Possibility	Units of butter	Units of guns
a	50	0
b	48	1
c	42	2
d	32	3
e	20	4
f	0	5

(a) Plot the PPF. (Put guns on the horizontal axis.)
(b) If the economy moves from combination c to combination d, what is the opportunity cost? (Hint: To produce the third unit of guns, the opportunity cost is 'X' units of butter.)
(c) If the economy moves from combination d to combination e, what is the opportunity cost?

(d) In general, what happens to the opportunity cost as the output of guns increases? Why?

(e) Suppose the PPF is a straight line. What does this imply about the opportunity cost and resources?

2. Show how each of the following 'events' will affect the PPF drawn for Question 1(a). Label the original frontier PPF$_1$ and the new frontier PPF$_2$.

(a) a new, easily exploited energy source is discovered;

(b) a large number of skilled workers emigrate from the country;

(c) a new invention increases the output per worker in the butter industry;

(d) a new law is passed compelling workers who could previously work as long as they wanted to retire at 60 years of age.

MULTI-CHOICE QUESTIONS

1. Which of the following statements describes the neoclassical view concerning the appropriate role of government?

(a) Government should redistribute income through the income tax and social welfare system.

(b) Government should intervene to stabilise economic fluctuations.

(c) Government co-operates with the bourgeoisie to exploit labour.

(d) The role of government is important but limited.

(e) None of the above.

2. Marxian and institutional economists agree that:

(a) government should intervene to stabilise economic fluctuations;

(b) capitalist economies are inherently unstable;

(c) capitalism should be replaced by a classless society;

(d) the capitalist system ensures even distribution of goods and services;

(e) none of the above.

3. Which of the following statements accurately describes the deductive model?

(a) It begins with theory that is tested with data.

(b) All definitions and assumptions are stated.

(c) If the data do not support the theory, the model is amended or discarded.

(d) It is transparent.

(e) All of the statements above describe the deductive model.

4. The inductive model:

(a) is unrealistic;

(b) is the 'model of choice' for neoclassical economists;

(c) moves from general to specific;

(d) begins with data;

(e) none of the statements above describe the inductive model.

5. When the government chooses to use resources to build a dam, those resources are no longer available to build a road. This illustrates the concept of:

(a) a market mechanism;
(b) an opportunity cost;
(c) exploitation of the working class;
(d) co-operation;
(e) none of the above.

6. Consider the production possibility frontier shown in Figure 1.6.

FIGURE 1.6: PRODUCTION POSSIBILITY FRONTIER

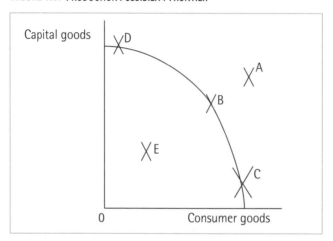

Which combination of goods and services may be produced *during a recession*?
   (a) A
   (b) B
   (c) C
   (d) D
   (e) E

TRUE OR FALSE (SUPPORT YOUR ANSWER)

1. According to Veblen, individuals make independent choices concerning the goods and services that they purchase.

2. Economic decision-making involves comparing costs to benefits, at the margin.

3. Pareto efficiency means that the goods and services produced by an economy are evenly distributed.

4. A problem with a deductive model is that the appropriate data are not always available.

5. The opportunity cost of a cup of tea in the college canteen is a cup of coffee *and* a Mars Bar.

6. An assumption of the PPF is that all resources are productive.

CASE STUDY

Extract from *The Irish Times*
Harney tackles labour crisis
by Arthur Beesley

Failure to address the labour shortage could 'destroy' the Republic's economic growth, the Tánaiste has warned . . .

Stating that the booming economy would need 200,000 additional workers by the time the National Development Plan was completed in 2006, Ms Harney said such demand would require increased immigration by Irish people living abroad and by others within and outside of the European Economic Area (EEA).

The EEA comprises the 15 EU members – and Norway, Iceland and Liechtenstein. Citizens of states in this zone do not need visas or permits to work in the Republic.

Such authorisations are required by non-EEA citizens. Ms Harney said about 18,000 work permits were issued this year, in addition to 1,000 work visas . . .

The Government intends infrastructure built in the plan to provide the foundation for the State's future economic development. In this context, Ms Harney said she would encourage Irish construction contractors to take foreign staff and to form partnerships with firms based outside of the state . . .

When asked whether the high cost of accommodation and property, in Dublin particularly, would deter people from coming to live in the Republic, Ms Harney said many Irish-based firms were offering relocation packages to workers with high qualifications. It was common also for groups of workers to share rented accommodation, she said.

In addition to labour from outside of the State, the Government saw employment opportunities from Irish women aged more than 35 years and among long-term unemployed . . .

Another element of Government policy was to provide training to upgrade the skills of the people already in the workforce. Certain multinationals with Irish operations have embarked on in-house 'upskilling' programmes . . .

Source: *The Irish Times*, 22 December 2000.

Questions

1. What is a production function? What are the factors of production and how are they related to an economy's output?
2. According to Mary Harney, what factor of production is limiting economic growth? What policies does she describe to overcome this problem? What effect will these policies have on the production possibility frontier?
3. Can you see other problems that may occur as a result of these policies? One is mentioned in the article but there may be others.

PART I

MICROECONOMICS

Introduction to Microeconomics

Microeconomics studies individual choice. Consumers and firms are the subjects of the analysis. Each is studied in isolation from the other before they interact in a particular product (or factor) market. The purpose of the study is to develop an understanding of the behaviour and actions of individual agents in the economy.

We begin our analysis of microeconomics in the market place characterised by voluntary exchange. The voluntary interaction between consumers and producers is the essence of the market system. The study of microeconomics will be divided into a number of topics.

Chapter 2 deals with consumers and producers (suppliers) interacting in a market for a particular product (i.e. a good or service). The price mechanism, a central feature of the market system, is explained. A brief account of price controls concludes the chapter.

In Chapter 3 we examine the sensitivity (in percentage terms) of market demand and supply to changes in price (or other indepenedent variables, e.g. income). This concept is called 'elasticity' and has important implications for the pricing strategy of firms seeking to maximise revenues.

Chapter 4 concentrates on the role of the individual consumer in the market place. We begin with the neoclassical assumption that each consumer acts as if s/he is attempting to maximise her or his utility or satisfaction. The negative relationship between price and quantity is explained in terms of utility. The demand curve for different categories of products is examined.

We begin a more intensive investigation of producer behaviour in Chapter 5. In traditional neoclassical economics, we assume that firms act as if they are attempting to maximise profit. We will see that both productivity and costs influence a firm's production decision.

In Chapter 6, we examine different types of market structure. The environment within which a firm operates determines a firm's specific behaviour. More specifically, the pricing and output decision of the firm is largely influenced by the degree of competition facing the firm. Game theory and the concept of a Nash equilibrium is shown to be particularly informative in the context of there being a small number of independent firms present in the market.

The initial chapters deal with the markets for final products. In Chapter 7, we focus on the market for factor inputs. Land, labour, capital and enterprise are all key inputs into the production process. This chapter also includes material on the Irish minimum wage.

In a mixed economy where both the market and the state play vital roles in the economy and society more generally, market failures and state failures occur. Microeconomic aspects of markets versus states are discussed in Chapter 8. For example, the market system does not in general price external effects. These external effects can be positive (e.g. public goods) or negative (e.g. externalities, such as pollution). To address these effects, extensive government involvement in the economy through expenditure, taxation and regulatory policies is required. However, government or state failure is also possible and its likely effects should also be considered.

Part 1 of the textbook concludes with applied microeconomic policy. Chapter 9 includes three topics that are particularly relevant to Ireland in the new millennium, namely taxation policy, competition policy (including regulatory policy) and national partnership agreements (e.g. national wage agreements).

CHAPTER 2

Demand, Supply and Market Equilibrium

'*The price of ability does not depend on merit, but on supply and demand.*'[1]

GEORGE BERNARD SHAW

'*We might as reasonably dispute whether it is the upper or the under blade of a pair of scissors that cuts a piece of paper, as whether value is governed by utility or cost of production.*'[2]

ALFRED MARSHALL (1842–1924)

CHAPTER OBJECTIVES

Upon completing this chapter, the student should understand:
- demand and the demand curve;
- supply and the supply curve;
- factors influencing demand and supply;
- the price mechanism and market equilibrium;
- price controls.

OUTLINE

2.1 **Demand and consumers**
2.2 **Supply and producers**
2.3 **Market equilibrium and the price mechanism**
2.4 **Price controls**

INTRODUCTION

Why do consumers pay €7.50 for a kilogram of Irish beef and €40 for a haircut? The answer lies in the analysis of 'the market'. We begin our analysis by looking at the market for a particular product (i.e. good or service) like beef or haircuts. The willingness of consumers to purchase a particular product is the basis of market demand. The willingness of producers or suppliers to produce or provide a particular product is the basis of market supply. The interaction of consumers and producers determines the market price for a product. While Chapter 2 focuses on the market demand curve, Chapter 4 examines an individual consumer's demand curve.

After considering the components of a market and the way in which price is determined, we will look at price controls. These are actions taken by government to promote the interests of either the producer or the consumer or society more generally (i.e. some combination of consumers and producers).

2.1 DEMAND AND CONSUMERS

If you were asked to provide an example of a 'market' your description might vary from a stock exchange, to a website (e.g. eBay), to a corner shop. In an economic context, we usually discuss the market for a particular product like a chocolate bar or a haircut. In this case, the 'market' is not a place, but a theoretical concept or model.

> **Definition**
>
> *The market is any institutional arrangement that facilitates the buying and selling of a product.*

Broadly interpreted, the term 'product' can encompass factors of production (e.g. labour) and future commitments (e.g. futures market) as well as goods, services or commodities. Generally, there is also a time dimension. This recognises that market conditions of demand and supply for a particular product last for only a limited period of time. The appropriate length of time varies with the particular product. Developments in oil-producing countries mean that the price of a barrel of oil on the world market is constantly changing. We may want to look at the market for oil on a daily or even hourly basis. The market for chocolate bars is more stable. It may be possible to look meaningfully at a market for this product over a longer period of time – a month or even a year.

The model of the market shows the interaction of consumers and producers. Consumers generate the demand for a product.

> **Definition**
>
> *Demand is the quantity of a product that consumers are willing to purchase at each conceivable price during a particular time period.*

Demand relates not to what consumers want, but to what they want and can afford. Sometimes this is called 'effective' demand. It is the desire for a product backed up by an ability to pay.

Demand does not refer to a particular quantity, but to a whole range of quantities. The reason we associate a particular price with a product is because in a market system, price is determined by the interaction of the consumers and the suppliers. If we observe consumers in isolation, we are then faced with a range of prices, and subsequently with a range of quantities.

What determines the level of demand? Why do consumers demand a small or large quantity of a product? One of the key factors which determine demand is the price of the product. We can write this relationship in mathematical form:

$$Qd = f(P)$$
[2.1]

where: Qd = Quantity demanded; P = Price.

This relationship can be expressed in a number of different ways. For example,

Quantity demanded is a function of price

or

Quantity demanded depends on price

or

Each level of quantity demanded is associated with its own price

Equation 2.1 is called the demand function. It involves two variables where a variable is defined as a symbol that can represent any unspecified number or value. Price is the explanatory variable in that it serves to explain the specific level of quantity demanded. Price is autonomous or independent. Quantity demanded is the dependent variable. It is conditional on the level of price.

We can examine the relationship between price and quantity for a product by considering a demand schedule.

> **Definition**
>
> *A demand schedule is a schedule or table which indicates the quantity of a particular product which consumers are willing to purchase at various prices during a specified time period.*

In this definition, we implicitly assume that any other factors which could conceivably influence the quantity demanded do not change during the relevant time period. Using the terminology of the economist, we say that a demand schedule examines the relationship between price and quantity demanded, *ceteris paribus.*

> **Definition**
>
> *Ceteris paribus is a Latin phrase which means 'other things being equal'. In the study of economics, this phrase is used to mean that the relationship between two variables can be examined, assuming that other factors are not changing.*

The factors which are held constant when we consider the demand schedule include the prices of related products, consumers' income and their tastes (e.g. the incidence of vegetarianism).

Table 2.1 shows the demand schedule for beef measured in kilograms for a one-month period. For each price, there is a corresponding level of quantity demanded.

TABLE 2.1: THE DEMAND SCHEDULE FOR BEEF (PER MONTH)

Price, P (Euros)	Quantity demanded, Qd (thousands of kilograms)
5.00	2,625
5.50	2,500
6.00	2,375
6.50	2,250
7.00	2,125
7.50	2,000
8.00	1,875
8.50	1,750
9.00	1,625
9.50	1,500

We can see from this schedule that when price increases from €7.00 per kilogram to €7.50 per kilogram, the quantity demanded falls from 2,125,000 kilograms to 2,000,000 kilograms.

This demand schedule is a specific example of a general relationship. With few exceptions, as the price of a product falls, the quantity demanded of that product rises. This relationship is observed so frequently that we call it the principle of demand.

Definition

The principle of demand refers to the inverse or negative relationship between price and quantity demanded, ceteris paribus.

Generally, we illustrate this relationship using a two-dimensional graph. It is customary to represent price on the vertical axis and quantity on the horizontal axis. We plot the points from the demand schedule and join them together to form the demand curve.

Figure 2.1 illustrates the demand curve for beef described by the demand schedule. Because the relationship between price and quantity is negative, the demand curve is downward sloping.

FIGURE 2.1: THE DEMAND CURVE FOR BEEF

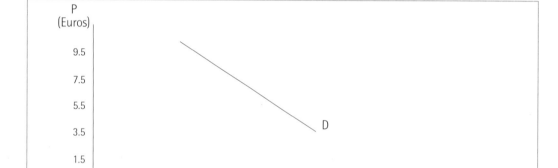

The demand curve alone cannot tell us the actual selling price or the quantity sold in the market. This information is only determined when the consumers (represented by the demand curve) interact with producers (represented by the supply curve) to form a functioning market.

At this stage we only offer an intuitive explanation as to why the demand curve is generally downward sloping. Recall that when we discussed the principle of demand, we stated that other factors that affect demand are 'held constant'. Among those factors are the prices of related products. A number of products can be substituted for beef – chicken or lamb, for example. As the price of beef increases, some consumers will purchase substitute goods in place of beef. Therefore, as the price of beef rises, the quantity of beef demanded falls. Alternatively, if the price of beef falls, it becomes cheaper relative to other types of meat, or food more generally. People will purchase more beef at a lower price instead of chicken or lamb. We offer a more detailed explanation of the downward sloping individual consumer's demand curve, and examine possible exceptions, in Chapter 4.

When the demand curve is a straight line, it can be represented in a simple linear form, as follows:

$$Qd = a - bP \qquad [2.2]$$

where: Qd = Quantity demanded; P = Price; a and b = constants.

Equation 2.2 shows the general form of a linear relationship between price and quantity demanded. The negative relationship between the two variables is reflected in the minus sign before price, the independent variable. The demand schedule for beef, which we have been discussing, is based on a linear demand relationship. The equation for this specific relationship is:

$$Qd = 3,875,000 - 250,000P$$

A demand curve is not always a straight line. A convex demand curve which is bowed towards the origin is shown in Figure 2.2.

The exact shape of the demand curve depends on the nature of the relationship between the change in price and the subsequent change in quantity demanded. We will examine this in greater detail in Chapter 3.

FIGURE 2.2: A CONVEX DEMAND CURVE

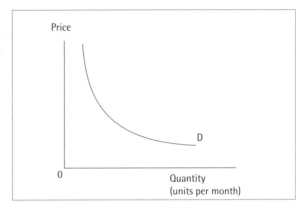

Exceptions to the downward sloping demand curve

There are a few exceptional cases where the demand curve is not downward sloping. For a limited number of products and over a limited range of prices, the demand curve may be 'perverse' or upward sloping as shown in Figure 2.3.

FIGURE 2.3: A 'PERVERSE' DEMAND CURVE

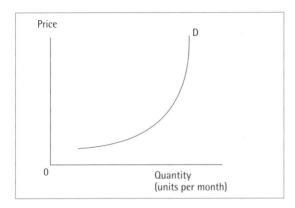

Arguably, one exception is provided by a snob or Veblen good. The demand curve of a Veblen good is upward sloping over a range of prices. The behaviour that underlies this demand curve was coined 'conspicuous consumption' by Thorstein Veblen, the American Institutional economist and author of *The Theory of the Leisure Class* (1899). He argued that certain sections of society, in particular the 'leisure' class, may not act like the consumers whom we have just described.

Veblen suggested that the ownership of goods that are expensive and frivolous confers status on the owner because others realise that these 'ostentatious' goods can only be purchased by members of the upper economic class. Status increases when the price of the good increases. If the price of the good falls, the 'snob' value also falls, since it is now less expensive and more affordable to lower classes. In some circumstances the demand for the 'snob' good may actually fall when the price falls, resulting in an upward sloping demand curve. Rolex watches and BMWs are possible examples, albeit only over a limited range of prices.

However, many economists argue that a snob or Veblen good should not really be regarded as an exception as the nature of the good and, in particular, tastes for the good change as its price changes, i.e. the *ceteris paribus* assumption does not hold.

A clearer exception to the principle of demand is provided by a Giffen good. The 'Giffen paradox' was described by Sir Robert Giffen (1837–1910) who, it is said, observed that an increase in the price of bread in nineteenth-century London, '. . . makes so large a drain on the resources of the poorer labouring families . . . that they are forced to curtail their consumption of meat and the more expensive farinaceous foods: and, bread being still the cheapest food which they can get and will take, they consume more, and not less of it'.[3]

This quotation suggests that the observation of a Giffen good requires a very specific set of circumstances. First, income levels must be low and the good must constitute a significant part of a consumer's purchases. Second, the good in question must have few affordable substitutes. Even so, an increase in demand in response to an increase in price will probably only occur over a very narrow range of prices. In western economies, characterised by relatively high levels of income and the existence of numerous substitutes, most economists believe that the Giffen paradox is no longer relevant.

In summary, although a 'perverse' market demand curve is theoretically possible, this relationship is seldom if ever observed. In general, we can rely on the negative relationship between price and quantity demanded described by the principle of demand.

Other factors influencing demand

In reality there is a wide range of factors that determine the level of quantity demanded. Here we focus on the more important determinants or, as they are sometimes referred to, underlying conditions of demand. Until now, these determinants were 'held constant' according to the *ceteris paribus* condition.

1. The price of related products
If two products are related, they are either substitutes for, or complements to, each other.

Definition
Two products are substitutes if consumers consider each product as an alternative for the other product. If the price of either product falls, demand for the other product falls and if the price of either product rises, the demand for the other product rises.

Beef and lamb, butter and margarine, tea and coffee, and bus and rail transport are likely examples of substitute goods and services. If the price of a return ticket on a bus between Galway and Dublin falls, we expect the demand for railway tickets for the same journey to fall. If we test this hypothesis and find that this relationship exists, we consider these products to be substitutes.

> ### Definition
>
> *Products which are complements are bought and consumed together. This implies that if the price of either product falls, demand for the other product rises and if the price of either product rises, the demand for the other product falls.*

Plausible examples of complementary products include beef and horseradish sauce, CDs and CD players, personal computers and printers, airline tickets and hotel accommodation, automobiles and automobile insurance. Consider CDs and CD players. When they first appeared on the market, CD players were reasonably priced but CDs were expensive. Subsequently, the demand for CD players increased dramatically when the price of CDs fell significantly, indicating that these products are complements.

2. Consumers' income (Y)

Income was also 'held constant' when we considered the demand schedule. However, it is another explanatory variable. This means that if income changes, it will usually have an effect on demand. Normal and inferior goods are defined in terms of income.

> ### Definition
>
> *For a normal good, there is a positive relationship between income and demand. Demand for a normal good increases as income increases and decreases as income decreases.*

There are many types of beef. Round steak and sirloin are better cuts of beef. The demand for superior cuts or organic beef increases with income. Most goods (or, more generally, products, i.e. goods and services) from a iPod to an automobile are examples of normal goods.

> ### Definition
>
> *For an inferior good, there is a negative relationship between income and demand. Demand for an inferior good decreases as income increases and increases as income decreases.*

Minced beef and bus rides, albeit only over a limited range of income, are examples of inferior goods. Consider minced beef. If income increases, consumers sometimes substitute a better grade of meat for minced beef. By establishing a negative relationship between demand for minced beef and income, we classify minced beef as an inferior good.

3. Consumers' tastes (T)

Tastes and preferences for the product also affect demand. Taste, in this context, is a broad concept. It is shaped by time, custom, tradition, fashion, location and social attitudes.

Economists generally believe that tastes change slowly over time. Therefore, they are comfortable with the assumption that consumers' preferences 'can be held constant' when the price/quantity relationship is examined. However, as the case study at the end of this section illustrates, the health scare caused by contaminated pork products in 2008 had an immediate impact on the demand for Irish pork products.

4. Other factors (O)

Advertising, expectations about future market conditions and access to foreign markets are some additional factors that lead to changes in demand for a particular product. For example, as a result of 'Mad Cow Disease', beef trade with Russia was curtailed and beef trade with Iran was discontinued. This led to a deterioration in the conditions of demand for Irish beef.

Hence, the quantity of a product demanded is determined by the price of the product itself and by the price of related products, by the consumers' income, by the consumers' tastes and by a range of other factors. The complete mathematical representation for our demand function is in the form of:

$$\boxed{Qd = f(P, \text{Related goods}, Y, T, O)}$$ [2.3]

where: Qd = Quantity demanded; P = Price; Y = Income; T = Tastes; O = Other factors.
In this demand function, as in the original demand function, quantity demanded is the dependent variable. The variables within the parentheses represent independent variables.

Suppose we want to examine the relationship between quantity demanded and price. We can show this using the demand function:

$$Qd = f\,(P, \overline{\text{Related goods}}, \overline{Y}, \overline{T}, \overline{O})$$

There is a line over all of the independent variables with the exception of price. The line indicates that underlying variables or the conditions of demand are held constant. We can interpret this function in the same way that we interpreted the original demand function. Quantity demanded depends on price, *ceteris paribus*.

We now examine the distinction between a movement along the demand curve and a shift of the demand curve.

A movement along the demand curve

A movement along the demand curve is caused by a change in price. Because of the *ceteris paribus* clause, all other factors influencing demand are held constant. For example, a move along the demand curve from A to B, as in Figure 2.4, is caused by a fall in price. As price falls from €7.50 to €6.00 per kilogram, the quantity of Irish beef demanded increases from 2,000,000 to 2,375,000 kilograms per month. Similarly, a movement from B to A is caused by an increase in price.

FIGURE 2.4: A MOVEMENT ALONG THE DEMAND CURVE

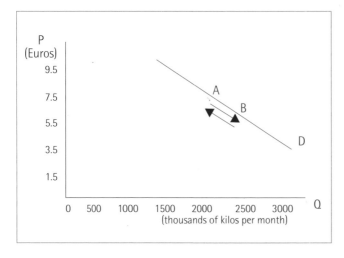

A shift of the demand curve

Suppose that one of the conditions of demand changes. For example, assume that income rises and beef is a normal good.

We can show this using the demand function:

$$Qd = f\,(\overline{P}, \overline{\text{Related goods}}, Y, \overline{T}, \overline{O})$$

In this case, there is a line over all of the independent variables except for Y, which represents income, the variable which is changing.

If one of the underlying variables changes, then each single point on the demand curve moves either out to the right or in to the left. Figure 2.5 shows the original demand curve, D. The second demand curve, D^1, reflects the increase in income. Every conceivable price corresponds to a higher level of demand. For example, at price P^0, demand increases from Q to Q^1. An improvement in the conditions of demand leads to a rightward shift of the demand curve.

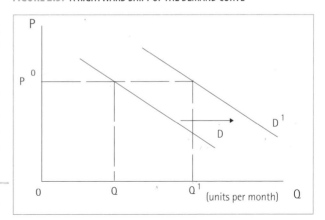

FIGURE 2.5: A RIGHTWARD SHIFT OF THE DEMAND CURVE

FIGURE 2.6: A LEFTWARD SHIFT OF THE DEMAND CURVE

If income had fallen for a normal good the shift would have been to the left. A deterioration in the conditions of demand leads to a leftward shift of the demand curve. This is shown in Figure 2.6.

Table 2.2 contains a number of possible changes in underlying factors which would result in either a rightward or a leftward shift of the demand curve. Draw these for yourself.

TABLE 2.2: CHANGES IN INDEPENDENT VARIABLES THAT CAUSE SHIFTS OF THE DEMAND CURVE

Independent variable	Rightward shift of demand curve	Leftward shift of demand curve
↑P substitute good	√	
↓P substitute good		√
↑P complement good		√
↓P complement good	√	
↑Y (normal good)	√	
↓Y (normal good)		√
↑Y (inferior good)		√
↓Y (inferior good)	√	
Preference improves	√	
Preference disimproves		√

CASE STUDY

Extract from *The Irish Independent*
Food firms 'must test for dioxins': Safety boss signals stricter regulations
for businesses after pork scare
by Aideen Sheehan

Food businesses in Ireland will be expected to test for dioxins in meat products in future, the Food Safety Authority of Ireland (FSAI) said yesterday. FSAI Deputy Chief Executive Alan Reilly told an Oireachtas Agriculture Committee looking into last month's pork contamination scare that Ireland historically had very low dioxin levels in the environment and in food, but its low-risk assessment would have to be reviewed. 'From now on, the FSAI would expect dioxins to be a hazard that is actively controlled in meat and meat products by . . . supplier control and testing by food business operators,' he said. Defending the proportionality of the total recall of Irish pork products, Mr Reilly said dioxins could cause cancer, disruption of the reproductive and immune systems, and damage to the skin in humans, and the more of them you put in your body, the greater the risk. 'Are we going to expose our children to these levels?' he said. People would not want to buy Irish pork containing 200 times the legal limit for dioxins when they could buy a competitive product below the legal threshold, he added. The FSAI concluded that ongoing exposure to the level of dioxins found in Irish pork during the crisis would have put consumers' health at risk.

The European Food Safety Authority calculated that the concentration of dioxins in the human body could have increased by 10% for an average consumer during the limited timescale of the incident, which affected Irish pork from September to December 2008. Dr Claudia Heppner of EFSA told the committee that, as effective measures had been taken, they considered this increase was of no concern. People who ate large amounts of contaminated pork throughout the period would not necessarily suffer adverse health effects, she added.

Mr Reilly stressed that the FSAI's remit extended from the farm gate onwards, with animal feed controls and inspections the responsibility of the Department of Agriculture.

Fine Gael Agriculture spokesman Michael Creed asked if a single agency should have control over the entire food and feed industry. Mr Reilly said that might be one of the topics considered in a review of the incident. The reason all Irish pork had to be withdrawn was that it was it impossible to distinguish between contaminated and uncontaminated pork at slaughterhouses, despite full traceability of individual pigs before slaughter, he added. The legislation could be amended to require full traceability but there would be likely to be a cost involved, he said. Committee Chairman Johnny Brady said the committee would produce its report on the scare in the coming weeks.

Source: The Irish Independent, 15 January 2009.

Questions

1. On one diagram, show the demand curve for Irish pork products before the pork scare and immediately after the pork scare. What changing variable caused the change in demand?
2. Did the above-mentioned change in the market for Irish pork products have 'knock-on' effects in any other markets? Explain your answer.
3. Consider the market for fish. Using the demand function, identify changes to underlying conditions which affected demand for this product. Show these changes on a diagram.

Answers on website

2.2 SUPPLY AND PRODUCERS

Supply and the quantity supplied can be analysed in a similar fashion to that of demand and the quantity demanded.

Definition

Supply is the quantity of the product that sellers are willing to offer at each conceivable price during a particular period of time.

It is not a particular quantity, but a whole set of quantities. Whereas demand is related to wants (supported by the ability to pay), supply is related to the use of resources. The time period may be hours, weeks, months or years.

Resources are 'inputs' which are used to produce products. These inputs or factors of production are land (or natural resources more generally), capital (or previously manufactured resources, e.g. machinery), labour and enterprise (or entrepreneurship). It is the cost of these factors of production that underlie the supply curve. This will be discussed in greater detail in Chapters 5, 6 and 7.

Again, we begin with price as the main explanatory variable. Quantity supplied is the dependent variable. This relationship can be written in a mathematical form, as follows:

$$Qs = f(P) \qquad [2.4]$$

where: Qs = Quantity supplied; P = Price.

This equation states that the quantity supplied depends on price. It is a function of price. There is a positive relationship between price and quantity supplied. We can examine the relationship between these two variables by looking at a supply schedule for beef.

Definition

A supply schedule is a schedule or table which indicates the quantity of a particular product which producers are willing to supply at various prices, over a particular period of time.

In this case, the factors that we are 'holding constant' include the wage of labour, the price of raw materials, the state of technology and government regulations (e.g. safety and environmental regulations). Table 2.3 shows the supply schedule for beef.

TABLE 2.3: THE SUPPLY SCHEDULE FOR BEEF (PER MONTH)

Price, P (Euros)	Quantity supplied, Qs (thousands of kilograms)
5.00	1,000
5.50	1,200
6.00	1,400
6.50	1,600
7.00	1,800
7.50	2,000
8.00	2,200
8.50	2,400
9.00	2,600
9.50	2,800

From the table, we can see that there is a positive relationship between price and quantity supplied. At €6.00 per kilogram, 1,400,000 kilograms of beef are supplied to the market. If the price increases to €7.50, producers are willing to supply 2,000,000 kilograms of beef to the market.

Again, we illustrate this relationship by plotting a supply curve on a two-dimensional graph. By plotting the range of prices on the vertical axis and the levels of quantity supplied on the horizontal axis, we can derive the upward sloping supply curve. Figure 2.7 illustrates the positive relationship between the two variables.

FIGURE 2.7: THE SUPPLY CURVE OF BEEF

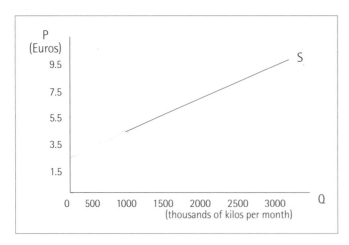

At this point, we will only offer an intuitive explanation about why the supply curve is upward sloping. A more rigorous explanation will be advanced in Chapter 6.

Notice that the supply curve starts above the origin. We can interpret this as meaning that if the price is less than €2.50 per kilogram, beef will not be supplied to the market. Producers must pay for inputs that include feedstuffs for cattle, fertiliser and machinery. At a price below €2.50, even the most efficient producer cannot cover costs and make a profit. Applying a concept we discussed in Chapter 1, the opportunity cost of producing beef is too high. Since we assume that producers attempt to maximise profits, we expect them to divert resources whenever possible to markets where they can do this. Farmers may move into tillage or sheep production until market conditions for beef improve.

At a price above €2.50, beef manufacturers begin production. As price increases, production expands. In doing so, resources may have to be diverted from the production of other goods to produce beef.

The supply curve can be represented in a linear form, as follows:

$$Qs = c + dP \qquad [2.5]$$

where: Qs = Quantity supplied; P = Price; c and d = constants.

Equation 2.5 is the general form of a linear relationship between price and quantity. The plus sign before the price variable reflects the positive relationship between the price and the quantity supplied. As price increases, so does the quantity supplied. The supply schedule for beef, which we have been discussing, is based on a linear relationship. The specific equation for this example is:

$$Qs = -1,000,000 + 400,000P$$

A supply curve may not be a straight line, depending on the nature of the producers' costs. A non-linear upward sloping supply curve is shown in Figure 2.8.

Exceptions to the upward sloping supply curve

The positive relationship between price and quantity supplied holds true for most products produced in competitive markets (see Chapter 6 for further details). There are, however, exceptions to this rule. One example is illustrated below.

FIGURE 2.8: A NON-LINEAR UPWARD SLOPING SUPPLY CURVE

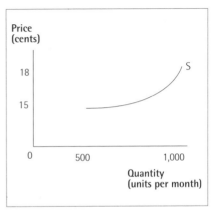

FIGURE 2.9: AN EXCEPTION TO THE UPWARD SLOPING SUPPLY CURVE

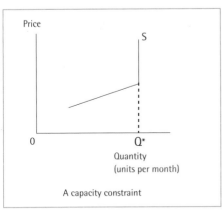

A capacity constraint

Figure 2.9 depicts a 'kinked' supply curve. The supply curve is upward sloping over a range of production. Then the supply curve changes and is vertical. Beyond Q*, firms operating in this market cannot respond to an increase in price because of limitations imposed by plant size, non-access to raw materials or the non-availability of skilled labour. The vertical part of the supply curve reflects maximum production capacity. It is impossible to produce beyond output level Q* because of this capacity constraint.

Factors such as the level of technology, the price of inputs or raw materials and the extent of government regulations will affect the position and shape of the supply curve.

Other factors influencing supply

1. Technology (T)
A supply curve is drawn for a particular technological process. A technological improvement means that suppliers can use inputs more efficiently, and the cost of producing a unit of output

falls. A technological improvement can result from improved machinery. It can also result from different work practices that make labour more efficient. Often, a technological improvement involves both new machinery and changing work practices.

2. Input prices (I)
Output is produced by using a certain combination of inputs, including labour, raw materials and machinery. A supply curve is drawn for a particular price (or cost) level for these factors of production. A reduction in input prices (e.g. lower wages, lower fertiliser costs, lower rental prices for machinery) induces farmers to supply more output at each price. Higher input prices, making production less profitable at each conceivable price, results in less output.

3. Government regulations (G)
Government regulations can positively or negatively affect producers' costs. Safety regulations that reduce accidents and safeguard the health of workers may be cost-reducing (e.g. the ban on smoking in the workplace). Compliance with restrictions and environmental regulations legislated by government can also increase the costs of firms operating in particular markets. Depending on the nature of the regulation, supply can be either positively or negatively affected.

4. Taxes (Tx)
Taxes on wages, property, utilities or other inputs increase the costs of production. A reduction in taxes decreases the costs of production.

5. Subsidies (Sy)
Government subsidies to producers decrease the cost per unit of output. Farmers have received extensive subsidies from the Irish government and the European Union. These were generally designed to supplement farm income so as to encourage people to remain in farming.

6. Other factors (O)
Other factors influencing the level of quantity supplied include the price of other commodities, expectations of the future, weather or climatic conditions and other unpredictable events.

The extended supply function is of the form:

$$\boxed{Qs = f(P, T, I, G, Tx, Sy, O)} \qquad [2.6]$$

where:　Qs = Quantity supplied; P = Price; T = Technology; I = Input costs;
　　　　G = Government regulations; Tx = Taxes; Sy = Subsidies; O = Other Factors.

Suppose we want to examine the relationship between quantity supplied and price. We can show this using the supply function:

$$Qs = f\,(P, \overline{T}, \overline{I}, \overline{G}, \overline{Tx}, \overline{Sy}, \overline{O})$$

There is a line over all of the independent variables with the exception of price. The line indicates that underlying variables or the conditions of supply are held constant. We can interpret this function in the same way that we interpreted the original supply function. Quantity supplied depends on price, *ceteris paribus*.

We now examine the distinction between a movement along the supply curve and a shift of the supply curve.

A movement along the supply curve

A movement along the supply curve is caused by a change in price. This is illustrated in Figure 2.10. The move along the supply curve from A to B is caused by an increase in price. As price rises from €5.00 to €6.50, quantity supplied rises from 1,000,000 to 1,600,000 units. Similarly, a decrease in price from €6.50 to €5.00 results in a fall in the level of quantity supplied. This is represented by a movement from B to A.

FIGURE 2.10: A MOVEMENT ALONG THE SUPPLY CURVE

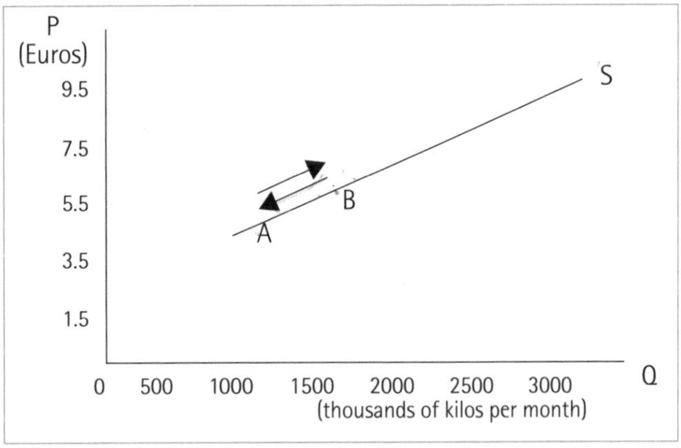

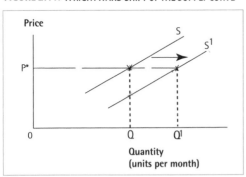

A shift of the supply curve

Suppose that one of the conditions of supply changes. For example, suppose the price of hay, which is used to feed cattle in the winter, falls. Hay is one input used in the production of beef. We can show this change using the supply function.

$$Qs = f\,(\overline{P}, \overline{T}, I, \overline{G}, \overline{Tx}, \overline{Sy}, \overline{O})$$

In this case, there is a line above all of the variables with the exception of I, which represents the price of an input which is changing. Because the price of the input falls, farmers can supply cattle, which are used for beef, at a lower cost.

FIGURE 2.11: A RIGHTWARD SHIFT OF THE SUPPLY CURVE

We can illustrate this improvement by a rightward shift of the supply curve, as shown in Figure 2.11. Because of the change in an underlying variable, the supply curve shifts from S to S¹. If we hold the quantity constant, we observe that Q units of beef can be produced at a lower cost per kilogram.

This rightward shift indicates an increase in supply. For example, at price P*, the quantity of beef supplied increases from Q to Q¹. At each price, more kilos of beef are produced.

Alternatively, suppose that the European Union decides to eliminate a subsidy payment on cattle. We can show this change using the supply function:

$$Qs = f\,(\overline{P}, \overline{T}, \overline{I}, \overline{G}, \overline{Tx}, Sy, \overline{O})$$

In this case, the line is above all of the variables with the exception of Sy, which represents the subsidy which is changing.

Figure 2.12 shows the original supply curve (S) which reflects beef production with the subsidy in place. Supply curve S¹ illustrates the new supply curve reflecting the elimination of the subsidy. This model predicts that if the subsidy on cattle is eliminated, it will lead to a reduction in the supply of beef.

Table 2.4 contains a number of possible changes in the underlying factors that result in either a rightward or a leftward shift of the supply curve. Draw the supply curves for yourself.

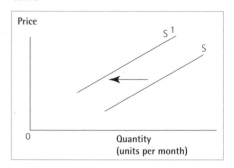

FIGURE 2.12: A LEFTWARD SHIFT OF THE SUPPLY CURVE

TABLE 2.4: CHANGES IN UNDERLYING FACTORS THAT CAUSE SHIFTS OF THE SUPPLY CURVE

Independent variable	Rightward shift of supply curve	Leftward shift of supply curve
Technological improvement	√	
↑ I	√	
↓ I	√	√
G (cost saving)	√	
G (cost increasing)		√
↑ Tx	√	√
↓ Tx	√	√
↑ Sy	√	√
↓ Sy	√	√

2.3 MARKET EQUILIBRIUM AND THE PRICE MECHANISM

So far, we have looked at consumers and producers separately. In a market, the (market) demand curve, which represents the collective purchasing decisions of all consumers for a particular product, interacts with the (market) supply curve, which shows how much of the same product firms produce. When consumers and firms interact, as reflected in the intersection of the demand curve and the supply curve, price and quantity are established, as we will soon demonstrate.

Market equilibrium

Alfred Marshall (1842–1924), the economist most noted for bringing demand and supply to the forefront of economic thinking, compared demand and supply to the blades of a pair of scissors (see Appendix 2.1). The demand curve shows the negative relationship between price and quantity demanded. The supply curve shows the positive relationship between price and quantity supplied.

In a market economy, price is determined by both sides of the market.

> **Definition**
>
> *Price can be defined as that which is given in exchange for a product.*

It is impossible to say whether it is (market) demand or (market) supply that determines the market price, just as it is impossible to say which blade of Marshall's scissors does the actual cutting. Price is determined by the interactions of consumers and producers. Theoretically, the consumer and the producer are equally important participants in the market.

It is the interaction of the demand curve and the supply curve that determines the quantity that will be traded in the market and the price that will be charged. There is one price and one quantity where the actions of the buyers and sellers coincide. We call this point equilibrium, a concept used frequently by economists.

> **Definition**
>
> *Equilibrium implies a state of balance, a position from which there is no tendency to change.*

At equilibrium, the market 'clears' in the sense that the quantity demanded equals the quantity supplied. At all other prices, either quantity demanded is greater than quantity supplied (excess demand) or quantity supplied is greater than quantity demanded (excess supply).

The equilibrium price does not reflect equity or fairness or any other moral concept. It simply reflects the positions of the demand and supply curves, which, in turn, represent the interaction of the two basic economic agents in the marketplace.

The role of price

The role of price in a market economy is very important. Price can signal, allocate and motivate. Think of how much information is conveyed by this single piece of information. In most cases, we do not have to conduct a market survey to see if consumers like a product or if they value it in comparison to other products. Similarly, we do not have to contact all possible producers to examine their production methods. Instead, price is the information link between buyers and sellers. Buyers indicate that a price is too high if they do not purchase a product, causing inventories to accumulate. Similarly, producers may deduce that a price is too low if inventories are depleted and consumers are left waiting for a product. Price is the signal used to communicate information between buyers and sellers.

Price also has an important role in allocating society's resources. Figure 2.13 illustrates the price mechanism at work in the market. By observing a change in consumer preferences from product X to product Y, we can clearly see the important role of price.

The falling price of product X and the higher price paid for product Y signals a change in the market, which is communicated from the consumers to current and potential producers. The potential for higher profits causes a reallocation of resources away from the production of product X and towards the production of product Y. It is profit which is assumed to act as the motivating force in a market economy. This means that more of the scarce resources of society are being allocated to the production of product Y, the product preferred by consumers.

FIGURE 2.13: THE ROLE OF PRICE IN THE ALLOCATION OF RESOURCES

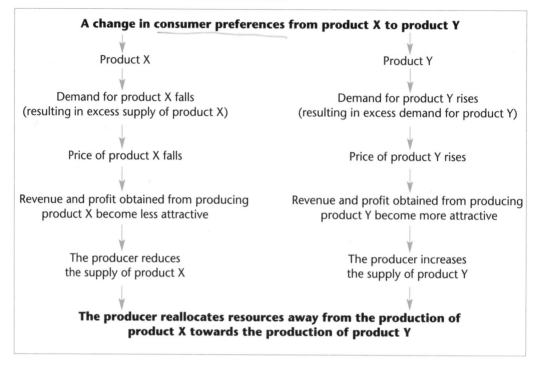

A change in consumer preferences from product X to product Y

Product X   Product Y

Demand for product X falls   Demand for product Y rises
(resulting in excess supply of product X)   (resulting in excess demand for product Y)

Price of product X falls   Price of product Y rises

Revenue and profit obtained from producing   Revenue and profit obtained from producing
product X become less attractive   product Y become more attractive

The producer reduces   The producer increases
the supply of product X   the supply of product Y

**The producer reallocates resources away from the production of
product X towards the production of product Y**

In all economies and societies, some form of mechanism must exist in order to allocate resources. In a pure market economy, it is the price mechanism that addresses the three basic questions in economics: what is produced, how it is produced and for whom it is produced. The price mechanism is an automatic process. No central agency is required to signal, allocate or motivate. The market, through adjustments in prices, carries out these functions.

This does not mean that we can rely on the price mechanism to ensure that all the products that we value as a society are produced. In particular, in many cases, the demand curve and the supply curve do not convey all the important information needed to allocate society's resources. We will discuss externalities, the provision of public goods and market failures more generally in Chapter 8.

Figure 2.14 illustrates a market for beef. The demand curve is represented by D and the supply curve is represented by S. It is the intersection of the consumers' demand curve D with the producers' supply curve S which determines the equilibrium price and quantity E in this market. The intersection is at a price of €7.50. This is the only price where quantity demanded (2,000,000 kilograms) is equal to quantity supplied (2,000,000 kilograms). In equilibrium, there is neither excess demand nor excess supply.

The equilibrium price and quantity (P, Q) can also be derived mathematically from a pair of linear equations. The general format of the two-variable demand and supply equations is as follows:

$$Qd = a - bP$$
[2.2]

$$Qs = c + dP$$
[2.5]

We can solve for price and quantity using these equations. In general, the equilibrium condition is as follows:

$$Qd = Qe = Qs \qquad [2.7]$$

where: Qe = equilibrium quantity.

The demand curve for beef was given by the equation Qd = 3,875,000 – 250,000P, whereas the supply curve was given by Qs = –1,000,000 + 400,000P. Solve for price and quantity using these simultaneous equations as follows:

$$3,875,000 - 250,000P = Qe = -1,000,000 + 400,000P$$

Solving for the unknown P, we get:

$$3,875,000 - 250,000P = -1,000,000 + 400,000P$$
$$4,875,000 = 650,000P$$
$$P = 7.50$$

If P = 7.50, then we can solve for the unknown Qe. This is solved by substituting P = 7.50 into either the demand or the supply equation since, in equilibrium, the quantity demanded equals the quantity supplied.

$$Qe = 3,875,000 - 250,000(7.50) = 3,875,000 - 1,875,000 = 2,000,000$$

The equilibrium price and quantity is (7.50, 2,000,000). This is the same equilibrium which is illustrated using the demand curve and the supply curve in Figure 2.14.

FIGURE 2.14: THE MARKET FOR BEEF

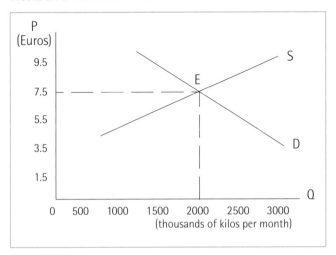

Tending towards market equilibrium

At all prices above the equilibrium price, quantity supplied is greater than quantity demanded. This is illustrated in Figure 2.15.

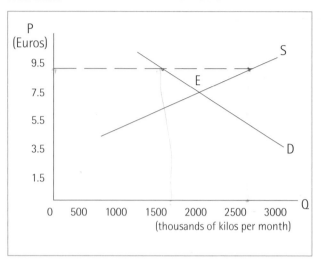

FIGURE 2.15: EXCESS SUPPLY IN THE MARKET FOR BEEF

At €9.00, suppliers are willing to supply 2,600,000 kilos, whereas consumers demand only 1,625,000 kilos. At this price there exists excess supply or surplus. We can actually estimate the amount of excess supply. At a price of €9.00 there is an excess supply of 975,000 kilos of beef (2,600,000 – 1,625,000).

In order for the market to clear, quantity demanded must equal quantity supplied. In this particular case, suppliers cut price in order to eliminate the excess inventory or surplus. Price continues to fall. As price falls, quantity supplied falls whereas quantity demanded rises. Thus, as price adjusts downwards, the excess is eliminated.

Remember, in a market economy, prices are allowed to adjust in order for markets to clear. Prices are continually cut until the excess is eliminated. In this particular market, price must fall to €7.50 before the excess is completely eliminated. At €7.50 the beef market returns to equilibrium.

At all prices below the equilibrium price, quantity demanded is greater than quantity supplied. This is illustrated in Figure 2.16.

At €6.00, consumers demand 2,375,000 units, but suppliers are only willing to supply 1,400,000 units. In this example there exists excess demand or a shortage. We can estimate the actual amount of excess demand. At a price of €6.00 there is excess demand of 975,000 kilos of beef (2,375,000 – 1,400,000).

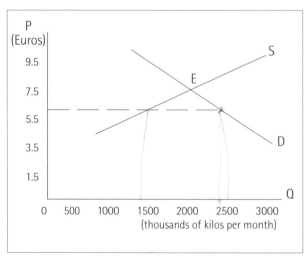

FIGURE 2.16: EXCESS DEMAND IN THE MARKET FOR BEEF

In order for the market to clear, quantity demanded must equal quantity supplied. Suppliers increase price, and by doing so the excess demand or shortage is eliminated. As price rises, quantity supplied rises and quantity demanded falls. Price continues to rise until quantity demanded is equal to quantity supplied. At €7.50 the market returns to equilibrium.

These two cases illustrate how market pressures or market forces, operating through the price mechanism, lead to equilibrium. The speed of the adjustment in prices depends on a number of factors. The size of transaction costs, the number of competitors in the market and the availability of information influence the speed of adjustment. The equilibrium level of price and quantity remains constant unless there is a change in either the conditions of demand or supply or a combination of both.

A change in the conditions of demand

Figure 2.17 illustrates an equilibrium position, E, with quantity demanded equal to quantity supplied.

Suppose income rises. For a normal good, an increase in income shifts the demand curve out and to the right from D to D^1. Equilibrium is no longer at E. A new equilibrium is reached at E^1. The diagram indicates an increase in equilibrium price and an increase in equilibrium quantity. We need to explain the adjustment process by which we move from E to E^1.

FIGURE 2.17: A CHANGE IN THE CONDITIONS OF DEMAND

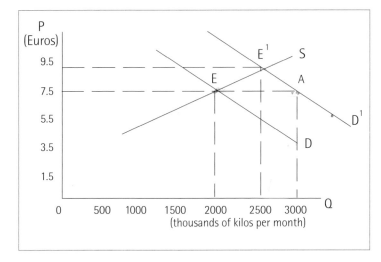

At the old equilibrium price of €7.50, quantity demanded is equal to quantity supplied. However, as income increases the quantity demanded increases at that particular price (and at all other price levels). At €7.50, the new level of quantity demanded is 3,000,000 kilos. Quantity supplied is still at the old level of 2,000,000 units. At the old equilibrium price there is excess demand. This is shown by the segment marked |EA| in Figure 2.17. The actual amount of excess demand is 3,000,000 − 2,000,000 = 1,000,000 kilos.

In a market economy, excess demand signals disequilibrium. Price adjusts in order for equilibrium to be restored. Suppliers respond to excess demand by increasing price. As price rises from €7.50, quantity supplied rises and quantity demanded falls. Price continues to be pushed up until all the excess demand disappears. As price approaches €9.00 the excess demand is eliminated. At €9.00 the market clears. The new equilibrium quantity is 2,600,000 kilos. Due to an increase in income, both equilibrium price and equilibrium quantity increase.

A change in any factor that results in a rightward shift of the demand curve leads to an increase in the equilibrium price and quantity. Similarly, a change in any factor which results in a leftward shift of the demand curve leads to a decrease in both equilibrium price and quantity.

A change in the conditions of supply

Figure 2.18 illustrates an equilibrium position E.

Suppose that technology improves. This means that, in theory, the same amount of inputs can now produce more output. In graphic terms an improvement in technology shifts our supply curve to the right. Equilibrium is no longer at E. A new equilibrium is reached at E¹. The diagram indicates a decrease in equilibrium price and an increase in equilibrium quantity. What is the adjustment process?

At the old equilibrium price of €7.50, the equilibrium quantity is 2,000,000 kilos. However, due to the technological improvement the quantity supplied increases at that particular price (and at all other price levels). The new

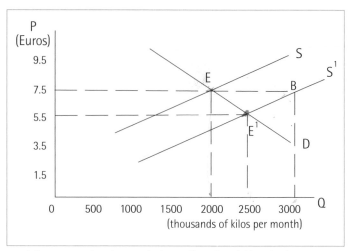

FIGURE 2.18: A CHANGE IN THE CONDITIONS OF SUPPLY

level of quantity supplied is 3,000,000 kilos. Quantity demanded is still at the old level of 2,000,000 kilos. At the old equilibrium price there exists excess supply. This is shown by the segment marked |EB| in Figure 2.18. The actual amount of excess supply is 3,000,000 – 2,000,000 = 1,000,000 kilos.

Price adjusts in order to restore equilibrium. Suppliers respond to excess supply by reducing prices. As price falls from €7.50, the quantity demanded rises and the quantity supplied falls. Price continues to be pushed down until all the excess supply is eliminated. At €5.50 the market clears.

E¹ represents the new equilibrium. Equilibrium price is €5.50 and the equilibrium quantity is 2,375,000 kilos. Due to the improvement in technology, the equilibrium price falls and the equilibrium quantity rises. Any factor that results in a rightward shift of the supply curve leads to a decrease in the equilibrium price and an increase in equilibrium quantity. Similarly, any factor that causes a leftward shift of the supply curve results in an increase in equilibrium price and a decrease in equilibrium quantity.

A change in the conditions of demand and supply

In the market for beef, the conditions of demand and supply are constantly changing. Consider the following scenario. Suppose there is decrease in the price of lamb, a substitute product for beef. The demand function for beef shows that the quantity of beef demanded is a function of the price of a related product, *ceteris paribus*. This variable is changing while all of the other variables are remaining constant.

$$Qd = f\,(\overline{P}, \text{Related goods}, \overline{Y}, \overline{T}, \overline{O})$$

A decrease in the price of the substitute product shifts the demand curve for beef to the left.

At the same time, an outbreak of tuberculosis requires that a significant percentage of the national herd be destroyed. This extraordinary event is shown by a change in 'other factors'.

$$Qs = f(\overline{P}, \overline{T}, \overline{I}, \overline{G}, \overline{Tx}, \overline{Sy}, O)$$

This calamity leads to a leftward shift of the supply curve for beef.

What can we deduce about the new equilibrium? We can say, unambiguously, that the equilibrium quantity will decrease. The shift of either curve to the left will lead to that result. But can we be as certain about price? Consider Figure 2.19.

FIGURE 2.19: ALTERNATIVE SCENARIOS FOR DEMAND AND SUPPLY CURVE SHIFTS IN THE MARKET FOR BEEF

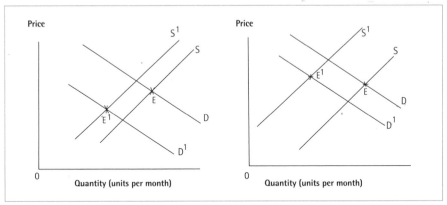

The left panel of Figure 2.19 is drawn to show a demand curve shift which is far greater than the supply curve shift. As a result, equilibrium price falls. The right panel of Figure 2.19 is drawn to show a relatively small demand curve shift and a relatively large supply curve shift. In this case, equilibrium price has risen. We cannot predict the direction of change of the equilibrium price unless we have more information about the magnitude of the changes in both demand and supply.

This simple example exposes one of the limitations of this type of analysis. We can confidently predict the direction of change of the market equilibrium, if – and only if – one change occurs.

2.4 PRICE CONTROLS

In a market economy, price is determined by demand and supply. In a planned economy, this is not the case. It is government, through a particular department or pricing authority, that decides not only which products to produce, but also what prices to charge.

Involvement by the state in the market is not restricted to planned economies. Authorities in the European Union and the United States have regularly intervened in certain markets (e.g. agricultural markets) with a variety of mechanisms designed to maintain domestic production levels and to supplement income. More generally, tax incentives and grants are frequently used by the Irish government to promote certain kinds of activity (such as training and research and development) or to attract certain types of industry (such as multinational manufacturing subsidiaries). Many types of intervention are quite complex and at times it is difficult to disentangle their likely effects on the market for a particular product. Indeed, all real-world economies are mixed economies containing many elements of a market economy and many elements of a planned economy.

One of the easiest and most transparent forms of market intervention is price controls.

Definition

Price controls are government regulations which limit the ability of the market to determine price.

In the presence of price controls, the price level will generally not equate market demand with market supply. An adjustment towards market equilibrium will not result because prices are fixed.

Two common types of price control are price ceilings and price floors.

Price ceilings

> **Definition**
>
> *A price ceiling is a maximum price on a product legislated by the government.*

When implemented, the supplier cannot charge above this 'maximum' price. Its basic purpose is to help consumers. It is usually imposed in times of scarcity. Without the imposition of a price ceiling, scarce supply would usually result in a high equilibrium price. The government may regard this high price level as undesirable, particularly in a market for basic products such as food, fuel and accommodation.

In order to make these products more affordable, the government sets a price below this high equilibrium price. It does so by imposing a price ceiling, which is legislated by the authorities at a price below the market clearing level. We know from the previous section that any price level below the equilibrium results in excess demand. However, prices will not adjust upwards in order for the market to clear. Prices are fixed at this level. It is illegal for suppliers to increase price in order to eliminate excess demand. This excess demand, or shortage, can become a permanent feature of the market.

Price controls are particularly common during periods of crisis like wars or natural disasters. During the Emergency (World War II), price controls were placed on many products, including tea.

Figure 2.20 shows the market for tea. In the absence of price controls, the price of tea would have been unaffordable to many Irish households. This price is represented by P^0. The government intervened and legislated that the price of tea could not exceed 3 shillings and sixpence per pound weight. This was approximately one sixth of a pound before decimalisation, or about €0.22. This is represented by P^* in Figure 2.20.

However, because of the lower price, quantity demanded increases whereas quantity supplied decreases. The net result is excess demand at this new price level. The shortage caused by the price ceiling is indicated on the diagram as the distance between point A and point B.

FIGURE 2.20: IMPOSITION OF A PRICE CEILING

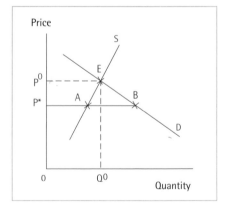

To mitigate the problems caused by the scarcity of tea, the government opted for a system of rationing. Rationing means that the government restricts the amount of a commodity that consumers are allowed to buy. During the Emergency, every man, woman and child was entitled to purchase 1.5 ounces of tea per week from their grocer.

A system of price controls and rationing often leads to the emergence of a 'black market'. In this instance, the black market refers to illegal activities of buyers and sellers who trade for prices above the legislated price ceiling. The 'black market' price of tea during the Emergency was 'a pound for a pound'. This price was approximately six times higher than the price ceiling imposed by the government. At today's prices (2011), a pound of tea on the black market would cost over €30!

To summarise, although there may be reasons to impose price controls in conditions of scarcity of essential commodities, there are a number of negative side effects. Organising the price control and a system of rationing is expensive, particularly if there are large numbers of consumers and suppliers. Shortages eventually lead to black market activities. If the controls are to be taken seriously, the government must police the market and prosecute offenders. All of these costs, both explicit and implicit, must be added together and matched against the benefits that consumers and society will receive. Unless the need is very compelling, the opportunity cost may be too high. For this reason, governments in developed countries rarely impose price controls.

Price floors

> **Definition**
>
> *A price floor is a minimum price legislated by government on a product.*

When a price floor is implemented, the seller is not legally permitted to sell the product below this price. The basic purpose of a price floor is to help producers (although a ban on below-cost selling of alcohol may represent an exception). In order for the supplier to attain a price higher than the market price, the government can impose a price floor above the market level. Any price level above the market price results in excess supply. However, since prices are fixed they cannot adjust downwards in order for the market to clear. The resulting excess supply or surplus can become a permanent feature of the market. The surplus is generally purchased by a government agency or exported.

A relatively recent example of a price floor was the intervention price within the Common Agricultural Policy (CAP). This price floor was imposed by the EU in some agricultural markets. In theory, if price fell below a particular price, EU agencies 'intervened' and bought the surplus stocks of agricultural products.

Figure 2.21 illustrates the beef market and the imposition of intervention prices.

With no price controls the market price would be P^0. However, because of CAP, suppliers (farmers) were guaranteed fixed prices which were above the market price. This was operated by setting a price floor at P^*. This minimum price resulted in excess supply represented by the distance between points A and B. The surplus, however, was not eliminated through a downward adjustment of prices. The suppliers knew that the surplus would be purchased by EU intervention agencies and put into storage. It was the imposition of price floors that explained the existence of the infamous 'wine lakes' and 'butter mountains', as well as the beef surplus. Up to €3.7 billion worth of food stocks were, at one time, in intervention.[4]

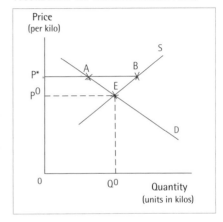

FIGURE 2.21: CAP AND INTERVENTION PRICES

In the example above, we can see that the benefits received by farmers imposed a cost on other sectors of society. First, the consumers were paying P*, which was higher than the market equilibrium price. Second, the intervention bureaucracy was expensive to operate. Various EU and national government agencies were involved in the inspection of produce and the payment of subsidies. Also, any surplus had to be stored or exported. The higher price of food was absorbed by EU consumers. The cost of administering the programme was paid for by EU taxpayers. When we look at it this way, we can see that a price floor is really a method of income redistribution from one section of society (consumers and taxpayers) to another (producers).

SUMMARY

1. Demand is a specific term used by economists to explain consumers' wants, supported by the ability and desire to pay, for a product. The demand curve illustrates the negative relationship between price and quantity demanded. It is drawn on the assumption that all other factors are held constant. There is an important distinction between a change in quantity demanded (a movement along the demand curve) and a change in demand (a shift of the demand curve).
2. Supply is a specific term used by economists to explain the amount of a product supplied to the market. The implicit assumption is that the motivating force behind production is profit. There is a positive relationship between price and quantity supplied and this is represented by an upward sloping supply curve. All other factors are assumed to be held constant. There is a distinction between a movement along the supply curve (change in quantity supplied) and a shift of the supply curve (change in supply).
3. Consumers and producers interact in the market and, in doing so, determine a market-clearing price. This market price, in graphic terms, occurs at the intersection of the demand curve and the supply curve. Adjustment to equilibrium is an automatic process in the market system. Any excess demand results in a price rise whereas any excess supply leads to a price fall.
4. Central to the market economy is the price mechanism. Prices play many key roles: they allocate resources, provide incentives, signal changes and reward economic agents.
5. Demand and supply analysis is a very useful tool in the study of economics. Changes in demand and supply conditions and intervention by the state affect the market price and can be analysed using basic demand and supply diagrams.
6. Even in market economies, some prices are legislated by government in the form of price controls. Price ceilings (maximum) and price floors (minimum) are two types of price control. Some elements of price controls can be found in market economies, e.g. rent controls, various alcohol price controls and, albeit in a slightly different context, minimum wage regulations.

KEY TERMS

Market	Supply
Demand	Factors of production
Quantity demanded	Quantity supplied
Demand schedule	Supply schedule
Ceteris paribus	Price
Principle of demand	Equilibrium
Demand curve	Price mechanism
Veblen good	Surplus
Giffen good	Shortage
Substitutes	Price controls
Complements	Price ceilings
Normal good	Price floors
Inferior good	

REVIEW QUESTIONS

1. Explain the principle of demand. Describe possible exceptions to the downward sloping demand curve. In particular, consider the case of housing. Is there an upward sloping demand curve for housing in Ireland? Explain your answer.
2. Explain why the supply curve has a positive slope. Describe a possible exception.
3. What does the concept 'equilibrium' mean? How do markets which exhibit excess demand and excess supply 'clear' or return to equilibrium?
4. Explain the following economic terms:
   (a) substitute
   (b) complement
   (c) normal good
   (d) inferior good
   (e) Veblen good
   (f) Giffen good.
5. (a) Explain what effect an improvement in preferences or tastes would have on the equilibrium price and quantity of a product.
   (b) Explain what effect a decrease in the price of inputs would have on the equilibrium price and quantity of a product.
6 How does the price mechanism within a market economy differ from that which would operate in a planned economy? In what way does a price ceiling or a price floor interfere with the price mechanism? Why might they be imposed?

WORKING PROBLEMS

1. Consider the following equations:

$$Qd = -2P + 40$$
$$Qs = 6P - 20$$

(a) Find the equilibrium using simultaneous equations. $Qd = Qs$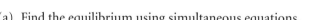

$Qd = 24$ (b) On a diagram, sketch the demand curve and the supply curve.

$Qs = 28$ (c) Suppose P = 20. Calculate the shortage or surplus. $Qd = 0$

surplus of   (d) Suppose P = 8. Calculate the shortage or surplus. $Qs = 100$

4

$Qs > Qd =)$ Surplus of 100.

2. Consider the market for opera shown in Figure 2.22. C

FIGURE 2.22: MARKET FOR OPERA

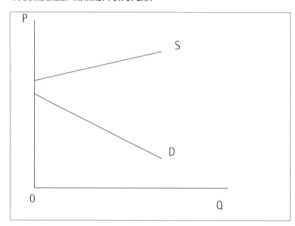

(a) If the government does not intervene in this market, will opera be supplied to the market? No

(b) Will a form of price control be effective in this situation? No

(c) Will a subsidy to suppliers be effective in this situation? Yes

(d) Why might a government intervene in this type of market?

MULTI-CHOICE QUESTIONS

1. Which of the following 'events' will cause a rightward shift in the demand curve for wine (assume that wine is a normal good)?
   (a) an increase in the price of beer;
   (b) a decrease in income;
   (c) an increase in the price of cheese (assume that cheese and wine are complements);
   (d) none of the above.

2. Which of the following 'events' will cause the supply curve for wine to shift to the right?
   (a) a frost kills half of the grape crop;
   (b) there is an improvement in technology;
   (c) there is an increase in the wage paid to labour;
   (d) a study is produced which confirms that drinking wine improves your health;
   (e) none of the above.

3. The price of coffee will tend to fall if:
   (a) there is a surplus at the current price;
   (b) the current price is above equilibrium;
   (c) the quantity supplied exceeds the quantity demanded at the current price;
   (d) all of the above;
   (e) none of the above.

4. A technological improvement lowers the cost of producing coffee. At the same time, a study is published that states that drinking coffee causes heart disease. In response to these 'events', the new equilibrium quantity of coffee will:
   (a) rise;
   (b) fall;
   (c) remain the same;
   (d) rise or fall, depending on the relative shifts of the demand and supply curves.

5. Suppose the market for milk is described by the following equations:

$$Qd = 150 - P$$
$$Qs = -50 + P$$

Q = quantity (litres of milk per day)
P = price (cents)

Further, suppose the government implements a price floor at P = 120. What can we predict will happen in this market?

   (a) there will be shortage of 70 litres;
   (b) the market will clear;
   (c) there will be a surplus of 70 litres;
   (d) there will be a surplus of 40 litres;
   (e) it is impossible to say with the information given.

6. Which of the following statements accurately describes a price ceiling?
    (a) it is generally designed to help producers;
    •(b) it is generally designed to help consumers;
    (c) a surplus may be a permanent feature of this market;
    (d) a shortage may be a permanent feature of this market;
    (e) both statements (b) and (d) accurately describe a price ceiling.

TRUE OR FALSE (SUPPORT YOUR ANSWER)

1. The demand curve for a Giffen good slopes downwards from left to right.
2. Maximimising revenue is the motivating force behind production and supply.
3. An increase in the costs of production reduces supply and, in turn, forces up the market price.
4. Excess demand in a market economy would force prices down towards the equilibrium level.
5. A price floor is a form of price control generally designed to help the consumer.
6. A price ceiling is set below market equilibrium.

CASE STUDY

Extract from *The Irish Times*
U2 tickets go on sale
by Daniel Attwood

Some 160,000 tickets for U2's Croke Park concerts this summer went on sale at 8 a.m. in Dublin this morning. Unprecedented demand to see the band perform to a home crowd is expected to ensure they are quickly sold out. According to Justin Green, spokesman for promoter, MCD, demand for the tickets will be unparalleled. 'The reaction to this tour has been unprecedented, we have never seen anything like this before.' The tickets for the Irish leg of the Vertigo world tour are priced at €59.50, €70, and €80. The promoters are hoping to arrange a third concert.

The Vertigo tour has sold out at each venue throughout the world as soon as tickets became available. In Britain, 260,000 tickets were sold within hours of them becoming available. In Brussels, 53,000 tickets were sold in less than four hours. In the US, 370,000 tickets have been sold for the gigs there.

However, sales have been marred by a controversy surrounding the pre-selling of some tickets that were offered to subscribers to the band's website. Even though they only became officially available at 8 a.m. today, pre-sold tickets were already being offered last night for both the June 24th and 25th dates in Croke Park. One British website was offering seated tickets for €335 each. The band has asked fans to report resellers. 'Some of these touts have posed as genuine U2 fans, taken out a subscription and bought tickets in the pre-sale only to re-advertise them for huge sums,' said U2's website.

Source: The Irish Times, 4 February 2005.

Questions

1. From an economics perspective, were official U2 tickets under-priced or over-priced? Explain your answer.
2. Why might promoters of popular events (e.g. pop concerts or sporting events) deliberately under-price tickets?
3. If it is expected that tickets for popular events (e.g. pop concerts or sporting events) will be under-priced, what actions might be expected of and by (a) genuine fans; and (b) ticket touts? What reasonable actions might be expected of the promoters of these events? What reasonable actions might be expected of government?

APPENDIX 2.1: THE HISTORY OF DEMAND AND SUPPLY ANALYSIS

Most textbooks today explain the price mechanism with the aid of demand and supply analysis. Changes in the market price are explained by changes in the conditions of demand and/or supply. This analysis is simplified further by the use of the two-dimensional demand/supply diagram. However, this was not always the case.

At certain times throughout history different theories of price and value have been espoused. Some economists focused primarily on the demand side of the market and the concept of utility. These include W. Stanley Jevons (1835–82) and Leon Walras (1834–1910) of the neoclassical school of economic thought. In contrast, the classical school, led by David Ricardo (1772–1823) and John Stuart Mill (1806–73), concentrated on the supply side and the costs of production. The economist primarily responsible for bringing consumers and producers together, for studying the interaction of demand and supply and for ultimately pushing this analysis to the forefront of economic thinking was the Professor of Political Economy at the University of Cambridge, Alfred Marshall. The familiar demand and supply diagram appeared in Marshall's book *Principles of Economics* in 1890. The actual drawing is reproduced below in Figure 2.23.

FIGURE 2.23: ALFRED MARSHALL'S ORIGINAL DEMAND AND SUPPLY DIAGRAM

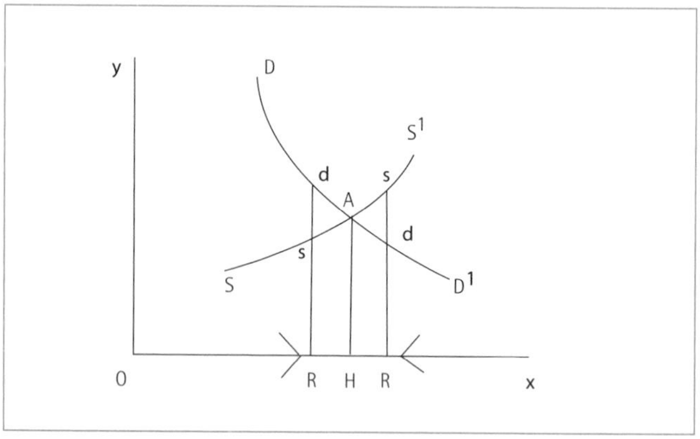

Source: Alfred Marshall, *Principles of Economics*, 8th edition.

CHAPTER 3

Elasticities of Demand and Supply

'Tax the rich until the pips squeak'.

ATTRIBUTED TO DENIS HEALEY (1917–)[1]

'It is clear that economics, if it is to be a science at all, must be a mathematical science.'[2]

W. STANLEY JEVONS (1835–82)

CHAPTER OBJECTIVES

Upon completing this chapter, the student should understand:

- the concept of price elasticity of demand;
- determinants of price elasticity;
- the relationship between price elasticity and total revenue;
- cross-price elasticity and income elasticity;
- price elasticity of supply.

OUTLINE

3.1 Price elasticity of demand
3.2 Cross-price elasticity of demand
3.3 Income elasticity of demand
3.4 Elasticity of supply

INTRODUCTION

The demand curve illustrates the negative relationship between price and quantity demanded. Therefore, if price increases, we can confidently predict that the quantity demanded will fall, *ceteris paribus*. In Chapter 2, we described this relationship as the principle of demand. Although the principle is useful, from a producer's point of view, it is not enough. The producer would like to know the sensitivity or responsiveness of quantity demanded to changes in price. Why? Total revenue depends not only on price, but also on the quantity sold. The producer would like to know if the additional revenue generated from the price increase will more than offset the revenue lost arising from the subsequent or associated decrease in sales.

The relevant economic concept is elasticity. This term was first used in an economic context by the British economist Alfred Marshall.

Definition

Elasticity measures the percentage change in one variable in response to a percentage change in another variable.

Elasticity should be carefully distinguished from slope or gradient, which measures the (absolute) change in one variable in response to the (absolute) change in another variable, i.e. percentages are not considered.

A producer is particularly interested in the percentage change in quantity demanded that results from a percentage change in price. This is one of three forms of elasticities of demand. Specifically, they include:

*   Price elasticity of demand, ε, which measures the sensitivity (in terms of percentages) of quantity demanded to changes in price.
*   Cross-price elasticity of demand, $\varepsilon_{A,B}$ which measures the sensitivity (in terms of percentages) of quantity demanded of product A to changes in the price of product B.
*   Income elasticity of demand, η, which measures the sensitivity (in terms of percentages) of quantity demanded to changes in income.

The first three sections of this chapter examine these three elasticities of demand. The final section provides a brief explanation of the price elasticity of supply. This considers the degree of responsiveness (in terms of percentages) of quantity supplied to changes in price.

3.1 PRICE ELASTICITY OF DEMAND

Definition

Price elasticity of demand measures the responsiveness (in terms of percentages) of quantity demanded to changes in the price of the same product.

It is sometimes referred to as own-price elasticity of demand. The additional term 'own' distinguishes it from cross-price elasticity. The formula for calculating the price elasticity of demand is as follows:

$$\varepsilon = \frac{\%\ \textbf{Change in Quantity Demanded}}{\%\ \textbf{Change in Price}} = \frac{\frac{Q_2 - Q_1}{Q_1} \times 100}{\frac{P_2 - P_1}{P_1} \times 100} = \frac{\frac{\Delta Q}{Q} \times 100}{\frac{\Delta P}{P} \times 100} \qquad [3.1]$$

where Q_1 = original quantity demanded; Q_2 = new quantity demanded; ΔQ = change in quantity demanded; P_1 = original price; P_2 = new price and ΔP = change in price.

We can make much sense of this formula by way of example.

The Cake Shop in Clifden is the only location in town that sells locally baked bread. The owner checks her records and notices that she sells 250 loaves per week at a price of €1. She increases the price to €1.10. The level of demand falls to 200 loaves. What is the price elasticity of demand, the single numeric value which describes the responsiveness (in terms of percentages) of quantity demanded to changes in price for this particular example? It is explained in the following few steps:

Step 1

$$\frac{P_2 - P_1}{P_1} \times 100 = \frac{1.10 - 1.00}{1.00} \times 100 = \frac{.10}{1.00} \times 100 = 10\%$$

Calculate the percentage change in price.
There is a 10% change (increase) in price.

Step 2

$$\frac{Q_2 - Q_1}{Q_1} \times 100 = \frac{200 - 250}{250} \times 100 = \frac{-50}{250} \times 100 = -20\%$$

Calculate the percentage change in quantity demanded.
There is a 20% change (decrease) in quantity demanded.

Step 3

$$\varepsilon = \frac{\%\ \text{Change in Quantity Demanded}}{\%\ \text{Change in Price}} = \frac{\frac{\Delta Q}{Q} \times 100}{\frac{\Delta P}{P} \times 100} = \frac{-20\%}{10\%} = -2$$

Calculate the price elasticity of demand.
A 10% increase in price results in a 20% decrease in quantity demanded. The percentage change in quantity demanded is twice as large as the percentage change in price. The single numeric value which explains the sensitivity of quantity demanded to a change in price in this example is –2 (or 2 if, for the sake of simplicity, we omit the minus sign and work with absolute values).

Because we measure elasticity as a percentage divided by a percentage, we eliminate the problem of different units of measurement. For example, the demand for milk, at retail, is measured in terms of price (in cents) per litre. Fabric, on the other hand, is measured in terms of price (in euros) per metre. If we calculate elasticities (as opposed to slopes or gradients) we can directly compare the price elasticity of demand for milk with the price elasticity of demand for fabric. It is for this reason that we refer to elasticity as a 'unit free' measure of response. The numeric value, in this case –2, is called the coefficient of

TABLE 3.1: THE DEMAND FOR CINEMA TICKETS

Price, P (€)	Quantity, Q (thousands)
15.00	0
12.00	15
9.00	30
6.00	45
3.00	60
0.00	75

elasticity. Another example is illustrated in Table 3.1.
Consider two price levels and their respective quantity levels.

Suppose price falls from €12 to €9. As a result quantity demanded rises from 15,000 to 30,000 units. For calculation purposes, let

$P_1 = €12.00$ and $Q_1 = 15,000$
$P_2 = €9.00$ and $Q_2 = 30,000$

$$\varepsilon = \frac{\frac{Q_2 - Q_1}{Q_1} \times 100}{\frac{P_2 - P_1}{P_1} \times 100} = \frac{\frac{30,000 - 15,000}{15,000} \times 100}{\frac{9 - 12}{12} \times 100} = \frac{\frac{15,000}{15,000} \times 100}{\frac{-3}{12} \times 100} = \frac{100\%}{-25\%} = -4$$

We now derive the price elasticity of demand for this particular example.
In this example a 25% change in price results in a 100% change in quantity demanded. The percentage change in quantity demanded is four times greater than the percentage change in price. The elasticity coefficient is –4 (or 4).

The six points that form the demand curve have their own respective measures of elasticity.

TABLE 3.2: ELASTICITY MEASURES FOR CINEMA TICKETS

Price, P (€)	Quantity, Q (thousands)	Elasticity measures (numeric values)
15.00	0	–infinity
12.00	15	–4.0
9.00	30	–1.5
6.00	45	–0.67
3.00	60	–0.25
0.00	75	–0.00

FIGURE 3.1: THE DEMAND CURVE FOR CINEMA TICKETS

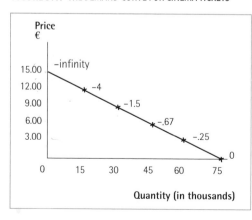

Quantity (in thousands)

Table 3.2 shows the various elasticity measures at each price.

The demand curve, with the respective elasticity measures, is shown in Figure 3.1.

As we move down the linear demand curve the absolute values for the price elasticities decline. This applies in the specific case, as shown above, and in the general case, as shown in Figure 3.2. Why? Each successive fall in the price level, down along the vertical axis, represents a larger percentage fall in price. Therefore, the denominator in the formula for price elasticity of demand increases in size.

Likewise, each successive rise in the quantity level, from left to right along the horizontal axis, represents a smaller percentage rise in quantity. The numerator in the formula for price elasticity of demand reduces in size. Hence, as we move down the demand curve the fractional measure of elasticity approaches zero.

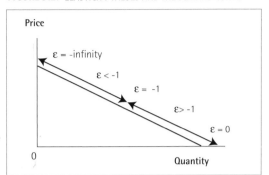

FIGURE 3.2: ELASTICITY VALUES AND THE DEMAND CURVE

It is important to note that each point on the demand curve has its own unique elasticity measure. It may appear strange that a straight line, with a constant slope (or gradient) in mathematical terms, can have a set of elasticity measures. The answer lies in the fact that we measure elasticity at different prices and subsequently examine the proportionate change in demand. This gives us a different elasticity measure at each price level on the demand curve (see Appendix 3.1 for an explanation of arc elasticity).

However, there are a small number of exceptions. Three of these exceptions are shown in Figure 3.3. In each of these cases, price elasticity is the same at each point along the demand curve.

FIGURE 3.3: THREE SPECIAL CASES OF PRICE ELASTICITY

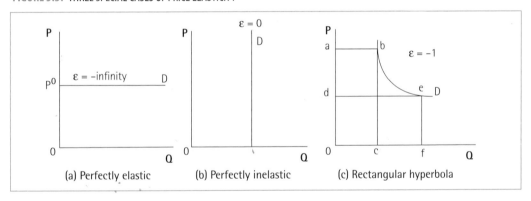

(a) A horizontal demand curve is perfectly (infinitely) elastic and has an elasticity coefficient equal to minus infinity. Demand is infinite (or, more precisely, very large and appears to be infinite from the individual producer's perspective) at price P^0. The demand for an individual farmer's wheat in the USA is an example of a perfectly elastic demand curve. If the farmer charges a price above P^0, there will be no demand for her product. Demand is perfectly responsive to a change in price. The market for agricultural commodities features perfectly elastic demand curves (from the individual producer's perspective) and is a good example of what economists call a 'perfectly competitive' market. We will discuss different market structures in greater detail in Chapter 6.

(b) A vertical demand curve is perfectly inelastic and has an elasticity coefficient equal to zero. Price has no effect on the quantity demanded. For example, the demand for insulin by diabetics is perfectly inelastic (at least over a certain price range). A certain quantity is required regardless of the price (at least over a certain price range). Market demand, at least over a certain price range, is unresponsive to a change in price.

(c) A demand curve in the shape of a rectangular hyperbola has an elasticity coefficient equal to minus one. In this case, any percentage change in price is matched by an equal percentage change in quantity demanded. It is drawn so that the areas of all rectangles under the demand curve are equal. For example, the area of rectangle [abc0] is equal to the area of rectangle [def0].

Categories of price elasticity

There are three categories of price elasticity: elastic, inelastic and unit elastic.

> **Definition**
>
> *The demand for a product is price elastic if the percentage change in quantity demanded is greater than the percentage change in price.*

Numerically, the price elasticity of demand is less than −1. (This is equivalent to the absolute value being greater than 1.) The demand for a product with an elasticity equal to minus infinity is defined as perfectly elastic.

> **Definition**
>
> *The demand for a product is price inelastic if the percentage change in quantity demanded is less than the percentage change in price.*

Price elasticity of demand falls between 0 and −1. The demand for a product with an elasticity equal to zero is defined as perfectly inelastic.

> **Definition**
>
> *The demand for a product is unit elastic if the percentage change in quantity demanded is equal to the percentage change in price.*

Numerically, the price elasticity of demand is equal to −1.

A summary of the different categories of price elasticity is presented in Table 3.3.

TABLE 3.3 SUMMARY OF PRICE ELASTICITIES

Category	ΔP compared to ΔQ (in percentage terms)	Price Elasticity
Perfectly Elastic	$\Delta P < \Delta Q$	$\varepsilon = -\text{infinity}$
Elastic	$\Delta P < \Delta Q$	$\varepsilon < -1$
Unit Elastic	$\Delta P = \Delta Q$	$\varepsilon = -1$
Inelastic	$\Delta P > \Delta Q$	$\varepsilon > -1$
Perfectly Inelastic	$\Delta P > \Delta Q$	$\varepsilon = 0$

The number line provides us with another mechanism for examining the different price elasticities. This is presented in Figure 3.4.

FIGURE 3.4: USING THE NUMBER LINE TO DISTINGUISH BETWEEN THE CATEGORIES OF PRICE ELASTICITIES

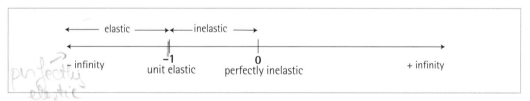

The determinants of price elasticity

The price elasticity of demand for any product is influenced by a number of different factors, which are examined below.

1. The number and availability of substitutes

The demand for products that have a large number of readily available and close substitutes is likely to be highly elastic. For example, the owner of the Cake Shop in Clifden found that the demand for her bread was elastic. Why? Numerous, at least fairly acceptable, substitutes are available from Irish Pride, Pat the Baker, etc.

Conversely, if few substitutes are available for a particular product, demand for that product is likely to be inelastic. For example, a product whose demand had, in the past, a low elasticity measure because of the scarcity of readily available substitutes is oil. The Organisation of Petroleum-Exporting Countries (OPEC), being aware that many consumers were heavily dependent on oil as their major energy source, took the opportunity to increase the price of oil by over 300% in 1973–74. The inelastic nature of the demand for oil meant that the fall in demand was not excessive.

2. The width of the product definition

The narrower the definition of the product the higher its elasticity measure, and the broader the definition of the product the lower its elasticity measure. For example, the demand for Guinness stout has a higher elasticity measure than the demand for stout or beer and the demand for trousers or even jeans has a lower elasticity measure than the demand for Levi 501s. In general, the demand for a particular brand of a product is more elastic than the demand for the product as a whole.

3. The time dimension

In general, demand is inelastic over a short time period and is elastic over a long period of time. In many cases it takes time for consumers to adjust their patterns of consumption to changes in price. Again, oil is a good example. The initial response to the increase in the price of oil was conservation. Consumers turned down the thermostat to use less oil. However, they could not immediately switch from oil to other fuels because that would require a change in heating systems. Over time, consumers did adapt or change their heating systems, often to combinations of oil, gas, electricity and solid fuels. Over the longer term, they were better able to switch from oil to other heating substitutes and their demand for oil became more price elastic.

4. Proportion of income spent on the commodity

If the price of a product is inexpensive, relative to income, demand is likely to be inelastic. For example, consumers are unlikely to change their demand for paperclips even if the price increases. On the other hand, demand is likely to be elastic if the price of a product requires a large percentage of the consumer's income. For example, if a consumer wishes to purchase a personal computer, she might watch the relevant advertisements very carefully. Although some people may purchase the latest model at the highest price because it is 'state of the art', others will wait a few months until the price falls. Demand for this expensive product is 'elastic' because consumer demand is responsive to a change of price.

Other factors influencing the price elasticity of demand include the durability of the product and the habit-forming or addictive nature of the product.

Although the measurement of price elasticity of demand seems to be quite straightforward, in reality it is not. Table 3.4 shows a sample of price elasticities for consumer products in Ireland. These were calculated by different researchers over a seventeen-year period. Notice the variations in the estimations for each classification.

TABLE 3.4: PRICE ELASTICITIES IN IRELAND

Good	elasticity estimation by		
	O'Riordan (1976)	Conniffe & Hegarty (1980)	Madden (1993)
Food	−0.43	−0.42	−0.57
Alcohol	−0.48	−0.56	−0.65
Tobacco	–	–	−0.35
Clothing and footwear	−1.01	−0.70	−0.69
Petrol	–	–	−0.19
Fuel and power	0.11	−0.06	−0.17
Durables	−0.48	−0.84	−1.05
Transport and equipment	−1.59	−1.02	−1.06
Other goods	−0.76	−0.35	−0.69
Services			−1.01

Source: David Madden, 'A New Set of Consumer Demand Estimates for Ireland', *The Economic and Social Review,* 24 January 1993.

Although in certain classifications, such as food and alcohol, the elasticity estimates are quite consistent, other classifications, such as transport and equipment and durables, show considerable variation.

Part of this variation may be caused by actual changes in consumer behaviour over time. However, much of the variation is probably due to differences in data and techniques. The earlier studies covered shorter estimation periods and the products included in each classification have changed over time. Also, the mathematical techniques used to measure elasticity changed with each new study. Indeed, Madden, the author of the article, actually calculated fifteen different sets of estimates.

This shows us that we cannot simply accept that single numbers, such as elasticities, provide anything more than an estimate. If we want to use the elasticities for taxation policy or revenue projections, we must be quite certain that we understand the method (and the associated uncertainties) by which the elasticities were calculated.

Elasticity and total revenue

There is an important relationship between price elasticity and total revenue (TR). Total revenue is simply defined as price (P) multiplied by quantity (Q) and can be written as follows:

$$TR = P \times Q$$ [3.2]

Total revenue is normally represented by a shaded area, as shown in Figure 3.5. Continuing with the example of cinema tickets, if price is €6, quantity demanded is 45,000 tickets and total revenue is €6.00 x 45,000 = €270,000. This is represented by the shaded area in Figure 3.5.

A change in price results in a change in quantity demanded, which may result in a change in total revenue.

The price elasticity of the demand for the product indicates the extent to which a change in price affects total revenue. This information can be used by the firm to decide if price should be changed. We can say pricing policy depends largely on the elasticity of demand. Two alternative cases are discussed below.

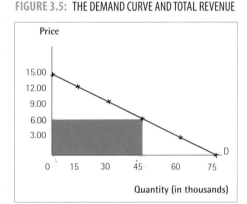

FIGURE 3.5: THE DEMAND CURVE AND TOTAL REVENUE

Case 1: A price increase

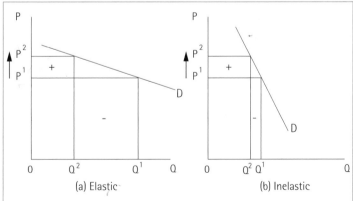

FIGURE 3.6: CASE 1: A PRICE INCREASE

A producer is considering an increase in the price of a product. The producer knows that if she increases price, the consumers will respond by reducing the level of quantity demanded. However, it is the magnitude of the change in quantity that determines whether total revenue rises or falls.

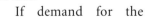

If demand for the product is elastic (or at least elastic between two particular prices), the subsequent drop in demand in percentage terms is large relative to the price change in percentage terms. This is illustrated in Figure 3.6(a).

The small box, denoted by (+), represents the revenue gained from the increase in price. The large box, denoted by (−), represents the revenue lost from the subsequent fall in demand. The revenue lost due to the fall in demand is greater than the revenue gained from the price increase. When demand is elastic, total revenue falls as a result of the price increase.

If demand for the product is inelastic (or at least inelastic between the two prices involved), the subsequent fall in demand in percentage terms is small relative to the price change in percentage terms. This is shown in Figure 3.6(b). The magnitude of the price change is the same as for the elastic demand curve. However, the revenue gained from the increase in price (+) outweighs the revenue lost from the subsequent fall in demand (–). When demand is inelastic, total revenue rises as a result of the price increase.

To summarise, when revenue maximisation is the objective, the producer will increase price if the demand for the commodity is price inelastic over the relevant price range, *ceteris paribus*.

Case 2: A price decrease

A producer considers a decrease in price. The producer knows that if she decreases price, consumers will respond by increasing the level of quantity demanded. However, will revenue increase or decrease as a result of this price cut? Again, the answer depends on the elasticity of demand. Figure 3.7(a) shows a price decrease for a product represented by an 'elastic' demand curve.

The additional revenue gained from the increase in demand (+) outweighs the revenue lost from the fall in price (–). By cutting price, the producer increases total revenue.

FIGURE 3.7: CASE 2: A PRICE DECREASE

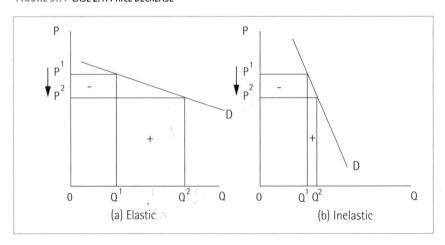

(a) Elastic   (b) Inelastic

Figure 3.7(b) is the demand curve for a product represented by an 'inelastic' demand curve. The size of the price decrease is the same as with the elastic demand curve. However, the revenue gained due to the increase in demand (+) is less than the revenue lost due to the decrease in price (–). Total revenue falls as a result of the price decrease.

If revenue maximisation is the objective, the producer should decrease price if demand is elastic.

Table 3.5 presents the change in total revenue in response to price changes. Different demand elasticities are considered.

TABLE 3.5: SUMMARY TABLE OF ELASTICITY AND TOTAL REVENUE

Price elasticity of demand	Price change	Total revenue change
Elastic	Increase Decrease	Fall Rise
Inelastic	Increase Decrease	Rise Fall

Price elasticity and maximum total revenue

The upper part of Figure 3.8 shows that demand is elastic along the upper segment of the demand curve and inelastic along the lower segment of the demand curve. The point of unit elastic demand $(\varepsilon = -1)$ separates the elastic and inelastic segments.

The lower part of Figure 3.8 shows the change in total revenue as price falls. Along the elastic portion of the demand curve, if price falls, total revenue increases. Along the inelastic portion of the demand curve, if price falls, total revenue falls. Total revenue reaches the maximum at the point of unit elastic demand.

At the point of unit elastic demand, where $\varepsilon = -1$, the total revenue curve is at its highest point. This indicates the specific price level, P*, and corresponding quantity level, Q*, where total revenue is maximised. If revenue maximisation is the producer's objective, (P*,Q*) is the desired price and output combination.

FIGURE 3.8: PRICE ELASTICITY AND MAXIMUM TOTAL REVENUE

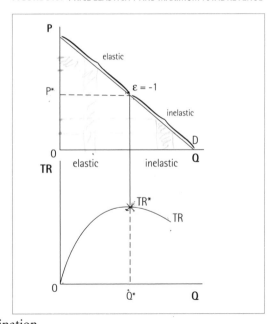

Government revenue and price elasticity

Governments as well as producers are interested in price elasticity of demand. Much government revenue is generated through levying taxes on goods and services. In 2009, value added tax (VAT) and excise duties accounted for approximately 47% of the tax revenue collected by the state.

Definition

Value added tax (VAT) is an integrated sales tax levied (on a percentage basis) at each stage of production and distribution.

> **Definition**
>
> *Excise duties are imposed in order to: (i) discourage the production and consumption of goods and services which have detrimental effects on individuals other than direct producers or consumers; and/or (ii) collect taxation revenue.*

Table 3.6 shows the amount of tax levied on a packet of twenty cigarettes between the years 2000 and 2009.

TABLE 3.6: INCIDENCE OF EXCISE DUTY AND VAT PER PACKET OF TWENTY CIGARETTES (ALL PRICES IN €)

Year	Excise duty	VAT	Total tax content	Retail price
2000	2.94	0.83	3.77	4.78
2001	3.00	0.81	3.81	4.88
2002	3.14	0.90	4.04	5.20
2003	3.58	1.01	4.59	5.83
2004	3.80	1.07	4.87	6.16
2005	3.81	1.09	4.90	6.25
2006	3.84	1.11	4.95	6.40
2007	4.27	1.22	5.49	7.02
2008	4.95	1.37	6.31	7.88
2009	5.19	1.48	6.67	8.35

Source: Revenue Commissioners Statistical Report, 2009.

In 2009, the average retail price of cigarettes was €8.35. Excise duty and VAT accounted for €6.67, which was 80% of the retail price.

The next section deals with cross-price elasticity of demand and the difference between substitutes and complements.

3.2 CROSS-PRICE ELASTICITY OF DEMAND

> **Definition**
>
> *Cross-price elasticity measures the sensitivity (in terms of percentages) of quantity demanded of one product to a change in the price of another product.*

If two products are related, they are either substitutes for or complements to each other.

The formula for cross-price elasticity is very similar to the one used for own-price elasticity. It is the percentage change in quantity demanded of one product divided by the percentage change in the price of the other (related) product. For two products, A and B, cross-price elasticity $\varepsilon_{A,B}$ can be expressed as follows:

$$\varepsilon_{A, B} = \frac{\text{\% Change in Quantity Demanded of Product A}}{\text{\% Change in Price of Product B}} \quad\quad [3.3]$$

$$\varepsilon_{A, B} = \frac{\dfrac{\Delta Q}{Q} \times 100 \text{ of Product A}}{\dfrac{\Delta P}{P} \times 100 \text{ of Product B}}$$

If two products are related to each other, the relationship is in either of two forms.

One possibility is for products A and B to be substitutes for each other. Likely examples include beef and pork, apples and oranges, heating oil and natural gas. Let us suppose the price of apples increases. The percentage change in the price of apples is positive. As apples and oranges can be regarded as substitutes for each other, consumers consequently consume fewer apples and more oranges. The percentage change in the quantity demanded of oranges is also positive. If both the numerator and the denominator are positive, then the quotient is also positive.

A positive numeric value also results if the price of apples falls. In this situation, the percentage change in the price of apples and the percentage change in the quantity demanded of oranges are both negative. In summary, if products are substitutes for each other, their cross-price elasticity is positive.

A second possibility is for products A and B to be complements to each other. Likely examples include petrol and cars; pencils and erasers; cigarettes and lighters. Let us suppose the price of pencils increases. The percentage change in the price of pencils is positive. As pencils and erasers are consumed together, consumers subsequently demand fewer pencils and, in turn, fewer erasers. The percentage change in the quantity demanded of erasers is negative. If the numerator is negative and the denominator is positive then the quotient is negative.

A negative value also results if the price of pencils falls. In this situation, the percentage change in the price of pencils is negative but the percentage change in the quantity demanded of erasers is positive. In summary, if products are complements to each other, their cross-price elasticity is negative.

The above analysis can be clearly illustrated by means of a number line, as Figure 3.9 shows.

FIGURE 3.9: USING THE NUMBER LINE TO DISTINGUISH BETWEEN DIFFERENT CROSS-PRICE ELASTICITIES

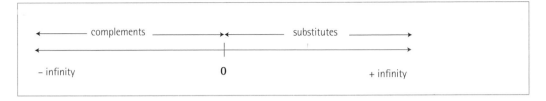

If cross-price elasticity of demand is zero or very close to zero, the two products are not related. For example, an increase in the price of apples is unlikely to affect the demand for flowers in any significant manner.

As the magnitude of the number increases, so does the strength of the relationship between the two products. For example, blocks of ice cream and wafers are often bought together. We expect a large percentage increase in the price of the ice cream block to result in a large percentage decrease in the demand for wafers, *ceteris paribus*. This large negative number indicates that the two products are 'strong' complements.

CASE STUDY

Extract from the Institute for Fiscal Studies
The revenue effect of changing alcohol duties
by Zoe Smith

... For any particular good, the relationship between the tax rate and tax revenues depends on total expenditure on the good, the current tax rates and how responsive consumers are to a change in the price of the good (the price elasticity of demand). Other things being equal, the more responsive people are to a change in the price of a good, the more likely it is that a cut in duty will lead to an increase in revenue. This is because, for a given fall in price after a tax cut, the more responsive people are, the larger the increase in sales, so the more likely it is that the extra revenue from the increase in sales will outweigh the loss per unit sold.

It is also important to consider the effect that cutting duty on one type of alcohol would have on the demand for, and therefore the revenue from, other types of alcohol and all other goods. A change in the price of, say, beer will lead to a reallocation of spending between beer and all other goods. The effect is likely to be greatest on the demand for other types of alcohol because of the similarity between different types of alcohol.

If beer and wine are complements to each other, then when the price of beer falls (following a tax cut) people buy more beer and also more wine. This means there will be an increase in revenue from wine, so we are more likely to see an increase in total tax revenue following a tax cut on beer. If beer and wine are substitutes for each other, a fall in the price of beer will lead to an increase in sales of beer but a fall in sales of wine. The result would be a fall in revenue from wine, so we are less likely to see an increase in total revenue following a tax cut

on beer. The responsiveness of demand for one good with respect to a change in the price of another good is called the cross-price elasticity of demand.

... In order to determine whether cutting duty would lead to an increase or a decrease in revenue, we need to know expenditure, current tax rates and own- and cross-price elasticities. We know current tax rates and expenditure and we use data from the Family Expenditure Survey from 1976 to 1996 (about 120,000 households) to estimate elasticities.

... [The table opposite] summarises the effect that cutting duty on one type of alcohol would have on its own sales and revenue and on the sales and revenue of the other types of alcohol.

A cut in beer duty will lead to an increase in sales of beer, but beer is not very price-responsive and so the increase in sales is not enough to outweigh the fall in duty on each unit sold. Thus a cut in beer duty would lead to a fall in revenue from beer. But we also have to take into account the effect that a cut in beer duty would have on wine and spirit revenue. Beer is a complement to wine, so a cut in beer duty would lead to an increase in sales of wine and so an increase in revenue from wine. Beer is also a complement to spirits, so again a cut in beer duty will lead to an increase in sales of spirits and this means an increase in revenue from spirits. The increase in revenue from wine and spirits would offset the loss of beer revenue but not completely. Overall, we find that a cut in beer duty would lead to a fall in indirect tax revenue.

	Cut in beer duty		Cut in wine duty		Cut in spirits duty	
THE EFFECT OF CUTTING DUTY ON ALCOHOL						
	Sales	*Revenue*	*Sales*	*Revenue*	*Sales*	*Revenue*
Beer	Increase	Decrease	Increase	Increase	Increase	Increase
Wine	Increase	Increase	Increase	Increase	Decrease	Decrease
Spirits	Increase	Increase	Decrease	Decrease	Increase	Increase
Overall		**Decrease**		**Decrease**		**At maximum**

Source: Institute for Fiscal Studies, Briefing Note No. 4, November 1999.

Questions

1. Using the contents of the table above, describe the effect of a cut in wine duty on: sales of wine; wine revenue; sales of beer; beer revenue; sales of spirits; spirits revenue; and total revenue.
2. Using the contents of the table above, describe the effect of a cut in spirits duty on: sales of spirits; spirits revenue; sales of beer; beer revenue; sales of wine; wine revenue; and total revenue.
3. The above case study focuses attention on the likely effect of changes in alcohol duties on total revenue from alcohol duties. Consider other possible arguments in favour of, and against, changing alcohol duties.

Answers on website

3.3 INCOME ELASTICITY OF DEMAND

Definition

Income elasticity of demand measures the responsiveness (in terms of percentages) of quantity demanded to changes in income.

When discussing the role of the consumer and demand in Chapter 2 we distinguished between a normal and an inferior good. Both goods were defined, not in terms of the effect of changes in price, but in terms of the effect of changes in income.

Economists attempt to determine whether a good is normal or inferior using the following formula for income elasticity of demand:

$$\eta = \frac{\% \text{ Change in Quantity Demanded}}{\% \text{ Change in Income}} = \frac{\frac{\Delta Q}{Q} \times 100}{\frac{\Delta Y}{Y} \times 100}$$

[3.4]

For a normal good (or service), η is a positive number. This is because income and demand are moving in the same direction.

Suppose we want to test to see if a good is normal. We could consider a range of increasing incomes. In this case, the denominator is a positive number. We then check to see if demand for a particular good is increasing over this range of incomes. If so, the numerator is a positive number. The quotient of a positive number divided by a positive number is a positive number.

If income is falling, the denominator is a negative number. If demand for a good is decreasing over this range of incomes, the numerator is also a negative number. Both the numerator and denominator are negative which means that the quotient, representing η, is positive. In summary, as long as income and demand are moving in the same direction, income elasticity is positive and the good is normal.

Conversely, for an inferior good (or service), η is a negative number. As income changes, demand for the inferior good changes in the opposite direction (albeit only over a range of income).

The relationship between income and quantity demanded can be shown diagrammatically. It is called the Engel curve, after the German statistician Ernst Engel (1821–96) who carried out extensive research on the effect of changes in household budgets on household expenditures. Figure 3.10 illustrates the Engel curves for normal goods and inferior goods.

FIGURE 3.10: ENGEL CURVES

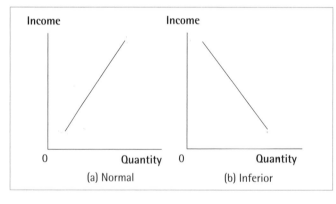

(a) Normal   (b) Inferior

Figure 3.10(a) shows the positive relationship between income and quantity demanded which we associate with a normal good. By definition, as income increases, the demand for the normal good increases. The Engel curve for the normal good is upward sloping. Figure 3.10(b) illustrates the Engel curve for an inferior good. When income increases (over some income range), we expect consumers to substitute goods of higher quality for the inferior good. The relationship between income and quantity demanded for the inferior good is negative. Hence, the Engel curve for the inferior good is downward sloping.

The above analysis can also be illustrated by the use of the number line as shown in Figure 3.11.

FIGURE 3.11: USING THE NUMBER LINE TO DISTINGUISH BETWEEN NORMAL AND INFERIOR GOODS

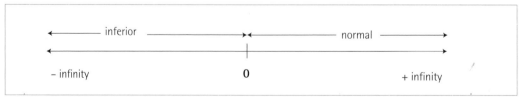

The number line shows that negative numbers (η<0) are associated with income elasticities for inferior goods and positive numbers (η>0) are associated with income elasticities for normal goods. However, a further distinction can be made within the 'normal' classification.

All normal goods, by definition, have positive income elasticity. Further, a good is regarded as a 'luxury' or superior good if the percentage change in quantity demanded is greater than the percentage change in income. It has an elasticity coefficient greater than one. Likely examples include yachts, expensive cars and jewellery.

A good is a 'necessity' if the percentage change in quantity demanded is less than the percentage change in income. The elasticity coefficient is between zero and one. Likely examples include basic toiletries.

Figure 3.12 shows the numerical values of necessities ($0 < \eta < 1$) and luxuries ($\eta > 1$), the two categories of 'normal' goods.

FIGURE 3.12: USING THE NUMBER LINE TO DISTINGUISH BETWEEN DIFFERENT INCOME ELASTICITIES

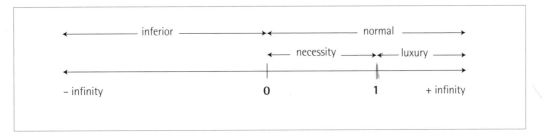

A sample of income elasticities is listed in Table 3.7.

TABLE 3.7: INCOME ELASTICITIES IN IRELAND

Good	Income elasticity estimation by		
	O'Riordan (1976)	Conniffe & Hegarty (1980)	Madden (1993)
Food	0.58	0.68	0.50
Alcohol	1.15	1.51	0.65
Tobacco	–	–	0.03
Clothing and footwear	1.75	1.37	1.74
Petrol	–	–	1.10
Fuel and power	1.61	1.66	0.29
Durables	1.67	1.72	1.95
Transport and equipment	2.12	3.52	2.31
Other goods	0.92	0.67	2.03
Services			0.90

Source: David Madden, 'A New Set of Consumer Demand Estimates for Ireland', *The Economic and Social Review*, 24 January 1993.

Again, we observe considerable variation between the three sets of income elasticities. We notice in looking at these broad classifications that there are no inferior goods. Only food and tobacco can be classified as necessities. According to the findings, clothing and footwear, durables, and transport and equipment are luxuries. The other categories of goods vary between necessities and luxuries, depending on the study.

This reinforces the point that we made earlier. Indeed, if anything, there is greater variation in the estimation of income elasticities than there was for price elasticities. This variation may be due to differences in consumer behaviour over time, differences in the data collection procedures and/or differences in techniques utilised.

3.4 ELASTICITY OF SUPPLY

The analysis of the relationship between price and quantity applies equally well to supply as it does to demand.

> **Definition**
>
> *The price elasticity of supply measures the responsiveness (in terms of percentages) of quantity supplied to changes in price.*

The elasticity coefficient is positive, reflecting the conventional upward sloping supply curve. Terms such as 'elastic' and 'inelastic' are also used to describe the degree of sensitivity between changes in price and the corresponding changes in quantity supplied.

Factors such as the availability of inputs, the state of technology and the level of excess capacity affect the price elasticity of supply. Time is also an important factor. We can distinguish between three different periods of supply. They are illustrated in Figure 3.13 and we will discuss the periods using the example of The Cafe, a cafe owned by Monica.

FIGURE 3.13: PERIODS OF SUPPLY

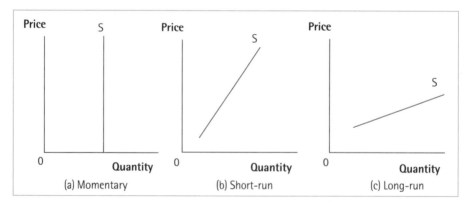

Momentary (market) supply

This period is so short that the firm does not have time to respond to price changes. In effect, the supply is fixed and this is reflected in a vertical supply curve. The momentary supply curve, shown in Figure 3.13(a), is perfectly inelastic with an elasticity coefficient equal to zero.

For example, consider the situation that confronts Monica. She owns a small cafe that is popular with hikers in the summer. Monica works alone and her business is generally scattered throughout the opening hours.

One day, a bus stops outside her door and forty hikers, ready to begin their excursion, pour into her tiny cafe. What can she do? Her friend Bridgid, who stopped in for a quick latte, gives her a hand, but there are only two of them. The cafe has a limited number of tables and the stock of food is finite. With the resources at her disposal, she is simply unable to cater for the tourists' needs. 'On the day', the number of meals that Monica can serve from her cafe is perfectly inelastic, limited by the resources that are immediately at hand.

Short-run supply

This period of time allows for some inputs to be varied while others remain unchanged. The short-run supply curve, as represented in Figure 3.13(b), illustrates how quantity supplied responds to changes in price with the possibility that some alterations in the production process can be made. The short-run supply curve has a positive elasticity coefficient.

Returning to The Cafe: Michelle, the local archaeologist, tells Monica that she is scheduling a tour for hikers to the local area for each weekday throughout the summer. Monica, always looking for new opportunities, organises the household that very night. They clean out the stock room and gather extra tables, chairs and cutlery from their friends and relations. Monica convinces two neighbours, Billie and Pat, to work for a few hours each day preparing food and serving the hikers. Monica calls her suppliers to increase the food order, to be delivered the following morning.

These inputs can be varied in the short run, but Monica is still limited by the size of her cafe and the capacity of her appliances. These particular inputs require planning permission and financing and cannot be changed in the short run.

Long-run supply

This period of time is long enough to allow for the full adjustment of all of the inputs involved in the production process. The long-run supply curve, as represented in Figure 3.13(c), shows how quantity supplied responds to price changes allowing for the possibility of adjustments of all inputs used in the production of the product. It also has a positive elasticity coefficient. The long-run supply curve is flatter than the short-run supply curve because more adjustments can be made in response to price changes in the long run.

At the end of the summer, Monica applies for planning permission and borrows money to finance construction to expand her cafe and to upgrade her appliances. By the beginning of the next tourist season, she has adjusted all of the inputs to cope with the changes in demand.

The length of these time periods varies from market to market. For Monica, 'momentary' was up to a day and the 'long run' was beyond a year. For the automobile industry, momentary may be up to a week, since it is more difficult to schedule labour and organise the other necessary inputs. The long run may be five years, the time that it takes to design and construct a new manufacturing facility.

Only a brief discussion on the price elasticity of supply is given here. Supply and its price elasticity are largely influenced by costs and their responsiveness to output changes. This is analysed in greater detail in Chapter 5.

SUMMARY

1. Elasticity of demand explores the direction and the magnitude of percentage changes in quantity arising out of percentage changes in economic variables. There are three elasticities of demand: price, cross-price and income.

2. Price elasticity of demand measures the responsiveness (in terms of percentages) of quantity demanded to changes in price. This sensitivity can be expressed in the form of a numeric value. The price elasticity is usually negative. Each point on the demand curve has an elasticity measure. There are three categories of price elasticity: elastic, inelastic or unit elastic. Factors which influence price elasticity include the time period, the number of substitutes available, the width of the definition and the proportion of income spent on the good or service.

3. The price elasticity of demand determines the extent to which a change in price affects total revenue where total revenue is price multiplied by quantity. In order to maximise total revenue, a producer will only increase price if demand is inelastic and, likewise, will only decrease price if demand is elastic. Total revenue is maximised at the point of unit elastic demand.

4. Cross-price elasticity of demand measures the sensitivity (in terms of percentages) of quantity demanded of one product to changes in the price of another product. Substitute products have a positive cross-price elasticity of demand. Complementary products have a negative cross-price elasticity of demand.

5. Income elasticity of demand measures the sensitivity (in terms of percentages) of quantity demanded to changes in income. A positive income elasticity reflects a normal good. An inferior good has negative income elasticity. We also use income elasticities to classify goods as either necessities or luxuries, depending on the magnitude of the positive response to a change in income.

6. Price elasticity of supply measures the responsiveness (in terms of percentages) of quantity supplied to changes in price. The price elasticity of supply is usually positive. Its magnitude depends on the availability of inputs.

KEY TERMS

Elasticity	Perfectly inelastic
Elasticity of demand	Perfectly elastic
Price elasticity	Total revenue
Cross-price elasticity	Engel curve
Income elasticity	Luxury
Elastic	Necessity
Inelastic	Elasticity of supply
Unit elastic	

REVIEW QUESTIONS

1. Explain the difference between the terms 'slope' and 'elasticity'. How are these terms related to the theory of demand and supply?
2. What is the connection between the three different measures of elasticity of demand? What are the differences between each measure?
3. Explain the difference between point elasticity of demand and arc elasticity of demand (see Appendix 3.1).
4. What factors influence the price elasticity of demand for a product and in what ways?
5. How is price elasticity useful when analysing the effect of price changes on total revenue?

6. Explain why both cross-price elasticity and income elasticity can result in either positive or negative values, whereas price elasticity is usually limited to negative values.

WORKING PROBLEMS

1. The demand for Solero Ice, a popular ice cream, is shown in Table 3.8.

TABLE 3.8: DEMAND FOR SOLERO ICE

Price (€)	Quantity (thousands per year)
1.80	20
1.50	30
1.20	40
0.90	50
0.60	60

(a) Sketch the demand curve for Solero Ice.
(b) Estimate a measure of price elasticity at all five points on the demand curve.
(c) Explain why these values (in absolute terms) decline as the demand curve slopes downwards from left to right.
(d) At which price is total revenue maximised? Explain your answer.

2. The set of data in Table 3.9 was processed over a five-year period. It has been confirmed that there was no change in the preferences of the household in question. Also, there were no changes recorded in the price of any other product.

TABLE 3.9

Year	1	2	3	4	5
Price of A (€)	72	60	60	66	72
Price of B (€)	36	28	22	28	36
Household income (€000 per year)	170	250	250	250	265
Quantity of A demanded (per year)	60	75	85	70	65
Quantity of B demanded (per year)	130	150	180	170	160

From the above data, calculate:
(a) the price elasticity of demand for product A;
(b) the price elasticity of demand for product B;
(c) the income elasticity of demand for product A;
(d) the cross-price elasticity of demand for product A;
(e) the cross-price elasticity of demand for product B.
Interpret your answers.

MULTI-CHOICE QUESTIONS

1. The demand curve for a product is inelastic when:
   (a) the amount of income spent on the product is small;
   (b) there are few substitutes;
   (c) quantity demanded is very responsive to a change in price;
   (d) consumers have sufficient time to adjust to changes in price;
   (e) none of the above.
2. Price elasticity of demand for a particular service is $\varepsilon = -1$. At this point:
   (a) demand is elastic;
   (b) demand is inelastic;
   (c) demand is unit elastic;
   (d) total revenue is maximised;
   (e) both (c) and (d) are correct.
3. Suppose price elasticity of demand for an iPod is $\varepsilon = -1.5$. We can interpret this number as meaning that:
   (a) if price increases by 10%, quantity demanded decreases by 15%;
   (b) this is an inferior good;
   (c) this is a normal good;
   (d) if price increases by 10%, quantity demanded increases by 15%;
   (e) revenue is maximised at this price.
4. Mars bars and Kit Kats are substitutes. This means that:
   (a) as the price of Mars bars increases, the demand for Kit Kats decreases;
   (b) as the price of Mars bars increases, the demand for Kit Kats increases;
   (c) as the price of Mars bars decreases, the demand for Kit Kats decreases;
   (d) as the price of Mars bars decreases, the demand for Kit Kats increases;
   (e) both statements (b) and (c) are true.
5. Suppose income increases by 10% and the demand for digital TVs increases by 12%. Digital TVs are:
   (a) an inferior good;
   (b) a normal luxury;
   (c) a normal necessity;
   (d) price inelastic;
   (e) none of the above.
6. The momentary supply curve is:
   (a) perfectly inelastic;
   (b) inelastic;
   (c) elastic;
   (d) perfectly elastic;
   (e) none of the above.

TRUE OR FALSE (SUPPORT YOUR ANSWER)

1. Price elasticity of demand measures the responsiveness (in terms of percentages) of price to changes in quantity demanded.
2. A 15% rise in price with a subsequent 5% fall in quantity demanded results in a price elasticity coefficient of −3.

3. A product that has few or no substitutes is likely to have a relatively steep demand curve.
4. The cross-price elasticity of demand for Daniel O'Donnell tickets and Eminem tickets is likely to be high and positive.
5. All necessities are normal goods but not all normal goods are necessities.
6. The longer the time period, the more elastic is supply and the flatter the supply curve.

CASE STUDY

Extract from *The Irish Times*
Minister rules out ESRI advice on fuel carbon tax
by Christine Newman

Minister for the Environment Dick Roche yesterday ruled out the introduction of a carbon tax on fossil fuels as suggested in an Economic and Social Research Institute (ESRI) report. The ESRI said in its report, *Aspects of Irish Energy Policy*, that unless such a tax was considered for certain sectors, it was unlikely the Republic would meet its emissions targets. In light of recent oil prices, a 'sensitive approach' in this area was needed. Yesterday, however, the Minister ruled out the introduction of carbon tax, saying the decision was made in 2004 and it was inopportune to revisit it now.

Meanwhile, SIPTU general president Jack O'Connor called for an immediate reduction in excise duty to reduce the impact of higher energy costs on the cost of living. He said the Government must learn from the lessons of the past and act on fuel costs now. Mr O'Connor made his remarks as petrol prices continued to rise toward the €1.30-a-litre mark for unleaded fuel. 'I am flabbergasted at the complacency of the Government response to the clear evidence of a serious crisis developing before our eyes. The 9 per cent surge in the price of home heating oil in the month of July alone has been followed this past week by a 7 to 8 per cent increase in prices facing the average motorist at the petrol pumps. There has been an overall increase of 25 per cent in petrol prices alone since January,' Mr O'Connor said.

He said it was a repeat of the crisis in the second half of 2000 when a resumption of rising inflation almost led to the collapse of the then national pay agreement. Mounting demands by SIPTU calling for a review of Government policy and an anti-inflation package were only yielded to after the December 2000 budget, when it was almost too late.

'Consumer prices should be eased by reducing excise duty and by the Government forgoing its own unexpected windfall resulting from the surge in prices,' he said. In this context, the ESRI call for increased carbon taxes was ill-timed and had unfortunately detracted from the more positive comments the ESRI report had made in favour of the greater use of public transport, he added. Working people must be offered enhanced public transport provision, he also said.

Filling stations nationwide reported heavy demand and even queues over the weekend, in advance of price increases. Oil industry sources said the US hurricane was unlikely to have any lasting effect on Irish petrol supplies. On international markets, oil prices fell sharply on Monday – the drop started on Friday after the release by industrialised nations of emergency oil stocks to prevent a fuel crisis in the US.

Source: *The Irish Times*, 8 September 2005.

Questions

1. Do you think that the demand for oil products (e.g. home heating oil, petrol) is elastic or inelastic? What elements of the article could be used to support your answer?
2. What factors might lead to the ESRI, the government and SIPTU having similar or different positions with respect to the appropriate excise (or carbon) tax on oil products?
3. Using the appropriate tables from the most recent Statistical Report of the Revenue Commissioners (available at www.revenue.ie), find (in percentage terms) the total tax take on: a litre of unleaded petrol; a litre of auto diesel; a packet of twenty cigarettes; a pint of stout; a pint of lager; a standard measure of whiskey; and a bottle of whiskey. Do you think that the aim of government in imposing excise duties on each of these products is: to (a) discourage production and consumption; and/or to (b) maximise taxation revenue? Explain your answers.

APPENDIX 3.1: ARC ELASTICITY

The definition of price elasticity used in this chapter is often referred to as point elasticity. It measures the elasticity at every point along the demand curve. Each elasticity coefficient is calculated from an initial point or base. This base reflects the starting price and the corresponding quantity level. Consequently, the result varies as the initial price changes.

Arc elasticity measures the elasticity of demand over a price range using the midpoint or average price as the base. In graphic terms, it is the elasticity over the length of a segment or arc of the demand curve. Hence, it is called arc elasticity. The formula for arc elasticity is expressed as follows:

[3.5]

$$\frac{\dfrac{\Delta Q}{.5(Q_1 + Q_2)} \times 100}{\dfrac{\Delta P}{.5(P_1 + P_2)} \times 100} = \frac{\dfrac{\Delta Q}{Q_1 + Q_2} \times 100}{\dfrac{\Delta P}{P_1 + P_2} \times 100}$$

where Q_1 = original quantity demanded; Q_2 = new quantity demanded; ΔQ = change in quantity demanded; P_1 = original price; P_2 = new price and ΔP = change in price.

An example is shown below using the same price levels and quantity levels as in the earlier example of cinema tickets.

Price, P (€)	Quantity (thousands)
12.00	15
9.00	30

Let $P_1 = €12.00$
       $Q_1 = 15,000$
       $P_2 = €9.00$
       $Q_2 = 30,000$

Thus,

$$\frac{\dfrac{Q_2 - Q_1}{.5(Q_1 + Q_2)}}{\dfrac{P_2 - P_1}{.5(P_1 + P_2)}} = \frac{\dfrac{30,000 - 15,000}{.5(15,000 + 30,000)}}{\dfrac{9 - 12}{.5(12 + 9)}} = \frac{\dfrac{15,000}{22,500}}{\dfrac{-3}{10.5}} = -2.33$$

The elasticity coefficient using the arc formula is –2.33. As expected, it is between the values of –4 (this is the point elasticity with a base of $P_1 = €12.00$ and $Q_1 = 15,000$) and –1.5 (this is the point elasticity with a base of $P_1 = €9.00$ and $Q_1 = 30,000$).

The arc elasticity method provides a measure at neither the start nor the end price but at an average price. Thus, the elasticity coefficient using the arc method lies between the two relevant point elasticity measures.

CHAPTER 4

The Consumer and Demand

'Value in use cannot be measured by any known standard; it is differently estimated by different persons.'[1]

DAVID RICARDO (1772–1823)

'Value depends entirely on utility.'[2]

W. STANLEY JEVONS (1835–82)

CHAPTER OBJECTIVES

Upon completing this chapter, the student should understand:
- marginal utility and the principle of diminishing marginal utility;
- the equi-marginal principle;
- indifference curves and budget lines;
- substitution and income effects;
- differences in the demand curves for normal, inferior and Giffen goods;
- the differences between the two main theories of, or approaches to, demand.

OUTLINE

INTRODUCTION

In Chapter 2 we gave an intuitive explanation as to why the market demand curve slopes downwards from left to right. This chapter provides us with a more rigorous explanation of the theory of demand. It examines the behaviour of individual consumers in the market and how they react to price changes. Its purpose is to explain the downward sloping nature of the individual consumer's demand curve and hence the downward sloping market demand curve as described in Chapter 2.

We begin with an historical account of the theory of demand. This is followed by an analysis of the two main theories of consumer behaviour. The concept of consumer surplus is also examined.

4.1 AN HISTORICAL PERSPECTIVE

Marginal utility analysis

There are two main theories of demand. The first is the marginal utility or cardinalist analysis. Central to this approach is the assumption that satisfaction can be measured in absolute terms like weight or height.

This approach was instrumental in elucidating the paradox of value, which remained unresolved for many centuries and left scholars from Plato to Adam Smith baffled. The paradox of value means that some products, for example water and salt, have a high value in use but a low value in exchange, while others, such as diamonds and gold, have a low value in use but a high value in exchange.

In the 1770s Adam Smith asked the question, 'How is it that water, which is so essential to human life, has a low market value whereas diamonds, which are relatively trivial, have a high market value?'[3] This paradox remained unanswered until the marginal utility revolution of the 1870s. Economists including W. Stanley Jevons in England, Carl Menger (1840–1921) in Austria and Leon Walras in Switzerland were independently responsible for bringing the marginal utility approach to the forefront of economic thinking.

The 'marginalists', as they were later identified, claimed that the market value of a product (i.e. good or service) is determined by its utility to the consumer. The marginalists' key contribution was to distinguish between total utility and marginal utility. Total utility is the pleasure or satisfaction that an individual receives from consuming a particular product. Marginal utility is the additional utility that a person receives from consuming one more unit of a particular product. While total utility increases with consumption, the addition to utility (or marginal utility) almost inevitably diminishes as each extra unit is consumed.

The distinction between total and marginal utility was central to the solution to the water-diamond paradox. Water is essential. Therefore, the total utility that we receive from consuming water is very high. However, the extra amount of satisfaction obtained by consuming an additional unit of water (or its marginal utility) is low because we consume such a large volume. On the other hand, because we consume such a small amount of diamonds, we obtain a high amount of satisfaction at the margin. The few units of diamonds that we do consume each has a very high marginal utility. The application of marginal utility was the first step in explaining the paradox of value.

Indifference-preference analysis

The marginalists, particularly Jevons, believed that a method for measuring utility would ultimately be discovered. An absolute measure of happiness has not been found and this deficiency limits the usefulness of this approach. A second approach, called the indifference-preference or ordinalist analysis, relies on ranking or ordering preferences, rather than assigning absolute values to the level of utility gained from consumption. This approach entered the mainstream of economic theory through the efforts of John R. Hicks (1904–89) and Roy G. Allen (1906–83).

Although the second approach dominates consumer theory, it is to at least a certain extent a modification rather than a replacement of the utility approach. Hence, we will begin our examination of consumer theory with the marginal utility analysis and then discuss the indifference-preference analysis.

4.2 THE MARGINAL UTILITY ANALYSIS

An outline of utility theory

Classical economists, particularly David Ricardo, believed that the value of a product was determined by the wages paid to labour. This is called the labour theory of value. This explanation focuses on the supply side of the market. The marginalists, on the other hand, argued that utility was the basis of value. Their discussion focused on the consumer, or the demand side of the market. In terms of the theory of price determination as we know it today (and as explained in Chapter 2), each of the groups mentioned above was looking at only one half of the story. We will now look at the marginalists' contribution to our understanding of the demand side of the market. We begin by defining a few of the relevant terms.

Definition

Utility is the satisfaction or pleasure that is derived from consuming a product.

Definition

Total utility (TU) is the total satisfaction that a consumer gains from the consumption of a given quantity of a product.

Definition

Marginal utility (MU) is the extra or additional satisfaction that a consumer gains from consuming one extra unit of a product.

The difficulty with this approach is the measurement of utility, which is both abstract and subjective. This problem can be overcome conceptually by defining a unit of measure called a 'util'. A util is an imaginary unit which measures satisfaction or utility. If a person consumes a particular product, the satisfaction that is received is measured in utils.

Using the util as a unit of measure, we can examine the relationship between total utility and marginal utility. Table 4.1 shows the total utility and marginal utility derived by an individual from eating apples.

TABLE 4.1: CONSUMER'S UTILITY FROM CONSUMING APPLES

Quantity	TU (utils)	MU (utils)
0	0	
		7
1	7	
		4
2	11	
		2
3	13	
		1
4	14	
		0
5	14	
		−2
6	12	

To calculate total utility, we add the utils for each unit consumed. Marginal utility is the utility gained from consuming one more unit. The marginal utility gained from consuming the first unit is 7 utils. The marginal utility gained by consuming the second unit is 4 utils (11 utils–7 utils), and so on.

This information is shown in Figure 4.1. Satisfaction, measured in utils, is the variable on the vertical axis. The number of apples consumed (Q) is the variable on the horizontal axis.

Typically, total utility curves are in the shape of an inverted U (our example illustrates only the first six units consumed). For the first few units total utility increases but at a decreasing rate. It is rising but at a slower and slower rate. Total utility then reaches a maximum. The level of satisfaction derived from consuming the particular product is at its highest; satiation has been attained. After this total utility declines, i.e. slopes downwards. The consumption of more units of the product has a negative impact on total utility. These extra units yield dissatisfaction or what economists term disutility.

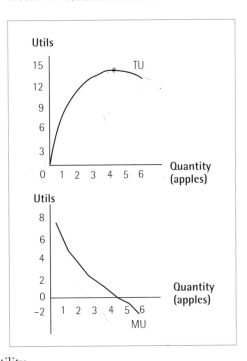

FIGURE 4.1: TOTAL AND MARGINAL UTILITY

The marginal utility curve slopes downwards. The first unit consumed gives the greatest satisfaction or the highest number of utils. The consumer gains less utility from each additional apple consumed. This example demonstrates an issue that is so fundamental that we call it the principle of diminishing marginal utility.

> **Definition**
>
> *The principle of diminishing marginal utility: the consumption of the first unit of a product provides the consumer with the highest level of marginal utility. Each additional unit yields lower and lower levels of marginal utility.*

In other words, the marginal utility curve declines as consumption increases. Initially the total utility curve increases at a decreasing rate and the marginal utility curve slopes downwards but the values are still positive. The marginal utility curve intersects the quantity axis when total utility is at a maximum; satiation has occurred. Finally, as the total utility curve slopes further downwards reflecting disutility, the marginal utility curve is below the quantity axis reflecting negative values. We now turn to the consumer's objective, which economists assume to be utility maximisation.

Utility maximisation and consumer equilibrium

We begin with the assumption that the consumer aims to maximise utility subject to constraints. The two constraints that limit the choices of the consumer are income and prices.

The utility-maximisation equilibrium condition is best illustrated with an example.

Kieran drives to Dundalk every Saturday to do his weekly shopping. He has €48, which he spends on three items: bread, meat and cigarettes. Bread costs €2 per unit (i.e. loaf), meat costs €4 per kilogram and cigarettes cost €6 per pack of 20. Table 4.2 presents the total utils that Kieran gains by consuming each of these products.

TABLE 4.2: KIERAN'S TOTAL UTILITY

Bread		Meat		Cigarettes	
Q	TU	Q	TU	Q	TU
0	0	0	0	0	0
1	24	1	48	1	60
2	46	2	92	2	114
3	66	3	132	3	162
4	84	4	168	4	204
5	100	5	200	5	240
6	114	6	228	6	270

The marginal utilities are presented in Table 4.3. For the purpose of comparison we divide the marginal utility for a unit of product by its price to calculate the marginal utility per euro (MU/€).

TABLE 4.3: MAXIMISING UTILITY BY EQUALISING MUs PER EURO SPENT

Bread				Meat				Cigarettes			
Q	TU	MU	MU/€	Q	TU	MU	MU/€	Q	TU	MU	MU/€
0	0			0	0			0	0		
		24	12			48	12			60	10
1	24			1	48			1	60		
		22	11			44	11			54	9
2	46			2	92			2	114		
		20	10			40	10			48	8
3	66			3	132			3	162		
		18	9			36	9			42	7
4	84			4	168			4	204		
		16	8			32	8			36	6
5	100			5	200			5	240		
		14	7			28	7			30	5
6	114			6	228			6	270		

We will find the best bundle that Kieran can afford by applying the equi-marginal principle.

> **Definition**
>
> *The equi-marginal principle states that utility is maximised when the utility for the last euro spent on each product is equalised.*

Assuming that all of the consumer's income is spent, this principle ensures that the consumer will not find it possible to increase utility by switching a euro's worth of expenditure from one product to another.

For two products X and Y, the equi-marginal principle can be expressed in algebraic terms, as shown in Equation 4.1.

$$\frac{MU_X}{P_X} = \frac{MU_Y}{P_Y} \qquad\qquad [4.1]$$

In the example above, the utility-maximising rule holds for four different combinations:

Combination 1 = (3 bread, 3 meat and 1 cigarettes)
Combination 2 = (4 bread, 4 meat and 2 cigarettes)
Combination 3 = (5 bread, 5 meat and 3 cigarettes)
Combination 4 = (6 bread, 6 meat and 4 cigarettes)

Total cost and total utility for these four combinations are calculated in Table 4.4.

TABLE 4.4: FOUR POSSIBLE COMBINATIONS

	Combination 1	Combination 2	Combination 3	Combination 4
Bread at €2 ea.	€ 6	€ 8	€10	€12
Meat at €4 ea.	€12	€16	€20	€24
Cigarettes at €6 ea.	€ 6	€12	€18	€24
Total cost	€24	€36	€48	€60
Total utility	258	366	462	546

Combinations 1 and 2 do not satisfy the condition that all income is used. Thus, the consumer is not maximising utility with either of these combinations. The income limit of €48 is exceeded in the choice of combination 4. The consumer maximises utility when he chooses combination 3. All income is spent and total utility is equal to 462 utils.

The following is the utility-maximising combination subject to the €48 budget constraint:

$$\frac{16}{2} = \frac{32}{4} = \frac{48}{6}$$

Similarly, we can consider other combinations that will use all of Kieran's available income, but that do not satisfy the principle that the utility for the last euro spent is equal for all available products. We will compare combination 3 (the utility-maximising combination of bread, meat and cigarettes) with two other affordable combinations:

Combination 3 = (5 bread, 5 meat and 3 cigarettes)
Combination 5 = (4 bread, 4 meat and 4 cigarettes)
Combination 6 = (5 bread, 2 meat and 5 cigarettes)

Total cost and total utility for these three combinations are calculated in Table 4.5.

TABLE 4.5: THREE AFFORDABLE COMBINATIONS

	Combination 3	Combination 5	Combination 6
Bread at €2 each	€10	€ 8	€10
Meat at €4 each	€20	€16	€ 8
Cigarettes at €6 each	€18	€24	€30
Total cost	€48	€48	€48
Total utility	462	456	432

All of these combinations are affordable, but only combination 3 maximises utility. This is the only one of the three combinations where marginal utility divided by price is equal for the last unit of each product consumed.

Combination 3 is the best combination that Kieran can afford. He cannot increase utility by switching a euro's worth of expenditure from one product to another. Since there is no tendency to change, it is an equilibrium position.

This analysis can be used to explain why the individual's demand curve is negatively sloped. For example, let us concentrate on the utility derived from the consumption of meat. At the existing price level of €4 the utility-maximising rule indicates that Kieran will purchase five kilos of meat. Suppose the butcher cuts the price of meat. As a result Kieran will switch consumption away from both bread and cigarettes to the lower-priced meat. The utility-maximising rule will yield a new combination in equilibrium. The new combination will include a higher quantity of meat at the lower price. This suggests a negative relationship between the price and the quantity demanded, which is reflected in a downward sloping demand curve for this product.

Synopsis of the marginal utility approach

The assumptions

1. The consumer can measure satisfaction by utils.
2. Consumer choices are limited by income and prices.
3. The principle of diminishing marginal utility applies.

The theory

The consumer wishes to maximise utility, given income and price constraints.

The predictions

Consumer equilibrium is achieved with the combination of products that satisfy the equi-marginal principle, provided that all income is spent. In other words, the consumer will maximise utility where the utilities for the last euro spent are equal for all products, and all income is spent.

The weaknesses

1. There is no way of measuring utility.

2. Interpersonal utility comparisons are not possible.

We now turn to the second approach.

4.3 THE INDIFFERENCE-PREFERENCE ANALYSIS

The problems associated with measuring utility led to the development of the indifference-preference approach. This approach acknowledges the difficulties involved in attempting to measure utility. These difficulties can be overcome or simply avoided by the adoption of an ordinal approach which merely requires that the consumer be able to rank or order different alternatives according to his or her preference. It does not depend on allocating specific numerical values to different levels of satisfaction.

A number of assumptions apply to the consumer's preferences.

1. The consumer ranks alternatives according to tastes and preferences that do not depend on income or prices. A consumer's tastes and preferences change slowly over time and therefore we can consider them as 'constant' at a particular moment in time.
2. The consumer prefers more to less. This observation excludes what we call 'bads' (e.g. pollution), where the consumer prefers less to more.
3. Any two consumption bundles can be compared. This is known as the axiom of completeness. A consumer must either prefer combination A to combination B or prefer combination B to combination A or be indifferent between combination A and combination B.
4. Preferences must satisfy the law of transitivity, i.e. if a consumer chooses combination A over combination B and also chooses the same combination B over combination C then the consumer must be consistent by choosing combination A over combination C.

The first assumption makes reference to the two constraints, income and prices. These constraints are represented by a budget line which we will discuss later. We begin our analysis with a look at another new concept – an indifference curve.

The indifference curve

> **Definition**
>
> *An indifference curve shows all the bundles or combinations of two products that give the same level of utility to the consumer.*

Although all points on an indifference curve represent different combinations of products, the consumer is indifferent between all the combinations. We could say that utility is constant along any given indifference curve. Indifference curves reflect the consumer's tastes and preferences for the products.

There are a number of properties of indifference curves. These are listed here and discussed in greater detail in Appendix 4.1.

1. Indifference curves slope downwards from left to right.
2. Indifference curves are normally convex to the origin.
3. Indifference curves do not intersect.
4. There is a multiple set of indifference curves, called a preference map.

5.   The higher the indifference curve, the higher the level of utility.

FIGURE 4.2: AN INDIFFERENCE CURVE

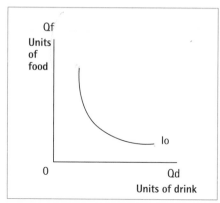

An indifference curve is illustrated in Figure 4.2.

The horizontal and vertical axes represent units of drink and food.

   Indifference curves reflect individual tastes and preferences. For example, a consumer may consume both food and drink but have a relative preference for drink, i.e. prefer one unit of drink to one unit of food. This set of preferences is indicated in Figure 4.3(a). The indifference curve is relatively steep. To gain an additional unit of drink, the consumer is willing to give up several units of food. Alternatively, Figure 4.3(b) shows a relatively flat indifference curve. In this case, the consumer is willing to give up several units of drink in order to gain an additional unit of food. This particular indifference curve indicates that the consumer has a relative preference for food over drink.

   The slope of an indifference curve at a particular point represents the consumer's willingness to trade between the two products, i.e. the consumer's trade-off between the two products. The slope of an indifference curve is determined by tastes and preferences. Economists refer to the slope of an indifference curve at a particular point as the marginal rate of substitution (MRS) between the two products.

FIGURE 4.3: INDIFFERENCE CURVES AND PREFERENCES BETWEEN TWO PRODUCTS

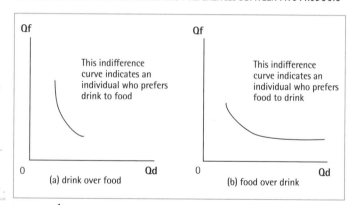

Definition

The marginal rate of substitution (MRS) for an individual consumer between two products X and Y represents the maximum number of units of product Y that the consumer is willing to sacrifice for an extra unit of product X.

If the two products are food and drink then the MRS is given by the number of units of food that the consumer is willing to sacrifice in order to gain an extra unit of drink. This is expressed in Equation 4.2.

$$MRS = \frac{-\Delta Q_f}{\Delta Q_d}$$

[4.2]

The income of the consumer and the prices of the products limit the endless wants of the consumer. These constraints are reflected in our second new concept, the budget line.

The budget line

> **Definition**
>
> *The budget line illustrates the various maximum combinations of two products that the consumer can purchase, given income and prices.*

It constrains the consumer's choices. In effect, it splits the two-dimensional space into two parts, the affordable and the unaffordable. The feasible alternatives are located on or inside the budget line, whereas the much larger range of unfeasible alternatives is found outside the budget line. The two constraints, income and prices, determine the position and the slope of the budget line. A change in either or both of the constraints results in a new budget line.

The position of the budget line is determined by the level of income, as illustrated in Figure 4.4. As income increases, the budget line moves away from the origin and, as a result, the affordable space increases. At a higher income, the consumer can afford more units of food and more units of drink. If income falls, the budget line moves closer to the origin and the affordable space contracts.

FIGURE 4.4: THE BUDGET LINE AND CHANGES IN INCOME

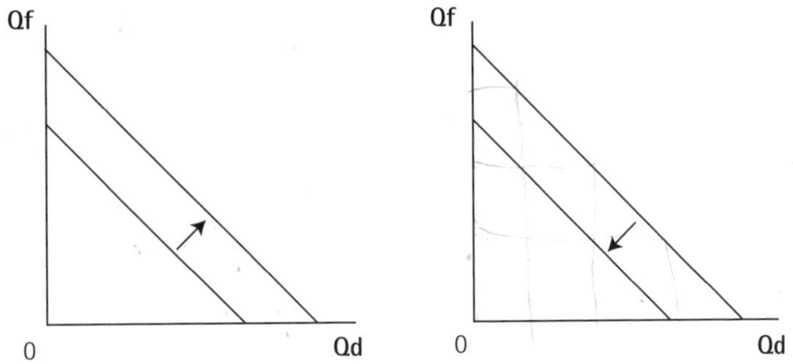

(a) An increase in income   (b) A decrease in income

The slope of the budget line is determined by the relative prices of the two products. The slope measures the opportunity cost of one product, food, in terms of another product, drink. For example, suppose that drink costs €2 per unit and food costs €1 per unit. In order to consume an extra unit of drink, the consumer must forgo two units of food. The opportunity cost of an extra unit of drink is two units of food. As such, the budget line indicates the trade-off between the two products from society's perspective. Formally, the slope of the budget line is equal to the negative of the ratio of the two prices. Equation 4.3 states this in mathematical form.

$$\text{Slope of the budget line} = \frac{-P_d}{P_f} \qquad\qquad [4.3]$$

where: P_d = price of drink; P_f = price of food.

If the product on the vertical axis is expensive in relation to the product on the horizontal axis, the budget line is relatively flat. Conversely, if the product on the horizontal axis is expensive in relation to the product on the vertical axis the budget line is relatively steep. This is shown in Figure 4.5.

FIGURE 4.5: RELATIVE PRICES AND THE SLOPE OF THE BUDGET LINE

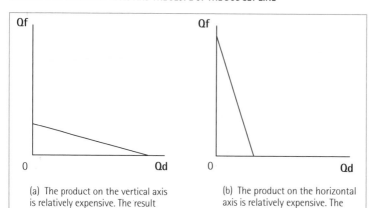

(a) The product on the vertical axis is relatively expensive. The result is a flat budget line.

(b) The product on the horizontal axis is relatively expensive. The result is a steep budget line.

CASE STUDY

Inflation and the purchasing power of people on 'fixed incomes'

Inflation is a rise in the general price level. It will be discussed in greater detail in Chapter 17. However, in this case study, we will look at the effect of inflation for people on 'fixed incomes'. These are people who, for example, receive jobseeker's benefits, state pensions or other social welfare payments. Their budget is 'fixed' in the sense that often their entire income consists of the money which they receive from the state in the form of a weekly payment which changes only annually. Increases to social welfare payments are announced by the Minister for Finance on budget day (usually in early December). Table 4.6 shows the standard (maximum) payments for various social welfare categories for 2010 and 2011.

Consider the pensioner who is under 80 years of age and receiving the maximum contributory pension. 'Contributory' means that this person previously paid pay related social insurance (PRSI). In effect, the state collected this money when the person was employed and returns it after the person retires. In 2010, this pensioner received €230.30 per week. This amount remained unchanged in nominal terms for 2011. However, for the year 2011, the government expected an increase in the price level of approximately 2.0%. If this inflation estimate was correct, the pensioner could purchase approximately 2.0% less products in 2011 than in 2010, i.e. the pensioner's real purchasing power would have decreased by approximately 2.0%.

TABLE 4.6: MAXIMUM RATES OF SOCIAL WELFARE PAYMENTS				
	2010	**2011**	**% Change**	**% Real Change**
State pension (weekly)				
Contributory				
Under 80	€230.30	€230.30	0.0	−2.0
80 or over	€240.30	€240.30		
Non-contributory				
Under 80	€219.00	€219.00		
80 or over	€229.00	€229.00		
Jobseeker (weekly)				
Jobseeker's benefit	€196.00	€188.00		
Jobseeker's allowance				
25+	€196.00	€188.00		
22–24	€150.00	€144.00		
18–21	€100.00	€100.00		
Carer (weekly)				
Carer's benefit	€213.00	€205.00		
Carer's allowance (under 66)	€212.00	€204.00		
Child Benefit (monthly)				
First child	€150.00	€140.00		
Second child	€150.00	€140.00		
Third child	€187.00	€167.00		

Questions

1. Complete the '% Change' and '% Real Change' columns. Between 2010 and 2011, which social welfare categories received (a) the biggest real increase; and (b) the smallest real increase?

2. If 'real change' is defined with respect to changes in average earnings (as opposed to inflation) and if average earnings between 2010 and 2011 are assumed to have decreased by 1.5% during 2010, which categories received a real increase in payment?

3. Using the internet (e.g. www.cso.ie) or otherwise, attempt to find estimates for the change in average earnings for different broad categories (e.g. for industrial workers or for public sector workers) between 2010 and 2011. Which of these estimates do you think is most appropriate for measuring or estimating average earnings in Ireland? Explain your answer.

Answers on website

Consumer equilibrium

Consider Pauline, who can choose between only two products, food and drink. In Figure 4.6 the quantity of food, Qf, is depicted on the vertical axis and the quantity of drink, Qd, is depicted on the horizontal axis. A set of indifference curves and a budget line are drawn.

Pauline chooses the combination of food and drink that maximises her utility and uses all her income. Graphically, this is where the budget line, reflecting the budget constraint, is tangent to the highest possible indifference curve, reflecting the consumer's preferences. Equivalently, this is the point at which the slope of the budget line is equal to the slope of the indifference curve.

Point X is the optimal consumption bundle. Recall that the slope of the indifference curve is the marginal rate of substitution (MRS) whereas the negative of the ratio of prices is the slope of the budget line. Equation 4.4 states that they are equal at X, the point of tangency, which is the optimum bundle the consumer can afford.

FIGURE 4.6: MAXIMISING CONSUMER UTILITY CONSTRAINED BY INCOME AND PRICES

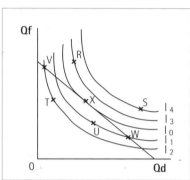

$$MRS = \frac{-P_d}{P_f}$$ [4.4]

Let us examine other consumption bundles. Bundles R and S are desirable but unattainable. They are desirable because they are on higher indifference curves: they are unattainable because they are outside the budget line. Pauline does not have sufficient income to purchase either of these combinations. In contrast, bundles T and U are attainable but undesirable. Pauline can afford them because they are inside the budget line. They are undesirable because it is possible for Pauline to reach a higher level of utility if she spends all of her income. Neither V nor W is the optimal consumption bundle because it is possible to reach a higher indifference curve and still remain on the budget line.

Point X, and only point X, is the optimal consumption bundle. This point is called consumer equilibrium. Like any equilibrium, when the consumer is at this point, there is no tendency to change. Pauline is at the highest level of satisfaction possible given her income and the prevailing prices. This is the best bundle that Pauline can afford.

Income change analysis

In the analysis above, income and prices were held constant. Now we will consider a change in equilibrium arising out of a change in income with prices held constant. We will observe that the changes in the equilibrium positions will differ, depending on whether the goods (or more generally products) are normal or inferior.

Two scenarios are illustrated in Figure 4.7. Figure 4.7(a) shows a budget line for two normal goods, food and drink. Figure 4.7(b) shows a budget line drawn for food (a normal good) on the vertical axis. Bus rides, an inferior good, is represented on the horizontal axis. In both cases income increases and the budget line shifts out and to the right. Since prices do not change, the new budget line is parallel to the original budget line.

FIGURE 4.7: A CHANGE IN INCOME

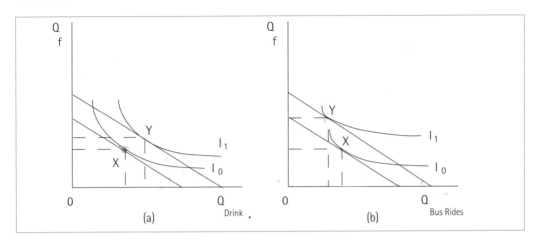

| (a) | (b) |

Consider Figure 4.7(a). Before the income change, the consumer was in equilibrium at point X. The consumer is now in equilibrium at the optimal consumption bundle Y. This bundle contains more units of both food and drink. If both goods are classified as normal, an increase in income results in an increase in the consumption of both goods.

Now consider Figure 4.7(b). Again, the point of consumer equilibrium, after income increases, is represented by point Y. In this case, an increase in income results in the consumption of more of the normal good, food, but less of the inferior good, bus rides.

We can now see that an increase in income affects consumer equilibrium differently, depending on whether a good is normal or inferior. If a good is normal, more of that good will be consumed if income increases. On the other hand, if a good is inferior, less is consumed if income increases. We will now turn our attention to the effect of a change in price on consumer equilibrium.

FIGURE 4.8: A CHANGE IN PRICE

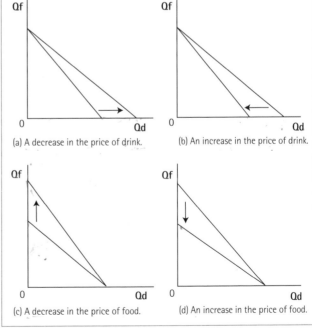

(a) A decrease in the price of drink.

(b) An increase in the price of drink.

(c) A decrease in the price of food.

(d) An increase in the price of food.

Price change analysis and the demand curve

A change in price alters the equilibrium position. We begin by examining the effect of a change of price on the budget line. Different price adjustments are illustrated in Figure 4.8.

The slope of a budget line is equal to the negative of the ratio of prices. A change in the price of one good alters the slope of the budget line. When this occurs, the budget line pivots around one or other of the intercept points, outwards or inwards depending on whether there is a price decrease or price increase, respectively. All four possible cases are presented above.

Suppose the price of drink decreases. What happens to the consumption of drink? Any change in consumption arising out of a change in price can be separated into two separate components. The first is called the substitution effect, and the second the income effect.

Definition

The substitution effect is the change in demand that is caused by the change in the relative prices of the two goods (or services), holding utility or real income (i.e. purchasing power) constant.

If the price of drink falls, food becomes relatively more expensive in comparison to drink. The consumer reacts to the change in relative prices by consuming more drink and less food.

Definition

The income effect is the change in demand that is caused by the change in real income (i.e. purchasing power) alone.

When price falls, the consumer is wealthier in the sense that the decrease in the price of drink has increased real income. From Figure 4.8(a), we can see that the affordable space is larger as a result of the decrease in price. The purchasing power of the consumer has increased.

From the previous section, we know that the consumer does not respond uniformly to a change in income. The consumer's response depends on whether the good, as defined in economic terms, is normal or inferior.

Therefore, when price decreases, two separate effects are evident. The substitution effect results in an increase in quantity demanded. The consumer will purchase more of the good which is relatively cheaper. The income effect varies depending on whether the good is normal or inferior.

The addition of these two effects amounts to the total change in quantity and is called the total price effect. This is expressed in Equation 4.5.

$$\textbf{Total price effect} = \textbf{substitution effect} + \textbf{income effect} \qquad [4.5]$$

First, we consider the case of a normal good.

A case of a normal good

Figure 4.9 shows the price change and its effect on the consumption of food and drink. Both food and drink are normal goods. X is the original equilibrium bundle. As the price of drink decreases, the budget line rotates around the vertical intercept and moves out to the right along the horizontal axis. The new budget line reflects the change in price and, as a result, has a different slope. The new equilibrium is at bundle Z, the point of tangency between the new budget line and the highest possible indifference curve. More units of drink are consumed at bundle Z than at bundle X. This suggests that there is a negative relationship between price and quantity demanded.

How do we know that bundle Z lies to the right of bundle X and thus reflects a higher level of quantity demanded? The move from X to Z can be divided into two separate parts. First, there

FIGURE 4.9: THE SUBSTITUTION AND INCOME EFFECT FOR A NORMAL GOOD

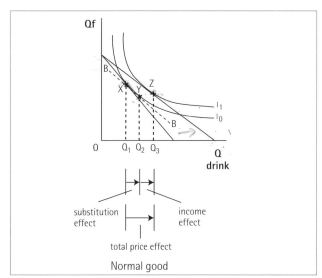

is the substitution effect. This can be illustrated by drawing a hypothetical budget line, BB, which is parallel to the new budget line but is tangent to the original indifference curve, at point Y. Recall that the level of utility is constant along a particular indifference curve. The move from X to Y is the substitution effect. The consumer is changing the consumption bundle in response to the change in relative prices alone, i.e. utility is being kept constant. Consumption of drink is higher at Y than at X.

Second, there is the income effect. As the price of drink decreases, the purchasing power (i.e. real income) of the consumer increases. Since drink is a normal good, as income increases the consumer demands more drink. The income effect is the move from Y to the new bundle Z which must lie to the right of Y in order to reflect the fact that drink is a normal good.

The total price effect is the move from X to Z with Z lying to the right of X and thus reflecting higher units of drink consumed. As price decreases, quantity demanded increases.

Figure 4.10 shows how this analysis combined with a price consumption curve can help in the graphical derivation of an individual consumer's demand curve. The upper figure shows three budget lines, which correspond to decreasing prices of drink. Each new budget line pivots to the right. There is a unique equilibrium (X, Z and U) associated with each budget line. As the affordable space increases, the consumer can move to higher indifference curves.

FIGURE 4.10: THE PRICE CONSUMPTION CURVE AND THE DEMAND CURVE FOR A NORMAL GOOD

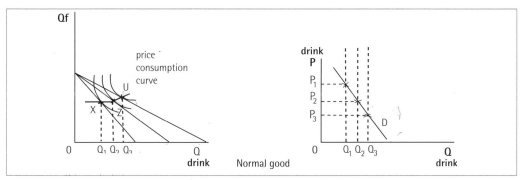

There is a line called the 'price consumption curve', which joins these three equilibria. This curve shows the consumer's preferred combinations given a fixed nominal income and the change in relative prices.

The diagram on the right shows the consumer's demand curve for drink. We are looking at the 'price consumption' relationship for a single good. The three price levels, shown on the vertical axis, correspond to the falling price of drink which caused the budget line to pivot to the right. The horizontal axis shows the units of drink consumed at each price level. The consumer responds to the change in the price of drink by increasing the consumption of drink. The demand curve slopes downward from left to right.

The analysis above applies to a normal good. We now turn our attention towards an inferior good.

A case of an inferior good

We will now consider a decrease in the price of an inferior good, bus rides. The substitution effect is always the same, regardless of whether a good is normal, inferior or Giffen; when the price of a good falls, the demand increases for that good as a result of the substitution effect. In this case, when the price of bus rides falls, we expect the consumer to react to the change in relative prices by using buses more often as a means of transport, holding utility or purchasing power constant.

The income effect is the change in consumption which arises from a change in real income. For a normal good, as price decreases real income increases and, consequently, consumption increases. However, for an inferior good, as real income increases consumption decreases. In this case, as a response to the increase in real income, we expect that the consumer will demand fewer bus rides, an inferior good.

We now have an increase in consumption arising from the substitution effect and a decrease in consumption arising from the income effect. One effect offsets, to at least some extent, the other effect and since the total price effect is the addition of the two, it is unclear whether consumption increases or decreases.

In fact, the decrease in quantity due to the increase in income is generally relatively small so that it does not generally outweigh the increase in quantity that arises from the substitution effect. The substitution effect outweighs the income effect for an inferior good (with the exception of the Giffen good, which is explained later). The increase in quantity arising from the substitution effect (reflected in the move from X to Y) is greater than the decrease in quantity arising from the income effect (reflected in the move from Y to Z). The total price effect (shown by the move from X to Z), which is the addition of the substitution and the income effect, is still an increase in quantity. This is shown in Figure 4.11.

As price decreases for an inferior good the quantity consumed increases but not by as much as it would for a normal good. The demand curve for an inferior good is downward sloping but, on account of the smaller change in quantity consumed, the demand curve is relatively steep. The price consumption curve for the inferior good is shown in Figure 4.12.

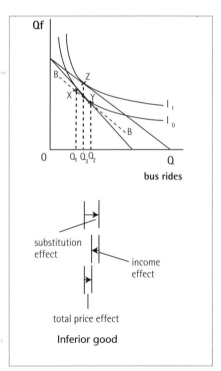

FIGURE 4.11: THE SUBSTITUTION AND INCOME EFFECT FOR AN INFERIOR GOOD

The difference between the normal good and the inferior good is reflected in the respective slopes of the demand curves. The demand curve for the inferior good is steeper than the demand curve for the normal good.

FIGURE 4.12: THE PRICE CONSUMPTION CURVE AND THE DEMAND CURVE FOR AN INFERIOR GOOD

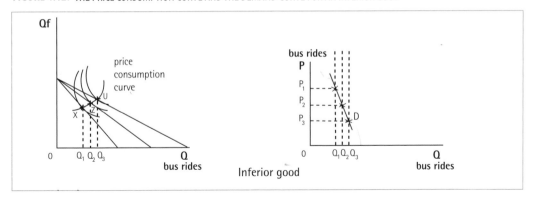

Inferior good

A case of a Giffen good

Definition

A Giffen good has an upward sloping demand curve over a range of prices. As price decreases, the quantity demanded of a Giffen good also decreases. A Giffen good is a very inferior good.

We need to consider the effect of a price change on a Giffen good. The Giffen good received its name from Sir Robert Giffen who, it is believed, claimed that during the Irish famine of the 1840s, the consumption of potatoes increased even though the price increased.[4] Theoretically, this strange phenomenon can be explained using substitution and income effects.

The substitution effect is always the same. However, in the case of a strongly inferior or Giffen good, the (unusual) income effect actually outweighs the substitution effect. In the case of a Giffen good, a decrease in the price results in an increase in demand that stems from the substitution effect (as always), but a stronger decrease in demand that stems from the unusual income effect. Overall, as price decreases, demand decreases (albeit only over a limited range of price changes). The demand curve for the Giffen good is upward sloping (over a limited range of prices).

Figure 4.13 shows the substitution and income effects for a price fall for a Giffen good. The increase in quantity arising from the substitution effect (X to Y) is smaller than the decrease in quantity arising from the income effect (Y to Z). At the new consumer equilibrium, point Z, the consumer is consuming less of the Giffen good than before.

FIGURE 4.13: THE SUBSTITUTION AND INCOME EFFECT FOR A GIFFEN GOOD

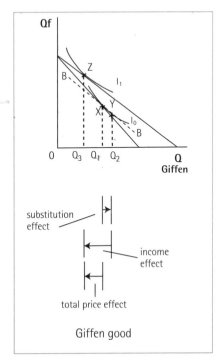

Figure 4.14 shows the backward-bending price consumption curve. As price falls, the quantity consumed decreases. The price-quantity relationship is positive and this is reflected in an upward sloping demand curve.

A complete summary of the price changes and the subsequent quantity changes for all three categories of goods is presented in Table 4.7.

FIGURE 4.14: THE PRICE CONSUMPTION CURVE AND THE DEMAND CURVE FOR A GIFFEN GOOD

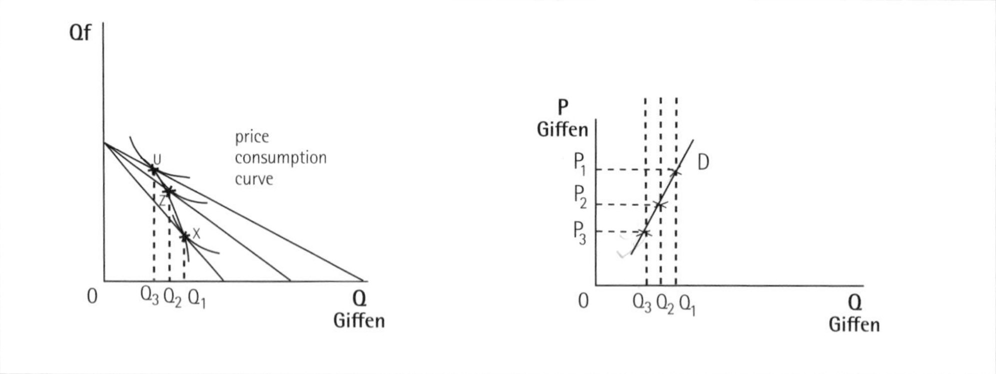

TABLE 4.7: SUMMARY OF PRICE CHANGES AND QUANTITY CHANGES

Price change	Type of good	Substitution effect	Income effect	Total effect
Decrease	Normal	Qd increases	Qd increases	Qd increases
	Inferior	Qd increases	Qd decreases	Qd increases
	Giffen	Qd increases	Qd decreases	Qd decreases
Increase	Normal	Qd decreases	Qd decreases	Qd decreases
	Inferior	Qd decreases	Qd increases	Qd decreases
	Giffen	Qd decreases	Qd increases	Qd increases

Synopsis of the indifference-preference approach

The assumptions

1. The consumer ranks alternative combinations of products according to preferences.
2. The consumer's choices are limited by income and prices.
3. The principle of diminishing marginal utility applies.

The theory

The consumer wishes to maximise satisfaction subject to income and price constraints.

The predictions

The optimal consumption bundle is found where the budget line is tangent to the highest possible indifference curve. At this tangency point, the respective slopes of the budget line and indifference curve are equal.

The weaknesses

1. Indifference curves are difficult, if not impossible, to observe or even derive in the real world.
2. The assumptions which underlie the theory are restrictive and sidestep or even ignore actual apparently irrational (but real world) consumer behaviour.

4.4 CONSUMER SURPLUS

In *Principles of Economics* Alfred Marshall defined consumer surplus as the '. . . excess of the price which he would be willing to pay rather than go without the thing, over that which he actually does pay . . .'[5]

> Definition
>
> *Consumer surplus is the excess of what a consumer is prepared to pay for a product over what the consumer actually pays.*

Sometimes this concept is referred to as the social benefit accruing to the consumer who purchases the product. This term is used to describe the operation of the price mechanism that allows consumers to acquire products at a lower price than they are willing to pay.

Before we look at a market consisting of many consumers, we begin with the consumption decision of a single consumer. Consider Jack, a hat lover. Figure 4.15 shows Jack's demand curve for hats.

We can see that Jack is willing to pay €8 for the first hat that he purchases. This is the hat from which he derives the highest marginal utility; therefore he is willing to pay the most for it. However, the market price is only €4 per hat. Therefore, although Jack is prepared to pay €8 for this hat, he only has to pay €4. His consumer surplus is €4 for the first unit. Because of diminishing marginal utility (and hence side-stepping any addictive behaviour that might lead to Jack actually having an increasing need for extra hats), Jack is willing to pay only €7 for the second hat.

FIGURE 4.15: JACK'S DEMAND CURVE FOR HATS

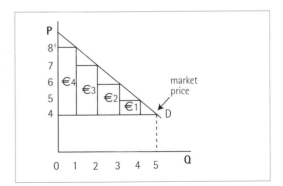

For this unit, his consumer surplus is €3. Jack continues to consume until the consumer surplus on the last unit purchased equals zero. In this example, the market price of €4 equals the price that Jack is just willing to pay for his fifth hat.

From Figure 4.15, we can see that Jack is willing to pay €30 for five hats (=€8+€7+€6+€5+€4). To put this in another way, we can say that Jack is gaining €30 worth of pleasure or benefit from his purchase of hats. Jack's total expenditure is €20 (5 x €4). Jack's total consumer surplus for hats is the amount that he is willing to pay less the amount that he has to pay (the total expenditure). The consumer surplus in this example is €10 (the sum of €4+€3+€2+€1).

The market demand curve is derived by adding individual demand curves. We can think of the market demand curve for hats as representing the amount that consumers collectively are willing to pay for a particular quantity of that product. Consider Figure 4.16.

FIGURE 4.16: MARKET DEMAND CURVE FOR HATS

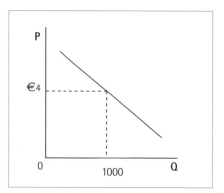

If 1,000 hats are available for sale, consumers are willing to pay €4 per hat. This is the market price. However, there are some consumers who are willing to pay more for those hats. Since they only have to pay €4 per hat, some consumers pay less than they are willing to pay. In other words, just as with Jack, we can identify consumer surplus for the market. It is the difference between the market price and the price that consumers are willing to pay.

Figure 4.17 shows consumer surplus for the market.

Suppose that the market price for hats is P^0 and at this price the market demands Q^0 hats. The total benefit or satisfaction received by the market is represented by the area [$0AXQ^0$]. This is the total amount that consumers are willing to pay for Q^0 hats. The total expenditure on hats is represented by the area [$0P^0XQ^0$]. The difference between the total benefit and the total expenditure is represented by the shaded triangle P^0AX. This is the area of consumer surplus.

FIGURE 4.17: CONSUMER SURPLUS

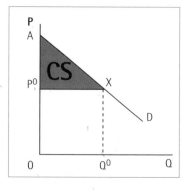

Consumer surplus is a very important concept in economics and has many valuable applications. These include cost-benefit analysis, the efficiency and distribution effects of tax changes and subsidies and competition policy.

SUMMARY

1. There are two main approaches to the theory of consumer behaviour and demand. The first is the marginal utility theory. It is based on the assumption that utility is measurable. A marginal utility curve is derived which slopes downward and reflects the principle of diminishing marginal utility. The consumer maximises utility if the marginal utility per euro spent on each product is the same. This is called the equi-marginal principle.
2. The second approach is the indifference-preference theory. It requires the ordering of different alternatives according to the consumer's preferences. The preferences of the consumer are reflected in indifference curves whereas the constraints are reflected in the budget line.
3. The consumer maximises satisfaction where the budget line is tangent to the highest possible indifference curve. At this point, called consumer equilibrium, the negative of the ratio of prices of the two products is equal to the marginal rate of substitution between the two products.
4. The demand curve for a good can be derived by separating the quantity change into two separate components. The substitution effect is the change in demand arising out of the change in relative prices. It is in the same direction for all categories of goods. The income effect is the change in demand arising out of the change in real income. Its direction varies depending on whether the good is normal or inferior.
5. The substitution and income effect analysis is useful when deriving the demand curve for the three standard categories of goods. The demand curve for a normal good conforms to the principle of demand by sloping downwards from left to right. The demand curve for an inferior good also slopes downwards but it is steeper on account of the (unusual) income effect which partially offsets the substitution effect. The exception is the Giffen good, whose demand curve has a positive slope (over a range of prices).
6. Consumer surplus arises from the difference between the price consumers pay for the product and the price they are willing to pay. In effect, it is a benefit to consumers. It has many useful applications in economics.

KEY TERMS

Marginalists	Marginal rate of substitution	Indifference curve
Utility	Relative prices	Budget line
Total utility	Optimal consumption bundle	Preference map
Marginal utility	Substitution effect	
Util	Income effect	
Diminishing marginal utility	Price consumption curve	
Equi-marginal principle	Giffen good	
Preferences	Consumer surplus	

REVIEW QUESTIONS

1. Briefly explain the main differences between the marginal utility approach and the indifference-preference approach to consumer choice theory.
2. Using the marginal utility approach, explain how the consumer maximises utility. Show how this approach and, in particular, the concept of marginal utility is related to the principle of demand and the conventional downward sloping demand curve.

3. List and briefly explain the assumptions of consumers' preferences and the properties of both the budget line and indifference curves.

4. Using the indifference-preference approach, explain how the optimal consumption bundle is derived.

5. Suppose we have a two-good model with both goods classified as normal. The price of the good whose quantity is represented on the horizontal axis increases. Use the substitution and income effect analysis to explain why consumption decreases in response to this price increase.

6. Suppose the good, whose quantity is represented on the horizontal axis, is a Giffen good. Consider a price increase. Derive the price consumption curve that is associated with this change in price. How does this vary from the price consumption curve for a normal or inferior good? Explain the reason for the difference.

WORKING PROBLEMS

1. Sara spends a day on the beach. She has an income of €22 and can spend this budget on some combination of mineral water, ice cream and soft drinks. Mineral water sells for €4, ice cream for €2 and soft drinks for €1. The hypothetical marginal utility values are presented in Table 4.8.

TABLE 4.8: SARA'S THREE ALTERNATIVES: MINERAL WATER, ICE CREAM AND SOFT DRINKS

Mineral water		Ice cream		Soft drinks	
Q	MU	Q	MU	Q	MU
	36		30		32
1		1		1	
	24		22		28
2		2		2	
	20		16		20
3		3		3	
	18		12		14
4		4		4	
	16		10		8
5		5		5	
	10		4		6
6		6		6	
	6		2		4
7		7		7	

What combination yields Sara maximum utility?

2. Ellie and Moe each receive €150 per week for their retirement pensions. They purchase two products, bread and tea. Bread costs €1.50 per loaf and tea costs €3.00 per 250g weight. On two separate diagrams, draw a budget line for Ellie and Moe. Ellie prefers bread and Moe prefers tea. Draw an indifference curve for each budget line which reflects the difference in preferences for these two women.

MULTI-CHOICE QUESTIONS

1. According to the marginal utility approach:
    (a) the substitution effect and the income effect confirm that consumption responds positively to price changes;
    (b) real income changes allow for the possibility of an upward sloping demand curve;
    (c) the consumer maximises utility where the utility for the last euro spent on each product is the same;
    (d) indifference curves slope downwards from left to right;
    (e) none of the above.

2. The substitution effect of a price change:
    (a) is in the same direction for all products;
    (b) is the change in demand due solely to the change in relative prices;
    (c) is the change in demand which results from a change in income;
    (d) differs depending on whether a good is normal, inferior or a Giffen good;
    (e) both (a) and (b) above.

3. Which of the following is not a property of indifference curves?
    (a) Combinations of products on the one indifference curve yield the same level of satisfaction to the consumer;
    (b) Indifference curves reflect the income and price constraints;
    (c) The slope of an indifference curve is the marginal rate of substitution;
    (d) Indifference curves usually slope downwards from left to right;
    (e) Indifference curves do not intersect.

4. Suppose Kathleen, an old age pensioner, received an increase of €10 per week immediately following the budget announcement. *Ceteris paribus,* her new budget line for tea and bread will:
    (a) be parallel to her old budget line;
    (b) show an increase in the amount of tea that she can buy but a decrease in the amount of bread that she can buy;
    (c) show that her 'affordable space' has decreased;
    (d) be the same as her old budget line;
    (e) none of the above.

5. Figure 4.18 shows consumer equilibrium for Jack, whose income is €300 per week. From this diagram we know that:

    (a) the price of tea is €1.50;
    (b) the price of bread is €1.00;
    (c) the slope of the budget line is −0.67;
    (d) the marginal rate of substitution between the two products is −0.67;
    (e) all of the above.

FIGURE 4.18

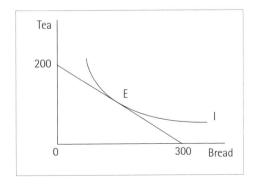

6.   The difference between the price consumers pay for a product and the price they are willing to pay for the product is called:
     (a) substitution effect;
     (b) marginal utility;
     (c) marginal rate of substitution;
     (d) consumer surplus;
     (e) none of the above.

TRUE OR FALSE (SUPPORT YOUR ANSWER)

1.   Diminishing marginal utility means that the second Mars Bar tastes better than the first.

2.   The marginal utility approach states that utility is maximised when marginal utility for the last euro spent on each product is equal.

3.   The consumer surplus is the difference between the market price of a product and the price at which suppliers are willing to supply the products.

4.   The optimal consumption bundle is the tangency point between the highest possible indifference curve and the given budget line.

5.   The demand curve for an inferior good is positively sloped.

6.   For a Giffen good the income effect is stronger than the substitution effect and this produces an upward sloping demand curve.

CASE STUDY

Thinking about Transitivity

The following two examples focus on the assumption of transitivity. The reader should consider to what extent, if any, each example undermines the transitivity assumption.

Example 1: Consider the rather unusual arrangements of numbers on the following three dice: (A) 1 1 4 4 4 4; (B) 3 3 3 3 3 3; and (C) 5 5 2 2 2 2. The reader can verify that the mean (i.e. average) of the six numbers on each die is 3. Consider the following 'game'.
Step 1 Your friend is allowed to choose any die.
Step 2 You can choose either of the remaining two dice.
Step 3 Each of you rolls your die.
Step 4 The highest number wins and a small payment is made by the loser to the winner.
    Let us assume that your 'friend' initially decides to choose die (A). Which of the remaining dice should you choose? The answer is (C) as (C) will beat (A) on 20 out of 36 occasions in the long run. Die C only loses when 2 loses to 4. The probability of this occurring is 2/3 (2 appears on die (C)) multiplied by 2/3 (4 appears on die (A)), i.e. 4/9. Die (C) is preferred by you to die (A). Let us assume that your friend initially chooses die (B). Which of the remaining dice should you choose? The answer is (A) as (A) will beat (B) on 24 out of 36 occasions in the long run. Die (A)

is preferred by you to die (B). Let us assume that your friend initially chooses die (C). Which of the remaining dice should you choose? The answer is (B) as (B) will beat (C) on 24 out of 36 occasions in the long run. Die (B) is preferred by you to die (C).

To summarise: you prefer die (A) to die (B); you prefer die (B) to die (C) but you also prefer die (C) to die (A). Notwithstanding your (at least apparently) intransitive preferences you win in the long run. Of course, your friend will win on many occasions but this should be enough to ensure that your friend remains in the game long enough to guarantee your overall success (and perhaps becomes your ex-friend).

Source: Paul Anand, 'The Philosophy of Intransitive Preferences', *The Economic Journal*, Vol. 103, March 1993, pp. 337–46.

Example 2: Consider three voters (A, B and C) and three policy options (x, y and z). Assume that voter A has the following ranking of policies: x, then y and then z; voter B has the following ranking of policies: y, then z and then x; and voter C has the following ranking of policies: z, then x and then y. It is assumed that each voter also has transitive preferences.

From the collective perspective, however, x is preferred to y (as two voters prefer x to y), y is preferred to z (as two voters prefer y to z) but z is preferred to x (as two voters prefer z to x). In summary, collective preferences can be intransitive despite individual preferences being transitive. This example is generally referred to as the voting paradox.

Conduct within a conflict setting is sometimes argued to provide a real-world example of the voter paradox. Consider x as 'engage in all-out conflict', y as 'engage in limited conflict' and z as 'refuse to engage in conflict'. It seems plausible to suggest that the collective will might rationally prefer x to y, y to z but z to x. The level or scale of US involvement in the Vietnam War is sometimes cited as an example.

The politically astute reader will no doubt recognise other possible policy implications. For example, x could be 'fairly unrestricted access to abortion facilities in Ireland'; y could be 'restricted access to abortion facilities in Ireland' and z could be 'no abortion facilities in Ireland'. However, as only two options are generally put to the electorate, each of the three options could be advantaged by being put against an appropriate alternative.

APPENDIX 4.1: THE PROPERTIES OF INDIFFERENCE CURVES

The properties of indifference curves were listed in Section 4.3. A more detailed explanation is provided below.

1. Indifference curves slope downwards from left to right

FIGURE 4.19: INDIFFERENCE CURVES SLOPE DOWN FROM LEFT TO RIGHT

Consider bundle a in Figure 4.19. Now compare this bundle with other possible bundles. Let us begin with the quadrant to the northeast of a. Compared to bundle a, bundle b offers more of both products, bundle c offers more food and the same amount of drink whereas bundle d offers more

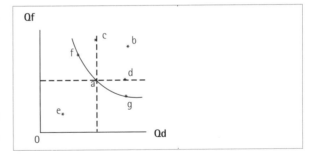

drink and the same amount of food. All of these bundles are preferred to bundle a as the consumer prefers more to less. Hence, these cannot form a locus of points with bundle a which maintains constant utility. This rules out all the possible bundles in the northeast quadrant.

A similar analysis can be applied to the southwest quadrant. All bundles in this quadrant contain less food and/or less drink than are included in bundle a. Since more is preferred to less, the consumer prefers bundle a to any bundle in the southwest quadrant. Bundle e and similar bundles do not lie on the same indifference curve as bundle a.

The only options left are areas to the northwest and southeast of bundle a. Bundles like f and g could possibly be on the same indifference curve. In comparison to bundle a, bundle f contains more food but less drink. Bundle g, on the other hand, contains more drink and less food. It is possible that the consumer is indifferent between bundles a, f and g. Therefore, they can form a meaningful indifference curve which slopes downwards from left to right.

2. Indifference curves are normally convex to the origin

Figure 4.20 indicates that as we move down and to the right along the indifference curve the MRS declines or diminishes. The indifference curve is said to exhibit a diminishing marginal rate of substitution. As we move down the indifference curve, less food and more drink is consumed. A rational consumer is now willing to give up less and less food in order to obtain an extra unit of drink. The MRS diminishes. In the example below, the MRS declines from 3 units to 1 unit.

Diminishing marginal rate of substitution means that indifference curves are usually drawn convex to the origin. However, there are some exceptions to the rule of convexity. Three exceptions are shown in Figure 4.21.

FIGURE 4.20: THE SLOPE OF THE INDIFFERENCE CURVE AND THE MARGINAL RATE OF SUBSTITUTION

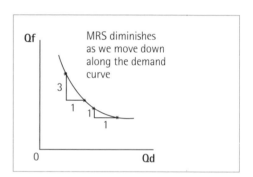

FIGURE 4.21: A SAMPLE OF INDIFFERENCE CURVES

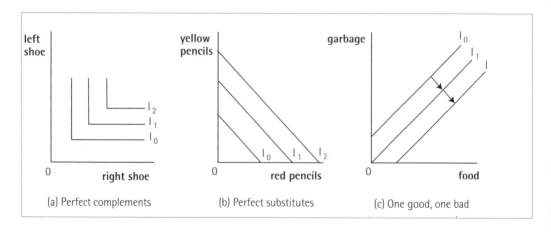

(a) Perfect complements   (b) Perfect substitutes   (c) One good, one bad

Case (a) represents perfect complements; two products that are consumed together in fixed proportions. The indifference curves for such products are L-shaped. An example of perfect complements, for most individuals, is provided by left shoes and right shoes. An individual with one left shoe is no better off if she has two (or three or four) right shoes. Additional right shoes will leave her at the same level of utility (I_0) as the original pair. To move the consumer to a higher level of utility (I_1) she must have a second pair of shoes.

Perfect substitutes, such as red pencils and yellow pencils, are represented by case (b). Here the indifference curves are straight lines with negative slopes equal to –1. The typical consumer is willing to exchange one red pencil for one yellow pencil. In this case, the marginal rate of substitution is constant, rather than diminishing.

Case (c) shows the indifference curve for a good and a 'bad'. A 'bad' is a commodity that the consumer does not like. In order to accept more of the 'bad', which leads to increasing disutility, the consumer must be compensated with more of the 'good', which increases utility. Therefore, the indifference curve has a positive slope. Higher utility is achieved as the curves move from garbage towards food.

3. Indifference curves do not intersect

To establish the validity of this property we use the 'proof by contradiction' method which is used frequently in mathematics and increasingly in economics. In this particular case there are only two possible alternatives; the indifference curves either intersect or they do not intersect. These are mutually exclusive outcomes. Let us presuppose that they do intersect (the idea is to end up with a contradiction which then implies that the only other alternative must be true).

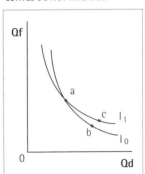

FIGURE 4.22: INDIFFERENCE CURVES DO NOT INTERSECT

Two indifference curves are drawn, intersecting at point a, as in Figure 4.22. Consider I_0. The consumer is indifferent between bundle a and bundle b as both lie on I_0. Consider I_1. The consumer is also indifferent between bundle a and bundle c as both lie on I_1. If she is indifferent between bundles a and b, and also indifferent between bundles a and c then transitivity implies that she is also indifferent between bundle b and bundle c. However, Figure 4.22 clearly shows that bundle c offers more of both products than bundle b. The consumer is not indifferent between these two bundles and opts for bundle c over bundle b. Thus, we have a contradiction that implies that the original proposition was incorrect. The alternative must be true. Indifference curves do not intersect.

FIGURE 4.23: A PREFERENCE MAP

4. There is a multiple set of indifference curves, called a preference map

Every bundle represents some level of satisfaction to the consumer. Hence, every point is on an indifference curve. There is a set of indifference curves. This set is called a preference or indifference map and is drawn in Figure 4.23. For every two consumption bundles there is a third between them. Consequently, for every two indifference

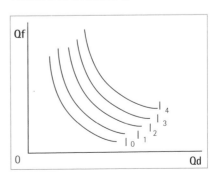

curves there is a third between them. Therefore, there is a multiple set of indifference curves.

5. The higher the indifference curve, the higher the level of utility

Figure 4.24 illustrates three indifference curves. Consider bundles a, b and c. Bundle c offers more of both products compared to bundle b. Consequently, bundle c is preferred to bundle b. Likewise, bundle b is preferred to bundle a. The same applies to indifference curves. Indifference curves which are further from the origin are preferred to indifference curves which are closer to the origin. For example, I_2 is preferred to I_1 which, in turn, is preferred to I_0.

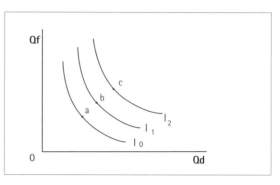

FIGURE 4.24: A SET OF INDIFFERENCE CURVES, EACH REFLECTING A HIGHER LEVEL OF UTILITY THAN THE PREVIOUS (LOWER) ONE

CHAPTER 5

The Firm and Supply

'*Whatever may be the abundance of the source of production, the producer will always stop when the increase in expense exceeds the increase in receipts.*'[1]

AUGUSTIN COURNOT (1801–77)

'*Normal profits are simply the supply price of entrepreneurship to a particular industry.*'[2]

JOAN ROBINSON (1903–83)

CHAPTER OBJECTIVES

Upon completing this chapter, the student should understand:

- short-run production and the law of diminishing returns;
- long-run production and returns to scale;
- opportunity cost and normal profit;
- short-run and long-run costs;
- fixed and variable costs;
- the output decision for the profit-maximising firm.

OUTLINE

5.1 The objectives of the firm
5.2 Production
5.3 Costs
5.4 Profit-maximising output level

INTRODUCTION

Whereas the theory of demand is primarily concerned with the consumer and utility, the theory of supply is related to the producer (supplier) and the costs of production. Costs are the main determinants used by producers to decide what amount of output is to be supplied at the different possible prices. We begin the chapter by examining the traditional, neoclassical objective of profit maximisation. Other plausible objectives are briefly mentioned. The theory of production and an analysis of costs follow. This is followed by a description of the output decision for profit-maximising firms.

5.1 THE OBJECTIVES OF THE FIRM

A firm's behaviour depends largely on its aims. By this we mean that the output produced and the price charged by the firm depend largely on the objective of the firm. For example, the price and output decision of a profit-maximising firm is likely to be different from that of a revenue-maximising firm because of their different objectives. A few of these alternative objectives and their associated models are discussed below.

The traditional neoclassical theory is based on the assumption that the objective of the firm is to maximise profits. It differs from the 'managerial' model which emphasises the differences between ownership and control in modern corporations. Firms are owned by shareholders. Decisions on the operation of the firm are made by managers and implemented by other employees. Although the shareholders may want the firm simply to maximise profits, managers (and other employees) may choose to maximise other objectives such as sales revenue, market share or their own remuneration (e.g. via bonuses or share options).

Another alternative to the traditional neoclassical model is the behavioural model developed by Simon (1955) and Cyert and March (1963). The behavioural model is based on the idea that a firm is comprised of groups or coalitions who have their own objectives. Workers demand better pay, job security and improved working conditions. Shareholders, seeking maximum return for their investment, demand higher profits. There are other demands made from outside the firm by the government, consumers' associations and various other interest groups. This model is different from the traditional neoclassical model which sees the firm as an individual entity (the so-called 'black box') with only one objective, profit maximisation.

The managerial and behavioural models are important contributions to the theory of the firm. However, the traditional neoclassical model, based on profit maximisation, continues to dominate microeconomic theory. We will examine this traditional model in detail. It should be noted at this stage, however, that more recent neoclassical models of the firm no longer treat the firm as a 'black box'. Indeed, the newer (and more complex) neoclassical models of the firm are much more compatible with the managerial and behavioural models.

5.2 PRODUCTION

Any production process involves the transformation of inputs into units of output. Inputs, or factors of production, are usually classified into four categories: labour, land, capital and enterprise. The relationship between these inputs and the output which they generate can be presented in the form of a production function for an economy as demonstrated in Chapter 1. At a more micro level, the production function can also refer to the inputs employed and the outputs produced by an individual firm.

> Definition
>
> *The production function shows the relationship between the amounts of inputs used and the maximum amount of output generated.*

The production function can be expressed in algebraic form as follows:

$$\text{TP} = f(\text{L, Land, K, Enterprise}) \qquad [5.1]$$

where: TP = total product or output; L = number of workers employed; K = capital including plant and machinery.

Literally, this expression means that the amount of a product a firm can produce depends on the amount of inputs used in the production process. Labour, land, capital and enterprise are the independent variables and total product is the dependent variable. In the examination of production that follows, we distinguish between the short run and the long run.

Production in the short run

To begin our discussion, we must explain a few relevant terms.

> **Definition**
>
> *The short run is a period of time where there is at least one factor of production that cannot change.*

The quantity of a 'fixed' factor does not (and cannot) vary as the level of output varies. The fixed factor is generally land, plant or machinery, with the latter falling into the general classification of capital.

In order to discuss production, we will consider a business developed by Sara, an entrepreneur from County Mayo. Sara owns a small firm called Key Chains Ltd. She began producing key chains and selling them from the boot of her jeep. As her business expands, Sara finds that she cannot produce enough key chains to meet all of her orders. Therefore, she hires one employee, then a second and a third. We will consider how each additional worker affects Sara's output.

For this example, we will use a simple short-run production function with only two inputs: capital (i.e. machines) and labour. To produce key chains, Sara uses two machines. These machines represent capital and this factor is fixed in the short run. In contrast, labour is a variable input. Table 5.1 presents the changes in output which result from increasing the number of employees. We can see by looking at the total product column that production begins with the addition of labour. In this case, Sara is the first labourer and, working on her own, she can produce 100 key chains per week. The total product continues to increase as Sara hires more staff. However, with the addition of the eighth worker, total product actually falls.

TABLE 5.1: KEY CHAIN PRODUCTION PER WEEK

(1) Number of workers	(2) K	(3) Total product (TP)	(4) Average product (AP)	(5) Marginal product (MP)
0	2	0	0	
				100
1	2	100	100	
				220
2	2	320	160	
				310
3	2	630	210	
				410
4	2	1040	260	
				360
5	2	1400	280	
				340
6	2	1740	290	
				220
7	2	1960	280	
				−120
8	2	1840	230	

The same information is shown in Figure 5.1. The upper diagram shows the total product curve. It shows the relationship between the variable input, labour and output or total product. Labour is represented on the horizontal axis and total product is represented on the vertical axis. The total product curve shows the same relationship that we described above. Production begins with the addition of the first labourer. The upward sloping curve indicates that output increases until we add the eighth worker. Then the total product curve slopes downward.

The total product curve separates space into attainable output and unattainable output. Levels of output which are above the curve are unattainable using the available labour. For example, three labourers could not produce 700 key chains. All output possibilities inside and on the TP or total product curve are attainable. Those on the curve reflect the maximum attainable output levels. In this example, three labourers could produce 630 key chains (on the curve) or fewer then 630 key chains (inside the curve).

FIGURE 5.1: PRODUCTION: TOTAL PRODUCT, AVERAGE PRODUCT AND MARGINAL PRODUCT

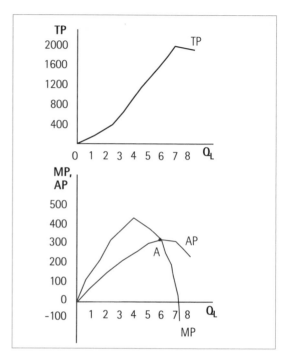

It is clear from the diagram that the production level changes by a different amount with each additional worker because the total product curve is not a straight line. Variations in the total product curve are explained more explicitly using the concept of marginal product.

Definition

The marginal product is the change in total output obtained from using an additional unit of a variable input, holding other inputs constant.

In this example, the marginal product of labour is the extra output derived from the addition of one extra worker while capital is held constant. This relationship is described in Equation 5.2:

$$MP = \frac{\Delta TP}{\Delta Qv} \qquad [5.2]$$

where: Δ = change; MP = marginal product; TP = total product; Qv = quantity of variable input.

Column 5 of Table 5.1 presents the data for the marginal product of labour. Output begins with the addition of the first unit of labour. The marginal product of the first worker is 100 key chains, the number of units that Sara can produce if she works on her own. To find the marginal product of the second employee, we subtract the total product of one worker from the total product of two workers (320 – 100 = 220). Since the change in labour is one, we divide 220 by 1, which equals 220 key chains. This means that the addition of the second worker has increased total product by 220 key chains.

The bottom diagram of Figure 5.1 shows the marginal product of labour curve. We can see that the marginal product curve rises sharply with the addition of each labourer until four individuals are hired. In other words, each additional labourer is adding more to total output than the last. With the addition of the fifth worker, the marginal product of labour begins to fall. After the fourth worker, the marginal product curve is downward sloping.

To understand why the marginal product of labour rises and falls, we will return to Key Chains Ltd and look specifically at Sara's production process. Initially, Sara did everything herself. Before she hired her first employee, Sara made a list of all the tasks required to produce and sell key chains. She broke the process into seven stages:

1. order and receive materials;
2. cut design (machine 1);
3. laminate design (machine 2);
4. cut chain;
5. assemble ring, chain and laminated design;
6. inspect finished product; and
7. sell.

Each of these tasks can possibly be completed by a different person who specialises in that task. Adam Smith, in *An Inquiry into the Nature and Causes of the Wealth of Nations*, provided the famous example of the pin-maker in order to illustrate the productivity gains that can stem from the specialisation of labour.[3] Alone, the pin-maker would have had great difficulty in making even one pin, as pin-making itself consisted of a number of separate trades, e.g. drawing out the wire, straightening the wire, cutting the wire, pointing the wire and grinding the wire for receiving the head, the making of which also required a number of separate tasks. The number of separate tasks, and hence potential separate trades, in pin-making appeared, according to Smith, to lie between eighteen and twenty-five, although in practice one manufacturer visited by Smith employed ten (as opposed to between eighteen and twenty-five) people to perform the totality of these potentially separate tasks. Smith identified improved dexterity, saving of time and the application of specialised machinery as representing the underlying causes of the improved productivity associated with the specialisation of labour. Smith went on to argue that the specialisation that would lead to increased productivity would also facilitate the production of new types of machinery that, in turn, would facilitate even greater specialisation of labour.

In summary, the division of labour generally increases productivity, even in the presence of a fixed number of machines, i.e. a fixed factor of production. This feature of the production process is referred to as increasing marginal returns.

> **Definition**
>
> *Increasing marginal returns means that an additional unit of a variable factor adds more to total product than the previous unit.*

In other words, if labour is the variable factor, the additional worker adds more to the total product than the previous worker. This is what happens when Sara hires William, who worked as a machine operator in Dublin for a few years before returning home to Mayo. She trains him to use the machines, to cut the chain and to assemble the key chains. Sara continues to order materials, to inspect and to sell the key chains.

The addition of William causes output per week to more than double, from 100 key chains to 320 key chains per week. The marginal product, caused by adding another worker, is 220 units. William concentrates on the production of key chains while Sara specialises in ordering and selling.

A few months later, Sara decides to hire another person. Frances, a former assembly line worker, has recently been made redundant. Because of her previous experience, Sara divides the manufacturing process between William and Frances. William continues to work on the machines, while Frances cuts the chain and assembles the pieces. Total product almost doubles. The marginal product attributed to the addition of the third worker (Frances) is 310 units.

Pleased with the increases in output, Sara hires a fourth worker. Daragh assumes the tasks of ordering materials and inspecting the finished product. The addition of this worker results in an increase of 410 units per week.

Sara adds a fifth, sixth and seventh worker. She continues to divide the tasks. However, she finds that while total product continues to rise, the marginal product is falling. Increasing marginal returns ends with the addition of the fourth worker.

Perplexed by this development, Sara decides to take a day off from selling, to observe the operation. She notices that the two machine operators are constantly working. However, they do not produce enough of the laminated design to keep the other members of the staff constantly occupied. In short, there is a bottleneck in the system. Sara can see that the problem is with the machines, not the operators. In addition, the odd breakdown of machinery suggests that the machines are being used to capacity.

The problem that Sara observes occurs so regularly that it is called the law of diminishing returns.

Definition

The law of diminishing returns means that if at least one factor is fixed, a point is reached where an additional unit of a variable factor adds less to total product than the previous unit.

In other words, if labour is the variable factor, an additional worker adds less to total product than the previous worker. In this case, where Sara's capital is limited to two machines, with the addition of the fifth worker, marginal product diminishes.

Sara decides that given the limitations imposed on the production process by the machinery, she will not hire any additional workers in the short run. Indeed, we can see from Table 5.1 that the addition of the eighth worker would actually cause the total product to fall; labourers are literally getting in each other's way.

The 'law of diminishing returns' was identified by the classical economist John Stuart Mill (1806–73), who, when describing agricultural production said, '. . . the state of the art being given, doubling the labour does not double the produce'.[4] The law of diminishing returns is widely observed in practice and characterises many production activities.

We can come to a further understanding of the total product curve by comparing it to the marginal product curve. When the marginal product curve is rising, the total product curve is becoming steeper. This means that marginal returns are increasing; each worker is contributing more to total product than the last.

When the marginal product curve begins to fall, the total product curve becomes flatter. In other words, when the marginal product is falling, the total product curve is increasing at a decreasing rate. This means that marginal returns are decreasing; each worker is adding to total product, but by less than the previous worker.

When the marginal product curve cuts the horizontal axis, the marginal product of labour becomes negative. The additional worker is causing the total product to fall. At this point, the total product curve begins to slope downwards.

Next we will consider the average product and its relationship with the marginal product.

> **Definition**
>
> *The average product is the total output divided by the number of units of the variable input utilised.*

For example, the average product of labour is the total output divided by the total units of labour. Equation 5.3 states this relationship in algebraic form.

$$AP = \frac{TP}{Qv} \qquad [5.3]$$

where: AP = average product; TP = total product; Qv = quantity of variable input.

Column 4 of Table 5.1 presents the data for the average product of labour. If three workers produce 630 key chains, the average product of labour is 630/3, which equals 210. Notice that the average product of labour also rises and then falls. Both the average product of labour and the marginal product of labour are derived by looking at the relationship between total product and labour. But is there a particular relationship between the AP and the MP?

A simple example may clarify this relationship. Suppose that a footballer has an average score over three games of 1 goal per match. Consider two possibilities for the fourth match.

First, suppose that the footballer scores 2 goals in the fourth game. The 'marginal' score is 2. This is the number of goals that she adds to her total by playing in the fourth game. The footballer's average increases to 1.25 goals per game. We can think of the marginal goals as dragging up the average goals. Now consider the possibility that the footballer fails to score in the fourth game. The 'marginal' score is 0, which is below the average score of 1. This drags down the average to 0.75. If the marginal score is above the average score, the average score is dragged up. Conversely, if the marginal score is below the average score, the average score is dragged down.

We can see this same relationship in the bottom frame of Figure 5.1. When the marginal product of labour is above the average product of labour, the average product of labour is rising. However, when the additional labourer fails to add more to total product than the previous worker, the marginal product of labour falls. When the marginal product of labour is below the average, the average product of labour falls. Hence, the marginal product curve must cut the average product curve at its highest point, labelled point A.

We will end this discussion with one final comment on the short run. The short run is not a particular length of time: it varies from market to market. For example, the short run may last for only a few months in the food business. If, say, Lemon wants to expand, the management must find a new location, arrange for financing and prepare the site before they can open. This period of time will be far shorter than the time it would take, say, Bord na Móna to open a new production site. Finding a suitable location, applying for planning permission, arranging for financing and determining the technological processes might take years, rather than months.

Production in the long run

We observed that at Key Chains Ltd, the level of output was limited by the machinery. In the short run, Sara's capital was fixed. In the long run, it is possible for Sara to increase the number of machines, the size of the plant and the production process. In the long run, all inputs can be varied.

> **Definition**
>
> *The long run is a period of time when all the factors of production can be varied in quantity.*

The long-run production function shows combinations of inputs and the quantities of output produced. There are three possible relationships between inputs and outputs. Indeed, the long-run production function may exhibit all three relationships over the range of production.

1. Increasing returns to scale mean that the increase in output is proportionately greater than the increase in inputs. For example, if we double the amount of inputs, the level of output will more than double.
2. In the case of constant returns to scale, the increase in output matches the increase in inputs. In this situation, a doubling of inputs is matched exactly by a doubling of output.
3. Decreasing returns to scale mean that the increase in output is proportionately smaller than the increase in inputs. Therefore, if inputs double, output will increase but by less than a factor of two.

These cases relate to the scale of production, which requires further discussion.

Increasing returns to scale are closely related to the concept of economies of scale where an increase in the scale of production leads to lower costs per unit of output produced. Where there are constant returns to scale, changing the level of output over a range of production does not affect the (average) cost per unit. Decreasing returns to scale are closely related to the concept of diseconomies of scale where an increase in the scale of production results in higher unit costs.

There are a number of reasons why a firm experiences increasing returns to scale over a range of production. As firms produce large numbers of units of output, more labour is hired and employees become increasingly specialised in the tasks which they perform. In the long run, large firms can purchase dedicated machinery and train their employees to operate it very efficiently.

In addition, firms that produce high levels of output can in general expect to purchase inputs at a discounted price. Large firms put intense pressure on their suppliers to reduce the cost of inputs, particularly if they are a major customer.

Another source of increasing returns to scale is indivisibilities. Some capital investments are only suitable for high levels of output and when used in those circumstances are very efficient. A combine harvester can be used to reap and thresh thousands of acres of wheat or corn. However, this type of machinery is 'indivisible'. It is impossible to purchase anything less than a whole combine harvester and it is very expensive to operate one at low levels of output.

Finally, there is a group of costs incurred by the firm which are called 'overheads'. These are some of the operating expenses of a firm that do not arise from the production of the good or service. They include the costs of advertising, insuring, marketing and research and development. The cost of overheads decreases as they are spread over more units.

It is recognised that firms can experience decreasing returns to scale beyond a certain range of production. When a firm grows beyond a certain size, the cost of managing the firm may increase disproportionately. The decision-making process may become slower and more complex. Staff morale problems, which in turn lead to production problems, are more likely to occur. Firms may experience problems in co-ordinating production activities. All of these factors may cause the cost per unit of production to increase or at least not to decrease further beyond a certain level of output.

The relationship between the scale of production and the long-run cost of production will be discussed further in the next section.

5.3 COSTS

Costs are payments for the use of factors of production. Labour receives wages, rent is paid for the use of land, interest is the cost of capital and profit is the payment for enterprise.

At this point, a student of accounting may be particularly confused. Why does the economist consider profit as a cost while the accountant considers profit as the difference between revenues and costs? The answer is that accountants and economists define costs differently.

Economists are interested in economic costs, which include both the explicit costs like wages, rent and interest recognised by accountants, and opportunity costs discussed in Chapter 1. The opportunity cost is the economist's way of acknowledging that all factors of production, including enterprise, can be used in alternative ways.

Consider Sara, the owner of Key Chains Ltd. Sara could use her many talents in a number of different ways. She could produce something else besides key chains or she could work for another firm. Economists believe that Sara will continue to produce and sell key chains, if and only if she makes (at least) a 'normal' profit.

> **Definition**
>
> *Normal profit is the amount (or percentage) of profit which the entrepreneur requires to supply entrepreneurship.*

From an opportunity cost perspective, normal profit is the amount of profit that the entrepreneur could earn in the next best alternative business. It is a cost to the firm in the sense that production will cease (at least in the long run) if the normal profit is not earned by the entrepreneur. Economic costs include the explicit costs which are found in the Profit and Loss Account like cost of sales, operating costs, interest charges and taxation. However, economic costs also include a 'normal profit' for the entrepreneur.

It is possible that the entrepreneur will earn more than a normal profit. Economists refer to this as supernormal profit.

> **Definition**
>
> *Supernormal profit is the difference between revenue and economic costs (including normal profits).*

Supernormal profit is also referred to as economic profit, excess profit or abnormal profit. All of these terms are also closely related to the concepts of producer surplus (see Section 5.4) and economic rent (see Section 7.3).

An example showing the difference between accounting profit and economic profit is shown in Table 5.2.

TABLE 5.2: ACCOUNTING VERSUS ECONOMIC PROFIT

The accountant's interpretation			
Total revenue			600,000
Total cost			380,000
			————
Profit			220,000
The economist's interpretation			
Total revenue			600,000
Economic costs			570,000
of which:	Explicit costs	380,000	
	Opportunity cost	190,000	
		————	————
Supernormal or economic profit			30,000

We will now consider costs in greater detail. As with inputs, we will distinguish between the short run and the long run.

Short-run costs

You will recall from our discussion of factor inputs that the short run is the length of time when at least one factor input is fixed and other factor inputs are variable. Factors of production must be paid. If the factor of production is fixed in the short run, we consider the cost to be fixed as well. Fixed costs are the payments to fixed factors of production. They remain constant as output varies.

We will return to the example of Key Chains Ltd. Recall that Sara initially uses two machines to manufacture key chains. The machines are Sara's fixed input. If we were considering a more complex production function, fixed costs might also include rent, insurance premiums and the price of the fixed line phone connection.

You will also recall that other inputs, such as labour and raw materials, vary with the level of production. Variable costs are the payments to variable factors of production. They are incurred with the first unit of production and increase as production increases.

For Key Chains Ltd, labour is the only variable input and therefore wage is the variable cost. Other variable costs might in reality also include monies paid for the materials used to produce the key chains and the charge for telephone calls. As with wages, these costs will change with the level of production.

The short-run total cost is equal to the sum of the fixed costs and the variable costs. This relationship is expressed in the following equation:

$$STC = SFC + SVC \qquad [5.4]$$

where: STC = short-run total cost; SFC = short-run fixed cost; SVC = short-run variable cost.

Table 5.3 shows the details of the short-run costs for Key Chains Ltd.

TABLE 5.3: SHORT-RUN COSTS (€ PER WEEK) FOR KEY CHAINS LTD $\frac{\Delta STC}{\Delta Q}$

(1) Labour	(2) Q	(3) SFC	(4) SVC	(5) STC	(6) SMC	(7) SAFC	(8) SAVC	(9) SATC
0	0	100	0	100		–	–	–
					2.00			
1	100	100	200	300		1.00	2.00	3.00
					0.91			
2	320	100	400	500		0.31	1.25	1.56
					0.65			
3	630	100	600	700		0.16	0.95	1.11
					0.49			
4	1040	100	800	900		0.10	0.77	0.87
					0.56			
5	1400	100	1000	1100		0.07	0.71	0.79
					0.59			
6	1740	100	1200	1300		0.06	0.69	0.75
					0.91			
7	1960	100	1400	1500		0.05	0.71	0.76

Column 3 shows the fixed costs, which are constant regardless of the level of output. The variable costs, shown in column 4, increase with the level of production. Column 5 shows the total costs. Since total costs include both fixed and variable costs, they increase as the quantity of output increases. The curves drawn in the left-hand panel of Figure 5.2 are based on the short-run fixed, variable and total costs.

FIGURE 5.2: SHORT-RUN COST CURVES FOR KEY CHAINS LTD

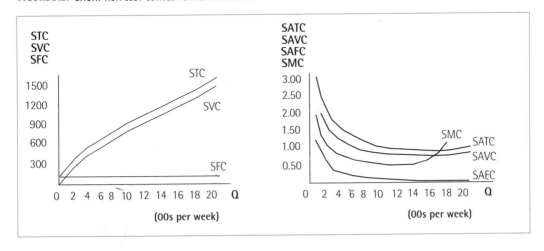

Fixed costs are independent of the level of production. These costs are incurred even if no output is produced. Therefore, the short-run fixed cost curve (SFC) is a horizontal line at €100 (the cost of machinery). Variable costs are incurred when production begins and increase as production increases. In this example the wage per worker equals €200. Therefore, the short-run variable cost curve (SVC) begins at the origin and is upward sloping.

The short-run total cost curve (STC) is the vertical summation of the other two curves; it begins at €100. The fixed costs are the only costs incurred before production begins. The STC curve is upward sloping and is always above the SVC curve by an amount equal to the value of the fixed costs. In the short run, fixed costs always separate the STC curve from the SVC curve.

We can examine other important economic concepts more conveniently by looking at the cost per unit. We will begin by defining the average cost and the marginal cost.

Definition

Average total cost or average cost is total cost divided by the number of units produced.

We can calculate average variable costs and average fixed costs. The addition of average fixed cost and average variable cost is average total cost.

$$\text{SATC} = \text{SAFC} + \text{SAVC} \qquad [5.5]$$

where: SATC = short-run average total cost; SAFC = short-run average fixed cost; SAVC = short-run average variable cost.

The key to understanding how much a firm will produce and sell is its marginal cost, which is probably the most important of all cost concepts, at least for economists.

Definition

The marginal cost is the extra cost incurred from producing an additional unit of output.

In the short run it is expressed as follows:

$$\text{SMC} = \frac{\Delta \text{STC}}{\Delta \text{Q}} \qquad [5.6]$$

where: Δ = change; SMC = short-run marginal cost; STC = short-run total cost; Q = level of output. The short-run marginal cost is equivalent to the short-run marginal variable cost as the short-run marginal fixed cost, by definition, is zero.

The marginal and average costs for this example are calculated in columns 6 through 9 of Table 5.3. We notice immediately that the short-run average fixed costs are falling as the costs are spread over more units. All of the other short-run costs fall initially and then rise again. These relationships can be examined more easily by looking at a diagram.

The right-sided frame of Figure 5.2 shows the short-run average fixed cost curve (SAFC), the short-run average variable cost curve (SAVC), the short-run average total cost curve (SATC) and finally the short-run marginal cost curve (SMC). Notice that the SAFC curve is downward sloping. As production expands, the average fixed costs fall. Both the SAVC and the SATC curves fall initially and then rise. The SMC curve also falls and then rises.

We can relate the changes in the marginal cost to our discussion about marginal product in Section 5.2. Remember that in the simplified production function for Key Chains Ltd, labour is the only variable input. Therefore, wage is the only variable cost. With the addition of each of the first four workers, the marginal product increases. Assuming that all workers are employed at the same wage, if the marginal product of labour is increasing, the marginal cost to produce key chains falls. However, with the addition of the fifth worker at Key Chains Ltd, labour becomes less productive. Therefore, the marginal cost of producing a unit of output increases.

To summarise this relationship, if the marginal product of labour is rising, its marginal cost is falling, but if the marginal product of labour is falling, its marginal cost is rising.

The relationship between 'average' and 'marginal' described in Section 5.2 also applies to costs. Both the short-run average total cost and short-run average variable cost 'follow' the short-run marginal cost. When the marginal cost is below the average, the average costs fall. When the marginal cost is above the average, the average costs rise. In terms of the diagram, the SMC curve intersects both the SATC curve and the SAVC curve at their lowest points.

As a final point, it should be noted that as costs change, the position of all of the relevant cost curves must also change. For example, if the cost figures in Table 5.3 increase, in order to reflect an increase in wages (i.e. the cost of labour), all of the relevant cost curves in Figure 5.2 must shift upwards to the appropriate extent, in order to reflect these increased costs.

CASE STUDY

Extract from the *Sunday Business Post*
Controls needed to cut costs in claims culture

The extent to which many small and budding businesses are affected by the claims culture in Irish society has increased in recent years, according to Tony Briscoe, IBEC's assistant director for social policy.

The problem of insurance claims is not lost on small business entrepreneurs during the set up phase when they go shopping for insurance cover. They are frequently shocked to learn that the third and fourth most costly element of their list of . . . costs (including wages, materials and premises) is the cost of indemnity cover; to provide for potential claims by the public or by future employees.

This is a cost which has no direct or proportional relationship to their levels of production, sales or profit. Additionally, it is money which has to be paid over often before the business receives any sales revenue. In some areas of work, because of their level of exposure to claims, the initial premiums many small firms have to pay can be as much as equivalent of four months payroll cost.

'The potential for somebody suing them, particularly for business involved in the services area where they deal with the public, is quite considerable,' said Briscoe.

Among the measures proposed by IBEC and the SFA (Small Firms Association) to . . . bring about some realism in the cost of insurance are:

- Greater account being taken by the legal system for contributory negligence by persons bringing claims.
- A book of quantum, providing realistic values for general damages awards.
- A reduction in the period within which a claim for personal injuries may be brought, to six months (currently three years).
- Severe penalties for fraudulent, spurious and exaggerated claims.

Source: *Sunday Business Post.*

Questions

1. What is the difference between 'variable' costs and 'fixed' costs?
2. What are the four largest costs for a new enterprise? Which are variable and which are fixed?
3. How would the proposed changes help the entrepreneur? Explain your answer in the context of fixed and variable costs.

Answers on website

Long-run costs

The long run is a period of time which is long enough to vary all factors of production. Since all inputs can be used with greater flexibility in the long run, we do not differentiate between variable and fixed costs. We will begin by discussing the shape of the long-run average cost curve (LAC).

The LAC curve shows the relationship between output and the lowest attainable average cost per unit of output when all inputs are variable. A downward sloping LAC curve reflects declining unit costs as production increases. This indicates the presence of economies of scale. The straight line (parallel to the quantity axis) LAC curve reflects constant returns to scale. An upward sloping LAC curve indicates the presence of diseconomies of scale where the cost per unit of production increases as the level of output increases. In theory, the LAC curve can be in any of three forms or, indeed, in some combination of all three. Figure 5.3 shows all three cases.

FIGURE 5.3: THE SLOPE OF THE LONG-RUN AVERAGE COST CURVE

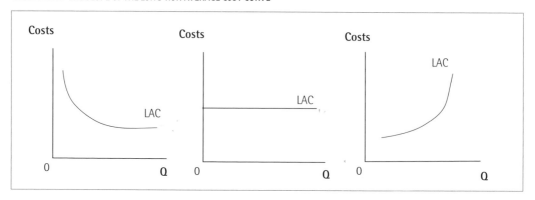

The typical long-run average cost curve is thought to be a combination of these three curves. The U-shaped LAC curve supposedly captures realistic trends in costs relative to output levels. It is shown in Figure 5.4.

Initially, the LAC curve is downward sloping, which means that the average cost per unit is falling over a range of production. As previously stated, economies of scale are associated with the use of specialised labour and machinery. Large firms can decrease their cost per unit of output because of their ability to negotiate for discounts for the purchase of inputs, to efficiently use 'indivisible' capital assets and to spread 'overhead' costs over a large number of units.

FIGURE 5.4: THE U-SHAPED LONG-RUN AVERAGE COST CURVE

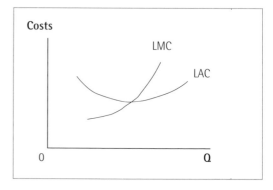

The LAC curve is relatively flat over a range of production. This means that the firm can expand production with little change in the cost per unit of output. Over this range of production, the firm experiences constant returns to scale.

Eventually the LAC curve is upward sloping, which means that the average cost per unit of output increases with output. Diseconomies of scale are associated with managerial problems that firms experience when they increase in size. At the bottom of the LAC curve, costs per unit of production are at their lowest. This level is called the minimum cost production level. It is of particular significance and is explained in greater detail in the next chapter when we discuss different market structures.

The relationship between average costs and marginal costs also applies in the long run. In other words, when the marginal cost is below the average cost, the average costs fall. When the marginal cost is above the average cost, the average costs rise. As in the short run, the long-run marginal cost curve (LMC) cuts the LAC curve at the lowest point. The LMC curve is also shown in Figure 5.4.

The envelope curve

The long-run average cost curve can be explained in terms of short-run average total cost curves. This is shown in Figure 5.5.

A set of SATC curves is reproduced in Figure 5.5. Each short-run average total cost curve is U-shaped because of the law of diminishing returns. The LAC curve is said to 'envelope' the SATC curves. Each point on the LAC curve is a point of tangency with respective points on corresponding SATC curves. There is a tendency to match the points on the LAC curve with minimum points on the SATC curves; this is incorrect.[5]

Point x is the minimum point of the LAC curve. Each point to the left is a tangency point with a point on the falling part of the respective SATC curves. Each point to the right is a tangency point with a point on the rising part of the respective SATC curves. Only at the minimum point x on the LAC curve is the corresponding SATC curve also at a minimum. This suggests that to the left of point x the plants are not working to full capacity whereas to the right of point x the plants are overworked. At point x the plant is optimally employed, in the sense that it is producing at the lowest possible cost per unit.

FIGURE 5.5: THE ENVELOPE CURVE

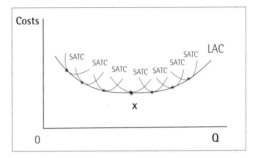

This completes the discussion of the derivation of short-run and long-run cost curves. We will now discuss the way that we use these cost curves to identify the firm's profit-maximising level of output.

5.4 PROFIT-MAXIMISING OUTPUT LEVEL

The objective of the firm in the traditional neoclassical model is profit maximisation. In this section we will derive the profit-maximising output level using two methods. These methods are essentially the same, though each looks at revenues and costs from a slightly different perspective.

The first approach requires values for total revenue (TR) and total cost (TC) for each level of production. The output level where the difference between total revenue and total cost is the largest is the profit-maximising output level. The second approach is based on marginal revenue (MR) and marginal cost (MC) values. By comparing marginal revenue and marginal cost we can derive the same profit-maximising output level as in the first approach.

We will use another example to illustrate the relevant concepts. Liam from County Meath produces organic potatoes. Again, we will consider only two inputs for the short-run production function. Land is a fixed factor of production and rent is the associated fixed cost. Labour is the variable input and wage is the associated variable cost. Column 4 of Table 5.4 shows the total cost (fixed cost plus variable cost) associated with the different levels of output of potatoes.

TABLE 5.4: TOTAL REVENUE, TOTAL COST AND PROFIT FOR THE PRODUCTION OF POTATOES

(1) Q (tons)	(2) P (€00)	(3) TR (€00)	(4) TC (€00)	(5) Profit (€00)
0	–	0	36	–36
1	33.0	33	50	–17
2	31.5	63	62	1
3	30.0	90	73	17
4	28.5	114	82	32
5	27.0	135	92	43
6	25.5	153	105	48
7	24.0	168	119	49
8	22.5	180	144	36
9	21.0	189	171	18

Although Liam is always conscious of his costs, that is only half of the story. Over the years, he notices that to sell more potatoes, he must sell his potatoes at a lower price per ton. In other words, the demand curve for his product ('Liam's Organic Potatoes') is downward sloping.

There is a particular price associated with each level of output. The price per ton of output is shown in column 2 of Table 5.4. Liam is interested in the total revenue that he will receive at each level of production. We know from Chapter 3 that total revenue is the price of the good times the quantity of output sold.

Total revenue is calculated in column 3 of Table 5.4.

Profit is the difference between total revenue and total cost. Recall that a normal profit is included in the calculations for (economic, as opposed to accounting) cost. Therefore, if profit is zero, the firm (or in this case Liam) is making a normal profit. Any profit which is greater than zero is supernormal profit. Profit is calculated in column 5 of Table 5.4.

In this example, the difference between total revenue and total cost is maximised when seven tons is produced. At this level of output, profit is €4,900.

As mentioned earlier, this profit-maximising level of output can also be identified by comparing the marginal revenue and the marginal cost.

Definition

Marginal revenue is the change in total revenue resulting from a one unit change in output.

Algebraically, we can describe this relationship in the following way:

$$MR = \frac{\Delta TR}{\Delta Q}$$

[5.7]

where: Δ = change; MR = marginal revenue; TR = total revenue; Q = level of output.

Marginal revenue is calculated in column 3 of Table 5.5, Consider the additional revenue Liam gains by producing and selling the seventh ton of potatoes. When he produces and sells six tons, he earns €15,300 in revenue. For the production and sale of seven tons, Liam earns €16,800. The difference between the two is €1,500. Since one additional ton is produced, we divide this total by one. In this example, the marginal revenue gained from the production and sale of the seventh ton is €1,500.

We have already defined the marginal cost as the additional cost incurred from producing and selling one unit of output. The marginal cost is calculated in column 5 of Table 5.5.

The total cost of producing seven units is €11,900. However, producing the first six units costs the farmer €10,500. Therefore, the marginal cost of the seventh unit is (€11,900 − €10,500)/1 which is €1,400.

TABLE 5.5: TOTAL REVENUE, MARGINAL REVENUE, TOTAL COST AND MARGINAL COST

(1) Q (tons)	(2) TR (€00)	(3) MR (€00)	(4) TC (€00)	(5) MC (€00)	(6) MR–MC (€00)	(7) Output decision
0	0		36			
		33		14	19	Increase
1	33		50			
		30		12	18	Increase
2	63		62			
		27		11	16	Increase
3	90		73			
		24		9	15	Increase
4	114		82			
		21		10	11	Increase
5	135		92			
		18		13	5	Increase
6	153		105			
		15		14	1	Increase
7	168		119			
		12		25	−13	Decrease
8	180		144			
		9		27	−18	Decrease
9	189		171			

The last two columns of Table 5.5 help us to determine the profit-maximising output level for Liam. Marginal revenue is greater than marginal cost from the first unit of production to the seventh unit of production. As output increases by one unit the additional revenue is greater than the additional cost incurred. This means that Liam can earn additional profits by increasing production. Since we assume that Liam wants to maximise profits, output should be increased.

Marginal revenue is less than marginal cost beyond the seventh unit of production. The extra revenue is not large enough to cover the extra cost incurred. Production should not be increased beyond seven units. A profit-maximising firm (Liam) will continue to produce as long as the difference between the marginal revenue and marginal cost is positive. The difference is calculated in column 6 above. In this example the difference is positive up to seven units of production.

In summary, when marginal revenue is greater than marginal cost, the level of output should be increased and when marginal revenue is less than marginal cost, output should be reduced. Consequently, a firm produces at the profit-maximising output level when marginal revenue is equal to marginal cost.

However, this is a necessary, but not sufficient condition for profit maximisation. An examination of the second condition will be covered after we compare the profit-maximising output level using total revenue and total cost with the level of output determined using marginal revenue and marginal cost. Figure 5.6 shows the relationship between the two approaches.

In the top frame of Figure 5.6, we have drawn the curves for total revenue (TR) and total cost (TC). When the gap between the TR and TC curves is the greatest, profits are maximised. As we saw in the table, this occurs at a production level of seven units.

In the bottom frame, we can see the relationship between marginal revenue (MR) and marginal cost (MC). Consider a production level of six units. From the diagram, we can clearly see that the MR curve is above the MC curve. Therefore, the firm can increase profits by producing and selling more units. Now consider the production level of eight units. On the diagram, we can see that the MC curve is above the MR curve. If the firm produces at this level, total profits will fall. Therefore, the profit-maximising level of production is between six and eight units of production. The profit-maximising firm will produce seven units. This is where the MR curve intersects the MC curve. Refer to Appendix 5.1 to see how this is related to cost minimisation and the least-cost production technique.

FIGURE 5.6: PROFIT MAXIMISATION WITH TOTAL REVENUE AND TOTAL COST, MARGINAL REVENUE AND MARGINAL COST

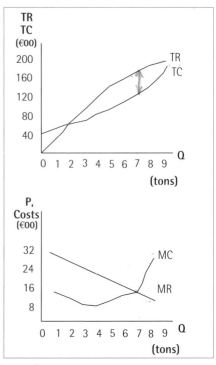

Using either approach, the profit-maximising level of output is the same.

In the example of the potato-producing farmer, the profit-maximising decision was to produce, i.e. to operate. This is not always the case. In some situations, firms operate at a loss, at least in the short run. The owner of the firm may decide that losses can be minimised by producing where marginal revenue equals the marginal cost. Alternatively, the owner may decide that it is better to shut down, and pay only the fixed costs. In other words, it is costing the owner more to produce than it would to shut down. We will extend our analysis to show how the owner of a profit-maximising firm makes that choice both in the short run and in the long run.

The output decision of the firm in the short run

There are two conditions for short-run equilibrium. First, we have already discussed the marginal condition. A profit-maximising firm which is going to produce will choose a production level where marginal revenue equals short-run marginal cost (MR = SMC). However, there is a second condition which must also be met; it is the average condition. A firm will produce this level of output if, and only if, average revenue or price is no less than short-run average variable cost (P ≥ SAVC).

> **Definition**
>
> *Average revenue is a firm's total revenue divided by the quantity sold.*

It is simply the price of the good.[6]

This second condition implies that in order to produce any output, the firm must at least cover its variable costs. This equilibrium position is illustrated in Figure 5.7.

The marginal condition, where MR = SMC, is met at output level Q* in Figure 5.7. Given the present market conditions and the short-run costs, the profit-maximising output level is Q*. However, this condition alone is not enough to determine the firm's optimal production decision as it does not provide for the possibility of not producing at all. This requires the second condition. The average condition involves comparing average revenue with average cost, at Q*. Given the nature of costs in the short run, three distinct possibilities arise.

If average revenue or price exceeds the short-run average total cost resulting in a supernormal

FIGURE 5.7: OUTPUT DECISION IN THE SHORT RUN

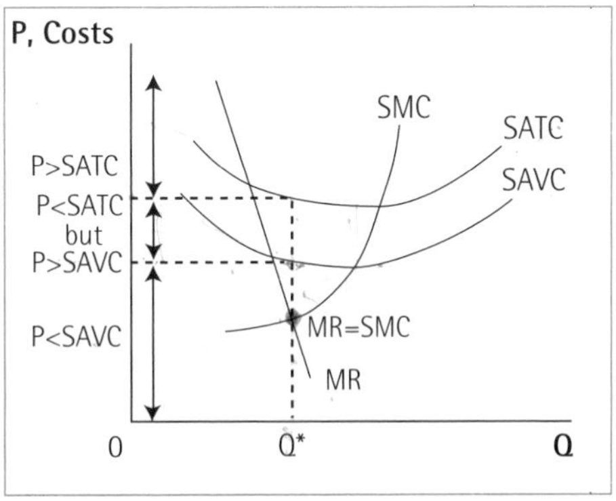

profit, the firm will continue to produce at this output level. If the price level falls between the SATC and the SAVC curves, the firm is operating at a loss. However, it is covering its variable costs and making some contribution to the fixed costs which, by definition, must be paid even if production is halted. Under this condition, the firm will continue to produce because it will lose even more if it closes. The firm is minimising losses and hence maximising profits. Of course, a favourable change in market conditions could turn short-run losses into profits.

If price is lower than the short-run average variable cost, the situation is more serious. In this case the firm is not covering its variable costs. The day-to-day expenses such as labour costs, tax bills, social insurance and so on are not met. At Q* the variable cost per unit of production exceeds the price received for each unit. The firm minimises losses by shutting down. A shutdown is preferred to continued production at Q*.

In brief, a firm that is not making profits will attempt to limit short-run losses. The decision to produce in the short run requires that both the marginal and average conditions are met. Ultimately any profit-maximising firm produces in the short run as long as it covers its variable costs.

In the short run, we have seen that a firm may continue production, even if it is not making a normal profit. In the long run, the owner of the firm can make a number of choices, which include switching resources to another form of enterprise where at least a normal profit can be made. We now explore the output decision for a profit-maximising firm in the long run.

The output decision of the firm in the long run

There are two conditions for long-run equilibrium. The first condition states that the profit-maximising firm will produce where marginal revenue equals the long-run marginal cost (MR = LMC). The marginal condition is met at the output level of Q* as illustrated in Figure 5.8.

As before, this condition is not sufficient as it does not consider the alternative of not producing at all. The second condition states that a firm will produce in the long run if price is greater than or equal to the long-run average cost (P ≥ LAC). This condition implies that the firm will only produce in the long run if it can cover all of its costs. In the long run, two cases arise.

FIGURE 5.8: OUTPUT DECISION IN THE LONG RUN

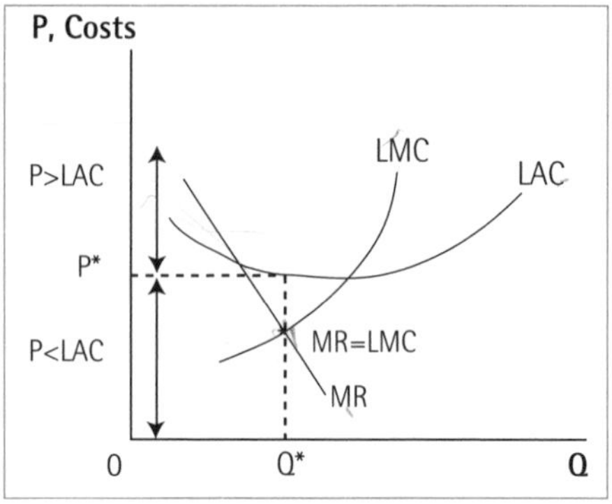

If price equals or exceeds the long-run average cost, the firm will continue to produce where marginal revenue equals marginal cost. If the price obtained for the product is P*, shown in Figure 5.8, the firm is covering its costs and making a normal profit. If price is greater than P*, the firm is making supernormal profits. In either situation, the firm will continue to produce in the long run.

Alternatively, if price is lower than P*, then losses result. Since a firm must cover all of its costs in the long run, it will have no choice but to stop production and close down. In this case, we would expect the factors of production to be released for use in activities which will earn at least a normal profit.

In brief, the long-run output decision requires that both the marginal and the average conditions are met. Ultimately all costs must be covered in the long run.

Producer surplus

In Section 4.4, consumer surplus was identified with the benefit that the individual consumer or consumers receive from being able to purchase a product at a price that is often significantly below the price(s) that the individual consumer or consumers are willing to pay. The analogous concept from the supply side of the market is producer surplus.

Definition

Producer surplus is the excess in revenue that a producer receives for a product over the minimum revenue that the producer would have accepted for the product.

In the short run, producer surplus is the difference between total revenue and total variable cost. Provided that the producer is covering variable cost, the producer is willing to continue operating in the short run. It is important to note that in the short run, producer surplus is not equivalent to economic (i.e. supernormal) profit. Indeed, provided that there are at least some fixed costs, producer surplus will always exceed economic profit in the short run as producers are willing to accept some (short-run) losses. In the long run, as all costs are variable, producer surplus is equivalent to economic profit.

As with consumer surplus, producer surplus is a very important concept in economics and has many valuable applications, e.g. cost-benefit analysis, the efficiency and distribution effects of tax changes and subsidies, and competition policy. The comparison between outcomes associated with perfect competition and monopoly in Section 6.2 provides an example of the application of consumer surplus and producer surplus.

SUMMARY

1. The production process involves the transformation of inputs or factors of production into output. The production function shows the maximum amount of output that can be produced employing different amounts of land, labour, capital and enterprise.
2. The short run is a period of time when at least one input is 'fixed' or does not change. The marginal product is the change to total output from an additional unit of a variable input, holding other inputs constant. Increasing marginal returns means that an additional unit of a variable input adds more to total output than the previous unit, *ceteris paribus*. The law of diminishing returns means that if at least one factor is fixed, a point is reached when an additional unit of a variable factor adds less to total product than the previous unit.
3. In the long run, the levels of all inputs can be varied. We consider the relationship between inputs and outputs in the long run in terms of 'returns to scale'. Increasing returns to scale means that if all factor inputs double, outputs increase by a factor of more than two. Constant returns to scale means that doubling inputs exactly doubles outputs. Decreasing returns to scale means that doubling inputs leads to an increase of outputs, but by a factor of less than two.
4. Economists include a 'normal' profit as a cost of production. This is the opportunity cost of the entrepreneur. Variable costs are the costs associated with employing variable factors of production. They begin with production and increase as production increases. Fixed costs are the costs associated with employing fixed factors of production. They are constant (i.e. fixed) in the short run, regardless of whether or not a firm produces. Supernormal profit is the difference between total revenue and economic costs which include variable costs, fixed costs and a normal profit.
5. Marginal cost is the additional cost incurred if output is altered by one unit. Marginal revenue is the change in total revenue arising from a one unit change in output. In the short run, a profit-maximising firm produces where marginal revenue equals marginal cost so long as it has covered all of its variable costs. If a firm does not cover its variable costs, it minimises its losses in the short run by shutting down.
6. In the long run, a firm must make at least a normal profit. A profit-maximising firm produces where MR = LMC, if it at least covers its long-run average cost. If the firm does not cover its long-run average costs, it exits the industry.

KEY TERMS

Profit maximisation	Increasing marginal returns	Total cost
Factors of production	Law of diminishing returns	Economic profit
Production function	Average product	Producer surplus
Short-run production	Long-run production	Opportunity cost
Fixed input	Increasing returns to scale	Average revenue
Variable input	Constant returns to scale	Normal profit
Total product	Decreasing returns to scale	Marginal revenue
Marginal product	Variable costs	Indivisibilities
Economies of scale	Average cost	Fixed costs
Diseconomies of scale	Marginal cost	
Specialisation of labour	Envelope curve	

REVIEW QUESTIONS

1. What are the objectives of a firm? What is the objective of the firm in the traditional neoclassical theory?
2. Explain the difference between short-run production and long-run production. What is the difference between the 'law of diminishing returns' and 'returns to scale'?
3. List the three possibilities for the basic shape of the long run average costs curve. What are possible sources of economies of scale and diseconomies of scale?
4. How is the economist's interpretation of costs different from the accountant's interpretation of costs? What is the difference between accounting profit and economic profit?
5. What two conditions must be met in order for a profit-maximising firm to produce? How is the output decision in the short run different from the output decision in the long run?
6. Explain the relationship between diminishing returns to the variable factor (in the short run) and the shape of the firm's short-run marginal cost curve. What does this suggest about the theory of production and the theory of costs?

WORKING PROBLEMS

1. This is a weekly production schedule for mushrooms.

TABLE 5.6

Land	Labour	Output	Average	Marginal
20	0	0		
20	1	1		
20	2	3		
20	3	6		
20	4	10		
20	5	16		
20	6	20		
20	7	21		
20	8	20		
20	9	18		

    (a) What are the inputs used in this production process?
    (b) How do you know that this is a short-run production function? Which inputs are fixed and which are variable?
    (c) Sketch the total product curve.
    (d) Complete the table for the AP and MP of labour.
    (e) Explain why the MP of labour declines.
    (f) Where does the MP of labour curve cut the AP of labour curve? Explain your answer.

2. The cost of land is €50 per acre and the cost of labour is €100 per worker per week.
    (a) Complete Table 5.7.
    (b) Sketch the cost curves.
    (c) Will the SATC curve and the SAVC curve ever intersect?
    (d) Where will the SMC curve cut the SAVC and the SATC curves? Explain your answer.

TABLE 5.7

Land	Labour	Output	SFC	SVC	STC	SMC	SAFC	SAVC	SATC
2	0	0							
2	1	1							
2	2	3							
2	3	6							
2	4	10							
2	5	16							
2	6	20							
2	7	23							
2	8	25							
2	9	26							
2	10	24							

MULTI-CHOICE QUESTIONS

1. Diseconomies of scale:
   (a) arise due to indivisibilities and the division of labour;
   (b) exist when the average cost per unit of production rises as the level of output rises;
   (c) exist when the LAC curve falls as output rises;
   (d) arise due to increasing layers of bureaucracy and problems with management-staff relations;
   (e) both (b) and (d) above.

2. The law of diminishing returns:
   (a) is reflected in the slope of the total product curve;
   (b) is a short-run concept;
   (c) sets in when the marginal product of the variable factor begins to decline;
   (d) occurs when production is constrained by fixed factors of production;
   (e) all of the above.

3. The short-run marginal cost curve:
   (a) reflects the law of diminishing returns;
   (b) cuts the SATC and SAVC curves at their lowest points;
   (c) is a mirror image of the marginal product curve;
   (d) both (a) and (c) above;
   (e) (a), (b) and (c) above.

4. The profit-maximising output level in the short run is given by:
   (a) $TR = TC$ and $AR = SAVC$;
   (b) $MR = SMC$ and $AR \geq SAVC$;
   (c) $TR > TC$ and $MR > SMC$;
   (d) $MR = SMC$ and $AR < SATC$;
   (e) none of the above.

5. Economic costs:
   (a) are no different from accounting costs;
   (b) include the opportunity cost of the entrepreneur;
   (c) are equal to the explicit costs of production;
   (d) guarantee that normal profit and economic profit are equal;
   (e) none of the above.

6. The standard neoclassical treatment of the firm is based on the assumption of:
   (a) sales maximisation;
   (b) revenue maximisation;
   (c) growth maximisation;
   (d) profit maximisation;
   (e) none of the above.

TRUE OR FALSE (SUPPORT YOUR ANSWER)

1. When the total product curve is upward sloping and increasing at a decreasing rate the marginal product of the variable input is declining.

2. One reason for decreasing returns to scale are discounts which large firms receive for purchasing large quantities of inputs.

3. The two conditions for a profit-maximising firm are the average and marginal conditions.

4. Normal profit is a cost of production.

5. A firm will only continue to produce in the long run if the market price covers both fixed and variable costs.

6. The LAC curve is formed by the envelope of the minimum points of the SATC curves.

CASE STUDY

Extract from *The Irish Times*
Personal injuries board to save €60m legal costs
by Carol Coulter

More than €60 million will be saved in litigation costs on the first 15,000 claims processed by the Personal Injuries Assessment Board (PIAB), according to its chief executive Patricia Byron. Ms Byron was speaking at the publication of PIAB's first annual report yesterday. She said that in 2004 it had met all its targets, including setting up the organisation, recruiting management and staff, publishing a Book of Quantum and opening its doors to new claimants. This began in July last year.

The PIAB was set up by the Government to process claims for personal injuries where the question of liability is not contested by the respondent. Where it is contested, the case must go to court. However, the claim first goes to the

PIAB, from where it is released to the courts.

The awards made by the PIAB are based on court awards, and the range of awards for specific injuries are published in the Book of Quantum. Claimants fill in a form and submit it to the board with a medical report. The PIAB charges the respondent for processing the claim.

Three out of every four claimants were happy with the awards made, she said. The total amount awarded so far was just €2.7 million, but this was expected to rise substantially as more claims were processed. So far, 13,000 claims have been received, the majority of them in 2005. Of these 5,000 have either been settled upfront between the parties, or claim papers are now being submitted by the claimant. She said that about 2,000 claims were settled between the parties without the involvement of the PIAB.

Ms Byron said the cost of making the €2.7 million in awards was €185,000, less than 10 per cent of the amount being assessed. According to the report of the Motor Insurance Advisory Board two years ago, litigation costs ran at 46 per cent of the cost of awards. Therefore awards were being made by PIAB at a quarter of the cost. They were also being made within nine months, she said, which was three times quicker than through the courts. She said she expected the PIAB to be self-financing by the end of the year.

Projecting future savings from these figures, Ms Byron said that 15,000 awards were expected to result in a cost to respondents of €169.2 million. If PIAB continued to cost 10 per cent of the value of the award, this would amount to €16.9 million, compared to a projected €77.8 million if all of these claims were litigated, a saving of more than €60 million.

She pointed out that in 2004, the last year before all claims had to go first to PIAB, 15,293 cases were lodged in the High Court. Figures are not yet available for the number lodged in the Circuit Court, but these normally run at about twice those lodged in the High Court. Asked if any respondents had rejected the level of award, she said she knew of only one, and this was a company based outside the country. Asked what was happening to the promised reduction in insurance costs, the chairwoman of the PIAB, Dorothea Dowling, said this was not the responsibility of the board. However, the statistics showed there had been a reduction so far in insurance premiums of 24 per cent. She said that initially about half of all claimants were represented by solicitors. Following a High Court judgment that the PIAB could not refuse to deal with a claimant through his or her solicitor, this had risen to 75 per cent. She pointed out that solicitors could not claim their costs from the PIAB, and that it was illegal for them to claim a percentage of the award.

Source: The Irish Times, 14 September 2005.

Questions

1. Compare the scale of litigation costs with the scale of the costs of the PIAB. To what extent is like being compared with like? Explain your answer.
2. What is the likely impact of the PIAB on solicitors' earnings? The Law Society represents solicitors. What arguments do you think could be used by the Law Society against the PIAB?
3. What mechanisms, other than the PIAB, might be expected to reduce insurance costs?

APPENDIX 5.1: COST MINIMISATION USING ISOQUANTS AND ISOCOST LINES

A more detailed analysis of the theory of production requires the use of concepts and techniques similar to those used in the theory of consumer choice. By the use and application of these new concepts we can derive the least-cost technique of producing a certain level of output.

FIGURE 5.9: AN ISOQUANT

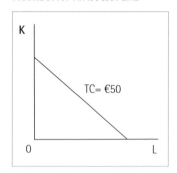

An isoquant is a locus of points, showing the various combinations of two inputs that can be used to produce a given level of output. The most common combination of inputs discussed in neoclassical theory is labour (L) and capital (K). Therefore, the isoquant is drawn on a diagram with capital on the vertical axis and labour on the horizontal axis. A single isoquant is shown in Figure 5.9.

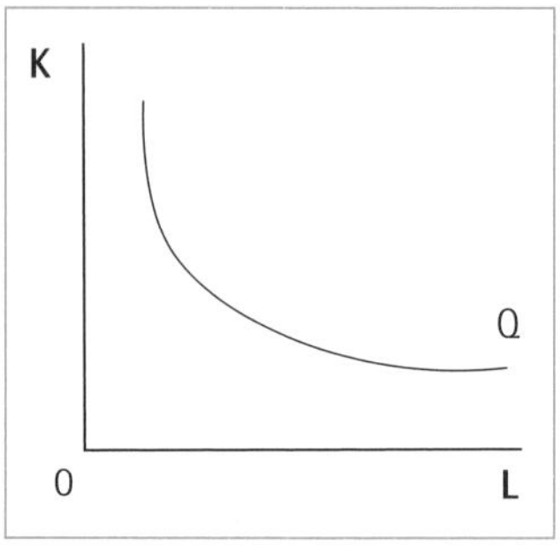

The slope of an isoquant is called the marginal rate of technical substitution (MRTS) which is equal to the amount of an input that can be replaced by one unit of another factor input without changing the level of output. It measures the technical trade-off between two factors of production. Equation 5.8 states this in algebraic terms.

$$MRTS = - \frac{\Delta K}{\Delta L}$$ [5.8]

An isoquant has similar properties to an indifference curve. Isoquants slope downwards from left to right; they are usually drawn convex to the origin; there is an isoquant map with each isoquant representing a different level of output; the higher the isoquant, the higher the level of output. The slope is the MRTS. It diminishes as we move down the isoquant from left to right.

FIGURE 5.10: AN ISOCOST LINE

The isocost line reflects the cost of the inputs and available monies to be expended on costs. The isocost line shows all the combinations of the two factors that can be employed for a ceratin amount of money. Figure 5.10 illustrates an example of an isocost line.

Higher isocost lines are associated with higher costs. Likewise, lower costs are reflected in isocost lines closer to the origin. The slope of an isocost line is equal to the negative of the factor price ratio, $-\frac{P_L}{P_K}$, the price of labour over the price of capital.

A change in relative prices results in change in the slope of the isocost line.

A profit-maximising firm chooses the particular combination of inputs that minimises cost. The least-cost technique of production is the combination of inputs that minimises the total cost of producing a given level of output. It is determined by superimposing a set of isocost lines onto a given isoquant. This is shown in Figure 5.11.

FIGURE 5.11: THE LEAST-COST INPUT COMBINATION

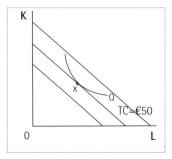

The optimal level, where the profit-maximising firm will minimise costs, is given by the tangency point between the isoquant and the lowest possible isocost line. At this point x the respective slopes are equal. This is expressed in algebraic form in Equation 5.9.

$$\text{slope of isoquant} = \text{MRTS} = \frac{-\Delta K}{\Delta L} = \frac{-P_L}{P_K} = \text{slope of isocost line}$$

[5.9]

This approach is similar to the analysis used in consumer choice theory. The similarities are outlined in Table 5.8.

TABLE 5.8: DUALITY BETWEEN CONSUMER CHOICE THEORY AND PRODUCTION THEORY

Consumer theory	Production theory
Each indifference curve reflects a different level of utility.	Each isoquant represents a different level of output.
Constraints reflected by budget lines.	Costs reflected by isocost lines.
The consumer maximises utility subject to the price and income constraints.	The producer produces a certain level of output by using the least-costly combination of inputs available.
Utility maximisation occurs where	Cost minimisation occurs where
$MRS = -\dfrac{P_d}{P_f}$	$MRTS = -\dfrac{P_L}{P_K}$

CHAPTER 6

Market Structures

'By perfect competition I propose to mean a state of affairs in which the demand for the output of an individual seller is perfectly elastic.'[1]

JOAN ROBINSON (1903–83)

'People of the same trade seldom meet together, even for merriment and diversion, but the conversation ends in a conspiracy against the public, or in some contrivance to raise prices.'[2]

ADAM SMITH (1723–90)

CHAPTER OBJECTIVES

Upon completing this chapter, the student should understand:

- the supply curve of the perfectly competitive firm;
- efficiency;
- monopoly power and barriers to entry;
- product differentiation and monopolistic competition;
- mutual interdependency between oligopolistic firms;
- game theory and the concept of a Nash equilibrium;
- the differences between various market structures.

OUTLINE

INTRODUCTION

The theory of the firm was outlined in Chapter 5. However, there are many aspects of a firm's behaviour that remain unaddressed. Relative to costs, will the price charged to the consumer by the firm be high or low? Will the profits be high or low? Will the level of output be large or small? Will the firm produce efficiently from society's perspective? The answers to many of these questions depend on the market environment in which the firm operates and, in particular, on the degree of competition facing the firm. For example, there may be only one firm in the market. If so, the market outcome is likely to be different from the outcome in a market in which there are a large number of competitors.

It is traditional at this stage of our analysis to divide markets into categories according to the degree of competition and market power available to the individual firm. Market power signifies the degree of control that a firm or a group of firms has over market price. There are four broad categories: perfect competition; monopolistic competition; oligopoly; and monopoly. The term 'imperfect competition' is sometimes used to denote a market that is not perfectly competitive. The differences between each case depend on a number of key characteristics. These characteristics are:

- the number of firms (i.e. sellers) in the market;
- the nature of the product, whether it is differentiated (heterogeneous) or undifferentiated (homogeneous);
- the extent of information available to market participants;
- the freedom of entry and exit, depending largely on the existence (or otherwise) of barriers to entry.

Throughout our discussion of the different market structures, we assume that there are a large number of consumers whose actions are unco-ordinated, except through the standard market place. In other words, consumers are not grouping together to exert pressure on firms in the market. Also, we assume that the objective of all firms is profit maximisation. The profit-maximising level of output for firms is explained in terms of the marginal condition and the average condition examined in the previous chapter.

We begin in Section 6.1 by examining perfect competition. Monopoly, monopolistic competition, oligopoly and game theory are examined in Sections 6.2, 6.3, 6.4 and 6.5, respectively. An overall summary of the complete market structure spectrum is given in Section 6.6.

6.1 PERFECT COMPETITION

Perfect competition lies at one end of the market spectrum. The model of the perfectly competitive market is based on strict and fairly unrealistic assumptions, which we will discuss below. The markets for certain raw materials, agricultural products and the stock exchange are usually cited as examples of perfectly competitive markets, but in reality it is very difficult to find real-world examples of (truly) perfectly competitive markets.

With so few examples, a student might be forgiven for asking why so much time and energy is spend in understanding this market structure. Perfect competition and monopoly are located at the two ends of the market spectrum. If we understand the extreme cases, we can use them as a basis of comparison for other commonly observable market structures which lie between the two extremes. Also, at the end of this section, we will define and discuss efficiency. We examine perfect competition as the benchmark of efficiency and later discuss how other market structures compare with perfect competition in regard to efficiency.

Perfect competition has a number of identifying characteristics:

1. There are a large number of firms and the output of any firm is very small (i.e. negligible) relative to the market output. Because its output is small, each firm is a price taker and cannot influence price.

2. The market product is homogeneous. The product produced by one firm is identical to the product produced by any other firm in the market and this is recognised by all consumers.
3. There is perfect information. Consumers are aware of market prices and firms are aware of the actions of their competitors.
4. There is complete freedom of entry to and exit from the market.

The fact that the firm is a price taker (because there are so many firms in the market) has very important implications for the shape of the demand curve confronting the firm.

Let us consider an example. Molly is a street trader on Moore Street. The price of apples is 25 cent each. Molly can sell as many apples as she likes at this market price; hence, there is no incentive to cut price. Likewise, there is no incentive to increase price. Her three sisters Margie, Annie and Bridie, along with the other street traders, are all selling apples for the same price. If Molly increases her price she will not be able to sell any apples, as customers will go elsewhere. In summary, her individual actions will have no effect on the market price of apples, which is determined by the total market demand and supply on any given day.

In terms of price, the demand for Molly's apples is perfectly elastic. The demand curve that Molly and other street traders face for their product is horizontal. This is illustrated in Figure 6.1.

The left-hand panel of Figure 6.1 illustrates the market for apples on any given day on Moore Street. The equilibrium price is 25 cent. It is determined by market demand and market supply. The market demand is the aggregate of all the individual consumers' demand curves whereas the supply curve is the sum of all the street traders' supply curves. Any change in market demand or market supply will affect the equilibrium price.

FIGURE 6.1: THE PERFECTLY COMPETITIVE MARKET

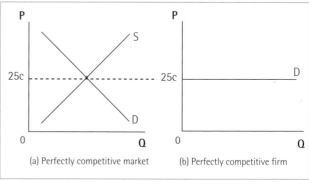

(a) Perfectly competitive market   (b) Perfectly competitive firm

For example, an influx of tourists into Dublin will increase the demand for apples. Hence, the market demand is pushed right, resulting in an increase in the price.

The right-hand panel illustrates the demand curve facing the perfectly competitive firm; in this case, Molly. Molly is a price taker. She sells her apples for 25 cent. On this day, all other things being equal, she will neither increase price nor cut price. The demand curve is horizontal. We say demand is perfectly elastic at a price level of 25 cent.[3]

A horizontal demand curve has important implications for the relationship between price and marginal revenue. Before we consider a numerical example for a firm operating in a perfectly competitive market, we will briefly recall some of the definitions discussed in detail in Chapter 5.

Total revenue is the amount a firm receives for selling its products. It is calculated by multiplying price by quantity ($TR = P \times Q$). Marginal revenue is the change in revenue which a firm receives if it sells one more unit ($MR = \frac{\Delta TR}{\Delta Q}$). Average revenue equals total revenue divided by quantity sold ($AR = \frac{TR}{Q}$). If we multiply both sides of this equation for AR by Q, we are left with another formula for TR ($AR \times Q = TR$). Comparing this with the first equation, we see that $P = AR$. This result will hold regardless of whether a firm's demand curve is horizontal or downward sloping.

However, if a firm is operating in a perfectly competitive market, marginal revenue is also equal to price and to average revenue. We will illustrate this with an example. Table 6.1 shows the demand schedule confronting an individual firm in perfect competition.

TABLE 6.1: PRICE, MARGINAL REVENUE AND AVERAGE REVENUE

Q	P	TR	MR	AR
0	10	–		
			10	
1	10	10		10
			10	
2	10	20		10
			10	
3	10	30		10
			10	
4	10	40		10

It is clear from the table that this firm is operating in a perfectly competitive market because it does not have to lower its price in order to sell more output. Regardless of the quantity the perfectly competitive firm chooses to sell (subject to the condition that the firm remains very small relative to the size of the market), the last unit will be sold at the market price of P = 10. Hence, the marginal revenue received from selling additional output is equal to the price received, i.e. MR = P.

In terms of a diagram, the marginal revenue curve and the demand curve are one and the same for a firm in a perfectly competitive market. This is shown in Figure 6.2.

The output decision in the short run

How much will a firm in a perfectly competitive industry produce in the short run? From our discussion in Chapter 5, we know that if a firm is going to produce a positive level of output, the profit-maximising level of output is where marginal revenue equals marginal cost. This is also illustrated in Figure 6.2.

We can see from Figure 6.2 that the profit-maximising level of output is at Q* where MR = SMC. Moreover, at Q*, MR = SMC = P for a firm in a perfectly competitive market. We will see in

FIGURE 6.2: MARGINAL REVENUE AND MARGINAL COST

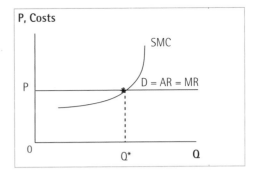

the next sections that this result differs for firms which operate in other, less competitive market structures.

We know from Chapter 5 that MR = MC is a necessary but not sufficient condition for producing at the profit-maximising output level. The second condition relates to average revenue and average cost. The short-run cost curves which we derived in Chapter 5 are reproduced below. Four possible cases are presented in Figure 6.3.

FIGURE 6.3: FOUR SCENARIOS FOR A PERFECTLY COMPETITIVE FIRM

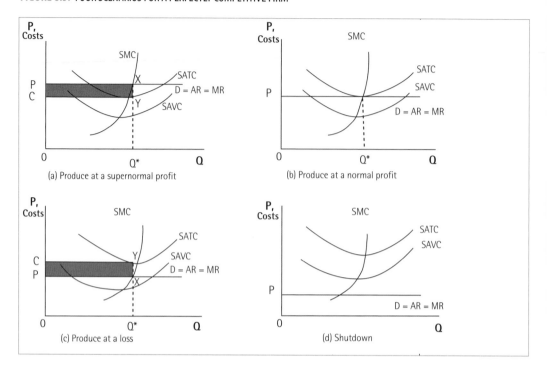

In panel (a), price is above the short-run average total cost. This is presented by drawing the demand curve above the short-run average total cost curve. The first condition is met at Q* where MR = SMC. Second, at this output level, price is greater than average total cost. From our discussion in the previous chapter, we know that a 'normal' profit is included as a cost of production. Since the AR curve is above the SATC curve, at the profit-maximising level of production, this firm is making a <u>supernormal profit</u>. The supernormal profit per unit is measured by the distance between the SATC curve and the AR curve at Q*. This is shown on the diagram by line segment IXYI.

The shaded area on the diagram is the area of supernormal profits. We identify this area by subtracting the area of total cost from the area of total revenue. On the diagram, total revenue is defined by the area of the rectangle [PXQ*0]. Total cost is shown by the rectangle [CYQ*0]. The difference between the two areas is the shaded rectangle [PXYC] which represents the total supernormal profits received by the firm.

In panel (b) the profit maximising output is Q*, where the marginal revenue equals the short-run marginal cost. The AR curve is tangent to the SATC curve. At this point, the firm is making a <u>normal profit</u>.

In panel (c) price is below the short-run average total cost but above the short-run average variable cost. This is presented by drawing the AR curve above the SAVC curve but below the SATC curve. <u>Because we assume that firms will maximise profits (or equivalently minimise losses)</u> <u>we conclude that a firm that faces this situation will produce at Q* in the short run.</u> The alternative is to cease production and pay all of the fixed costs. At Q*, the firm is covering its variable costs and making some contribution to its fixed costs. The loss per unit is shown by the line segment IYXI, which represents the difference between average total cost and price. The area of economic loss is shown by the shaded rectangle [CYXP]. This is the area which remains when total revenue, represented by the area [PXQ*0] is subtracted from total cost, represented by the rectangle [CYQ*0].

In panel (d) price is below the short-run average variable cost. This is presented by drawing the AR curve below the SAVC curve. The market price does not cover the variable costs of the firm. The firm in this situation minimises losses (and hence maximises profits) by discontinuing production immediately.

Deriving the short-run supply curve

The above analysis can also be used to derive the short-run supply curve for a firm in a perfectly competitive market. Let us begin with a market price of P_0. At P_0 the firm will produce at Q_0 where MR = SMC. Both the marginal condition and the average condition are met. This gives us point X, the first point on the supply curve.

FIGURE 6.4: DERIVATION OF THE SHORT-RUN SUPPLY CURVE

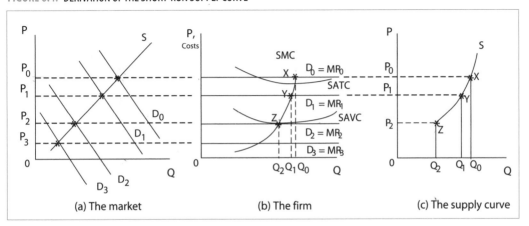

(a) The market   (b) The firm   (c) The supply curve

Suppose there is a change in market conditions. In panel (a) the demand curve shifts downwards to the left (from D_0 to D_1). The firm reacts to the lower price by cutting production to Q_1 where MR_1 = SMC. Point Y is another point on the supply curve. As price falls, less is supplied.

Suppose the fall in demand reduces the market price to P_3. For the firm, this price level is below both the average total cost and the average variable cost. The firm minimises its losses by discontinuing production immediately and paying its fixed costs. There is no corresponding output level for this price, or any price below P_2.

At P_2, price is equal to average variable cost. The AR curve is tangent to the SAVC curve. A price at or below P_2 is a shutdown price.

> **Definition**
> *A shutdown price is a price at or below the short-run average variable cost of production.*

At P_2, the firm will produce Q_2 units of output, shown as point Z on Figure 6.4, panel (b). Below this price, the firm will not supply output.

We can see from panel (c) of Figure 6.4 that the SMC curve beginning at point Z is the supply curve for the firm in the short run. All profit-maximising firms produce where MR = SMC. For a firm in a perfectly competitive market, marginal revenue is equal to the price. Therefore, a firm in this market will produce where P = SMC, as long as the average variable costs are covered.

What can be implied from the above? Under perfect competition, the firm's supply curve in the short run is its marginal cost curve above the highest shutdown price. Hence, the amount the firm supplies to the market depends primarily on its costs of production.

The short-run supply curve for the competitive market is simply the horizontal sum of the supply curves of all individual firms. It shows the sum of all the quantities produced by all firms at each given price in the short run. This is the same (market) supply curve that we discussed in Chapter 2.

The output decision in the long run

The analysis in the long run is a little more complex. It is based on the assumption that firms are free to enter and exit the market. Let us begin by looking at two possibilities: the long-run equilibrium following short-run losses and the long-run equilibrium following short-run (supernormal) profits.

Figure 6.5 depicts the long-run equilibria following short-run losses. Panel (a) illustrates the market demand and supply conditions whereas the firm's position is depicted in panel (b).

We assume that all firms maximise profits. However, we have seen that in the short run, a firm may operate at a loss, provided that its variable costs are covered. From our discussion in the last chapter,

FIGURE 6.5: THE LONG-RUN POSITION FOLLOWING SHORT-RUN LOSSES

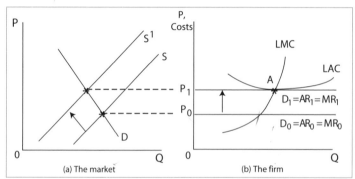

(a) The market   (b) The firm

we know that in the short run, some inputs to the production process are fixed. In the long run, all inputs are variable. Therefore, a firm can exit a market in the long run, and channel its assets into another market where it can earn at least a normal profit. If losses are incurred by firms in a perfectly competitive market in the long run, we confidently predict, based on this model, that those firms will exit the market.

As the number of suppliers in the market falls, the supply curve shifts to the left. This is reflected in panel (a). As a result of this shift, price is driven up. The price continues to rise until market equilibrium is attained.

Panel (b) depicts the position for the individual firm. At P_0 losses result (the difference between average revenue and long-run average cost). In a perfectly competitive market all individual firms are price takers. Hence, as price rises due to the change in market conditions, the price that the individual firm can charge also rises. The AR curve continues to shift upwards until it touches the LAC curve at a tangency point, A. The firms which remain in the perfectly competitive market will earn (only) a normal profit in the long run.

Figure 6.6 depicts the long-run equilibria following short-run supernormal profits. Panel (a) illustrates the market demand and supply whereas the firm's equilibrium position is depicted in panel (b).

In the short run, firms in the perfectly competitive market can earn supernormal profits. However, because of the assumption of perfect information, other firms are aware of the supernormal profits in the market. Also, we assume that firms are free to enter the market. An increase in the number of firms shifts the market supply curve to the right from S to S^1 as shown in panel (a). Price falls until an equilibrium is reached.

Panel (b) depicts the position for the individual firm. Supernormal profits are made at P_0. As market price falls, the price that the individual firm can charge also falls. In this case, prices will continue to fall until all supernormal profits are 'competed' away. The AR curve continues to shift downwards until it touches the LAC curve at a tangency point, A. The result is normal profit. The inflow of new firms decreases as supernormal profits diminish.

FIGURE 6.6: THE LONG-RUN POSITION FOLLOWING SHORT-RUN PROFITS

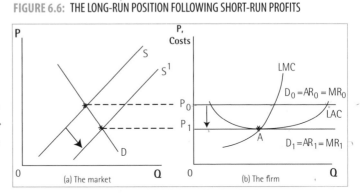

Panel (b) in both Figure 6.5 and Figure 6.6 illustrate long-run equilibrium for a firm in a perfectly competitive market. At point A, the firm is producing at the minimum point of the long-run average cost curve. The firm is said to be making optimum use of its resources since it is producing at the least possible cost per unit of output. In addition, at equilibrium, the firm is making (only) a normal profit.

This is very desirable from the point of view of the consumer and society as a whole. The firm is producing in its most efficient manner while at the same time the consumer is being charged no more than the marginal cost of production. This is an example of efficiency, a concept that requires further explanation. When markets are perfectly competitive, the amount of a product produced is socially optimal. Another way to say this is that equilibrium in a perfectly competitive market is Pareto efficient. By Pareto efficient, we mean that no other level of output can make any individual better off without making at least one other individual worse off (see Section 1.2).

FIGURE 6.7: PERFECTLY COMPETITIVE MARKETS AND EFFICIENCY

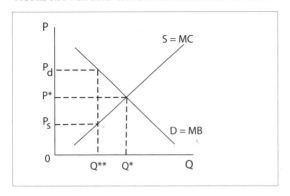

Figure 6.7 shows long-run equilibrium in a perfectly competitive market. The supply curve is derived by adding together the marginal cost curves of all firms producing for this market. In long-run equilibrium, all firms in a perfectly competitive market are covering their costs and making a normal profit. We can think of the supply curve as showing the amount that producers are willing to supply at each price.

The market demand curve is derived by adding together individual demand curves based on the marginal utility that a consumer gains from the consumption of this product. The demand curve represents the amount that consumers are willing to pay for different amounts of this product. They are willing to pay for a product, as long as the marginal benefit which they receive from consuming the product is greater than or equal to the price of the product.

In Figure 6.7, the market equilibrium level of output is Q* and the market clearing price is P*. Suppose the amount of output is Q**. This amount of output is not efficient. Suppliers are willing to accept P_s for Q** units of output and consumers are willing to pay P_d. As long as one consumer is willing to pay more than the marginal cost, a producer benefits from increasing production. Both parties are better off.

By contrast, at an output level that is greater than Q*, consumers are not willing to pay the producers' marginal cost. Additional output will only make a consumer better off at the expense of a producer. This is not efficient.

We therefore conclude that Q* is the socially optimal and efficient amount of output. At Q*, consumers are willing to pay the marginal cost to the producers. All gains from trade are exhausted. (For further discussion of efficiency in perfectly competitive markets, see Sections 8.1 and 9.2.)

6.2 MONOPOLY

Monopoly is another form of market structure, which is identified by the following characteristics:

1. There is only one firm (seller) in the market. In effect, the firm is the market.
2. A unique product is sold. There are no close substitutes.
3. There are barriers to entry which preclude the possibility of new firms entering the market, even if the monopolist is making supernormal profits.

Most Irish monopolies were (and in some cases remain) state-owned, but they have declined significantly in number. They included Aer Lingus, Aer Rianta, An Post, Dublin Bus, the Electricity Supply Board (ESB), Iarnród Éireann and Telecom Éireann (subsequently eircom). Previously protected markets have been opened up to at least some competition. Some have been privatised and some have become take-over targets or have entered into joint ventures with foreign-owned firms.

Barriers to entry are the main source of monopoly power, or more generally market power. The various types of barriers to entry and the factors which account for their strength are detailed in Table 6.2. Barriers to entry are also discussed in Section 9.2.

TABLE 6.2: BARRIERS TO ENTRY

Type	Description	Low barrier	High barrier
Type of asset	Specific assets have more value in their current use than in the next best alternative. General assets can be shifted to alternative activities.	general	specific
Excess capacity	Incumbents are able to produce more output at an equal or lower price. Can be caused by cyclical demand or adopted as a strategy to deter new entrants.	insignificant excess capacity	substantial excess capacity
Reputational effects	Based on history of retaliation against new entrants and/or the resources available to incumbents to retaliate.	no retaliation anticipated	retaliation expected
Precommitment contracts	Long term contracts: with suppliers to purchase input at favourable rates; with distributors to give the product a favourable location; and with consumers to provide and maintain their product.	none or few	extensive
Pioneering brand advantage	Consumer loyalty given to first entrant into market.	quality of product can be judged prior to purchase	product must be purchased before testing
Cost of entry	Set-up costs required for a firm to enter a market.	low	high
Economies of scale	Minimum viable scale is the minimum amount of output required to produce a product at a cost that is very close to the competitors' cost per unit.	MVS at low % of industry output	MVS at high % of industry output
Government regulations	Licensing agreements are required before a firm can enter some markets. Patents legally restrict firms from copying an innovation for 17 years. Other regulations are designed to ensure product quality and/or consumer safety.	unregulated	regulated
Learning curve effects	Incumbents operating in a market benefit from knowledge which allows them to produce at a lower cost per unit.	small cost advantage	large cost advantage
Cost of exit	Exit barriers are factors that keep firms competing in a market. Sources of barriers include labour agreements, government intervention and emotional attachment to a market, location or employees.	low	high

Single-price monopolist

Since the monopolist is the only firm in the market, the demand curve that it faces is the downward sloping market demand curve. If the demand curve is downward sloping, marginal revenue is less than price. This point is best illustrated with an example. In this example, we are considering the behaviour of a 'single-price' monopolist, i.e. all of the monopolist's customers are charged the same price. Table 6.3 is the demand schedule for the monopolist.

TABLE 6.3: PRICE, MARGINAL REVENUE AND AVERAGE REVENUE

Q	P	TR	MR	AR
0	10	–		
			9	
1	9	9		9
			7	
2	8	16		8
			5	
3	7	21		7
			3	
4	6	24		6

In order to sell more products, the monopolist must lower price. In this example, to increase sales from two units to three units, the monopolist cuts its price from €8 to €7. Let us consider what happens to the marginal revenue. At P = €8, the monopolist sells two units, collecting total revenues of €16. The total revenue increases to €21 when the monopolist charges €7 per unit. However, the marginal revenue falls to €5 per unit. Why? Because to sell the extra unit, the single-price monopolist must cut the price for all units sold. The monopolist has gained revenue by selling more units, but has lost revenue because the price per unit is lower. For this reason, marginal revenue is always less than price if the demand curve is downward sloping. Notice, however, that the average revenue equals price, for reasons which were explained in the previous section.

On a two-dimensional graph, the marginal revenue curve is drawn below the demand curve. Since price equals average revenue, the demand curve and the average revenue curve are identical. The revenue curves are illustrated in Figure 6.8.

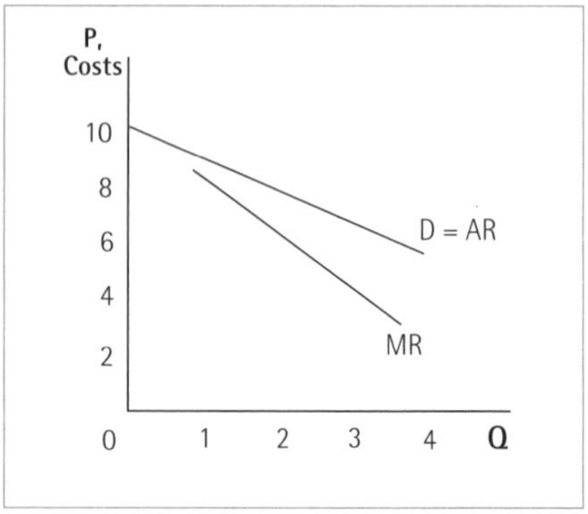

FIGURE 6.8: THE DEMAND CURVE AND THE MARGINAL REVENUE CURVE

We will now examine the equilibrium for the monopolist.

Short-run equilibrium

Figure 6.9 illustrates the equilibrium position for the monopolist.

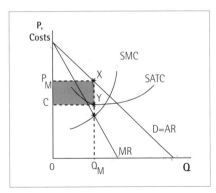

The demand curve D is downward sloping with the marginal revenue curve drawn below it. The cost structure of the firm is given by the average total cost curve, SATC, and the marginal cost curve, SMC. The two profit-maximising conditions are the marginal condition and the average condition. These two conditions must be met in order for the monopolist to produce in the short run.

The marginal condition is met at output level Q_M. At this level of production, marginal revenue is equal to marginal cost. The second condition requires that the average revenue is no less than the average variable cost at this output level.

In Figure 6.9 the difference between price and SATC is (supernormal) profit and is given by the vertical distance |XY|. The total profit made by the monopolist is the profit per unit multiplied by the total quantity sold. In Figure 6.9 it is given by the area $[P_MXYC]$, the difference between the total revenue area $[P_MXQ_M0]$ and the total cost area $[CYQ_M0]$. This shaded area represents supernormal profits.

The distinction between the long run and the short run is less important for the monopolist who is making supernormal profits. Unlike the firm in a perfectly competitive market, competition via new entry will not drive down price and profit. Supernormal profits, as shown in Figure 6.9, can persist in the long run.

However, there is no guarantee that a monopolist will make supernormal profits. Regardless of market structure, profits depend on both demand and cost conditions. Panel (a) of Figure 6.10 shows a monopolist who is making (just) normal profits. In panel (b), the monopolist is operating at a loss.

FIGURE 6.10: MONOPOLIST EARNING A NORMAL PROFIT; SUSTAINING A LOSS

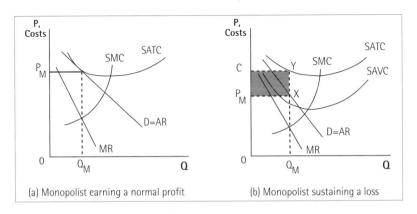

(a) Monopolist earning a normal profit

(b) Monopolist sustaining a loss

In panel (a) the marginal condition is fulfilled when Q_M units of output are produced. However, at this level of output, the average revenue curve is tangent to the average total cost curve. Therefore, the monopolist is making only a normal profit.

The monopolist in panel (b) is sustaining a loss. The level of output is Q_M, determined by the intersection of the marginal revenue curve and the marginal cost curve. In this situation, in the short run, the monopolist will produce at a loss because the price is greater than the average variable cost. In other words, the monopolist minimises losses by producing, rather than closing down and paying fixed costs. The loss per unit is shown by the segment |YX|. The total loss is shown by the shaded rectangle $[CYXP_M]$.

If a monopolist is operating at a loss in the short run, we expect the owner to close if variable costs are not being covered. In the long run, we expect a monopolist who cannot make a normal profit to exit. However, state-owned or state-subsidised companies could operate if price were less than short-run average variable cost or long-run average costs.

It is evident from Figure 6.9 and Figure 6.10 that the monopolist does not produce at the lowest point of its average cost curve. In addition, price always exceeds marginal cost. This is due to the existence of monopoly power which is reflected in the downward sloping demand curve. With price exceeding marginal cost, the consumer pays more for the product than the marginal cost associated with producing the product. As such, there is inefficiency from society's perspective.

Price discriminating monopolist

In the discussion above, the monopolist charged the same price to all consumers. Under some circumstances, a monopolist may charge different prices for the same product.

> **Definition**
> *Price discrimination occurs when a firm charges different prices to different customers for the same product for reasons other than differences in costs.*

There are two conditions necessary for price discrimination:

1. Separate markets featuring demand curves with different price elasticities must be identified. In other words, the seller must be able to classify consumers into separate groups.
2. The markets must be separated so that the products cannot be resold (i.e. no arbitrage).

Separate markets can be identified by classification of customer, geographically or by time. Iarnród Éireann, for example, offers cheaper train tickets to students than to other travellers. A traveller who purchases a return ticket from Galway to Dublin may also pay less than one who purchases a return ticket from Dublin to Galway.

The monopolist is attempting to charge as close as possible to the maximum that the consumer is willing to pay. A monopolist who can practise price discrimination can increase profits, beyond what is earned by a single-price monopolist.

There are different categories or methods of price discrimination. The most common forms are called third degree and first degree price discrimination.

> **Definition**
> *Third degree price discrimination occurs when a firm separates consumers into a small number of classes and establishes a different price for each class.*

The ESB charges different rates to its commercial and residential customers; eircom charges different rates at different times, as do the mobile phone companies in general. The highest charge per minute generally occurs during 'business' hours. In the evenings and at weekends when people are more likely to make discretionary calls, the charge per minute decreases substantially. Cinemas offer cheaper tickets for their matinee performances to attract senior citizens and other people who are not working (in the paid labour market) or studying. In the evenings, when most people are free to attend the cinema, the price increases. These are all forms of third degree price discrimination.

The firm that engages in first degree price discrimination must have very detailed knowledge of the preferences of each and every consumer.

> **Definition**
> *First degree price discrimination occurs when every consumer is charged the maximum price that he or she is willing to pay.*

Customised financial or legal services are examples where the seller of the service may be able to charge the maximum price. The consumer must believe that the product offered by the monopolist is unique in order to purchase under these circumstances. Either form of price discrimination results in higher profits because the monopolist is capturing all or part of the consumer surplus. (See Section 4.4 to review consumer surplus.)

We will consider an example involving first degree price discrimination. Table 6.4 is a demand schedule for the price discriminating monopolist.

TABLE 6.4: DEMAND SCHEDULE FOR THE PRICE DISCRIMINATING MONOPOLIST

Q	P	TR	MR
0	10	–	
			9
1	9	9	
			8
2	8	17	
			7
3	7	24	
			6
4	6	30	

This table is similar to the table we used for the single-price monopolist – with one important difference. To sell the second unit, the producer does not have to cut the price on the first unit. The monopolist sells the first unit for €9 and the second unit for €8.

This leads to the collection of higher total revenue with the marginal revenue per unit sold higher for the price discriminating monopolist than it was for the single-price monopolist. In this case, the marginal revenue is equal to price. (Review Table 6.3 to see that the marginal revenue is lower than price for the single-price monopolist.) Therefore, the demand curve and the marginal revenue curve are the same for the price discriminating monopolist.

Now we will consider the difference in the quantity produced between the two types of monopolist. Consider Figure 6.11.

If the monopolist is charging a single price, its marginal revenue curve is below the demand curve. Profit maximisation requires that it produce where marginal revenue equals marginal cost. This is indicated by the level of output Q_1.

For the monopolist engaging in first degree price discrimination, the demand curve and the marginal revenue curve are equivalent. The profit-maximising level of output is Q_2. You can see from the diagram that the level of output increases if the monopolist practises price discrimination.

FIGURE 6.11: PROFIT-MAXIMISING LEVELS OF OUTPUT FOR THE SINGLE-PRICE MONOPOLIST AND THE PRICE DISCRIMINATING MONOPOLIST

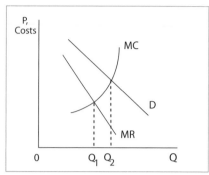

The absence of a supply curve

One important characteristic of a monopoly is the absence of a supply curve. For a perfectly competitive firm, the marginal cost curve (above the highest shut-down price) is its supply curve. For a monopoly, supply is affected by cost considerations and also by demand conditions. Hence, it is impossible to draw a supply curve which is determined independently of demand. This is illustrated in Figure 6.12.

FIGURE 6.12: THE ABSENCE OF A SUPPLY CURVE

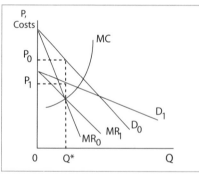

Figure 6.12 is similar to Figure 6.9 above. The demand curve D_0 is drawn downward sloping with the marginal revenue curve MR_0 drawn inside it. The marginal cost curve, MC, is upward sloping.

Let us now superimpose another set of demand and marginal revenue curves onto the diagram. The marginal cost curve cuts both sets of marginal revenue curves at the same point. At output level Q^*, price can either be P_0 or P_1 depending on the conditions of demand. Q^* is sold at P_0 when the demand curve is D_0, and at P_1 when the demand curve is D_1. Hence, for a given level of output, different demand conditions give rise to different prices. There is no unique relationship between price and quantity supplied. In conclusion, there is no identifiable or meaningful supply curve for the monopolist.

Students tend to think initially that a monopolist can charge any price and produce any quantity of output that it wants. In other words, it has an unlimited ability to extract supernormal profits. From the discussion above, we can see that this is not true. Like the perfectly competitive firm, the monopolist will maximise profit by producing where MR = MC. The maximum price that can be charged is limited by the demand curve which the monopolist faces for the product.

Comparing the perfectly competitive market with the single-price monopolist

It is a very useful exercise to compare the equilibrium position of the perfectly competitive market with that of the monopolist. To do this, we (hypothetically) join all the firms in the perfectly competitive market together to form one single firm. Further, we assume that the demand and cost conditions remain the same notwithstanding the market structure changes. We then compare the price and output decision of the perfectly competitive market with that of the single-price monopolist. This is illustrated in Figure 6.13.

FIGURE 6.13: PERFECT COMPETITION AND MONOPOLY COMPARED

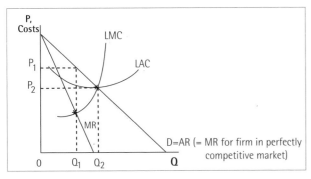

For the perfectly competitive market, the equilibrium in the long run is given by the equation MR = MC = AC = AR. In this case, the output level is Q_2 and the price charged is P_2. The single-price monopolist produces where MR = MC. The output level is Q_1 and the price is P_1. Since barriers to entry preclude the entry of new firms to the market, this equilibrium can persist into the long run. The single-price monopolist is producing less output and charging a higher price than the perfectly competitive market.

With regard to efficiency, when the market structure is characterised by monopoly, the level of output produced in this market is not efficient. The level of output will be below its socially optimal level and the price charged for that output will be above the socially optimal level.

Figure 6.14 shows market equilibrium for a single-price monopolist. At market equilibrium, the additional cost of producing an extra unit of output (MC_1) is less than what consumers are willing to pay for an extra unit of output (P_1). Since the price that consumers are willing to pay must reflect the utility to them of the extra unit of the product, then increasing output beyond Q_1 adds more to consumer utility than it adds to producers' cost. However, since the monopolist is charging only one price, P_1 and Q_1 is the profit-maximising combination. If the monopolist drops price for one customer, the price that the monopolist gets for all other units sold will also fall.

So the potential gain to the monopolist from increasing output beyond Q_1 is wiped out by the loss in earnings on the existing level of output Q_1, as a result of the fall in market price. If it were possible for consumers to share some of their gains (from higher output and lower prices) with the producer, both could be made better off.

If the market structure were perfectly competitive, then output would be at its socially efficient level Q_2. The area BCE represents the net gain to society from increasing output from the monopoly level to the level that would occur in a perfectly competitive market.

FIGURE 6.14: MONOPOLY EQUILIBRIUM AND EFFICIENCY

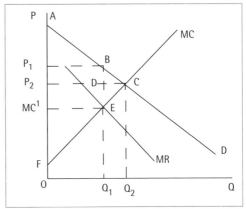

There are also distributional effects. Recall that consumer surplus is the amount which consumers are willing to pay, over and above what consumers actually have to pay, while producer surplus is the amount that producers receive over and above the minimum amount necessary to keep them in the market. In the perfectly competitive market, the area of consumer surplus is shown by the triangle (ACP_2) in Figure 6.14. With the single-price monopolist, the area of this triangle shrinks to (ABP_1). Part of the area of original surplus is appropriated by the monopolist as revenue (P_1BDP_2). The rest of the consumer surplus (BCD) is lost to both parties because of the pricing strategy followed by the monopolist. In the perfectly competitive market, the area of producer surplus is shown by the triangle (CFP_2) in Figure 6.14. With the single-price monopolist, producer surplus changes to the area (P_1BEF).

The area (DCE) represents the lost producer surplus that is not appropriated by consumers. The total loss to society is BCE.

Comparing the single-price monopolist with the monopolist practising first degree price discrimination

A monopolist practising first degree price discrimination charges each consumer exactly what the consumer is willing to pay. We saw in Table 6.4 that marginal revenue equals price, which means that the demand curve and the marginal revenue curve are equivalent (as they are in a perfectly competitive market).

This monopolist will produce at Q_2 (Figure 6.14) the same level of output as the perfectly competitive market. There is no unique price level because price changes with every unit of output that is sold. The level of output is socially optimal. The total gains to society in the market for the monopolist practising first degree price discrimination are the same as they are in the perfectly competitive market. However, the gains are distributed differently. Because each consumer pays exactly what the consumer is willing to pay, there is no consumer surplus. The entire area under the demand curve (ACQ_2) is appropriated by the monopolist as revenue. The consumer is worse off since all of the gains are appropriated by the monopolist.

CASE STUDY

Extract from *The Irish Times*
Dairy Board urged to set up 'OPEC for milk producers'
by Sean MacConnell

The Irish Dairy Board was asked to pursue the possibility of setting up a global group similar to OPEC [Organisation of Petroleum-Exporting Countries] to represent milk producers, with other big international companies or State agencies. Hugo Maguire, a town of Monaghan co-operative delegate, proposed his idea to Kevin Lane, chief executive of the dairy board at the annual conference of co-operative societies yesterday. Mr Maguire asked Mr Lane if it would be feasible to link up with international dairy marketing giants like Fonterra in New Zealand and Campina in Europe to meet the challenges from multinational retailers. 'We should try set up an organisation to do what the oil producers do in OPEC for milk producers and processors worldwide,' he said at the Irish Co-operative Organisation Society's national conference.

Mr Lane said he was in the process of meeting other major global marketing companies on a range of issues and it was possible the issue might arise. He said fragmented marketing of Irish dairy products internationally was costing money and a unified marketing arm was needed rather than individual companies competing in markets and driving down the price. He also put a cost on increasing the milk output by 50 per cent here in 10 years' time as set out in the *Harvest 2020* report at over €800 million. He said it would cost processors €400 million. There would be a need for up to €300 million in working capital, finance and storage facilities, and marketing infrastructure and investment in acquisitions and growth would cost a further €200 million. Mr Lane said the expected growth in the dairy sector was a potential 'good news' story at a critical time, but there were still many obstacles to overcome.

The society, which represents 150 co-operative businesses, also put forward its figures on the cost of expanding milk output. It said it would cost those increasing their milk output dramatically 30 cent per litre of annual capacity. The society said the time was right to re-establish the link between milk supply and co-operative shareholding, which had been weakened by the imposition of EU milk quotas and co-ops diversifying into non-dairy areas. It also proposed establishing a minimum shareholding by all members relative to their supply.

Source: *The Irish Times*, 22 November 2010.

Questions

1. Research the activities of OPEC, especially in the 1970s. Describe briefly the consequences of OPEC's activities for oil-exporting countries and for oil-importing countries such as Ireland.
2. Discuss briefly the likely effects of the setting up of an OPEC-like organisation for milk producers and processors on: (a) milk producers (i.e. dairy farmers); (b) milk processors; (c) retailers; and (d) consumers (including Irish consumers).
3. Should Ireland and/or the European Union support the setting up of such an organisation? Explain your answer.

Answers on website

6.3 MONOPOLISTIC COMPETITION

The standard model of monopolistic competition was independently developed in the 1930s by the American economist Edward Chamberlin (1899–1967) and the English economist Joan Robinson. Some credit must also go to Piero Sraffa (1898–1983), who was unhappy with the existing market set-up in the 1920s and who subsequently began the search for alternative market structures.[4]

Monopolistic competition incorporates features of both perfect competition and monopoly. It is similar to perfect competition in that there are a large number of firms in the market. There is also freedom to enter and exit. However, it differs from perfect competition in that the products produced are heterogeneous, or differentiated, as opposed to homogeneous. Product differentiation means that in the short run, firms have some degree of market power (with respect to their own particular products or brands) resulting in the possibility of supernormal profits.

> **Definition**
> *Product differentiation means that the product produced by one firm is different from the products produced by the firm's competitors.*

There are close but not perfect substitute products or brands available.

Differentiation is achieved through various strategies, which include product design, customer service, packaging and advertising. Examples of monopolistically competitive markets include book publishers, filling stations, retail outlets and restaurants.

Product differentiation has implications for the demand curve that the firm faces. Recall that the demand curve for the firm in the perfectly competitive market is perfectly elastic because the products are perfect substitutes. The demand curve for the monopolist is downward sloping because there are no close substitutes. A firm in a market classified as monopolistically competitive faces competitors who are producing similar, but not identical, products or brands. Therefore, the demand curve faced by this firm is downward sloping, but more elastic than the demand curve of the monopolist.

The short-run equilibrium position for the monopolistically competitive firm is illustrated in Figure 6.15.

FIGURE 6.15: A MONOPOLISTIC COMPETITOR'S SHORT-RUN EQUILIBRIUM

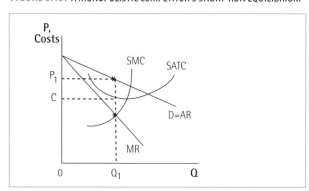

The firm's demand curve is downward sloping with the marginal revenue curve lying below the demand curve. The standard short-run average cost and marginal cost curves are superimposed onto Figure 6.15. The profit-maximising firm in a monopolistically competitive market must meet the same conditions as firms in other markets.

The firm will produce at output level Q_1, where marginal revenue is equal to marginal cost, (MR = SMC). It will charge a price based on its demand or average revenue curve. In this case, the price is P_1. At this price, average revenue exceeds average cost. The difference, given by the distance between P_1 and C, is profit per unit of output. This profit per unit of output multiplied by the quantity sold gives us the supernormal profits earned by the firm.

In the short run, the firm in the monopolistically competitive market can earn supernormal profits. However, it cannot maintain this equilibrium position or continue to earn supernormal profits in the long run.

The long-run equilibrium position is illustrated in Figure 6.16.

In the long run, because of the absence of entry barriers, new firms will enter the market, attracted by the presence of supernormal profits. These new entrants will produce very close substitutes for the existing products. The overall market supply rises, causing the market price to fall. In addition, the demand for the existing firm's product falls as its share of the market demand declines. The existing firm's demand curve becomes more elastic because new firms produce very similar products.

Supernormal profits are 'competed away' with the influx of new firms. Equilibrium in the long run is achieved when participating firms are making normal profits only. There is no further incentive for other firms to enter the market. In graphic terms, this occurs when the firm's average revenue curve is tangent to its average cost curve. Long-run equilibrium is achieved at point A in Figure 6.16. Hence, the monopolistic competitor is not producing at the point of full productive capacity. The difference between Q_2 and Q^* represents excess capacity.

FIGURE 6.16: A MONOPOLISTIC COMPETITOR'S LONG-RUN EQUILIBRIUM

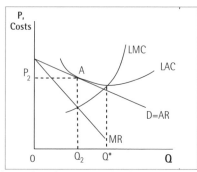

The long-run equilibrium condition for a monopolistic competitor is MR = MC and AR = LAC. It is evident from Figure 6.16 that the firm under conditions of monopolistic competition does not produce at the lowest point on its average cost curve. In this regard, monopolistically

competitive markets compare unfavourably to perfectly competitive markets. Furthermore, on account of product differentiation and the subsequent market power that exists, price exceeds marginal cost. This market structure does not exhibit efficiency from society's perspective.

Part of the explanation for such inefficiencies lies in the fact that advertising, branding and other forms of product differentiation constitute additional costs to the firm. The generally positive aspect of monopolistic competition is the wider product choice it offers to the consumer. Benefits such as improved quality and service may also result from non-price competition. Unfortunately we gain variety at the expense of efficiency. More advanced textbooks attempt to measure the advantages of product variety against the disadvantages of the standard inefficiency caused by the imbalance between marginal cost and price.

6.4 OLIGOPOLY

Another commonly observed market structure is oligopoly. It is another form of imperfect competition. An oligopolistic market consists of a small number of firms (sellers), each with some ability to affect the market price. The most important feature of this market structure is the recognition of interdependence between firms.

Firms in other market structures act independently of each other when choosing market strategies. In oligopoly, the reaction of competitors to a change in price or some other market strategy (e.g. quantity or quality) is critical. Firms are said to be mutually dependent. The level of price in this market structure is generally higher than in the perfectly competitive market, and the level of output is lower than in the perfectly competitive market. For example, if the firms decide to (explicitly) collude, they act in the market as a monopolist.

Products are either homogeneous or differentiated. In some oligopolistic markets, products are identical. Examples include the oil market and basic commodity markets, e.g. tin, copper, steel etc. In others, products are differentiated. Examples include the automobile, newspaper and beer markets.

Unlike the other market structures studied so far (i.e. perfect competition, monopoly and monopolistic competition), there is no generally accepted single theory of oligopolistic behaviour. This is because oligopolies exhibit a wide variety of different types of economic behaviour. The most important models, however, are briefly outlined below. They differ because of the assumptions made about an individual firm's behaviour and its reaction to its rivals' strategies.

The collusion model

One option potentially available to firms in oligopoly is that of explicit collusion. This occurs when firms get together and collude over price and output strategies. In such cases, the equilibrium position regarding price and output is identical to the monopoly. The equilibrium position is illustrated in Figure 6.17.

The market demand curve is drawn downward sloping with the market marginal revenue curve drawn below it. Profits are maximised at the output level where MR = MC. The total market output Q_1 is shared out in a number of different ways. For example, a quota system may be in place where each respective firm is allotted a sales quota. The results of

FIGURE 6.17: COLLUSIVE OLIGOPOLY

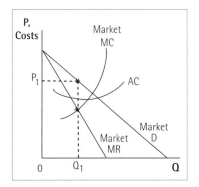

collusion are higher prices, higher profits and lower output than would otherwise be the case. The name given to these formal groupings is a cartel.

> **Definition**
> *A cartel is a group of firms in a particular market who collude on price and output decisions in an effort to earn monopoly profits.*

Cartels are outlawed in most countries in order to protect consumers and society. However, the illegal actions of cartels are often difficult to investigate and successfully prosecute. As difficult as it is to uncover and prosecute national cartels, international cartels, like the Organisation of Petroleum Exporting Countries (OPEC) often act without fear of reprisal.

In general, once a cartel is formed, there is an incentive for each individual participant to cheat. The benefits of cheating on a collusive agreement as compared to adherence to the agreement (where joint profits are maximised) come in the form of higher output levels and higher profits for the 'cheating' firm at the expense of its rivals. Furthermore, some cartels face competition from non-members who are not bound by any formal agreement.

The price leadership model

The price leadership model demonstrates a tacit (or implicit) form of collusion compared to the explicit collusion of the cartel. It is based on the existence of a generally recognised dominant firm. This firm sets price and the other firms follow. Although other firms in the market are technically free to choose whether or not to 'follow the leader', their freedom is limited by the ability of the dominant firm to retaliate. Examples of dominant firms arguably include Kellogg's (breakfast cereals), Goodyear (tyres), Intel (semiconductors) and Coca Cola (soft drinks).

Figure 6.18 illustrates the equilibrium position for the price leadership model with a dominant firm.

Market demand is represented by the demand curve, D. The quantity supplied by the smaller firms is given by the supply curve, s. The demand curve facing the dominant firm is the difference between these two curves. In graphic terms, we subtract the quantity supplied by the smaller firms at each price from the total quantity demanded in the market. The difference at each price is the dominant firm's demand curve and is labelled Dd. Take, for example, the price P_1. At P_1 the smaller firms' supply curve intersects the market demand curve. This means that at this price the total market demand is met entirely by the smaller firms. As a result, the quantity demanded of the dominant firm is zero. Hence, at P_1 the dominant firm's demand curve intersects the price axis.

FIGURE 6.18: THE PRICE LEADERSHIP MODEL WITH A DOMINANT FIRM

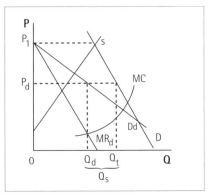

Knowing the demand curve for the dominant firm, we can now derive its marginal revenue curve. If a firm's demand curve is drawn downward sloping, its marginal revenue curve is drawn below it. The dominant firm's marginal revenue curve is labelled MR_d.

The profit-maximisation output level for the dominant firm is attained by producing a quantity at which its marginal revenue is equal to its marginal cost. The output level is Q_d and the price charged by all firms is P_d. The total quantity demanded in the market at P_d is given by the output level Q_t. This comprises Q_d which is the amount supplied by the dominant firm, and Q_s, the amount supplied by the other smaller firms.

The dominance of the price leader depends on its costs, its financial assets, its excess capacity and, perhaps most important, its reputation for retaliation. If its marginal costs are substantially lower than its competitors, it can temporarily charge a price which is lower than the average variable costs of its competitors, forcing them to shut down, at least temporarily. Although the collusion between the dominant firm and its many smaller competitors is 'tacit', under certain circumstances the threat posed by the dominant firm to its smaller competitors can be quite persuasive.

The kinked demand curve model

This model was developed by Paul Sweezy in the USA and by R. Hall and C. Hitch in the UK in the 1930s.[5] The model is used to explain why the price in an oligopolistic market, once established, tends to remain the same, even if cost conditions change quite significantly. It assumes asymmetrical reactions by competitors in a market to a change in price by one firm. For example, if one firm increases price, the others will tend not to respond or not to respond to the same extent. As such, the action of increasing price results in a sharp decrease in demand for the initiating firm. In contrast, if the firm cuts price, the others will tend to follow, and to the same extent. As such, only a small increase in the quantity demanded for its product will result for the firm who initiated the price cut. The kinked demand curve outlined in Figure 6.19 results from the asymmetrical responses of market competitors.

The oligopolistic firm's kinked demand curve is drawn in Figure 6.19. Suppose that the market price for the product supplied by the market is P_1. If one firm increases price above P_1, the other firms will not follow. As a result, the firm loses most of its market share. Consumers purchase the product at a lower price from the firm's competitors. The demand curve for the firm is elastic above the price of P_1.

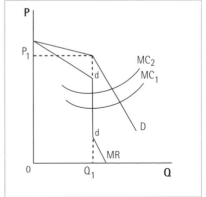

FIGURE 6.19: THE KINKED DEMAND CURVE

Alternatively, suppose that the firm cuts price so that it is below P_1. Its competitors react by cutting their prices to the same extent. The price change does not significantly increase demand for the firm's product. The demand curve for the firm is inelastic below the price of P_1.

Above P_1 the demand curve is relatively flat. Below P_1 the demand curve is relatively steep. At P_1, the demand curve is said to be 'kinked'. A kinked demand curve will result in a discontinuous marginal revenue curve. At Q_1, there is said to be a 'jump' in the marginal revenue curve.

This model of oligopoly is used to explain price rigidity and the absence of price wars in oligopolies even when there is no explicit collusion. In particular, the discontinuous part of the MR curve (the segment dd) provides an explanation for price rigidity. Along this segment, marginal cost could change significantly without affecting the profit-maximising output or price level. In effect, the oligopolist absorbs the change in costs and, by doing so, maintains the existing price level. This partly explains the price stickiness or inflexibility which is sometimes associated with oligopolies.

This model is based on the assumption made about the reactions of firms to changes in price by a competing firm. However, it omits a whole range of other possible reactions and consequently results in a rather restrictive model. In particular, and crucially, it fails to explain how the initial price is reached. In explaining the reason behind price rigidity, it fails to account for other possible explanations such as the administrative expenses involved in changing prices. In addition, the model has not stood up well to empirical tests.

To address the criticisms directed at these models and their assumptions regarding firms' behaviour and pricing strategies, economists began to use a particular branch of mathematics called 'game theory', which focuses on the interdependent decision-making of firms in a market. It is applied to firms operating under conditions of oligopoly and in particular those firms which anticipate rivals' reactions.

6.5 GAME THEORY

Game theory is a mathematical technique used to analyse strategic interaction. It was first developed in the 1940s by the mathematician and physicist John von Neumann and the economist Oskar Morgenstern to analyse the behaviour of firms in oligopolistic markets.[6]

A game consists of rules, players (decision-makers), strategies (actions) and payoffs (scores). In any single game, the players are allowed to make certain moves, as defined by the rules of the game. The player tries to maximise his or her own payoff.

One of the most famous games in game theory is the prisoners' dilemma.

The prisoners' dilemma

Michael and Jean are charged for committing a lewd act in public. They are remanded in custody, each facing a possible sentence of up to one year in jail. On meeting the two prisoners, the sergeant immediately suspects them of involvement in another crime committed recently in the locality: the robbing of local church funds.

He places the prisoners in separate rooms. Each prisoner is made aware of the sergeant's suspicion of their involvement in the more serious crime of robbery. They are told that if both confess to the crime, the jail sentence will be four years. Each is also told that if only one of them confesses to the crime, the confessor's sentence will be quashed while the accomplice will receive an eight-year jail sentence. If neither confesses, both prisoners will spend only one year in jail for the lesser offence.

This can be presented as a game with two players, each player having two strategies – to deny the charge or to confess to the crime. With two players and two strategies, there are four possible outcomes:

- neither Michael nor Jean confesses to the more serious crime;
- both Michael and Jean confess to the more serious crime;
- Michael confesses, Jean denies involvement;
- Jean confesses, Michael denies involvement.

We use a payoff matrix to tabulate the possible alternative strategies of both players. Table 6.5 shows the payoff matrix for Michael and Jean.

TABLE 6.5: THE PRISONERS' DILEMMA PAYOFF MATRIX

		Michael's strategies	
		Confess	Deny
	Confess	M. 4 years	M. 8 years
		J. 4 years	J. Free
Jean's strategies	Deny	M. Free	M. 1 year
		J. 8 years	J. 1 year

Each square shows the payoffs for the two players (M for Michael and J for Jean) for each possible strategy. We begin with the top left-hand box. If both confess, they each get a four-year jail sentence. In contrast, if both deny the charge, they each get a one-year jail sentence. This latter possibility is recorded in the bottom right-hand box. The more interesting payoffs are to be found in the two remaining boxes. If Michael confesses and Jean denies, the court will free Michael but will hand down an eight-year jail sentence to Jean. This possibility is presented in the bottom left-hand box. The other possibility is for Jean to confess and for Michael to deny. This combination will involve freedom for Jean but the much longer sentence of eight years for Michael.

It is evident from the above analysis that the two players are faced with a dilemma. Neither player knows what the other's decision will be. Should Michael confess in the hope that Jean denies the charge? Likewise, should Jean confess hoping to minimise the amount of time she spends behind bars? The answers to these and other questions are to be found in the 'equilibrium' for the game. The equilibrium for this particular type of game is called the Nash equilibrium. This is the result of all participating players playing their best strategy given the (best) actions of their competitors. It is named after John Nash, the American mathematician who introduced this concept in 1951.

In the case of the prisoners' dilemma, the equilibrium occurs when Michael makes his best choice given Jean's choice and, likewise and simultaneously, when Jean makes her best choice given Michael's choice. However, the Nash equilibrium for the prisoners' dilemma is a special case. No matter what Jean does (or is expected to do), Michael's best choice is to confess. Likewise, no matter what Michael does (or is expected to do), Jean's best choice is to confess. Hence, the equilibrium of the prisoners' dilemma is that both players confess. This equilibrium, where there is a unique best action regardless of what the other player does (or is expected to do), is called a dominant strategy equilibrium.

From the prisoners' joint or collective viewpoint, however, this is a bad outcome. If both denied the charges, they would receive only a one-year jail sentence. Unfortunately, they have no way of communicating to each other. Yet they do know that, despite the action of the other individual, their best unilateral choice is to confess. On confessing, a bad outcome is delivered.

Similar techniques can be applied to firms in oligopolistic markets. Such firms may decide to alter output levels or prices, depending on the (expected) actions of others. Assumptions are made about the behaviour of their rivals. All possible strategies can then be analysed in the same way as above.

The application of game theory to the study of a firm's behaviour in oligopolistic markets has been one of the most outstanding recent developments in the field of economics. In recognition of this, the 1994 Nobel Prize in Economics was awarded to three economists for their work in this field. The recipients were John Nash (of Nash equilibrium fame), John Harsanyi and Reinhard Selten, who introduced time and uncertainty to game theory models.

More recently, the 2005 Nobel Prize in Economics was awarded to two other game theorists, Robert Aumann and Thomas Schelling. Aumann specialises in the theoretical study of repeated games, where players (e.g. firms) continuously encounter a similar environment. In such an environment, co-operation may be expected to evolve naturally. Schelling specialises in the study of strategies that may be expected to be adopted by players in real-world 'games', e.g. conflicts or wars. For example, it may sometimes be rational for an army to eliminate its own fallback or retreat options in order to convince the enemy of its total commitment, i.e. its determination to fight to the end.

INFORMATION BOX 6.1

A troubled mind that found some equilibrium
by William Reville

John Forbes Nash Jnr, along with two others, shared the Nobel Prize in Economics in 1994, in recognition of his contribution to game theory. After a brilliant early career in mathematics, Nash suffered a protracted period of mental instability from which he eventually recovered. His story is the subject of the book *A Beautiful Mind* by Sylvia Nasar (Simon and Shuster, 1998), and also of a recent movie starring Russell Crowe.

John Forbes Nash Jnr was born on June 13th 1928 in Bloomfield West Virginia. A sister, Martha, was born in 1930. His father was an electrical engineer and his mother was a teacher. Although he was brought up in a loving household, he did not relate emotionally to other boys, seeming remote and confrontational. Nash first showed an interest in mathematics at the age of 14, inspired by the book *Men of Mathematics* by ET Bell. He was also very interested in chemistry.

Nash entered the Carnegie Institute of Technology in 1945 to study chemical engineering. His teachers recognised his mathematical skills and persuaded him to change to mathematics. He continued to have poor relations with his fellow students, many of whom sensed he had a mental problem. Nash behaved at times in a very odd manner, for example, playing a single piano chord over and over. Nash was awarded a BA and an MA in mathematics in 1948. He was accepted into the postgraduate programme at Princeton in September 1948. Nash took an interest in a broad range of mathematics – topology, algebraic geometry, game theory and logic. The point in game theory is to find the best rational strategy to use when your opponents make no mistakes and always pursue their own best outcome. The simplest games have two players and a zero-sum payoff rule, which means that one player's gain is the other player's loss. John von Neumann had shown in the 1920s that optimal strategies exist for such players and that such games reach equilibrium where none of the players can improve their position. Von Neumann's argument couldn't be extended to multiplayer games or to non-zero-sum games.

Nash developed game theory to include multiple players in non-co-operative situations where each player must play his best game in response to his opponent's best strategy. Nash showed there is also a point of equilibrium for those games for which the rational strategies of all players are in balance. This is called the Nash Equilibrium Theory.

Equilibrium Theory has wide applicability in many fields. The economist P. Ordeshook has written: 'The concept of the Nash Equilibrium is perhaps the most important idea in non-co-operative game theory. Whether we are analysing candidates' election strategies, the causes of war, agenda manipulation in legislatures, or the actions of interest groups, predictions about events reduce to a search for a description of equilibria. Put simply, equilibrium strategies are the things that we predict about people.'

Nash received his doctorate from Princeton in 1950. He moved to the Massachusetts Institute of Technology (MIT) in 1952. Between 1950 and 1958 Nash published many significant mathematical contributions. Many believe that game theory was not his best work, pointing to his major contributions in topology and other areas.

In 1952 he established a romantic relationship with a nurse, Eleanor Stier. However, he concealed her existence from his family and most colleagues at MIT. When she became pregnant, Nash apparently made no offer of marriage and after his son was born, Eleanor had difficulty supporting the boy. Eventually she was forced to enrol her son in an orphanage.

The second woman in Nash's life is Alicia Larde who was a student in his calculus class. They married in 1957. Shortly afterwards their son John was born and around this time also Nash's mental state became very disturbed. He appeared at a New Year's party dressed only in a nappy and spent the evening curled up on his wife's lap. He declared that the *New York Times* contained encrypted messages from outer space that were meant only for him. He was diagnosed as schizophrenic and Alicia had him involuntarily committed to a hospital. On his release, Nash resigned from MIT and went to Europe where he intended to renounce his US citizenship. Alicia had him deported back to the US.

Alicia settled with Nash in Princeton, but his illness continued and he spent most of his time hanging around the campus behaving strangely. He made temporary recoveries followed by further treatment. Alicia divorced Nash in 1962 but in 1970 she took him into her house again because no one else would have him. They are together still but have not re-married.

Ever so slowly Nash regained his lucidity. He claims that his recovery was partly an act of will, saying: 'I began to intellectually reject some of the delusional lines of thinking which had been characteristic of my orientation.' Nash resumed his research at Princeton. A colleague once asked Nash how, as a man devoted to reason and logic, he could believe that extraterrestrials were sending him messages. 'Because the ideas I had about supernatural beings came to me the same way that my mathematical ideas did. So I took them seriously,' he replied.

Source: *The Irish Times, Under the Microscope,* 7 August 2003.

Examples of games and Nash equilibria

Economists are particularly interested in a number of types of games that appear to have specific relevance for settings in which a small number of firms interact, e.g. oligopoly. More generally, these games can also offer insights into strategic interactions between any economic or social agents, for example: central bankers and wage setters; employers and employees; lecturers and students; partners in a relationship; potential partners; parent and child, etc.

The following four games provide examples that allow us to highlight certain issues and difficulties associated with the concept of a Nash equilibrium. For ease of exposition, not all of the games refer to economic issues, but readers should try to apply the issues to economics. Table 6.6 provides a more economics-based example of a game very similar in nature to the prisoners' dilemma. In terms of payoffs, i.e. profits, each of two tobacco firms would ideally like to advertise and for its competitor not to advertise. In addition, advertising by both firms leads to lower payoffs relative to advertising by neither firm.

TABLE 6.6: ADVERTISING GAME

		Firm j	
		Advertise	Don't Advertise
Firm i	Advertise	(i = 2, j = 2)	(i = 4, j = 1)
	Don't Advertise	(i = 1, j = 4)	(i = 3, j = 3)

The numbers in Table 6.6 are merely illustrative, but the rankings are important. The Nash equilibrium is for both firms to advertise. As before, this Nash equilibrium (Advertise, Advertise) is also a dominant strategy equilibrium. From an economic perspective, however, it is interesting to consider how things might change if the game is played repeatedly over time. There are at least two new considerations. First, we might expect co-operation to evolve naturally over time and for the firms to curtail their advertising. In practice, perhaps one firm might reduce or eliminate its own advertising for one period and wait to see whether or not its competitor reciprocated. Second, and perhaps more interesting, there is the possibility that the government might ban tobacco advertising, i.e. the rules of the game might change. Given the above payoffs, the tobacco firms would be 'delighted' if the government banned tobacco advertising. Indeed, rather paradoxically, one could envisage the tobacco firms campaigning (perhaps covertly) for such a change in the law. (Of course, we are not suggesting that such a thing actually happened/happens; the example is purely illustrative.)

Table 6.7 provides the payoffs associated with two friends eating out. Because the relevant mobile phone network is down, the friends cannot communicate with each other. However, they had previously arranged to eat out in one of two restaurants, located at different ends of town. In terms of payoffs, i.e. utility, the friends want to eat together but person i has a preference for Chinese food while person j has a preference for Italian food. Of course, the worst scenarios would be for the two friends to guess differently and for both to end up eating alone.

TABLE 6.7: EATING OUT GAME

		Person j	
		Chinese	Italian
Person i	Chinese	(i = 4, j = 2)	(i = 1, j = 1)
	Italian	(i = 1, j = 1)	(i = 2, j = 4)

Again, the numbers in Table 6.7 are merely illustrative but the rankings are important. What is the Nash equilibrium? If the two friends decide to go to the Chinese restaurant, we have a Nash equilibrium. But if the two friends decide to go to the Italian restaurant, we also have a Nash equilibrium, albeit a different Nash equilibrium. A fundamental issue, even problem, in game theory is the simultaneous existence of multiple Nash equilibria. Which of the two (or perhaps more) equilibria should economists expect to occur and why? There is no obvious solution. Of course, should the game be repeated, it is possible that the friends will be able to develop some solution to their predicament. For example, a focal point may exist or emerge over time.

Table 6.8 provides the payoffs associated with the 'game' of chicken. Two drivers drive rather quickly towards each other. For each driver, victory is achieved by not swerving while the opponent does swerve. In addition, two swerves are better than no swerves, which at least provides some element of rationality to the setting.

TABLE 6.8: CHICKEN GAME

		Driver j	
		Swerve	Don't Swerve
Driver i	Swerve	(i = 2, j = 2)	(i = 1, j = 4)
	Don't Swerve	(i = 4, j = 1)	(i = 0, j = 0)

Again, we are confronted by the presence of multiple equilibria. Driver i might be reassured to note that it is a Nash equilibrium for him (or her, at least in theory although probably unlikely in practice) not to swerve while his opponent swerves. However, he should also realise that it is also a Nash equilibrium for his opponent not to swerve while he swerves. An interesting twist is provided by the possibility that one driver might detach his steering wheel and hang it out the window in order to highlight one Nash equilibrium over another, i.e. in order to create a focal point for the 'game'. The economist would see such a move as one player attempting to pre-commit to a particular strategy, perhaps in the context of a price war between two firms, where one firm suddenly offers to commit to its current low prices for a certain extended period in an effort to drive its opponent from the market. However, the rather nasty possibility also exists that both drivers might simultaneously follow the strategy of flaunting their detached steering wheels (and brake pedals).

Finally, Table 6.9 provides the payoffs associated with the game of matching pennies. Two players simultaneously call out either 'heads' or 'tails'. Player i wins a penny if both calls are identical, while player j wins a penny otherwise.

TABLE 6.9: MATCHING PENNIES GAME

		Player j	
		Heads	Tails
Player i	Heads	(i = 1, j = −1)	(i = −1, j = 1)
	Tails	(i = −1, j = 1)	(i = 1, j = −1)

In this zero-sum game, there appears to be no Nash equilibrium. There is always an incentive for at least one player to deviate from any proposed outcome. Although there is no (pure strategy) Nash equilibrium to this game, there is what is termed a mixed strategy Nash equilibrium in which each player randomises between the two possible calls. Readers may be more familiar with the somewhat more three-dimensional version of this game, 'scissors, rock, paper' in which it generally pays to randomise equally between the three possible calls. Of course, over time if you find that your opponent deviates from this randomising strategy, by for example, favouring rock, you should be prepared to lean towards paper. As such, it is clear that in repeated games, opportunities for learning and creating reputations become crucially important.

6.6 MARKET STRUCTURE SPECTRUM

We have now completed our analysis of the different market structures. One useful way of comparing one structure with another is by examining the market structure spectrum. The market structure spectrum is similar to any other spectrum such as the spectrum of light or colour. The different market structures are presented in a line from left to right. It is primarily the degree of competition (i.e. number of firms or sellers) which explains the differences between the market structures.

On one extreme of the spectrum we have 'perfect' competition. Monopoly is the other extreme where there is no competition. Most markets, in reality, lie somewhere in between these two extreme cases. It is monopolistic competition and oligopoly that lie between these two polar extremes, with the former being generally known as 'competition among the many' and the latter being generally referred to as 'competition among the few'. In these two cases there are varying degrees of competition between the respective firms.

FIGURE 6.20: THE MARKET STRUCTURE SPECTRUM

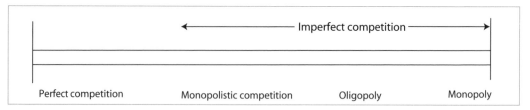

Figure 6.20 illustrates the market structure spectrum. The various market structures include perfect competition, monopolistic competition, oligopoly and monopoly. As previously indicated, the last three market structures are sometimes grouped together and referred to as 'imperfect competition' because in each of these structures an individual firm has some ability to influence price. A summary of the different market structures and their characteristics is given in Table 6.10.

It is often difficult to classify firms into a specific market structure, e.g. motor fuels. Also, the framework which we have discussed is often criticised because the models are simple and static while the actual behaviour of firms is complex and dynamic. However, the more realistic and dynamic models developed by economists are reactions against these comparative static models. A thorough knowledge of the standard models is essential to understand and appreciate the models of the critics.

TABLE 6.10: THE CHARACTERISTIC DIFFERENCES BETWEEN MARKET STRUCTURES

	Perfect competition	**Monopolistic competition**	**Oligopoly**	**Monopoly**
No. of firms	Many	Many	Few	One
Type of product	Identical	Differentiated	Identical or differentiated	Unique
Barriers to entry	No	No	Yes/No	Yes
Pricing strategy	Price taker	Price maker	Interdependent	Price maker
Long-run profits	Normal	Normal	Possibility of Supernormal	Possibility of Supernormal
Examples	Agricultural markets Capital markets	Service stations Restaurants	Automobile fuel Cement	Rail-transport Airport management

SUMMARY

1. A firm's behaviour depends largely on the degree of competition it faces and hence the level of market power it possesses. We examined four market structures in detail: perfect competition, monopolistic competition, oligopoly and monopoly. They differ in relation to the number of firms in the market, the nature of the product sold, the difficulties associated with entry to and exit from the market and, finally, the availability of information.

2. Perfect competition is a model which describes idealised economic conditions that are rarely met in practice. It consists of a large number of small firms with no single firm large enough to influence price. Each firm is a price taker. There is freedom of entry and exit on account of the absence of entry barriers. A standardised product is sold. Perfect knowledge exists with consumers and firms accurately informed about costs, prices, profits and quality. As a result, perfectly competitive firms cannot make supernormal profits in the long run.

3. A monopolist is the sole seller in the market. It is a price maker. There are barriers to entry. A unique product is sold with no close substitutes readily available. As a result, the monopolist can make supernormal profits even in the long run. Compared to perfect competition, the single-price monopolist charges a higher price and produces less output. There is no well-defined supply curve for the monopolist. A monopolist can also increase its profits by engaging in price discrimination.

4. Monopolistic competition is similar to perfect competition, with one important exception: it assumes that products are differentiated. Products are close rather than perfect substitutes for each other. This allows for the possession of some market power. The short-run equilibrium in monopolistic competition is similar to the monopoly equilibrium. A firm in this market can earn supernormal profits in the short run, but freedom of entry ensures that only normal profits are earned in the long run. A firm in this market does not produce at the lowest possible cost per unit. Its failure to exhibit efficiency is at least partly offset by the wider choice it offers to the consumer.

5. Oligopoly is another example of imperfect competition. In oligopoly, the actions of firms are interdependent. Each firm tries to anticipate the actions and reactions of its competitors

when formulating and implementing its own strategy. The standard oligopoly models are broadly divided into two: those that assume collusion and those that assume competition. Collusion may be open (explicit) or tacit (implicit). Game theory is the study of strategic interactions. As such, oligopoly can be viewed as an economic application of game theory. More generally, the insights offered by game theory can be applied across the whole market structure spectrum. There is a Nash equilibrium when each and every player is (simultaneously) doing her/his best (i.e. following her/his best strategy) given the strategies pursued by the other players. The prisoners' dilemma offers the most famous example of a Nash equilibrium.

6. The market structure spectrum highlights the differences between the market structures. The amount of competition ranges from 'pure' competition in a perfectly competitive market to a complete absence of any competition in a monopoly. The other cases exhibit varying degrees of competition. Monopolistic competition, oligopoly and monopoly are sometimes called 'imperfect competition' to distinguish them from perfect competition. One characteristic common to all imperfectly competitive markets is a degree of market power (at least in the short run), reflected in a downward sloping demand curve.

KEY TERMS

Market power	Third degree price discrimination
Perfect competition	First degree price discrimination
Monopolistic competition	Product differentiation
Oligopoly	Interdependency
Monopoly	Concentration ratios
Price taker	Collusive oligopoly
Barriers to entry	Cartels
Short-run supply curve	Dominant firm
Shutdown price	Kinked demand curve
Efficiency	Game theory
Single-price monopolist	Nash equilibrium
Price discriminating monopolist	Imperfect competition

REVIEW QUESTIONS

1. (a) Derive the firm's short-run supply curve under conditions of perfect competition.
   (b) Explain why the perfectly competitive firm produces at the minimum point of the average cost curve in the long run. What does this suggest about perfect competition?
2. Outline the short-run equilibrium position for a monopoly. Why is it not possible to draw a well-defined supply curve for the monopolist?
3. (a) Outline the differences and similarities between perfect competition and monopolistic competition.
   (b) Sketch the short-run and long-run equilibrium positions of the monopolistic competitor.
4. Using the kinked demand curve model, explain one rationale for price rigidity.
5. Explain the main differences between perfect and imperfect competition. Provide examples of each.
6. Describe the concept of a Nash equilibrium. Provide a real-world example of an economic game and the associated Nash equilibrium.

WORKING PROBLEMS

1. Figure 6.21 shows the cost curves of a firm competing in a perfectly competitive market. Complete Table 6.11.

FIGURE 6.21

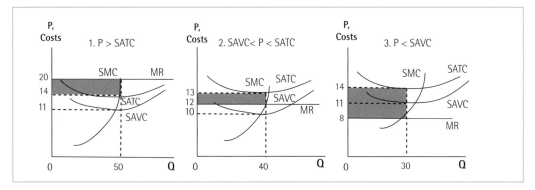

TABLE 6.11

TR = €	TR = €	TR = € . . . .
TVC = €	TVC = €	TVC = € . . . .
TFC = €	TFC = €	TFC = € . . . .
TC = €	TC = €	TC = € . . . .
Profit =	Profit =	Profit =
Production	Production	Production
Decision	Decision	Decision . . . .

2. Figure 6.22 shows two equilibrium positions in the long run. Which equilibrium is for a perfectly competitive firm and which is for a monopolistically competitive firm? Explain. What are the main differences between the two market structures at equilibrium? What are the similarities of the two market structures at equilibrium?

FIGURE 6.22: LONG-RUN EQUILIBRIUM

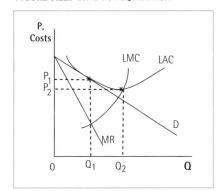

MULTI-CHOICE QUESTIONS

1. Firms act independently of each other in the following market structures:
   (a) perfect competition and imperfect competition;
   (b) perfect competition, oligopoly and monopolistic competition;
   (c) monopolistic competition and oligopoly;
   (d) perfect competition and oligopoly;
   (e) perfect competition and monopolistic competition.

2. Figure 6.23 illustrates a short-run equilibrium position for a perfectly competitive firm where price is less than average total cost.
   If the loss is equal to €75, the market price x must be equal to:
   (a) 48;
   (b) 46;
   (c) 45;
   (d) 47;
   (e) none of the above.

FIGURE 6.23

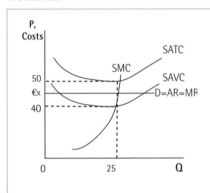

3. The long run condition that holds in perfect competition but that does not hold in a monopoly is:
   (a) MR = MC;
   (b) AR = D;
   (c) P = MC;
   (d) ATC = AVC;
   (e) none of the above.

4. Assuming identical demand and cost conditions, a monopolist, compared to a perfectly competitive market, charges:
   (a) a higher price for a higher output;
   (b) a higher price for a lower output;
   (c) a lower price for a lower output;
   (d) a lower price for a higher output;
   (e) none of the above.

5. Figure 6.24 illustrates the equilibrium position for the profit-maximising single-price monopolist.
   The single-price monopolist charges price equal to:
   (a) P_4;
   (b) P_3;
   (c) P_2;
   (d) P_1;
   (e) none of the above.

FIGURE 6.24

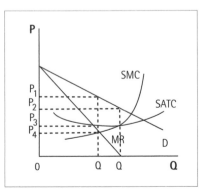

6. Which model in oligopoly is useful in explaining price rigidity?
    (a) price leadership model;
    (b) single-price monopolist;
    (c) collusion model;
    (d) kinked demand curve model;
    (e) none of the above.

TRUE OR FALSE (SUPPORT YOUR ANSWER)

1. The market demand curve in perfect competition is downward sloping from left to right.

2. The supply curve for the perfectly competitive firm in the short run is its marginal cost curve above the highest shutdown price.

3. Price discrimination involves charging different prices for different products to different consumers.

4. The demand curve for the monopolistic competitor is more elastic than the demand curve for the monopolist because of the absence of available substitutes.

5. At equilibrium in the long run, the firm under conditions of monopolistic competition produces at the output level where MR = MC = AR = AC.

6. Once a cartel is formed, there is no incentive for any individual firm to cheat.

CASE STUDY

Extract from www.rte.ie
One year price freeze on drink prices

Publicans have announced a one-year freeze in drink prices with immediate effect. The announcement was made by the Vintners Federation of Ireland, which represents about 5,000 publicans outside Dublin, and the Licensed Vintners Association, which represents 700 publicans in Dublin. The two organisations said 2009 is going to be a challenging year for the drinks industry and the move was made to provide value for money to customers at a difficult time.

Source: www.rte.ie/news/2008/1202/alcohol.htl, 1 December 2008 (accessed 1 December 2008).

Extract from www.rte.ie
Judge finds against publicans over freeze

The High Court has found the two main publicans' organisations to be in contempt of court because they recommended a price freeze to their members in breach of previous court orders. The Competition Authority has welcomed the judgement, while the publicans said they were disappointed.

The Competition Authority had claimed that an announcement in December last by the Licensed Vintners Association and the Vintners Federation Ireland of a one-year price freeze was in breach of previous undertakings given to the court in settlement proceedings over alleged drink price fixing. The authority

→

claimed a price freeze during a recession was likely to result in substantial harm to the consumer and breached the 2002 Competition Act. Both publican groups denied the claims.

In his ruling, Mr Justice Liam McKechnie found the publicans to be in contempt of court for recommending a price freeze to members because they were in breach of previous High Court orders. Mr Justice McKechnie has given both sides until next Wednesday to decide what action will be taken.

Source: www.rte.ie/news/2009/0724/pubs-business.html, 24 July 2009 (accessed 10 February 2011).

Extract from *The Irish Times*
UK plans minimum alcohol pricing
by PA (Press Association)

British government plans to introduce a minimum price level for alcohol in England and Wales have been criticised by campaigners who say they will not resolve the problem of binge-drinking. Crime prevention minister James Brokenshire said the move was an important first step towards banning below-cost sales of alcohol. But critics said the ban did not go far enough, making it a 'green light for supermarkets to keep selling booze at pocket-money prices'.

The ban was promised as part of efforts to tackle alcohol-related crime and disorder which costs the taxpayer up to £13 billion (€15.5 billion) each year. But the much-touted move will see cost price defined as just duty plus VAT and will have little if any impact on cut-price supermarket deals, campaigners said. A can of lager will cost at least 38p (45c) and a litre of vodka at least £10.71 (€12.80) under the move. It will be seen as a retreat from the coalition government's pledge to ban the sale of alcohol below cost price and will stop short of setting a minimum price for the alcohol itself.

Mr Brokenshire said: 'By introducing this new measure we are sending a clear message that the Government will not stand by and let drink be sold so cheaply that it leads to a greater risk of health harms or drunken violence.' He went on: 'We know that pricing controls can help reduce alcohol-related violent crime and this is a crucial step in tackling the availability of cheap alcohol. In nearly half of all violent incidents the offender is believed to be under the influence of alcohol. That's why we believe it is right to tackle the worst instances of deep discounting.'

Source: The Irish Times, 18 January 2011.

Questions

1. With respect to the first extract ('One year price freeze on drink prices'), discuss the likely motivations and effects of the publicans' proposed one-year freeze on on-trade drink prices.
2. Do you agree with the basic judgment as outlined in the second extract ('Judge finds against publicans over freeze')? Explain your answer.
3. With regard to the third extract ('UK plans minimum alcohol pricing'), consider the likely impact of the UK policy on off-trade drink prices. Briefly consider other economic mechanisms by which the consumption of alcohol could be curtailed.

CHAPTER 7

Factor Markets

'*Wages are determined by the bitter struggle between capitalist and worker.*'[1]

KARL MARX (1818–83)

'*Profit is the result of risks wisely selected.*'[2]

FREDERICK B. HAWLEY (1843–1929)

CHAPTER OBJECTIVES

Upon completing this chapter, the student should understand:

- derived demand;
- marginal productivity theory;
- wage determination;
- the capital market and the cost of capital;
- economic rent;
- the sources of profits.

OUTLINE

INTRODUCTION

Until now, our analysis of markets has focused on the final output of products. We mentioned that land, labour, capital and entrepreneurship are combined in the production process and that rent, wages, interest and profit, respectively, constitute the costs of these factor inputs to the firm. However, when we mentioned the cost or price of these factor inputs, we took them as 'given'.

We will now look at each of the factor markets individually. We will attempt to explain how the rental rate, the wage rate, the interest rate and the profit rate are determined within their respective factor markets.

According to the traditional or neoclassical theory of distribution, factor prices can be explained in terms of standard demand and supply analysis. In the resource market, however, the roles of firms and households are reversed. The firms that supply the products in the product markets are now the source of the demand for the factor inputs. The householders, who demand final products, are now the suppliers of the factor inputs. In short, firms are the buyers of resources and households are the sellers of the same resources. We will use marginal productivity theory to provide us with an understanding of the demand for the various factor inputs.

Section 7.1 discusses the labour market. Capital, land and enterprise and their respective factor prices (interest, rent and profit) are discussed in Sections 7.2, 7.3 and 7.4 respectively. Although each market is explained separately, they are inter-related in practice; developments in one resource market affect other resource markets.

7.1 LABOUR AND WAGES

The labour market is comprised of a demand for and supply of labour. We begin by studying the demand for labour.

The demand for labour

A firm's demand for labour is a derived demand.

> Definition
> *A derived demand means that an input is not demanded for its own sake but for its use in the production of products.*

A farmer requires (or 'demands') labourers in order to produce foodstuffs; a car manufacturer requires workers to help on the production line; an insurance company requires staff to put together saleable products and to sell them to customers. The demand for labour stems from what the employment of labour can produce.

In order to understand the demand for labour we need to return to production theory in general (Section 5.2) and to marginal productivity theory in particular. This was developed by several economists including E. von Bohm-Bawerk (1851–1914) and J. Bates Clark (1847–1938) in the late nineteenth century.[3] This theory postulates that wages, as well as other factor payments, depend largely on the productivity of the factor input. The existence of perfectly competitive markets is an underlying assumption of this theory.

Before we consider an example, recall a few of the terms that were defined in Chapter 5. We are considering the production function of a firm in the short run, which means that at least one input (usually assumed to be capital) is fixed while other inputs (e.g. labour) are variable. Total product (TP) is the total output produced during a specified time period, using particular amounts of inputs. Marginal product (MP) is the additional output generated by the addition of one more unit of a variable input. The declining productivity of labour reflects the law of diminishing returns. The law states that in the short run, when capital is fixed, an additional worker will eventually produce less output than the previous worker.

We can also look at the contribution of an additional worker in monetary terms.

> Definition
> *The marginal revenue product (MRP) of labour is the addition to revenue from the employment of an extra worker.*

Equation 7.1 states this in algebraic form:

$$MRP = \frac{\Delta TR}{\Delta Q_L} \qquad [7.1]$$

where: Δ = change; MRP = marginal revenue product;
            TR = total revenue; Q_L = number of workers.

The MRP of labour measures the monetary value of the extra output generated from the employment of an additional worker. The MRP of labour can also be calculated by multiplying the marginal product by the marginal revenue earned per unit. In simple terms:

$$MRP = MP \times MR$$ [7.2]

where: MRP = marginal revenue product;
MP = marginal product; MR = marginal revenue.

We will now apply these concepts using an example in an effort to understand the hiring decision of the firm. Hibs (Ireland) Ltd is a manufacturing company. The relationship between the number of workers employed and the total output generated by the workforce is recorded in Table 7.1. Because Hibs is producing a product for a perfectly competitive market, its marginal revenue is equal to price, i.e. MR = P.

TABLE 7.1:   DAILY PRODUCTION SCHEDULE FOR HIBS (IRELAND) LTD

(1) Labour (wkrs)	(2) TP (units)	(3) MP (units)	(4) MR = P (€)	(5) MRP (€)	(6) Wage (€)	(7) Contribution (€)	(8) Wage (€)	(9) Contribution (€)
0	0							
		55	4	220	100	120	48	172
1	55							
		43	4	172	100	72	48	124
2	98							
		33	4	132	100	32	48	84
3	131							
		25	4	100	100	0	48	52
4	156							
		18	4	72	100	−28	48	24
5	174							
		12	4	48	100	−52	48	0
6	186							
		5	4	20	100	−80	48	−28
7	191							
		1	4	4	100	−96	48	−44
8	192							

How many workers will Hibs Ltd employ? Column 5 records the extra revenue that each additional worker contributes to the business. The cost to the firm of hiring each worker is recorded in column 6. Because the labour market is perfectly competitive, all labourers can be hired for the same wage. The difference (column 7) between the two is simply the net contribution that each additional worker makes to the firm. In other words, this is what the labourer produces, in excess of her or his wage.

For example, if the (let's say daily) wage rate is €100 and the marginal revenue product of the first worker is €220, the net contribution of the first worker is €120 (€220 – €100). The contribution from the second worker is €72 (€172 – €100) and so on. In this example the first four workers each makes a positive net contribution, i.e. MRP ≥ W. The contributions from the employment of a fifth worker, a sixth worker, a seventh and so on are all negative (MRP < W). Hence, Hibs Ltd employs until MRP = W. In this example, if the wage rate is €100, Hibs Ltd employs four workers.

If the wage rate falls from €100 to €48, will Hibs Ltd increase or decrease the size of its workforce? This scenario is shown in columns 8 and 9 of Table 7.1. For a wage rate of €48, the first six workers contribute positively to the firm. In this case, MRP = W when six workers are employed. Thus, if the wage rate falls, this model predicts that the profit-maximising firm will employ more workers. The opposite is true if the wage rate rises.

In general, the lower the wage rate the more workers will be employed.

Derivation of the demand curve for labour

Hibs Ltd employs workers up to the point where the MRP = W. In other words, the profit-maximising firm will employ an additional labourer if the amount that the labourer produces is at least sufficient to pay the labourer's associated wage.

Figure 7.1 plots the relationship between the marginal revenue product of labour and the number of workers employed as described in columns 1 and 5 of Table 7.1.

We can see from the figure that the MRP of the fourth worker is €100 while the MRP of the sixth worker falls to €48. However, we can interpret this diagram in another way. We can ask, 'If the wage is €100, how many employees will Hibs Ltd employ?' At a wage rate of €100, we predict, using this model, that Hibs Ltd will hire four workers. If the wage rate falls to €48, the firm will hire six employees. At a lower wage rate, firms can afford to hire additional workers.

For Hibs Ltd and for all other profit-maximising firms, workers will be employed up to the point where the marginal revenue product equals the wage paid to labour, i.e. MRP = W. Therefore, the MRP curve is the firm's demand curve for labour. Figure 7.2 depicts the same curve as Figure 7.1. However, we have substituted wage for the marginal revenue product on the vertical axis. The horizontal axis continues to represent the number of workers employed.

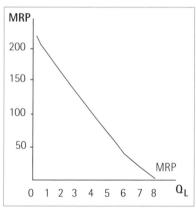

FIGURE 7.1: MARGINAL REVENUE PRODUCT CURVE FOR HIBS LTD

Figure 7.2 shows the amount of labour that Hibs Ltd will hire at each wage rate. It is downward sloping, depicting the negative relationship between the wage rate and the number of workers employed. It is drawn holding other variables constant, including the technological process and the level of training of the labour force. Also, because the demand for labour is 'derived', factors which affect the product market will also affect the labour demand curve. A change in any of the underlying variables which affects the price of a product will also cause the position and/or the slope of the demand curve for labour to change.

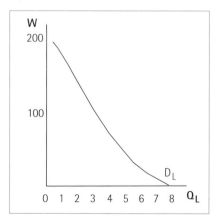

FIGURE 7.2: THE DEMAND CURVE FOR LABOUR FOR HIBS LTD

In summary, we have used the marginal productivity theory to derive the marginal revenue product for labour. For a profit-maximising firm, workers will be hired up to the point where W = MRP of labour. Hence, the marginal revenue product curve for labour is the demand curve for labour. It is derived from the productivity of labour, the wage paid to labour and the price of the product.

Derivation of the market demand curve for labour

In order to obtain the market demand curve for labour we need to sum all the individual firms' demand curves for labour. The market demand curve for labour shows the quantity of labour demanded at each wage rate by all firms in the market. In graphic terms this market demand curve can be derived by 'adding' or aggregating the firms' individual demand curves. This exercise is illustrated in Figure 7.3.

FIGURE 7.3: DERIVATION OF THE MARKET DEMAND CURVE FOR LABOUR

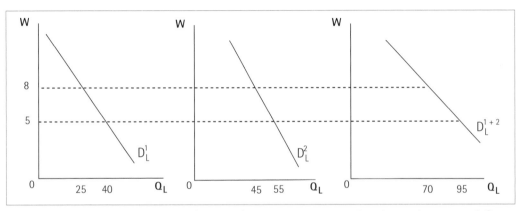

Two individual demand curves, $D_L{}^1$ and $D_L{}^2$, are drawn. The market demand curve, $D_L{}^{1+2}$, can be derived by summing up the separate levels of labour demanded at each wage rate. Technically, we are summing the demand curves horizontally. If, for example, the wage rate is €5, the total number of workers demanded would be 95 (40 + 55). At a wage level of €8, the total number demanded would be 70 (25 + 45). This exercise is repeated for each wage level. The result is a downward sloping market demand curve for labour.

We now turn our attention to the supply of labour.

The supply of labour

An individual's decision regarding the supply of labour is related to the wage rate. An increase in the wage rate generally increases the incentive to work. As a result, the quantity of hours worked increases. Hence, the supply curve for labour for an individual is upward sloping. This is depicted in Figure 7.4.

The individual supply curve for labour shows the number of hours offered for work at any given wage rate. At a wage rate of W, the quantity of hours worked is Q_H. At the higher wage rate of W^1, the number of

FIGURE 7.4: THE INDIVIDUAL SUPPLY CURVE FOR LABOUR

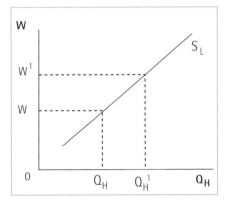

hours worked increases to $Q_H{}^1$. As the wage rate increases, the number of hours worked generally increases.

An interesting aspect of an individual's labour supply is the possibility that the supply curve could be backward bending. This can be explained by examining the trade-off between work and leisure for an individual. According to this theory, individuals work to earn the money to purchase products. At lower wage levels, any increase in the wage rate is likely to elicit an increase in the number of hours worked. At lower levels of wages, the labour supply curve is upward sloping. However, the opportunity cost of labour is to forgo leisure activities. As wages continue to increase, individuals may resist a further increase in the number of hours worked, preferring leisure to labour. Hence, as wages increase, the number of hours worked eventually declines. This is reflected in the backward bending labour supply curve depicted in Figure 7.5.

If the wage rate increases from W to W^1, the individual is prepared to increase the number of hours worked from Q_H to $Q_H{}^1$. Beyond this wage level, however, the individual is not prepared to work longer hours. If wage levels increase beyond W^1, the individual will 'sacrifice' work in return for consuming more leisure. For example, if wages increase from W^1 to W^2, the number of hours worked declines from $Q_H{}^1$ to $Q_H{}^2$.

The backward bending supply curve can be explained using substitution and income effects. The substitution effect is caused by a change in the relative prices of work and leisure. At higher wages, more products can be purchased. The opportunity cost of leisure time (which is the wage forgone) increases with the wage rate. The substitution effect suggests that labour will be substituted for leisure under these conditions.

FIGURE 7.5: A BACKWARD BENDING LABOUR SUPPLY CURVE

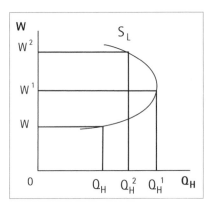

The income of the worker increases with the wage rate. Leisure activities are considered to be 'normal' products. Therefore, the demand for these products increases with income. More time allocated to leisure activities means that less time is available for work. The income effect suggests that more time will be allocated to leisure (and less to labour) as income increases. In the context of the demand for leisure activities and a change in the price of labour, the substitution effect and the (standard, i.e. normal) income effect operate in opposite directions; as such, this context should be recognised as being slightly different from the standard environment covered in Chapter 4.

Initially, it is generally accepted that the substitution effect outweighs the income effect and the first portion of the labour supply curve is upward sloping. However, beyond a certain wage, the income effect is stronger than the substitution effect. This part of the labour supply curve is backward bending.

In this instance, we cannot conclude that what is true for an individual can be applied to the market. Empirical evidence suggests that the labour supply curve for the market is upward sloping, even over the wide range of incomes that we observe in modern, developed economies. As wages increase, the extra workers who enter the (paid) labour market more than offset the effects of the backward bending individual supply curve.

Therefore, while admitting that the backward bending supply curve of labour is a theoretical possibility that could be observed, we will assume that the market labour supply curve is upward sloping in line with the empirical evidence. This is drawn in Figure 7.6.

FIGURE 7.6: MARKET SUPPLY CURVE FOR LABOUR

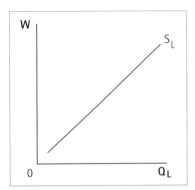

This positive relationship is depicted in an upward sloping market supply curve for labour. The supply curve for labour considers the relationship between wages and the number of people working, *ceteris paribus*. The variables that are held constant include the tax and social welfare system, educational policies, the degree of unionisation (see Information Box 7.1) and the size of the labour force. If any of these underlying variables changes, the position and/or the slope of the labour supply curve will change.

INFORMATION BOX 7.1

The trade union movement in Ireland

The purpose of a trade union is to represent workers and to maximise their power in the workplace. They also play a wider role in the social and political arena. Trade union power is based largely on the solidarity between workers.

Although trade unions existed in Ireland in the eighteenth century, they were first legalised in 1871 when the first Trade Union Act was passed. Almost twenty-five years later, in April 1894 the Irish Trade Union Congress (ITUC) was founded: 119 delegates from different labour organisations were present, representing 21,000 trade unionists directly and a further 39,000 indirectly through the trade councils. The first President of Congress was Thomas O'Connell. Other famous trade unionists included William O'Brien, James Larkin and Louie Bennett.

The Irish Transport and General Workers Union (ITGWU) was founded in 1909 by James Larkin. On his return from the USA in 1910, James Connolly joined and worked as a full-time official in Belfast. The next few years were both eventful and traumatic for the labour movement in Ireland.

The Irish Labour Party was formed in 1912. In its infancy, membership was restricted to trade unionists. Two years later, the great Dublin lock-out occurred. Even with the massive publicity which surrounded the lock-out, it had a detrimental impact on the union movement in the short term. Less than two years later, James Connolly was executed after the 1916 Easter Rising. Connolly had been the chief organiser of the ITGWU in Ulster as well as one of the founding members of the Irish Labour Party. His loss to the trade union movement was immense.

Although membership of the ITGWU had increased to 100,000 in 1922, it subsequently fell to below 16,000 by the end of the decade. The ITUC membership also fell, from 189,000 in 1922 to 92,000 in 1929. The economic conditions during the Depression, in addition to government policy, were contributing factors to the decline in union membership.

The last eighty-five years have witnessed great changes in the trade union movement in Ireland. In 1959, the Irish Congress of Trade Unions (ICTU), the co-ordinating body for trade unions in Ireland, was established. In 1990, the country's two largest unions – the ITGWU and the FWUI (Federated Workers' Union of Ireland) – were amalgamated to form the Services, Industrial, Professional and Technical Union (SIPTU).

A number of other smaller unions also merged. However, there are currently over seventy unions listed on the Registrar of Friendly Societies.

The 1980s was a particularly difficult decade for the trade union movement. Spiralling inflation led to increased wage demands. Union members voted with their feet. Between 1981 and 1987, an average of over 350,000 workdays per year were lost due to industrial disputes.

At the end of that decade, ICTU, under the leadership of Peter Cassells, entered into negotiations with the social partners for the first national partnership agreement. This was the beginning of a new era of industrial relations. Although there will always be issues that separate labour and management, the national and local partnership agreements provide a framework for discussing those issues in a forum which is less combative than other industrial relations models.

Trade union membership rose to well over 500,000 in 2009 and approximately one-third of employees in Ireland are members of a trade union. However, there is a much higher rate of union membership among full-time workers (approximately 37%) compared to part-time workers (approximately 20%). In addition, it is noteworthy that union membership is much higher among Irish nationals compared to non-Irish nationals with much of the difference being explained by the different economic features of the sectors and sub-sectors in which these groups tend to participate. There is also a significantly higher rate of union membership among the public sector compared to the private sector; indeed, many private sector (including multinational) firms do not actively encourage union membership. It is clear that the recent prolonged recession has presented many issues both for, and within, the Irish trade union movement.

Using the demand curve and the supply curve, we now consider the labour market.

Labour market equilibrium

Figure 7.7 depicts the labour market with a downward sloping demand curve and an upward sloping supply curve. The intersection of the demand curve and the supply curve determines the equilibrium wage rate and the equilibrium quantity of labour. At W*, the quantity demanded of labour is equal to the quantity supplied. W* is the wage rate that clears the labour market.

At all other wage levels, there is either a shortage or a surplus of labour. At wage rates above the equilibrium level, an excess supply of labour exists. This surplus labour results in downward pressure on wages. At wage rates below the equilibrium level, an excess demand for labour results. Such a shortage of workers puts upward pressure on wage levels. W* is the equilibrium wage rate. At W* the quantity demanded and quantity supplied of labour are equal.

As we discussed previously, the labour demand curve and supply curve are drawn holding other variables constant. A change in one of the underlying variables will cause the demand curve or the supply curve to shift. Any shift of the demand curve or the supply curve of labour results in a change in the equilibrium wage rate and the quantity of labour.

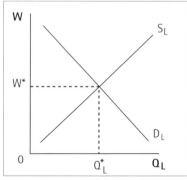

FIGURE 7.7: LABOUR MARKET EQUILIBRIUM

For example, suppose we examine demand and supply conditions for labour in the construction industry. In a recession, severe economic conditions can adversely affect the construction industry. In response to worsening economic conditions, construction companies reduce their demand for labourers. The effects of such a change are shown in Figure 7.8.

Equilibrium is initially at (W, Q_L). The adverse economic conditions force the construction companies to cut their workforce. Fewer labourers are required to work on the construction sites. This reduction in demand is illustrated in graphic terms as a leftward shift of the demand curve for labour. The excess supply of labour arising from the fall in demand forces wage levels downwards. As wage levels fall, fewer workers are willing to supply their services. Equilibrium is restored at (W^1, Q_L^1), the intersection of the old supply curve, S_L and the new demand curve, D_L^1. The net result is a lower equilibrium wage level combined with a lower quantity of labour. Conversely, an improvement in demand conditions will result in higher wages and a higher quantity of labour.

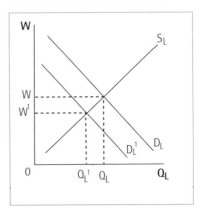

FIGURE 7.8: A CHANGE IN LABOUR DEMAND

The neoclassical model of the labour market and minimum wage legislation

In Section 2.4, we discussed price controls. Minimum wage legislation is a form of price control for the labour market. It is legislated by governments to ensure that wages will not fall below a certain level. Proponents of the minimum wage argue that it is the single most effective policy to decrease the range of income distribution and to lift workers out of poverty. By putting a floor under wages, it moves some of those in employment into higher income brackets. They argue that the enforcement of minimum wage legislation reduces the exploitation of labour by those employers who refuse to pay a wage which will allow an adequate living standard.

Many economists take at least a slightly different view. Figure 7.9 shows a very basic model of the labour market after the imposition of a minimum wage.

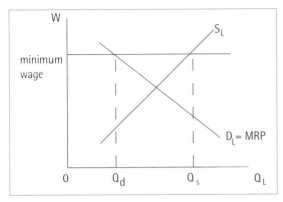

FIGURE 7.9: LABOUR MARKET WITH A MINIMUM WAGE

Generally, the minimum wage is set above the labour market equilibrium. This model predicts that, as a result of the minimum wage legislation, there will be a surplus of labour or unemployment in the labour market. The supply of labour, or the number of people who are willing to work at the minimum wage, is greater than the demand for labour. Unemployment will persist because the wage rate cannot adjust to 'clear' the market.

The economics profession has been fairly united in its condemnation of radical minimum wage legislation.[4] Rather than improving the living standards of the working poor, who are supposed to benefit from this legislation, they argue that it benefits those who can find employment at the expense of those who are 'involuntarily' unemployed. These are individuals who are willing to work for less than the minimum wage. Profit-maximising employers cannot hire these workers because the amount that they are producing (as measured by the marginal revenue product) is less than the minimum wage.

In spite of the opposition of the economics profession, minimum wage legislation has been implemented in a number of countries. The United States passed the Fair Labour Standards Act in 1938. France enacted its first minimum wage legislation over fifty years ago. The Irish government adopted a minimum wage on 1 April 2000.

Minimum wage legislation in Ireland

The merits of minimum wage legislation have been discussed in Ireland for many years, particularly by trade unions and organisations attempting to combat poverty. Employers' organisations and the government were less enthusiastic. Their attitudes were possibly shaped by economists' predictions that the imposition of a minimum wage would lead to higher levels of unemployment. Until the late 1990s, the rate of unemployment in Ireland was above the EU average. Policy-makers were unwilling to risk enacting a policy that could make a bad situation worse.

By the end of the 1990s, the labour market situation had changed. Instead of unemployed labour, there were labour market shortages in many sectors. The Fianna Fáil and Progressive Democrats coalition included a commitment to implement a national minimum hourly wage as one of the objectives of the government's Action Programme for the New Millennium. They appointed a National Minimum Wage Commission. Their terms of reference were:[5]

1. to advise the best way to implement minimum wage legislation with regard to improving the situation of the low paid;
2. to examine existing mechanisms to recommend changes to ensure compliance with minimum wage legislation by employers;
3. to examine any adverse impact on competitiveness, particularly with regard to small and medium-sized enterprises; and
4. to consult with the social partners before the finalisation of the report.

Based on the work of the Commission, the Inter-Departmental Group was formed with representatives from various government departments. The Group's task was to find ways to implement the Commission's recommendations. For a policy which is theoretically simple, the implementation of a minimum wage is complex.

For example, the Commission was concerned about the effect of the minimum wage on people who are under 18 years of age. Research pointed to two possible effects. First, students, attracted by jobs paying the minimum wage, might discontinue their studies. From the point of view of the teenager (at least in the longer term) and society, the Commission did not consider this to be a beneficial outcome. An individual's future earning capacity is far greater if the individual completes second-level education and proceeds to training or third-level education. Second, employers might not be willing to pay the minimum wage to employ teenagers. Generally, unemployment among teenagers is high relative to other age groups.

The actual rate to be set was another contentious issue. The Commission recommended a rate of £4.40 (approximately €5.60) per hour. The Irish Congress of Trade Unions (ICTU) and the Irish National Organisation of the Unemployed (INOU) argued that a rate of £5 (approximately €6.35) per hour was the minimum required to improve the quality of life of the low paid. They stated that market conditions already made £4.40 (approximately €5.60) lower than the wage rate paid for cleaning staff and fast food operators, particularly in urban areas. In response to this, the Small Firms Association (SFA) conducted a survey of its members.[6] If a minimum wage of £5 (approximately €6.35) per hour were imposed, the survey showed that one in three firms would let staff go and half of the respondents would place expansion plans on hold. The director of the SFA stated that employers would replace unskilled workers with more highly skilled workers, implying that those without skills were not productive enough to earn £5 (approximately €6.35) per hour. He concluded that unskilled workers would be 'permanently locked out of jobs'.

In April 2000, the minimum wage was implemented under the terms shown in Table 7.2. Notice that the government established rates for workers under 18 years of age and for those in training that were lower than the rate set for 'experienced' adults. The minimum wage of £4.40 (approximately €5.60) for experienced adults pleased employers rather than unions. On the other hand, labour unions and other organisations that had lobbied for years for this legislation were pleased that the principle was adopted.

TABLE 7.2: MINIMUM WAGE RATES IN IRELAND (2000–11)

	Rates of pay	
Employee	**2000** **(1 April)**	**2011** **(1 Feb)**
Adult experienced (€)	€5.59	€7.65
Under 18	70% of adult hourly rate = €5.36	
Over 18 in structured training or directed study:*		
1st period	75% of adult hourly rate = €5.74	
2nd period	80% of adult hourly rate = €6.12	
3rd period	90% of adult hourly rate = €6.89	

* Each period is one-third of the training period. A period must be at least one month and no longer than 12 months.

Source: Department of Enterprise, Trade and Innovation.

CASE STUDY

Extract from *The Irish Times*
Ferries bring global wage pressure home
by Marc Coleman

Industry and unions both will have to adapt old mindsets to survive in changing international competitive environment. The Central Statistics Office recently told us that 6000 jobs were lost in manufacturing in the year to May of this year. Many were relocated in parts of the world where wages are far lower than those offered to its workforce by Irish Ferries. While their loss was lamented, there were no cries of outrage, nor calls for government intervention.

Irish Ferries is different. Employment in the ferry industry links workers from Latvia, where a house can be purchased for less than €100,000, with workers from Ireland, where

→

you'd spend that money on a coal shed. Like textiles, the ferry industry chooses those workers from countries where Ireland's minimum wage amounts to a reasonable, if modest, income. But whereas the textile industry migrates to China and is forgotten, Irish Ferries stays Irish and docks in port every day to remind us of what happened. Thus it becomes a political problem.

By dint of what it does, the ferry industry is an internationally open industry. Some important facts about it need analysis, however, boring as this is for the polemicists. Firstly, the day of passenger ferry traffic is not quite over, but its heyday is. A revolution in the aviation sector has made air fares much cheaper relative to ferry fares ... Secondly, the boon of duty free shopping – once a major pull for the Irish ferry industry – is no longer with us. Thirdly, local authorities in Brittany subsidise French Ferries on the grounds that it encourages tourism. This has given Irish Ferries' competitors an unfair advantage on its Normandy route. Fourthly, the rising cost of holidays in rural Ireland has scared off the kind of tourist who wants to drive a car – the kind that uses ferries ...

Fifthly, and most importantly, globalisation and EU enlargement mean that wage rates needed to live decently are far higher in western European countries than Latvia or Lithuania ... . For this last reason many of Irish Ferries' competitors have been forced to outsource their workforces, including the Seacat ferry from Northern Ireland to Scotland, P&O Ferries and the Isle of Man steam packet. Irish Ferries has been forced to respond. A question that must be asked is whether it has responded reasonably ..

Now, Irish Ferries is proposing a redundancy package to workers on the Irish routes. Workers can accept lower rates of pay, or can opt for redundancy with eight weeks of pay for each year worked ...

Those are the facts. What judgments and solutions can be taken from them? Irish Ferries has managed its company reasonably well and the pressure for it to reduce its cost base is understandable. But the salary awarded to the chief executive Eamonn Rothwell, in excess of €600,000, is an issue. Japan has maintained good industrial relations between workers and management because of a system whereby managers of troubled companies impose cuts on their own pay before asking workers to do so.

In Ireland, we should develop partnership structures along these lines, so that workers and management share both good times and bad. Apart from improving worker-manager solidarity, such an approach is good for the bottom line ...

But the key issue in this dispute relates to the downward pressure on wages from globalisation. One of the saner contributions on this issue has recently come from Labour MEP Proinsias de Rossa. He recently asked whether the EU Commission would take action to safeguard the international rights of seafarers. Yesterday he got the following answer: the EU Commission will support the development of the first ever code of maritime labour standards, due to be finalised by the International Labour Organisation convention on maritime labour standards. This means that common standards of employment will apply worldwide.

Source: The Irish Times, 30 September 2005.

Questions

1. There appear to be at least two alternative responses to competitive pressures: export the jobs (e.g. manufacturing jobs to China); or lower the wages dramatically (e.g. jobs in Irish shipping and on Irish construction sites). Comment on the economic and other aspects of these alternatives.
2. Comment on alternative mechanisms for lowering a firm's wage cost base.
3. Using the internet or other sources, comment upon the outcome and longer-term consequences of the Irish Ferries dispute.

Answers on website

Conclusions and criticisms of the neoclassical model of the labour market

The neoclassical model of the labour market continues to influence the thinking of economists and policy-makers. The student, when reading this section, should recognise the similarities between the model of the product market and the model of the labour market. We have essentially adapted the 'tools of the trade' and used them to analyse a different market.

While one may question many of the assumptions of the product market, applying them to the labour market seems to be inappropriate in a number of respects. We speak of a labour market as if labour is homogeneous. We discuss workers as if they were interchangeable. While wheat may be homogeneous, labourers are not: workers differ in their training and their ability. There are huge differences in the education and training required for various occupations and professions. However, we lump everyone together to discuss the 'labour market'.

The labour demand curve is based on marginal productivity. Workers are not uniformly productive, either when compared to each other or in comparison with themselves over time; changes in health and personal circumstances cause the productivity of even the most 'stable' workers to vary significantly.

Also, although firms may be willing to vary their output decision fairly quickly, they are unlikely to change their employment levels, particularly if their workers are skilled. 'Derived demand' for labour suggests that if demand for a product increases, firms will demand more labour. Workers with sufficient skills may not be available. Similarly, if demand for a product falls, management may be reluctant to make labour redundant. Recognising the hardship caused by unemployment and the problems in reassembling a skilled group of employees, they may prefer to maintain their labour force in the hope that the demand for their product will increase. In summary, the labour market may not respond as quickly or as predictably as the product market to a change in demand or supply.

In product markets, we expect a fairly uniform price for fairly similar products. Wage differentials in sectors of the labour market occur for many different reasons. These include working conditions in certain sectors, trade union power, workers' qualifications and skills, geographic immobility and discrimination (e.g. based on race, sex). Even in a given market, in a particular firm, one employee may be paid more than another to do the same job, simply because the employer values that employee more.

Alternative labour market models have been offered by Barbara Bergmann, Gary Becker, Victor Fuchs and others. Students who are interested in the criticisms above are encouraged to read more about this complex and important topic.

7.2 CAPITAL AND INTEREST

We will now look at the market for capital. In this instance, we are looking at the relationship between the interest rate which is the payment for capital, and the amount of capital goods which are demanded and supplied by firms and households. We will begin by defining some relevant terms.

Definition

Capital goods are durable assets used during the production process.

Durable means that the assets are useful for a significant period of time. Capital goods include plant, machinery, tools and factories.

> **Definition**
> *The capital stock includes all of the capital goods controlled by a firm.*

We measure the capital stock of a firm or of a country at a point in time. The capital stock of a firm loses value over time. This is called depreciation.

> **Definition**
> *Depreciation refers to the decline in value of the capital stock over a certain period of time due to its use in production or its age.*

In order to maintain its capital stock, a firm must replace its capital goods as they wear out. Investment changes the capital stock.

> **Definition**
> *Investment refers to additions to the capital stock purchased or leased over a particular time period.*

Investment is a flow. Gross investment is the total increase in the capital stock over a period of time, including the additions necessary to replace depreciating assets. Net investment constitutes an increase over and above the replacements needed to maintain the capital stock at its current level.

Demand for capital goods

As in the labour market, the demand for capital goods is a derived demand. Firms invest in capital assets based on current demand for their products and, perhaps even more important, anticipated future demand for their products. The relevant time span for investment decisions may be considerably longer than a single period of time, such as a year.

Marginal productivity theory can also be used to derive the demand curve for capital goods.

> **Definition**
> *The marginal revenue product of capital is the extra revenue generated by an addition to the capital stock.*

In this case, if the size and training of the labour force is held constant and units of capital are added, additional units of capital eventually become less productive than the previous units.

For a profit-maximising firm, the addition to revenue which results from buying or leasing the capital asset must be greater than or equal to the cost of the capital asset. The process of determining when the two are equal is more difficult than in the labour market because a capital good is more durable. The benefits accrue over a number of years. Therefore, we have to estimate the revenue stream generated over the life of the asset and compare that with the cost of the asset.

Present value and future value

We will try to clarify this process by looking at an example. We return to the owner of Hibs Ltd who is thinking of purchasing a new piece of machinery valued at €10,000. Ms Hibs anticipates that the asset will last for two years and will have no salvage value. She expects the asset to generate the following revenue stream:

Year	Revenue
1	€6,000
2	€7,000

She begins by estimating the present value of this revenue stream.

> **Definition**
> *Present value is the estimate of what the revenue stream of a capital asset is worth today.*

To grasp this concept, we can consider an alternative decision that Ms Hibs could make. Instead of purchasing a new piece of machinery, she could buy bonds, which would earn a rate of interest of 10% per annum, compounded annually. In this case, we are considering the future value of the €10,000. If she invests this money today, what will it be worth in one year, in two years? We can use the future value formula to calculate the value of €10,000 in one year.

$$FV = PV\,(1+i) \tag{7.3}$$

where PV represents the present value and FV represents the future value of this sum at the interest rate of i. In this example, with a 10% rate of interest, the future value of €10,000 at the end of the first year will be €11,000.

Since the interest is compounded annually, the interest from year one is added to the principal. In year two, Ms Hibs will earn 10% interest on €11,000. At the end of two periods, Ms Hibs would receive a sum of €12,100.

The general form if there is more than one period is:

$$FV = PV(1+i)^t \tag{7.4}$$

where t represents the number of time periods (e.g. years) over which the sum is invested.

Suppose that Ms Hibs discovers that she will receive €12,100 in two years. She wants to know how much that sum is worth today, in other words, what is the present value of the €12,100? The general form of the equation used to solve this problem is derived from the future value formula. We simply solve for the present value.

$$PV = \frac{FV}{(1+i)^t} \tag{7.5}$$

If the market rate of interest is 10%, the present value is $\frac{€12,100}{(1+0.1)^2}$ or €10,000, as expected. In this case we are discounting the future value.

> **Definition**
> *Discounting is the process of reducing the future value of a sum of money or a flow of revenues to the present value.*

The problem that confronts us with the revenue stream of the capital asset is slightly more complicated because the revenues for each year must be considered separately. To calculate the present value, we will use the following equation:

$$PV = \sum \frac{R_t}{(1 + i)^t} \qquad [7.6]$$

where R_t represents the additional revenue earned by the asset in period t. The notation Σ means that we add together the discounted revenue for each of the t periods. We can use this equation to calculate the present value of the revenue stream which the new piece of machinery will generate.

$$PV = \frac{6,000}{(1 + 0.1)} + \frac{7,000}{(1 + 0.1)^2} = €11,240$$

Now, we compare this amount with the cost of the machinery. Obviously, €11,240 is significantly greater than €10,000. In this case, Ms Hibs will clearly benefit from purchasing this asset. Indeed, she would still purchase the asset if the present value was €11,000 or €10,500. We would expect Ms Hibs to invest in capital goods up to the point where the present value of the revenue generated by the asset is equal to the cost of buying the asset.

Rate of return on capital and the interest rate

We will now look at this problem from a slightly different perspective. We will try to determine the minimum rate of return which Ms Hibs must earn in order for her to decide to acquire an additional capital asset.

> Definition
> The rate of return on capital is a measure of the productivity of a particular capital asset.

We can calculate the rate of return using the following formula:

$$C = \frac{R_1}{(1 + r)} + \frac{R_2}{(1 + r)^2} \qquad [7.7]$$

where C is the cost of the asset, R_1 and R_2 are the revenues earned in periods 1 and 2 respectively and r is the rate of return on the asset. Substitute the figures for the asset purchased by Hibs Ltd into Equation 7.7 and solve for r.

$$10,000 = \frac{6,000}{(1 + r)} + \frac{7,000}{(1 + r)^2}$$

The rate of return equals 0.19 or 19% for this asset. By comparing the cost of the asset to the present value of the anticipated revenue stream, we realised that Ms Hibs, as the owner of a profit-maximising firm, will purchase this asset. We reach the same conclusion by comparing the rate of return on capital to the interest rate. Using this form of analysis, we can see that Ms Hibs will buy or lease the asset because the rate of return on capital is greater than the 10% interest rate. Further, as long as the rate of return on capital is greater than the interest rate, we assume that a profit-maximising firm will continue to invest in capital assets.

Interest rates and the demand for capital goods

Finally, we can consider the relationship between the interest rate and the demand for capital goods. From our discussion above, we assume that capital becomes less productive as more capital is employed, *ceteris paribus*. We also know that a profit-maximising firm will acquire additional capital goods if the rate of return on capital is greater than or equal to the interest rate. What happens if the interest rate falls?

As interest rates fall, *ceteris paribus*, firms will acquire more capital goods. Although the new acquisitions are less productive than previous capital goods, the lower interest rate means that money invested in bonds will earn lower returns. Even less productive capital assets will earn more than the market rate of interest. The relationship between interest rates and the demand for capital goods is negative. As interest rates fall, the demand for capital goods increases. Figure 7.10 shows a downward sloping demand curve for capital goods.

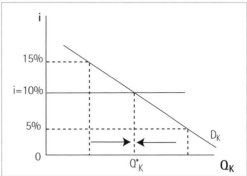

FIGURE 7.10: THE DEMAND CURVE FOR CAPITAL GOODS

D_K represents the demand curve for capital goods. It is downward sloping: the lower the interest rate, the larger the amount of capital goods demanded. We can think of this curve as representing, for any interest rate, the amount of capital goods demanded by profit-maximising firms, *ceteris paribus*. What variables are held constant? Among others, they include the size and level of training of the labour force, the taxation system and firms' expectations about the future.

The supply curve for capital goods

Funds are needed to finance capital goods. Whereas the labour supply curve is influenced by the labour/leisure trade-off, the supply curve for capital goods is influenced by the trade-off between consumption and savings. Savings can be viewed as deferred or postponed consumption. Individuals and households provide the funds for capital goods. As interest rates increase, the supply of capital tends to increase. At higher rates of interest, individuals and households tend to be more willing to forgo present consumption in favour of future consumption. Hence, as present consumption is more expensive in terms of future consumption the supply curve for

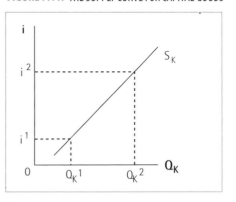

FIGURE 7.11: THE SUPPLY CURVE FOR CAPITAL GOODS

capital (S_K) is upward sloping as depicted in Figure 7.11.

At an interest rate of i^1, Q_K^1 is supplied. As interest rates rise, the supply of capital increases. With a higher interest rate of i^2, Q_K^2 is supplied.

Equilibrium in the capital market

The demand curve for capital D_K is derived from the demand for final output produced in the goods market. It is downward sloping. The supply curve for capital shows the quantity of capital at any given interest rate. It is upward sloping. The equilibrium interest rate is determined by the demand for and supply of capital. In graphical terms, equilibrium occurs at the intersection of the demand curve D_K and the supply curve S_K. The interest rate represented by i^* is the return on capital that clears the market for capital goods. This is shown in Figure 7.12.

Adjustment to equilibrium is an automatic process in the market for capital goods. For example, suppose the market interest rate is above i^*. At any rate above the equilibrium interest rate there exists an excess supply of capital. The actions of savers and investors in the capital market will eventually push interest rates downwards. The interest rate continues to fall until it reaches i^* where the market is in equilibrium. The inverse is true for interest rates below equilibrium where adjustments will occur upwards from positions of excess demand.

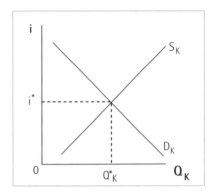

FIGURE 7.12: CAPITAL MARKET EQUILIBRIUM

Conclusions and criticisms of the neoclassical model of the capital market

In this analysis, we assume that firms have perfect or near-perfect knowledge of their present and future revenue streams. This assumption is very questionable in the short run. In the long run, over the lifetime of a durable asset, it is also probably fairly unrealistic. Today, all companies are concerned that new technologies will make capital goods obsolete before they are fully depreciated. Firms must begin the decision-making process concerning the acquisition of capital goods based on an estimate of the additional revenue that each asset will generate. Although firms face considerable uncertainty, economists rationalise this by saying that firms act 'as if' they have perfect or near-perfect knowledge.

In addition, the analysis of the capital market presents a single interest rate established through market competition. In reality, interest rates offered to firms differ for a number of reasons. One of the main reasons why interest rates differ is risk. If the lender is concerned that the loan may not be repaid, s/he will charge a higher rate of interest as a premium against that risk. Interest rates also vary depending on the duration of the loan.

7.3 LAND AND RENT

Rent is the return on land. The term 'rent' can be quite confusing as it means different things to different people.[7] In particular, it is often confused with another term frequently used by economists, 'economic rent'.

> **Definition**
> *Economic rent is a payment to a factor of production in excess of the opportunity cost.*

Economic rent is a surplus payment to any factor in excess of the minimum payment needed to keep a factor in its present use (see Appendix 7.1). This minimum payment is known as transfer earnings because if earnings fall below this level, the factor input would be withdrawn, i.e. it would be transferred to some other activity.

> **Definition**
>
> *Transfer earnings are what a factor of production could earn in its best alternative use. It is the opportunity cost of employing a factor of production.*

The essential feature of economic rent is that it is a surplus. Hence, its payment is not necessary to guarantee the supply of a particular factor.[8]

FIGURE 7.13: ECONOMIC RENT AND TRANSFER EARNINGS

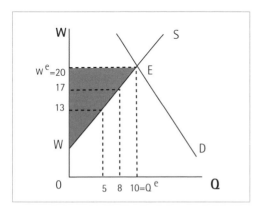

The terms 'economic rent' and 'transfer earnings' can be applied to all factor resource markets. We will attempt to clarify these terms in the context of the labour market shown in Figure 7.13.

Let us suppose that the actual market wage is €20. In the above market, the fifth worker is willing to work for a wage of €13. This amount is equal to her transfer earnings and her economic rent is the surplus, i.e. €7. If the eighth worker is willing to work only at the higher wage of €17, her economic rent is only €3 (€20 – €17). The tenth worker is the final addition to the workforce. Her transfer earnings amount to €20 with no surplus or economic rent.

In Figure 7.13 transfer earnings is given by the area under the supply curve [0WEQ^e]. The shaded area [WW^{e}E] between the supply curve and the factor price [W^e] is equal to economic rent.

In reality, most factor earnings are a composite of transfer earnings and economic rent. It is the elasticity of supply of the factor input that determines the relative size of each component of total income. If the supply curve for a factor input is perfectly elastic (i.e. a horizontal supply curve), all of factor earnings will be transfer earnings. As the supply curve becomes increasingly inelastic, the area of economic rent increases.

In terms of land, economic rent is specifically the price paid for the use of land and other fixed resources. It is this fixed supply which distinguishes rental payments from other factor payments.

As with all other economic resources, rent can be explained in terms of demand and supply analysis. The demand for fixed resources is a derived demand: it stems from the products produced on the land. Figure 7.14 shows the market for land. In this market, we are looking at the relationship between rent, the price of land, and the quantity of land that is demanded and supplied.

The downward sloping demand curve for land is derived from the marginal revenue product of land. In turn, the marginal revenue product of land is determined by the physical productivity of the land and the marginal revenue of the product produced on the land.

The demand curve is downward sloping because land exhibits diminishing marginal returns. The first units of land that are employed are the most productive.

Referring again to Figure 7.14, we observe that the supply curve for land is perfectly inelastic. This is because the supply of land is virtually fixed.[9]

The equilibrium rent R is determined by the intersection of the demand curve D and the supply curve S. With a fixed supply of land at Q*, the amount of economic rent is given by the shaded area [0REQ*].

In the market for land, the entire rental price is an economic rent. Why? Since land is a natural resource, fixed in supply and provided free by nature, the cost of production or supply cost is zero. Hence, the opportunity cost of supplying a fixed amount of this resource is zero. Since there are no transfer earnings, the entire price of land is an economic rent.

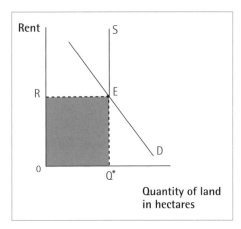

FIGURE 7.14: THE MARKET FOR LAND

If the economic rent is reduced or even removed, the supply of land remains the same.[10]

Given that the supply of land is fixed, demand becomes the sole 'active' determination of rent. A change in demand will cause a change in the rental price. For example, agricultural land along the west coast of Ireland was bought by developers to build holiday homes. This constituted a 'change in demand'. The marginal revenue product of land used for development was higher than the marginal revenue product of land devoted to agriculture. The demand curve for land shifted out to the right and rental prices increased. The subsequent higher rental prices did not induce landlords to increase supply. The only effect of the increase in demand was a rent increase.

The inverse (as we now know so well) is true for a decline in the demand for land. Changes in population, economic prosperity and property tax are examples of the factors which influence the demand for land and natural resources.

7.4 ENTREPRENEURSHIP AND PROFIT

A fourth category of factor inputs is entrepreneurship. It is distinct from other resources in the economy in the sense that it is difficult to define and perhaps impossible to measure. The entrepreneur receives profit as a payment.[11]

Profit is different from other factor prices because it is a residual; it is paid out to the entrepreneur after all other factor payments are made. Also, profit is not guaranteed. In fact, it may be negative in the short run.

As we mentioned in Chapter 5, the use of the term 'profit' can be quite misleading (see Section 5.3 for a more complete discussion). In particular, accountants and economists define the word differently. Profit, as defined by the accountant, is simply the difference between total revenue and total cost. However, the economist includes normal profit as an economic cost. A normal profit is the opportunity cost of the entrepreneur. Therefore, if total revenues equal total economic costs, the firm has made a 'normal' profit. For the economist, if total revenues exceed economic costs, the firm makes a 'supernormal' or economic profit. In terms of the difference between normal profit and supernormal profit, the former can be regarded as the entrepreneur's transfer earnings and the latter as the entrepreneur's economic rent.

There are several explanations for the existence of economic profits. We will consider three. Economic profits can be considered as:

1. a reward for uninsured risk;

2. a reward for innovation; and/or
3. the result of a monopolistic market structure.

A brief explanation follows.

A reward for uninsured risk

For Frank Knight and many other economists, profit is the reward entrepreneurs receive for taking risks in times of uncertainty.[12] Uncertainty arises from dynamic changes in the economy. Profit is the reward for a risk successfully taken. Knight distinguished between insurable and uninsurable risks. Insurable risk is covered (or coverable) by insurance premiums, he argued. Uninsurable risks are the source of profit. 'Business ability' is also a factor in the determination of profit.

A reward for innovation

Others define profit as a payment for innovation, which can be defined as the application of invention to industry. The famous Austrian economist Joseph Schumpeter was the main exponent of this theory (see Information Box 7.2). The act of innovation as described by Schumpeter was to be distinguished from the act of invention. Schumpeter's innovator, called the 'entrepreneur', was responsible for the dynamic characteristic of the capitalist system.

For Schumpeter, successful innovation depended on leadership rather than intelligence. The result of successful innovation was profit, which was a central feature of the capitalist system.

INFORMATION BOX 7.2

Joseph Schumpeter (1883–1950)

Joseph Schumpeter was born and educated in Austria. While at the University of Vienna he studied under Bohm-Bawerk (refer to Section 7.1 and marginal productivity theory). He began teaching economics at the University of Czernowitz and later at the University of Graz. He was also the Austrian Minister of Finance for a brief period after World War I. Between 1925 and 1932 he held the Chair of Public Finance at Bonn. After emigrating to the USA in 1932 he became a professor at Harvard University where he remained until his retirement in 1950.

One of Schumpeter's greatest contributions to economics was his economic character, the 'entrepreneur'. The entrepreneur played a central role in the capitalist system, argued Schumpeter. He was the agent largely responsible for change and for economic development. For Schumpeter, the entrepreneur's role was vastly different from that of the labourer, landowner, capitalist and so on. The entrepreneur was the person who innovates, the person who creates 'new combinations' in production.

Schumpeter identified several types of innovation. They include the creation of a new product, the creation of a new method of production, the opening of new markets, the discovery of a new source of supply and new organisations of industry.

Schumpeter was a strong supporter of enterprise, capitalism and the *laissez-faire* doctrine. Within a capitalist system, economic development is both a dynamic and erratic process, he argued. He openly acknowledged the dangers (arising not from its weaknesses but rather from its strengths) that inherently exist in a capitalist system. He discussed 'creative destruction', i.e. the implementation

→

of new combinations that perpetuate economic change. He recognised that this was a disruptive process which required limited government intervention to reduce inequalities, control monopolies, smooth out the business cycle and so on. However, he believed that continuous intervention by the state would eventually undermine the role of the entrepreneur. The performance of the economy would begin to falter, he argued. In the long run, Schumpeter predicted that capitalism would decay and be replaced with socialism.

Schumpeter's major works include *Theory of Economic Development* (1912), written when he was 28 years old. *Business Cycles* (1939) has been rediscovered in recent years, and recognised as an important work concerning an economic phenomenon which is constantly discussed but poorly understood. The entrepreneur plays a central role in Schumpeter's model of the business cycle. *History of Economic Analysis* (1954) was published posthumously. In it, Schumpeter critically reviews the work of economic scholars including Smith and Marshall.

Schumpeter is not as widely known as Keynes nor did he hold Keynes in high esteem. His economic works are even further removed than Keynes' from the neoclassical tradition. Still, both economists are undoubtedly among the greatest economists of the twentieth century. Many current writers, particularly in the area of business economics, owe an intellectual debt to Schumpeter. He recognised that the individual contributed more than her marginal revenue product. The entrepreneur was the central figure in economic development.

A more recent account of innovation has been given by Michael Porter (see Information Box 7.3).

INFORMATION BOX 7.3

Michael Porter and Innovation

Michael Porter is regarded as the world's leading authority on competitive advantage. By competitive advantage, he is referring to the ability of certain firms to create and sustain a dominant position in particular industries for a significant period of time. Central to this theory is the importance of innovation.[1]

The factor conditions referred to by Porter move beyond the traditional endowments of land, labour and capital emphasised by the classical economists. Factors vital to economic growth are created, not inherited. The stock of factors is less important than the rate at which they are upgraded.

Porter groups factors into broad categories including human resources, physical resources, knowledge resources, capital resources and infrastructure. Competitive advantage is based on the efficient employment of factors which may be basic or advanced. Basic factors are internationally mobile and are attracted to where they are most efficiently employed. Advanced factors require sustained investment and are necessary to achieve higher-order competitive advantages which are difficult for other firms to duplicate.

For Porter, innovation is the key to achieving and maintaining competitive advantage. He defines innovation as 'improvements in technology and better methods or ways of doing things' that are 'commercialised'. He goes on to say that innovation can manifest itself in many different ways. They include product changes, process changes, new approaches to marketing, new forms of distribution and new conceptions of scope (notice the similarity to Schumpeter's 'new combinations'). Innovation grows out of pressure, challenges and change. Whereas many view change as unwelcome, Porter sees it as both necessary and desirable. Innovation and change are inextricably linked.[2]

Once innovation is achieved (more likely in a mundane manner rather than in any radical fashion), continuous improving must follow so that the advantage is not lost to competitors who attempt to imitate any improvement.

Finally, 'innovation is the result of unusual effort' which ultimately must lead to unnatural acts by firms if the advantage achieved from innovation is to be sustained. This behaviour is inherent in 'leaders', i.e. in firms or individuals that recognise the dynamics of an industry and the importance of embracing and institutionalising change rather than avoiding it. Of course, sixty-five years ago Schumpeter said the same thing!

1 For a short summary of the book (*The Competitive Advantage of Nations*), read the article 'The Competitive Advantage of Nations' by M. Porter, *Harvard Business Review*, March–April 1990.
2 A leading guru on innovation and entrepreneurship is Peter Drucker. To understand why he views entrepreneurship as a practice which can be successfully managed, read his 1985 best-seller *Innovation and Entrepreneurship*.

The result of a monopolistic market structure

Until now, we have discussed factor markets under conditions of perfect competition. Consider the case of a monopoly. A monopoly is a sole producer in an industry. Its ability to restrict output, control price and deter entry allow supernormal profits to persist. If the demand for the monopolist's product is high, profits will also remain high. Profits arising from a monopoly position are viewed as socially less desirable than profits sourced from risk and from innovation. And unlike the other two sources, government action may be taken in order to restrict monopoly profits.

SUMMARY

1. The factors of production are the inputs used in the production process that result in final output. There are four factor inputs – labour, capital, land and entrepreneurship. Wage is the return to labour, interest is the reward to capital, rent is the return on land and profit is the reward to entrepreneurship.
2. According to the neoclassical theory of distribution, factor prices (at least in the long run) can be explained by standard demand and supply analysis.
3. The demand curve for labour is derived using marginal productivity theory. Profit-maximising firms will employ workers up to the point where MRP of labour = W. The MRP curve is the demand curve for labour, showing the number of workers employed at any given wage rate. It is downward sloping, showing that the lower the wage rate, the larger the number of workers who will be employed. The supply curve for labour shows the number of hours offered for work at different wage rates. It depends on the trade-off between work and leisure. It is generally upward sloping. The demand for, and supply of, labour simultaneously determine the equilibrium wage rate and quantity of labour.
4. The interest rate is the opportunity cost of capital. In deciding whether to purchase new capital, the firm must weigh the future benefits accruing from the investment against the cost of the investment. The demand curve for capital goods is downward sloping. The supply curve for capital goods is influenced by the trade-off between consumption and savings (i.e.

future consumption). The equilibrium interest rate is the cost of capital that clears the market for capital goods.

5. Transfer earnings is the portion of total earnings that is required to keep a factor in its present use. Economic rent is the portion of earnings in excess of transfer payments. Economic rent is paid on any factor of production that is in fixed supply. In terms of land, rent is the price paid for the use of land and other fixed resources. It is this fixed supply of land which distinguishes rental payments from other factor payments. The entire rental price is an economic rent.

6. Entrepreneurship is difficult to define and to measure. The reward to enterprise is profit. Unlike other factor payments, profit is a residual. It is received (if at all) after all other factor payments are made. There are several different sources of economic profit. One, it is the reward for uninsurable risk in the face of uncertainty. Two, it arises from acts of innovation carried out by the entrepreneur. Three, monopoly profits arise from output restriction, high prices and barriers to entry.

KEY TERMS

Labour	Present value
Wage rate	Discounting
Derived demand	Rate of return
Marginal productivity theory	Interest rate
Marginal revenue product	Land
Demand curve for labour	Economic rent
Supply curve of labour	Transfer earnings
Backward bending supply curve	Entrepreneurship
Wage differentials	Profit
Capital goods	Uninsurable risk
Capital stock	Innovation
Depreciation	Entrepreneur
Investment	

REVIEW QUESTIONS

1. Explain the term 'factors of production'. What are the four standard factors of production? What are their rewards?
2. Explain the derivation of the individual firm's downward sloping labour demand curve.
3. What effect would a decrease in labour supply have on the equilibrium price and quantity in the labour market?
4. 'An investment is worthwhile if the present value of the future benefits exceeds the cost of the investment.' Explain.
5. 'The equilibrium interest rate clears the market for capital goods.' Explain.
6. (a) Explain the sources of economic profit.
    (b) Outline the contributions of Frank Knight and Joseph Schumpeter to the theory of profit.

WORKING PROBLEMS

1. A number of entries in Table 7.3 have been omitted. Using marginal productivity theory, answer the following questions.
   (a) Complete the table.
   (b) According to the marginal productivity theory, how many workers will be employed if the wage rate is €40?
   (c) If the wage rate rises to €50, how many workers will be employed?

TABLE 7.3

Labour (wkrs)	TP (units)	MP (units)	P (€)	MRP (€)	Wage (€)
0	**0**				
		–	5	60	40
1	–				
		–	5	–	40
2	27				
		13	5	–	40
3	–				
		–	5	50	40
4	–				
		9	5	–	40
5	–				
		–	5	–	40
6	65				

2. A hypothetical labour market is depicted in Figure 7.15. With respect to Figure 7.15 fill in the blanks below:
   (a) total labour earnings are given by the area [ ]
   (b) transfer earnings are given by the area [ ]
   (c) economic rent is given by the area [ ]
   (d) transfer earnings for worker X are equal to ———
   (e) economic rent for worker X is equal to ———

FIGURE 7.15: THE LABOUR MARKET

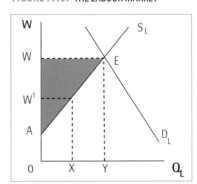

MULTI-CHOICE QUESTIONS

1. Under conditions of perfect competition, the MRP of labour:
    (a) is equal to the MP of labour multiplied by the marginal revenue of the product;
    (b) is the additional revenue due to employing an extra unit of labour;
    (c) curve falls because of the short-run law of diminishing returns;
    (d) curve is the demand curve for labour;
    (e) all of the above.

2. A derived demand for labour:
    (a) can be explained using the marginal productivity theory;
    (b) is derived from the demand for the product which labour produces;
    (c) can be represented by a downward sloping demand curve;
    (d) all of the above;
    (e) none of the above.

3. The present value of €5,000 two years from now at an interest rate of 6% is:
    (a) €5,618;
    (b) €5,600;
    (c) €4,450;
    (d) higher than €5,000;
    (e) both (a) and (d) above.

4. Figure 7.16 shows the labour market for university postgraduates. The economic rent for university graduates is given by the area:
    (a) $[AEQ_L*0]$;
    (b) $[W*EQ_L*0]$;
    (c) $[W*EA]$;
    (d) $[WEQ_L*0]$;
    (e) none of the above.

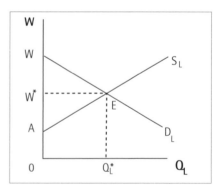

FIGURE 7.16: THE LABOUR MARKET FOR UNIVERSITY POSTGRADUATES

5. The more inelastic the supply curve for a factor of production becomes:
    (a) the more transfer earnings is paid;
    (b) the more economic rent is paid;
    (c) the less economic rent is paid;
    (d) both (a) and (c) above;
    (e) none of the above.

6. Profit is different from the other resource prices because:
    (a) it is a residual;
    (b) it can be negative;
    (c) it is easy to measure;
    (d) both (a) and (b) above;
    (e) both (a) and (c) above.

TRUE OR FALSE (SUPPORT YOUR ANSWER)

1. Resource prices serve as an allocative mechanism.

2. The declining MRP of labour reflects the law of diminishing returns; an additional labourer always produces more output than the previous labourer.

3. The higher the interest rate, the lower is the present discounted value of the future MRPs and the smaller the number of capital goods demanded.

4. Transfer earnings is the opportunity cost of employing a factor of production.

5. A factor of production does not earn economic rent if its supply curve is perfectly elastic.

6. Profit is the return to the entrepreneur.

CASE STUDY

Opinion from *The Irish Times*
Migrant workers need protection

Most foreign workers are well treated in Ireland. But recent events have revealed a pattern of gross exploitation and law-breaking by a minority of unscrupulous employers that cannot be tolerated by the Government. Reform of the work permit system, the employment of extra inspectors and the imposition of heavy fines for breaches of minimum pay legislation would all contribute to a more equitable situation. But, above all, there has to be a change in an official mindset that adopts a security-based approach to migrant workers.

Socialist Party TD Joe Higgins has contributed significantly to the current debate in the Dáil by championing the cause of non-EU workers employed by the Turkish construction company, Gama. And while the company has denied mistreating its employees and secreting their money in Dutch bank accounts, it was found to have destroyed important records and to have underpaid its workers. Minister for Enterprise, Trade and Employment, Micheál Martin, has directed that further inquiries be instituted.

The economy needs foreign workers to generate wealth. But there is an official reluctance to improve their conditions, lest they become permanent residents. Non-EU workers are most vulnerable because their work visas are granted to a particular employer and, if they complain, they can be threatened with the sack and deportation. The recent case of Filipina beauticians, employed by a foreign company on behalf of Irish Ferries, was a good example. And the resolution of the case reflected well on Siptu officials. The Churches, the trade unions and various immigrant organisations have all asked that non-EU workers be given the freedom to change their employers, but the Government has resisted. At the same time, mechanisms designed to protect the rights of EU workers are seriously deficient.

As our Industry and Employment correspondent, Chris Dooley, writes elsewhere, the Labour Inspectorate charged with enforcing the law and preventing the abuse of workers has been compromised as a result of staff shortages, inadequate resources and a lack of enforcement powers. It is not good enough. Twenty-one inspectors have no hope of enforcing statutory employment conditions throughout the State.

$\longrightarrow$

An estimated 50,000 Polish citizens are now registered here and, since last year, they do not require temporary work visas. Because of that, they are increasingly likely to complain of exploitation. Some are instantly dismissed. Their embassy advises them to get another job or to contact a trade union with their complaints, rather than resorting to the slow and cumbersome process of official channels. It is a damning indictment of the quality of State support for such people.

Mr Martin has promised new work permit legislation. He needs to do more than that to protect basic human dignity. This is also an issue on which the trade union movement needs to initiate concerted action.

Source: The Irish Times, 8 April 2005.

Questions

1. Describe the effectiveness or otherwise of minimum wage legislation from the perspective of migrant workers, both EU and non-EU, in Ireland.
2. Using the internet or other sources, describe the general conditions of employment for non-EU workers, e.g. rights to welfare payments, rights with respect to changing employers. How do they differ from EU workers?
3. Using the internet or other sources, describe recent or suggested changes in respect of the treatment of migrant workers in Ireland.

APPENDIX 7.1: DAVID RICARDO AND ECONOMIC RENT

The theory of economic rent was developed in the nineteenth century by the British economist, stockbroker and MP, David Ricardo (1772–1823) in his book *The Principles of Political Economy and Taxation* (1817). His theory arose from the Napoleonic wars and the rising corn (grain) prices which occurred at the same time as the rise in land rents. It was argued at the time that the high corn prices were a direct result of the landlords' policy of high land rents. Ricardo disagreed strongly with such an analysis. He saw the cause and effect in reverse. High rents were an effect and not a cause of high corn prices, he argued. In his own words 'Corn is not high because a rent is paid, but a rent is paid because corn is high.'[13]

The Napoleonic wars were directly responsible for a shortage of corn. The subsequent rise in the price of corn, he argued, forced landlords to seek out more land in order to take advantage of profitable corn production. Subsequent high demand for land in turn forced up the land rents. For Ricardo, rent was price determined and not price determining.

The above analysis can be described in the context of the demand for and supply of land. The supply of land is fixed, with land having only one use: to grow corn. The demand for land is a derived demand, stemming from the demand for corn. The payment to land is a surplus. This surplus payment is rent, according to Ricardo.

CHAPTER 8

Markets and States

'It is not from the benevolence of the butcher, the brewer, or the baker that we expect our dinner, but from their regard to their own interest. We address ourselves, not to their humanity, but to their self-love.'[1]

ADAM SMITH (1723–90)

'... the market needs a place and the market needs to be kept in its place.'[2]

ARTHUR OKUN (1928–80)

CHAPTER OBJECTIVES

Upon completing this chapter, the student should understand:

- perfectly competitive markets and market efficiency;
- market failures, such as externalities, public goods and distributional considerations;
- possible remedies for market failures;
- the public finance and public choice perspectives on the state;
- state failures, such as regulatory capture.

OUTLINE

INTRODUCTION

There is an ongoing economic, political and social debate in Ireland between advocates and opponents of the market as a mechanism for the allocation of resources. While from the perspective of the twenty-first century it may appear that the broader and more internationally based philosophical and political debate between capitalism and communism should be viewed almost historically, it is clear that many feel significant unease about the expanding scope of the market in society. For example, in an Irish context, there is tension with respect to the appropriate role of the market in the provision of education, health, financial services and prison services.

Proponents of the market highlight its efficiency, while opponents of the market highlight its failures, particularly with respect to considerations of equity or equality. Notwithstanding the extent of disagreement between the two sides, both sides in general agree that there should be some role for both the market and the state with respect to the allocation of society's resources. The difference between the two sides is one of degree.

Adopting the standard starting point for this discussion, this chapter begins by reviewing the efficiency characteristics of perfectly competitive markets. It is these efficiency attributes that lend support to the pro-market stance adopted by market advocates. Moving away from the highly theoretical world of perfect competition, however, allows us also to focus attention on the failures of the market. These failures can be split into efficiency failures and failures with respect to equity or equality considerations. Efficiency failures manifest themselves in the incorrect allocation of resources (e.g. factor inputs) while equity failures appear in the very unequal distribution of final products.

Market failures that create inefficiencies can be addressed by private remedies (e.g. a suitably expanded market), public remedies (e.g. direct state provision) or some combination of the two (e.g. public private partnerships (PPPs)). Advocates of private remedies highlight the robustness of the market mechanism and argue that (apparent) market failures merely highlight the need for greater institutional supports for the market (e.g. more clearly defined property rights) while advocates of public remedies can be divided into those who support public provision and those who support some combination of the state and the market (e.g. PPPs in an Irish context). Market failures with respect to equity considerations inevitably imply the need for state involvement in the economy although market advocates differ among themselves, as well as with state advocates, with respect to the appropriate scope and size of the social security 'safety net'.

Within the last twenty-five years, there has been increasing recognition of failures associated with state provision. At the most benign level, these failures can be viewed as being inefficiencies inevitably associated with distortions caused by the presence of taxation, which is required to finance state expenditure. However, at another level, it is increasingly acknowledged that the 'state' consists of many agents (e.g. politicians and bureaucrats), each with separate, although difficult to identify exactly, objectives. The so-called school of public choice is recognised as being the first group to address from both a theoretical and applied perspective the possible policy implications of viewing the state as being diferent from a benevolent social planner. At its most sinister level, these state failures stem from the corruption and bribery generally associated with the breakdown of the state. Given the generally accepted presence of both market failures and state failures, it is clear that the policy issue is not market or state but how much market and how much state.

8.1 MARKET EFFICIENCY

Sections 6.1 and 6.2 examined the market characteristics and outcomes associated with perfect competition and monopoly, respectively. In Section 6.2, it was also demonstrated that the aggregation of consumer surplus and producer surplus in a particular market is maximised under conditions of perfect competition. Figure 8.1 also provides support for the proposition that perfect competition maximises societal welfare.

In the perfectly competitive market equilibrium (P*, Q*), where market demand is equal to market supply,

FIGURE 8.1: EQUILIBRIUM IN A PERFECTLY COMPETITIVE MARKET

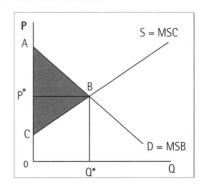

consumer surplus is represented by the area of the triangle ABP*, while producer surplus is represented by the area of the triangle CBP*. As such, total societal welfare is measured by the area of the triangle ABC. Any increase in output above Q*, and hence an associated decrease in market price below P*, would result in a decrease in societal welfare as the marginal increase in cost to society MSC (as captured by the marginal area under the supply curve) would outweigh the marginal increase in benefit to society MSB (as captured by the marginal area under the demand curve). Similarly, any decrease in output below Q*, and hence an associated increase in market price above P*, would also result in a decrease in societal welfare as the marginal decrease in benefit to society MSB (as captured by the marginal area under the demand curve) would outweigh the marginal decrease in cost to society MSC (as captured by the marginal area under the supply curve).

The equivalence between price or marginal social benefit (MSB) and marginal costs or marginal social cost (MSC) that occurs in a perfectly competitive market is referred to as allocative efficiency (see also Section 9.2), as society's resources are being allocated efficiently to that market. In contrast, in monopoly, price is greater than marginal cost and the market is allocatively inefficient as too little of the product is being produced from society's perspective.

More generally, if it is assumed that all product markets satisfy the conditions or assumptions underlying perfect competition (i.e. many sellers and buyers, homogeneous product, perfect information and freedom of entry and exit), it can be shown that the market system has some very important economy-wide or society-wide characteristics. These characteristics are summarised in the two standard theorems of welfare economics.

The first welfare theorem states that if all markets are perfectly competitive, then the resulting market allocation of resources will be Pareto-efficient in the sense that starting from that allocation no individual can be made better off by re-allocating resources without making at least one other individual worse off. In essence, the first welfare theorem provides theoretical support for Adam Smith's invisible hand metaphor: ' . . . and by directing that industry in such a manner as its produce may be of the greatest value, he intends only his own gain, and he is in this, as in many other cases, led by an invisible hand to promote an end which has no part of it. By pursuing his own interest he frequently promotes that of the society more effectually than when he really intends to promote it.'[3]

In summary, it is the first welfare theorem and Adam Smith's invisible hand that offers comfort to market adherents' enthusiasm for the market.

Although not nearly as well known, or as well championed, as the first welfare theorem, there is also a second welfare theorem. The second welfare theorem focuses on equity considerations, in contrast to the first welfare theorem's focus on efficiency considerations. Consider a hypothetical world with just two individuals and a fixed amount of two products. Although the market may guarantee Pareto efficiency in this world, there are numerous Pareto-efficient outcomes or allocations. For example, one individual having all of both products would constitute a Pareto-efficient allocation, as would an alternative world in which the other individual has all of both products. However, neither of these allocations would probably correspond to any even mildly objective individual's sense of equity. Enter the second welfare theorem.

The second welfare theorem states that any specific Pareto-efficient allocation can be provided by the market, supported by appropriate lump sum taxes and subsidies. From a theoretical perspective at least, the second welfare theorem allows society to choose between the many (actually infinite number of) possible Pareto-efficient allocations available. Some economists refer to the chosen Pareto-efficient allocation as being Pareto optimal. The second welfare theorem is not as well known as the first welfare theorem primarily because of the restrictive nature of the assumption surrounding the availability of lump-sum taxes and subsidies. In particular, it is difficult to envisage the actual existence of either taxes or subsidies that do not in some way distort at least one individual's decision-making process. For example, labour taxation causes a substitution effect away from the provision of labour and capital taxation causes a substitution effect away from savings, while even a head tax or poll tax that is based on the electoral register causes at least some individuals to avoid registering on the electoral register; the infamous UK poll tax of the late 1980s that arguably led to Lady (Margaret) Thatcher's demise provides an example of the latter. In summary, it is claimed that the second welfare theorem is not as useful as the first welfare theorem because the underlying assumptions of the second welfare theorem are too unrealistic.

However, this argument should also highlight the very restrictive nature of the assumptions underlying the first welfare theorem. Indeed, the so-called second best theorem (as distinct from the second theorem of welfare economics) demonstrates that when even one market is not perfectly competitive, it is no longer necessarily appropriate to strive for perfect competition in all of the other markets in order to maximise societal welfare. In practice, the second best theorem highlights the non-robust nature of the first theorem of welfare economics and undermines to at least some extent the market adherents' faith in the market from a theoretical perspective.

It is essential to examine the different types of market failure that undermine the assumptions underlying the first welfare theorem and hence in themselves justify significant state involvement in the economy.

8.2 MARKET FAILURES

It is possible to identify market failures under the two general headings of efficiency failures and equity failures. Efficiency failures are, in general, associated with the presence of some effect that is not incorporated or internalised into the price paid by consumers and/or the cost incurred by producers. If the market price does not internalise these effects, these effects are not considered appropriately by either the consumers and/or the producers. These effects are generally referred to as externalities, although this term also has a narrower meaning, as will be demonstrated below. Even if the market is granted its efficiency characteristics, it is highly likely that society will not like the equity implications of the efficient allocation that the market 'chooses'. As such, society in general deems that the market generally fails with respect to equity or equality considerations.

Efficiency failures

It is instructive to consider efficiency failures under a number of separate headings: externalities (narrowly defined), public goods, informational failures and market power. As previously argued, it is also possible to regard each of these separate failures as being caused by the presence of external effects or externalities (broadly defined) that are not captured by the price, and hence market, mechanism.

1. Externalities

Externalities can be either negative or positive and can stem from either production or consumption decisions.

> **Definition**
> *Externalities are positive or negative non-priced by-products of production or consumption decisions.*

Pollution represents the standard example of a negative production externality. In general, at least until recently, a producer did not have to pay the full costs associated with polluting the environment. There is thus a divergence between marginal private cost (i.e. the standard MC curve that the producer is confronted by, and responds to) and marginal social cost, which incorporates the marginal private cost and the marginal external cost that is imposed on the rest of society by the pollution that is produced by the producer as a by-product.

Figure 8.2 represents the situation graphically. The market equilibrium (P_1, Q_1) is located at the intersection of the market demand curve and the market supply curve, with the latter being constructed from the summation of the relevant segments of the perfectly competitive firms' marginal cost curves. However, the presence of the non-priced pollution by-product means that the marginal social cost curve is above the marginal private cost curve. The appropriate equilibrium, from society's

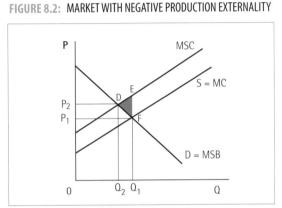

FIGURE 8.2: MARKET WITH NEGATIVE PRODUCTION EXTERNALITY

perspective, would be represented by (P_2, Q_2); the market produces too much and charges too little. The monetary size of the welfare loss associated with the market equilibrium is given by the triangle DEF.

Of course, the above negative production externality represents just one type of externality. The other possibilities are positive production externalities, negative consumption externalities and positive consumption externalities.

The standard setting for the presence of positive production externalities is provided by an environment with orchards and honey-producing bees.[4] Neither the operator of the orchard nor the keeper of the honey-producing bees is likely to take into account the positive effect of his or her activity on the other's activity. The market outcome is likely to result in too little of each activity. Figure 8.3 represents the situation graphically.

The presence of the non-priced by-product or by-products (namely, apples as bees' food and/or bees as pollinators of apple blossoms) means that the marginal social cost curve is below the marginal private cost curve. The welfare loss associated with the market equilibrium is given by the area of the triangle HGQ. From society's perspective, too little is being produced and too high a price is being charged for the product or products that produce positive production externalities.

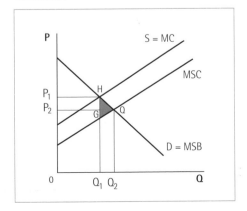

FIGURE 8.3: MARKET WITH POSITIVE PRODUCTION EXTERNALITY

Similar results hold for the case of consumption externalities. A standard example of a negative consumption externality is provided by rush-hour drivers who in general do not take into account the effect of their decision to drive on the associated increased congestion costs imposed on other drivers. As a result, too many rush-hour trips are likely to be taken. Figure 8.4 represents this situation.

The presence of the non-priced by-product (namely, the effect of each car on other drivers' experiences of congestion) means that the marginal social benefit curve is below the marginal private benefit curve. The welfare loss associated with the market equilibrium is given by the area of the triangle MNO. From society's perspective, too much is being consumed of the product or products that produce negative consumption externalities.

FIGURE 8.4: **MARKET WITH NEGATIVE CONSUMPTION EXTERNALITY**

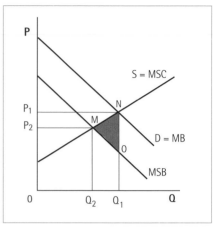

FIGURE 8.5: **MARKET WITH POSITIVE CONSUMPTION EXTERNALITY**

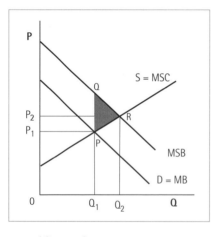

Finally, a standard example of a positive consumption externality is provided by the consumption of flu vaccines. The MMR vaccine for children would provide a similar example. Consumers of vaccines in general do not internalise the positive effect of their decisions on others, so too few vaccines are likely to be consumed within the market setting.

Again, the presence of the non-priced by-product (namely, the effect of each flu vaccine shot on others' reduced likelihood of contracting flu) means that the marginal social benefit curve is above the marginal private benefit curve. The welfare loss associated with the market equilibrium is given by the area of the triangle QRP. From society's perspective, too little is being consumed of the product or products that produce positive consumption externalities.

2. Public goods

Public goods (or services) have two key characteristics that distinguish them from private goods. There is non-rivalry in the consumption of public goods and the consumption of public goods is non-excludable in nature. In contrast, there is rivalry in the consumption of private goods, in that if one individual consumes a specific unit of a private good no other individual can also consume that specific unit of the private good. In addition, the existence of the price mechanism for private goods implies that individuals who do not demand private goods can be excluded from the consumption of private goods.

Definition

Public goods are consumed by all consumers to the same extent (non-rivalry) and no one can be excluded from consumption (non-excludable).

National defence provides the standard example of a public good. Access to the benefits of national defence by one individual within a certain territory almost certainly implies access to the same level of national defence by all other individuals within that territory. In addition, it is difficult, if not impossible, to envisage excluding any individual within that territory from the benefits of national defence. Other standard examples of public goods include street lighting, free-to-air television and radio broadcasts and lighthouses.

The market failure associated with public goods is one of under-provision. Figure 8.6 facilitates an understanding of this market failure.

MB^1 represents the first individual's demand and hence willingness to pay for the public good, while MB^2 represents the second individual's demand and hence willingness to pay for the (same) public good. Given the non-rivalry consumption attribute of public goods, the total market demand and willingness to pay for the public good is given by the vertical, as opposed to the horizontal, summation of the individuals' demand curves. The appropriate market willingness to pay is $MSB = MB^1 + MB^2$, and the appropriate output is Q^*. However, in a market system, each individual has an incentive to free-ride on the other individual's demand for the public good. In particular, in Figure 8.6, where the first individual is less willing to pay for the public good than the second individual, the first individual will likely demand no public good and wait for the second individual to demand, and hence provide, for all, a more than ample amount of the public good. Of course, the second individual may well respond to this situation by reducing stated willingness to pay and hence stated and actual demand for the public good. It is clear that the market system will not provide the appropriate quantity of the public good (i.e. Q^*), i.e. there is a market failure.

It is also possible to view public goods as providing an example of an externality, broadly defined, as the market fails because individual consumers produce (positive) external effects for which they are not compensated. Indeed, public goods can be viewed as being positive consumption externalities. As in the case of a product with positive consumption externalities, the market produces an insufficient amount of the public good.

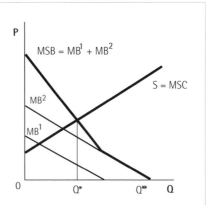

FIGURE 8.6: CONSTRUCTING THE APPROPRIATE DEMAND CURVE FOR A PUBLIC GOOD

3. Incomplete information

One of the assumptions in perfectly competitive markets is the availability of perfect information. In particular, it is assumed that all buyers and sellers have access to all relevant market information, e.g. the prices offered by the different sellers and the exact quality of the products.

However, it is clear that in the real world there is often a significant level of uncertainty, at least on the buyer side, with respect to the exact quality of the sellers' products. Consider the market for second-hand cars. Most buyers of second-hand cars are not expert car technicians and hence are unaware of the exact quality of the second-hand cars. In addition, it may be difficult for the sellers to provide such exact information, even if they, in turn, had such information. In such an environment, it is unrealistic to expect an appropriately sized market to develop for high-quality second-hand cars, as potential buyers rationally believe that part of the reason that a car is being sold into the second-hand car market is because it turned out to be a non-high-quality car (sometimes referred to as a 'lemon'). The underlying informational problem is referred to as 'adverse selection' or 'hidden information'; in particular, non-high-quality second-hand cars tend to drive out high-quality second-hand cars from the second-hand car market.[5]

> **Definition**
>
> *Adverse selection characterises the situation where hidden information leads to incomplete or missing markets.*

Providers of private health insurance in Ireland, who are forced by law to accept (more or less) all applicants and charge the same premium to all subscribers, face a somewhat similar problem in that they rationally expect only the relatively unhealthy to be attracted by the premium offered. Therefore, the market for private health insurance policies for relatively healthy individuals is probably underdeveloped, i.e. the market does not produce socially optimal results.

A somewhat different informational problem, referred to as 'moral hazard' or 'hidden action', also arises in the insurance sector where sellers of insurance need to take account of possible changes in behaviour by individuals subsequent to the taking out of insurance. For example, a cyclist's behaviour with respect to safeguarding his/her bike against theft could easily change after the cyclist takes out bicycle insurance. In particular, it may be possible in the extreme that no bicycle insurance market will exist for this reason. The underlying problem is that the sellers cannot easily observe the buyers' possible behavioural changes. In summary, the market fails as a result of the presence of asymmetric information, i.e. information that is known by only one side to the potential agreement or trade.

> **Definition**
>
> *Moral hazard characterises the situation where hidden action leads to incomplete or missing markets.*

More generally, there is a large economics literature on principal agency problems, which focuses on the informational problems that affect the economic relationship between an economic principal (e.g. shareholder, patient, voter, student) and its economic agent (e.g. board, doctor or dentist, elected official or government, lecturer). Conceptually at least, the principal appoints the agent to perform some role (e.g. run the firm, check health status, operate the state mechanism or lecture a course in economics). However, the principal must be aware that the agent probably has its own interests, which to some extent at least will diverge from or conflict with the principal's interests. The presence of informational problems will likely imply that the market for certain types of task will not be efficient, i.e. certain welfare-increasing transactions will not occur.

4. Market power

One of the assumptions in perfect competition is the presence of a large number of buyers and sellers. Any relaxation of this assumption, on either the seller or buyer side, leads to the presence of market power and consequently a divergence between the market outcome and the socially optimal outcome. Chapter 6 focused exclusively on the seller side of the market by covering, for example, monopoly and oligopoly. In each case, it was shown that either a divergence between the market allocation and the socially optimal allocation either existed (i.e. monopoly) or could easily exist (e.g. temptations with respect to collusion within oligopoly). More generally, it can be shown that any relaxation in the assumption that there are a large number of buyers present in the market also leads to the existence of market power (e.g. monopsony, where only one buyer exists) and hence market failure.

Again, it is possible to view the presence of market power as providing an example of an externality, broadly defined, as the market fails because individual sellers or buyers impose a cost on others for which they are not charged.

Equity failures

Even if efficiency failures are simply assumed away, it is clear that the market can fail with respect to equity considerations. Many economists, perhaps especially neoclassical economists, feel uneasy discussing equity because the issue does not easily lend itself to formal analysis or resolution (e.g. what is the exact meaning of equity?). The underlying difficulty is the inevitable need to measure, compare and aggregate utilities, happiness, well-being or welfare across different individuals. Economists' inability to measure utility, let alone compare utility or aggregate utility across individuals is the reason that economists approach demand theory from an indifference curve perspective (see Chapter 4). Even if it is assumed that utilities can be measured, compared and aggregated across different individuals, many different but perhaps equally plausible claims to an 'equitable' allocation of resources present themselves.

Alternative approaches to how society's utility or welfare can be maximised are outlined and described in alternative social welfare functions. For example, a so-called 'utilitarian' social welfare function suggests that society's aim should be to maximise the sum of all individuals' utilities, while a so-called 'Rawlsian' social welfare function suggests that society's aim should be to maximise the utility of the worst-off individual.[6]

Theoretically, if one adopts any of the available approaches, say the utilitarian approach, one then simply chooses the Pareto-efficient allocation of resources that maximises the sum of all individuals' utilities and hence achieves, by definition, both an efficient and equitable outcome. Indeed, from a public policy approach, it may also appear reasonable to argue that in the process of electing a government, society is in effect choosing between alternative social welfare functions. However, very few political parties explicitly put themselves forward on the basis of a stated social welfare function, and many individuals do not vote in elections; in addition, there are many potential problems associated with aggregating individuals' votes across different policy options (e.g. see the case study at the end of Chapter 4). At best, one can see the political process as an imperfect mechanism for choosing between different menus of policies, including policies with respect to different concepts of equity. In summary, it is unlikely that the market when acting alone – or even when supplemented by the political process – can successfully achieve equity, however defined.

8.3 THE STATE AND REMEDIES FOR MARKET FAILURES

Given that there are significant market failures with respect to both efficiency and equity, it is clear that the market cannot be expected to perform in isolation from the state. Even the most fervent proponent of the market sees a role for the state in providing institutional support for the market. For example, the state can define, and enforce where necessary, the property rights that are crucial to facilitating the smooth operation of the market. Beyond this so-called 'nightwatchman' role for the state, market proponents differ with respect to the extent to which they believe that the market can independently address apparent market failures. In contrast, opponents of the market see a very large role for the state. Indeed, some proponents of the state insist that the state is the appropriate institution or mechanism for allocating and distributing resources even if there were no market failures.

As before, it is instructive to address remedies for market failures under the two headings of efficiency failures and equity failures. In addition, in each case, it is useful to consider both private and public solutions, as well as combined public and private solutions.

Private solutions

Assuming that the state exists in a nightwatchman form, some market proponents believe that the market itself is capable of addressing almost all, if not all (apparent) market failures. The Coase theorem summarises the standard position.[7] Provided that the relevant economic agents are aware of the apparent market failures and can negotiate with each other, previously well-defined property rights can be traded until the apparent market failure simply disappears.

Taking the standard negative production externalities case summarised above in Figure 8.2 as an example, it is argued by Coase and his many followers that it is 'incomplete' to compare the (apparent) market outcome $(P_1, Q_1,)$ with the optimal outcome (P_2, Q_2). At the (apparent) market equilibrium (P_1, Q_1), those polluted would have an incentive to talk to, and trade with, the polluter. Indeed, provided that negotiations were feasible and that transactions costs were negligible (e.g. there were small numbers of individuals involved), it is claimed that the relevant economic agents (i.e. the polluted and the polluter) would negotiate themselves to the optimal outcome (P_2, Q_2). Why? Because any outcome other than (P_2, Q_2) would be inefficient and hence there would be an incentive to negotiate away from that temporary inefficient outcome.

For those who find the implications of the Coase theorem surprising, it will be even more surprising that these implications carry over into much, if not all, of the above examples of market failures associated with efficiency considerations. For example, ship operators can negotiate with each other with respect to the provision of appropriately located lighthouses, while beekeepers and orchard owners can negotiate with respect to appropriately sized side-payments, either in monetary terms or in kind (e.g. apples for honey). Even in the context of the standard monopoly versus perfect competition comparison, the Coase theorem appears. Consumers, it is argued, who would have bought the product in perfect competition but who are apparently priced out of the market in monopoly can subsequently offer to buy the product from the monopolist at individually negotiated prices (that are limited to lie somewhere between the monopolist's marginal cost of production and the individual consumer's willingness to pay).

Although it is difficult to see how the Coase theorem can overcome the inefficiencies and associated market failures associated with informational problems, it is unlikely that the market will be passive in the presence of these problems. For example, second-hand car dealers can at least attempt to overcome the adverse selection problem by offering extended warranties on high-quality second-hand cars. In addition, insurance companies can at least attempt to overcome the moral hazard problem by insisting on full police reports on claimed robberies and by offering suitably structured policy excesses and no claims bonuses. The latter, in particular, offer a way to align the incentives of the insurance companies and the insured individual. More generally, contractual terms such as bonuses and commissions (e.g. linkages between wages and profits) can offer part resolution of the principal agency problem, although recent experiences in the financial services sector suggest strongly that these incentives can cause, rather than solve, market failure.

As with all theorems, the Coase theorem can be accused of being rather tautological; provided that its assumptions are true, the results of the theorem must follow. As such, there is nothing to be gained in trying to 'disprove' the Coase theorem. However, it may be enlightening to focus on the assumptions underlying, and the equity implications of, the Coase theorem. In the presence of ill-defined property rights or significant negotiation or transactions costs (e.g. the presence of many individuals), there may be no movement away from the standard market outcome (e.g. (P_1, Q_1) in Figure 8.2 above). In addition, even with perfectly defined property rights and zero negotiation and transactions costs, it is possible that economic agents will not actually attain the mutually beneficial agreements that are at least in theory available. In particular, each agent may hold out for too large a slice of the economic rents available (e.g. the area of the triangle DEF in Figure 8.2 above). For example, in the monopoly example, the extra potential consumers may hold out for a price closer to the monopolist's marginal costs, while the monopolist may hold out for a price closer to the consumers' average willingness to pay. Indeed, in this monopoly versus perfect competition example, matters might be even worse as the consumers who previously paid the monopoly price may refuse to purchase the product, believing that the monopolist would later sell the product at a lower price to consumers who did not pay the monopoly price. The market outcome in reality might be even worse than the monopoly outcome.

Even when the Coase theorem does provide an actual solution, as opposed to a theoretical solution, to the market failures associated with inefficiencies, the assigning of property rights will have significant distributional effects. For example, even if the assigning of the property rights to clean air to the polluted might eventually lead to the same level of pollution as the assigning of property rights to pollute to the polluter, it is clear that the equity implications would be very different. The polluted would gain from being assigned the initial property rights (by the state) from being paid by the polluter for the favour of being allowed to pollute a little, while the polluter would gain from being assigned the initial property rights (by the state) from being paid by the polluted for the favour of not being polluted too much.

More generally, with respect to equity considerations, it is sometimes argued, though not by too many, that the market can address (apparent) equity failures through the process of charitable donations. Indeed, to the extent that one individual's concern for other individuals' utility goes so far as to warrant or even demand inclusion of the other individuals' utilities in his/her utility function, it would be efficient as well as equitable for there to be private donations from that individual to the others. Some, although again not too many, even argue that the market outcome is by definition fair, provided that there is a very basic form of equality of opportunity available to all. In general, however, almost all, including economists, agree that private solutions alone to the market failures associated with equity considerations would be very inappropriate. However, as previously indicated, there is considerable disagreement with respect to the appropriate extent of the social security safety net.

Public solutions

Proponents of the state mechanism as a response to efficiency-based market failures differ with respect to the required level of state involvement. At one level, some argue that state provision always provides the most appropriate economic and political mechanism. For example, education and health should, it is argued, be provided exclusively by the state under this approach. Even small residual roles for private education and private health (e.g. private hospitals) would be ruled out as they would be seen to undermine the services provided by the state. Similarly, when viewed from this perspective, the solution to the natural monopoly or monopoly problem is simply nationalisation. To the extent that externalities would not be met with the nationalisation solution, so-called command-and-control regulations, as opposed to market-based incentives, would be utilised, i.e. the polluter would simply be told not to pollute or the polluted would simply be told to put up with being polluted.

From an equity or equality perspective, proponents of the state mechanism view the market with particular suspicion. Indeed, some proponents of the state mechanism see the existence of the state itself as being primarily in response to failures associated with equity as opposed to efficiency considerations. Followers of this approach are particularly critical of the assumption of a pre-existing consensus that efficiency considerations are more important than equity considerations.[8] In short, the emergence of the state (and its subsequent non-disappearance) indicates the primacy of the state over the market and the primacy of equity over efficiency considerations. Proponents of this view are supported by the near-universal observation that the state is the central, and by far the largest, institution in almost all countries with respect to the allocation of society's resources.

Public and private solutions

In practice, most supporters of the state mechanism see at least some role for the market, even if it is only in offering some supporting role to the state. However, given the shift in favour of the market that has been experienced across the world in the past thirty years, it is useful to consider more market-based 'public' solutions to market failures associated with both efficiency and equity considerations.

Within the context of narrowly defined externalities, for example, the state could choose to utilise market-based solutions. Returning to Figure 8.2, a tax in the order of magnitude |EF| which is imposed on each unit of output (and the associated amount of pollution) would shift upward the private marginal cost (MC) curve until it coincided with the marginal social cost (MSC) curve. With the tax internalised into the market price, the new market outcome, where the new marginal private cost curve intersects the marginal social benefit curve, would be at (P_2, Q_2). From both a US and an EU public policy perspective, there has been a shift towards the use of tax-based instruments to reduce pollution. For example, in Ireland, the new EU carbon tax regime is implemented via the issuing of permits that allow a certain level of pollution: polluters then face the alternative of reducing pollution by adopting the appropriate abatement technology or having to purchase permits that allow for the previous level, or even an increased level, of pollution.

A similar market-based solution presents itself in the case of positive production externalities, where a subsidy (i.e. a negative tax) in the order of magnitude |HG| would be required in Figure 8.3 in order to shift downward the marginal private cost curve until it coincided with the marginal social cost curve. Consumption externalities could also be internalised by the appropriate implementation of consumption taxes or subsidies.

The under-provision of public goods by the market could also be addressed by market-based instruments such as production or consumption subsidies (e.g. tax breaks) or vouchers (e.g. education or health) that allow the holder to choose between different private providers. Within the context of market power-based market failures (e.g. monopoly versus perfect competition), the state could even choose to auction off the rights to be the monopolist (see Section 9.2) as well as retain the rights, via an appropriate state agency, to regulate the resulting market outcome.

In the context of public goods such as education, health care and public roads, even if a decision is taken by the state that state provision is preferable to market provision, it could still be the case that the market mechanism might be used to build and/or operate the associated institutions/activities, with the resulting outputs perhaps being provided free to all users. Increasingly, public private partnerships are being used in Ireland (and elsewhere, to varying degrees, in the EU) to fund road infrastructure and local area regeneration projects. The details can differ considerably between the various public private partnerships but it is clear that they represent a middle ground between exclusive private provision, operation and ownership, and exclusive public provision, operation and ownership.

From an equity perspective, the state can supplement the market and/or replace the market with respect to the appropriate level of redistribution depending on one's perspective. To the extent that some might argue that the market would provide at least some redistribution if only the providers could be sure that others would not free-ride on their 'contributions', the state, via compulsory taxation (and the related social welfare payments), provides, or acts as what might be regarded as, a co-ordination mechanism. More generally, to the extent that it is believed that few would 'contribute' towards redistribution even if others did not free-ride on their 'contributions', the state can simply redistribute through the use of income taxes and associated transfers as well as through the use of social expenditures (e.g. the provision of housing, education or health services).

CASE STUDY

Lighthouse – public good or private good?

' . . . The question remains: how is it that these great men [John Stuart Mill, Henry Sidgwick, A.C. Pigou and Paul A. Samuelson] have, in their economic writings, been led to make statements about lighthouses which are misleading as to the facts, whose meaning, if thought about in a concrete fashion, is quite unclear, and which, to the extent that they imply a policy conclusion, are very likely wrong? The explanation is that these references by economists to lighthouses are not the result of their having made a study of lighthouses or having read a detailed study by some other economist. Despite the extensive use of the lighthouse example in the literature, no economist, to my knowledge, has even made a comprehensive study of lighthouses finance and administration. The lighthouse is simply picked out of the air to serve as an illustration.'

Source: R.H. Coase, 'The Lighthouse in Economics', *Journal of Law and Economics*, Vol. 17, 1974.

' . . . Instead of a dichotomy between private and government provision, we might imagine a continuum between the poles of pure private provision with no government support to full governmental provision out of general revenues. In the case of lighthouses, it might include these different points: (1) private provision with no government enforcement of property or contract rights; (2) private provision with government enforcement of property or contract rights; (3) private provision with government fixing rates, granting monopolies, and enforcing collection of specified user levies; (4) government provision from collection of specified user levies; and (5) government provision from general revenues. In fact, the lighthouses that have existed fall into categories 3, 4 or 5. They existed because the government was able to provide a feasible technology to address the excludability and small numbers problems.

'Those problems did not necessitate that the government "own" the lighthouses or provide lighthouses out of general revenues as some economists suggest. As Coase points out, many lighthouses were "owned" by private individuals in the sense that private individuals supplied the capital to build the lighthouses . . . There are, however, no examples of lighthouses operating in the pristine "private" world (category 2) in which the government only protected property entitlements and enforced consensual deals.

'In almost every case, the government did much more. It granted the lighthouse owner a monopoly on the provision of lighthouse services at a particular location; it set and enforced a fixed schedule of "light dues"; and it assisted the lighthouse operator in collecting his light dues against nonconsenting ship captains. The only exceptions to this generalization were the lighthouses provided by religious persons or entities; in those cases, while the government was not always involved, it is likely that similar socially coercive devices were used to overcome the particular problems of the lighthouses . . .'

Source: D.E. Van Zandt, 'The Lessons of the Lighthouse: "Government" or "Private" Provision of Goods', *Journal of Legal Studies*, Vol. 22, January 1993.

Questions

1. After reading the above two extracts, do you view the lighthouse as a public good or as a private good? Support your answer.
2. National defence and street lighting represent two other standard examples of public goods. After reading the above two extracts, do you now consider these products as being public goods or private goods? Support your answer in each case.
3. Van Zandt uses a five-point continuum for categorising products. In an Irish context, provide examples of products that correspond at least somewhat closely to each of these five points.

Answers on website

8.4 STATE FAILURES

In the study of public sector economics within neoclassical economics, the state was for many years generally presented and analysed as if it were equivalent to a benevolent social planner (or benevolent dictator). The literatures on stabilisation policy (macro-based) and optimal taxation (micro-based) provide two specific examples of this so-called public finance approach or perspective that held sway from the early 1950s into at least the early 1980s. In essence, in much of this literature, the state was viewed as being the appropriate institution or mechanism to step in when the market mechanism was demonstrated to have failed. In particular, the state was represented as attempting, via stabilisation policy and/or optimal taxation policy, simply to maximise societal welfare; it was assumed that neither the state nor its constituent parts (e.g. the government or the state bureaucracy) had separate objectives to those of its members (i.e. citizens or residents). The literature's goal was to discover the technical solutions to the quantitative problems that were used to represent economic problems confronting the state, e.g. the appropriate amount of capital investment by the state or the optimal labour and capital tax rates. In summary, the state was expected to do what the state should do, i.e. the public finance approach was basically normative – what should the state do?

From the early 1960s onwards, however, there was a growing movement that began with a small number of economists (e.g. James Buchanan, Ronald Coase and Gordon Tullock) who differed fundamentally in their perspective from the public finance approach. In particular, the public choice school insisted that it was completely inappropriate to simply assume that the incentives of the state coincided with the incentives of its members. Notwithstanding the difficulties associated with identifying the exact motivations of, say, the specific government in power and the state bureaucracy more generally, it was imperative at least to recognise that their incentives could be diametrically opposed to the interests of the members of society. In summary, the state was expected to pursue its own interests, i.e. the public choice approach was basically positive – what does the state do?

In the context of addressing possible state failures, it is instructive to take both a public finance and a public choice approach.

Public finance perspective

Given that the public finance approach assumes that the state acts benevolently, it may appear that there can be no failures with respect to either efficiency or equity considerations. However, taxation, which is required to finance state expenditure, by its very nature distorts market signals (see Section 9.1 for further details); as such, the state imposes an efficiency cost on society or, more specifically, the market. The optimal taxation literature attempts to minimise these distortions, but on the reasonable assumption that state expenditure is not negligible, these distortions cannot be completely eliminated. These distortions manifest themselves, for example, in distorted labour decisions, caused by the tax wedge between the gross cost of labour to the employer and the net wage received by the employee, and distorted savings and investments decisions, caused by the tax wedge between the pre-tax rate of return and the post-tax rate of return on savings and investments. In addition, the costs of administering the tax system should also be regarded as inefficiencies, both for taxpayers and tax collectors.

From an exclusively equity perspective, it is true that from a public finance perspective, the state does not fail. However, to the extent that an increased emphasis on equity or equality considerations generally requires higher levels of taxation and expenditure, it is clear that the pursuit of an increased level of equality may have an associated efficiency cost. Arthur Okun used the analogy of the leaky bucket to describe the claimed efficiency–equality trade-off: 'The money must be carried from the rich to the poor in a leaky bucket. Some of it will simply disappear in transit, so the poor will not receive all the money that is taken from the rich.'[9]

To the extent that efficiency considerations and equality considerations are viewed as distinct and separate concepts, Okun's metaphor is relatively straightforward. The pursuit of an increased level of equity involves not just taking money in the form of increased levels of taxation from one group and giving this same money in the form of increased levels of transfers to another group (which could in theory and most likely does in practice contain many members from the first group, e.g. child benefit), but it also involves the imposition of distortions on the market, e.g. on the labour market. In addition, there are costs associated with administering the taxation and social welfare systems. These costs and distortions create a welfare cost in terms of reducing the total level of consumer surplus plus producer surplus. As such, improvements in equity must come at the expense of efficiency.

However, many economists have questioned the assumption that efficiency considerations and equity considerations should be viewed as being distinct and separate concepts. Efficiency-enhancing measures can have positive effects on equity and equity-enhancing measures can have positive effects on efficiency. For example, given that capital markets are inevitably imperfect, the relatively poor generally find it difficult to borrow funds for the purposes of improving their human capital; the introduction of free second-level education in Ireland in the late 1960s is generally agreed to have had both equity-enhancing and efficiency-enhancing effects, both in the short run and in the long run. Overall, it is clear that untangling the complex relationships between economic growth, economic efficiency, redistribution and equity is too difficult a task to be summarised with the leaky bucket metaphor.

Public choice perspective

The divergence between the view of the state as a benevolent social planner and the view of the state as consisting of multiple economic agents, each with its own incentives, represents the underlying difference between the public finance perspective and the public choice perspective. This divergence between private incentives and society's incentives can create its own inefficiencies on top of the standard inefficiencies outlined above. For example, consider politicians and bureaucrats separately. Although it may be appropriate to represent some politicians' objectives as simply being the implementation of their previously stated public policy manifestos, it is probably more realistic to incorporate the desire to be re-elected as being at least part of the average politician's objective. To some extent, these objectives do not conflict, as in order to implement policy one has to be elected and/or re-elected. However, the chances of being re-elected appear to be positively related to economic conditions, perhaps particularly those in the run-up to elections. To the extent that incumbent politicians have some control over the economy, they may be expected to at least attempt to fine-tune it in a way that increases their chances of being re-elected. In recent years, a great deal of academic research has been directed to the area of the relationship, if any, between economic business cycles and political business cycles. In an Irish context, the term 'election budget' is probably familiar to most readers.

The incentives of bureaucrats (e.g. civil servants or regulators) may also differ considerably from the incentives of society more generally. Pursuit of a quiet life and pursuit of a maximised budget represent two possible objectives, each with its own inefficiencies from the broader societal perspective. Indeed, if politicians and bureaucrats both find it in their own interests to increase their budgets, the overall economy may fall victim to Wagner's law, i.e. continual growth in the relative size of the state in the economy.

Within the specific context of regulators, it has been argued that the process of regulation can fall victim to regulatory capture, whereby the regulators, either consciously or subconsciously, begin to represent the interests of the regulated as the latter tend to be very well organised and consumers tend to be less well organised. In the Irish context, it is clear that the regulation of the financial services sector contributed significantly to the extent of the recent economic crash in Ireland.

From an equity perspective, once it is recognised that the state can pursue its own objectives, the state can be viewed as imposing the views of one group onto other groups. Taken narrowly, this perspective would be fairly compatible with a Marxist perspective, with the state representing the interests of the capitalist class at the expense of the working class. More generally, the battle between the various groups' interests should be seen as more dynamic and somewhat less one-sided, with one group winning on some issues and other groups winning on other issues.

8.5 MARKETS AND STATES

It is clear that there exist both market failures and state failures; neither institution on its own can be expected to be the appropriate sole or unique mechanism for the allocation and distribution of society's resources. In practice, there is a policy trade-off between attempting to assign comprehensive property rights and leaving it to the market mechanism (i.e. voluntary private negotiation) to allocate and distribute all resources, and attempting to put in place a wise and benevolent state apparatus that can then cajole society into producing, allocating and distributing the appropriate resources.[10]

From an efficiency perspective, it appears possible, at least in theory, to reach a compromise between the market and the state. Where there are no standard market failures present, it appears reasonable to utilise the market mechanism. Indeed, even if there are standard market failures present, but private voluntary negotiation can be viewed as being reasonably expected to negotiate itself around these failures, then perhaps the market can also be utilised. In general, this might be expected to cover situations in which there is some private information, but the small number of economic agents concerned has both the ability, and the incentive, to negotiate its own way out of the market failure. In all other cases, however, the state should be expected to play a significant role in the allocation of resources. Typical situations would cover the existence of widespread private information and/or the presence of many economic agents. In summary, from an efficiency perspective, it appears possible not only to identify but perhaps also to limit the policy differences between market adherents and supporters of the state.

From an equity perspective, however, it appears that there will be still a sizeable gap between market adherents and supporters of the state. For example, market adherents tend to associate themselves with something close in spirit to the concept of equality of opportunity (i.e. some version of liberalism) while supporters of the state as distributor tend to associate themselves with something close in spirit to the concept of equality of condition or outcome (i.e. some version of egalitarianism).

In practice, and in an Irish, UK and even broader European context, the starting point for the market versus state debate appears to have moved towards a presumption in favour of the market. In particular, opponents of the market appear increasingly to find themselves in the rather defensive position of having to attempt to explain why the market cannot do something better than the state as opposed to simply explaining why the state should be expected to perform some function or role. More generally, however, it is essential to remember that the state still represents by far the largest economic agent in almost all if not all countries. As such, the ongoing policy debate between the market and the state will continue into the future, notwithstanding temporary ebbs and flows in favour of one side or the other.

SUMMARY

1. The first welfare theorem demonstrates that if all markets are perfectly competitive the resulting market allocation of resources will be Pareto-efficient in the sense that starting from that allocation no individual can be made better off by re-allocating resources without making at least one other individual worse off. It is the first welfare theorem that provides support for market followers' enthusiasm for the market place.

2. The second welfare theorem demonstrates that any specific Pareto-efficient allocation can be attained by the market supported by the appropriate lump sum taxes and subsidies. From a theoretical perspective, the second welfare theorem allows society to choose between the many possible Pareto-efficient allocations available.

3. The second best theorem demonstrates that when even one market is not perfectly competitive, it is no longer necessarily appropriate to strive for perfect competition in all of the other markets in order to maximise societal welfare. In practice, the second best theorem highlights the importance of market failures, which encompass externalities, public goods, incomplete information and market power, as well as equity considerations.

4. Market failures that create inefficiencies can be addressed by private remedies (e.g. more clearly defined property rights or a suitably designed tax or subsidy), public remedies (e.g. direct state provision or command-and-control regulations) or some combination of the two (e.g. public private partnerships (PPPs)). Market failures with respect to equity considerations inevitably imply the need for state involvement in the economy.

5. From the perspective of the school of public finance, the state is represented as maximising societal welfare. In particular, it is assumed that neither the state nor its constituent parts (e.g. the government or the state bureaucracy) has separate objectives to those of its members (i.e. citizens or residents). From the perspective of the school of public choice, it is regarded as inappropriate to simply assume that the incentives of the state coincide with the incentives of its members. In particular, the state is expected to pursue its own interests.

6. Given the generally accepted presence of both market failures (e.g. externalities and market power) and state failures (e.g. regulatory capture), it is clear that the policy issue is not market or state but how much market and how much state.

KEY TERMS

Market mechanism
State mechanism
Efficiency considerations
Equity considerations
Market failures
State failures
Public finance perspective
Public choice perspective
Perfect competition
Allocative efficiency
Pareto efficiency
Invisible hand
First welfare theorem

Second welfare theorem
Second best theorem
Externalities
Public goods
Adverse selection
Moral hazard
Principal-agency problems
Market power
Utilitarian social welfare function
Rawlsian social welfare function
Coase theorem
Transactions costs
Property rights

REVIEW QUESTIONS

1. From both a theoretical and policy perspective, discuss briefly the implications of the first and second welfare theorems and the second best theorem.

2. Describe plausible Irish examples, different from those discussed in the text, of the various types of market failure, i.e. externalities, public goods, incomplete information and market power.

3. Describe plausible responses to, and possible remedies for, your examples of market failures. Your answer should encompass both market-based and state remedies.

4. Evaluate the Coase Theorem from a policy perspective. In particular, how realistic is it to expect private negotiations to overcome apparent market failures?

5. From an Irish public policy perspective (e.g. using Irish-based examples), contrast the approach of the public finance school with the approach of the public choice school.

6. Within the following broad categories of public expenditures, describe whether there is, in your opinion, too little or too much public expenditure: education; health; and housing.

MULTI-CHOICE QUESTIONS

1. Adam Smith's invisible hand metaphor is:
   (a) related to Adam Smith's successful career as a conjurer;
   (b) related to the market mechanism's ability to co-ordinate economic actions;
   (c) related to Adam Smith's description of economists' tendency to begin many sentences with the expression 'on the one hand ...';
   (d) none of the above.

2. A situation in which a market left on its own fails to allocate resources efficiently is defined as:
   (a) monopoly;
   (b) market failure;
   (c) oligopoly;
   (d) market power.

3. In the case of positive production externalities:
   (a) too little of the product is produced and too high a price is charged;
   (b) too much of the product is produced and too low a price is charged;
   (c) too little of the product is produced and too low a price is charged;
   (d) too much of the product is produced and too high a price is charged.

4. In the case of negative consumption externalities:
   (a) too little of the product is produced and too high a price is charged;
   (b) too much of the product is produced and too low a price is charged;
   (c) too little of the product is produced and too low a price is charged;
   (d) too much of the product is produced and too high a price is charged.

5. Public goods display:
   (a) rivalry and non-excludability in consumption;
   (b) non-rivalry and non-excludability in consumption;
   (c) non-rivalry and excludability in consumption;
   (d) rivalry and excludability in consumption.

6. Regulatory capture highlights:
   (a) bribery;
   (b) the influence of the private sector on regulators;
   (c) the restraining influence of regulators on the private sector;
   (d) none of the above.

TRUE OR FALSE (SUPPORT YOUR ANSWER)

1. The first theorem of welfare economics addresses equity considerations, while the second theorem of welfare economics addresses efficiency considerations.
2. Adam Smith's invisible hand metaphor suggests that there is no need for private sector involvement in the economy.
3. The Rawlsian social welfare function, relative to the Utilitarian social welfare function, places a higher weight on the less well-off in society.

4. Public private partnerships represent a private-based solution to problems caused by the existence of market failures.
5. The public choice perspective is somewhat suspicious of state involvement in the economy.
6. Arthur Okun's leaky bucket metaphor suggests that there should be no redistribution from rich to poor.

CASE STUDY

Extract from *The Irish Times*
Public-private partnerships to expand
by Gabrielle Monaghan

Public-private partnerships (PPP) will increasingly be used [to] address the issue of scarce government resources, according to a new report by PricewaterhouseCoopers.

The Government has announced plans to set up a new centre of expertise responsible for the procurement of all new PPP projects, with the exception of road and rail, and intends to spend almost €5 billion by 2008 on PPP projects. Indeed, PPPs are a growing element of public sector procurement processes across Europe, PWC said.

'We now have a unique opportunity to build on these solid foundations by applying the lessons learnt to new PPP projects in the education, health, transport, justice and social housing sectors,' said Shane Lyons, the director of PWC's corporate finance unit.

Ireland's first national conference centre, to be built at Spencer Dock in Dublin, will also be constructed as a PPP.

Minister for Transport Martin Cullen expects to raise €240 million from PPPs, he said earlier this month. That is on top of the €1.3 billion that his department has budgeted for road improvements and the €55 million for road maintenance. The N4/N6 road from Dublin to the north-west was the first PPP road project signed as part of the €52 billion National Development Plan for 2000–2006. Four PPP road projects have closed in the Republic in the past five years with a further six in procurement, according to the Pricewaterhouse report.

About 25 per cent of the Transport 21 programme announced earlier in November will be funded through PPPs. Of the €8 billion financed through PPPs, €2 billion will be toll-based road investment.

The State's experimentation with PPPs dates to 1999, when the Government introduced eight pilot PPP projects. By the end of 2001, more than 100 projects were earmarked for procurement through PPP.

Source: The Irish Times, 26 November 2005.

Extract from *The Irish Times*
IBEC seeks to usher in glorious PPP era
by Cantillon (Inside the world of business)

IBEC [the Irish Business and Employers Confederation] wants a new quango. It's calling it the National Infrastructure Development Agency. It wants this agency to usher in a glorious new age of jobs-producing Public Private Partnerships (PPPs).

Haven't we got one of those already? Well, we have the National Development Finance Agency (NDFA), which has a quiet life under the auspices of the National Treasury Management Agency, and has full responsibility for the procurement and delivery of PPPs in sectors other than transport and local authorities. IBEC proposes that the NDFA be merged with National Roads Authority and the Rail Procurement Agency. It also wants the next government to begin an audit of all planned infrastructure projects within the first 100 days of coming to power, with a view to prioritising those that can be funded through PPPs.

The rationale for giving the private sector 'a more extensive role both in the provision and funding of a range of services and infrastructure' lies, on the surface, in the fact that exchequer funding for capital projects is tightening rapidly. The outgoing government envisaged a 60 per cent drop in funding for the public capital programme over the next four years.

But can IBEC really blame anyone in public administration for adopting what the business body claims is an 'uneven' commitment to the PPP funding model? Recent property crash history has yielded many stories of failed PPPs involving developers such as Bernard McNamara (social housing projects) and Pierse (public sector offices).

Of course, the days of Irish developers attempting to cash in on infrastructure projects traditionally in the realm of the exchequer are over. The suction of foreign capital is what IBEC desires. Whether this aim, if achieved, manages to provide the 'significant boost for economic recovery' that IBEC claims it will remains to be seen.

Source: *The Irish Times*, 8 February 2011.

Questions

1. Comment on the recent scale and scope of investments in public private partnerships in Ireland.
2. Should public private partnerships be viewed as being closer to a pure public good or being closer to a pure private good? Explain your answer.
3. Using the internet and other resources as necessary, compare and contrast Ireland's recent experiences with public private partnerships with other EU countries' experiences with public private partnerships.

CHAPTER 9

Microeconomic Policy Issues in Ireland

'The hardest thing in the world to understand is the income tax.'

ALBERT EINSTEIN (1879–1955)

'The Supreme Power who conceived gravity, supply and demand, and the double helix must have been absorbed elsewhere when public utility regulation was invented.'

F. M. SCHERER

CHAPTER OBJECTIVES

Upon completing this chapter, the student should understand:

- the reasons for, and the canons of, taxation;
- the scale and sources of taxation;
- the structure of different types of tax and the political and social importance of taxation;
- the process of competition and the concept and indicators of market power;
- the framework of competition policy in Ireland;
- the natural monopoly problem and possible regulatory solutions;
- public ownership, privatisation and market liberalisation;
- regulation and the Irish banking crisis;
- national partnership agreements and national wage agreements in Ireland.

OUTLINE

9.1 Taxation policy
9.2 Competition policy and regulation
9.3 National Partnership Agreements

INTRODUCTION

There has been a growing awareness in Ireland in recent years of the importance of microeconomic policy issues. For example, recent changes in what may be termed microeconomic tax policy have had large economic, as well as political and social, effects (e.g. the tax treatment of property investments). Similarly, the decisions to open up previously closed sectors of the economy to competition (e.g. telecommunications, postal services) have had a significant impact upon almost every Irish household.

It is also true, of course, that the increased awareness of the importance of microeconomic policy issues has been driven by the realisation that the scope for large-scale macroeconomic policy decision-making has been reduced significantly by the increased role of the European Union (and more specifically the European Central Bank) in monetary policy and by the more recent increased role of the European Union and the International Monetary Fund (IMF) in Irish fiscal policy. Of course, microeconomic policy issues and macroeconomic policy issues should never have been viewed as separate matters. In particular, macroeconomic policy objectives have been, and are, generally pursued through what could be termed as a combination of suitably designed changes in microeconomic policy instruments.

This chapter covers three broadly defined microeconomic policy issues: taxation, competition (including regulation) and national partnership agreements. The chapter begins by reviewing taxation policy. The second part of the chapter deals with competition policy and regulation. The related policy issues of the regulation of specific markets or sectors of the economy, market liberalisation and privatisation are also discussed. The third part of the chapter deals with Ireland's recent experience with national partnership agreements and more specifically with national wage agreements. In respect of each issue, the interested reader is directed to the business and economic media for more up-to-date information.

9.1 TAXATION POLICY

Reasons

There are at least three reasons for the existence of significant levels of taxation in Ireland. First, the state needs to finance the provision of public services, i.e. public goods (e.g. roads, education and health). Second, the state needs to generate funds in order to redistribute income (e.g. jobseekers' payments). Third, the state may use taxes in order to alter behaviour (e.g. carbon taxes). Indeed, if successful this latter motive may lead to the collection of little tax revenue; in this regard, the reader should consider the motivations behind the taxation of alcohol, hydrocarbon oils and tobacco products.

Canons of taxation

Adam Smith developed his so-called canons of taxation in *An Inquiry into the Nature and Causes of the Wealth of Nations* (1776). Given that the significance of taxation has increased dramatically in the intervening two centuries, Smith's canons of equity, certainty, convenience of payment and economy of collection are even more important today. Smith's canons are now generally referred to under the headings of equity, efficiency and effective administration.

1. *Equity* The ability-to-pay principle, which underlies the majority of tax systems, relates an individual's tax payment to the individual's ability to pay, which in practice is generally taken as the individual's level of income. This principle generally suggests the adoption of a progressive tax system. A progressive (regressive) tax structure implies that an individual's average tax payment – the individual's tax payment as a proportion of the individual's income – should increase (decrease) with income. For example, the Irish income tax system's basic structure at least appears progressive; the individual is confronted with tax rates of increasing magnitude (i.e. 0%, 20% and 41%) as the individual's income increases. In contrast, the basic structure of Value Added Taxation (VAT) appears proportional (i.e. neither progressive nor regressive).

2. *Efficiency* Taxes place a wedge between the price received by the seller and the price paid by the buyer. As such, taxes distort market transactions by distorting market signals (i.e. prices). For example, income tax contributes to the wedge between the buying price of labour (the total cost of labour to the employer) and the selling price of labour (the net wage received by the employee). It is likely that many potentially beneficial economic transactions do not take place because of the existence of this so-called tax wedge. Efficiency requires that the distortions that are inevitably caused by the existence of taxation should be as small as possible, subject to meeting the government's revenue requirement.

More technically, the presence of a tax causes an income effect and a substitution effect. The income effect is unavoidable as it relates to the reduction in purchasing power caused by the existence of the tax. For example, if the government collects an extra €100m in excise duties on tobacco products then there is an extra cost of €100m imposed on consumers (or producers and their employees and shareholders) of tobacco products. As such, the income effect can be viewed as arising from a financial transfer from taxpayers to the relevant tax authority (e.g. the Office of the Revenue Commissioners in Ireland). The substitution effect measures the response by consumers to the change in relative prices (i.e. market signals) caused by the tax. For example, smokers react to the presence of excise duties on tobacco products by reducing (to some extent) their consumption of tobacco products. Tax efficiency requires that substitution effects be minimised, subject to meeting the government's revenue requirement. As a general principle, tax efficiency requires that low (high) taxes be placed where economic responses are large (small). For example, it is often argued that low taxes on corporate profits in Ireland are justified from an efficiency perspective as corporations, especially when foreign-owned, are rather mobile. Conversely, it is sometimes argued that high excise duties on alcohol, hydrocarbon oils and tobacco products are justified from an efficiency perspective, as consumers of these products do not appear to be particularly responsive to the high taxes. It should be apparent to the reader that the demands of tax efficiency and tax equity may not work in the same direction.

3. *Effective administration* The effective administration of a tax system requires that the compliance costs of the tax authorities and taxpayers be minimised, subject to meeting the government's revenue requirement. Effective administration also requires the minimisation of tax code uncertainty. Ineffective administration is characterised by the presence of widespread tax evasion and tax avoidance. Tax evasion refers to the illegal non-declaration of taxable monies whereas tax avoidance refers to the legal circumvention of the tax system. A former British Chancellor of the Exchequer, Denis Healey, was quoted as saying 'The difference between tax avoidance and tax evasion is the thickness of a prison wall.'

Scale and sources

It is important to have some knowledge of the scale of taxation and the relative importance of the different types of taxation in Ireland. In the absence of such knowledge, media discussion may give a false impression about the significance of a specific proposed tax change. Expressing total taxation revenue as a proportion of a country's gross domestic product (GDP) is a frequently used measure of the overall scale of taxation in a country. Of the thirty-four members of the Organisation for Economic Co-operation and Development (OECD), only seven countries rank below Ireland in terms of this measure although it should be noted that the use of GDP, as opposed to gross national product (GNP), underestimates the overall scale of taxation in Ireland. However, notwithstanding this and other cross-country comparison difficulties, Ireland cannot (at least at present – early 2011) be classified as a high tax country in overall terms.

Figures on the overall scale of taxation, however, can mask important differences between countries with respect to the composition of taxation revenue. Social security contributions by employees and employers account for a relatively small proportion of Irish tax revenue compared with the mean EU or OECD figure, while taxes on goods and services, which include VAT and excise duties, account for a relatively large proportion of Irish tax revenue compared with the mean EU or OECD figure. Differences between Ireland and other EU/OECD members reflect different national features (e.g. age profiles) and priorities (e.g. treatment of foreign investment). However, in an increasingly integrated European market, at least some of these differences may be expected to decline (e.g. taxes on goods and services or perhaps, and much more controversially from an Irish perspective, corporation tax).

Types of tax

Income tax

Income tax is charged on income accruing to all residents in the Irish state, whether arising within or outside the state, and on the income of non-residents generated within the Irish state, to an extent which depends on the double taxation agreements between Ireland and the home country of the non-resident. Income is taxed according to two main schedules in Ireland. Income from an office, employment or pension (Schedule E) is taxed on a Pay As You Earn (PAYE) basis with the employer typically deducting tax from the employee's gross income. Profits from trade, professions, etc., rental income, interest income and income from abroad is taxed according to Schedule D; this category encompasses the income of the self-employed.

Income taxes are imposed according to a given table, which is typically subject to change in the annual Budget, which is usually presented by the Minister for Finance in early December. The present system in Ireland, as of 1 January 2011, has two tax rates: a standard rate of 20% and a higher rate of 41%. The standard rate applies as soon as the individual's tax-free credits are used up. The automatic personal tax credit is €1,650 for an individual and €3,300 for a married couple; there is also an extra PAYE tax credit of €1,650 available to those individuals taxed under Schedule E. The width of the standard rate tax band is €32,800 for an individual, €41,800 for a one-income married couple and a maximum of €65,600 for a two-income married couple. The distinction between two-income and one-income married couples represents partial individualisation of the standard rate band; the introduction of this policy caused significant political controversy.

A number of important discretionary (i.e. not automatically available to all) tax credits and tax allowances are also available and these can significantly reduce the individual's income tax payment and affect the progressiveness of the income tax code. Perhaps the most important of these are the allowances against tax of contributions to pension funds and superannuation schemes, which are intended to encourage individuals to provide for retirement.

Pay Related Social Insurance and Universal Social Charge

Social insurance contributions by both employees and employers are used to support so-called social provisions (e.g. state pensions). Social insurance contributions are referred to in Ireland as Pay Related Social Insurance (PRSI). The PRSI system is complex, with a variety of rates and conditions applying to different classes of insured individuals. Most employees, including the self-employed, contribute 4% of gross income, with a weekly (non-cumulative) allowance of

€127. In addition, employees earning less than €352 per week are exempt from employee PRSI. The standard rate of employer contribution is 10.75% on all incomes. However, the employer rate for incomes at or below €356 per week is reduced to 8.5%, with the rate jumping to 10.75% on all income once income rises above this threshold.

The newly introduced Universal Social Charge, which has replaced the health levy and the income levy, applies on all incomes (although those earning less than €4,004 will be exempt). A rate of 2% applies on the first €10,036; a rate of 4% applies on the earnings between €10,036 and €16,016; and a rate of 7% applies on earnings above €16,016.

Value Added Tax and excise duties

The Value Added Tax (VAT) system is a highly integrated sales tax, where the tax is levied at each stage of production and distribution and where companies at each stage are required to account for the tax. VAT is imposed upon a large range of goods and services in Ireland at rates up to the standard rate of 21% (which is due to increase to 22% in 2013 and 23% in 2014 as a result of Ireland's austerity measures). Some foods, children's clothing and children's footwear are among a small number of products that are zero-rated while a small number of other products (e.g. residential childcare) are exempt from VAT. The allocation of products between the 13.5% reduced rate and the 21% standard rate appears somewhat arbitrary but was influenced in the past by employment considerations. For example, the lower rate was probably imposed in garage services and hairdressing so as to encourage employment in these areas.

Excise duties are imposed across a small range of products in Ireland. The major excisable products are alcohol, hydrocarbon oils, motor vehicles and tobacco products. These products have in the past been collectively referred to as 'sin' goods. Perhaps this partially explains why approximately 80% of the price of a packet of cigarettes is accounted for by a combination of VAT and excise duties. Equivalent figures for a litre of (unleaded) petrol, a pint of stout and a pint of lager are approximately 61%, 29% and 28%, respectively.

Corporation tax

A key feature of the Irish corporate tax system used to be its dual rate structure. There was a standard rate of corporation tax, which was at times, even within the past decade, levied at a rate of over 30%; and a preferential rate of 10% on profits in manufacturing and certain internationally traded service activities. However, the different rates were unified at 12.5% from the beginning of 2003. The original rationale for the lower rate of 10% in manufacturing was so as to encourage the expansion of employment, particularly by the influx of foreign investment.

The rationale for unifying the various rates at 12.5% was twofold. First, it is unlikely that the EU would have allowed a lower rate to apply only to internationally mobile sectors in the future; other EU countries would be likely to lose out in such a scenario. This factor supported the unification of rates across sectors. Second, there appears to have been a consensus within Irish society that capital, relative to labour, had become increasingly mobile. This factor supported a low tax being imposed on capital. However, it appears that a number of other EU countries would like Ireland to increase the 12.5% rate significantly.

Policy Areas

Income tax and social welfare

Although taxation and social welfare may warrant separate administrative units in Ireland, it is not possible to evaluate separately the effects of the social welfare and taxation systems on equity and efficiency.

For the unemployed, the social welfare safety net takes the form of jobseeker's assistance/benefits together with other allowances such as differential rent and medical cards (which entitle the holder to free medical care). For the employed on a low income, the social welfare safety net may take the form of family income supplement (FIS) for those with children, together with other allowances such as differential rent and medical cards. Interactions between the tax and social welfare systems almost inevitably lead to the existence of unemployment and poverty traps, particularly for households with a relatively large number of children (see Chapter 17 for more details). An unemployment trap is said to exist when an individual or household is as well off, in monetary terms, unemployed as employed. A poverty trap is said to exist when an individual or household faces a marginal tax and benefit withdrawal rate of at least 100%, i.e. an increase in gross income gives rise to a decrease in net income. Significant improvements in this area have been made by relating family income supplement payments more closely to net, as opposed to gross, income.

In addition, and from a broader perspective, both the income and social welfare systems will likely be forced in the near future to address the related issues of individualisation of the tax and social welfare codes and the relative treatment of married and unmarried couples.

Tax harmonisation

With the increased openness of world economies many countries are under pressure to follow taxation and expenditure patterns established elsewhere. Within the context of the EU, for example, rather strict tax harmonisation guidelines have been issued with respect to VAT. Looser guidelines have also been issued in the area of corporation tax, with EU member states being somewhat more comfortable with the harmonisation of tax bases as opposed to the harmonisation of tax rates. These guidelines, together with other considerations, have led the Irish government to equalise corporation tax rates across the different sectors of the Irish economy. Even when there is an absence of formal guidelines, arbitrage opportunities place some limits on the extent of tax differences between countries. Indeed, variations in the levels of excise duties imposed on alcohol, hydrocarbon oils and tobacco products across countries within the EU have decreased considerably in the past twenty years.

Property and wealth taxes

Ireland is rather unusual in that it collects a very small proportion of its taxes from what can be broadly termed property and wealth taxes. Up until 1977 Ireland had a very broad-based system of property taxes or rates that financed local authorities' expenditures; in that year those taxes attaching to residential property were abolished. Not only did this result in a significant reduction in revenue, it also removed the economic underpinnings of local government in Ireland. The re-introduction of a residential property tax in the 1980s was very controversial, despite the tax rate being very low and applying only above a very high property value threshold (at the time). The residential tax was abolished in 1997. The likely re-introduction of a property tax in Ireland is certain to provoke much political controversy.

There have been no taxes imposed on wealth *per se* in Ireland since 1977. However, some revenue is collected from the taxation of capital transfer between individuals, in particular the capital acquisitions tax. The capital acquisitions tax is a tax levied on the recipient of the transfer of assets belonging to a recently deceased individual. The tax is supported by the taxation of transfers (gifts) between living individuals.

9.2 COMPETITION POLICY AND REGULATION

Competition

Other sections of this textbook address in detail the issue of the importance of market structure; the reader should review these sections as appropriate. In these other sections, the market characteristics and outcomes associated with perfect competition are contrasted with the market characteristics and outcomes associated with monopoly; perfectly competitive markets are seen generally to perform well relative to monopolistic markets.

Allocative efficiency

In particular, perfectly competitive markets have the characteristic of being allocatively efficient, as firms are forced by their own self-interests to price at marginal cost, i.e. $P = MC$.[1] This equality between price and marginal cost is regarded as highly desirable by economists as price represents the value placed by society on the marginal unit of the product while marginal cost represents the cost to society of producing that marginal unit. Consider the two alternatives: (i) price is greater than marginal cost (i.e. $P > MC$); and (ii) price is less than marginal cost (i.e. $P < MC$). If price is greater than marginal cost, then the marginal value (or benefit) to society of an extra unit is greater than the marginal cost to society of producing that extra unit. As such, more of the product should be produced; society's resources are being allocated inefficiently. Indeed, the primary disadvantage associated with a monopolistic market structure is that the monopolist produces a level of output at which price is greater than marginal cost (i.e. $P > MC$). Alternatively, if price is less than marginal cost, then the marginal value (or benefit) to society of the last unit produced is less than the marginal cost to society of producing that last unit. As such, less of the product should be produced; society's resources are again being allocated inefficiently. However, if price is equal to marginal cost (i.e. $P = MC$), society requires neither more nor less of the product; society's resources are being allocated efficiently.

    The state is seldom given a stark choice between choosing a perfectly competitive structure or a monopolist structure for a particular market. However, the state can attempt to facilitate the conditions or characteristics that encourage outcomes associated with perfectly competitive markets. In short, the state can encourage the competitive process. Broadly defined, a state's competition policy attempts to protect and enhance the process of competition. The process of competition, although difficult to define, is facilitated by the presence of effective competition and/or potential competition. Effective competition focuses particular attention on the degree of interbrand, and intrabrand, competition between firms within a particular market. Interbrand competition refers to competition between sellers of different products or brands within a given market; for example, Coca-Cola and PepsiCo may be said to compete within the soft drinks (or even cola) market. Intrabrand competition refers to competition between sellers of the same product or brand; for example, Tesco and Dunnes Stores compete to sell Coca-Cola to consumers. Potential competition focuses particular attention on the ability of potential entrants, via the threat of entry, to dissuade incumbent firms from abusing their market position.

Market power

The presence of market power does not support the process of competition. An individual firm is said to have market power when it has the ability to price above marginal cost. A perfectly competitive firm does not have market power, as it cannot (profitably) price above marginal cost; in contrast, a monopolist has market power as it can (profitably) price above marginal cost. As noted above, pricing above marginal cost is inefficient (from society's perspective) as it means that too little of the product is being produced. In practice, almost all firms have some degree of market power. However, it is generally accepted that the process of competition is only threatened when a firm (or a small number of firms acting collectively) has substantial market power, i.e. the firm has the ability to price significantly above marginal cost.

Ideally the existence, or otherwise, of substantial market power could be identified by a close inspection of data on a firm's own-price elasticity of demand. As described in detail in Chapter 3, a firm's own-price elasticity of demand measures the percentage decrease in demand that would follow from a percentage increase in the price of the firm's product. A low own-price elasticity (in absolute terms) signals the possession of substantial market power as the firm has the ability to significantly increase price without losing significant market share.[2] The general non-availability of data on own-price elasticities of demand, however, leads to the need for indirect indicators of the existence, or otherwise, of substantial market power. Typical indicators include data and information on market shares and market concentration, entry barriers into and exit barriers from the market and the competitive environment within the market. These indicators attempt to identify the presence, or otherwise, of substantial market power in the context of a previously well-defined market. The first step, therefore, is the defining of the relevant market. As an example, the reader should consider whether cola constitutes a relevant market for the purposes of competition policy, or whether the relevant market should be broader and encompass (at least) other soft drinks.

Market power and market definition

The relevant market, for competition policy purposes, is thought of as representing the minimum set of products over which a (hypothetical) firm would have to have monopoly control before it could be sure of exercising a given degree of market power. In practice, this 'given degree of market power' is generally perceived of as the ability to profitably raise prices (above competitive levels) by 5% for a significant period of time (say, a year).[3]

The European Commission and the Irish Competition Authority have, in the past, adopted the following somewhat simpler, but more intuitive, approach to market definition and market power. A market is said to be composed of those products that are regarded as interchangeable or substitutable by the consumer, by reason of the products' characteristics and their intended use. Market power, in turn, is defined as a position of economic strength enjoyed by a firm that enables it to hinder the maintenance of effective competition on the relevant market by allowing it to behave to an appreciable extent independently of competitors and ultimately of consumers.

Market power and market concentration

Once the market has been established the market shares of the market participants and overall market concentration should be estimated. Regulatory authorities have commonly adopted two alternative approaches for this purpose – concentration ratios and the Herfindahl-Hirschman Index (HHI).

Definition

A concentration ratio measures the total market share of a given number of the largest firms.

For example, the C_4 ratio measures the total market share of the four largest firms in a market.

> **Definition**
> *The Herfindahl-Hirschman Index is defined as the sum of the squared percentage shares of all firms of the relevant variable (sales, assets . . .) in the market.*

As such, the HHI varies between just above 0 (corresponding to a market with a very large number of very small firms) and 10,000 (corresponding to a market with a single firm, i.e. a pure monopoly). For example, a market consisting of only two equally sized firms would have an HHI of 5000 (= $50^2 + 50^2$) whereas a market consisting of five equally sized firms would have an HHI of 2000. A market with an HHI below 1000 is generally regarded as a non-concentrated market and, hence, as a market in which market power issues are unlikely to arise. A market with an HHI above approximately 2000 is generally regarded as a concentrated market and as a market in which significant market power issues may arise.

Market power and barriers to entry

Market power is only likely to exist when there is both high market concentration and high entry barriers. Without entry barriers, any attempt by an incumbent firm or incumbent firms to abuse an apparent position of market power is likely to simply attract entry by other firms. The definition of entry barriers, however, provokes the greatest degree of disharmony between protagonists of the so-called Chicago and Harvard Schools. The Chicago School tends to view entry barriers as being restricted to '. . . costs that must be borne by an entrant that were not incurred by established firms.'[4] In the extreme, so-called Chicago economists only accept restrictive licensing schemes as being valid examples of entry barriers. Within an Irish context, legal barriers against entry into the markets for the provision of certain postal services (e.g. standard letter post) or certain bus services (e.g. many commuter routes in Dublin) would be regarded as being examples of entry barriers. Harvard and the majority of other economists have a broader definition of entry barriers in mind. The Harvard School defines entry barriers as any '. . . factors that enable established firms to earn supra-competitive profits without threat of entry'.[5] Economies of scale, excess capacity, lower average costs as a result of experience (learning-by-doing), brand proliferation, restrictive distributional agreements and product differentiation (perhaps as a result of excessive advertising) represent some of the major examples of entry barriers as at least potentially justified by this broader definition of entry barriers.

Market power and competitive environment

The overly mechanical reliance on summary statistics on market concentration (and entry barriers, where available) is fraught with some danger. The existence or otherwise of a non-competitive environment within a market should also be considered. By non-competitive environment is meant the market conditions that would facilitate tacit or explicit price co-ordination between competitors. The presence of a trade association may, for example, be indicative of conditions that would facilitate tacit or explicit price co-ordination between competitors. Although difficult to quantify precisely, a non-competitive market structure that facilitated the altering of pricing (and other dimensions of competition, say advertising) strategies at exactly the same point in time, in the same direction and by the same magnitude is not conducive to the restraint of market power.

Example: the Irish Competition Authority's *Interim Report of the Study on the Newspaper Industry* (1995) provided a number of interesting details on the pricing policies of market participants within the newspaper market(s): '*The Irish Times* and *Irish Independent* have repeatedly increased prices on the same day and by the same amount while constantly maintaining a price differential of 5p between them,' and '. . . prices of the *Evening Herald* and *Evening Press* have repeatedly changed simultaneously over the period since 1984. Throughout this period the retail price of both titles were identical.'

More generally, when reviewing the issue of co-ordination between competitors, there is an examination of the market for the presence, or absence, of the following features (whose presence would tend to be supportive of tacit collusion): product homogeneity; firm structure homogeneity; symmetry in market shares; stability in market shares; transparency with respect to trading conditions (and, in particular, transparency with respect to prices), low price elasticity of demand (reducing the incentive to 'cheat' on any implicit understanding); the non-existence of maverick firms; the non-existence of strong buyers; and the non-existence of excess capacity.

Competition policy in Ireland

Legislation to prohibit restrictive business practices in Ireland was first enacted in 1953 with the Restrictive Trade Practices Act that established the Fair Trade Commission. Legislation was based on the 'control of abuse' principle with restrictive practices considered on a case-by-case basis. The Minister (for Industry and Commerce), on the advice of the Commission, could issue a Restrictive Practice Order to cover a particular trade. A failing of competition policy in Ireland over past decades was that it was Order-led; for sectors of the economy not covered by an Order, it remained legal to engage in price-fixing and market-sharing. Repeated enquiries were carried out into the behaviour of several trades as new anti-competitive practices emerged. Policy towards mergers and monopolies was dictated by a separate piece of legislation – the Mergers, Take-overs and Monopolies (Control) Act 1978. The Minister for Enterprise, Trade and Employment had sole jurisdiction over acquisitions and mergers. Although this Act could also have been used to impose severe sanctions on monopolies, no such sanctions were imposed.

The Competition Acts

The Competition Act 1991 introduced a prohibition-based system of competition law to Ireland. Anti-competitive agreements between undertakings (firms) and restrictive trade practices are prohibited under Section 4 and the abuse of a dominant position (e.g. predatory pricing or unjustified price discrimination) is prohibited under Section 5. The Competition Authority was established under the Act to play a supportive and advisory role; it had no enforcement powers. The passing into legislation of the Competition (Amendment) Bill 1996 represented a significant change in emphasis. The primary aim of this legislation was to provide more effective enforcement of competition policy. It became a criminal offence not to comply with the conditions of a licence granted by the Authority. This Act also criminalised certain anti-competitive behaviour and allowed for prison sentences of up to two years and fines of up to 10% of a firm's world-wide turnover. New powers of search and greater rights of discovery, including the right to conduct a 'dawn raid', were granted to the Competition Authority and the ability to initiate prosecutions, both civil and criminal, was given to the Authority. Furthermore, it could carry out studies without being requested to do so by the Minister. The Competition Act 2002 represented a further significant piece of legislation. Almost total responsibility for mergers was transferred to the

Authority, penalties for hardcore cartel cases were increased and the Authority's search powers were increased. The Competition Act 2006 was designed to prevent certain business practices in the Irish groceries sector.

Regulation policy

Competition policy is complementary to the process of competition as it attempts to facilitate the market conditions that give rise to market outcomes associated with perfectly competitive markets. For example, competition policy attempts to facilitate ease of entry into (and exit from) a market and attempts to create the conditions generally associated with a competitive environment. Competition policy does not replace, or substitute itself for, the process of competition. More specifically, competition policy does not dictate the number of firms within a market or the price (output) that individual firms can charge (produce).

In contrast, regulation policy generally substitutes directly for the process of competition. Regulation policy tends to dictate the number of firms within a market and/or the price (output) that individual firms can charge (produce). Electricity, natural gas, telecommunications and transportation represent just some examples of the many markets that are, or have recently been, regulated in this sense in many countries.

From an economic perspective, the major justification for the use of regulation policy, as opposed to competition policy, is the existence of so-called natural monopolies. However, regulation policy may also be used for other purposes; the 'public interest' has been used to justify the use of regulation policy in many contexts. For example, the state has asserted a public interest in the existence of a concentrated transportation market in Ireland in the past. In addition, the case study at the end of this section considers the regulation of the financial services sector.

Definition

A market is said to be a natural monopoly if its total output can be produced more cheaply by a single firm than by two or more firms.

Technically, a natural monopoly exists if $C(Q) = C(Q_1 + \ldots + Q_N) < C(Q_1) + \ldots + C(Q_1)$, where Q represents total output, $C(Q)$ represents the total cost of producing Q and N represents the relevant number of firms.[6] A natural monopoly exists if there are very significant economies of scale. In such a case, an individual firm's marginal cost (MC) and average cost (AC) curves decline continuously and the firm's marginal cost (MC) curve will be below its average cost (AC) curve over the relevant range of output. From an economics perspective, the existence of a natural monopoly gives rise to serious concerns. The natural monopolist, being a monopolist, has an incentive to maximise profits by producing a level of output at which price is greater than marginal cost, i.e. resources are allocated inefficiently. The natural monopolist can be regulated in a number of ways.

Marginal cost pricing

The regulator can apparently achieve allocative efficiency by simply insisting that the natural monopolist produce a level of output at which price is equal to marginal cost. There are at least two problems with this proposed solution. First, the regulator may not have enough information to be able to determine the output level at which price is equal to marginal cost and it would not be in the natural monopolist's interest to help in this regard. Second, if the natural monopolist produces the allocatively efficient level of output, it will sustain losses. Pricing at marginal cost implies pricing below average cost as the marginal cost curve of the monopolist lies below the average cost curve of the natural monopolist. One possible solution to this latter problem is for the regulator to provide the natural monopolist with a subsidy to offset the losses associated with achieving allocative efficiency. However, these subsidies must be financed by increased taxes elsewhere; these increased taxes, of course, also lead to inefficiencies. It may also be difficult politically to provide a natural monopolist with a subsidy.

Average cost pricing

The problems associated with implementing marginal cost pricing have tended to lead regulators towards the adoption of some form of average cost pricing. Setting price at average cost avoids the problem of having to subsidise the natural monopolist but at the expense of sacrificing allocative efficiency. Pricing at average cost ensures that the natural monopolist makes neither economic profits nor economic losses. However, average cost pricing regulation suffers from the problem of dampening cost-reducing incentives. For example, if the natural monopolist succeeds in reducing costs by 10%, the regulator may respond by insisting that prices are also reduced by 10%. Indeed, the natural monopolist has no obvious reason not to allow costs to actually increase.[7] In practice, average cost pricing is often adapted so as to encourage innovation by allowing for some profits. This type of regulation – adjusted average cost pricing – is referred to as rate-of-return regulation. More recently, regulators have tended to impose limits on future price increase; these limits are often linked to future inflation rates. For example, so called 'CPI-X' regulation limits the future price increase to X percentage points below the future inflation rate. Should the natural monopolist decrease costs by more than X percentage points, the natural monopolist is allowed to keep the supernormal profits, at least until the next price review.

Franchise bidding

Rather than regulating the natural monopolist on an ongoing basis, it may be preferable to auction the (franchise) rights to be the natural monopolist in the first place. If the auction is done on the basis of the highest bid winning, the outcome is likely to be equivalent to a standard monopoly outcome. However, the monopoly profits are transferred to the state as a result of the bidding process as the bidders would find themselves forced to bid higher and higher amounts until almost no net profits could be gained. A possible alternative is for the auction to be done on the basis of bidders committing to charging a certain price to customers in the future. The results of this process are likely to be close to the results obtained by average cost pricing regulation, as bidders would find themselves forced to offer lower and lower prices until almost no net profits could be expected. A further possibility is for the 'auction' to be done on the basis of a number of criteria; 'bidders' would then compete on the basis of quality as well as price considerations. This latter possibility is often referred to as a 'beauty contest'. Most real-world auctions consist of a combination of the above types of auction.

Public enterprise and privatisation

Rather than the state attempting to regulate the natural monopolist, many governments, particularly in Europe, have in the past elected to actually be the natural monopolist. The distinctive feature (and advantage or disadvantage depending on one's political, economic and social perspective) of this approach is that the objective of the natural monopolist is no longer necessarily the maximisation of private profits. The management of a public enterprise must ultimately be somewhat accountable to voters as opposed to shareholders and, as such, it is possible that the management's goal will be the maximisation of public welfare as opposed to private profit. Within an Irish context, airport management, electricity, telecommunications and transportation provide just four of the many possible recent examples of state ownership. However, a sustained movement away from public ownership and enterprise and towards privatisation began in the early 1980s. Within a European context, the UK government led by Margaret Thatcher was at the forefront of this movement; the privatisation of British Telecom (1984) and British Gas (1986) represented very significant economic and political events.

Ireland and market liberalisation

Many of the large privatisations in the UK were followed by the subsequent setting up of specialist independent regulatory agencies (e.g. Oftel and Ofgas), as public monopolies were simply being replaced by private monopolies. The over-riding lesson from the UK privatisation experience appears to have been that the creation of market conditions suitable for facilitating the process of competition or the continued or renewed regulation of a natural monopoly was at least as important as the actual nominal ownership structure (i.e. public or private enterprise).

Arguably, given other countries' mixed fortunes with respect to privatisation (see Chapter 19), it was fortuitous that Ireland came relatively late to privatisation. After successfully selling its stakes in Irish Life and the Irish Sugar Company (now Greencore) in 1991, the state privatised eircom (previously known as Telecom Éireann) in 1999. Initially, the privatisation proved to be a political success as eircom's share price increased by over 20% above its flotation price. However, eircom's share price subsequently fell back to well below the flotation price. Indeed, eircom's share price remained well below the flotation price for the remainder of its initial spell as a public limited company. The eircom share price experience has had significant repercussions (e.g. lengthy and ongoing postponements) for other proposed privatisations in Ireland, e.g. the VHI.

More generally, however, it appears that in Ireland the high level debate no longer surrounds the exclusive public ownership versus exclusive private ownership issue as opposed to the micro details of continued market liberalisation. In particular, within the context of goods and services previously provided by the public service, exclusive public ownership/provision no longer appears to be the preferred option for any of the social partners as, for example, the public sector unions appear focused on the details of the associated employees share ownership plans (ESOP). In addition, so-called public private partnerships (PPPs) have been set up to fund and provide major infrastructural projects (e.g. roads and local area redevelopments).

Market liberalisation, via continued deregulation – or what should more accurately be referred to as re-regulation – continues apace in Ireland. One obvious example is provided by the very significant changes in the regulation of taxis, and in particular in the huge increase in the number of taxi plates (e.g. in Dublin). Other examples include the abolition of the Groceries Order, which restricted retailers from passing on certain (i.e. off-invoice) discounts to consumers and the abolition on restrictions on the location of retail pharmacies. Somewhat more controversial examples include the entry of the private sector into domestic refuse collection and the provision of a national car testing service. The latter examples highlight the need for the state to place appropriate safeguards on the behaviour of private firms once these private firms find themselves in at least temporary monopoly situations. Again, the central issue appears to be the appropriate regulation of a natural monopolist, as opposed to the identity (i.e. public or private) of the natural monopolist.

CASE STUDY

The Irish Banking Crisis: Regulatory and Financial Stability Policy 2003–2008
Chapter 1: Summary and Conclusions

Consider the following extracts from Chapter 1 of the report on the Irish banking crisis (also and more generally known as the 'Honohan Report')

Section 1: Introduction

1.1 This Report covers the period from the establishment of the FR [Financial Regulator] in 2003 to the end of September 2008 when the provision of exceptional Government support, in the form of the comprehensive State Guarantee for the liabilities of the Irish domestic banking system was announced. It deals with two distinct aspects: crisis prevention (in the years before 2008); and crisis containment (starting with the onset of the global liquidity crisis in August 2007).

1.2 The Report seeks to answer two questions. First, why was the danger from the emerging imbalances in the financial system that led to the crisis not identified more clearly and earlier and headed-off through decisive measures? Secondly, when the crisis began to break, were the best containment measures adopted?

. . .

Section 4: Overall Conclusions

. . .

1.30 Apart from the CBFSAI [Central Bank & Financial Services Authority of Ireland], banking practice and Government policy both clearly played a role in contributing to the crisis:

i) there is prima facie evidence of a comprehensive failure of bank management and direction to maintain safe and sound banking practices, instead incurring huge external liabilities in order to support a credit-fuelled property market and construction frenzy, and

ii) macroeconomic and budgetary policies contributed significantly to the economic overheating, relying to a clearly unsustainable extent on the construction sector and other transient sources for Government revenue (and encouraging the property boom via various incentives geared at the construction sector). This helped create a climate of public opinion which was led to believe that the party could last forever. A less accommodating and procyclical policy would have greatly reduced the need for preventive action from the CBFSAI.

1.31 As regards the CBFSAI, the root causes appear to have been threefold:

i) a regulatory approach which was and was perceived to be excessively deferential and accommodating; insufficiently challenging and not persistent enough. This meant not moving decisively and effectively enough against banks with governance issues. It also meant that corrective regulatory intervention for the system as a whole was delayed and timid. This was in an environment which placed undue emphasis on fears of upsetting the competitive position of domestic banks and on encouraging the Irish financial services industry even at the expense of prudential considerations.

ii) an under-resourced approach to bank supervision that, by relying on good governance and risk-management procedures, neglected quantitative assessment and the need to ensure sufficient capital to absorb the growing property-related risks.

iii) an unwillingness by the CBFSAI to take on board sufficiently the real risk of a looming problem and act with sufficient decision and force to head it off in time. 'Rocking the boat' and swimming against the tide of public opinion would have required a particularly strong sense of the independent role of a central bank in being prepared to 'spoil the party' and withstand possible strong adverse public reaction.

Source: *A Report to the Minister for Finance by the Governor of the Central Bank*, 31 May 2010.

Questions

1. Using the above material as well as other sections of the above report, as well as any other sources that you deem appropriate, describe the following regulatory terms: light-touch regulation; principle-based regulation; rules-based regulation; and regulatory capture.
2. Outline your opinion as to which factor was most to blame for the Irish banking crisis.
3. Briefly discuss the (to some extent ongoing) resolution of the Irish banking crisis. In particular, describe the present structure of the Irish banking sector and compare it briefly with the structure from, say, five or ten years ago.

Answers on website

9.3 NATIONAL PARTNERSHIP AGREEMENTS

The neoclassical model of the factor markets is very useful in explaining and predicting events in large economies such as the United States. Ergas (1984) suggests that in the United States, market changes which lead to the reallocation of the factors of production are generally perceived of as being legitimate. In particular, there is a strong 'exit' mechanism tradition, with labour (and capital) resources, when dissatisfied, having the ability to vote with their feet.[8] For example, if steel cannot be produced cheaply enough in Pittsburgh to compete on the world markets, the owners of the mills can move production to another state or (albeit more controversially) another country where steel can be produced more cost-effectively. The unemployed steelworkers can, to some extent at least, move to a new sector in Pittsburgh, or leave the area to find more suitable employment. Because the country is very large and the economy is highly diversified, there is scope for movement of the factors of production as well as a strong belief in the efficiency and even fairness of the market.

In contrast, Ergas argues that western European economies rely on 'voice' rather than 'exit'. Ergas claims that in Europe, 'change is induced through consensus and through the conscious societal weighting of interests and options, buttressed by mechanisms for redistributing income between winners and losers'.[9] Ergas argues that Europeans do not have the same 'faith' in the legitimacy of market outcomes and notes that, '. . . it can be argued that the Western European economies, being considerably smaller, could not smoothly absorb the levels of social conflict tolerable in large, geographically mobile and diverse societies like the United States'.[10]

Compared to the US economy, however, the Irish economy is both 'small' and 'open'. Ireland is also small in comparison to many of the other EU economies. It is open in the sense that both imports and exports are very large in relation to national income. This means that the Irish economy is very exposed and vulnerable to disruptions in international markets. The neoclassical model is probably a rather poor starting point to discuss the Irish factor markets, particularly the labour market since 1987, as the Irish government has been actively involved with representatives of business, labour unions, the farming community and the voluntary sector in establishing an economic and social framework called the national partnership agreement (NPA). Seven such agreements were negotiated since 1987. A brief history of the national partnership agreements follows, with some details on the associated seven national wage agreements.

History of the national partnership agreements

In the 1980s, the Irish economy was in crisis. During a prolonged recession, and in spite of massive emigration, the unemployment rate approached 18%. The spectre of national insolvency loomed as the debt to GNP ratio approached 130%. To pay for government spending and to service the debt, tax rates had to be increased significantly. The high income tax rates combined with a high inflation rate meant that the living standards of workers were falling. Many emigrated to the United Kingdom and the United States. Workers who remained 'took to the streets' for higher pay and lower income taxes.

In 1986, the National Economic and Social Council (NESC), an advisory board comprising organisations representing employers, trade unions and farming organisations, together with civil servants, published *A Strategy for Development*. This formed the basis of the first of seven national partnership agreements. The agreements were negotiated between the social partners. The composition of the social partners for the first three agreements included the government and organisations representing trade unions, employers and farming interests. Beginning with the second partnership agreement, submissions were considered from organisations representing children, parents, women, religious denominations, various trade interests and the unemployed. From the fourth partnership agreement onwards, the composition of the social partners expanded to include formally and explicitly the community and voluntary sector.

As the membership expanded, so too did the number of topics included in the agreements. One of the principal initial reasons for entering into the agreement was to break the 'wage/price' spiral that caused labour unrest and contributed to inflation in the 1980s. Periodic increases in wages were negotiated as part of all of the agreements. The social partners also outlined the broad parameters of tax reform, social welfare payments and government spending. They agreed to changes to improve the industrial relations machinery and to modernise the public sector. The agreements were negotiated with various governments and survived changes in government but (apparently) not the recent recession.

The national wage agreement (NWA) was a cornerstone of each of the partnership agreements. Generally, this was the part of the agreement that received the most coverage in the national press. A partnership agreement was generally deemed a success if the provisions of the pay agreement were negotiated and subsequently (more or less) maintained. However, the most cursory examination of the latter partnership agreements reveals that a partnership agreement was more than just a wage agreement. It was a general framework for economic and social progress.

The national wage agreements

The general thrust of each of the wage agreements was to increase 'take-home pay' while restraining 'nominal pay'. In other words, gross pay, or the amount paid by firms, increased by relatively small amounts each year. However, and simultaneously, the government, particularly in the earlier partnership agreements, implemented changes to personal taxation so that the net pay of workers increased significantly.

Maintaining moderate increases in gross wages meant that firms could retain profits. This provided the source of funds needed to increase investment. Particularly in 1987, when the first agreement – the Programme for National Recovery (PNR) – was negotiated, the lack of growth in investment was a cause of great concern. The social partners agreed that this had to change so as to support higher levels of employment in the future.

The duration of each of the first six agreements was approximately three years, with the planned maximum duration of the seventh agreement – Towards 2016 – being ten years. Annual percentage increases in the basic wage ranged between 2% and 7.5% for the eighteen-year period associated with the first six agreements. An 'inability to pay' clause was introduced in the second agreement – Programme for Economic and Social Progress (PESP). It stated that increases should be negotiated through industrial relations machinery, considering the competitive circumstances of the firm. Also beginning with PESP, there were special considerations designed to increase the basic wage of the very low paid. ICTU (Irish Congress of Trade Unions) expressed a desire to implement a minimum wage in the PESP published in 1991. This became a reality in 2000, as discussed in Section 7.1. A local bargaining clause that allowed for a small additional increase in the basic wage was a feature of the second, fourth and sixth agreements.

The fourth agreement – Partnership 2000 – promoted the development of 'enterprise partnership'. One of the topics discussed was 'financial involvement'. The ambiguity of language allowed business and labour to interpret this as a local bargaining clause. An enterprise, in compliance with the national wage agreement, could increase the basic wage by the amount specified in the national wage agreement and in addition implement an employee participation scheme in the form of gain sharing (e.g. sharing of productivity gains and cost savings), profit sharing and employee share ownership schemes. Trade unions published local partnership agreements featuring employee participation schemes, providing models for other firms to follow.

One might wonder why at least some of the social partners did not object to this interpretation of the agreement. During Partnership 2000 (1997–2000), the unemployment rate was falling and skills shortages were developing in many sectors. It is likely that the social partners believed that the national wage agreement, and hence the national partnership agreement, would unravel if enterprises did not have a way of increasing employee remuneration to attract and maintain their staff. The latter agreements maintained this ambiguity.

Negotiations for the fifth agreement – Programme for Prosperity and Fairness (PPF) – which was published in 1999 were particularly difficult. Labour market shortages meant that firms in some sectors, particularly those dominated by multinational corporations, were offering wage increases at the end of Partnership 2000 which were well above the agreed limits to attract and retain staff. These increases were in excess of what other sectors, often dominated by indigenous firms, could afford to pay. Workers were concerned that they were not benefiting sufficiently from the economic boom. The wage increases for the PPF were higher than for any other agreement. However, when the inflation rate increased to 6% during 2000, it completely wiped out the value of the 5.5% increase negotiated for that year. ICTU used the review clause that was part of the agreement to insist that the pay increase be renegotiated. After another round of intensive negotiations, unions and employers' organisations agreed to an additional 2% increase to be paid from April 2001 and a 1% once-off lump sum to be paid from April 2002. The government had already signalled significant tax cuts to 'copper-fasten' the agreement.

Did the agreements work?

In other chapters we discuss the spectacular performance of the Irish economy during the 1990s.

Most commentators believe that the national partnership agreements helped at least to some extent in establishing the conditions for the recovery of the Irish economy. In this section we approach this question from the specific perspective of the labour market. Did the national wage agreements improve the situation of Irish labour? One important labour market indicator is the unemployment rate. This is the number of unemployed people divided by the number of people in the labour force (see Section 17.2 for more information). Table 9.1 shows the numbers unemployed and the corresponding unemployment rates between 1988 and 2010.

TABLE 9.1: UNEMPLOYMENT IN IRELAND 1988–2010

Year	Numbers unemployed (thousands)	Unemployment rate (%)
1988	217.0	16.3
1989	196.8	15.0
1990	172.4	12.9
1991	198.5	14.7
1992	206.6	15.1
1993	220.1	15.7
1994	211.0	14.7
1995	177.4	12.2
1996	179.0	11.9
1997	159.0	10.3
1998	126.4	7.8
1999	96.9	5.7
2000	74.5	4.3
2001	65.1	3.6
2002	77.0	4.2
2003	82.1	4.4
2004	84.2	4.4
2005	85.6	4.2
2006	95.0	4.4
2007	99.9	4.5
2008	122.6	5.5
2009	256.6	11.6
2010	284.7	13.2

Source: Central Statistics Office.

As can be seen from Table 9.1, the unemployment rate remained persistently high until the mid-1990s. The years between 1990 and 1993 were particularly disappointing because the growth in national income as measured by GNP actually coincided with an increase in the unemployment rate.

The unemployment rate dropped steadily after 1994. The drop in the unemployment rate was even more impressive because the size of the labour force was increasing as emigrants returned home. Also, the percentage of 'long-term' unemployed (unemployed for more than one year) fell from 10.4% of the labour force in 1988 to 1.6% of the labour force in 2000. The policy of the social partners to award low wage increases and to spread the benefits of employment throughout the labour force appeared to have worked.

A second issue concerns the adherence of firms to wage increases negotiated under the partnership agreements. One can legitimately ask the question, if firms or the public sector do not adhere to the terms of the agreement, should they have been negotiated in the first place? For one thing, the opportunity cost of negotiations was high as it took many months to conclude a deal. More importantly, the process itself loses credibility if participants do not 'follow the rules'. Further, the sectors (often unionised) that maintain the wage increases negotiated under the national wage agreement lose ground to sectors (e.g. the non-unionised multinational sector) that do not. The largest gap emerged at the end of Partnership 2000 (1998–99). During that period, there were shortages in many sectors of the labour market. It appears that compliance with the terms of the national wage agreement broke down as firms increased wages to attract and retain staff. Another statistic, which helps to shed light on the 'mood' of the labour market, is the number of days lost due to industrial disputes; when workers 'vote with their feet', it shows their dissatisfaction with pay and working conditions. The number of days lost because of industrial disputes was highest during the early and mid-1980s. This period preceded the first agreement, the Programme for National Recovery (1987–90). However, at the end of 2000, the country experienced a 'winter of discontent' when teachers, taxi drivers, train and airline personnel 'took to the streets'. The increase in labour disputes in 1999 and 2000 indicated that the limitations placed on wage increases, negotiated as part of the national partnership agreements, were no longer acceptable to labour.

Why was labour dissatisfied? Two reasons come to mind. First, the percentage increases in wages were much lower than the percentage increases in national income. During the 1990s, the gap between the increase in GNP and the average manufacturing wage widened. The social partners realised that limiting wages would increase the share of profits. They followed this policy initially to promote investment. Retained earnings are one of the primary sources of funds used by firms to finance the purchase of machinery. The social partners believed that increased investment would lead to employment growth. Indeed, they were right. Investment did grow during the period of the wage agreements. This is a factor that contributed to Irish employment growth during the 1990s. However, a policy that made a great deal of sense initially, when business confidence was low, was not as necessary or appropriate when the economy was booming (and later busting).

Second, at the end of 1999, the inflation rate started to increase. The inflation rate is a measure of changes in the price level (see Section 17.1). If prices increase more rapidly than income, the real purchasing power of consumers falls. This is exactly what happened during 2000, the first year of the PPF. The negotiated wage increase of 5.5% for the first year of the PPF was completely eroded by an inflation rate of 6%. Employees were slightly better off than they had been in the previous year in terms of 'take-home pay' because of tax reductions. However, many sectors clearly felt that they were not benefiting enough from the 'Celtic Tiger' economy. This led the unions to renegotiate wage increases in the PPF.

The initial phase of the seventh partnership agreement – Towards 2016 – covered the period 2006 to 2008. Although not all unions actively participated in the process, various pay increases, much greater enforcement of, and commitment to, existing labour standards and a ten-year commitment by the government to improved state and welfare services were successfully negotiated. The second phase of Towards 2016 was agreed by the employers and unions towards the end of 2008 but it quickly became apparent that the national wage agreement, if not the national partnership agreement itself, had run its course. For example, the Construction Industry

Federation (CIF) withheld consent as it had already attempted to introduce a pay freeze in the face of the collapse of the construction bubble.

SUMMARY

1. Taxation finances the provision of public services, facilitates the redistribution of income and alters economic behaviour. A tax can be judged according to its contribution to equity, efficiency and effective administration. Ireland is a low tax economy. The size of the tax rate and the width of the tax base determine tax revenue.
2. Relative to other members of the European Union, Ireland places high taxes on consumption and low taxes on property and wealth. Ireland's corporate tax structure is unusual by international standards.
3. Competition policy and regulation policy attempt to facilitate allocative efficiency. Competition policy attempts to facilitate the conditions necessary for the creation of effective and potential competition. Regulation policy attempts to address the natural monopoly problem. Regulation policy attempts to set the number of firms and/or the prices (outputs) that individual firms can charge (produce).
4. Privatisation alters the ownership structure of a firm; it does not necessarily alter the market's competitive environment. Market liberalisation attempts to introduce and/or enhance competition in previously regulated markets.
5. Seven national partnership agreements (NPAs) were negotiated between the social partners from 1987. They provided an economic and social framework, based on consensus, to facilitate the country in meeting the challenges of a rapidly changing environment. One important part of each NPA was the national wage agreement.
6. The NPA came under increasing pressure because of a general concern that a 'one size fits all' policy was no longer appropriate for a rapidly changing economy and society.

KEY TERMS

Taxation policy
Equity
Ability-to-pay principle
Progressive tax
Regressive tax
Proportional tax
Efficiency
Income effect
Substitution effect
Effective administration
Tax evasion
Tax avoidance
Pay As You Earn
Pay Related Social Insurance
Value Added Tax
Excise duties
Corporation tax

Capital acquisitions tax
Competition policy
Perfect competition
Monopoly
Allocative efficiency
Market power
Own-price elasticity of demand
Market definition
Concentration ratio
Herfindahl-Hirschman Index
Entry barriers
Competitive environment
Competition Authority
Natural monopoly
Economies of scale
Marginal cost pricing
Average cost pricing

Unemployment trap
Poverty trap
Tax harmonisation
Local authority rates
Residential property tax

Franchise bidding
Public enterprise
Privatisation
National partnership agreement
National wage agreement

REVIEW QUESTIONS

1. Discuss the progressiveness, or otherwise, of the Irish tax system. Discuss the progressiveness, or otherwise, of at least two individual components of the Irish tax system. How important are these components? How has the progressiveness of the Irish tax system been affected in recent budgets?
2. Describe some general aspects of the Irish tax system that are shaped by the European Union. Describe some individual components of the Irish tax system that are shaped by the European Union. How important are these aspects and components?
3. Describe possible advantages and disadvantages associated with using the Herfindahl-Hirschman Index for assessing market concentration.
4. Consider a number of concentrated markets in Ireland. Is there scope for improved competition within these markets? Is regulation of these markets necessary? Explain your answers.
5. What were the national partnership agreements (NPAs)?
6. Discuss the contributions of the NPAs to the Irish economy.

TRUE OR FALSE (SUPPORT YOUR ANSWER)

1. Irish taxation revenue as a proportion of Ireland's GNP is lower than Irish taxation revenue as a proportion of Ireland's GDP.

2. Efficiency requires that high taxes be placed on products with high price elasticities of demand and that low taxes be placed on products with low price elasticities of demand.

3. Expenditure taxes (i.e. VAT and excise duties) in Ireland are high compared to other member states of the European Union.

4. Allocative efficiency requires that price be less than marginal cost.

5. A Herfindahl-Hirschman Index (HHI) of 5000 implies the existence of a highly concentrated market.

6. The major justification for the existence of regulation policy, as opposed to competition policy, is the existence of natural monopolies.

CASE STUDY

Extract from www.rte.ie
EU moves against minimum cigarette prices

European Union governments cannot set minimum prices on cigarettes, the bloc's executive arm warned today. It said it was taking legal action against Ireland, Greece, France, Belgium, Italy and Austria. Public authorities setting the minimum price on cigarettes distorted competition and impaired the right of the manufacturer or importer of cigarettes in the 25-nation EU to determine the selling price, the European Commission said. 'Introducing minimum retail prices for cigarettes is against community law and mainly benefits manufacturers who are able to protect their profit margins,' Tax Commissioner Laszlo Kovacs said in a statement. The Commission said if governments wanted to discourage smoking through high cigarette prices, they should raise excise taxes. 'I strongly support member states in their efforts to implement new health policy. However, this must respect community law,' Kovacs said.

Source:
www.rte.ie/news/2006/0410/cigarettes-business.html, 10 April 2006 (accessed 16 February 2011).

Extract from www.rte.ie
Cigarette price-fixing infringes EU law

The Court of Justice of the European Union has ruled that Irish legislation fixing a minimum retail price for cigarettes infringes EU law. The legislation here breaches Directive 95/59 which has rules on excise duty

affecting the consumption of tobacco products. The court says imposing a minimum price on cigarettes can undermine competition by preventing some manufacturers taking advantage of lower cost manufacturing prices, so as to offer more attractive retail selling prices. The court says that while the Directive [95/59] ensures health protection, it does not prevent member states from combating smoking.

In a statement, cigarette manufacturer PJ Carroll welcomed the ruling saying: 'The reality is the set minimum price for cigarettes has become irrelevant. Packs of cigarettes are being purchased up and down the country for as little as €3.50 on the black market. This is under half the current minimum price of €7.75.' However, the Irish Cancer Society say they are disappointed with the ruling by the European Court of Justice which found Irish legislation fixing a minimum retail price for cigarettes infringed EU law. Head of Advocacy with the Irish Cancer Society, Kathleen O'Meara, said they are disappointed with the potential impact of the ruling because it could mean a reduction in the price of cigarettes here. Anti-smoking group ASH also said it was concerned with the ruling. Dr Angie Brown, ASH, said: 'We will be in contact with the government on this vitally important matter. Ireland has and is permitted to have a separate tax regime to all other EU countries – and it is our view that the Government has every right to apply taxes which ensures that tobacco is sold at current and even higher prices.'

Source:
www.rte.ie/news/2010/0304/cigarettes.html, 4 March 2010 (accessed 4 March 2010).

Extract from *The Irish Times*
Pall Mall cigarette price cut
by Ciaran Hancock

After about 30 years of steady price increases, Irish smokers will see the cost of a packet of 20 Pall Mall cigarettes cut by 50 cent from February 7th. Tobacco manufacturer PJ Carroll has told retailers that it is reducing the recommended retail price (RRP) for Pall Mall to €7.25 from €7.75 from next Monday. This move follows a ruling last March by the European Court of Justice, which found that the Government's fixed minimum pricing of tobacco products violated EU law.

PJ Carroll, which is owned by British American Tobacco, said it is also a response to the growth in cigarette smuggling. It is estimated that 27 per cent of cigarettes smoked here are sourced from the black market. 'PJ Carroll is committed to returning stability to the legal tobacco market and to supporting retailers who stock legitimate tobacco products,' said Chloe Campen, head of corporate and regulatory affairs at PJ Carroll. 'We hope retailers welcome the RRP change. We believe we have shown leadership in this move.' The move is expected to cause controversy with anti-smoking groups, who oppose the sale of tobacco on health grounds. Pall Mall will now be the cheapest cigarette for sale here.

Source: The Irish Times, 3 February 2011.

Questions

1. Drawing on the first extract ('EU moves against minimum cigarette prices'), outline the basic advantage and disadvantage of imposing a price floor with respect to the retail price of cigarettes in Ireland.
2. Drawing on the second extract ('Cigarette price-fixing infringes EU law'), consider the impact of cigarette smuggling on the arguments for and against the imposition of a price floor on the retail price of cigarettes in Ireland.
3. Using the third extract ('Pall Mall cigarette price cut'), as well as any other resources you deem appropriate, consider various possibilities with respect to future public policy towards the regulation of cigarette consumption.

PART II

MACROECONOMICS

Introduction to Macroeconomics

Macroeconomics is concerned with the operation of the economy as a whole. In this branch of economics, we deal with aggregate variables such as national output, the general price level and total employment. Arising out of our study of macroeconomics is an appreciation of policy issues.

Our starting point in macroeconomics is the measurement of economic activity. Chapter 10 examines the different ways of measuring economic activity. The problems associated with the National Accounts are also discussed.

The two main doctrines of economic thought are outlined in Chapter 11. The classical school of economics dates back to Adam Smith. The Keynesian revolution challenged the existing economic orthodoxy of the time.

In Chapter 12, the Keynesian model of income determination is explained. The policy implications arising out of the Keynesian model are also discussed. The chapter ends with an account of the Irish experience with Keynesian economics.

In a non-barter economy, transactions are facilitated by money. The money stock and interest rates are important variables in any modern economy. Monetary policy is a policy instrument used by the authorities to achieve various economic objectives. Chapter 13 examines the role of money in the economy, both in the context of the Irish economy and in the euro area.

A model of the macroeconomy is presented in Chapter 14. The IS/LM model is a useful framework to explain fiscal and monetary policies and to examine the divergent views of Keynesians and monetarists.

Chapter 15 introduces open economy macroeconomics. Our examination of macroeconomics until now has been largely within the confines of a closed economy. This chapter analyses the effect which factors such as external trade, foreign interest rates and flexible exchange rates have on the economy. It also examines Ireland's experience and performance within the European Monetary System. Economic and Monetary Union, the European Central Bank and the euro are all discussed.

A more complex model of the macroeconomy is examined in Chapter 16. Prices and output are determined in the AD/AS model. This framework can be used to analyse macroeconomic problems and policy options.

Chapter 17 examines a number of important macroeconomic issues. Unemployment, inflation and international trade are discussed in the context of a small open economy on the periphery of Europe. Some policy options are also examined.

Chapter 18 examines the issue of economic growth and long-run changes in both economic activity and the living standards of a nation. A simple model explaining economic growth is presented. Factors that might explain an economy's growth, both in an international and domestic context, are outlined. The chapter ends with a critical account of Ireland's economic growth, both during and after the Celtic Tiger years, culminating in the 2010 EU–IMF bailout.

Economic issues and policies pertinent to developing and transition countries are outlined in Chapter 19. The problems facing the developing countries of Africa, Asia and Latin America and the transition economies of the ex-socialist countries of Central and Eastern Europe, the former Soviet Union and China are some of the greatest challenges currently confronting economists and policy-makers alike. These problems and challenges are examined in this final chapter.

CHAPTER 10

Measuring the Macroeconomy

'Among the most effective measures of the economic performance of a nation is its total net product, or national income – the sum of all goods produced during a given period . . .'[1]

SIMON KUZNETS (1901–85)

'For, unlike many measurements in the physical sciences, there is no unique way of measuring either the size of an economy at a particular point in time, or its growth over time.'[2]

PAUL ORMEROD

CHAPTER OBJECTIVES

Upon completing this chapter, the student should understand:

- the circular flow model of economic activity;
- the different ways of measuring economic activity;
- the meaning of gross domestic product (GDP) and other similar measures of economic activity;
- the shortcomings of GDP as a measure of economic activity;
- the Irish National Accounts.

OUTLINE

INTRODUCTION

This chapter begins with the circular flow model of economic activity. Although it is a very simple model, it introduces all of the principal agents in the economy: households, firms, financial institutions, the state and foreign markets. The model also explains how these sectors interact.

We use this model to introduce the three ways by which economic activity is measured. Gross domestic product (GDP), the most common measure of economic activity, is explained in detail. GDP is often used as a measure of national economic activity and as a basis of international comparisons. Its defects as a measure of prosperity are also discussed.

The chapter ends with an analysis of the Irish National Accounts as published by the Central Statistics Office (CSO).

10.1 THE CIRCULAR FLOW OF ECONOMIC ACTIVITY

The circular flow is a simplified model of the economy showing the movement of resources between consumers and producers. The French economist François Quesnay (1694–1774) is credited with its discovery.[3] It is believed that he modelled it on William Harvey's famous circulation of blood diagram.

A modern economy is very complex. There are many different sectors (households, firms, government, financial, foreign) with each sector comprised of many interacting individual units. In order to understand this sophisticated system we need to begin with a simple model.

We begin with a model of the private sector: households and firms. These are identifiable not by who they are but by what they do: households consume whereas firms produce. In a simple, closed economy the only transactions are between households and firms. The result is a model of the economy which shows the transactions between households and firms. This model is called the circular flow and is illustrated in Figure 10.1.

FIGURE 10.1: THE CIRCULAR FLOW BETWEEN HOUSEHOLDS AND FIRMS

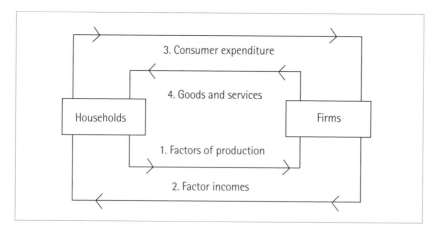

It is the households who own the basic factors of production. These inputs are supplied to the firms (1) in order to produce goods and services. The firms pay the households factor incomes for the use of these inputs (2). There is a special term given to each return on the different factors of production: wages are the return on labour, interest on capital, rent on land and profit on enterprise. Households receive the factor incomes and use them to buy goods and services from the firms (3). These goods and services are supplied by the firms to the households (4).

The transactions between households and firms are reflected in the loops drawn above. There is a distinction between the inner loop and the outer loop. Flows 1 and 4 (the inner loop) reflect the transfer of real or non-monetary resources. Flows 2 and 3 (the outer loop) reflect the transfer of money or monetary payments.

In this simple model all output is sold (output = expenditure) and all income is spent (income = expenditure). Thus, output must equal income (output = income). These equalities are discussed again in the next section of this chapter.

The transactions, in terms of the agents involved, are summarised in Table 10.1.

TABLE 10.1: SUMMARY OF TRANSACTIONS BETWEEN HOUSEHOLDS AND FIRMS

Households	Firms
Supply factors of production to firms.	Use factors of production to produce goods and services.
Receive factor income in return for inputs.	Pay households for use of inputs.
Spend income on goods and services.	Sell goods and services to households.

The simple circular flow can be modified to include the financial sector. In the above analysis, the households spend all of their factor incomes on goods and services. In Figure 10.2 the households are faced with two options: to spend on goods and services or to save. One of the functions of the banking system in the circular flow is to facilitate savings. However, savings is a leakage or a withdrawal from the circular flow. A leakage is simply a movement of funds out of the circular flow. This can diminish the level of economic activity in the economy. A simple example is illustrated below.

FIGURE 10.2: THE CIRCULAR FLOW, SAVINGS AND INVESTMENT

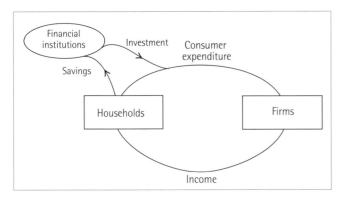

Let us suppose income is equal to €10,000 and households save 20% of their income. Spending is now limited to €8,000 (80% of €10,000). In these circumstances there are no economic incentives for firms to continue producing €10,000 worth of goods since their sales on the domestic market (no foreign sector exists so there is no possibility of exporting goods to foreign markets) are limited to the €8,000 which households are prepared to spend.

The value of output produced is limited to €8,000. Consequently the income generated is limited to €8,000. If we assume that households still save 20% of their income, spending in the next round is reduced to €6,400 (80% of €8,000). This process continues with the level of economic activity diminishing further with every round. This appears quite alarming and we might question whether there is any escape from this vicious circle. An escape exists in the form of 'investment expenditure', which is an injection into the circular flow. An injection is a movement of funds into the circular flow: it is an addition to economic activity. The term 'investment' was defined in Chapter 7. It is corporate or business expenditure on machinery, fixtures and fittings, equipment, vehicles and buildings. It also includes inventory build-ups of raw materials, semi-finished and finished goods. Firms may finance investment expenditure by borrowing from the very same financial institutions which facilitated those households who had surplus funds and decided to save a percentage of their income. The borrowing facility is the other main function of the banking system. Financial institutions serve as intermediaries to bring together those who have excess funds (households) and those who are in need of funds (firms).

If savings are greater than investment in money terms the level of economic activity diminishes. However, if investment is greater than savings the level of economic activity increases. The level of economic activity remains unchanged if savings are matched by investment: the economy is said to be in equilibrium. See Appendix 10.1 for more material on this subject.

The circular flow with savings and investment is now adjusted to include the government or the public sector. The government is involved in spending large amounts of money on defence, security, education, health services and so on. It also spends money on transfer payments.

Definition

Transfer payments redistribute wealth rather than provide a unique good or service. They include pensions, unemployment benefits, disability allowances and other payments.

All of these forms of expenditure are injections into the circular flow. However, these expenditures need to be financed. It is government revenue, primarily in the form of taxation, which finances such expenditure. Taxes are usually divided into two categories, direct and indirect. The former is a tax on income. Examples include personal income tax and corporate tax. Indirect tax is a tax on expenditure. Excise duties and VAT are examples. Taxation, both direct and indirect, is a leakage from the circular flow. Direct taxes are a leakage from the income loop; indirect taxes are a leakage from the expenditure loop. The adjusted circular flow is illustrated in Figure 10.3. Government spending and taxation is incorporated in the circular flow model.

There is one final adjustment to be made to the circular flow model. International trade between countries is a very important part of total expenditure. The analysis to date was applied to a closed economy. We now adjust the model to include foreign markets. Exports are Irish goods and services purchased by non-residents. Export earnings are a monetary flow from the foreign market into the domestic market. Hence, it is an injection into the circular flow. Imports are goods and services purchased by Irish households and firms from foreign-based firms. Payment for imports is a monetary flow from the domestic market into the foreign market: it is a leakage out of the circular flow. The difference between exports and imports is referred to as net exports. Its value is positive if the value of exports exceeds the value of imports. It is negative if the value of imports exceeds the value of exports.

FIGURE 10.3: THE CIRCULAR FLOW INCLUDING THE GOVERNMENT

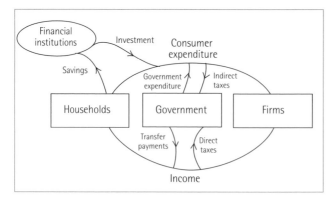

FIGURE 10.4: THE COMPLETE CIRCULAR FLOW

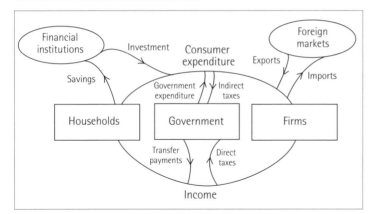

Figure 10.4 is the complete version of the circular flow diagram. All agents and their transactions with each other are included. A more complete explanation is now required.

On receipt of the factors of production from the households, the firms engage in the production of goods and services. The income which the firms pay out for the use of the factor inputs is reflected in the lower loop of the diagram.

In a simple model without government intervention or a banking sector, as represented in Figure 10.1, the households receive and, in turn, spend all of the national income. However, the introduction of the government sector ensures that the households do not receive all of the national income. The amount which the households actually receive is referred to as disposable income. This is national income supplemented by transfer payments but excluding taxes. On receipt of this income, the households allocate a certain amount to savings. The rest is allocated to consumer expenditure.

The upper loop shows that consumer expenditure is only one form of expenditure. Others include investment expenditure by the corporate sector, public expenditure by the government, expenditure on domestic goods and services by non-residents and expenditure on foreign goods and services.

There were no leakages or injections in our simple model. The analysis is a little more complicated when we extend the model to include other sectors. In Figure 10.4 savings, taxation and imports constitute the leakages whereas investment, government expenditure, transfer payments and exports constitute the injections. Economic activity depends largely on the relative size of these injections and leakages.

National income is one measure of economic activity. An important difference between the leakages and the injections is their respective relationship with national income. Leakages are endogenous variables. This means that they vary with one of the other components of the model. In this particular case, savings, taxation and imports will all increase when national income increases. There is a functional relationship between these variables and national income.

In contrast, all four injections are independent of the income level. They are exogenous. They are part of the model in that they affect the level of national income. However, their values are determined by variables which are outside the model. For example, investment depends on expectations about the future and the interest rate. Government spending and transfer payments are determined within the political process. Exports increase or decrease with foreign income. These variables are not a function of national income. This subtle difference between leakages and injections is fundamental to the stability of the economy. This issue will be discussed in greater detail in Chapter 12.

In relation to the leakages and injections in the economy three possibilities arise and are summarised in Table 10.2.

TABLE 10.2: INJECTIONS, LEAKAGES AND THEIR EFFECT ON ECONOMIC ACTIVITY

Effect on economic activity:			
Decreases, if	Injections	<	leakages
Increases, if	Injections	>	leakages
Unchanged, if	Injections	=	leakages

If the leakages are greater than the injections, in money terms, the level of economic activity diminishes. If the injections are greater than the leakages the level of economic activity increases. The level of economic activity remains unchanged if the leakages and the injections are equal. The economy is said to be in equilibrium.

This completes our study of the circular flow model. We will now examine the ways in which economic activity is actually measured.

10.2 THE THREE METHODS FOR MEASURING ECONOMIC ACTIVITY

There are three approaches to measuring the economic activity of a country. These are portrayed in Figure 10.5.

FIGURE 10.5: A SIMPLIFIED VERSION OF THE CIRCULAR FLOW

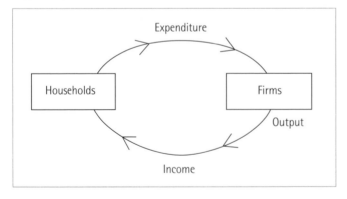

Figure 10.5 is a simplified version of the circular flow. It highlights the three approaches for measuring national economic activity. It indicates that the factors of production are combined to produce *output*. In turn, the factors of production are paid *income* which then becomes *expenditure*. These are the three methods for measuring a nation's economic activity. As we will see later they are defined in such a way that they should yield the same result. In practice they usually give slightly different results due to measurement errors which arise from the difficulty in collecting and tabulating all of the data involved.

Explanations for all three are provided below. In Ireland, the income and expenditure methods are widely used. Estimates for the two methods will differ as they arise from different data sources. The income and expenditure approaches are published annually by the CSO in the publication entitled *National Income and Expenditure*. For our purpose the most important is the expenditure approach because many subsequent chapters in this textbook incorporate material which is largely based on this method of calculation.

Expenditure method

National expenditure is the sum of the expenditures of consumers, firms, government and the foreign sector on domestically produced goods and services. More specifically, we add household spending on consumer goods and services, spending by firms and households on capital goods, government purchases of goods and services and finally, net exports. Imports are substituted because consumption, investment and government spending cover both domestically produced goods and foreign-produced goods. Exports are added in order to get a value for total expenditure on domestic production.

Table 10.3 shows the calculation of national income using the expenditure approach for the calendar year 2009. The numbers in the column on the left-hand side are the item numbers used by the CSO.

TABLE 10.3: MEASURING ECONOMIC ACTIVITY IN IRELAND USING THE EXPENDITURE METHOD

		€m
79	Personal consumption of goods and services	84,331
80	Net expenditure by central and local government on current goods and services	27,718
81	Gross domestic fixed capital formation	24,731
82	Value of physical changes in stocks	–2,284
83	Exports of goods and services	144,782
84	less Imports of goods and services	–120,380
12	Statistical discrepancy	748
86	Gross domestic product at current market prices	159,646
87	Net factor income from the rest of the world	–28,405
88	Gross national product at current market prices	131,241
28	less Provision for depreciation	–14,784
	Net national product at market prices	116,457
30+33	less Taxes	–18,372
31+34	plus Subsidies	2,571
15	Net national product at factor cost	100,655

Source: CSO, *National Income and Expenditure 2009,* August 2010.

Income method

Alternatively, national income is derived by adding the different incomes of the factors of production: remuneration of employees, income from the self-employed, profit of companies and rent of dwellings (imputed in the case of owner-occupied). In Ireland it is based on data collected by the Revenue Commissioners for the purpose of income tax assessment. The calculation of national income for the year 2009 as published by the CSO is shown in Table 10.4.

TABLE 10.4: MEASURING ECONOMIC ACTIVITY IN IRELAND USING THE INCOME METHOD

	Description	€m
	Income from agriculture, forestry and fishing:	
1	Income from self-employment and other trading income	1,632
2/3	Wages/contribution to social insurance	568
	Non-agricultural Income:	
4/5	Trading profits and self-employed earnings	46,763
6	Adjustment for stock appreciation	1,036
7/8	Rent	7,153
9	Wages and salaries	67,361
10	Employers' contribution to social insurance	5,295
12	Statistical discrepancy	−748
13	Net value added at factor cost	129,060
14	Net factor income from the rest of the world	−28,405
15	Net national product at factor cost	100,655

Source: CSO, *National Income and Expenditure 2009,* August 2010.

Output method

To arrive at a figure for national output, we add together the money value of the output produced from the various sectors of the economy. There is the danger of double or multiple counting when adopting this approach.

Definition
Double counting occurs if the expenditure on intermediate goods is included in the calculation of national output.

National output does not consist of the full value of every single item produced in the economy since the output of one good may be the input for another.

For example, a farmer may sell his cow at the market to a retail outlet for €800. The cow is slaughtered, packaged and sold for the retail value of €1,000. A straight summation of transactions suggests that national output has increased by €1,800. In this case, national output would be overstated because the value of the cow has been double counted. The cow is the input for the retail meat trade. The addition to national output is actually €1,000.

In order to avoid double counting one of two methods can be used. First, we can sum the value added at each stage of production. Second, the final value of all finished goods can be calculated with the value of all intermediate goods excluded. Since the sum of all the value added at each stage of production must equal the value of the final output produced, these two methods yield the same figure.

Table 10.5 shows economic activity in Ireland in 2009, by sector of origin.

TABLE 10.5: MEASURING ECONOMIC ACTIVITY IN IRELAND USING THE OUTPUT METHOD

	Description	€m
19	Agriculture, forestry and fishing	2,201
20	Industry (including building)	43,159
21	Distribution, transport and communication	19,884
22	Public administration and defence	6,372
23	Other services	58,192
12	Statistical discrepancy	−748
27	Net value added at factor cost	129,060
36	Net factor income from the rest of the world	−28,405
15	Net national product at factor cost	100,655

Source: CSO, *National Income and Expenditure 2009*, August 2010.

Figure 10.6 summarises graphically the three ways of measuring the level of national economic activity.

We will now define the various measures of economic activity which appear in the National Accounts.

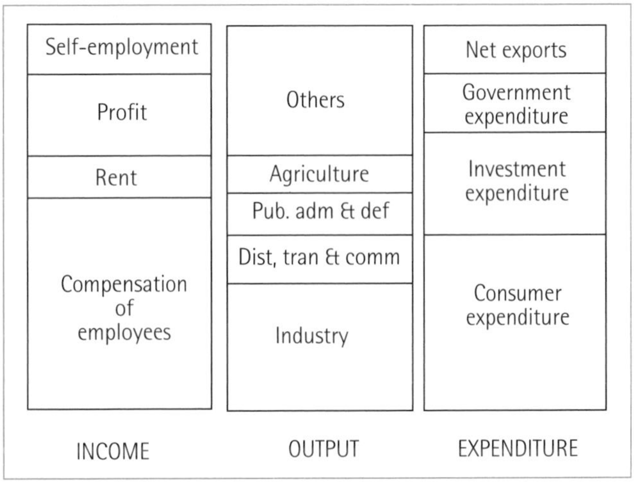

10.3 THE NATIONAL ACCOUNTS

Simon Kuznets of Harvard University developed the national income accounting system which provided the basic framework for measuring economic activity.[4] The key concept in the national income accounts and the most common measure of a country's economic performance is gross domestic product.

FIGURE 10.6: THE THREE METHODS OF MEASURING ECONOMIC ACTIVITY

Definition

Gross domestic product (GDP) is the value of all goods and services produced domestically in the economy, regardless of the nationality of the owners of the factors of production.

GDP for Ireland includes the value of output produced by subsidiaries of foreign multinationals operating in Ireland. The output of Irish multinationals operating outside the country is excluded. GDP is a flow concept, i.e. it is the value of goods and services produced over a particular time period. In Ireland it is measured on a yearly basis. In 2009 the CSO estimate for GDP was €159.6bn.

There are many different variations to GDP, outlined in Figure 10.7. The figure also highlights the differences between the calculation of GDP and disposable income, another economic measure which is frequently used. An explanation of Figure 10.7 follows.

FIGURE 10.7: FROM GDP TO DISPOSABLE INCOME

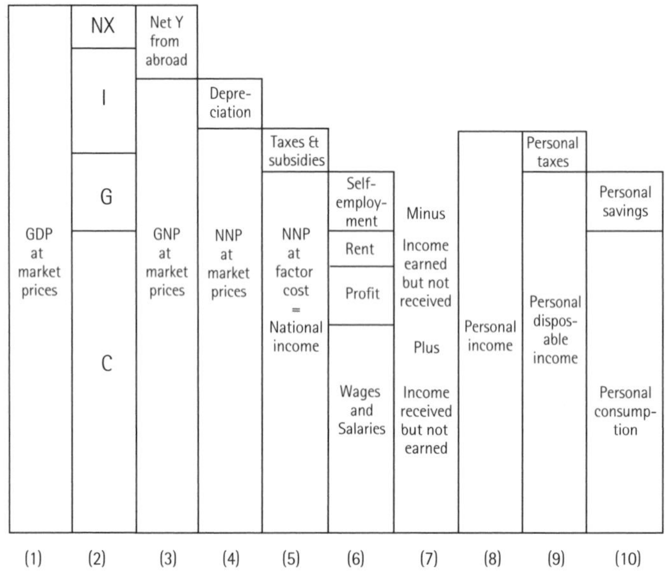

Composition of GDP

GDP is comprised of consumer expenditure, investment expenditure, government expenditure on goods and services and net exports (exports less imports), as shown in columns 1 and 2 in Figure 10.7.

*   Consumer expenditure, or simply consumption (C) is spending by the household sector on durable (e.g. furniture, cars, etc.) and non-durable (e.g. food, drink, etc.) goods and services. The CSO estimates that consumer expenditure for 2009 was €84.3bn, accounting for just 53% of GDP. It is by far the largest component of GDP. However, in comparison to other western economies, the percentage of total expenditure devoted to consumption in Ireland is not high. Table 10.6 shows comparable percentages for other developed countries, for 2008.
    Consumer expenditure is dependent on a range of factors including income, wealth, advertising, prices and expectations. These factors and their relationship with consumer expenditure are discussed in greater detail in Chapter 12.
*   Investment expenditure (I), or to use its full title gross domestic fixed capital formation, is the total outlay on all capital goods. This category of goods includes machinery, factories, vehicles and so on. All new buildings and all current construction work on roads, harbours, airports, forestry development and so on is included. It also includes new home spending. Although the contribution to a single year's GDP is small relative to consumption, investment expenditure is viewed as the key to long-run economic activity. In 2009 investment

TABLE 10.6: CONSUMPTION AS A PERCENTAGE OF GDP, 2008 (US$bn)

Country	GDP	Consumption/GDP
USA	14,369	70
UK	2,663	64
Spain	1,594	57
France	2,854	57
Germany	3,656	57
Canada	1,499	56
Estonia	24	55
Belgium	505	52
Ireland	266	50
Denmark	341	49

Source: World Bank.

expenditure was €24.7bn, accounting for 15.5% of GDP. This component of GDP is more volatile than any other and therefore more difficult to predict. Its volatility is primarily due to the factors which influence it. These include expectations and interest rates, two factors which are known to fluctuate considerably.

- Government expenditure, denoted by G, measures spending by the state on current goods and services. The CSO estimate for 2009 was €27.7bn. This accounts for just over 17% of GDP. It is important to note that transfer payments are excluded from this component as they do not involve payment in exchange for production. Government expenditure as a percentage of GDP varies significantly from economy to economy. For example, welfare states tend to have a high (general) government expenditure share of GDP. Examples include Sweden and Denmark where the respective ratios were 28% and 30%, in 2009. In contrast, the USA and Switzerland have low (general) government spending/GDP ratios. The relevant figures for 2009 were 17% and 11% respectively, as opposed to Ireland's 20% .

- Net exports, denoted by NX, is the difference between the exports and the imports of goods and services. Net exports can be positive, reflecting a trade surplus where the value of exports exceeds the value of imports; or negative, reflecting a trade deficit where the value of imports exceeds the value of exports. In Ireland the ratio of exports or imports to GDP is very high. In 2009 the ratio of exports (amounting to €144.8bn) to GDP was over 90% whereas the ratio of imports (amounting to €120.4bn) to GDP was 75%. This reflects the extreme openness of the Irish economy. As a result, Ireland is an economy which is very susceptible to changes in the international economic climate. This component of GDP is determined by a wide range of factors including the level of domestic and foreign income, exchange rates and relative inflation rates.

GDP is the sum of consumer expenditure, investment expenditure, government expenditure and net exports and can be expressed as follows:

$$\text{GDP} \equiv \text{C} + \text{I} + \text{G} + \text{NX} \qquad [10.1]$$

where the symbol $\equiv$ denotes an identity. An identity is something that is true by definition.

Variations of GDP

One variant of GDP is gross national product.

> **Definition**
> *Gross national product (GNP) is the value of all goods and services produced by a country's
> productive factors regardless of their geographical location.*

In 2009, Ireland's GNP was valued at €131.2bn.

Although GDP is used for comparison with other EU countries, GNP is probably a better
measure of Irish economic activity. GNP reflects only the part of economic activity that is
produced and shared by Irish nationals.

Column 3 of Figure 10.7 indicates that the difference between gross domestic product and
gross national product is net factor income from the rest of the world.

> **Definition**
> *Net factor income from the rest of the world is the outflows of income earned by foreigners
> operating in Ireland minus the inflows of income earned by foreign subsidiaries of Irish
> companies.*

There are more foreign multinationals operating in Ireland sending profits abroad than there
are Irish multinationals sending profits home.[5] The net repatriation of profits and the interest
payments on the national debt to non-residents are both outflows. In 2009, net factor income
from the rest of the world amounted to an outflow of €28.4bn. Hence, GDP is consistently larger
than GNP in Ireland. This was not always the case. Less than five decades ago, emigrants'
remittances and interest on the country's external assets meant that the net factor income from
abroad was positive. This resulted in GNP greater than GDP.

GNP plus EU subsidies minus EU taxes is equal to gross national income (GNI). In 2009,
GNI at current market prices was €132.6bn. Gross national disposable income (GNDI) is GNI
plus net current transfers from the rest of the world (excluding EU subsidies and taxes). These
payments are not in exchange for goods or services and they include, among others, emigrants'
remittances and overseas aid. These should be included in any accurate measure of Irish economic
activity. In 2009, current transfers accounted for a small outflow of €2.3bn. Taking this into
account, GNDI for 2009 was €130.3bn.

Columns 3 and 4 show that the difference between gross national product and net national
product (NNP) is a provision for depreciation. We defined depreciation in Chapter 7 as the value
of capital which has been used up during the production process. Whereas GNP does not account
for the capital depleted in the production process, NNP does. The CSO estimated that
depreciation for 2009 amounted to €14.8bn. Deducting depreciation from GNP meant that
NNP at market prices was valued at €116.5bn in 2009.

Columns 4 and 5 illustrate the difference between NNP measured at market prices and NNP
at factor cost. The difference is accounted for by indirect taxes and subsidies, or net taxes. To
calculate NNP at factor cost we deduct indirect taxes from and add subsidy payments to NNP
at market prices. In 2009, €18.4bn of indirect taxes were deducted from NNP at market prices
and €2.6bn of subsidies were added, giving us a figure of €100.7bn which represents NNP at
factor cost or, simply, national income.

NNP at factor cost is represented in Columns 5 and 6. It is simply the addition of payments
to the factors of production. These factor payments are wages, profits, interest and rent.

Column 7 of Figure 10.7 shows that the difference between national income and personal income is accounted for by what economists call 'income earned-but-not-received' and its counterpart 'income received-but-not-earned'. An example of the former is retained earnings of companies. Transfer payments are an example of the latter. In 2008 (latest figures available) personal income was €123.4bn.

The last term to be explained is personal disposable income, which is sometimes referred to as take-home or after-tax income. Personal disposable income is defined as personal income minus personal taxes, as shown in columns 8 and 9 of Figure 10.7. An individual or household divides disposable income between personal consumption and personal savings. This is shown in column 10 of Figure 10.7. In 2008, disposable income was €100bn. Of this amount, over €94.8bn was spent on personal consumption while €5.2bn was reserved for personal savings.

The differences between national income and personal consumption for 2008 are shown in Table 10.7.

TABLE 10.7: FROM NATIONAL INCOME TO PERSONAL CONSUMPTION

		€m
119	Net national product at factor cost before adjustment for stock appreciation	117,837
120	less Government trading and investment income	–2,725
121	plus National debt interest	2,482
122	plus Transfer income	24,576
124	less Undistributed profits of companies before tax	–18,727
125	Personal income	123,443
127	less taxes on personal income and wealth	–23,438
	Personal disposable income of which	100,006
126	Personal consumption of goods and services	94,825
129	Personal savings	5,181

Source: CSO, *National Income and Expenditure 2009,* August 2010.

GDP can be measured in two ways.

Definition
Nominal GDP or GDP at current prices is a measure of economic activity based on the current prices of the goods and services produced.

Definition
Real GDP or GDP at constant prices measures economic activity in the prices of a fixed or base year.

Increases in nominal GDP can arise for two different reasons: an increase in the quantity of goods and services produced, or an increase in the price of these goods and services. Increases in real GDP (see Figure 10.8) arise from only one source: an increase in the quantity of goods and services produced. By measuring production in constant terms, we separate the actual changes in the quantity of goods and services produced from the change in the price level. In effect, we isolate the production change from the price change.

FIGURE 10.8: REAL GDP GROWTH RATES 2000–2010

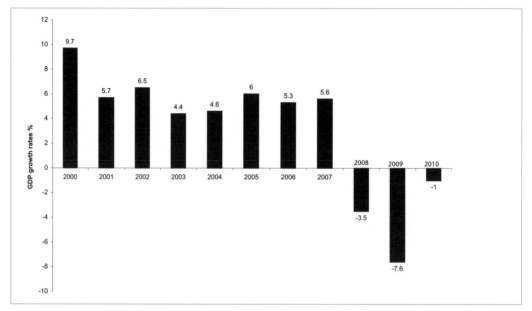

Two conclusions apply here. One, GDP at constant prices is a better measure of a country's economic performance. Two, in terms of the source of higher income and output levels, an increase in the quantity of goods and services produced is preferred to an increase in their price.

GDP at current prices can be converted to GDP at constant prices by means of a price index called the GDP deflator.

Definition

The GDP deflator is the ratio of nominal GDP to real GDP expressed as an index.

Price indices and their construction are discussed in Chapter 17.

Let us take an example to highlight the difference between the two measures. It is estimated that between 1979 and 1986 the Irish economy, measured in terms of increases in nominal GNP, grew by 130%. However, the increase over the same period measured in real GNP terms was only 3%. This suggests that the increase recorded in nominal GNP during this period was due to changes in the price level with no significant increase in production recorded.

What about GDP (or any measure of national income) comparisons across countries rather than over time? We confront a similar measurement problem here as any two countries are likely to have different price levels. Using GDP, or GDP per capita, is misleading as these (unadjusted) measures do not account for relative purchasing power. Purchasing power parities (PPP) are the rates of currency conversion that allow for differences in price levels between countries. Because goods and services may cost more, or less, in one country than in another, PPP allows us to make more accurate comparisons of living standards across countries. PPP rates are normally expressed in national currency units per US dollar. For example, suppose a basket of goods costs $100 in the USA and 2,500 roubles in Russia. This indicates that one dollar has the same purchasing power as 25 roubles. The PPP exchange rate is defined here as US$1 = 25 roubles. For various reasons, the actual exchange rate is likely to differ from the PPP rate (see Chapter 15 for more on exchange rates and PPP). In Table 10.8 below, it is the 2008 GDP (and GDP per capita) data, in US$, *adjusted for PPP*, that are reported.

In order to take into account the size of or changes in the population of a country, GDP per capita is used. This measure is expressed in Equation 10.2.

$$\textbf{GDP per capita = GDP/population} \qquad \textbf{[10.2]}$$

This is a better measure of a country's standard of living than GDP itself. For example, two countries with similar values for GDP may have very different standards of living because of variations in the size of their respective populations. In this case, GDP per capita is a more suitable measure.

Table 10.8 depicts GDP and GDP per capita for 2008 for a small sample of countries. It is evident that GDP can be quite misleading at times. In Table 10.8, this is particularly true in the case of India (and less so China) whose GDP appears relatively high but because of its vast population its GDP per capita is relatively small.

TABLE 10.8: GDP, POPULATION AND GDP PER CAPITA, 2008 (PPP US$)

Country	GDP 2008 (bn)	Population 2008 (m)	GDP per capita 2008
Malawi	11.9	14.8	807
Cambodia	28.4	14.6	1.954
India	3,356.3	1,140.0	3,032
China	7,903.2	1,324.7	6,195
Brazil	1,976.6	192.0	10,367
Czech Rep.	256.9	10.4	25,828
Greece	329.9	11.2	30,285
UK	2,178.2	61.4	37,317
Ireland	185.2	4.4	43,658
USA	14,591.4	304.4	47,210

Source: United Nations; World Bank.

Furthermore, any increase in GDP recorded may be offset by an increase in the size of the population. In this case, as above, GDP per capita is a more suitable measure.

We now consider the following case study in order to highlight some of the issues which we have already explained.

CASE STUDY

Extract from *The Sunday Business Post*
Consumer spending and investment drive economy
by Cliff Taylor

It is the boom that never ends, or so it would appear from the latest growth figures from the Central Statistics Office. We are in the mature phase of an economic expansion with consumer spending and investment surging ahead. So far two interest rate increases and the threat of more to come have not slowed the economy. On the contrary, all the signals are that growth accelerated towards the end of last year and that the economy has been at full steam in the early months of 2006. Economic growth – as measured by the increase in gross national product (GNP) – was 5.4 per cent last year, according to last week's CSO figures.

While quarterly breakdowns need to be treated with caution, all the signs are that growth accelerated as the year went on. GNP growth averaged 4.3 per cent in the first half of the year and 6.5 per cent in the second half. What is most astonishing about the figures is the strength of the domestic economy. For years, growth was driven by multinational exports in sectors such as electronics and pharmaceuticals.

Last year, however, imports actually grew more rapidly than exports. Growth was driven by consumer spending – up 5.6 per cent on the year – and capital investment, which rose by an extraordinary 13.1 per cent, powered by the housing market. Both consumer-spending growth and the rise in investment spending accelerated towards the end of the year, as growth gathered even more momentum. Encouragingly, NCB stockbrokers report that investment in machinery and equipment was one reason why investment spending accelerated towards the end of the year – in other words, money is going into places other than bricks and mortar.

How long can it go on? Who knows, but so far there is no sign of any slowdown. On the contrary, the latest data shows a 9 per cent rise in new car sales in the first two months of the year; the volume of retail sales in January was also up 9 per cent on the previous year, while borrowing from banks and building societies continues to storm ahead, running almost 30 per cent ahead of 2005 levels. Stockbrokers are now talking of growth of 5.5 per cent to 6 per cent this year, which would be the highest since the extraordinary 9.5 per cent growth recorded in 2000, at the very peak of the last boom.

Our huge reliance on the property market is the obvious point of exposure of our economy. This means that the main danger in the short term would be if the German economy started to enter a period of sustained growth, leading to a rapid increase in European Central Bank interest rates. There are also background concerns about the US economy, where any upheaval would be bound to have serious repercussions here. However, for the moment it appears to be a case of carry on borrowing and spending.

Source: *The Sunday Business Post*, 2 April 2006.

QUESTIONS

1. Define the term gross national product. Explain how it is different from (a) gross domestic product; (b) gross national disposable income. Using CSO data (www.cso.ie), report, in current prices, the value of, and annual percentage change in, all three measures for 2005. Repeat the exercise for the more recent recessionary year of 2009. Comment on the differences between the two years, as reflected in the respective growth rates.

2. 2006 was one of the last years of the Celtic Tiger boom. Using the expenditure components of GDP, report the annual percentage change over 2005 levels. In contrast, 2009 was the trough of the recession. Again, but for 2009, report the annual percentage changes in the GDP constituents. Comment on the differences. In both cases, report the volume (real) change.
3. We know that the boom did end, and with a terrible bang. In particular, during the recessionary years domestic demand collapsed whereas exports were reasonably resilient. Using CSO volume data, report the annual percentage change in both consumption and investment expenditure during the period 2007–2009. As a comparison, report the annual percentage real change in exports for the same period. What factor(s) might account for the difference(s)?

Answers on website

In brief, the national accounts do more than just describe the overall level of economic activity in the economy. Economists, policy-makers, interest groups and others are concerned with a whole range of issues such as the level of consumer spending, taxes, savings and other important components of the circular flow model. Notwithstanding the importance of these individual aspects of the national accounts, its overall contribution to economics is in its ability to measure a country's economic performance, either from year to year or in comparison to other economies. The collection of this data has greatly facilitated research into macroeconomic issues.

Any measure of economic activity is subject to criticism for what it includes or what it fails to include. We will now examine some of the shortcomings of GDP.

10.4 LIMITATIONS OF GDP AS A MEASURE OF ECONOMIC ACTIVITY

GDP is not a perfect measure of a country's economic performance: it has many weaknesses. Listed below is a comprehensive, although not exhaustive, record of transactions which are omitted from GDP. In addition, GDP does not measure or account for many aspects of a modern economy. A list of these is also included below.

Omissions

- *Transactions within the 'shadow' economy*   These include illegal activities such as drug-trafficking and prostitution and legal activities which are not reported to avoid tax payment. It is very difficult to estimate the value of such transactions. Estimates vary significantly from country to country. For example, in the USA estimates of the unofficial economy share in GDP range from 10–15%, while in Italy the range is 20–25%. In contrast, estimates for the UK and Switzerland, for example, are usually less than 10%. Using a currency–demand approach where it is assumed that shadow transactions take place in the form of cash, one estimate of the share of the unofficial economy in Ireland gives a figure of 7.8%.[6] It is common for a large shadow or hidden economy to exist in developing and transition countries. While this suggests that their national income statistics significantly underestimate the value of economic activity in these regions, their standard of living is still far below the average for western European countries.[7]

- *Externalities* These are side-effects generated in the production or consumption of commodities (see Chapter 8). They can be either positive, generating an external benefit, or negative, generating an external cost. Positive examples include education, inventions and attractive lawns. Pollution, congestion and waste disposal are examples of negative externalities. It is very difficult to calculate accurate values for these 'spillover' items. The omission of positive externalities from the National Accounts results in a GDP figure which underestimates the level of economic activity. Likewise, the exclusion of negative externalities results in an overestimated value of GDP.
- *Non-monetary transactions*   These are activities which, although economically beneficial, are undertaken by individuals primarily for their own benefit and not sold to the market. They include household work, gardening and DIY. Another example is the work done by voluntary, community or charity organisations. The reason for the omission of such activities is the difficulty in obtaining accurate figures for the value of the product or service involved. The omission of these non-monetary transactions results in a value of GDP which underestimates the level of economic activity.
- *Non-marketable goods and services*   Examples include state education and health care, defence and justice. These contribute to economic activity but, by their very nature, are not priced by market forces. These economic activities are included in the calculations for GDP but are done so at cost price whereas if a private body undertook the same service it would be included at market price. These activities are particularly important when making international comparisons.

GDP is neither a measure of, nor accounts for, the following:

- It is not a measure of economic well-being or welfare.[8] Arthur Pigou (1877–1959) argued that there is a close correlation between the level of national income and the level of economic welfare. At times, many would argue that the relationship is not very close. By definition, GDP measures only the value of goods and services produced. In preference to GDP, the United Nations (UN) uses a composite socio-economic measure called the human development index (HDI). Its constituents are GDP per capita, knowledge and education attainment, and life expectancy at birth. Table 10.9 shows the HDI for a small sample of countries (more in Chapter 19).
- It is not a measure of the competitiveness of an economy or its workforce. Competitiveness is measured annually by the International Institute for Management Development (IMD), which publishes the World Competitiveness Yearbook. The survey looks at 327 criteria, of which a number are background information and are not used in the calculations of the overall rankings. Of the remainder, about two-thirds is 'hard' data. This is information collected from international, regional and national sources, like the *National Income and Expenditure* report. The rest of the information comes from survey data collected from a panel of experts. The categories of criteria are: an assessment of a country's economic performance; government efficiency; infrastructure; and business efficiency. Ireland was ranked twenty-first in 2010, behind countries such as Singapore (first), the USA (third), Sweden (sixth), the Netherlands (twelfth) and Israel (seventeenth), but ahead of the UK (twenty-second) and France (twenty-fourth).
- Per capita GDP does not reflect disparities in income distribution. Although per capita income is increasing, distribution of that income is becoming more skewed. A number of relevant studies have been conducted by the Economic and Social Research Institute (ESRI), considering changes in 'relative poverty' among Irish households. Measures of relative poverty

TABLE 10.9: THE HUMAN DEVELOPMENT INDEX, 2010

Country	HDI	HDI Rank
Norway	0.938	1
Australia	0.937	2
USA	0.902	4
Ireland	0.895	5
UK	0.849	26
United Arab Emirates	0.815	32
Portugal	0.795	40
Malaysia	0.744	57
Jordan	0.681	82
India	0.519	119
Lesotho	0.427	141
Zimbabwe	0.140	169

Source: UNDP, *Human Development Report 2010.*

differ from measures of absolute poverty. For example, one measure of absolute poverty is the minimum amount of income required to pay for the food, clothing and shelter necessary to keep a person alive. In 'real' terms, this amount changes very little over time. Measures of relative poverty are 'moving targets'. As an economy develops, the basic requirements to participate socially and economically change. Items that were considered luxuries forty years ago, like telephones and televisions, are found in almost every household in Ireland today. Households that cannot afford these goods and services are relatively deprived, though strictly speaking, they can live without them. The ESRI classifies a household as living below 'poverty lines' if its disposable income (income from all sources, after tax is deducted) is less than 40%, 50% and 60% of the mean (average) income for all Irish households. During the early years of the Celtic Tiger, surveys revealed that there was an increase in the number of households living below the 50% poverty line, from 18.6% in 1994 to 24.6% in 1998. In the later years of the Celtic Tiger, between 2004 and 2007, the proportion falling below the poverty line (set at 60% of median income) actually fell, from 19% to 16%.[9] Overall, the rising tide of the Celtic Tiger economy did not lift all boats: increasing per capita GDP masks increasing inequality in the distribution of Irish income. A measure of income inequality is the Gini coefficient. Its range, as it is normally expressed, is between zero and one. Zero reflects no inequality. One reflects maximum inequality (all of the nation's income received by a single household). Two different sources from the 1990s gave Ireland a Gini coefficient of between 0.330 and 0.320.[10] While acknowledging the difficulties in measuring income inequality (cross-country comparison, in particular), it would appear that income inequality in Ireland, as measured by the Gini coefficient, did not change all that much in the 1990s and early 2000s, hovering close to, but above, the 0.30 level. According to Nolan and Maître (2007), '. . . rapid growth has not greatly affected the Irish ranking in terms of income inequality: Ireland continues to have a high degree of economic inequality in comparative terms after the boom, just as it did beforehand'.[11] Of course, all this may have changed during the economic crisis of the late 2000s.

It does not take into account differences in the composition of GDP. A common example compares countries with similar values for GDP. One nation is engaged in the production of weapons while the other is involved in the production of food. There is a very large difference in terms of relative economic well-being yet the relative data for GDP would not detect this difference. Let us take one further example.

Consider the relative importance of consumption and investment in terms of their respective contributions to the long-term prosperity of an economy. Some would argue that an increase in economic activity which arises out of greater expenditure on investment is more desirable than a similar increase in economic activity that arises out of greater expenditure on consumption. It is not coincidental that the countries which have achieved the fastest growth rates in recent times, the newly industrialised countries (NICs) for example, have proportionately more expenditure on investment relative to other countries. For example, in 2007 investment expenditure accounted for 23% and 29% of GDP in Japan and Korea respectively. This compares to a range of 15–18% for the UK and the USA.[12]

Unfortunately a straightforward comparison of the respective GDPs would not detect these and other subtle but important differences.

- It does not take into account the quality of the goods produced or improvements in quality over time. For example, a calculator purchased in 1970 was both more expensive and less sophisticated than a calculator purchased today.

In response to the criticisms which the economics profession faced on account of these omissions a number of alternatives to GDP as a measure of a country's economic performance have emerged. For example, in 1972 Professors James Tobin (1918–2002) of Yale University and William Nordhaus (b. 1941) estimated a value of net economic welfare (NEW).[13] They argued from the outset that GNP, which measures production, is not the ideal measure and should be replaced with some measure of consumption. They adjusted the GNP figure by subtracting the following set of activities: health and educational spending which were considered capital expenditure, 'disamenities' and 'regrettable necessities'. A value of non-market activities and leisure were added to give us the NEW. Between 1929 and 1965 in the USA it was estimated that the NEW grew at an annual rate of 1.1% per capita whereas an annual 1.7% per capita was recorded for the more conventional measure, NNP.

Notwithstanding the deficiencies listed above, GDP is still the most common measure used by the economics profession today. It is reasonably accurate given the complexities of a modern economy. Moreover, it is consistent from year to year and this facilitates yearly comparisons. It is likely to remain as the measure of economic activity for the foreseeable future.

This chapter concludes with a brief account of certain aspects of the Irish National Accounts.

10.5 THE IRISH EXPERIENCE

Although the National Accounts appear to be quite technical and tedious, the controversies which arise from them are lively and interesting.

Most of the tables in this section are taken from the annual CSO publication entitled *National Income and Expenditure*. Reports of this kind provide the 'raw materials' of economic research and are the sources of data used in most studies. The annual editions of these publications are always reported by the media and are available online from the CSO website.

In this section, we want to show how an economist uses these reports to understand what is happening in the national economy. First, we examine in some detail the difference between

GDP and GNP. We will then discuss the difference between GNP and GNDI. We conclude by examining the components of GNDI, and personal consumption in particular.

GDP vs GNP

As we stated earlier, for Ireland, GDP is greater than GNP. The two figures are separated by net factor income from the rest of the world. Table 10.10 shows the relevant data from the *National Income and Expenditure* publication.

TABLE 10.10: DIFFERENCE BETWEEN GDP AND GNP (AT CURRENT MARKET PRICES), €M

	2000	2001	2002	2003	2004	2005	2006	2007	2008	2009
GDP	105,018	117,136	138,464	140,008	149,344	162,314	177,343	189,374	179,989	159,646
Net factor income from the rest of the world	−15,488	−18,975	−23,696	−21,724	−22,879	−24,261	−23,264	−26,520	−25,317	−28,405
GNP	89,530	98,161	106,768	118,284	126,465	138,053	154,078	162,853	154,672	131,241

Source: CSO, *National Income and Expenditure 2009*, August 2010.

From this table we can see that net factor income from the rest of the world has increased in magnitude over time. Obviously, Irish nationals benefit more from the portion of national income that remains in the country than from the portion that leaves. Therefore, GNP is generally considered to be a better measure of Irish economic activity than GDP.

However, most international comparisons are based on GDP. More important, most comparisons within the EU are based on GDP. The reason is that for most developed countries, there is not much of a difference between GNP and GDP.

Table 10.11 shows the ratio of GNP to GDP for fourteen member states of the EU (before the 2004 and 2007 accessions). If the ratio is one, the two measures are essentially the same. This means that the outflows of interest and profits equal the inflows. A number greater than one indicates that

TABLE 10.11: RATIO OF GNP/GDP FOR 2009

Country	GNP/GDP
Austria	0.9949
Belgium	1.0131
Denmark	1.0260
Finland	0.9937
France	1.0096
Germany	1.0142
Greece	0.9586
Ireland	0.8063
Italy	0.9818
Netherlands	0.9949
Portugal	0.9519
Spain	0.9719
Sweden	1.0173
UK	1.0238

Source: World Bank.

the inflows are greater than the outflows. This could happen if a country is the home base for many multinationals that are sending their profits home or if the country lends more to other countries than it borrows. These inflows are added to the income of the nation. If the ratio is less than one, then the outflows exceed the inflows.

Most of the countries exhibit a ratio which is very close to one, with the exception of Ireland. Ireland has the dubious distinction of exhibiting the most disproportionate outflows.

Ultimately, this means that while Ireland did catch up to (and surpassed some of) her European partners, in terms of GDP, the standard of living did not catch up as fast.

In the Irish context, a better measure of the trend in living standards than either GNP or GDP is gross national disposable income (GNDI). As we explained in Section 10.3, GNDI is GNI plus net current transfers from the rest of the world. Table 10.12 reports GNDI for the period 2004–2009.

TABLE 10.12: GNP AND GNDI, 2004–2009, €M

	2004	2005	2006	2007	2008	2009
GNP	126,465	138,053	154,078	162,853	154,672	131,241
EU subsidies minus taxes	1,464	1,807	1,308	1,209	1,313	1,361
Net current transfers from the rest of the world	–1,071	–1,542	–1,813	–2,199	–2,467	–2,261
GNDI	126,858	138,318	153,574	161,863	153,518	130,340

Source: CSO, *National Income and Expenditure 2009*, August 2010.

Another advantage of this measure is that it can be decomposed into total consumption expenditure and total savings. In turn, total consumption expenditure can be either private (C) or public (G), as in Table 10.3. The decomposition of disposable income and of consumption expenditure in Ireland for the period 2004–2009 is in Table 10.13.

TABLE 10.13: GNDI AND ITS USE, 2004–2009, €M

	2004	2005	2006	2007	2008	2009
GNDI	126,858	138,318	153,574	161,863	153,518	130,340
Savings	34,805	38,252	43,976	41,103	29,497	18,291
Expenditure	92,053	100,066	109,598	120,761	124,021	112,049
of which						
Personal consumption of goods and services	71,478	77,820	85,044	93,436	94,825	84,331
Governmnent consumption of goods and services	20,575	22,246	24,554	27,324	29,196	27,718

Source: CSO, *National Income and Expenditure 2009*, August 2010.

We began this investigation of the Irish National Accounts with GDP, the international standard measure of economic activity. Table 10.14 reports a 1.3% annual increase in nominal GDP for the period 2004–2009. In this section, we noted that both GNP and GNDI are better measures of Ireland's economic activity. Interestingly, for the same period, the annual percentage increases in GNP and GNDI, of 0.7% and 0.5% respectively, are smaller than the GDP annual increase.

TABLE 10.14: ANNUAL PERCENTAGE INCREASES IN MAIN AGGREGATES

	2004–2009
Gross Domestic Product (GDP)	1.3
Gross National Product (GNP)	0.7
Gross National Disposable Income (GNDI)	0.5
Total consumption expenditure	4.0
of which	
Government consumption of goods and services	6.1
Personal consumption of goods and services	3.4

Source: CSO, National Income and Expenditure 2009, August 2010.

Yet another measure of a nation's economic success is the level of private consumption by its residents. The annual percentage increase in the personal consumption of goods and services was 3.4%. While this average annual growth rate (much of it debt financed) exceeds the GDP average annual growth rate, it still leaves Ireland, in terms of private consumption levels, behind some of its EU partners. This is shown in Table 10.15.

TABLE 10.15: PRIVATE CONSUMPTION EXPENDITURE

	IRL	UK	DK	IT	DE	AT
1980	80.4	91.7	101.8	101.7	123.0	112.3
1985	74.1	96.1	106.1	101.8	123.2	115.0
1990	77.8	102.5	93.8	101.8	118.0	110.8
1995	82.8	106.3	100.0	104.8	110.3	110.8
2000	93.9	115.4	92.8	103.6	103.2	106.5
2005	100.4	120.3	90.5	94.0	104.9	103.8
2009	101.0	115.9	90.6	93.1	104.8	104.8

Source: European Commission, European Economy, Spring 2010.
Note: IRL = Ireland; UK = United Kingdom; DK = Denmark; IT = Italy; DE = Germany; AT = Austria. The figures are adjusted for purchasing power.

Table 10.15 shows private final consumption expenditure at current prices per capita for a selection of EU countries, where EU-15 = 100. The phenomenal growth rates of the Celtic Tiger years have certainly reversed Ireland's position vis-à-vis other EU member states. By the mid-2000s only Luxembourg, UK, Austria and Germany had a private consumption expenditure level, per head of population, in excess of Ireland's. Of course, much of this was to change with the Great Recession and the fall in consumption in the late 2000s (see Chapter 18).

The point of this short exercise was to use the National Accounts to assess a country's economic activity. In addition, we have shown that measures of economic well-being other than GDP are worth considering and monitoring. This is particularly true in the case of Ireland.

SUMMARY

1. The circular flow diagram depicts the workings of a modern economy where transactions between households, firms, government, the banking system and the foreign markets are described. These transactions are real or monetary.
2. The three methods for measuring a country's economic activity are the income, output and expenditure approaches. They are defined so that each should yield the same result. In Ireland the data are published by the CSO in the annual *National Income and Expenditure* publication.
3. National income accounting is the system economists use to measure the economic activity of a country. The most common measure used is gross domestic product. All other terms used are simply a variation of this measure.
4. Nominal GDP is a measure of goods and services at current prices. Real GDP is measured at constant prices, by the use of a fixed or base year. Changes in GDP can come from two sources: price changes or production changes. Real GDP is a better measure because it isolates the production changes.
5. Although GDP is the most common measure of economic activity, it has a number of significant shortcomings. Both its omissions and its failure to capture changes in other economic variables have forced economists to look for alternative measures. The human development index (HDI), used by the United Nations, is a common alternative.
6. *National Income and Expenditure*, published by the CSO, is the main source of data for economists who are studying changes in Ireland's national income. More important, it reports on GDP, the measure of national income which is used for international comparisons.

KEY TERMS

Circular flow
Leakages
Injections
Investment
Transfer payments
Expenditure method
Income method
Output method
Double counting
Value added
National Accounts
Gross domestic product
Gross national product
Net factor income from abroad
Gross national disposable income
Net economic welfare

Net national product
Depreciation
Market prices
Factor cost
National income
Personal income
Disposable income
Nominal GDP
Real GDP
GDP deflator
GDP per capita
Shadow economy
Externalities
Human development index
Gini coefficient

REVIEW QUESTIONS

1. Explain, with the aid of a diagram, the complete circular flow model. List the injections and the leakages. Explain how these movements into and out of the circular flow can influence the level of economic activity.
2. Describe the transactions that occur between the following sets of agents: households and firms; households and government; firms and financial institutions; firms and government; firms and foreign markets.
3. List and briefly explain the three approaches to measuring economic activity. Using the circular flow diagram, explain why, in principle, they yield the same result.
4. Outline the differences between gross domestic product and national income. Explain all relevant terms used.
5. Do you think GDP is an underestimate or an overestimate of the level of economic activity in Ireland? Support your answer.
6. For Ireland, does GDP or GNP provide a more accurate measure of economic activity? Support your answer.

WORKING PROBLEMS

1. On the basis of the data below determine national income using:
   (a) income method;
   (b) output method;
   (c) expenditure method.

TABLE 10.16

Item	€bn	Item	€bn
Rent	450	Personal consumption	4,000
Interest	300	Transport and communication	1,500
Agriculture	100	Profits	300
Investment	600	Depreciation	300
Indirect taxes	800	Subsidies	400
Net income from abroad	250	Government expenditure	700
Exports	3,050	Industry	3,000
Public administration	650	Imports	2,400
Compensation of employees	4,200		

2. The information in Table 10.17 has been gathered for an imaginary economy. Using the data in the table calculate the following:
   (a) GDP;
   (b) disposable income;
   (c) savings;
   (d) net exports;
   (e) injections and leakages. Comment on their relative sizes.

TABLE 10.17

Item	€bn
Consumer expenditure (C)	250
Government expenditure (G)	500
Investment (I)	150
Taxes (TX)	350
Transfer payments (TR)	200
Exports (X)	360
Imports (M)	340

MULTI-CHOICE QUESTIONS

1. Within the circular flow model:
   (a) transactions are either real or monetary;
   (b) transfer payments are an injection and reflect current production;
   (c) economic activity will increase if injections exceed withdrawals;
   (d) both (a) and (c) above;
   (e) (a), (b) and (c) above.

2. Which of the following set of variables is an injection into the circular flow diagram?
   (a) exports, taxes and investment;
   (b) government expenditure, exports and investment;
   (c) investment, imports and subsidies;
   (d) imports, savings and taxes;
   (e) none of the above.

3. Which of the following is an example of a real flow from firms to households?
   (a) factors of production;
   (b) payments for goods and services;
   (c) goods and services;
   (d) payments for factors of production;
   (e) none of the above.

4. The three broad methods of measuring economic activity are:
   (a) GNP, GDP and NNP;
   (b) income, expenditure and output;
   (c) national income, personal income and disposable income;
   (d) budget, balance of payments and expenditure estimates;
   (e) none of the above.

5. The difference between gross national product and gross domestic product is accounted for by:
   (a) depreciation;
   (b) indirect taxes;
   (c) transfer payments;

(d) net factor income from abroad;

(e) personal taxes.

6. Which of the following is a better measure of the standard of living?

(a) GDP per employee;

(b) investment expenditure;

(c) GDP per capita;

(d) personal savings;

(e) GDP.

TRUE OR FALSE (SUPPORT YOUR ANSWER)

1. The circular flow model implies that the value of exports, a leakage, must be equal to the value of imports, an injection, in order for economic activity to remain unchanged.

2. The four factors of production are wages, interest, rent and profit. Workers are paid rent, lenders earn profit, landowners earn wages and interest is the residual.

3. The values for GNP and national income would be equal if depreciation, indirect taxes and subsidies were all valued at zero.

4. If two countries have the same GNP, then the standard of living is the same in both countries.

5. If over some period of time prices have doubled and real GDP has doubled, then nominal GDP has doubled.

6. The Irish GDP figure exceeds the GNP figure because outflows of factor income exceed inflows of factor income.

CASE STUDY

Extract from *The Irish Times*
Ireland technically out of recession
by Charlie Taylor

GDP grew slightly during the third quarter but the Central Statistics Office (CSO) has urged caution on calling an end to recession. The latest Quarterly National Accounts, which were published this morning, indicate that on a seasonally adjusted basis there was a 0.3 per cent increase in Gross Domestic Product (GDP) from July through to September. On an annual basis, GDP fell by 7.4 per cent in the year to the end of October, compared to a 7.9 per cent decline in the preceding quarter. Technically, given that the definition of recession is two quarters in a row of falling GDP, this means that Ireland has now exited recession. However,

at a press conference earlier today, assistant director general of the CSO Bill Keating refused to call an end to the recession, pointing out that much of the rise in GDP was attributed to profits from multinationals based in Ireland. Whether Ireland was out of recession or not was 'a matter of semantics', Mr Keating said. 'The general picture shows that on a seasonally adjusted basis there is a levelling off in GDP but GNP continues to decline, albeit at a slower pace than it has in previous quarters. Contributing to the GDP increase in a fairly major way was growth in the multinational sector,' he added.

$\longrightarrow$

Analysts also warned against declaring the end of what has been one of the worse recessions ever experienced in Ireland. GDP is the international method of calculating economic decline but in Ireland's case, the Economic and Social Research Institute (ESRI) and other local bodies prefer to focus on GNP (Gross National Product), a measure which strips out multinational profits, much of which usually leave the country. According to CSO, profits declared here by foreign-owned enterprises increased by €1,054 million during the year ending 31 October 2009. During the third quarter Gross National Product (GNP) showed a decline of 1.4 per cent on a seasonally adjusted basis. In the year to the end of October 2009, GNP was 11.3 per cent lower.

A breakdown of the latest CSO figures show that consumer spending was 7.3 per cent lower in the third quarter of 2009, compared to the same three-month period a year earlier. Capital investment declined by 35 per cent on an annual basis while net exports were 2,813 million higher than a year earlier. Over the year the volume of output of industry decreased by 9.6 per cent. Within this the output of the construction sector fell by 34.4 per cent. Output of distribution, transport and communications was down 9 per cent on an annual basis, while output of other services was 3.4 per cent lower, the figures show.

Alan McQuaid, economist at stockbroking firm Bloxham said, given that international commentators put so much emphasis on quarterly changes in GDP, we shouldn't downplay the third quarter increase. He said we should take some consolation that on this basis, Ireland came out of recession ahead of the UK. 'Overall, we continue to believe that the Irish economy is making progress and is heading in the right direction,' said Mr McQuaid. 'While GDP is set to contract by around 7.5 per cent in real terms in 2009, we still think the average fall in national output could be less than 1 per cent next year.'

Commenting on the quarterly figures, Ibec senior economist Fergal O'Brien said the latest data shows the economy is beginning to stabilise. 'In terms of the pace of contraction in the Irish economy, the worst is now clearly behind us. Most sectors of activity are showing signs of stabilisation, with the exception of the construction sector, which continued to lurch downwards in the third quarter,' he said. 'Today's numbers do not change our view that GDP will fall by about 7.5 per cent this year and will drop on an annual basis again in 2010. We can now see some light at the end of the tunnel, however, and the economy should begin to grow again around the middle of next year.' KBC's chief economist Austin Hughes also rejected the idea the recession was over, saying the quarterly GDP increase does not reflect the reality of the drop in incomes and employment experienced in Ireland over the past year.

Source: The Irish Times, 17 December 2009.

Questions

1. What two methods for measuring economic activity are implied by the article? What are the components of each method and how did they perform, in terms of real percentage growth rates, in Q3 2009?

2. The article refers to the technical terms 'seasonally adjusted' and 'recession'. Define both terms and explain how they are measured.

3. Using the most up-to-date data for the year 2009 from the CSO (www.cso.ie), report the following:
   (a) GDP, GNP and net factor income from abroad, all in constant prices;
   (b) GDP and GDP real growth rates;
   (c) C, I, G, X and M, both levels and growth rates, and all at constant prices.

APPENDIX 10.1: SAVINGS AND INVESTMENT

The classical doctrine of economics argued that the equality of savings and investment was an automatic process with the rate of interest playing the key role. This equality between savings and investment can be explained in mathematical form. Suppose there is no government and no foreign sector. The expenditure approach measures GDP as the sum of consumer expenditure and investment expenditure. This identity can be expressed as follows:

$$Y \equiv C + I$$ [1]

However, we can also view GDP as national income which is equal, in the absence of government, to disposable income. Disposable income in turn is either spent or saved. This can be written as follows:

$$Y \equiv C + S$$ [2]

Combine Identity 1 and 2

$$C + I \equiv Y \equiv C + S$$ [3]

The left-hand side of [3] shows the components of expenditure whereas the right-hand side shows the allocation of income. Subtracting consumption from both sides yields:

$$I \equiv S$$ [4]

Identity [4] shows that in a simple model of the economy investment and savings are equal. This was one of the basic tenets of the classical school which dominated economic thinking in the nineteenth century.

However, in the *Treatise on Money* Keynes argued that savings and investment were very different activities, carried out by two very different sets of people and, moreover, were not necessarily identical. In the next two chapters we will examine in greater detail Keynes' views on these activities.

CHAPTER 11

The Keynesian Revolution

'*The General Theory of Employment is the Economics of Depression.*'[1]

JOHN R. HICKS (1904–89)

'*Whenever I ask England's six leading economists a question, I get seven answers – two from Mr Keynes.*'[2]

WINSTON CHURCHILL

CHAPTER OBJECTIVES

Upon completing this chapter, the student should understand:

- the pre-Keynesian economic doctrine;
- the economic turbulence caused by the Great Depression;
- the contribution of Keynes to modern macroeconomics.

OUTLINE

11.1 The classical doctrine of economics
11.2 The life and works of John Maynard Keynes
11.3 The Keynesian revolution

INTRODUCTION

This chapter deals with the background to Keynesian economics. We begin with a description of the classical doctrine of economics. This is followed by a discussion on Keynes and his life, his ideas and his contribution to macroeconomics. The last section deals with the Great Depression of the 1930s and the emergence of the economics of Keynes.

11.1 THE CLASSICAL DOCTRINE OF ECONOMICS

Disagreement among economists is not new. In the seventeenth century, prior to the emergence of the classical doctrine, economics was not considered to be a distinct academic discipline. Even then, two groups, the mercantilists and the physiocrats, held radically different views about the way that the economy operates. Economic disagreements to this day, particularly about the appropriate role of government, date back to the mercantilist/physiocrat debate. These two groups helped to lay the groundwork for the discussion of economic issues.

The actual word 'mercantilism' had different meanings but was generally understood to mean 'the economics of nationalism'. According to followers of mercantilism the key to national economic prosperity was the accumulation of gold and silver. All policies were aimed towards building a positive balance of trade. Economic thinking was dominated by this policy concern.

Mercantilism was particularly strong in France. Jean Baptiste Colbert (1619–83) served as the Minister for Finance during the reign of Louis XIV. Under his guidance, every aspect of French production was state controlled. Manufactured products were promoted at the expense of agricultural products. All imports and exports were closely monitored.

Many of the writers of the day were merchant businessmen. Critics of mercantilism were quick to point out that the businessmen themselves were often the main beneficiaries of the policies which they advocated. At the time, many felt that the excessive regulations by government led to production inefficiencies. It is often said that the burden of taxation, unevenly spread, ultimately led to the French Revolution.

Not surprisingly, the main reaction against mercantilism also came from the French. While not advocating the overthrow of the monarchy, the physiocrats argued for a radical departure from the policy of state regulation. Physiocracy is derived from the French word 'Physiocrate' which means the 'rule of nature'. The physiocrats, and later the classical economists, believed that there was natural order in the economic system which was analogous to the laws of nature. The massive state intervention of the mercantilists was at best ineffective, and at worst served as a deterrent to economic growth.

François Quesnay was a prominent physiocrat. He attempted to explain and identify the general laws which govern economic behaviour. Quesnay and the physiocrats believed that the agricultural sector was the only productive sector of the economy. The export duties placed on grain by the mercantilists were both unnecessary and served as a disincentive to production. In this sense, the rule of government violated natural law. It is from the physiocrats that we inherit the ideological basis for *laissez-faire* which generally refers to an economic system which is characterised by free trade and low levels of state intervention.

Adam Smith (1723–90) is considered to be the father of economics and the founder of the classical school. His book, *An Enquiry into the Nature and Causes of the Wealth of Nations* was at one level a reaction against mercantilism. His thinking was obviously influenced by his acquaintance with François Quesnay. Like Quesnay, Smith attempted to understand the general principles which underlay economic growth.

For Smith, the basis of wealth was the division of labour. Production expands significantly as labour becomes more specialised. It is within this context that Smith adopted the free-trade doctrine of the physiocrats. A larger market expands the opportunities for specialised labour.

Smith also advanced the physiocrats' argument concerning 'deregulation'. He attempted to explain the economic forces which cause individuals, motivated by self-interest, to achieve objectives which are socially beneficial. The 'invisible hand' is often interpreted as the forces of competition. Consumers, acting independently of each other, nevertheless communicate their needs to producers. Producers, who are striving to make a living, attempt to satisfy consumer needs. This is the basis of the perfectly competitive market structure.

Smith observed that the mercantilist system promoted collusive agreements between merchants and politicians, often at the expense of the ordinary citizen. He argued that unregulated competition would ensure that goods were produced more efficiently and distributed more evenly among the population. Competition, in short, was a system that militated against a concentration of wealth and in favour of a more equitable distribution of resources.

Smith was one of a group of economists who came to be known as the classical school. Others include David Ricardo (1772–1823), Thomas Malthus (1766–1834) and John Stuart Mill (1806–73). They dominated economic thought in the hundred years following the publication of *The Wealth of Nations*. They were academics, with the exception of David Ricardo, who was a stockbroker by profession. This raised the tenor of the economic debate since they could no longer be accused of advocating particular policies which advanced their self-interest.

Although they ultimately became known as economists, their writings span many of the classical subjects including history, politics, physics, philosophy and jurisprudence. Political economy was originally taught under the chair of moral philosophy by Smith at the University of Glasgow. Needless to say, Smith's economic perspective was influenced by his study of philosophy.

The classical economists focused on the issues of growth, value and distribution. Unlike their successors, the classical economists never saw growth as an automatic process. Discussions focused not only on attempting to understand the conditions which promoted economic growth, but also on the type of policies which would foster these conditions. In this sense, *laissez-faire* should not be construed as the lack of government policy, but as a positive initiative to support competition.

The end of the nineteenth century was a period of transition. It was during this period that economics was firmly established as a distinct academic discipline. Many within the discipline attempted to align it with the natural sciences rather than with what were considered to be the less rigorous social sciences. A deductive methodology was adopted. Models were developed, based on restrictive assumptions, which are logical within their own framework. This approach may be traced back to Ricardo, but it is very different from the descriptive, historic approach which was more common to the other classical economists.

The 'Marginalists' were a group of economists who included W. Stanley Jevons (1835–82), Carl Menger (1840–1921) and Leon Walras (1834–1910). The work of these economists represented the transition between the classical and neoclassical schools. One of the unresolved issues of the classical school was the theory of value. This was partly because the classical economists concentrated on the supply side. They assumed that goods had some utility, otherwise nobody would want them. However, the value of goods was determined by the amount of labour which it took to produce them.

The contribution of the marginalists was to develop the downward sloping demand curve which was based on diminishing marginal utility. Goods had utility, as suggested by the classicals, but that marginal utility diminished as more of the good was consumed. Only falling prices could entice an individual to consume more of the same good.

This idea was later applied by neoclassical economists to the supply side. The upward sloping supply curve is based on the idea of diminishing marginal productivity which causes marginal costs to increase when more is produced. Part of the marginal cost curve is the supply curve for the perfectly competitive firm. The two curves combine to form a model of price determination. When price is set in the competitive market, based solely on the forces of demand and supply, it means that resources are efficiently diverted to the uses which achieve the highest possible utility for the consumer. The 'market' is the neoclassical model which conceptualises Adam Smith's 'invisible hand'.

In the decades which preceded the Great Depression, the neoclassical economists developed general equilibrium and partial equilibrium models which were mathematically difficult and aimed at a narrow range of consumption and production problems. They followed the thinking of the physiocrats and the classical economists, recommending a circumscribed range of government activity. Their emphasis on individual choice meant that they saw government as limiting the range of individual actions. Government spending meant that less money was available for private investment. It had to be paid for by taxation which limited the disposable income of consumers. Specific policy recommendations of the neoclassicals will be contrasted with Keynesian alternatives in Section 11.3.

11.2 THE LIFE AND WORKS OF JOHN MAYNARD KEYNES

Keynes is to economics what Freud is to psychoanalysis, Einstein is to physics and Darwin is to biology.[3] Mark Blaug in his work *John Maynard Keynes: Life, Ideas, Legacy* referred to the three great revolutions in modern economics: Adam Smith's support for unregulated markets, the 'marginal revolution' and finally the emergence of a new orthodoxy – Keynesian economics.

John Maynard Keynes was born in Cambridge, England in 1883. His parents were middle-class intellectuals. His father John Neville was a well-respected philosopher and economist who worked with Alfred Marshall in Cambridge. Keynes, with the help of scholarships, was educated at Eton and then King's College, Cambridge where he studied classics and mathematics, winning many college prizes in the process. At the time his other academic interests included philosophy and literature but, notably, not economics.

He graduated in 1905 at the age of 22 and opted for a career in the civil service. In order to prepare himself for the entry examinations he attended economics lectures in Cambridge. His lecturer was Alfred Marshall who taught Keynes the basic tenets of neoclassical economics. Little did he know that this son of a former colleague would question the very essence of what he and his contemporaries represented.

After briefly studying economics Keynes disappointed Marshall and others by joining the civil service. On completing his exams, it is said that he remarked, 'I evidently knew more about Economics than my examiners.'[4] This was not the last time that Keynes expressed self-belief, verging on arrogance.

His two-year experience in the India Office was the inspiration behind his first book on economics, *Indian Currency and Finance*. While working for the civil service, Keynes made significant progress with his thesis on probability. On the basis of this work, Keynes was offered a Fellowship at King's in 1909. He began teaching economics and within two years had become the editor of *The Economic Journal*, the most respected economics journal in the UK at the time. His *Treatise on Probability*, published in a revised form in 1921, was well received by his peers and particularly by philosophers.

Keynes' talents were also recognised outside academic circles. During World War I he had re-entered the civil service and by 1919 he had become the senior British Treasury representative at the Versailles Peace Conference. However, he became very disillusioned with the Allied treatment of the Germans and when the figure of £24bn in reparations was demanded, he resigned. On returning to England he wrote *The Economic Consequences of the Peace*, for which he received international acclaim. In the book Keynes was highly critical of the harsh economic terms agreed by the Allies and he predicted serious consequences for the future including the possibility of 'vengeance' in the form of a 'final civil war . . . before which the horrors of the late German war will fade into nothing . . .'

Keynes spent the next few years teaching, writing and speculating in financial markets. This latest interest made Keynes a millionaire although he was to lose heavily during the Wall Street crash of 1929. By 1936 he had recovered his losses and was worth approximately half a million pounds.

In 1923 *A Tract on Monetary Reform* was published. This marked a change in Keynes' view on economics and, particularly, on the role of government. Prior to its publication Keynes was regarded as a supporter of the classical doctrine of economic liberalism. He had advocated the reliance on market forces in preference to active government intervention. He was also a strong supporter of international free trade, which he saw as a necessary condition for economic prosperity.

In this publication Keynes advocated the active use of monetary policy in order to determine the price level. This was to be done within the context of a managed monetary system which was to replace the Gold Standard. This support for managing the economy, both in a positive and active fashion, was a shift away from the *laissez-faire* policies of the nineteenth century. However, it was not until 1936, with the publication of *The General Theory*, that the economics profession acknowledged the beginning of a revolution.

A Tract on Monetary Reform did make a significant impact but for a very different reason. In it Keynes argued against returning to the Gold Standard at the pre-war fixed exchange rate. He believed that price stability was more important than exchange rate stability with exchange rate policy ideally being subordinate to the needs of the domestic economy. In advocating this policy, Keynes argued against the conventional wisdom advocated by the economic and financial establishment of the day. The Treasury, bankers and business people, for various reasons, supported the reinstitution of the Gold Standard. Unlike Keynes, they applauded the decision by the Chancellor of the Exchequer, Winston Churchill, to rejoin in 1925 at the pre-war exchange rate.

Keynes wrote a number of pamphlets prior to 1936 which indicated his growing mistrust of the market system and his belief in tackling unemployment with the aid of government policies. By this time he was involved with the Liberal Party and had the job of advising its leader, Lloyd George. It was widely known that Keynes supported public works programmes in order to provide employment. As usual Keynes presented his argument in a graphical and emotive way: 'If the Treasury were to fill old bottles with bank-notes, bury them at suitable depths in disused coal mines which are then filled up to the surface with town rubbish, and leave to private enterprise . . . to dig the notes up again . . . there need be no more unemployment . . .'[5]

Some of Keynes' early work was criticised within the economics profession because it was not grounded in theory. Whereas the *Tract* was written for a general audience, the *Treatise on Money* (1930) was pitched at a more professional level. Nonetheless, it was severely criticised. Friedrich von Hayek (1899–1992) and D. H. Robertson (1890–1963), two contemporaries of Keynes, wrote less than favourable reviews of the book.

Yet many elements of this book re-appeared in *The General Theory*, which Keynes started shortly after the publication of the *Treatise* and took four years to complete. Valuable contributions were made by his Cambridge followers, including Richard Kahn (1905–89), Joan Robinson (1903–83), Piero Sraffa (1898–1983), Roy Harrod (1900–78) and James Meade (1907–95). His letter to George Bernard Shaw in 1935, in anticipation of the book's publication, is another example of Keynes' self-belief. He wrote '. . . I believe myself to be writing a book on economic theory which will largely revolutionise – not, I suppose, at once but in the course of the next ten years – the way the world thinks about economic problems.'[6]

The General Theory of Employment, Interest and Money of 1936 is generally agreed to be a very difficult book to read and understand. As the title suggests it is concerned almost exclusively with theory; this differentiates it from the *Treatise*. To this day, over seventy-five years later, economists and commentators argue over the precise meaning of many elements in the book. Essentially it is a book on unemployment, with the causes and solutions analysed in very obscure language. Terms such as the consumption function, the marginal propensity to consume and the multiplier confused many a reader. Yet most students of economics today are familiar with these and other Keynesian concepts. This illustrates the influence that *The General Theory* and more particularly Keynes has had on economics.

The pattern of his life was disturbed yet again by World War II. In 1939, he re-entered the Treasury as an adviser to the Chancellor of the Exchequer. *How to Pay for the War*, which was published in 1940, dealt not with the problems of deficiencies in demand, as *The General Theory* had, but with the problems arising out of excess demand. His influence was evident in both the British budget of 1941 and the UK White Paper on *Employment Policy* of 1944. The latter is of historical importance as it marks the first time in modern economic history that there was a government commitment to securing 'a high and stable level of employment'.[7]

In the same year Keynes was the head of the British delegation at the Bretton Woods Conference. Just prior to that, he put forward a plan, known as the Keynes Plan, which aimed to restore stability to the international economy and, in particular, to international trade which had been decimated by the break-up of the Gold Standard and the outbreak of World War II. The establishment once again rejected his ideas and opted instead for the less radical approach proposed by the American delegation. This led to the establishment of the International Monetary Fund (IMF) and the World Bank.

On Easter Sunday, April 1946, at the age of 62, he died at his Sussex farmhouse in Tilton. After such a fulfilling life his only regret was the wish that he had drunk more champagne.

11.3 THE KEYNESIAN REVOLUTION

Though educated by neoclassical economists, Keynes diverged from them both theoretically and in terms of his policy prescriptions. The catalyst for this change was the Great Depression.

Thursday, 24 October 1929 will always be remembered as Black Thursday, the day that the stock market on Wall Street crashed.[8] Panic and confusion reigned. It was reported that eleven speculators committed suicide during the crash. Wall Street did not recover in the subsequent months or years. By November 1929, the average price of fifty leading stocks had fallen to 50% of their September levels. In July 1932, the Dow Jones index of industrial companies was 90% below its value of September 1929.[9]

The Great Depression followed the Wall Street crash in both the USA and the UK. After a prosperous decade in the 1920s, aggregate economic activity in the USA reached a peak in August 1929. Real GNP fell by nearly 30% between the 1929 peak and the 1933 trough. The unemployment rate rose from about 3% or 1.5 million people to close to 25% or 12 million people. Investment expenditure fell by 75% during this period while consumer expenditure dropped by 20%. The UK suffered a similar fate. Unemployment reached over 22% in the winter of 1932 which meant that three million people were out of work.

Economists, politicians and journalists could not agree on the cause of the crash or on the preferred policy response.[10] The classical school of economics advanced policies based on the belief in the ultimate stability of the market and its ability to return to full employment. Keynes argued against this non-interventionist approach and proposed radical changes in economic policy. He suggested an urgent need for active and extensive government intervention. To understand the differences between the policy recommendations, we must first consider some of the theoretical distinctions which separate the classical and Keynesian schools.

Often, when we discuss the upheaval in the study of economics which we attribute to Keynes, we call it the 'Keynesian revolution'. To understand why Keynes was revolutionary, we will look at how his point of view differed from the classical position. We will begin with the theoretical differences and then discuss how these translated to differing policy recommendations.

Classical economists built on the foundation laid by the physiocrats. Their belief in the stability of the market led them to advocate minimum government intervention. Keynes, however, followed the mercantilists. He not only adopted some of their ideas, he advocated a much more prominent and active role for government. Keynes believed that the market was inherently unstable. Government policy could counter instability in the market.

Keynes began his theoretical attack by looking at the classical model of the labour market. For classical economists, this was the source of unemployment. Labour was demanded by firms and supplied by households. At the equilibrium wage rate, all labour that wanted to work could work: there was no involuntary unemployment. When confronted with the high unemployment which existed during the Great Depression, classical economists argued in favour of a cut in the wage rate to alleviate the excess supply of labour. Keynes had the advantage of learning from the US experience. In 1932–33, the wage rate fell but this did not lead to increased employment as classical theory predicts.

This led Keynes to look for a different explanation for unemployment. He thought that the cause of unemployment was a deficiency in the demand for goods. He argued that a cut in the wage rate would reduce consumer expenditure and lead to a deficiency in demand. This would create uncertainty among investors who would be less likely to undertake investment expenditure. As the demand for consumer and capital goods fell, so would the demand for labour. In short, the decrease of the wage rate actually exacerbated the problem of unemployment.

Moreover, there was little agreement between the classical school and Keynes on the flexibility of wages. Wage flexibility was an intrinsic part of the classical doctrine. In contrast, Keynes argued that wages may not respond quickly to changing market conditions. Institutional arrangements like labour contracts and unions keep wages rigid. In fact, he disputed the desirability of flexible wages. Since consumption is one source of demand, falling wages led to a decrease in consumer expenditure. Inflexible wages helped to maintain the level of demand in an economy.

Keynes continued his theoretical attack with a discussion of Say's Law which states that 'Supply brings forth its own demand.' This is an idea which is often depicted through the circular flow. Households provide the factors of production which are used by firms to produce goods. The households are paid income by the firms which they use to purchase the goods which the firms produced. To take this one step further, households can either consume or save their income. However, in the classical model, based on Say's Law, savings will always re-enter the circular flow in the form of investment. In other words, savings, a leakage from the circular flow, always equals investment, an injection into the circular flow. The classical economists advocated thrift. A high savings rate released labour and capital from producing consumer goods to producing investment goods. This increased the productive capacity of the economy.

Keynes disagreed with the classical analysis of savings and investment. He argued that savings and investment were very different activities, carried out by different people and influenced by different factors. There was nothing automatic about the process. Savings might sit as idle balances if investors were not inclined to use them. A high rate of savings reduced consumer expenditure which led to a reduction of national income. In this case, savings, the leakage from the circular flow, is greater than investment, the injection. The result is a slowdown of economic activity.

For classical economists, investment depends on the interest rate. The interest rate is determined in the market for loanable funds. The source of the supply of loanable funds is savings. Investors demand loanable funds for investment. The interest rate, which can be thought of as the price of borrowed funds, adjusts to bring the demand and supply into equilibrium.

Keynes believed that interest rates were determined in the money market. Money supply was determined by the monetary authorities. Money demand depended on income and the households' preference for holding money rather than interest-bearing assets. The interest rate was determined by the interaction of the demand for and supply of money.

Keynes did not deny that interest rates influenced firms' investment decisions. However, he argued that investment decisions depended mainly on their expectations for future profits. Even at very low rates of interest, firms would not invest if they did not feel that their revenues would cover the cost of borrowing money. From Keynes' perspective, investment was not simply a mathematical decision based on anticipated costs and revenues. The revenue prediction depended on the investors' belief of future business conditions. In his own words, 'Thus if the animal spirits are dimmed and the spontaneous optimism falters, leaving us to depend on nothing but a mathematical expectation, enterprise will fade and die; – though fears of loss may have a basis no more reasonable than hopes of profit had before.'[11]

Differences in theory naturally led to differing policy recommendations. The policy recommendations of the British Committee on National Expenditure which was set up in 1931 to address the problems of the Great Depression offered policy prescriptions which were neoclassical. The preoccupation over the balanced budget led the Committee, under the chairmanship of Sir George May, to recommend cuts in government expenditure and increases in taxation. They were concerned that government spending would 'crowd out' private investment.

Keynes argued against this non-interventionist approach. Unemployment, according to Keynes, resulted from a failure of demand. The policy recommendations of the Committee would aggravate this situation in two ways. Increased taxation decreases disposable income. With less income, households will spend less and consumer expenditure falls. A decrease in government expenditure directly decreases the demand in the economy.

According to Keynes, government spending was not a diversion of funds from the private sector. The public sector compensated for deficient demand which originated in the private sector. Keynes advocated fiscal policy measures, primarily government spending on public works projects, in order to generate employment. He said, 'I expect to see the State . . . taking an even greater responsibility for directly organising investment.'[12] As a consequence of this higher expenditure, the neoclassical rule of balancing the budget each year was abandoned. Adam Smith's advice that 'The only good budget is a balanced budget' became redundant. Keynes' ideas were adopted by Lloyd George, leader of the Liberal Party, who proposed an increase in the amount spent on public works programmes.

In addition, Keynes advocated using monetary policy to stimulate demand. This would translate into low interest rates which would induce new investment expenditure. However, he was sceptical of relying solely on monetary policy because, as was mentioned earlier, reduced interest rates alone might not be enough to entice investment. The use of both fiscal and monetary policy to stimulate demand and increase employment, is in sharp contrast to the *laissez-faire* policies advocated by neoclassical economists.

Figure 11.1 illustrates the relationship between the economic variables which were mentioned in *The General Theory*.

Output depends on total expenditure, which is comprised of consumer, government and investment expenditure. Consumer expenditure is explained by the consumption function which is described in the next chapter. Investment expenditure depends on the rate of interest and the expected rate of return on new investment. Finally, the rate of interest is determined by the quantity of money and what Keynes called the liquidity preference, i.e. the demand for money.

The Keynesian model which is outlined in the next chapter and the policy recommendations which follow are ultimately short-term in duration. Keynes' dismissive nature of the long run explains the absence of any long-term analysis. Such a view is epitomised in his famous line '*In the long run* we are all dead.'[13]

FIGURE 11.1: THE RELATIONSHIP BETWEEN THE VARIABLES IN THE KEYNESIAN MODEL

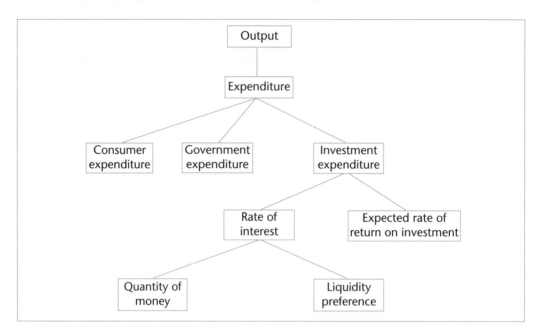

SUMMARY

1. The pre-Keynesian or classical school of economics believed that markets were inherently stable and would automatically tend towards full employment. Unemployment arose out of imperfections in the market system which over time would disappear. Hence, government intervention was unnecessary and, in some cases, counterproductive.
2. Keynes' early grounding in economics was of a neoclassical origin. One of his first teachers in economics at Cambridge was Alfred Marshall. On returning to Cambridge, Keynes began to question the economic orthodoxy of the time. This was evident in many of his great works and in particular *The General Theory*. Outside England, he is probably best remembered for his attack on the Versailles Treaty and, later, for his contribution to the setting up of the international organisations after World War II.
3. The Keynesian revolution emerged out of the Great Depression of the 1930s and challenged the orthodox classical economic doctrine of the time. For Keynes, an economy could be at an equilibrium which is below the full-employment level. Insufficient demand was the primary cause of low output and high unemployment. There was a role for government in ensuring sufficient demand.

KEY TERMS

Mercantilists
Physiocrats
Classical economics
Laissez-faire
Invisible hand
Marginalists

Keynesian revolution
Say's Law

REVIEW QUESTIONS

1. Briefly outline the main differences between the classical and the Keynesian schools of economic thought.
2. Assess J. M. Keynes' contribution to modern macroeconomics.
3. Why did the Keynesian revolution occur in the 1930s? What were the different explanations given to explain the Great Depression?

CHAPTER 12

The Determination of National Income

'After several years of plunging production, followed by a sluggish recovery, his decision to examine the forces that determined output made sense, but after even more decades of regarding prices as the proper object of enquiry for economists, the shift was not easy.'[1]

LORIE TARSHIS (1911–93)

'. . . if I were an Irishman, I should find much to attract me in the economic outlook of your present government towards greater self-sufficiency'.[2]

JOHN MAYNARD KEYNES (1883–1946)

CHAPTER OBJECTIVES

Upon completing this chapter, the student should understand:

- the assumptions of the Keynesian income determination model;
- aggregate expenditure and the equilibrium level of national income;
- the expenditure multiplier;
- the policy implications arising out of the Keynesian model;
- the experience with Keynesian economics.

OUTLINE

12.1 The model of income determination
12.2 The policy implications
12.3 The Irish experience

INTRODUCTION

Over seventy-five years after its inception, the Keynesian model of income determination is still considered to be at the core of modern macroeconomics. This chapter deals with the Keynesian model. We begin with the income determination model for a closed economy. The framework is then extended to an open economy model. The last two sections deal with the major policy implications arising out of the Keynesian model and the Irish experience.

12.1 THE MODEL OF INCOME DETERMINATION

We begin our analysis by constructing a simple model of the economy. We work with a two-sector economy with two primary sources of demand – households and firms. Households are engaged in consumption, denoted as C, whereas firms are engaged in (production and) investment, denoted as I. Initially, there is no government or foreign trade sector. Furthermore, we ignore the differences between the different measures of national income. Henceforth, we use national income, total output and GNP interchangeably.

A number of basic assumptions concerning the Keynesian income determination model are made. First, wages and prices are fixed, as it is a short-run model. Second, since price does not adjust to changes in demand, all of the adjustment is made by the quantity produced. In other words, suppliers produce what is demanded at the going price. Third, the economy can operate at less than full capacity: this means that there are unemployed resources. Because of this excess capacity, an increase in demand will increase output and employment but it will have no effect on price. Fourth, the monetary system is omitted from the model.

In order to fully understand the workings of the model we need to examine both consumer and investment expenditure in detail. We do so by introducing two new concepts – the consumption function and the investment function.

Consumption and the consumption function

Consumption is defined as household spending on consumer goods and services which include food, clothes, DVDs, washing machines and so on. In the pre-Keynesian era, the predominant view was that the interest rate determined savings and, in turn, consumption. In contrast, Keynes believed that the level of (current) income was the main explanatory variable. The relationship between consumption and income is described by the consumption function.

Definition

The consumption function shows consumer expenditure at different levels of income.

It can be written as an equation in the following form:

$$C = f(Y_d)$$

[12.1]

where C is planned household consumption and Y_d is aggregate disposable income. Disposable income was defined in Chapter 10 as national income plus transfer payments minus personal taxes. In terms of explaining changes in consumer expenditure, it is a better explanatory variable than national income. Equation 12.1 simply states that consumption depends on disposable income. It is a positive relationship.

Keynes argued that this is a stable relationship and as current income increases, expenditure on consumer goods increases. However, the increase in consumer spending is not as great as the increase in income because some of the extra income is saved. Keynes explained this tendency to consume in the following way: 'Our normal psychological law that, when the real income of the community increases or decreases, its consumption will increase or decrease but not so fast . . .'.[3] He called this the marginal propensity to consume.

> **Definition**
> *The marginal propensity to consume (MPC) is the fraction of each additional unit of*
> *disposable income that is spent on consumer goods and services.*

The consumption function can now be defined more specifically:

$$C = bY_d$$

[12.2]

where

$$b = \frac{\Delta C}{\Delta Y_d} = MPC$$

Furthermore,

$$0 < b < 1$$

b is less than one because only a portion of disposable income is spent on goods and services. The remainder is saved.

Let us consider an example. Table 12.1 provides a set of disposable income and consumption levels.

TABLE 12.1: THE CONSUMPTION FUNCTION

Disposable income, Yd	Consumption, C
0	0
100	75
200	150
300	225
400	300
500	375
600	450
700	525
800	600

As disposable income rises in increments of €100 (billion, for example) consumption rises in increments of €75. The MPC is equal to the change in consumption divided by the corresponding change in disposable income. Hence, in this example,

$$b = \frac{\Delta C}{\Delta Y_d} = \frac{75}{100} = 0.75$$

If disposable income increases, households will plan additional consumption equal to three-quarters of any increase in disposable income.

This particular consumption function is represented by the equation,

$$C = .75Y_d$$

For example, if disposable income increases by €100, planned consumption increases by the b × €100 which in this example is equal to 0.75 × €100 = €75.

This consumption function is represented in Figure 12.1.

FIGURE 12.1: THE CONSUMPTION FUNCTION, $C = .75Y_d$

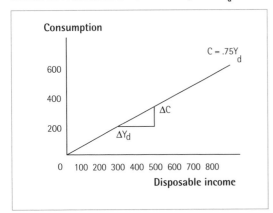

Figure 12.1 shows the specific consumption function $C = .75Y_d$ in diagrammatic form. This diagram can be drawn by substituting values for disposable income (Y_d) and solving for consumption (C). Alternatively, the points can be plotted directly from Table 12.1. By convention consumption, the dependent variable is positioned on the vertical axis. Disposable income, the independent variable, is on the horizontal axis. The line shows the positive relationship between consumption and disposable income; as disposable income increases, so does consumption. The slope of any line shows how the variable on the vertical axis changes relative to a change in the variable on the horizontal axis. The slope of the consumption function relates the change in consumption to the change in disposable income. This is the marginal propensity to consume.

The difference between disposable income and consumption is accounted for by savings. For example, at an income level of €100 consumption amounts to €75. The difference of €25 is accounted for by savings. As we will see, in every sense, the savings function is directly related to the consumption function.

Savings and the savings function

At a given level of income the household has two choices: either consume or save. This can be represented by the following identity:

$$Y_d \equiv C + S \qquad [12.3]$$

Rearranging the variables we can see that savings is, by definition, the difference between disposable income and consumption:

$$S \equiv Y_d - C \qquad [12.4]$$

The savings function, defined below, is usually written in the following format:

$$S = (1 - b)\, Y_d \qquad [12.5]$$

The derivation of the savings function is given in Appendix 12.1.

Definition

The savings function shows the relationship between savings and disposable income.

The relationship between the change in savings and the change in disposable income has a special name. It is called the marginal propensity to save.

> **Definition**
>
> *The marginal propensity to save (MPS) is the proportion of a change in disposable income that is saved.*

Since b represents the amount of additional disposable income that is spent on consumption, 1–b shows the amount of additional disposable income that is devoted to savings. Hence 1–b is the marginal propensity to save.

The consumption function reconsidered

In Table 12.1 and Figure 12.1 we assumed that consumption depends only on disposable income. Excluding all other factors is unrealistic as there are many others which affect the level of consumption. Expectations and aggregate wealth are examples of such factors. Thus, we must adjust our consumption function to allow for these other factors. An adjusted consumption function can be written in the following manner:

$$C = \overline{C} + bY_d$$ [12.6]

This new consumption function has two separate parts.

$\overline{C}$ is called the autonomous component. This is the part of consumption which is independent of income levels: it changes as other factors vary.

bY_d is called the income-induced component. This is the part of consumption which is solely determined by the level of disposable income. It changes as disposable income varies. It corresponds to our simple consumption function which was described above.

Let us take an example. Table 12.2 provides a set of disposable income and consumption levels.

TABLE 12.2: THE CONSUMPTION FUNCTION

Y_d	$\overline{C}$	bY_d	$C = \overline{C} + bY_d$
0	50	0	50
100	50	75	125
200	50	150	200
300	50	225	275
400	50	300	350
500	50	375	425
600	50	450	500
700	50	525	575
800	50	600	650

This particular consumption function is represented by the following equation:

$$C = 50 + .75Y_d$$

where €50 is the autonomous component and .75 is the marginal propensity to consume. We can use this equation to find the level of consumption at any level of disposable income.

For example, if the income level is €100, planned consumption is €50 + (b × €100) which is equal to €50 + (0.75 × €100) = €125.

This particular consumption function is graphically represented in Figure 12.2.

The position of the consumption function relative to the vertical axis depends on the value of $\bar{C}$. A change in the value of autonomous consumption will cause the consumption function to shift upwards or downwards. The slope of the consumption function depends on the value of b, the MPC. A small b results in a relatively flat consumption function whereas a large b results in a relatively steep consumption function.

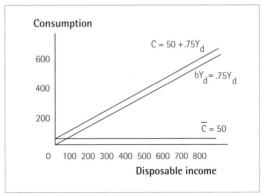

FIGURE 12.2: THE CONSUMPTION FUNCTION, $C = 50 + .75Y_d$

Investment and the investment function

Investment expenditure is planned spending by firms on capital or producer goods such as tools and machinery, vehicles, premises, factories and so on. In simple terms it is the addition to the capital stock of the economy. This component of total spending, denoted as I, is far more volatile and unstable than consumer expenditure. This is predominantly because of the role of expectations, or what Keynes referred to as 'animal spirits', in determining the level of investment expenditure.

In the simple Keynesian model we treat investment as autonomous. It is independent of the current level of income, and can be represented by the following equation:

$$I = \bar{I}$$ [12.7]

The case where investment expenditure is equal to €100 is illustrated in Table 12.3.

TABLE 12.3: THE INVESTMENT FUNCTION

Income, Y	Investment, $\bar{I}$
0	100
100	100
200	100
300	100
400	100
500	100
600	100
700	100
800	100

The equation for this particular investment function is as follows:

$$\bar{I} = 100$$

The corresponding diagram for investment expenditure is below.

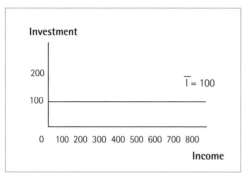

FIGURE 12.3: THE INVESTMENT FUNCTION, $\bar{I} = 100$

Investment expenditure is constant relative to income levels. The diagram shows that investment is €100, regardless of the level of income. It changes, however, as other factors vary. One key factor which determines investment spending is the rate of interest, where the rate of interest is the cost of borrowed funds. This applies whether firms borrow funds to finance investment projects or forgo interest by financing investment with their own funds. Other factors include innovation and technical change, corporate taxes and, finally, expectations (of future earnings, inflation, interest rates and so on). Changes in any one or a combination of these factors cause the investment function to shift upwards or downwards.

Aggregate expenditure and the aggregate expenditure function

In our two-sector economy, total planned spending comprises planned consumer spending by households and planned investment spending by firms. In the Keynesian model total expenditure or total spending is termed aggregate expenditure, AE (or aggregate demand, or, as Keynes wrote, effective demand).

> **Definition**
>
> *Aggregate expenditure is the amount that households and firms plan to spend on goods and services.*

For a two-sector model, it is usually written in the following format:

$$\mathbf{AE} \equiv \mathbf{C} + \bar{\mathbf{I}}$$

[12.8]

AE is simply the sum of planned consumer expenditure and investment expenditure. Table 12.4 shows a hypothetical example of an aggregate expenditure function which adds together the consumption and investment functions that were discussed above.[4]

TABLE 12.4: AGGREGATE EXPENDITURE

Y	C	$\bar{\text{I}}$	AE ≡ C + $\bar{\text{I}}$
0	50	100	150
100	125	100	225
200	200	100	300
300	275	100	375
400	350	100	450
500	425	100	525
600	500	100	600
700	575	100	675
800	650	100	750

We draw your attention to an important point. Disposable income, Y_d, was the explanatory variable used in the text up to this stage. With transfer payments and personal taxes accounting for the difference between disposable income and national income, it is reasonable to proxy 'Y_d' by Y, national income.

In algebraic form,

$$AE \equiv C + \overline{I}$$

where: $C = 50 + .75Y$ and $\overline{I} = 100$
Thus,

$$AE = (50 + .75Y) + 100$$
$$AE = 150 + .75Y$$

Figure 12.4 illustrates this particular aggregate expenditure function.

The diagram above clearly demonstrates that the AE function is simply the vertical summation of the consumption function and the investment function. It shows, at each level of income, the total planned expenditure by households and firms.

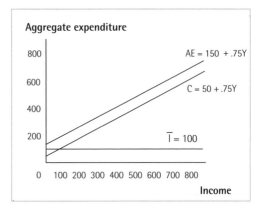

FIGURE 12.4: AGGREGATE EXPENDITURE, AE = 150 + .75Y

The equilibrium level of national income

Equilibrium is a state from which there is no tendency to change. In the context of the Keynesian model there is no tendency for income to either rise or fall at the equilibrium. Keynes argued that the equilibrium level of income was determined by the planned level of expenditure in the economy. At the equilibrium level of income, households and firms are spending what they had planned to spend. At this level, there is no unplanned change in the level of inventories.

Table 12.5 illustrates that equilibrium is achieved through changes in the inventories of firms.

TABLE 12.5: DETERMINING THE EQUILIBRIUM INCOME LEVEL

Y	C	$\overline{I}$	AE	Unplanned Δ in inventories	Change in Y
0	50	100	150	Falling	Increase
100	125	100	225	Falling	Increase
200	200	100	300	Falling	Increase
300	275	100	375	Falling	Increase
400	350	100	450	Falling	Increase
500	425	100	525	Falling	Increase
600	500	100	600	Constant	No change
700	575	100	675	Rising	Decrease
800	650	100	750	Rising	Decrease

The equilibrium level of income (column 1) is determined by the level of planned aggregate expenditure (column 4). In this example, the equilibrium level of income is €600. We explain why by using a trial and error approach.

Suppose Y = €400. When income is €400 planned expenditure is €450. Aggregate expenditure exceeds output. Firms will experience an unplanned fall in their stocks, and they will respond by increasing output. An income level of €400 cannot be the equilibrium level of income because of this tendency to change.

Suppose Y = €700. When income is €700 planned expenditure is only €675. Aggregate expenditure is less than output. Firms will experience an unplanned rise in their stocks. They will respond by reducing output. Hence, an income level of €700 cannot be the equilibrium level of income.

Suppose Y = €600. Planned expenditure is also €600. Aggregate expenditure equals output. This is the equilibrium level of income as there is no tendency to change. Equilibrium occurs when income is equal to (planned) aggregate expenditure. This is the equilibrium condition and it is expressed in the following equation:

$$\boxed{Y = AE}$$ [12.9]

There are ways of showing the equilibrium level of income other than by tabular form. It can be depicted graphically or derived algebraically. We first consider the graphical presentation. The algebraic derivation will follow.

The equilibrium level of income: a graphical presentation

The equilibrium level of income can be derived with the aid of a 45° line. A 45° line divides our two-dimensional space into two equal halves. All points on the 45° line are equidistant from both axes. Therefore, at any point on the 45° line, the value on the vertical axis equals the value on the horizontal axis.

In this example, the 45° line shows where expenditure and income are equal. In Figure 12.5, the 45° line is drawn with the aggregate expenditure line in order to derive the equilibrium level of income. The equilibrium point is where the 45° line intersects the AE line. Figure 12.5 is sometimes referred to as the Keynesian cross diagram.

The 45° line and the AE line intersect at point E where Y = AE at an equilibrium level of €600. To the left of point E the AE line is above the 45° line. Aggregate expenditure exceeds output; excess demand results. There is an unplanned fall in inventories. As a result, the response of firms is to increase output.

The AE line is below the 45° line to the right of point E. Aggregate expenditure is less than output; excess supply exists. There is an unplanned rise in inventories. A reduction in output is the response of firms.

FIGURE 12.5: THE EQUILIBRIUM LEVEL OF INCOME

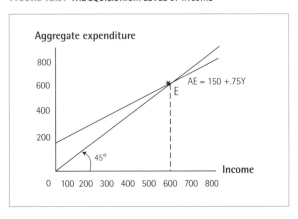

At point E, aggregate expenditure is equal to output and an equilibrium state exists. At the level of output where Y = €600 there is no tendency for change to occur.

The equilibrium level of income: an algebraic derivation

The equilibrium level of income can be determined algebraically using simultaneous equations. Although the solution is the same as the one obtained using the above two methods, this method is faster and more accurate. As previously stated:

$$AE \equiv C + \bar{I}$$ [12.8]

where consumption is defined as:

$$C = \bar{C} + bY$$ [12.6]

Substituting Equation 12.6 into 12.8, we get:

$$AE = \bar{C} + \bar{I} + bY$$ [12.10]

Group the autonomous components of expenditure together and substitute into Equation 12.10 above:

$$\bar{A} = \bar{C} + \bar{I}$$ [12.11]

$$AE = \bar{A} + bY$$ [12.12]

In equilibrium, income equals planned expenditure:

$$Y = AE$$ [12.9]

Equation 12.9 is the equation for the 45° line. Using simultaneous equations, substitute the right-hand side of Equation 12.12 for the right-hand side of Equation 12.9. The solution is the intersection of the aggregate expenditure line and the 45° line or the 'Keynesian cross'.

$$Y = \bar{A} + bY$$

Solve for Y:

$$Y = \bar{A} \times \frac{1}{1-b}$$ [12.13]

This is the equation for the equilibrium level of income. The equilibrium level of income can be calculated by substituting values for $\bar{A}$, the total level of autonomous spending, and for b, the MPC. In the example above,

$$\bar{A} = \bar{C} + \bar{I} = 50 + 100 = 150$$
$$b = .75$$

Thus,

$$Y = \bar{A} \times \frac{1}{1-b} = 150 \times \frac{1}{1-.75} = 150 \times 4 = 600.$$

€600 is the equilibrium level of income. This corresponds with the income level which we derived from both the tabular form and the graphical approach.

There is an alternative way of presenting the equilibrium level of income. Rather than focus on the income-expenditure approach as above, we can use the savings-investment approach. This is explained in Appendix 12.2.

The government sector

We now extend our model in order to include the government sector. Since this model is concerned essentially with the short run, we can assume that government spending is autonomous and is independent of national income.[5]

Thus,

$$G = \bar{G}$$
[12.14]

Table 12.6 illustrates the equilibrium level of income (similar to Table 12.5) but incorporating government expenditure equal to €40 (again, billion, for example).

TABLE 12.6: DETERMINING THE EQUILIBRIUM INCOME LEVEL WITH $\bar{G} = 40$

Y	C	$\bar{I}$	$\bar{G}$	AE	Unplanned Δ in inventories	Change in Y
0	50	100	40	190	Falling	Increase
100	125	100	40	265	Falling	Increase
200	200	100	40	340	Falling	Increase
300	275	100	40	415	Falling	Increase
400	350	100	40	490	Falling	Increase
500	425	100	40	565	Falling	Increase
600	500	100	40	640	Falling	Increase
700	575	100	40	715	Falling	Increase
760	620	100	40	760	Constant	No change
800	650	100	40	790	Rising	Decrease

The corresponding diagram is represented in Figure 12.6.

With the inclusion of government, aggregate expenditure now incorporates expenditure by the government on goods and services.

In algebraic form:

$$AE \equiv C + \bar{I} + \bar{G}$$
[12.15]

where $C = 50 + .75Y$, $\bar{I} = 100$ and $\bar{G} = 40$.

Thus,

$$AE = (50 + .75Y) + 100 + 40$$
$$AE = 190 + .75Y$$

Figure 12.6 shows the new aggregate expenditure function. The addition of government means that the intercept changes from 150 to 190. However, since government spending is autonomous, the slope of the line does not change. It is the marginal propensity to consume and still equal to .75.

The inclusion of government expenditure has important implications. First, its inclusion results in a higher level of income. The equilibrium level of income was originally €600 (but with no taxes). Incorporating government expenditure into the model, where $\bar{G} = 40$, increases the equilibrium level of national income to €760. This can be confirmed by applying the algebra formula which was derived earlier. In this case,

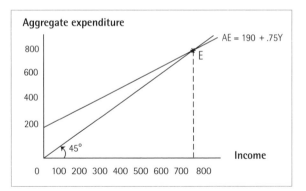

FIGURE 12.6: THE EQUILIBRIUM LEVEL OF INCOME WITH $\bar{G} = 40$

$$\bar{A} = \bar{C} + \bar{I} + \bar{G} = 50 + 100 + 40 = 190$$
$$b = .75$$

Thus,

$$Y = \bar{A} \times \frac{1}{1-b} = 190 \times \frac{1}{1-.75} = 190 \times 4 = 760.$$

Second, any fall-off in consumer or investment expenditure can be offset by an increase in government expenditure. Government expenditure can replace investment expenditure as a source of demand. Likewise, if the economy is below full employment (an assumption of the Keynesian model) an injection of government spending will increase output closer to the full-employment level.

We now consider changes in expenditure and analyse their effect on the equilibrium level of income.

Changes in aggregate expenditure: the multiplier effect

According to the Keynesian model, a change in aggregate expenditure results in a change in national income. Furthermore, the change in income is usually a multiple of the change in spending. Keynes described this concept stating that a '... definite ratio, to be called the *Multiplier*, can be established between income and investment ...'[6]
    The concept of the multiplier was first developed by Richard Kahn (later Lord Kahn) and Colin Clark (1905–89) in 1931. Kahn was regarded as Keynes' 'favourite pupil' and later became a colleague. Clark was a lecturer in statistics in Cambridge at the same time as Keynes. The early theory dealt with an employment multiplier, which explained how a change in public investment brought about a multiple expansion of employment. In *The General Theory* of 1936 Keynes focused attention on an expenditure multiplier and explained how a change in spending causes a multiple change in income. This multiple is called the Keynesian expenditure multiplier.

> **Definition**
> *The expenditure multiplier is the ratio of the change in income to the change in autonomous spending.*

Any injection of spending causes a multiplier or domino effect. Why so? An initial increase in aggregate expenditure generates extra income. The increase in income induces an increase in consumption, according to our analysis of the consumption function. Next, the increase in consumption generates a further increase in income which, in turn, leads to a further increase in consumption. This process continues.

Let us consider a simple example to illustrate the multiplier effect. Suppose a tourist spends €1,000 in a hotel. As a result of this additional income the hotel management upgrades the restaurant facilities by spending €750 on the purchase of tables and chairs. The furniture suppliers decide to hire an additional worker for the month on account of the extra business. They pay their new employee €562.50 a month. This new member of staff is from the locality and spends over €421 on food and drink from the local supermarket. In turn, the supermarket decides to buy in more foodstuffs and beverages to meet the extra demand. They spend an additional €316. This process, with each person's expenditure becoming someone else's income, continues.

The initial injection of spending has led to a successive series with the increases becoming successively smaller:[7]

$$€1,000 + €750 + €562.50 + €421.875 + €316.40625 + \ldots \ldots$$

This is illustrated in Figure 12.7.

FIGURE 12.7: THE MULTIPLIER WITH SUCCESSIVE INCREASES IN CONSUMPTION

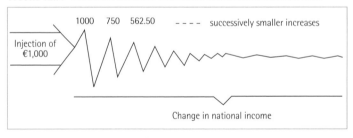

This is a convergent series which can be summed, in this case, to €4,000.[8] The initial €1,000 has now generated, in total, income of €4,000. The increase in income is four times greater than the increase in aggregate expenditure. The value of the multiplier is 4. This is an example of the Keynesian expenditure multiplier, or simply the multiplier, in action. This domino effect is illustrated in Figure 12.8.

Figure 12.8 illustrates the effect of an initial injection of expenditure on both consumption and on national income. The increase in expenditure of €1,000 induces additional increases in consumer expenditure equal to €3,000. Thus, the overall increase in total income is €4,000.

FIGURE 12.8: THE MULTIPLIER PROCESS

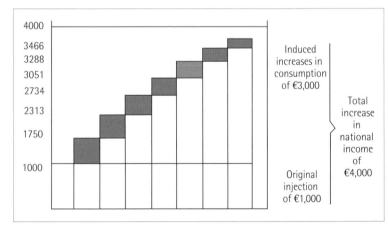

Example: Using the data from above

Continuing with the previous example, suppose that government expenditure increases by €50, from €40 to €90. Table 12.7 shows the effect on the equilibrium level of income.

TABLE 12.7: DETERMINING THE NEW EQUILIBRIUM INCOME LEVEL

Y	C	$\bar{I}$	$\bar{G}$	AE	Change in Y
0	50	100	90	240	Increase
100	125	100	90	315	Increase
200	200	100	90	390	Increase
300	275	100	90	465	Increase
400	350	100	90	540	Increase
500	425	100	90	615	Increase
600	500	100	90	690	Increase
700	575	100	90	765	Increase
800	650	100	90	840	Increase
900	725	100	90	915	Increase
960	770	100	90	960	No change
1000	800	100	90	990	Decrease

The table indicates that the increase of €50 in government expenditure, from €40 to €90, increases the equilibrium level of income by €200, from €760 to €960.[9] This increase of €200 suggests a multiplier of 4 $(\frac{200}{50} = 4)$. This can be verified by tabular form, by the multiplier formula, and by means of a diagram.

By tabular form:

The example above is presented in Table 12.8.
   Example: $\Delta\bar{G} = 50$ and $b = .75$

TABLE 12.8: THE MULTIPLIER PROCESS IN ACTION

	$\Delta\bar{G}$	C	AE
Round 1	50		50
Round 2		50 × .75	50 × .75
Round 3		50 × .75^2	50 × .75^2
Round 4		50 × .75^3	50 × .75^3
''		''	''
''		''	''
''		''	''
Totals	50	150	200

By the multiplier formula:

The multiplier formula is derived in Appendix 12.3. The multiplier is:

$$k = \frac{\Delta Y}{\Delta \overline{A}}$$

where $\overline{A}$ is autonomous spending. k is the symbol that Keynes used for the multiplier. k can also be calculated in the following manner:

$$k = \frac{1}{1-b}$$

where b is the marginal propensity to consume. In terms of this example, the multiplier is:

$$k = \frac{\Delta Y}{\Delta \overline{A}} = \frac{200}{50} = 4, \text{ or:}$$

$$k = \frac{1}{1-b} = \frac{1}{1-.75} = 4$$

We can use the multiplier to directly calculate the change in income using the following formula:

$$\Delta Y = k \times \Delta \overline{A}$$

In this example, k = 4 and $\Delta \overline{A}$ is the change in autonomous spending of €50.

$$\Delta Y = 4 \times 50 = €200.$$

Our familiar cross diagram can also illustrate the multiplier effect. We use the same example as above where government expenditure increases by €50.

By diagram:

Figure 12.9 shows the multiplier effect on national income. The increase in government expenditure causes a shift of the aggregate expenditure line from AE to AE[1]. The equilibrium level of income, as reflected in the intersection point between the 45° line and the AE line, changes from E to E[1]. The vertical distance between the two AE lines, AE and AE[1], is equal to $\Delta \overline{A} = \Delta \overline{G} = 50$. The horizontal distance between the

FIGURE 12.9: THE NEW EQUILIBRIUM LEVEL OF INCOME

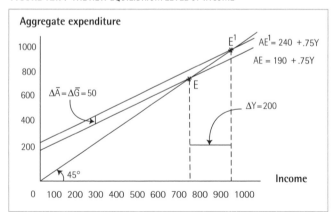

two income levels is equal to $\Delta Y = \Delta \overline{A} \times k = 50 \times 4 = 200$. In terms of length, the horizontal distance is four times the vertical distance. This reflects the multiplier which in this case is equal to 4.

The example above illustrates two important facts about the value of the multiplier. First, it depends on the size of the marginal propensity to consume. A large MPC results in a large multiplier; a small MPC results in a small multiplier. For example a MPC of .9 results in a multiplier of 10, a MPC of .75 results in a multiplier of 4 whereas a MPC of .6 results in a multiplier of 2.5.

Second, given that the MPC is less than one, the multiplier must be greater than one. This suggests than any increase in spending will lead to an increase in income of a greater amount. This has important implications for fiscal policy and its effectiveness in dealing with unemployment. This is discussed in greater detail in Section 12.2.

Most economists credit Keynes with the 'discovery' of the multiplier. However, its popularity, particularly in the United States, is due to the work of a Keynesian economist, Paul Samuelson (1915–2009). Samuelson's textbook, *Economics*, was first published in 1948. For the following thirty years, it was the principal text used at many universities in the USA. For this and many other contributions to the discipline of economics, Paul Samuelson was awarded the Nobel Prize in 1970.

It is important to note that the multiplier process is symmetric. Any decrease in expenditure causes a greater decline in national income because of the knock-on effect of lower induced expenditure. The failure of investment expenditure was the explanation given by Keynes to account for the Great Depression of the 1930s.[10]

Thus far, our analysis of the multiplier has been quite limited. First, the model has reflected a closed economy. Second, it has been expressed solely in terms of the MPC. We now redress these two shortcomings.

The foreign sector and a four-sector model

Our analysis so far has been almost entirely within the context of a closed economy. This is in line with Keynes' *The General Theory*. One reason for this was the major upheaval which was occurring in the international monetary system at the time *The General Theory* was written, after the collapse of the Gold Standard and before the Bretton Woods system was instituted. As a result, exchange rates floated freely on foreign exchange markets. Existing knowledge on flexible exchange rate regimes and how they influenced domestic economic variables was limited.

Another possible reason was the fact that foreign trade did not constitute a large percentage of GDP in either the USA or the UK. Relative to the Irish situation, this position still remains. Moreover, given the open nature of the Irish economy (see Chapter 10 for a discussion on the relative openness of the Irish economy), the foreign sector is particularly vital to our analysis. We now adjust our model to incorporate the foreign sector.

The foreign sector is incorporated into the model by including a value for net exports, denoted by NX, the difference between exports, X and imports, M.

The level of exports from the domestic economy depends on a number of variables including foreign income, the competitiveness of domestic goods in relation to similar goods produced by firms in other countries and exchange rates. The most important variable is foreign income. Because exports are domestically produced goods and services purchased by foreigners, demand for these goods and services varies with the income of a country's main trading partners. As exports are not related to national income we can treat them as autonomous.

$$X = \bar{X}$$ [12.16]

In this example, take $\bar{X} = €90$.

The amount of goods and services which are imported into the domestic economy is affected by some of the same variables including the relative competitiveness of domestic goods and exchange rates. However, the ability of an economy to import goods depends on national income. Therefore, imports are a function of income. As income increases imports increase. The import function is of the form:

$$M = mY$$

[12.17]

where m represents the marginal propensity to import.

In this example, let M = .15Y. This means that fifteen cents of each additional euro of national income is spent on imports. Table 12.9 shows hypothetical values for both exports and imports.

TABLE 12.9: EXPORTS, IMPORTS AND NET EXPORTS

Y	X̄	M	NX
0	90	0	90
100	90	15	75
200	90	30	60
300	90	45	45
400	90	60	30
500	90	75	15
600	90	90	0
700	90	105	−15
800	90	120	−30
900	90	135	−45
1000	90	150	−60

The net exports function is shown in Figure 12.10.

FIGURE 12.10: NET EXPORTS FUNCTION

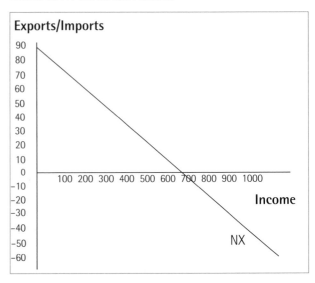

Table 12.10 illustrates the new equilibrium level of income with net exports varying as the level of income changes (and taking the initial level of government spending).

TABLE 12.10: DETERMINING THE EQUILIBRIUM INCOME LEVEL WITH NET EXPORTS

Y	C	$\bar{I}$	$\bar{G}$	NX	AE	Unplanned Δ in inventories	Change in Y
0	50	100	40	90	280	Falling	Increase
100	125	100	40	75	340	Falling	Increase
200	200	100	40	60	400	Falling	Increase
300	275	100	40	45	460	Falling	Increase
400	350	100	40	30	520	Falling	Increase
500	425	100	40	15	580	Falling	Increase
600	500	100	40	0	640	Falling	Increase
700	575	100	40	−15	700	Constant	No change
800	650	100	40	−30	760	Rising	Decrease
900	725	100	40	−45	820	Rising	Decrease
1000	800	100	40	−60	880	Rising	Decrease

The corresponding diagram is represented in Figure 12.11.

FIGURE 12.11: THE EQUILIBRIUM LEVEL OF INCOME WITH NET EXPORTS

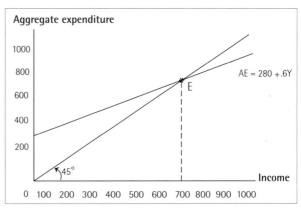

We can verify this equilibrium position algebraically. We begin with the expanded AE function, adding the foreign sector as follows:

$$AE \equiv C + \bar{I} + \bar{G} + \bar{X} - M \qquad [12.18]$$

where consumption and imports are defined as:

$$C = \bar{C} + bY \qquad [12.6]$$

$$M = mY \qquad [12.17]$$

Substitute Equations 12.6 and 12.17 into Equation 12.18 to get:

$$AE = \bar{C} + bY + \bar{I} + \bar{G} + \bar{X} - mY$$

Let $\bar{A} = \bar{C} + \bar{I} + \bar{G} + \bar{X}$, the autonomous components of AE, and substitute into the equation above:

$$AE = \bar{A} + bY - mY$$

Collect Y terms:

$$AE = \bar{A} + (b - m)Y \qquad \text{[12.19]}$$

In equilibrium:

$$Y = AE \qquad \text{[12.9]}$$

Substitute Y for AE in Equation 12.19 and solve for Y:

$$Y = \bar{A} \times \frac{1}{1 - b + m} \qquad \text{[12.20]}$$

This is the equation for the equilibrium level of income for the four-sector model of the economy. We can now use this derivation to find (a) the AE function and (b) the equilibrium level of income for our example.

(a) Equation 12.19 states that:

$$AE = \bar{A} + (b - m)Y$$

For our particular example:

$\bar{C} = 50$; $\bar{I} = 100$; $\bar{G} = 40$ (before the change in government expenditure); $\bar{X} = 90$; $b = MPC = .75$; $m = MPM = .15$. Substitute these values into Equation 12.19 to find the AE function:

$$AE = (50 + 100 + 40 + 90) + (.75 - .15)Y = 280 + 0.6Y$$

(b) Equation 12.20 states that:

$$Y = \bar{A} \times \frac{1}{1 - b + m}$$

where: $\bar{A} = 280$; $b = .75$; $m = .15$.

$$Y = 280 \times \frac{1}{1 - .75 + .15} = 280 \times 2.5 = €700$$

At this stage we need to examine the multiplier in an alternative form.

The multiplier reconsidered

It is possible to express the multiplier in terms of marginal propensity to save, MPS, rather than MPC. Since $MPC = 1 - MPS$, then the multiplier is the reciprocal of the MPS, or in equation form we can write it as follows:

$$\frac{1}{1 - b} = \frac{1}{MPS} \qquad \text{[12.21]}$$

This allows us to express the multiplier in terms of leakages. In the simple model of the economy the only leakage is savings. The higher the leakage, the smaller the multiplier. This is not surprising: a tendency to save limits the extent of consumer expenditure which, in turn, limits the final change in income. This format can be very useful when we extend the model to four sectors and when assessing the effectiveness of fiscal policy.

The extension of our model to include the foreign sector complicates not only the derivation of the equilibrium level of income but also the multiplier. Using the leakages format, the multiplier is equal to:

$$\frac{1}{MPS + MPM} \qquad [12.22]$$

where MPS is the marginal propensity to save and MPM is the marginal propensity to import. This multiplier is derived in Appendix 12.4.

If taxes are considered and treated as a function of income, a further complication arises in the form of the marginal propensity to tax.

Definition

The marginal propensity to tax (MPT) is the proportion of any increment in income paid in taxes.

It is a leakage. Assuming consumer expenditure depends on gross income and on taxation, the multiplier is of the form:

$$\frac{1}{MPS + MPM + MPT} \qquad [12.23]$$

The inclusion of the MPT, a leakage, further reduces the size of the multiplier.[11]

Earlier approximations for these parameters in the Irish economy were MPS = 0.26, MPM = 0.4 and MPT = 0.24.[12] This gives us a multiplier of approximately unity which is relatively low by international standards.[13] This has important implications for the effectiveness of domestic fiscal policy. The Irish experience with Keynesian economics in general, and fiscal policy in particular, is discussed in Section 12.3.

One final concept which requires explanation is the paradox of thrift.

Thriftiness or savings is normally treated as desirable. The paradox of thrift suggests otherwise. How so? An increase in the planned level of savings results in a reduction in the equilibrium level of national income and because savings depends on income, the actual level of savings may even decline. This suggests that although savings can be viewed individually as a virtue it becomes a vice when the analysis is extended to society. It is, yet again, a fallacy of composition: the assumption that what is true for a part is true for the whole.

As a corollary to the above, the classical school and Keynes had very different views on the virtues of savings. The classical economists were in favour of high levels of savings which would lead to lower interest rates and higher investment levels. Keynes disagreed on the basis that too much savings had adverse effects on expenditure and output.

The Keynesian model, as presented above, is incomplete: it excludes money and interest rates, wages and prices, and finally, supply-side effects. These are dealt with in subsequent chapters. As for the criticisms, there are many. Some criticise the underlying assumptions of the model (fixed prices, cyclical tendencies, undesirable equilibrium). Others are critical of the policy implications (government action, budget deficits) while the empirical evidence (consumption function, multiplier) has been the subject of harsh review. Despite all this, the Keynesian model remains an important part of macroeconomics. For the moment we turn our attention to the policy implications arising out of the Keynesian model and the Western economies' experience with Keynesian economics.

12.2 THE POLICY IMPLICATIONS

A number of important policy implications arise from the Keynesian model. With the possibility that the economy may settle at an income level below the full-employment level, Keynesians argued in favour of government intervention in order to narrow this deflationary gap between actual output and full-employment output. In *The General Theory* he called for public works programmes to provide jobs and to increase national income. He strongly supported demand management and, in particular, the active use of fiscal policy. There remains some controversy over his support for counter-cyclical policy.

The terms demand management, fiscal policy and counter-cyclical policy require explanations.

> Definition
>
> *Demand management is the collective term used to explain various government policies which influence the level of aggregate expenditure in the economy.*

These include fiscal and monetary policy. We will discuss monetary policy in the next chapter. Fiscal policy is described below.

Fiscal policy

> Definition
>
> *Fiscal policy refers to the use of government expenditure and taxation in order to influence aggregate expenditure and, in turn, national output.*

Irish fiscal policy was inherited from the British model and in both countries it is synonymous with budgetary policy. This is because fiscal policy in the UK is implemented primarily through the budget.[14] The budget is a record of what the government pays out in the form of expenditure and what it receives, usually in the form of tax revenue. It is the responsibility of the Minister for Finance.

In Ireland, each year's budget is divided into a current and a capital section. Current expenditure relates to spending on goods and services which are consumed during the fiscal year. For example, it includes wages and salaries of public servants and covers the operating expenses of public buildings. Current revenue is the income which accrues to the state from the day-to-day running of the economy. Examples include personal income tax, expenditure tax (e.g. VAT) and corporation tax.

Capital expenditure refers to spending on items which are not completely consumed during the fiscal year. Examples include expenditure on infrastructure and investment projects. The details of the government's capital spending are published each year in the Public Capital Programme (PCP). Capital revenue normally consists of interest on stocks owned by government, loan repayments and capital grants received from the EU.[15]

Measures of fiscal policy

Fiscal policy involves expenditure and the collection of tax and non-tax revenue. Within a single budget, expenditure can exceed revenue and if so, the government incurs a deficit. Alternately, if revenue exceeds expenditure, the budget is in surplus. If expenditure equals revenue, a balanced budget results.

There are two important measures of the relationship between revenue and expenditure. One measure is the Exchequer Borrowing Requirement (EBR) or Exchequer Balance. This was the measure most frequently used by economists and politicians in Ireland to evaluate the cumulative effect of fiscal policy changes in the annual budget.

> Definition
>
> *The Exchequer Borrowing Requirement (EBR) is the total amount of money that the central government borrows in any one fiscal year if current and capital expenditure exceeds current and capital revenue. If revenue exceeds expenditure, it is called an Exchequer Surplus.*

A budget, in a given year, is expansionary if the government incurs a deficit as measured by the EBR or if the size of the EBR increases. The budget is contractionary if the government cuts the size of the EBR or if it moves from a deficit to an Exchequer Surplus.

A broader measure, called the General Government Deficit, Surplus or Balance, is used by the EU to compare the fiscal stance of EU member states.

> Definition
>
> *The General Government Deficit (GGD) or Surplus (GGS) is calculated by adding the EBR or Exchequer Surplus to the balance of local authorities and non-commercial state-sponsored bodies.*

A budget, in a given year, is expansionary if the government incurs a deficit as measured by the GGD or if the size of the GGD increases. The budget is contractionary if the government cuts the size of the GGD or if it moves from a deficit to surplus as measured by the GGS.

Table 12.11 presents figures for these measures over the twenty-five-year period 1985–2009.

TABLE 12.11: MEASURES OF FISCAL POLICY (€M)

Year	Current Budget Deficit		Exchequer Balance		General Government Balance	
	€m	% of GNP	€m	% of GNP	€m	% of GDP
1985	−1,630	−7.4	−2,719	−12.3	...	...
1986	−1,751	−7.3	−2,722	−11.4	...	...
1987	−1,497	−5.9	−2,317	−9.1	...	...
1988	−404	−1.5	−835	−3.1	...	...
1989	−333	−1.1	−636	−2.2	...	...
1990	−193	−0.6	−620	−1.9	...	...
1991	−379	−1.1	−312	−0.9	...	...
1992	−566	−1.6	−915	−2.6	−1,184	−3.0
1993	−481	−1.2	−880	−2.3	−1,181	−2.7
1994	19	0.0	−854	−2.0	−914	−2.0

1995	−459	−1.0	−796	−1.7	−1,090	−2.1
1996	371	0.7	−554	−1.1	−62	−0.1
1997	767	1.3	−298	−0.5	765	1.1
1998	2,649	3.9	948	1.4	1,865	2.4
1999	4,367	5.7	1,512	2.0	2,461	2.7
2000	6,971	7.8	3,177	3.5	4,988	4.7
2001	4,729	4.8	653	0.7	1,023	0.9
2002	5,399	5.1	93	0.1	−472	−0.4
2003	4,410	3.7	−979	−0.8	544	0.4
2004	5,619	4.4	33	0.09	2,079	1.4
2005	6,353	4.6	−499	−0.4	2,691	1.7
2006	9,055	5.9	2,264	1.5	5,221	2.9
2007	6,991	4.3	−1,619	−1.0	261	0.1
2008	−3,069	−2.0	−12,714	−8.2	−13,198	−7.3
2009	−11,369	−8.7	−24,641	−18.8	−23,350	−14.6

Source: Department of Finance, *Budgetary and Economic Statistics 2010.*

Using the EBR as an indicator of fiscal policy, we can see that the budgets between the years 1985 and 1990 were largely contractionary. The EBR as a percentage of GNP fell steadily and then stabilised.

Although the EBR is often cited, it is a less than perfect indicator of changes in active fiscal policy. This is because the size of the EBR is influenced by automatic stabilisers which respond to changes in the economic environment. Examples include taxes and transfer payments. They are 'automatic' in the sense that they are built into the economy and do not require discretionary action by government. Their purpose is to reduce the impact of shocks that arise from cyclical fluctuations in the economy. If, for example, an economy is going into a recession, unemployment rises. Transfer payments increase because more people are receiving social welfare payments. The decline in national income means that tax receipts are likely to fall. The combination of higher expenditure and lower tax receipts results in a higher EBR. By the same logic, a lower EBR is likely to result during a boom period because of higher tax receipts and lower expenditures on transfer payments.

Therefore, changes in the EBR may reflect changes in the automatic stabilisers rather than deliberate action taken by the administration. Changes in the EBR which arise out of direct action taken by the government in order to move the economy in a given direction are called discretionary changes. The budget deficit (or surplus) which results from these government decisions is called the structural or discretionary budget deficit (or surplus). An increase in the personal tax rate or an increase in the rate of old-age pensions are two such examples.

In brief, the structural or discretionary change in the EBR is a better measure of fiscal policy as it reflects active and deliberate changes by the government.

A second, more accurate measure of fiscal policy is the primary budget balance. Interest payments on the national debt are included as an expenditure item in the annual budget. However, the national debt and the subsequent interest payments do not reflect current policy but arise out of past government policy. Thus, in order to arrive at a correct measure for current fiscal policy it is necessary to exclude the debt service. This adjusted measure is known as the 'primary budget balance'.

Whereas the unadjusted-for-interest-payments current budget was in deficit every year between 1980 and 1993, the current primary budget had been in surplus continually since 1986. The difference is accounted for by the high level of interest payments on the national debt.[16] More important, it suggests that fiscal policy during that period was even more contractionary than originally suspected.

Many economists argue that fiscal policy should be counter-cyclical. This is a restrictive use of fiscal policy. It means that the government should use the fiscal instruments available to it to boost the economy in times of recession and to deflate the economy in times of overheating. The government should increase spending and/or cut taxes to counter deficiencies in demand. This is the origin of the phrase 'spending your way out of recession'. During boom periods, when there is excess demand, the government cuts spending and/or increases taxes and thereby incurs a surplus. Over the lifetime of the business cycle the government budget would, in effect, be balanced, as the classical school endorsed, but with deliberate imbalances running counter-cyclically.[17] Terms such as 'pump-priming' and 'fine-tuning' the economy are also used to describe such a policy.

The question of whether domestic fiscal policy has been counter-cyclical has caused great debate among the economics profession. Throughout the 1970s and the 1980s there are examples of periods when policies were strongly pro-cyclical, i.e. the fiscal changes implemented by the incumbent governments were either expansionary during the upturn or contractionary during the downturn of the business cycle.

One such period was the mid-1970s. The world economy experienced an upturn in activity after 1976. On the back of this favourable international climate it was expected that the Irish economy would grow without any further stimulus from the state sector. Moreover, this was an opportunity to reduce borrowing and counterbalance the budget deficits of previous years. Yet domestic fiscal policy during these years was highly expansionary and pro-cyclical. This occurred partly because of the promises made during the general election of 1977 and partly because of deliberate action taken by the government on the advice of some economists. The expansionary fiscal policy of those years was justified on the basis of the 'self-financing' claim (see The Irish Experience in Section 12.3).

A second period was the early to mid-1980s when the international economic climate was unfavourable. Most Western economies were either in the depths of recession or else slowly emerging from one. Financial markets were highly volatile with high interest rates and fluctuating exchange rates. As a result international trade suffered. Advocates of counter-cyclical fiscal policies would argue that such adverse economic conditions warrant expansionary fiscal policy at home in order to counter low demand and rising unemployment. Yet domestic fiscal policy during these years was highly contractionary and pro-cyclical.

The rationale behind this pro-cyclical policy was the attempt to restore order to the public finances. By 1982 the EBR was 15.5% of GNP. Borrowing to finance day-to-day spending was almost 8% of GNP. Fears grew both at home and abroad about the sustainability of the debt. A consensus was reached, among economists and politicians, to reduce borrowing and improve the national debt/GNP ratio. Other economic aims, including unemployment, were seen as subordinate to this primary objective.

More recent examples of pro-cyclical fiscal policy can be taken from the 2000s. In the early part of the decade, the Irish economy was at, or close to, full employment. Yet, with a booming economy, a fiscal stimulus was provided in the form of large increases in current expenditure (particularly before the 2002 and 2007 general elections) and reductions in taxation (with, in particular, an increase in tax reliefs and tax expenditures). At the end of the decade, after three years of an economic downturn, actual output was well below its potential capacity. Yet, due to the mounting debt crisis and the inability to borrow abroad, the Irish authorities implemented a series of austere budgets aimed at restoring order to the public finances and improving Ireland's creditworthiness. Fiscal adjustments in the form of tax increases and public expenditure reductions were not only deeply unpopular with the electorate but further dampened economic activity at home. Unfortunately, both episodes of fiscal policy in the 2000s intensified the business cycle as opposed to reducing the worst excesses of boom and bust.

Another aspect of fiscal policy which featured during this period is the concept of crowding out. Suppose the government increases expenditure. Furthermore, let us assume that it will be financed by borrowing rather than by tax increases. This induced borrowing creates a demand for funds in the financial markets, leaving less funds available for the private sector. This may lead to higher interest rates and in turn decreases in private sector spending. In effect, the initial injection of public sector spending crowds out both consumer and investment expenditure. It is obvious from this simple explanation that crowding out has very important implications for the effectiveness of fiscal policy. Moreover, it appears from the above description that the expansionary fiscal policy adopted by the government may be far less effective than previously believed.

Opinions vary on the extent of crowding out. Supporters of fiscal policy, Keynesians included, argue that only partial crowding out occurs. Government spending is compensating for insufficient private investment. Critics of fiscal policy, monetarists for example, argue that full and complete crowding out is the norm. Government spending replaces private investment. The economy suffers as a result because private investment is more efficient than public investment, it is argued.

This discussion on fiscal policy has been limited to the confines of a closed economy. Little or no reference has been made to economic variables such as capital flows, foreign interest rates and output levels, fixed or flexible exchange rates. Changes in fiscal policy affect and are affected by these variables which play an important role in an open economy. Chapter 15 explains these international effects.

The Western economies' experience with Keynesian economics

The active use of public works programmes in modern times dates as far back as the 1930s when economies like Sweden, the USA (Roosevelt's 'New Deal') and even Germany, under Adolf Hitler, were using public investment to stimulate the economy. Hitler's Four-Year Plan to abolish unemployment, announced in 1933, depended largely on demand-side measures including the Reinhardt Programme of public works.[18]

In the UK, both the Labour and Conservative governments of the 1950s and 1960s advocated and implemented Keynesian demand-management policies. The government policies of that period appear to have had their desired effects on unemployment. However, on account of their tendency to influence the level of imports, they also led to periodic balance of payments crises. In the UK, the subsequent mix of contractionary and expansionary policies that followed became known as stop-go policies. Many economists were highly critical of such short-term policies and advocated strongly against the use of such policies in order to tackle rising unemployment.

Nineteen sixty-three is the year most often cited in the USA as the high point of Keynesian economics. The Kennedy administration advocated the use of Keynesian economic policies. Investment tax credits were introduced in 1962 in order to stimulate private sector spending and reduce unemployment. Many of the top economic advisers of the day, including the late J. K. Galbraith (1908–2006), the late James Tobin (1918–2002), the late Arthur Okun (1928–80),

Robert Solow (b. 1924), the late Walter Heller (1915–87) and Paul Samuelson were advocates of Keynesian economics.

Kennedy's successor, Lyndon Johnson, continued to adopt Keynesian-style policies early in his administration despite sufficient levels of demand and inflationary pressures arising from the US involvement in the Vietnam War. In 1964 Johnson persuaded Congress to enact personal tax cuts of 20% and a 10% cut for businesses. Notwithstanding the impact of the war, the results arising out of the Kennedy-Johnson experience with Keynesian economics were dramatic. Unemployment fell from 5.2% in 1962 to 4.8% in early 1965, and by 1966 it had fallen to 3.8%.

Support for Keynesian economics did not end with the Kennedy-Johnson administrations (1961–68). At the same time that the newly elected US President Richard Nixon was espousing the case for Keynesian economics with the infamous statement 'We are all Keynesians now', the UK Tory government under the leadership of Edward Heath was implementing similar Keynesian-style policies. The Chancellor, Anthony Barber, responding to the economic environment of the day which saw unemployment reach the one million figure for the first time in thirty years, increased public expenditure and cut taxes. What followed is commonly known as the 'Barber Boom' of the early 1970s. By the end of 1973 the unemployment figure was halved to 500,000. This dramatic improvement in the economy was attributed largely to the Keynesian-style policies adopted by the Chancellor.

However, things were to change in response to a number of factors. These included the economic environment of the time which was experiencing non-Keynesian trends of inflationary pressures in the face of deficient demand. Also, there was a growing dissatisfaction with Keynesian economics and the Phillips curve among the economics profession.[19] Finally, the ongoing economic research of the time focused less on the assumptions and conclusions of the Keynesian model and more on the microeconomic foundations of macroeconomics. Variables such as money, expectations and human capital were examined rather than the broad components of demand.

The economic environment of the 1970s was even more uncertain than the previous decade. The Bretton Woods system of regulating exchange rates broke down. There was an oil supply shock at the beginning and again at the end of the decade. There emerged a new phenomenon, called stagflation, which referred to rising unemployment accompanied by rising inflation. This phenomenon could not be explained within the framework of the basic Keynesian model.

In the UK, both the Tory government led by Edward Heath (in the later days of his administration) and, surprisingly, the Labour government of James Callaghan criticised the Keynesian economics of the past and adopted tough monetarist policies. Prime Minister Callaghan, addressing delegates at the 1976 Labour Party conference, said 'We used to think you could spend your way out of recession . . . I tell you in all candour that the option no longer exists and insofar as it did ever exist, it only worked by injecting demand into the economy.' However, it was the 1980s combination of Margaret Thatcher in the UK and Ronald Reagan in the USA which was primarily responsible for the emergence of an alternative to Keynesian economics, i.e. supply-side policies. Supply-side economics and how it differs from demand management is explained in Chapter 16.

The revival of Keynesian economics in the 1990s was largely in response to the Anglo-American recession and the general dissatisfaction with the supply-side policies of the previous decade. This re-emergence was partly reflected in the election of a Democratic President in the USA and the election of the Labour Party at home. Both parties in the past have supported and adopted Keynesian-style policies. It was believed that on the return to power they would re-introduce some demand-side policies.[20]

Keynes and supporters of Keynesian-style macroeconomic policies became popular again after the Great Contraction of the late 2000s. In the USA and elsewhere, governments increased deficit spending in order to counter the fall in world output and avoid a 1930s-style Great Depression. Supporters of Keynes claimed that the world economy, and unemployment, would have been much worse if it were not for the fiscal stimulus. Likewise, calls for austerity programmes were rejected by supporters of Keynesian economics, who claimed that deflationary policies would only lead to a double-dip recession. Despite concerns about rising budget deficits and debt levels, advocates of deficit spending and counter-cyclical fiscal policy argued that the over-riding problem at the end of the 2000s was not inflation, as some argued, but a lack of effective demand and rising unemployment.

In brief, the adoption of Keynesian-style policies both in the USA and the UK in the 1960s and early 1970s coincided with a period of prosperity and low unemployment. This compared with the high unemployment rates of the inter-war period and, likewise, the 1970s. Many attribute this success to the adoption of demand-management policies, but this is open to debate. What is probably less contentious is the significant contribution of a number of events other than the implementation of Keynesian economics. These include the decline in protectionism in favour of free trade, the importance of innovation, the adoption of new technologies and, finally, the stability of international financial markets.

Another contentious issue is the limits of Keynesian economics and the subsequent policy recommendations. Keynesian economics emerged out of the Great Depression, and the recommendations which followed were to apply to the economic environment of the time – one of mass unemployment, protectionism and floating exchange rates. The economic climate has changed dramatically over the past seventy-five years. Different periods with different problems require different solutions.[21] The adoption and success of Keynesian demand policies in the past does not necessarily require similar policies now or in the future.

This chapter concludes with a discussion on Keynesian economics within the context of Irish economic policy.

12.3 THE IRISH EXPERIENCE

Ireland was slow to adopt Keynesian economics. In the 1950s the authorities were more concerned with the substantial balance of payments deficits than with the unemployment trends. In the 1960s, policy was focused on attracting overseas industry and on building up the infrastructure in order to enhance the long-term development of the economy. Neither policy could be described as Keynesian which is in essence a short-term policy. However, if we lagged behind other European countries before the 1970s it is generally agreed that we surpassed these same countries in the twenty-five years that followed in our adoption of Keynesian demand management. The debate now centres on whether Keynesian policies were effective considering, in particular, the openness of the Irish economy.

The Irish experience with active use of fiscal policy began in earnest in the early 1970s.[22] Prior to this the Minister for Finance would balance his current budget every year, in accordance with sound accounting principles and, to a lesser extent, the classical economic doctrine. Nineteen seventy-two marks a watershed in Irish government policy. This was the year of the first planned current budget deficit in modern times. The Minister for Finance, Mr George Colley, admitted to taking a 'calculated risk' in opting for expansion in preference to stability. He went on to acknowledge '. . . a risk that I may be fuelling the fire of inflation rather than the engine of growth'.[23]

Unfortunately such a radical change in policy was overshadowed by the events of the following year when the world economy suffered an oil crisis which induced inflationary pressures throughout the Western world, including Ireland. Inflation was exacerbated even beyond what the Minister had feared. The difference, however, was in the cause and the extent of the rise in prices.

By 1975 the current budget deficit had increased to 6.8% of GNP. This was viewed by the incumbent government as being too high. According to the then Minister for Finance, Mr Richie Ryan, 'Borrowing for capital purposes is justifiable in the context of our long-term economic aims' but 'Borrowing to meet current deficits is not, no matter how desirable it may be by reference to immediately pursuing requirements.'[24] Taxes were raised and expenditure was curtailed in order to reduce the borrowing.

The general election of 1977 brought an abrupt end to this contractionary fiscal policy. Political parties promised tax cuts and expenditure increases although there was evidence of an economic recovery worldwide. The new government acted on its promises by abolishing rates on private dwellings, reducing motor tax, increasing tax allowances and creating over 11,000 new public-sector posts.

These and similar measures introduced by the government were justified on the basis that a fiscal stimulus would ensure a stable standard of living and a reduction in unemployment. In economic terms the policy was rationalised by reference to a self-financing fiscal boost. The then Minister for Finance, Mr Colley, aided by his economic advisers, argued that such a fiscal boost would ensure an increase in national income which, in turn, would generate sufficient taxes to self-finance the initial expansion. On account of these additional tax receipts, no substantial increase in borrowing would be necessary, it was argued. Unfortunately the results were somewhat different from the forecast.

Policy continued to be highly expansionary during a period when the economy, without any fiscal stimulus, was growing satisfactorily in real terms. Although this policy did manage to keep unemployment down and at the same time maintain a relatively high standard of living, it was also responsible for transforming the country into a net debtor, characterised by high annual budget deficits, external borrowing and a looming balance of payments crisis. This situation was exacerbated by the second oil crisis in 1979 and the subsequent world recession.

By 1981 the Exchequer Borrowing Requirement was 15.7% of GNP. Moreover, the government was borrowing over 7% of GNP to finance day-to-day expenditure. To make matters worse, the domestic political situation was far from stable with three elections within the space of eighteen months. Some commentators, unhappy with the domestic outlook, went so far as to call for assistance from the IMF. This would have been a highly unusual and embarrassing move for a developed Western economy.

The first step towards restoring some stability in the domestic economy was achieved when a consensus on the need for order in the public finances was reached among the main political parties. Fiscal rectitude, as it became known, took precedence over all other objectives, including a reduction in unemployment. The coalition government of 1982–86 set about tackling the problem primarily by increasing taxes and, to a lesser extent, curtailing capital expenditure.

Some commentators were very critical of such a policy mix. They argued that the higher tax rates acted as a disincentive to work and only succeeded in siphoning off legitimate work to the shadow economy. Capital expenditure, they argued, was a key element in the long-term development of the economy and did not warrant cutbacks. In addition, they postulated that cutting capital expenditure was an 'easy target' on the basis that it was politically more difficult to cut current expenditure and, second, a number of key investment projects were coming to an end at this time. Notwithstanding these criticisms, some credit must be given to the coalition partners for attempting to tackle the problem.

The highly deflationary policies which followed appeared to have more of an impact on unemployment than on the public finances. By 1986 the current budget deficit was 7.9% of GNP, the national debt/GNP ratio was 128% and the unemployment rate had increased to 17% of the labour force. On the positive side, inflation fell from 20% in 1981 to 3.8% in 1986. This was due to a combination of the deflationary policies of the administration and the international trend of lower prices.

The general election of 1987 and the subsequent change in government, with the support of the Tallaght Strategy, brought about another turn in policy and with it a dramatic improvement in both the public finances and the economy as a whole.[25] The cuts in current expenditure, the return to centralised wage bargaining with the Programme for National Recovery and the favourable international economic background all contributed to an economic performance over the period which surpassed even the most optimistic of forecasts.

In terms of the public finances, the austere measures introduced by the Minister for Finance, Mr Ray MacSharry, resulted in significant reductions in budget deficits and national debt/GNP ratios. Government expenditure was cut by 3.7% per annum on average between 1987 and 1989. The EBR was reduced from 12.1% of GNP in 1986 to 2.2% in 1989. Such draconian measures earned MacSharry the nickname of 'Mac the Knife'. What was even more extraordinary was the recorded growth rates in GNP during the same period. The increase was close to 3.6% per year on average, the highest growth rate recorded for any three-year period since the mid-1960s. Unfortunately, this did not translate into an equal growth in employment rates.

On reading the above account of the performance of the Irish economy during the period 1987–89 one might be led to believe that the remarkable transformation was due solely to the deflationary policies adopted by the government. However, the Keynesian model of income determination indicates that contractionary fiscal policy, as described above, deflates the economy and reduces national income. The Irish experience seems to suggest the opposite, that expenditure cuts can lead to increases in national income. This raised questions over the validity of the Keynesian model in the Irish context. It also gave rise to the phrase Expansionary Fiscal Contraction (EFC).[26] However, before we hastily disregard the work of Keynes, we need to look for possible explanations, other than the expenditure cuts, in order to explain the increases in GNP.

A detailed analysis of this period is beyond the scope of a basic textbook in economics. However, a number of possible, although not exhaustive, factors which contributed to the recovery are listed below. The occurrence of these raises doubts over the validity of EFC.

- The tax amnesty of 1987 which raised over IR£500 million in unpaid taxes. This extra source of income contributed to the reduction in the budget deficit which otherwise would have required further cuts in expenditure and/or hikes in tax rates. Furthermore, it is assumed the taxpayers who availed of the amnesty remained in the tax net and became an additional source of revenue in subsequent years.
- The 1980s was a boom period for the world economy. Higher income levels, lower inflation rates, stable exchange rates and lower interest rates all contributed to an environment which was conducive to external trade. Ireland, being a small open economy, availed of these conditions and recorded a strong export performance. The volume of Irish exports grew by 8.9% on average per annum between 1986 and 1989. Also, the recovery was export-led; improvements in domestic demand followed later.
- The credible economic policy adopted by the government, typified by the relatively low wage agreements contained in the Programme for National Recovery. Furthermore, financial

markets at home and abroad and, likewise, foreign investment both at home and abroad reacted positively to the change in policy.

· In 1986 the Irish pound was devalued by 8% within the EMS exchange rate mechanism. This benefited Irish exporters by making Irish goods cheaper in foreign markets. Furthermore, interest rates declined as the domestic environment improved. The interest rate differential between Ireland and our UK and German counterparts narrowed significantly. For example, the three-month interest rate differential with the UK fell from –2.8% approximately at the end of 1986 to +4.8% approximately at the end of 1988. Likewise, the interest rate differential with Germany fell, from 9% approximately to 3% approximately over the same period.

The period between 1987 and 1990 was followed by the Anglo-American recession of the early 1990s which slowed economic activity both at home and, in particular, in the UK and the USA. The subsequent decline in economic growth on the European continent and in the Far East was less severe. However, by 1993–94 both the UK and Ireland had clearly emerged from the recession and were recording very satisfactory growth rates. As a result, the Irish authorities were able to reduce borrowing, particularly for current purposes. In terms of GDP, they were recording one of the lowest budget deficits in the EU.

However, the one area of economic policy which concerned private-sector economists was the growth of public expenditure. It is estimated that between 1989 and 1993 current government spending increased by 31% whereas the inflation rate over the same four-year period was only 11.5%. The period from 1995 onwards was one of rising tax revenues (on the back of record economic growth) and ever-increasing budget surpluses. By 1999, the current budget was in surplus to the tune of 5.8% of GNP. By any standards, Ireland's public finances were in remarkable shape. The debt/GNP ratio, at 125% in 1987, was less than 55% in 1999. The turnabout was complete.

In the first five years of the new millennium the public finances remained in a healthy shape despite the economic slowdown both worldwide and, to a lesser extent, at home. Although public expenditure continued to grow steadily (particularly before the general election in 2002), tax revenues remained buoyant as the economy continued to outperform most of its EU partners. The tax and expenditure shares of national income, in the 30–35% range, are low by EU standards and more resemble levels in the Anglo-Saxon world. With a growing economy and relatively small annual fiscal deficits, Ireland's debt/GNP ratio, at close to 30% in 2004, was one of the lowest in the enlarged EU-25. At home, there was a trend toward rising indirect taxes (on the revenue side) and concerns over value for money with respect to spending on large infrastructural projects (on the expenditure side). As costs continued to rise in Ireland (clearly no longer the low-cost economy portrayed in the 1980s), these issues dominated debate for some time.

During the boom period of the 2000s, tax receipts were particularly buoyant – on the back of a construction boom and property-related transactions – and allowed government to continue increasing public spending. Although the budget remained in surplus, underlying problems were evident. Tax revenues were transitory, and highly dependent on the continued rise in residential and commercial property prices. In effect, the tax base had become too narrow, with, for example, a significant and growing proportion of workers not paying any income tax. With hindsight, the temporary surpluses were insufficiently large. When the world recession hit and the property bubble burst, the result was striking. The budget balance went from a surplus of 2.9% in 2006 to a deficit of 14.6% in 2009 (see Chapter 18 for more on the state of the public finances in the post-Celtic Tiger era). At a time when a fiscal stimulus was required, pressure from international debt markets, in view of the unsustainability of the Irish public finances and the increasing likelihood of a future sovereign debt default, resulted in the Irish authorities introducing a number of austere budgets in an attempt to reduce the deficit and placate the financial markets.

In brief, the consensus is that Keynesian-style policies were not very successful in Ireland in achieving their goals. On reflection, this is probably due more to the inappropriateness of fiscal policy in a small open economy like Ireland combined with the mismanagement by the authorities and institutional deficiencies relating to government decision-making rather than the ineffectiveness of Keynesian economics in general.

CASE STUDY

Extract from *The Economist*
Ireland's budget
Hard times: Ireland shows the rest of Europe what austerity really means

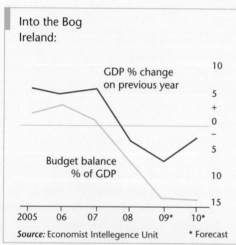

Into the Bog
Ireland:

GDP % change on previous year

Budget balance % of GDP

2005   06   07   08   09*   10*

Source: Economist Intelligence Unit   * Forecast

When the Irish finance minister, Brian Lenihan, in effect cut the pay of public-sector workers earlier this year by introducing a special 7% pension levy, he confessed that Ireland's European Union partners were amazed at the muted public reaction. There would, he said, have been riots in France. On 9 December Mr Lenihan presented his 2010 budget, inflicting even more pain by imposing steep pay cuts on public employees. This time, the response may not be quite so muted. The police are already threatening to defy a no-strike law in protest, and other public-sector workers are preparing to hold ballots on industrial action.

In a week when Greece and Spain both saw their credit ratings under attack, the budget at least gave the government an opportunity to reassure international investors that Ireland, unlike some other EU countries, is serious about controlling its budget deficit and public-debt burden. Mr Lenihan has done this with the toughest budget in his country's history. Public servants face pay cuts of 5–8% on salaries up to €125,000 ($190,000); higher earners (who will include the prime minister) will see their pay cut by 15% or more. Unemployment and welfare benefits have also been cut, though not pensions. Next year's budget deficit, at around 11.6% of GDP, will be similar to this year's.

The budget came against the background of a sharp contraction in economic activity, far greater than that experienced in other euro-area countries. GDP is projected to decline by 7.5% in 2009 and a further 1.3% in 2010. An unemployment rate of 12% this year is at least showing some signs of stabilising. But consumer confidence remains weak and households continue to save more and to spend less, thereby depressing tax revenues. Next year, almost half of all income earners will pay no tax. In an effort to widen the tax base, the government proposes to introduce a new property tax.

The budget will put the government into direct conflict with trade unions for the second time this year. The pension levy may have been accepted by the general public, but the unions still protested vociferously. In pre-budget talks, the government noted a hostile public reaction to the unions' proposal for a temporary pay cut for public-sector workers and a promise of big public-sector reform. It chose a permanent pay cut instead.

These measures mark the end of two decades of social partnership, based on a consensus approach to pay bargaining between government, employers and unions. Whether this will usher in a long period of industrial conflict will become clearer in the coming weeks. Public-sector unions are already giving warning of a sustained campaign of strikes. But in these hard times they may not win much support from the Irish public.

Source: The Economist, 10 December 2009.

Questions

1. Why, as shown by the graph, does a country's budget balance and GDP growth rate often follow a similar trend or pattern? More specifically, why did Ireland's budget balance deteriorate so rapidly at the end of the 2000s?
2. Using the Keynesian approach, how should austerity measures, in theory at least, affect the economy? According to its supporters, how is austerity linked to recovery and economy growth?
3. The article refers to Ireland's narrow income tax base. Using data from the Department of Finance (www.finance.gov.ie), report the total tax revenue figure for the four years 2007–2010, its composition and the annual change for the different headings. What did the 2009 Commission on Taxation report conclude in terms of new taxes and ways of widening the tax base?

Answers on website

SUMMARY

1. There are a number of assumptions to the Keynesian model of income determination. It is a fixed price model. It assumes that the economy is below full employment and that any increase in demand will increase output, and by a multiple.
2. The model incorporates many new concepts such as the consumption function, aggregate expenditure, the marginal propensity to consume and the multiplier. Output is determined by aggregate expenditure which is simply equal to total spending in the economy. Equilibrium exists at a point where aggregate expenditure equals output.
3. Any change in aggregate expenditure results in a greater change in output. This is explained by the multiplier process where the multiplier is simply the amount by which income changes as a result of an initial change in spending. The value of the Keynesian multiplier depends on the size of the leakages.
4. The Keynesian model can be extended to include both government and foreign sectors. If so, public expenditure and exports augment total spending by the private sector. Also, the value of the multiplier is affected by the marginal propensity to tax and import. As a result of these leakages, the multiplier in an open economy is smaller than the simple multiplier in the closed economy model.

5. Demand management is the collective term used to describe policies which aim to influence the level of demand and in turn the level of output in the economy. One example is fiscal policy which depends on the active use of government expenditure and taxes to influence demand. In Ireland, it centres on Budget day. Measures of active fiscal policy include the discretionary budget deficit and the primary budget balance.

6. Keynesian economics was very popular among economists, policy-makers and politicians after World War II and particularly in the 1950s and the 1960s. However, Ireland was relatively slow, by international standards, to adopt short-term Keynesian-style policies. The success of such policy in Ireland, possibly due to the open nature of the economy, has been limited.

KEY TERMS

Consumption	Paradox of thrift
Consumption function	Deflationary gap
Marginal propensity to consume	Demand management
Savings function	Fiscal policy
Marginal propensity to save	Exchequer Borrowing Requirement
Autonomous expenditure	General Government Deficit
Investment function	Automatic stabilisers
Aggregate expenditure	Structural budget deficit
Equilibrium	Primary budget balance
Inventory changes	Counter-cyclical policy
Keynesian cross diagram	Crowding out
Expenditure multiplier	Fiscal rectitude
Marginal propensity to import	Expansionary Fiscal Contraction
Marginal propensity to tax	

REVIEW QUESTIONS

1. Explain the significance of the consumption function in the Keynesian model of income determination.
2. What determines the equilibrium level of income in the Keynesian model? Explain, in words, how this position is reached.
3. What is the Keynesian multiplier? What factors influence its size? Explain how it is related to:
    (a) consumption function;
    (b) leakages;
    (c) fiscal policy.
4. Briefly explain the differences between the income determination model as applied to a closed economy and the model as applied to an open economy.
5. What policy recommendations arise out of the Keynesian model? When did support for Keynesian economics emerge? Why did it lapse in the 1970s?
6. Critically assess the success or failure of Keynesian economics in the context of the Irish economy.

WORKING PROBLEMS

1. The following equations are from a simple model of the economy:

$C = 110 + .8Y$
$\bar{I} = 300$
$\bar{G} = 150$
$\bar{X} = 250$
$M = .2Y$

(a) Calculate the equilibrium level of income for this model.
(b) Suppose the government decides to double its expenditure on goods and services. What is the new equilibrium income level?
(c) Calculate, and interpret the size of, the multiplier for this particular model.

2. Prove, using algebra, that the sum of the marginal propensity to consume and the marginal propensity to save is equal to 1.

MULTI-CHOICE QUESTIONS

1. The classical school of economics held the view that:
   (a) the economy was at or close to full employment;
   (b) large-scale government intervention was unnecessary;
   (c) large-scale government intervention was necessary;
   (d) both (a) and (b) above;
   (e) both (a) and (c) above.

2. If the marginal propensity to save increases from .2 to .25, then:
   (a) the slope of the consumption function steepens;
   (b) the marginal propensity to consume increases by the same proportion;
   (c) the expenditure multiplier increases from 4 to 5;
   (d) the savings function shifts downwards;
   (e) none of the above.

3. In the Keynesian cross diagram for the two-sector model:
   (a) investment is dependent on income levels;
   (b) when savings is less than investment output tends to decrease;
   (c) equilibrium is where $AE > \bar{I}$;
   (d) income is determined by the level of expenditure;
   (e) unplanned increases in stocks lead to an increase in output.

4. Due to a change in the pattern of consumption, the consumption function has flattened. This implies that the value of the multiplier has:
   (a) decreased since the marginal propensity to consume has increased;
   (b) decreased since the marginal propensity to consume has decreased;
   (c) increased since the marginal propensity to consume has increased;
   (d) increased since the marginal propensity to consume has decreased;
   (e) none of the above.

5. Suppose a model of the economy is represented by the following equations: $C = 120 + .8Y$, $\bar{I} = 280$, $\bar{G} = 300$. The equilibrium level of income is:
    (a) €700;
    (b) €3,500;
    (c) €560;
    (d) €140;
    (e) €584.

6. The government wants to increase national output by €300 million. Its economic advisers provide it with the following information: $S = .2Y$, $\bar{I} = 200$, $\bar{G} = 300$, $\bar{X} = 100$, $M = .2Y$. By how much should the government increase its spending on goods and services?
    (a) €120;
    (b) €300;
    (c) €750;
    (d) €1,500;
    (e) none of the above.

TRUE OR FALSE (SUPPORT YOUR ANSWER)

1. The classical school of economic thought argued that the self-adjusting mechanism of the market ensured the absence of any involuntary unemployment.

2. The autonomous component of the consumption function varies as income varies.

3. Unplanned decreases in inventories are a signal to firms to increase production.

4. The Keynesian multiplier is always greater than zero but less than one.

5. Adjusting the income determination model to include a value for exports and government expenditure (both autonomous) increases the equilibrium level of income.

6. Counter-cyclical fiscal policy implies the adoption of a budget deficit during a recession and a budget surplus during a recovery.

CASE STUDY

Extract from *Business and Finance*
Let's survive the Budget first
Our most urgent concern is the Budget and reassuring bond investors, not the deficit target in 2014
by Karl Whelan

Recent weeks have seen an intense focus on the question of whether the upcoming four-year budgetary plan should require the Government to maintain its commitment to meet the 3% deficit target in 2014. I believe that this focus has been misplaced and that not enough attention is being paid to the key issue: the size of adjustment required in the coming Budget. The focus on the 3% goal for 2014 – prompted by repeated references to this by ICTU and Sinn Féin, and also by recent comments from the ESRI – is misplaced for a number of reasons.

Firstly, one must take account of the European political environment. The euro zone has a guideline that deficits above 3% of GDP are considered excessive. Of course, this target has been blown past in every member state and there is widespread agreement that the Stability and Growth Pact simply did not achieve its goal of maintaining fiscal stability. Because of these past failures, there are proposals on the table for far stricter monitoring of member-state budgetary policies, proposals that Angela Merkel would like to formalise by changing the Lisbon Treaty. If anyone thinks there is room in this environment for the European Commission to agree to Ireland extending its 3% deadline target, they are seriously misreading the situation.

Secondly, we need to focus on the present because we can only take one step at a time: Worrying about the 2014 deficit is akin to setting tactics for how we're going to score our fifth goal when currently we're four-nil down. Brian Lenihan has more or less admitted that if we manage to get the deficit to 5% or 6% of GDP in later years, then the commission may be open to negotiating an extension on the 3%. In any case, it is unlikely to be the current Government taking decisions about fiscal adjustments in future years, so commitments to years beyond 2011 are unlikely to be credible.

Meanwhile, with all this focus on four years away, we've got to get through the next four months. Recent yields on government bonds have priced in a high likelihood of default. If this continues to be the case, then Ireland may not be able to continue borrowing on the sovereign bond market. The minimum goal of any upcoming Budget has to be to reassure bond investors that the budgetary actions taken have reduced the likelihood of default. If we fail to do that, then we can look forward to spending years debating the merits of EU-driven austerity because we'll have no choice. Meeting the 3% target by 2014 would be a minimum condition of any bailout from the European Financial Stability Facility. Unfortunately, instead of showing a steady and credible approach to reassure financial markets, the Government's handling of the upcoming Budget has been fairly shambolic. They have taken far too long to admit the scale of the fiscal problem that we are facing.

When last year's Budget was introduced, the plan for 2011 was to introduce €3bn in adjustments to reduce the budget deficit to €17bn which would be 10% of GDP. However, by spring, the Government knew that they would be issuing promissory notes for up to €30bn to pay for Anglo and Irish Nationwide and that these notes would have interest costs of €1.5bn that would count against the 2011 deficit. By summer, the Government knew that the CSO had revised the national accounts so that the GDP in 2011 was going to be closer to €160bn rather than €170bn and so the deficit target would have to be closer to €16bn, adding another billion to the adjustments required. Factoring in lower tax revenues and the effect of larger fiscal adjustments on GDP, it seems likely that the 10% target for 2011 can only be met with adjustments of €7bn (a figure that finance officials appear to have confirmed to Fine Gael's Michael Noonan). It seems clear, then, that the Government was clinging publicly to a figure of €3bn for adjustments in the upcoming Budget long after they must have known that this figure wasn't tenable. Moreover, at the time of writing, the Government have yet to publicly admit that a €7bn adjustment is likely to be required to meet its previous target for next year.

This should not be allowed to happen in the future. Budgetary figures and proposals should be drafted over the summer and debated in detail in the Dáil from September onwards. Is meeting the 10% target for 2011 really necessary if Ireland is to continue borrowing from the bond market? Might an adjustment of €4bn – perhaps getting us to about 12% of GDP – be ok if it was accompanied by an impressive-looking four-year plan? The answer is we simply don't know. Missing the 10% target might be shrugged off by the markets. However, given how concerned they have become about the possibility of default, I would be inclined to fear the worst. The current EU-agreed plan is already our second plan (there was a previous one in which we reached 3% in 2013). Ripping up this one, so we can start again with a third plan in which we've still only got as far as a 12% deficit next year, doesn't sound to me like the kind of plan that's going to work.

Source: Business and Finance, November 2010.

Questions

1. The budget deficit is the excess of expenditure over revenue. What is the rationale for a 3% deficit target as laid down by the European Commission?
2. Economic forecasting is not an exact science. Using the annual government budget as a source (from the Department of Finance website at www.finance.gov.ie), report the projected figure and actual outcome for the annual budget deficit (using the GGD measure) for the years 2007–2009. Do the same exercise for tax revenue, reporting both projected figures and actual outturns.
3. Write a brief note on the EU Stability and Growth Pact, outlining the rationale, the basic detail (and subsequent changes) and Ireland's record of compliance with the Pact (before the late 2000s crisis).

APPENDIX 12.1: THE SAVINGS FUNCTION

The following is the derivation of the simple savings function:

$$Y_d \equiv C + S \qquad \text{[12.3]}$$

which can be rewritten as:

$$S \equiv Y_d - C \qquad \text{[12.4]}$$

The consumption function is defined as:

$$C = bY_d \qquad \text{[12.2]}$$

Substitute bY_d for C in Equation 12.4:

$$S = Y_d - bY_d$$

Since Y_d is common to the two components, we can rewrite the right-hand side of the equation as follows:

$$S = (1 - b)Y_d \qquad \text{[12.5]}$$

We know from the previous discussion about the consumption function that b, the marginal propensity to consume, is a positive number which is greater than zero but less than one. The marginal propensity to save (1–b) must therefore also be a positive number which is greater than zero but less than one. Equation 12.5 shows that there is a positive relationship between disposable income and savings. As disposable income increases, savings increases by a fraction of that amount.

Let us take an example. Table 12.12 provides a set of disposable income and savings levels.

TABLE 12.12: THE SAVINGS FUNCTION

Disposable income, Y_d	Savings, S
0	0
100	25
200	50
300	75
400	100
500	125
600	150
700	175
800	200

As disposable income increases by increments of €100, savings increase by increments of €25. The MPS is equal to the change in savings divided by the corresponding change in disposable income. Hence:

$$MPS = \frac{\Delta S}{\Delta Y_d} = \frac{25}{100} = 0.25$$

If disposable income increases households will plan additional savings equal to one-quarter of any increase in disposable income. This particular savings function is represented by the following equation:

$$S = .25Y_d$$

Proof:
If MPC = .75

then MPS = 1 − b = 1 − .75 = .25
If C = .75Y_d

then S = (1 − b)Y_d = (1 − .75)Y_d = .25Y_d

For example, an increase in disposable income of €100 leads to an increase in planned savings of (1 − b) × €100 which is equal to 0.25 × €100 = €25. This particular savings function is graphically represented in Figure 12.12.

The upward sloping line shows that there is a positive relationship between savings and disposable income. The slope of the savings function is the marginal propensity to save.

The derivation for the more complicated savings function follows.

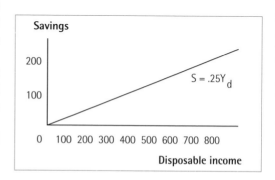

FIGURE 12.12: THE SAVINGS FUNCTION, $S = .25Y_d$

Beginning with Equation 12.4:

$$S \equiv Y_d - C$$ [12.4]

Recall that the consumption function can be defined as:

$$C = \bar{C} + bY_d$$ [12.6]

Substitute into Equation 12.4:

$$S = Y_d - \bar{C} - bY_d$$

This can be written as:

$$S = -\bar{C} + Y_d - bY_d$$

Grouping the Y_d variables together, we obtain the equation of the savings function:

$$S = -\bar{C} + (1 - b)Y_d$$ [12.24]

The savings function, in the general case, with an intercept of $-\bar{C}$ and a slope equal to $(1 − b)$ is illustrated in Figure 12.13.

At low levels of disposable income savings are negative. This means that past savings are being used to finance expenditure. Dissavings is the reason why consumer expenditure can be larger than disposable income levels, as they are in Table 12.2. At the point where the savings function crosses the horizontal axis, savings is zero; all disposable income is spent. In the text the consumption function is $C = 50 + .75Y_d$. With a $\bar{C} = 50$ and a MPC = .75 the savings function is $S = -50 + .25Y_d$. This is drawn in the bottom frame of Figure 12.14 in Appendix 12.2.

FIGURE 12.13: THE SAVINGS FUNCTION, $S = -\bar{C} + (1-b)Y_d$

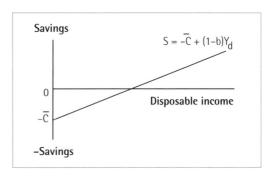

APPENDIX 12.2: THE SAVINGS-INVESTMENT APPROACH

In the income-expenditure approach, equilibrium occurs when income, Y, is equal to expenditure, AE. However, using the two-sector model we can also express equilibrium in terms of savings and investment.

Table 12.13 continues the example which we have been using throughout the chapter. The information from this table is depicted graphically in the bottom frame of Figure 12.14.

TABLE 12.13: THE EQUILIBRIUM LEVEL OF INCOME

Y	C	S	$\bar{I}$
0	50	−50	100
100	125	−25	100
200	200	0	100
300	275	25	100
400	350	50	100
500	425	75	100
600	500	100	100
700	575	125	100
800	650	150	100

By treating investment as autonomous, the investment function is drawn as a straight line. In our example it is equal to €100. The savings function is upward sloping. This reflects the positive relationship between savings and income. Savings equals €100 at an income level of €600. We can now compare the equilibrium levels of income from the income-expenditure approach and the savings-investment approach.

Figure 12.14 illustrates the equilibrium level of income. At €600, income equals expenditure (the top diagram) and savings equals investment (the bottom diagram).

We confirm this as follows. Below €600 planned investment exceeds planned savings. Any excess of injections over leakages causes an unplanned reduction in inventories which leads to an increase in national income. Above €600 planned savings exceeds planned investment. The excess of leakages over injections causes unplanned increases in inventories which leads to a decrease in national income. National income is in equilibrium where planned savings equal planned investment.

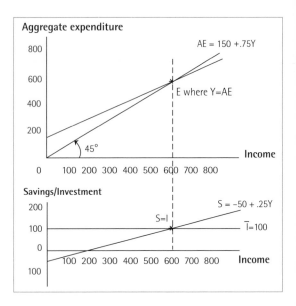

FIGURE 12.14: DERIVING THE EQUILIBRIUM LEVEL OF INCOME

APPENDIX 12.3: ALGEBRAIC DERIVATION OF THE TWO-SECTOR MODEL KEYNESIAN MULTIPLIER

We begin with Equation 12.13 from the text:

$$Y = \overline{A} \times \frac{1}{1-b}$$

[12.13]

where:

$$\frac{1}{1-b} = k$$

[12.25]

Substitute Equation 12.25 into Equation 12.13 above:

$$Y = \overline{A} \times k$$

[12.26]

If there is a change in the autonomous component of expenditure, we can adapt this equation to calculate the resulting change in income:

$$\Delta Y = \Delta \overline{A} \times k$$

Solve for k:

$$\frac{\Delta Y}{\Delta A} = k$$

[12.27]

Therefore k represents the multiplier. We can see that in this simple model, the magnitude of the multiplier is directly related to the marginal propensity to consume.

APPENDIX 12.4: ALGEBRAIC DERIVATION OF THE KEYNESIAN MULTIPLIER INCLUDING THE FOREIGN SECTOR

Begin with Equation 12.20 from the text:

$$Y = \overline{A} \times \frac{1}{1-b+m} \qquad [12.20]$$

If there is a change in autonomous expenditure, what is the corresponding change in income?

$$\Delta Y = \Delta \overline{A} \times \frac{1}{1-b+m}$$

Divide both sides by $\Delta \overline{A}$ to yield:

$$\frac{\Delta Y}{\Delta \overline{A}} = \frac{1}{1-b+m} \qquad [12.28]$$

In this situation the multiplier is:

$$k = \frac{1}{1-b+m} \qquad [12.29]$$

This multiplier is smaller than the simple multiplier $\frac{1}{1-b}$. Imports are a leakage from the circular flow. The inclusion of the marginal propensity to import causes the multiplier to decrease in magnitude.

CHAPTER 13

Money, Interest Rates, the Central Bank and Monetary Policy

'Money is the most important thing in the world.'[1]

GEORGE BERNARD SHAW

'How to have your cake and eat it too: lend it out at interest.'

ANONYMOUS

CHAPTER OBJECTIVES

Upon completing this chapter, the student should understand:

- what money is, what money does;
- how the banking system creates money;
- the different theories of interest rate determination;
- the functions of a central bank;
- how monetary policy works;
- the Irish experience of monetary policy;
- monetary policy in the context of EMU.

OUTLINE

13.1   Money, money supply and money creation
13.2   Interest rate determination
13.3   The role of a central bank
13.4   Monetary policy
13.5   The Irish experience

INTRODUCTION

In the words of the economist Milton Friedman, 'Money matters'. Money is indeed a very important feature of any modern state: it facilitates the workings of the economy. Its importance, however, is not confined to the day-to-day operations of an economy. Money and monetary policy play an important role in the macroeconomic management of the country. It can influence such variables as expenditure, output, employment and prices.

We begin this chapter with a discussion on money: its definition, characteristics, functions and how it is created by the banking system. This is followed by the theory of interest rate determination. Two main theories are explained. A short history of the evolution of the Central Bank in Ireland follows. Monetary policy and its role is also discussed. The chapter finishes with an examination of monetary policy in Ireland, pre- and post-1999, with the latter including a discussion of the European Central Bank and monetary policy in the eurozone.

13.1 MONEY, MONEY SUPPLY AND MONEY CREATION

Over the centuries, money has taken many different forms. Examples include whales' teeth in Fiji, rats on Easter Island, dogs' teeth in the Admiralty Islands, silk and salt in China, sea-shells in Africa and cattle in ancient Ireland.

'Money', regardless of the form it takes, has a number of desirable attributes: it should be easily recognisable and acceptable, durable and divisible, convenient, uniform and relatively scarce.

Above all else, money is anything that is generally accepted as a means of payment. Any means of payment has a number of functions.

Functions of money

According to John R. Hicks, 'Money is as money does.'[2] This suggests that the functions of money are more important than its form (dollars vs euros, gold vs silver). The real power of money is in what it does, rather than what it is. We will now explain the most important functions of money.

1. *A medium of exchange*   Money is used in a monetary economy in order to allow for exchange between buyers and sellers. A non-monetary or barter economy is one where there is no accepted medium of exchange. There is a direct exchange of one good for another good. Consequently, there must exist a 'double coincidence of wants', i.e. each person must possess what the other person requires. Each person involved in a transaction must be a buyer and a seller simultaneously.

For example, if you have apples but want chocolate ideally you must find somebody who has chocolate and is willing to exchange chocolate for apples. This 'coincidence of wants' involves a number of problems. They include the high level of transaction costs incurred if intermediate trades are necessary, and the indivisibility and non-standardisation of some commodities.

Using money as a medium of exchange is more efficient. You can sell your apples to Dunnes Stores and buy chocolate bars at the corner shop.

2. *A unit of account*   Money is the common unit of measurement which allows for prices to be quoted. Hence, the exchange value of different commodities such as chickens, clothes and cars can be compared to one another. In the USA, the prices of these and other goods are expressed in dollars. The pound sterling is the unit of account in the UK, and throughout the euro area the euro is the unit of account.

3. *A standard of deferred payment*   This is the same as the function above but with a time dimension added. Obligations for future payments like leases and contracts are denominated in money.

4. *A store of value*   Money, held rather than spent, can be used to make purchases in the future. Because of price inflation, money is not the best store of value. If it is not in an interest-bearing account, it is worth less in the future than it is worth today. Houses are the main store of value for most Irish families.

In the modern world, there are many forms of money. Examples include coins, banknotes, cheques (drawn on current accounts), credit cards (plastic money) and balances in deposit accounts. There is, however, a need to define the money supply more strictly.

Definitions of money supply

In Section 13.3, we will discuss the functions of the Central Bank in detail. For now, we will briefly mention that the Central Bank is responsible for controlling the money supply. We continue the discussion of money by explaining the definitions of the money supply used by the Central Bank.

The 'narrow money supply' includes the most liquid forms of money.

Definition

The narrow money supply is defined as the notes and coins in circulation plus current account balances at credit institutions.

It is labelled M1 by the Central Bank.

The broad money supply or M3E adds the narrow money supply to other forms of money that can be readily converted into cash.

Definition

The broad money supply is defined as M1 plus deposit account balances.

Any definition of the money supply is somewhat arbitrary because it is very hard to draw a distinction between 'money' and 'non-money'. For example, although credit cards can be readily used to purchase things, they are not included in these definitions. Furthermore, defining monetary aggregates has been made more complicated by the introduction of the euro in January 1999 and Ireland's participation in the euro area.

From January 1999 onwards, it is customary to refer to the 'Irish contribution to euro area money supply'. This entails the Irish credit institutions' contribution to various euro area monetary aggregates, including narrow money supply (M1) and broad money (M3). The main differences between M3 and M3E are that the new series, M3, has a maturity cut-off point of up to two years for deposits or debt securities, and includes deposits of Irish credit institutions from residents of other monetary union member states. Values for M1 and M3 of Irish contribution, all in euros, are reported in Table 13.1.

One final term which requires an explanation is high-powered money or the monetary base.

Definition

High-powered money (H) is equal to currency plus reserves held by the Central Bank.

These reserves play an important role in the creation of money. We now explain 'money creation'.

TABLE 13.1: MONETARY AGGREGATES OF IRISH CONTRIBUTION

	2008 (€m)	2009 (€m)	Year-to-year* (change, %)
Currency	8,084	11,173	
Overnight deposits	71,719	78,846	
M1	79,833	90,018	11.3
Deposits	117,725	99,983	
Debt securities	– 40,631	– 49,449	
Repurchase agreements	452	1,006	
Money market funds	59,899	56,877	
M3	217,277	198,436	– 2.1

Source: Various Central Bank of Ireland Quarterly Bulletins.   * = adjusted

Money creation

We know from the discussion of the circular flow that banks are financial intermediaries; they facilitate the transfer of purchasing power from lenders to borrowers. They are, however, also involved in other activities. In particular, banks can 'create' money. They do so by taking deposits, keeping a certain amount in reserve and lending out the remainder. This is known as the system of fractional reserves.[3] When they lend out these deposits, money is created. We will illustrate money creation with an example. In this particular example we assume that all the loans made by the bank are re-deposited.[4]

The Irish Bank (TIB) is the only financial institution on the island of Hibernia. A customer, Patricia O'Hara, deposits €1,000 in her local branch. The balance sheet of TIB Bank is presented in Table 13.2.

TABLE 13.2: THE BALANCE SHEET OF TIB BANK

Assets		Liabilities	
Cash	1,000	Deposit	1,000

The deposit is a liability of the bank because it must return that money to Ms O'Hara if requested. The bank manager, with many years of experience, knows that it is unlikely that Ms O'Hara will withdraw all of her savings at once. Only a small percentage of this deposit is needed to meet the customer's demand for money. The remainder can be lent to other customers and firms who require funds.

The manager decides to keep 10% in reserves (€100) and lends out the residual (totalling in this case €900) to another customer, Sean O'Shea.[5] The loan is an asset of the bank because it is owed to the bank by Mr O'Shea. The balance sheet reflects this transaction.

TABLE 13.3: THE BALANCE SHEET OF TIB BANK

Assets		Liabilities	
Reserves	100	Deposit	1,000
Loan	900		
	1,000		1,000

A couple of days later, Patrick Murphy, the owner of the local furniture store, deposits the €900 which Sean O'Shea has spent on a suite of furniture. The bank manager proceeds to lend out 90% of this amount and retains 10% or €90. Mrs O'Brien, the local greengrocer, borrows the €810 in order to pay the builder for the extension to her shop. The builder, Niall Burke, who is also from the locality, decides to deposit this amount in order to guard against a 'rainy day'. With only one financial institution on the island the loan of €810 has found its way back to the bank. The bank holds €81 as reserves and advances the remaining €729 to another credible client. This process continues with the loan amount diminishing every time.

The final picture, in terms of the bank's assets and liabilities including all of the transactions described above is presented in Table 13.4.

TABLE 13.4: THE BALANCE SHEET OF TIB BANK

	Assets		**Liabilities**	**Customer**
Reserves	100	Deposit	1,000	O'Hara
Loan	900			O'Shea
Reserves	90	Deposit	900	Murphy
Loan	810			O'Brien
Reserves	81	Deposit	810	Burke
Loan	729			
. . . .		. . . .		. . . .
Total reserves	1,000	Total deposits	10,000	
Total loans	9,000			

At the end of the process the liabilities equal the assets. An initial deposit of €1,000 with a required reserve ratio of 10% results in the bank's total deposits amounting to €10,000. The money creation process is depicted in Figure 13.1.

FIGURE 13.1: MONEY CREATION

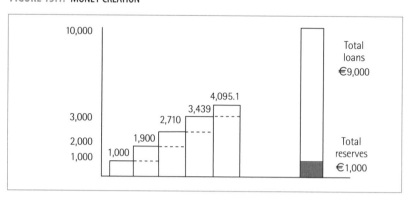

The deposits, loans and reserves amounts are recorded in Table 13.5.

TABLE 13.5: MONEY CREATION

Stages	Deposits (€)	Reserves (€)	Loans (€)
1	1,000	100	900
2	900	90	810
3	810	81	729
4	729	72.9	656.1
5	656.1	65.61	590.49
6 . . .			
7 . . .			
etc . . .			
Total	€10,000	€1,000	€9,000

In effect, there is a multiplier relationship at work. This multiplier is called the deposit multiplier.

Definition

The deposit multiplier is the multiple by which deposits will increase for every unit increase in reserves.

It can be expressed in the following form:[6]

$$\text{Deposit multiplier} = \frac{1}{r} \qquad \text{[13.1]}$$

where r equals the percentage of deposits which are held in reserve or the reserve ratio.

In this example, where 10% of deposits are held in reserve, the deposit multiplier is 1/0.1 and equals 10. Therefore, an increase in reserves will ultimately lead to a tenfold increase in deposits. The relationship between the change in reserves and the subsequent change in deposits can also be expressed in equation form:

$$\Delta D = \frac{1}{r} \Delta R \qquad \text{[13.2]}$$

where D represents deposits and R represents reserves.

For this example, we substitute 10 for the deposit multiplier and €1,000 for the change in reserves caused by Ms O'Hara's initial deposit. Substituting these values into Equation 13.2, we find that the total change in deposits is 10 × €1000 or €10,000. This is the same amount which we calculated by adding the total deposits in Table 13.5.

In summary, a change in reserves leads to a multiple change in bank deposits. The value of the multiplier depends on the reserve ratio. The larger the reserve ratio, the smaller the deposit multiplier; the smaller the reserve ratio, the larger the deposit multiplier. A more complicated version of this multiplier is derived in Appendix 13.1.

The money creation process is neatly summed up below.

Increase in reserves → increase in loans → increase in deposits
→ increase in money supply

The money creation process is also symmetric. Any withdrawal will lead to a decrease in reserves. As a result, banks reduce their lending, thus reducing the money supply. The reduction in the money supply will be a multiple of the fall in reserves.

This simplified analysis illustrates the power of a bank to create money. This analysis can also be extended to a two- or multi-bank system. Although the exercise is more difficult, the principle remains the same.

13.2 INTEREST RATE DETERMINATION

Again, we must begin this section by defining two important concepts.

> **Definition**
>
> *Interest is the amount that is paid on a loan or the amount that is received on a deposit.*

For example, Tomas borrows €2,000 from the bank to buy a second-hand car. At the end of the year his repayments to the bank equal €2,200. The principal is €2,000 and the interest is €200.

> **Definition**
>
> *The rate of interest is the interest amount expressed as a percentage of the sum borrowed or lent.*

In the example above, Tomas paid €200 in interest on a principal of €2,000. The interest rate is 10%.

In any economy there are many different rates of interest. They vary with time, risk, size and other factors.

There are two main theories of interest rate determination. The first is the classical approach where the interest rate is determined by the demand for and supply of loanable funds (or credit). This is called the loanable funds theory. The second is the Keynesian approach where the interest rate is determined by the demand for and supply of money. This is called the liquidity preference theory.

The loanable funds theory

For classical economists, interest was the 'price' paid for borrowing funds. According to this theory, if a firm is considering the purchase of a capital good, the total cost of that good increases with the interest rate. As the interest rate increases, fewer and fewer investment projects are considered because the revenue which they generate is not sufficient to cover the price of the investment. Alternatively, as the interest rate falls, more projects are viable. In short, there is a negative relationship between interest rates and investment.

Firms often finance the purchase or lease of capital goods by borrowing funds.[7] The relationship between the interest rate and the demand for loanable funds or credit is also negative. As interest rates rise, the price of capital goods rises

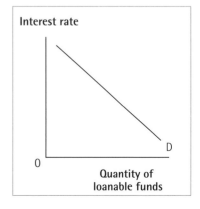

FIGURE 13.2: THE DEMAND CURVE FOR LOANABLE FUNDS

and firms are less likely to borrow money to finance an investment project. Alternatively, as interest rates fall, the demand for loanable funds increases. Therefore, the demand curve for loanable funds, D, is downward sloping as shown in Figure 13.2.

The supply of loanable funds is derived from the level of household savings. The classical economists argued that in order to persuade people to overcome the inclination to consume immediately, a reward in the form of interest had to be offered. The higher the rate of interest, the greater is the inducement to postpone current consumption, and so the greater is the supply of loanable funds. As the rate of interest rises, the supply of loanable funds increases.[8] Subsequently, the supply curve of loanable funds, S, is upward sloping, as drawn in Figure 13.3.

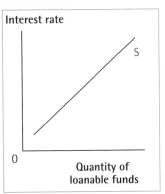

FIGURE 13.3: THE SUPPLY CURVE OF LOANABLE FUNDS

The rate of interest is determined by the demand for and supply of loanable funds. The function of the interest rate is to equate the demand for funds with the supply of funds in the same way that price adjusts to equate demand and supply in the goods market. The intersection of the demand and supply curves is the equilibrium rate of interest, i*. This is illustrated in Figure 13.4.

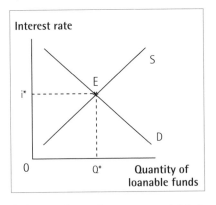

FIGURE 13.4: THE MARKET FOR LOANABLE FUNDS

Changes in the demand for loanable funds occur for a number of reasons. Since firms carry out investment projects in anticipation of making a profit, it follows that anything which changes the expected profitability of investment projects will change the demand for loanable funds. An increase in demand causes a rightward shift of the demand curve whereas a decrease in demand causes a leftward shift of the demand curve.

Since the supply of funds is provided by household savings, any change in attitude towards savings will change the supply of loanable funds. An increase in supply causes a rightward shift of the supply curve whereas a decrease in supply causes a leftward shift of the supply curve.

In conclusion, the decision to save, or to hold cash balances, depends on one variable in the classical model: the interest rate. The decision of firms to invest depends on the same variable. The combination of the demand for and the supply of loanable funds determines the market rate of interest.

The liquidity preference theory

Keynes and his followers argued that the rate of interest was not determined by the demand for and supply of loanable funds but by the demand for money and the existing money supply.

The demand for money

The demand for money in the Keynesian model is more complex than in the classical model. We begin by defining liquidity preference.

> **Definition**
>
> *Liquidity preference is the desire by households to hold assets in liquid form.*

According to Keynes, it is based on three motives which we will now explain. We will discover that the demand for money depends not only on the interest rate but also on the income of the household. In other words, the demand for money depends on two variables rather than just one as we discussed in the classical model.

1.   *Transactions demand*   A certain amount of money is required as a medium of exchange so that people can undertake day-to-day transactions such as the purchase of groceries, public transport and entertainment. The level of transactions demand depends on a number of factors. They include institutional factors such as the length of time between pay-days, the price level and, more importantly, the income level. The rate of interest has little or no effect on the transactions demand for money.

2.   *Precautionary demand*   A certain amount of money is held as a precaution against unforeseen contingencies such as illness or accidents. This desire to hold cash balances is related primarily to income. Other factors include the availability of overdraft facilities and the age of the economic agent involved.

     The transactions and precautionary motives are often combined. The addition of the two is sometimes referred to as the demand for 'active balances'; 'active' in the sense that these funds will be actively used to purchase goods and services. These two motives are directly related to the medium of exchange function of money.

     The demand for 'active balances' is drawn as a vertical line. This is shown in Figure 13.5.

     This means that it is interest rate inelastic; the demand for active balances does not change with the interest rate. Instead, the demand for active balances will change with income. An increase in income will shift the demand for active balances curve to the right. At higher income levels, more money is demanded for transactions and as a precaution against an uncertain future. If income levels fall, the demand curve will shift to the left.

FIGURE 13.5: THE DEMAND FOR ACTIVE BALANCES CURVE

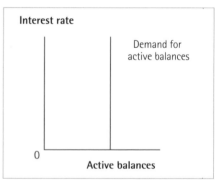

3.   *Speculative demand*   The final motive for holding money is to avoid losses from holding interest-bearing assets. For example, if investors had foreseen the Wall Street crash of 1929 they would have sold their interest-bearing assets and put the proceeds into bank accounts. This form of demand is sometimes called the demand for idle balances. It is related to the store of value function of money.

     Suppose an individual holds a portfolio of assets. Assume there are only two types of assets – money and bonds.[9] Money has the advantage of instant spending power or complete liquidity. However, it earns little or no interest. In contrast, bonds earn a rate of interest but suffer from being relatively illiquid.

     The individual must choose between holding money or holding bonds. The higher the rate of interest the more attractive it becomes to store wealth in bonds rather than money and with this the speculative demand for money declines. Hence, the speculative demand for money is inversely related to the rate of interest. If interest rates are high, the demand for bonds is relatively high whereas the demand for money is relatively low. A demand for 'idle balances' curve is drawn downward sloping, reflecting the inverse relationship between the speculative demand for money and the interest rate.

FIGURE 13.6: THE DEMAND FOR IDLE BALANCES CURVE

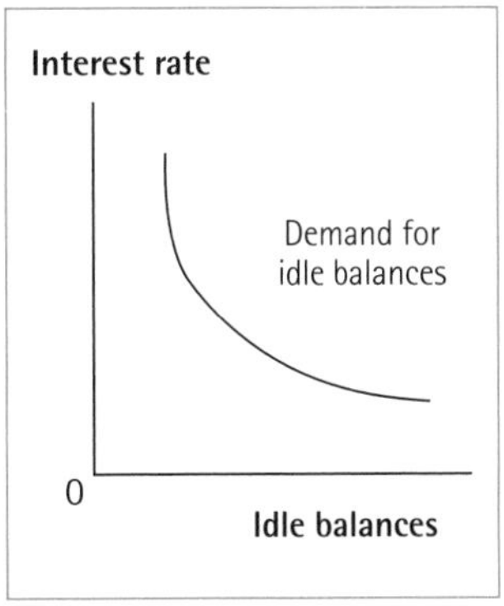

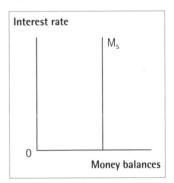

We can combine the demand for active balances curve with the demand for idle balances curve to yield the total demand for money curve. Keynes referred to this as the liquidity preference curve, denoted as L. It is the sum of the transactions demand, the precautionary demand and the speculative demand for money. The liquidity preference curve is downward sloping, reflecting the negative relationship between the total demand for money and the rate of interest. This inverse relationship arises largely from the speculative demand for money.

FIGURE 13.7: THE LIQUIDITY PREFERENCE CURVE

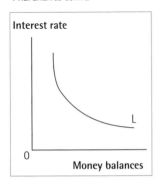

The liquidity preference curve, L, is drawn in Figure 13.7. Money demand also depends on the level of income. As income increases, the demand for money increases; as income decreases, the demand for money decreases. A change in the level of income causes a shift of the demand for money curve. An increase in income shifts the money demand curve to the right. The opposite is true for a fall in the income level.

The supply of money

In the liquidity preference theory of interest rate determination, the money supply is assumed to be controlled by the Central Bank. Remember, because of the nature of the banking system, commercial banks have the power not just to transfer purchasing power but also to create it. In turn, if the Central Bank can regulate the amount that the commercial banks hold on reserve, it can regulate the amount of money which they can create, thus controlling the money supply. Hence, the money supply curve is vertical, independent of the rate of interest. We say it is interest rate inelastic, at least in the short run. The money supply curve, M_s, is drawn in Figure 13.8.

FIGURE 13.8: THE MONEY SUPPLY CURVE

Money market equilibrium

Figure 13.9 shows a demand for money curve combined with a money supply curve. The interaction of the demand for and supply of money determines the interest rate. The rate of interest is the price of money and, like other prices, it is determined by the forces of demand and supply. In the words of J. M. Keynes it is 'the reward for parting with liquidity for a specified period'.[10]

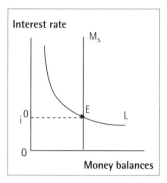

In Figure 13.9 the equilibrium rate of interest is i^0. At an interest rate above the equilibrium there exists an excess supply of money which leads to a downward movement of the interest rate. At an interest rate below the equilibrium there exists an excess demand for money which results in an upward movement of the interest rate.

Figure 13.10 illustrates the effect of an increase in the money supply. The money supply curve shifts to the right, from M_s to M_s^1. This results in an excess supply at the old rate of interest, i^0. Interest rates fall and continue to do so until the excess supply is eliminated. This adjustment process ends when the demand equals supply at a new and lower equilibrium rate of interest, i^1. Alternatively, a decrease in the money supply results in a higher equilibrium rate of interest.

FIGURE 13.10: AN INCREASE IN THE MONEY SUPPLY

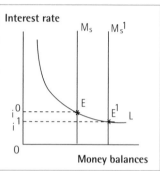

FIGURE 13.11: AN INCREASE IN THE DEMAND FOR MONEY

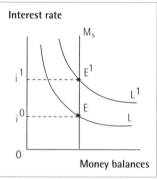

Figure 13.11 illustrates the effect of an increase in the demand for money (arising from an increase in income). The money demand curve shifts rightwards, resulting in excess demand at the old interest rate. Interest rates begin to rise and continue to do so until the excess demand is eliminated. Equilibrium returns to the money market at a higher interest rate, i^1, than before. Alternatively, a decrease in the demand for money results in a lower equilibrium rate of interest.

Finally, if interest rates are below 'normal', all market participants will expect a rise in interest rates. When explaining his liquidity preference theory, Keynes referred to the normal rate of interest, i.e. the rate of interest that is consistent with normal market conditions. If interest rates are low relative to the normal rate of interest, the market will expect an increase in the interest rate some time in the future. Due to the negative relationship that exists between interest rates and the price of bonds, we would expect a fall in the price of bonds.[11] In this case, investors would prefer to hold money to bonds because the holders of bonds will realise a capital loss.

Hence, at these 'low' interest rate levels, the demand for money may be perfectly elastic. This is illustrated by the horizontal part of the liquidity preference curve in Figure 13.7 above. Keynes referred to this as the liquidity trap. There is more discussion on the liquidity trap in the next chapter.

The two models suggest that the interest rate is determined in very different ways. In the loanable funds model, both the supply of funds and the demand for funds vary with the interest rate. In the liquidity preference theory, the interest rate is determined in the money market.

A more fundamental difference is that in the classical loanable funds theory, interest rate determination appears to be an automatic process. Funds become available from households as interest rates rise. Funds are demanded by firms as the interest rate falls. An adjustable interest rate clears the market. Keynes' speculative demand for money suggests that money is a 'safe' asset, preferred by investors, particularly in times of uncertainty. Equilibrium in the money market may be at very low rates of interest. Even at low rates of interest, firms are not enticed to put money to a productive use.

Finally Keynes suggests that in certain situations, the money supply can be used to affect the interest rate. Since the money supply is controlled by the government, policy-makers are able to adjust it to affect the interest rate and ultimately, private investment.

We finish this section with a brief explanation of the term structure of interest rates.

The term structure of interest rates relates the yield or interest rate on a security to the length of time until the security matures. It is reflected in the yield curve.

Definition

The yield curve shows the way in which the yield on a security varies according to its maturity or expiry date.

It is customary to represent yields (interest rates on security) on the vertical axis and maturities (time period) on the horizontal axis. The slope of the yield curve can vary. Among other factors, inflation and interest rate expectations can account for the differences in yield curve patterns.

The 'normal' shaped yield curve slopes up from left to right, as shown in Figure 13.12(a). This reflects the case where long-term interest rates are above short-term interest rates. This is viewed as the norm because the expectation of higher inflation over the long run will result in long-term securities offering higher yields than short-term securities.

Other types of yield curves are also shown in Figure 13.12.

FIGURE 13.12: DIFFERENT YIELD CURVES

In Figure 13.12(b) the yield curve is drawn as a straight line. A flat yield curve results when long-term and short-term interest rates are equal. When long-term interest rates are below short-term interest rates, a downward sloping yield curve is drawn, as in Figure 13.12(c).

Analysing the behaviour of the yield curve is quite common in financial markets.

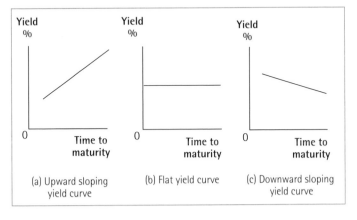

In particular, yield curves are used as a prediction tool. Market predictions about movements of short-term interest rates in the future are reflected in the slope of the yield curve. For example, a steep upward sloping yield curve means that short-term interest rates are expected to rise. In contrast, a flat or downward sloping yield curve means that short-term interest rates are expected to fall. Either way, yield curves reflect the prevailing expectations in the financial markets.

CASE STUDY

Extract from *The Irish Times*
Private sector credit falls by €3.2bn
by Laura Slattery

The use of credit by the private sector continued to fall in January, as consumers weaned themselves off credit card debt, the mortgage market contracted and lending to businesses declined. New figures from the Central Bank show that private sector credit fell by €3.2 billion during the first month of the year, further lowering the annual rate of change in private sector credit to 7.1 per cent. Just over half of the annual contraction is the result of writedowns by financial institutions, increased provisions for bad debts and the strengthening of the euro against other major currencies throughout the year. However, in the month of January, most of the decline in credit was due to repayments of credit exceeding fresh drawdowns.

The pace of decline in lending to businesses became more pronounced during the month, according to the Central Bank. Credit to this sector, adjusted for valuation effects, fell 4.3 per cent in the year to January. Household credit was 2.2 per cent lower in January 2010 compared with January 2009, while there was a 0.5 per cent monthly decline in total household credit compared to December 2009. Outstanding residential mortgage loans declined by €269 million during the month, bringing the annual rate of decline in mortgage lending to 0.7 per cent. The value of outstanding mortgages at the end of January 2010 was €147.4 billion. There was a 'more rapid' decline in the level of outstanding indebtedness on personal credit cards in January. Repayments exceeded new spending by €83 million during the month, taking the year-on-year change in credit card debt to minus 1.3 per cent.

Ireland's private sector credit data will be significantly affected by the transfer of toxic bank debt to the National Asset Management Agency (Nama), the Central Bank said yesterday. This is because the transfers are expected to trigger new writedowns of loans. Although some economists are hopeful that the establishment of Nama will pave the way for a functioning credit market, they do not expect a return to the expansionary credit markets of the boom years.

Source: The Irish Times, 27 February 2010.

Questions

1. Explain why private sector credit in Ireland continued to fall in 2009/2010. How is this concept related to the general state of the economy?
2. Using monthly data from the Central Bank of Ireland's Quarterly Bulletin (www.centralbank.ie), report the (unadjusted) year-to-year changes, in percentage terms, in private sector credit in 2008/2009. Compare this with private sector credit growth rates during the Celtic Tiger boom years by reporting, using monthly data, the year-to-year percentage changes for any two-year period between 2001 and 2006.
3. In terms of ownership, outline the changes that took place in the main Irish-controlled banks during the banking crisis. What was the purpose of NAMA and what does the agency do?

Answers on website

13.3 THE ROLE OF A CENTRAL BANK

The central bank is a very important component of any banking system. Yet, while some central banks are centuries old, others have been established quite recently.[12]

The first tentative step towards the establishment of a central bank in Ireland was taken in 1783 when Parliament established the Bank of Ireland. Its primary role was to issue banknotes. To a lesser extent, it acted as a bankers' bank and a lender of last resort.

The Bank of Ireland's role as central bank diminished following the Act of Union in 1801 when the Bank of England began to take on central bank activities in Ireland. However, the Bank of Ireland's role as a central bank effectively ended with the passage of the Bankers' Act of 1845. This Act promoted competition and relaxed restrictions concerning the issuing of banknotes. From this date on, the Bank of Ireland concentrated on commercial banking.

The most important financial event following political independence was the establishment of the Banking Commission called the Parker-Willis Commission, after its chairman Professor Henry Parker-Willis. It was established in 1926, in an environment which was hostile to the emergence of a central bank. In the following year, the Currency Act of 1927 introduced the Saorstat pound which was later renamed the Irish pound.[13] The Commission was also responsible for the regulation of the newly designed Irish notes and coins.

The Central Bank of Ireland was formally established in 1943, receiving its powers from the Central Bank Act of 1942. It was responsible for safeguarding the integrity of the currency and for controlling the amount of credit in the economy. New techniques and instruments for the purpose of implementing monetary policy were developed in the intervening decades. Notwithstanding these developments, the continuation of the sterling link confined the Central Bank of Ireland to a secondary role. All this changed in the 1970s.

In 1971 the Central Bank Act was passed. It was primarily concerned with the licensing and supervision of banks in the domestic market. This was to meet the structural changes which had occurred throughout the banking industry. Powers were further increased in 1989 when, among other things, building societies and all financial institutions in the International Financial Services Centre were placed under the regulation of the Central Bank. By 1993, the activities of the ICC Bank and the ACC Bank had also been brought under the supervision of the Central Bank. Since the early 1990s, events at home have been dominated by monetary developments in the EU, and in particular the establishment of the European Central Bank. Since the launch of the single currency in 1999, many of the functions of the Central Bank have been transformed from the Central Bank of Ireland to the European Central Bank.

Functions of a central bank

A central bank fulfils a number of functions. It issues and controls the currency, sometimes referred to as 'legal tender'. It acts as banker to the state.

A central bank is also the banker's bank. Reserves, required by law, are held for the commercial banking sector by the Central Bank. Since commercial banks operate with only a fraction of their deposits, the Central Bank ensures that they can obtain cash to meet any unexpected withdrawal of funds. Because of this role, the Central Bank is sometimes referred to as 'the lender of last resort'.

A central bank formulates and implements monetary policy which we will discuss in the next section. Adjusting the interest rate is the aspect of monetary policy which is most widely reported in the news.

Another function of the Central Bank is to manage the country's monetary system. It is usually responsible for the regulation and the supervision of all financial institutions.

We now examine one of its functions in more detail – the formulation and implementation of monetary policy.

13.4 MONETARY POLICY

> **Definition**
>
> *Monetary policy refers to the use of money supply, credit and interest rates to achieve economic objectives.*

We will discuss the use of credit guidelines and interest rates later. We begin, however, by looking at the supply of money in the economy.

In a closed economy, the supply of money can be controlled by the Central Bank which has a number of different options available. Three such options are described below. They are sometimes referred to as the tools or instruments of monetary policy.[14]

1. *Reserve requirements* All financial institutions are required to hold a certain amount of their deposits on reserve.

> **Definition**
>
> *The reserve requirement is the percentage of deposits which banks are legally obligated to lodge at the Central Bank.*

Changes in the rules that specify the amount of reserves a bank must hold to back up deposits can influence the money supply. For example, the higher the reserve requirement, the lower the deposit multiplier and subsequently the smaller the change in the money supply. Conversely, a decrease in the reserve requirement increases the amount of deposits that can be supported by a given level of reserves and will lead to an increase in the money supply.

2. *Open market operations*

> **Definition**
>
> *Open market operations involve the buying and selling of government securities or bonds.*

When the Central Bank buys securities, a cheque is drawn on the Central Bank as payment in favour of the client's commercial bank. When the cheque is presented for payment, bank deposits are transferred from the Central Bank to the commercial bank. Hence, the reserves of the commercial bank are increased. Moreover, its ability to create more deposits via the money multiplier process also increases. The end result is an increase in the money supply. In brief, an open market purchase expands the money supply; an open market sale reduces the money supply.

3. *Discount rate* As we discussed above, commercial banks must hold a percentage of their deposits as reserves. If their reserves fall below the legal limit, commercial banks borrow money from other banks, if possible, or from the Central Bank to make up the shortfall. The interest rate charged is called the discount rate.

> **Definition**
>
> *The discount rate is the rate which the Central Bank charges financial institutions that borrow from it for purposes of maintaining the reserve requirement.*

The lower the discount rate, the lower the cost of borrowing for reserves, the higher the amount of borrowing. As banks increase their borrowing from the Central Bank, the subsequent increase in bank reserves can support an increase in loans. We know from the money multiplier process that an increase in the money supply results. The opposite is true for a relatively high discount rate.

The discount rate is generally used as the base of all other interest rates. When the discount rate increases, all other interest rates on loans for firms and consumers generally follow. That is why announcements from the European Central Bank concerning their key interest rates are awaited with such interest by the financial markets.

One further possibility is for the Central Bank to make a formal request to the commercial banks to meet certain credit guidelines or to maintain a required reserve ratio. The request is sometimes accompanied with constraints. This practice of discouraging banks and other financial institutions is called moral suasion.

In conclusion, an increase in the money supply results from an open market purchase, a reduction in the discount rate and a reduction in the required reserve ratio. A sale of securities, an increase in the discount rate and a higher required reserve ratio lead to a reduction in the money supply.

This completes the operational aspect of monetary policy. We shall return to this later when we examine the ECB and how it influences liquidity and interest rates. We now outline the effects that monetary policy has on the macroeconomic variables of output and employment.

The effects of monetary policy

We will begin with an example which illustrates the relationship between the money supply, interest rates and national income.

Suppose the monetary authorities conduct an open market purchase. We know from our earlier discussion on the tools of monetary policy that the purchase of securities increases the money supply. This creates a disequilibrium (excess supply) in the money market which drives down the interest rate. The fall in the interest rate induces an increase in investment expenditure (and possibly consumer expenditure, particularly consumer goods bought on credit). Investment expenditure is one component of aggregate expenditure. The increase in aggregate expenditure will lead to an increase in national output, measured by GDP. If the link between economic growth and employment/unemployment is strong (see Okun's Law in Chapter 17), such increases in output will increase employment and reduce unemployment. In short,

$$\text{Increase in } M_s \rightarrow \text{decreases i} \rightarrow \text{increases I} \rightarrow \text{increases AE} \rightarrow \text{increases GDP} \rightarrow \text{decreases U}$$

The effects of monetary policy are illustrated in Figure 13.13.

FIGURE 13.13: MONETARY POLICY CHANGES

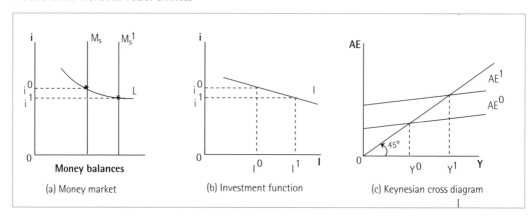

(a) Money market   (b) Investment function   (c) Keynesian cross diagram

The money market is represented in panel (a), the investment function in panel (b) and the Keynesian cross diagram in panel (c).[15] The increase in money supply shifts the money supply curve to the right. The equilibrium rate of interest falls from i^0 to i^1. Lower interest rates induce greater investment expenditure and this causes a movement down along the investment function (from I^0 to I^1). An increase in investment, one of the components of aggregate expenditure, shifts the AE curve upwards from AE^0 to AE^1, increasing the equilibrium income level.

We have shown that, using a Keynesian model, an increase in the money supply expands national income. Conversely, a reduction in the money supply contracts national income. Using the IS/LM framework, changes in monetary policy are discussed in more detail in the next chapter.

This short discussion on monetary policy illustrates its effects on economic variables and its importance in the context of achieving macroeconomic objectives. A discussion on inflation and how changes in the money supply affect the general price level are omitted; these are explained in Chapter 17.

Monetary policy as a policy instrument

The use of monetary policy became fashionable in the 1970s because economists and governments were concerned that government spending was not having the desired effect on unemployment. Rather, it was increasing the percentage of national income which was controlled by the public sector. Further, high levels of government spending combined with interest payments led to spiralling government debts.

The main attraction of monetary policy is that it affects the spending patterns of the private sector. A change in the money supply affects the interest rate. Changes in the interest rate lead to changes in both investment and consumer spending. Therefore, everyone in the private sector can potentially benefit from the change in the price of capital funds. The economy is stimulated or deflated by lowering or raising the interest rate. The emphasis of this policy is on the private sector; it does not directly affect public sector spending or the national debt.

Monetary policy became the preferred macroeconomic policy in the USA and the UK by the early 1980s. However, from the outset, the use of monetary policy to stabilise the economy was criticised by a group of economists called the 'monetarists'. Milton Friedman and Edmund Phelps were both early contributors to the debate.

They argued that the primary role of monetary policy is to maintain the price level which creates confidence in a national currency and ultimately in a national economy. They conceded that adjustments to the money supply might cause fluctuations in national output in the short run. However, they cautioned that the use of monetary policy to stabilise the economy leads to inflation and a weakening of the currency. Therefore, the use of monetary policy to stabilise the economy in the short run hinders the long-term growth of the economy.

We sometimes make the mistake of thinking that Keynesians advocate the use of fiscal policy, and monetarists advocate the use of monetary policy. In reality, particularly in the 1970s, Keynesians accepted and embraced the use of monetary policy.

In contrast, monetarists always believed in the importance of monetary policy but not in its use to stabilise the economy. Careful monitoring of the money supply ensures that inflation does not become entrenched in the national economy. For the monetarists, the role of monetary policy is to ensure price stability. This is much more limited than the role envisioned by the Keynesians.

Having discussed the two extreme positions on monetary policy, we will end with the observations of David Romer, who appears to be seeking the middle ground. He states that, 'The lesson I draw is that conducting monetary policy has always been difficult. The environment has been changing continually, the lags have been long, the uncertainty has been great. Thus, I would conclude that monetary policy should be conducted the way it always has been – using a mix of formal models, rules of thumb, shrewd observation, instinct, guesswork and prayer.'[16]

13.5 THE IRISH EXPERIENCE

The Irish experience pre-1999

From the comments above, we can see that for a closed economy, the role of monetary policy is debatable and even contentious. We will find that the scope of policy effectiveness is even narrower in a small open economy (SOE) such as Ireland.

> **Definition**
>
> *A small open economy (SOE) refers to an economy that is so small relative to the world economy that domestic economic events have no effect on the rest of the world. The domestic economy is a price taker: it accepts world prices. Also, external trade (exports and imports) represents a high proportion of the country's GDP.*

Ireland's economy exhibits these characteristics. Further, we find that Ireland, in common with other small open economies, exhibits particular behaviours which limit its ability to use monetary policy effectively. We will list these and then discuss their relevance in detail.

1. An SOE whose currency belongs to a fixed or semi-fixed exchange rate system does not control its money supply.
2. Domestic interest rates in the long term are determined primarily by external forces.
3. It may have some ability to manage the liquidity in the money market in the short term.

1. *Money supply*   The monetary authorities of an SOE cannot control its money supply to the same degree as other central banks.[17] Hence, there is little scope for an independent monetary policy. An example follows.

Independent of other central banks, suppose the Central Bank of Ireland decided (pre-1999) to increase the money supply in order to boost domestic spending. As the domestic money supply increases, interest rates fall. Because domestic interest rates are now lower than world interest rates, an outflow of capital results. In order to invest in other economies where interest rates are now relatively higher, the Irish pound is exchanged for foreign currencies. An excess supply of the Irish pound leads to a weakening of the Irish currency against foreign currencies which should cause a depreciation of the Irish pound. Because Ireland is a member of a semi-fixed exchange rate system, that is, the exchange rate mechanism of the European Monetary System, the Central Bank is obliged to maintain the value of the Irish pound between certain limits. The Central Bank intervenes by buying up and, in the process, eliminating the excess supply. On the purchase of the domestic currency, the money supply decreases and interest rates effectively revert to their original level. An independent monetary policy appears ineffective.

2. *Interest rates* Central banks in closed economies can 'set' their interest rate and adjust their money supply to support that interest rate. Interest rates in an SOE are determined largely by external factors, the most important of which is the level of foreign interest rates. As we explained above, investors will move capital to take advantage of higher interest rates in other economies. As a result, domestic interest rates cannot differ substantially from foreign interest rates if capital is mobile. Other external factors which affect the domestic interest rate work through the exchange rate. They include speculation and expectations concerning realignments of exchange rates.

This dependency on foreign interest rates is illustrated in the following example.

If the Bundesbank increased German interest rates (pre-1999), the Irish Central Bank was likely to follow. If it did not, an interest rate differential (a gap between German and Irish interest rates) would result. Given the absence of exchange controls, capital was likely to flow from Ireland to Germany where the return was now higher. As a consequence, the Irish pound would weaken against the German mark. This depreciation of the Irish pound would continue until the interest rate differential disappeared. This would happen only when the Irish Central Bank increased domestic interest rates or in the unlikely event of the Bundesbank rescinding its earlier decision.

3. *Liquidity* The above analysis seems to suggest the absence of any role for the Irish monetary authorities. This is not completely true. In the short term the Central Bank could influence liquidity levels by providing funds or withdrawing funds whenever necessary. Liquidity could be added to or drained from the domestic financial system by a number of different instruments. These are called liquidity management instruments. They included the following:

- *The short-term facility* The STF was an overdraft facility which the Central Bank provided to those financial institutions that were short of reserves. Funds were drawn down on a quota basis overnight and this facility was available for up to seven days. Frequent use of the STF reflected a shortage of liquidity.
- *Secured advances* The Central Bank provided a facility for banks to borrow funds on a longer-term basis against the security of government bonds. It was an extension of the STF and was normally only used when a bank's quota was filled. This seldom happened and, hence, this instrument was rarely used.
- *Foreign exchange (FX) swaps* A foreign exchange swap is a financial instrument whereby one party lends foreign currency to another party in exchange for domestic currency.[18] If the Central Bank wanted to add liquidity it could do so by swapping Irish pounds for foreign currency. Conversely, liquidity could be removed by swapping foreign currency for Irish pounds. This particular instrument provided liquidity for periods of up to four weeks.

- *Sale and repurchase agreements (REPOs)*   REPOs are financial instruments whereby one party agrees to buy a security on the condition that it will resell it to the other party at some future date. The Central Bank often bought securities from other financial institutions on the understanding that it would resell them back to the same banks on an agreed future date. Like swaps, REPOs provided liquidity for periods of up to one month.
- *Term deposits*   At times of temporary surplus liquidity, the Central Bank quoted rates for overnight and term deposits. Although the Central Bank could not add liquidity through this method, it could discourage banks from holding surplus liquidity by quoting unattractive rates for term deposits.
- *Changes in the reserve ratio*   Variations in the reserve ratio were used to add or withdraw liquidity. A reduction in the ratio allowed for greater liquidity; an increase permitted less liquidity. Variations in the reserve ratio were usually confined to periods where seasonal changes occur, e.g. Christmas.

In general, changes in one or more of these instruments allowed the Central Bank to add or remove liquidity from the domestic money market. Such action by the Central Bank aimed to avoid reductions in interest rates which would otherwise stem from excess market liquidity and, likewise, avoid increases in interest rates arising from shortages in liquidity in the market. In effect, the Central Bank attempted to smooth out changes in liquidity in order to prevent sharp movements in domestic interest rates.

The objective of monetary policy in Ireland

Pre-1999, monetary policy in Ireland was described in many different ways. Here is a small sample: '. . . the poor relation of economic policy in Ireland'; '. . . an unutilised instrument of public policy';[19] '. . . always there, exerting an influence, behind the scenes' and finally, the 'Hidden Stabiliser'.[20] The objective of Irish monetary policy was price stability, i.e. low inflation.[21]

Employing an exchange rate target strategy, the Central Bank tried to achieve price stability. By maintaining the value of the Irish pound within the Exchange Rate Mechanism (ERM), the Central Bank was able to sustain a low inflation rate. In order to maintain the exchange rate link with the German mark, it was, at times, necessary for the Central Bank to change interest rates. For example, a fall in the value of the Irish pound against the German mark might require a hike in interest rates, regardless of domestic economic conditions.

The 1992 Central Bank statement on monetary policy is a good summary of the aim of monetary policy at that time, 'The basic objective of monetary policy is to keep inflation as low as possible through the maintenance of a firm exchange rate for the Irish pound within the narrow band of the EMS.'[22]

The monetary policy experience in Ireland

An Irish financial system, independent from the UK, was established in the mid-1960s. In 1969 the Central Bank started a market for government securities. In the following year, a foreign exchange market was established. Assets which were owned by Irish commercial institutions but held in London were re-routed back to Ireland. The most significant change in the Irish monetary system occurred in 1979 when Ireland broke with sterling and joined the newly formed ERM of the European Monetary System. Prior to this, Irish interest rates were determined by factors such as UK interest rates, the value of sterling and the UK Treasury.

FIGURE 13.14: IRISH AND UK INTEREST RATES 1971–79

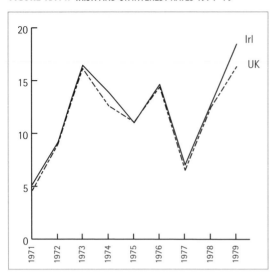

The close relationship between Irish and UK interest rates in the period up to 1979 is highlighted in Figure 13.14.

After 1979, UK interest rates and the value of sterling were no longer the dominant factors in the determination of Irish interest rates. This is not to suggest that the Irish monetary authorities were suddenly in charge of Irish interest rates: there was simply a change in the factors which determined Irish interest rates. Exchange rate and interest rate levels within the ERM became the most important factors in determining Irish monetary policy and, in particular, Irish interest rates. Moreover, it was the value of the German mark combined with German interest rates which became the dominant factor. This is because of the central role which Germany occupied within the exchange rate system. Irish, UK and German interest rates in the period 1980–99 are shown in Figure 13.15.

The large differential between Irish and German interest rates during the first few years of the EMS was unexpected and unwelcome. Fortunately, in the later period of membership the differential narrowed sub-stantially.

The Irish experience post-1999

The Treaty on European Union (see Chapter 15) and the new institutions that followed have changed the operation of monetary policy in Ireland and elsewhere. In January 1999, the Irish currency was fixed relative to other currencies of the EU countries that also adopted the euro. The euro interest rate is set by the European Central Bank. The Central Bank of Ireland plays a secondary role in the formulation and implementation of monetary policy. We begin our analysis by identifying the new institutions that are responsible for the single monetary policy in the euro area.

FIGURE 13.15: IRISH, UK AND GERMAN INTEREST RATES 1980–99

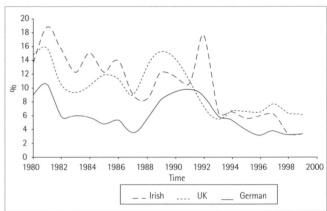

We begin with the European System of Central Banks (ESCB). The ESCB is composed of the European Central Bank (ECB) and the national central banks of all EU member states. As not all EU member states adopted the euro on its launch in January 1999, the term Eurosystem has been used to describe the ECB and the central banks of the EU member states that participate in the euro area.[23]

The decision-making bodies of the ECB comprise the Governing Council and the six-member Executive Board. The Executive Board comprises the ECB president, the ECB vice-president and four other members who are appointed by the heads of the participating states. The appointment is for an eight-year non-renewable term. The Governing Council comprises the members of the executive board and the governors of the national central banks participating in the euro area. In the context of membership of the Governing Council, governors of the participating national central banks (including the governor of the Central Bank of Ireland) are required to act in a personal capacity and not as national representatives. This supra-national responsibility was designed to ensure that governors are not subject to any instructions and are required to act in the best interests of the euro area as a whole.

It is the Governing Council that is the primary decision-making authority of the ECB. It formulates the single monetary policy for the euro area. Council decisions concerning monetary policy are made on the basis of a simple majority of votes, whereby each member has one vote. The role of the executive board is to manage the ECB and its primary function is to implement monetary policy in accordance with the guidelines and decisions laid down by the Governing Council. The national central banks take their instructions from the executive board and, by doing so, ensure a certain degree of co-ordination and decentralisation.

The provisions of the Maastricht Treaty attempt to ensure that the new ECB is independent from political interference. Article 107 states that neither the Community institutions nor national governments of the member states can interfere with or influence decisions of the ECB. The statutory powers of the ECB can only be altered by a revision of the Maastricht Treaty which, in itself, would require ratification by all EU member states. In theory, this makes the ECB even more independent than either the German Bundesbank or the US Federal Reserve (Fed). The purpose of this design or institutionalisation of Central Bank independence was to help establish the credibility and anti-inflation reputation of the new ECB. Despite the Treaty provisions regarding accountability (Article 109b), many view the new monetary institutions as undemocratic. Supporters of the ECB argue that the balance between independence and accountability is reasonable.

As stated in Article 105 of the Treaty, the primary objective of the single monetary policy in the euro area is price stability. In addition, the Treaty states that, 'Without prejudice to the objective of price stability, the ESCB shall support the general economic policies in the Community . . .'. For the euro area, the Governing Council of the ECB defined, in quantitative terms, price stability as an annual increase in the Harmonised Index of Consumer Prices (HICP) of below 2% (see Chapter 17 for a description of the HICP). With respect to a time frame, there is explicit reference to price stability thus defined 'to be maintained over the medium term'. The aim of this is to ensure a forward-looking, medium-term orientation for the single monetary policy. By any standards, including the admirable record of the Bundesbank and the Fed, achieving an inflation target of below (even if 'close to') 2% over the medium term, albeit undefined, is a difficult task.

Monetary policy strategy

In choosing a monetary policy strategy that will yield price stability, the ECB had a number of options available to it. These include the following;

- exchange rate targeting (as used by the Central Bank of Ireland);
- interest rate targeting;
- monetary aggregate targeting (as used by the Bundesbank);
- inflation targeting (as used by the Bank of England).

In each of these cases, the ultimate target of price stability is achieved by means of an intermediate target, namely the exchange rate (pegged to an anchor currency of a country with a strong anti-inflation reputation), a short-term interest rate, broad money or forecasted inflation respectively. In its 1997 report on alternative monetary policy strategies, the European Monetary Institute (the predecessor to the ECB) came out in favour of two strategies, namely monetary aggregate targeting and inflation targeting. With this in mind, the ECB announced the Eurosystem's stability-oriented monetary policy strategy in October 1998, details of which can be found in the ECB *Monthly Bulletin* January 1999 issue. A short description follows.

As expected, the monetary policy strategy preferred by the Eurosystem did not opt for a single intermediate target. Instead two 'pillars' or key elements are used in the pursuit of price stability. The first pillar, referred to as the 'monetary analysis', relates to a prominent role for money, in recognition of the monetary origins of inflation. Assessing medium- to long-term trends in inflation, it is in the form of a quantitative reference value (as opposed to a strict target) for broad money M3 growth, announced at 4.5% per annum.[24] In devising the strategy, cognisance was taken of the regime shift to EMU. In view of this regime change and the effect that it might have on the relationship between money and inflation, it was decided that deviations from the reference value would not automatically lead to a correction by the authorities. Also, the actual reference value of 4.5% could be changed in the future, if, for example, the trend growth in real GDP was to change. In view of this, a review of the reference value will take place on an annual basis. The second pillar, referred to as the 'economic analysis', is more broad-based, assessing the outlook for price developments and identifying short- to medium-term risks to price stability. A wide range of economic and financial indicators are used, including trends in output and wage levels, the exchange rate, bond prices and the yield curve. For example, if the inflation target was endangered by a sudden increase in wages arising from labour shortages, the ECB might respond by increasing short-term interest rates. A schematic presentation of the monetary policy strategy is given in Figure 13.16.

FIGURE 13.16: THE ECB'S MONETARY POLICY STRATEGY

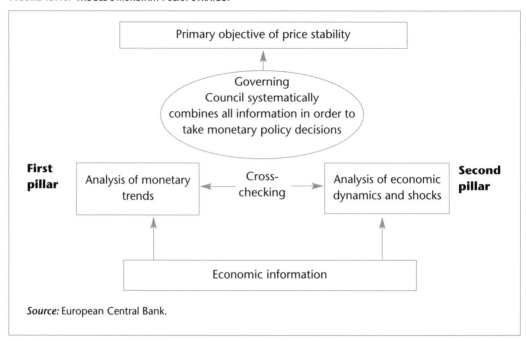

Source: European Central Bank.

Since the announcement of the monetary policy strategy, the ECB has been criticised for the confusion arising from the twin pillar strategy. Many have called for the abandonment of the quasi money-supply 'target' in preference for a strict inflation target.[25] Others have gone further and called for the ECB to 'target' not just inflation or money supply but asset prices and the level of the exchange rate. In response, the ECB reiterates that the two pillars are not targets but instruments which facilitate the achievement of its primary objective, namely price stability. In addition, the ECB draws attention to the complexity of monetary policy and to the new and unfamiliar format of its monetary strategy. The ECB did, however, clarify its definition of price stability in view of deflationary risks. The Governing Council reaffirmed its '... below 2% ...' definition, but agreed, after reviewing its strategy in 2003, '... to maintain inflation rates *close to* 2% over the medium term'.

The instruments of monetary policy

In the implementation of monetary policy in the euro area, there are a number of instruments available to the monetary authorities (see Section 13.4 for a general discussion on monetary policy instruments). The core elements of the operational framework are open market operations, standing facilities and minimum reserves.

Open market operations As explained earlier, open market operations are the buying and selling of government securities. Although there are a number of instruments available to the Eurosystem for the conduct of open market operations, the main refinancing operations (MRO) is the most important.

> **Definition**
>
> *Main refinancing operations are reverse transactions using tenders and are normally executed weekly, with a maturity of one week.*

The procedure is as follows. The ECB sets the interest rate that will be applied on the main refinancing operations. This is followed by a tendering procedure, where the tender can either be at a fixed rate or a variable rate. Bids are made by Monetary Financial Institutions (MFIs), seeking liquidity in return for the delivery of collateral. Following this, the ECB decides on the total allotment and distributes *pro rata.*

   The interest rate applied to the main refinancing operations is the Eurosystem's key interest rate. According to the ECB, the role of the MRO is to signal the monetary policy stance, steer short-term interest rates and provide the bulk of the liquidity to the banking system. By changing the interest rate and the size of allotments, the ECB can effect the market interest rate and the amount of liquidity. At the launch of the euro in January 1999, the refinancing rate was set by the ECB at 3%. During the financial crisis of 2008/9 it was reduced to 1%.

Standing facilities (credit lines) The function of standing facilities is to provide or absorb liquidity with an overnight maturity. Two such facilities are available, namely a marginal lending facility and a deposit facility. The marginal lending facility may be used to obtain overnight liquidity from the national central banks. The deposit facility is used to make overnight deposits with the national central banks. The interest rate on the marginal lending facility provides a ceiling for the overnight market interest rate. The interest rate on the deposit facility provides a floor for the market rate. In January 1999, the lending rate and the deposit rate were set at 4.5% and 2%

respectively. By 2008/9, at the peak of the financial crisis, rates were 1.75% and 0.25% respectively.

Minimum reserve requirements Reserve requirements allow MFIs to smooth out liquidity fluctuations. For example, a decrease in the reserve requirements reduces the liquidity shortage, tending to increase the money supply. Minimum reserves are applicable to all credit institutions in the euro area. The reserve requirement of each credit institution is calculated by applying a reserve ratio to selected liabilities of the balance sheet. The reserve ratio was set at 2% as from the start of stage three of EMU.

As for the operating target, namely the interest rate, there is some concern expressed over the sustainability of a 'one interest rate fits all' policy, especially in the context of the euro area where participating states are at different stages of the economic cycle. In the first couple of years of EMU, the biggest difference was between the smaller, fast-growing (at that time) economies of Ireland, Portugal and Finland and the bigger, sluggish economies of Germany and Italy. Given the economic and political realities of the euro area, the likelihood is that future monetary policy will reflect conditions in the bigger economies of France, Germany and Italy rather than in the peripheral economies of Ireland, Portugal and Greece.[26]

The ECB and monetary policy in the eurozone

In a monetary union there is one currency, one Central Bank and one monetary policy. In the context of EMU, the euro is the single currency and the ECB is the monetary authority. What has the ECB's record been since it assumed responsibility for monetary policy in 1999? What has the growth in the money supply been relative to the 4.5% reference value? What have short-term euro interest rates been for the first decade or so of the ECB reign? Let us begin our analysis with euro interest rates.

The ECB sets the short-term euro interest rate through three channels. It sets a ceiling (the marginal refinancing or lending facility whereby financial institutions can borrow from the monetary authorities), a floor (the deposit facility whereby financial institutions can make overnight deposits with the monetary authorities) and conducts regular auctions (the MRO) at the main refinancing interest rate (MRIR). The ECB's main refinancing rate moves closely with the key market interest rate, the euro overnight index average EONIA (which is a weighted average of overnight lending transactions in the eurozone interbank market) as both MRIR and EONIA are funding rates for the financial institutions and commercial banks. If, as financial institutions depend on the interbank market for funds, the EONIA is less than the MRIR, credit institutions would borrow in the interbank market, driving the EONIA upwards. Changes in the MRIR (and the ECB's marginal lending and deposit rates) will impact on the EONIA and, in turn, affect all the commercial interest rates. Hence, the ECB can change interest rates and engage in open market operations, thus forcing changes in liquidity and interbank rates, and, in turn, steering short-term interest rates throughout the eurozone.

Figure 13.17 shows ECB interest rates and the EONIA for the period 1999–2010. Between 2003 and 2005 the key euro interest rate remained constant, at 2%. Sluggish economic growth in the eurozone (and particularly in the bigger economies of France, Germany and Italy) prevented the ECB from increasing interest rates at a time when some ECB members wished to tighten monetary policy in view of higher interest rates elsewhere (especially in the UK and the USA) fear of inflationary pressures arising from higher oil prices and rising property prices in

FIGURE 13.17: ECB INTEREST RATES AND THE EONIA 1999–2010

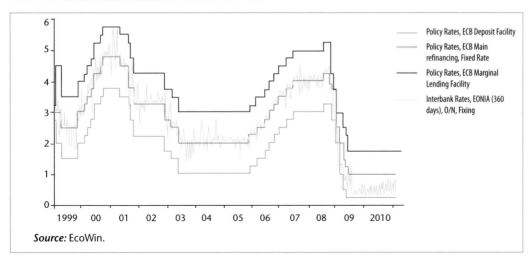

Source: EcoWin.

some eurozone member states (including Ireland) and to counteract the fiscal indiscipline arising from some member states' failure to abide by the Stability and Growth Pact and the subsequent loosening of the Pact's rules. In terms of money supply, the 4.5% M3 growth reference value has seldom been reached since the start of EMU. In some cases, the actual money supply growth rate has been well in excess of the reference value. However, the monetary policy strategy as outlined by the monetary authority did allow for deviations (that were neither significant nor protracted) and it is argued by many that the ECB wishes to give the impression that it does not conduct monetary policy in a mechanistic fashion. Although ECB interest rates did eventually rise, they were aggressively cut in the late 2000s in the light of the financial crisis and global recession. What have these levels of interest rates and rates of money supply growth meant for eurozone inflation? Figure 13.18 shows the inflation rate in the eurozone for the period 1999–2010.

FIGURE 13.18: EURO AREA INFLATION RATE 1999–2010

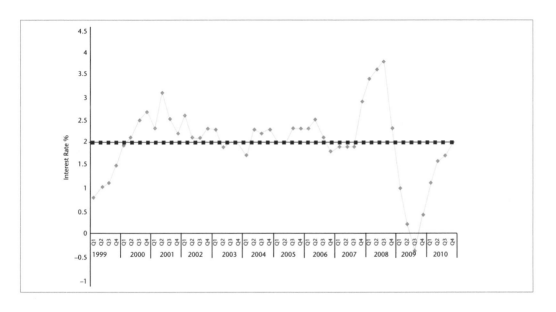

Although the inflation rate has been low, there were long periods in the early days when the rate was in excess of the price stability definition of an inflation rate of below 2% (partly prompting the clarification in May 2003 to below but close to 2%). The ECB's inflation objective was hampered in the first half decade of its reign by a number of events and economic shocks, including the dotcom bubble and its subsequent collapse, the 9/11 attack and aftermath, variable oil prices and volatile movements in the €/US$ exchange rate. Much worse was to follow in the late 2000s, as we will outline in Chapter 15.

SUMMARY

1. Money is anything that is accepted as a medium of exchange. It is also a unit of account, a standard of deferred payment and a store of value. Narrow money supply is defined as notes and coins and balances on current accounts. Broad money supply is defined as the narrow money supply plus balances on deposit accounts.
2. The banking system can create money. This phenomenon can be explained by the multiplier process. The deposit multiplier relates a change in reserves to the change in deposits. It depends inversely on the reserve ratio.
3. The classical loanable funds theory and the Keynesian liquidity preference theory are the two main models of interest rate determination. In the former, the interest rate is derived from the demand for and supply of funds. In the latter, it is the demand for and supply of money which determine the interest rate. For Keynes, the demand for money depends on the interest rate and the level of income.
4. The functions of the Central Bank are many and diverse. It is the government's and the banker's bank. It issues notes and coins. It regulates the financial institutions. It formulates monetary policy. The Central Bank of Ireland was formally established in 1943. Its powers were increased in 1971 and again in the late 1980s. The European Central Bank was established in 1998.
5. There are a number of ways by which the Central Bank can control the level of reserves and, in turn, the money supply. They include open market operations, changes in the discount rate and changes in the reserve requirements. Changes in these instruments affect the money supply and, in turn, other macroeconomic variables such as interest rates, output and employment.
6. The aim of monetary policy is price stability. Pre-1999, the Central Bank of Ireland employed an exchange rate targeting strategy. Since January 1999, there has been a single monetary policy in the euro area. The European System of Central Banks (ESCB), comprising the European Central Bank (ECB) and the national central banks, is responsible for the formulation and implementation of monetary policy.

KEY TERMS

Money	Lender of last resort
Medium of exchange	Monetary policy
Double coincidence of wants	Reserve requirement
Unit of account	Open market operations
Standard of deferred payment	Discount rate
Store of value	Moral suasion

Narrow money supply
Broad money supply
High-powered money
Reserve ratio
Deposit multiplier
Interest
Interest rate
Loanable funds theory
Liquidity preference
Transactions demand
Precautionary demand
Speculative demand
Yield curve
Active and idle balances
Liquidity trap

Monetarists
Small open economy
Liquidity
Short-term facility rate
Secured advances
Foreign exchange swaps
Sale and repurchase agreements
Term deposits
Price stability
European System of Central Banks
European Central Bank
Inflation targeting
Main refinancing operations
Standing facilities
Eurosystem

REVIEW QUESTIONS

1. What is 'money'? What are its functions? What are the different definitions of money supply in Ireland?
2. Explain how the banking system creates money.
3. Explain Keynes' three motives for holding money.
4. What are the functions of a central bank? How can a central bank influence the money supply?
5. Explain what effect an increase in the money supply has on the rate of interest and the level of output.
6. Explain the monetary policy strategy of the Eurosystem.

WORKING PROBLEMS

1. Patrick O'Hara deposits €5,000 with ABC Bank. The reserve requirement is 20%.
   (a) What is the value of the deposit multiplier?
   (b) What will be the increase in deposits?
   (c) Fill in the blanks in Table 13.6.

TABLE 13.6: MONEY CREATION

Stages	Deposits (€)	Reserves (€)	Loans (€)
1	5,000	———	———
2	4,000	800	———
3	———	———	2,560
4	2,560	———	———
5			
6 . . .			
etc. . .			
Total	€ ———	€ ———	€ ———

2. Suppose €400 falls from Milton's helicopter into the hands of Maria, a student. What is the minimum increase in the money supply that can result? What is the maximum increase that can result? (Assume the reserve ratio is 5%.)

MULTI-CHOICE QUESTIONS

1. Money:
   (a) is broadly defined as coins in circulation;
   (b) can be created by the banking system;
   (c) is equal to income;
   (d) both (a) and (c) above;
   (e) (a), (b) and (c) above.

2. A customer deposits €800 in AOB Bank. The required reserve ratio is 12.5%. What is the potential increase in the money supply?
   (a) €6,400;
   (b) €5,600;
   (c) €10,000;
   (d) € 8,750;
   (e) none of the above.

3. In the liquidity preference theory of money:
   (a) there are three motives for holding money;
   (b) the money supply is interest rate inelastic;
   (c) the interest rate is the price of money;
   (d) the demand for money is positively related to income;
   (e) all of the above.

4. An increase in the money supply results from:
   (a) an open market sale and a reduction in the reserve ratio;
   (b) a reduction in the discount rate and an increase in the reserve ratio;
   (c) an open market purchase and an increase in the reserve ratio;
   (d) an open market purchase and a reduction in the discount rate;
   (e) none of the above.

5. In a SOE:
   (a) interest rates are largely influenced by external factors;
   (b) an independent monetary policy is ineffective;
   (c) the monetary authorities control the money stock;
   (d) both (a) and (b) above;
   (e) both (b) and (c) above.

6. The primary objective of monetary policy in the euro area is:
   (a) price stability;
   (b) low interest rates;
   (c) a strong euro;

(d) stable money supply growth;

(e) none of the above.

TRUE OR FALSE (SUPPORT YOUR ANSWER)

1. There is no generally accepted means of payment in a barter economy.

2. Broad money supply is defined as notes and coins and current account balances.

3. The higher the reserve ratio, the greater the bank's ability to create money.

4. The liquidity preference is positively related to income and negatively related to interest rates.

5. A lowering of the discount rate increases the money supply.

6. The national central banks are responsible for the formulation of monetary policy in the euro area.

CASE STUDY

Extract from RTÉ News
ECB cuts rate to record low of 1%

The European Central Bank cut its main interest rate to a record low of 1%. But economists want to know how the ECB can boost bank lending further amid a deep recession. The decrease of 0.25% makes for a combined cut of 3.25% since early October, bringing it to the lowest level in the bank's history. The ECB lowered another reference rate, the marginal lending rate, to 1.75%, but left its deposit rate unchanged at 0.25%, a bank spokesman said. The main, or refinancing, rate is that paid by commercial banks to borrow ECB funds for up to six months, while the deposit rate is what the central bank pays commercial banks that deposit money with it overnight.

A number of financial institutions have said they will pass on today's quarter-point interest rate cut to homeowners with variable rate mortgages. The European Central Bank cut rates to an all-time low of 1% earlier today. The ECB rate cut has no impact for those with fixed rate home loans but reduces monthly tracker mortgage repayments by €13 for every €100,000 borrowed over 30 years. Since last October, the combined effect of rate cuts has reduced monthly repayments on a €300,000 mortgage by around €550.

Homeowners with variable rate loans from AIB, Irish Nationwide, Permanent TSB, Bank of Ireland, KBC Bank, ICS Building Society and EBS will benefit from today's cut. But Ulster Bank and First Active will not pass the reductions on to variable rate mortgage holders. Halifax /Bank of Scotland says only customers with variable loans incorporating the bank's 'price promise' element will see the reductions passed on. Others, including National Irish Bank and ACC, are reviewing the situation following the ECB announcement.

At a press conference following the ECB's decision to drop interest rates the bank's president Jean Claude Trichet announced a number of measures to help to improve market liquidity and ease funding conditions for banks. Mr Trichet said the ECB was adopting an 'enhanced credit support approach' for banks, allowing them longer-term refinancing operations. More details of this will be announced on 23 June. He said the European Investment Bank will become an eligible counterparty bank from 8 July. He also said the eurosystem was going to buy euro bonds issued in the euro area, more details of which will be released after the ECB governing council's next rates setting meeting on 4 June. The bond buying programme could be in the region of €60bn. Mr Trichet said he expects a further deterioration in labour markets this month and does not expect a recovery to begin until 2010. He said inflation would remain low because of the fall in commodity prices. Mr Trichet said there are 329 million people in the eurozone. 'This is a single market with a single currency, and these moves are appropriate for a single market, for all of the eurozone's fellow citizens,' he said.

Source: www.rte.ie/news, 7 May 2009.

Questions

1. Why did the European Central Bank cut rates in May 2009? Explain why ECB interest rates were at a 'record low of 1%'.
2. Using the ECB Monthly Bulletin (www.ecb.int) as a source, report the changes in ECB interest rates during the 2008/9 years of the financial crisis. As indicated in the article, what other actions has the ECB taken to support the economy and prevent a deterioration in economic activity?
3. What is the stated objective of the European Central Bank? How is its mandate different from that of the US Fed? How might cuts in interest rates affect the ECB's primary objective, particularly in the context of the 2008/09 global crisis and world recession?

APPENDIX 13.1: DERIVATION OF MONEY MULTIPLIER

In Section 13.1 we explained the deposit multiplier. The analysis was based on the assumption that no cash was held by the public and no excess reserves were held by banks. We now adjust our analysis to account for such possibilities. The result is a money multiplier which relates a change in the money supply to a change in high-powered money.

The broad money supply, M is defined as current and deposit account balances, D plus currency, C.

$$M = D + C \qquad [1]$$

High-powered money, H is defined as currency, C plus bank reserves, R.

$$H = C + R \qquad [2]$$

Dividing Equation [1] by Equation [2], we get the ratio of money supply to high-powered money:

$$\frac{M}{H} = \frac{D + C}{C + R} \qquad [3]$$

Dividing the numerator and the denominator by D, we get:

$$\frac{M}{H} = \frac{1 + \dfrac{C}{D}}{\dfrac{C}{D} + \dfrac{R}{D}}$$

[4]

Multiplying both sides by H results in:

$$M = \frac{1 + \dfrac{C}{D}}{\dfrac{C}{D} + \dfrac{R}{D}} H$$

[5]

If there is a change in the reserves component of H, we can adopt this equation to calculate the resulting change in money supply:

$$\Delta M = \frac{1 + \dfrac{C}{D}}{\dfrac{C}{D} + \dfrac{R}{D}} \Delta H$$

[6]

Divide both sides by ΔH to get:

$$\frac{\Delta M}{\Delta H} = \frac{1 + \dfrac{C}{D}}{\dfrac{C}{D} + \dfrac{R}{D}}$$

[13.3]

The left-hand side of Equation 13.3 is the change in money supply arising out of a given change in the reserves component of high-powered money. The right-hand side of Equation 13.3 is the money multiplier. Any change in the reserves leads to a multiple change in the money supply. Its value depends on the currency deposit ratio, $\frac{C}{D}$ and the reserve deposit ratio $\frac{R}{D}$. If $\frac{C}{D} = 0$, the money multiplier is equal to the simple deposit multiplier defined in the text.

CHAPTER 14

A Basic Framework for Macroeconomic Analysis – The IS/LM Model

'[The IS/LM diagram is] to macroeconomic textbooks what the benzene ring diagram is to textbooks of organic chemistry.'[1]

CHRISTOPHER BLISS

'A basic version of that model [IS/LM] remains the core of many introductory textbooks, which use it throughout to analyse the effects of changes in some exogenous macroeconomic variables and, in particular, the impact of alternative monetary and fiscal policies.'[2]

JORDI GALI

CHAPTER OBJECTIVES

Upon completing this chapter, the student should understand:

- the purpose, derivation, position and slope of the IS curve;
- the purpose, derivation, position and slope of the LM curve;
- how interest rates and national income are determined in the IS/LM model;
- fiscal and monetary policy in the context of the IS/LM model;
- the policy differences between Keynesians and monetarists.

OUTLINE

INTRODUCTION

Sir John R. Hicks, the 1972 Nobel Prize winner in economics, is credited with bringing the IS/LM model to the forefront of economic thinking. His famous article 'Mr Keynes and the Classics: a suggested interpretation', which first described an SI-LL (now commonly referred to as the IS-LM) framework, was published in the journal *Econometrica* in 1937. With the help of refinements from economists such as Hansen (1887–1975), Klein (b. 1920), Modigliani (1918–2003) and Patinkin (1922–95), the IS/LM model became the accepted framework for analysing macroeconomic concepts and policies.[3] It was the model which popularised many Keynesian ideas and, moreover, dominated macroeconomic theory until the 1970s. Notwithstanding the achievements of others, it was Hicks who converted many of his contemporaries to the Keynesian doctrine – a doctrine which many had failed to comprehend given the revolutionary nature of the ideas and the obscurity of the language used.

The IS/LM framework is an extension of the Keynesian income determination model which we introduced in Chapter 12. Many assumptions underlie both models. First, both are demand-side models with aggregate expenditure determining output and employment. Linked to this is the assumption that the economy is operating at less than full capacity, i.e. equilibrium is at less than full employment in both models. Second, prices are assumed to be exogenous, i.e. they are assumed 'fixed'.[4] Third, both are short-run static models, developed for a closed economy.

These assumptions can also be viewed as inherent weaknesses of the model. Other criticisms might include the absence of any reference to expectations and the supply-side of the economy where supply bottlenecks may exist. Notwithstanding these omissions, the IS/LM model has been described as the most successful textbook model in the history of macroeconomics.

The IS/LM framework differs in a number of ways from the simple Keynesian model. First, investment is now treated as a function of interest rates. Second, the money market is included. Moreover, it analyses the interaction between two markets: the goods market and the money market. Because both markets are included, the effects of fiscal and monetary policy on interest rates and income can be examined.

The outline to this chapter is as follows. We begin by analysing the goods market. A goods market equilibrium curve is derived. An analysis of the money market follows. Central to this is the derivation of a money market equilibrium curve. Following this, both markets and their respective curves are brought together to analyse the effects of fiscal and monetary policy changes on both interest rates and income levels. Finally, the differences in policy between Keynesians and monetarists are briefly discussed.

14.1 THE GOODS MARKET AND THE IS CURVE

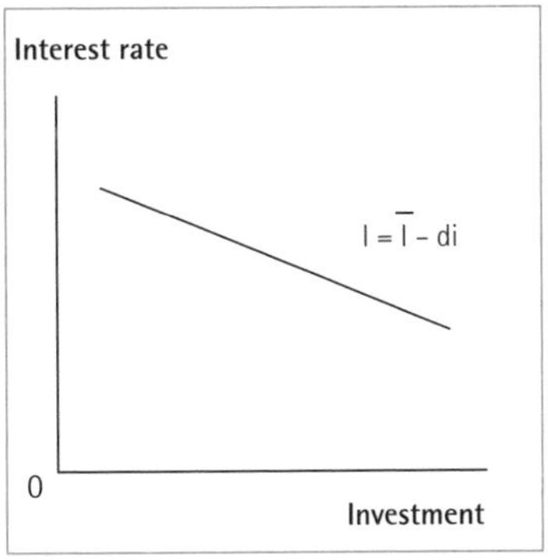

The IS (Investment/Savings) curve is the goods market equilibrium curve. The IS curve depicts the negative relationship between interest rates and income that exists in the goods market.[5] It can be derived from the Keynesian income determination model. However, we must first examine investment and its determinants in greater detail before we can derive the IS curve. In Chapter 12 we assumed that investment was independent of the explanatory variable, income. Investment was exogenous: it was determined by variables outside the model. We now adjust this in order to incorporate interest rates as an explanatory variable. With this adjustment to the model, investment is now a function of the interest rate. Figure 14.1 shows the relationship between interest rates and the level of investment when all other factors including expectations are held constant.

FIGURE 14.1: THE INVESTMENT FUNCTION

Interest rate

$I = \bar{I} - di$

0

Investment

The level of investment expenditure is related to the cost of borrowing investment funds. The investment function is downward sloping, depicting a negative relationship between interest rates and investment. Lower interest rates induce higher investment expenditure. Likewise, high interest rates induce businesses to defer or postpone investment decisions. A change in expectations for future corporate earnings causes the entire curve to shift.

Another possibility is for a firm to use its own funds to finance capital projects. However, if the market rate of return on these funds is high, there is an opportunity cost involved. The firm can place the funds into an interest-bearing account rather than undertake the investment project. The higher the rate of return, the less likely the investment project is to be financed from these funds. The negative relationship still holds.

The equation for the investment function is as follows:

$$I = \bar{I} - di \qquad\qquad [14.1]$$

where: I = total investment expenditure; $\bar{I}$ = autonomous investment expenditure; d = the investment sensitivity to interest rates; i = interest rates.

The position of the investment function is determined by the level of autonomous investment whereas the slope is given by the sensitivity of investment to interest rate changes, measured by d. This sensitivity measure plays an important role in the slope of the IS curve and the subsequent effectiveness of both fiscal and monetary policy.

Investment decisions must include interest rates as an explanatory variable in order to derive the IS curve. We begin with the Keynesian income determination model. Changes in interest rates will cause investment and ultimately income to change.

The IS curve: derivation, position and slope

The IS curve is derived from the Keynesian cross diagram as shown in Figure 14.2.

In the top diagram the AE curve, AE^0, is drawn for a particular level of interest rate, i^0.[6] This corresponds to an equilibrium level of income, Y^0. In equilibrium, expenditure is equal to income, $AE = Y$. This, in turn, gives us our first point in (i,Y) space.

Let us suppose interest rates decline, from i^0 to i^1. Lower interest rates increase the level of investment expenditure and, subsequently, aggregate expenditure. The higher AE function results in a new and higher equilibrium level of income, Y^1. This lower interest rate and higher income level gives us the second point in (i,Y) space. We could continue to change the interest rate and find corresponding levels of income. The locus of points results in a downward sloping curve (or line), illustrating the inverse relationship between interest rates and income.

FIGURE 14.2: DERIVATION OF THE IS CURVE

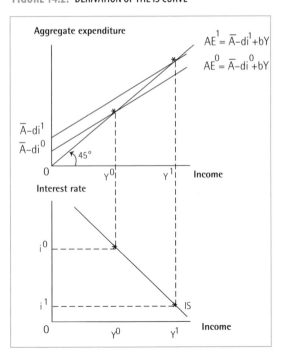

We know that when the aggregate expenditure curve crosses the 45° line, the goods market is in equilibrium. Therefore, since every point on the IS curve is derived from these equilibrium points, the goods market is in equilibrium at every point along the IS curve. In other words, this locus of points reflects equilibrium in the goods market.

Definition

The IS curve depicts the combination of interest rates and income levels that is consistent with equilibrium in the goods market.

The equation for the IS curve is derived algebraically in Appendix 14.1.

The position of any given IS curve is determined by the level of autonomous spending. $\bar{A}$, consisting of autonomous consumer, investment and government expenditure, remained constant throughout the derivation of the IS curve. Any discretionary change in $\bar{A}$ will result in a shift of the IS curve. An increase in $\bar{A}$ results in a rightward shift whereas a decrease in $\bar{A}$ results in a leftward shift. In terms of broad macroeconomic policies any change in fiscal policy, either expansionary or contractionary, results in a change in the position of the IS curve. This, in turn, helps us to analyse the effect of fiscal policy changes on the equilibrium level of interest rates and income. This is discussed in Section 14.4 below.

The two factors which largely determine the slope of the IS curve are the interest rate sensitivity of investment and the expenditure multiplier. For example, the IS curve is relatively steep when investment is insensitive to changes in interest rates and the multiplier is relatively small. The opposite is true for a relatively flat IS curve. The slope of the IS curve has important implications for the effectiveness of fiscal and monetary policy.

As an exercise, draw the relevant IS curves when the multiplier is low/high and for low/high interest rate-investment sensitivity measures.

We will now turn to the money market to derive the LM curve.

14.2 THE MONEY MARKET AND THE LM CURVE

The LM curve is the money market equilibrium curve. It depicts the positive relationship between interest rates and income that exists in the money market.

The LM curve: derivation, position and slope

The LM (Liquidity/Money supply) curve is derived from equilibrium points in the money market as shown in Figure 14.3. Here, the demand for money is inversely related to the interest rate. Therefore, the demand curve is downward sloping: as interest rates rise, the demand for money falls. The money supply is determined by the monetary authorities and is therefore independent of the rate of interest. Hence, the supply curve for money is $(\frac{M}{P})$vertical (denoted by M_S in Chapter 13).[7] At the intersection between the demand curve and the supply curve, the money market is in equilibrium. At this particular rate of interest, the demand for real balances equals the supply of real balances. This is shown in the right-hand panel of Figure 14.3 (see the money market as illustrated in Figure 13.9).

FIGURE 14.3: DERIVATION OF THE LM CURVE

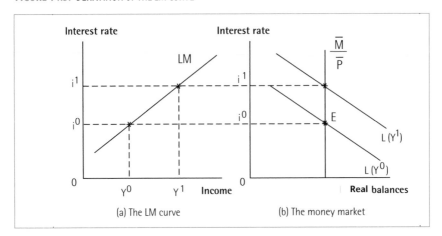

(a) The LM curve　　　　　　(b) The money market

The interest rate and the level of income at point E in the money market gives us our first point in (i,Y) space, (i^0,Y^0). The demand for money curve is drawn for a particular level of income.

Suppose that the level of income increases to Y^1. As a result, the demand for money increases. This is shown by a rightward shift of the money demand curve. If the supply of money is held constant, the subsequent excess demand of money pushes up equilibrium interest rates. Thus, as income increases, interest rates increase.

If we plot interest rates against income, we get the second point in (i,Y) space, (i^1,Y^1). We could continue to change the income level and find corresponding rates of interest. The locus of points results in an upward sloping curve illustrating a positive relationship between income and interest rates in the money market. This is the LM curve.

> **Definition**
>
> *The LM curve depicts the combination of interest rates and income levels that is consistent with equilibrium in the money market.*

The equation for the LM curve is derived algebraically in Appendix 14.1.

The position of the LM curve is determined by the real money supply. When we derived the LM curve, the real money supply was held constant. Any discretionary change in the real money supply, $\frac{M}{P}$ will result in a shift of the LM curve. For example, an increase in $\frac{M}{P}$ results in a rightward shift of the LM curve. Similarly, a decrease in $\frac{M}{P}$ results in a leftward shift of the LM curve. Monetary policy aimed at changing the real money supply will cause the position of the LM curve to change. This, in turn, affects the equilibrium level of interest rates and income. Section 14.4 below deals with these matters in greater detail.

The slope of the LM curve is largely determined by the income and the interest rate elasticities of money demand. A large income elasticity of money demand combined with a small interest rate elasticity of money demand results in a relatively steep LM curve. A relatively flat LM curve results from a combination of a small income sensitivity and a large interest rate sensitivity of money demand. The slope of the LM curve has important implications for the effectiveness of fiscal and monetary policy.

As an exercise draw the relevant LM curves for different combinations of income elasticities of money demand and interest rate elasticities of money demand.

14.3 EQUILIBRIUM IN THE IS/LM MODEL

The IS curve depicts the negative relationship that exists in the goods market between interest rates and income. At all points along the IS curve, the goods market is in equilibrium. The LM curve shows the combinations of interest rates and income at which the money market is in equilibrium. All points on the LM curve are points where money demand equals the stock of money. The IS and LM curves together determine the equilibrium interest rate and the equilibrium income level. We know from Chapter 12 that the equilibrium income level may not coincide with the full-employment output level: it is independent of the labour market. The market clearing position is illustrated in Figure 14.4.

In this diagram the IS and LM curves intersect at (i^0, Y^0). This point E represents the equilibrium interest rate, i^0, and equilibrium income level, Y^0. At this point, the goods market and the money market are in equilibrium simultaneously. The forces of excess demand and excess supply act together to move the economy towards this equilibrium position. Let us take an example.

FIGURE 14.4: EQUILIBRIUM IN THE IS/LM MODEL

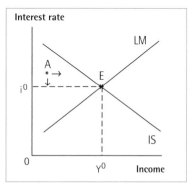

Consider point A in Figure 14.4. Point A is to the left of the IS curve. It is a point of excess demand in the goods market.[8] This excess demand will result in unplanned inventory depletions, and eventually to an increase in output. There is a subsequent move to the right, towards the IS curve.

In addition, point A is above the LM curve. It is a point of excess supply in the money market.[9] This excess supply of money will result in a downward movement of interest rates. There is a move towards the LM curve. Taken together, the economy moves from a point of disequilibrium to the one point where the goods market and the money market are in equilibrium simultaneously.

The separate analysis of the goods market (Section 14.1) and the money market (Section 14.2) is a deliberate exercise in understanding the framework to this model. In the real world, however, the goods market and the money market are dependent on each other. The interdependency between these two markets is explained in two examples below.

Example 1

The demand for money (a money market concept) is influenced by the level of income which is determined in the goods market.

Example 2

The level of investment expenditure (a goods market concept) is influenced by the rate of interest which is determined in the money market.

This interdependency has important consequences for government policy. For example, a policy which is targeted exclusively at the goods market may have implications for the money market. The inverse is also true.

Finally, any change in fiscal and/or monetary policy will change the position of the respective IS or LM curves and, in turn, affect the equilibrium interest rate and income level. A more detailed analysis follows.

14.4 FISCAL AND MONETARY POLICY

Fiscal policy is concerned with government expenditure and taxation and how they affect national output. Monetary policy refers to the use of money supply, credit and interest rates to influence national output. Changes in these policies and in particular their effect on interest rates and national income can be explained by using the IS/LM framework. Let us begin with a fiscal policy change.

Fiscal policy

Suppose the government decides to increase expenditure. We know from the Keynesian income determination model that an increase in expenditure will increase national income and do so by a multiple of itself. The increase in income may be quite large, depending on the size of the multiplier. However, this is a very simple model where interest rates are assumed to be fixed. The analysis is a little more complicated when interest rates are allowed to vary.

Figure 14.5 illustrates the effect of a change in government expenditure. The original equilibrium point reflects the old level of government expenditure. We know from our analysis of the IS curve that an increase in expenditure shifts the IS curve out and to the right. Interest rates rise, from i^0 to i^1. There is also an increase in the level of equilibrium income. A more detailed explanation is required.

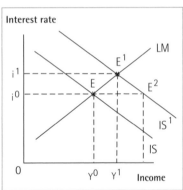

FIGURE 14.5: EXPANSIONARY FISCAL POLICY – AN INCREASE IN $\bar{G}$

The Keynesian model predicts an increase in income arising out of an increase in government expenditure. Higher income levels increase money demand. The subsequent excess demand for money forces up interest rates. Higher interest rates have a negative effect on investment expenditure. The decline in investment expenditure causes a reduction in national income. As a result the overall increase in national income is not as large as originally predicted. This knock-on effect is known as crowding out. The extent of the crowding out can be measured by the move from E^2 to E^1, in Figure 14.5. In summary, higher public expenditure and its subsequent effect on national income is crowded out by higher interest rates and lower private spending.[10]

Expansionary fiscal policy and its effect on economic variables is shown below.[11]

> Increase in $\overline{G}$ → increases Y → increases L → increases
> i → reduces I → reduces Y

In this example, the initial increase in government spending does increase national income, but by less than it would if the interest rate was fixed (as in the Keynesian model of income determination).

Belief in the effectiveness of fiscal policy has changed over the years. Fiscal policy was in the ascendancy after World War II and in particular (as we saw in Chapter 12) during the 1960s. Changes in public expenditure or taxes were believed to have a large influence on the level of aggregate expenditure and, in turn, on national output. The belief in the active use of fiscal policy was particularly strong in the USA and the UK.

In the 1970s most governments, with few exceptions (Ireland being one), abandoned fiscal policy as a method of increasing national output and employment. In the 1990s, the use of fiscal policy re-emerged as an alternative policy to the supply-side measures advocated by the followers of Reaganomics and Thatcherism. One of its prominent supporters was J. K. Galbraith (1908–2006) who strongly advocated the use of fiscal policy. It became even more popular in the 2000s with the advent of the Great Recession and the global financial crisis.

Monetary policy

A change in monetary policy is now considered. Suppose the monetary authorities decide to increase the supply of money in the economy. The effect of a change in the stock of money is shown in Figure 14.6. The original equilibrium point E reflects the old level of money stock. We know from our discussion in a previous section that an increase in the real money supply shifts the LM curve to the right. Interest rates fall, from i^0 to i^1. A higher level of equilibrium income (Y^1) also results. A more comprehensive explanation follows.

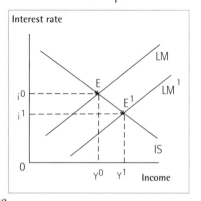

FIGURE 14.6: EXPANSIONARY MONETARY POLICY – AN INCREASE IN $\frac{M}{P}$

Lower interest rates induce higher investment expenditure. The increase in expenditure will contribute to an increase in national income. Higher income levels increase the demand for money, which puts upward pressure on interest rates. As a result the initial easing of interest rates may be partly offset by this subsequent increase.

Definition

The process where a change in monetary policy affects aggregate expenditure and national output is called the monetary transmission mechanism.

Expansionary monetary policy and its effect on economic variables is shown below.

Increase in $\frac{M}{P}$ → reduces i → increases I → increases Y

Monetary policy as a tool to control inflation became popular once again in the early 1970s with the advent of monetarism and the downfall of Keynesian economics. In more recent times, however, monetary policy has been used to help countries out of recession. For example, in the 1990s in both Japan and the EU, monetary policy was used as an instrument to boost spending and, ultimately, national income. More recently, at the outset of the 2008/9 financial crisis and subsequent global recession, monetary authorites in the USA, UK and euro area aggressively cut interest rates in an attempt to ease monetary conditions and stimulate economic activity.

A policy mix

A policy mix is the simultaneous use of fiscal and monetary policy. One example which is quite common among policy-makers is a monetary accommodation of a fiscal expansion. This is where the adverse effects of fiscal expansion, namely higher interest rates, are lessened by deliberate increases in the money supply.[12] National output increases but there is no corresponding rise in interest rates. This is illustrated in Figure 14.7.

FIGURE 14.7: A POLICY MIX – A MONETARY ACCOMMODATION OF A FISCAL EXPANSION

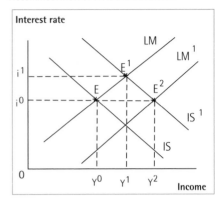

Expansionary fiscal policy shifts the IS curve rightwards, from IS to IS^1. As a result, income and interest rates rise, from Y^0 to Y^1 and from i^0 to i^1 respectively. To counteract the rise in interest rates, the Central Bank increases the money stock. This shifts the LM curve to the right, from LM to LM^1. This expansion of the money supply causes a further increase in income from Y^1 to Y^2 and a fall in interest rates from i^1 to i^0. The net effect of this particular policy mix is a relatively large increase in income from Y^0 to Y^2 combined with no change in the interest rate level. The monetary accommodation of the fiscal expansion keeps interest rates at the original level, i^0.

Monetary accommodation of fiscal expansion was used by the US authorities during the recessionary period 1974–75 and again in 1981–82.

CASE STUDY

Extract from *The Economist*
Up and down

Although Japan's economy is officially in recession again, it is stronger than it looks.

The Japanese economy is following in the footsteps of the Grand Old Duke of York. Having marched up the hill, earlier last year, it now appears to be marching swiftly down again. After the massive fiscal stimuli injected into the economy in recent years, along with near-zero short-term interest rates, Japan's latest slump suggests that the economy is even sicker than originally thought. Below the surface, however, there are reasons to believe that it is slowly on the mend.

In the first half of 1999, Japan's GDP grew at an annual rate of 5.1%. But it then shrank in the third quarter, and the head of the country's Economic Planning Agency has warned that GDP probably fell again in the fourth quarter of last year (official figures are not due until next month). Two consecutive quarters of contraction technically put Japan back into recession. However, Japan's GDP figures are notoriously unreliable, swinging wildly from quarter to quarter and subject to

large revisions. The official figures probably overstated growth during the first half of the year, and then overstated the slowdown in the second half. Some economists reckon that a better gauge is industrial production, which continued to expand throughout the second half of last year.

For 1999 as a whole, Japan's economy grew by an estimated 0.6%. Disappointing, yes, but better than the 1.1% decline expected by *The Economist*'s poll of forecasters in the middle of last year. This shows that fiscal policy does work. Indeed, one reason why growth stumbled in late 1999 is that by then the fiscal stimulus had been exhausted. The latest budget package will spur the economy again this spring. The snag is that with a budget deficit already at 8% of GDP, the path of Japan's public-sector debt now looks scary. Government borrowing cannot permanently prop up the economy; private-sector spending needs to revive.

Household spending has been depressed by continuing deflationary pressures: prices, wages and bank lending are all falling. Despite this, some on the Bank of Japan's policy board are talking about raising interest rates. Instead, the bank should be pursuing more aggressive monetary expansion, either through unsterilised foreign-exchange intervention or by buying government bonds. Not only would this help to take some of the strain off fiscal policy, but by adjusting the monetary and fiscal mix, it would also help to hold down the yen. The currency has in fact weakened over the past few weeks, but any renewed strength would risk choking exports.

Source: The Economist, 12 February 2000, p. 15.

Questions

1. Using the IS/LM model, outline the predicted effects of a fiscal stimulus and a monetary expansion. How has the Japanese economy actually performed?
2. Why does the author favour expansionary monetary policy instead of an interest rate increase? Explain using the IS/LM model.
3. Aside from foreign trade and the exchange rate issue, why is the IS/LM model more appropriate in analysing the Japanese economy rather than, say, the Irish economy, at the start of the new millennium?

Answers on website

14.5 THE KEYNESIAN–MONETARIST DEBATE

How effective fiscal and monetary policies are can be explained by the slopes of the IS and LM curves. The slopes in turn are determined largely by a range of sensitivity measures which were outlined in Sections 14.1 and 14.2 above.

Fiscal policy is more effective when the LM curve is flat and the IS curve is steep. We know from our discussion of the IS curve that a steep IS curve results from investment expenditure which is insensitive to interest rate changes. Likewise, it is the particular combination of a demand for money which is insensitive to income and highly sensitive to interest rates which results in a flat LM curve. The inverse is true for the case of ineffective fiscal policy.

Monetary policy, in contrast, is relatively effective when there is a flat IS curve and a steep LM curve. When the sensitivity of investment to changes in interest rates is high, the subsequent IS curve is relatively flat. A steep LM curve results from a demand for money which is sensitive to income and insensitive to interest rates. The opposite is true for ineffective monetary policy.

This rather technical discussion prepares us for the debate between the Keynesian view and the monetarist view of either policy.

Keynesians argue that the IS curve is relatively steep, and is so because investment is insensitive to changes in interest rates. A steep IS curve results from investment pessimism. A change in interest rates does not entice investors to undertake new projects which would lead to an increase in economic activity. Of greater importance is their belief in a relatively flat or, in the extreme case, a horizontal LM curve.

This hypothetical situation is known as the liquidity trap which, in theory, could exist at very low interest rates where the demand for money may be infinitely large. In effect, people are willing to hold any amount of money at this given interest rate. However, even Keynes himself doubted the very existence of such a case. Nonetheless, since it was felt that the IS curve was relatively steep and the LM curve relatively flat, fiscal policy was preferred to monetary policy.

In contrast, monetarists argued that the IS curve is relatively flat, reflecting investment expenditure which is highly responsive to changes in interest rates. Their belief in a relatively steep LM curve, and vertical in the extreme, is a return to the classical doctrine. The vertical LM curve arises from an absence of any speculative demand for money. The demand for money does not change in response to changes in interest rates. Any increase in output which results directly from a rise in public expenditure is offset by subsequent increases in interest rates which have an adverse effect on private spending. This possibility is known as crowding out. In these circumstances, fiscal policy is largely ineffective.

The Keynesian/monetarist controversy is illustrated in Figure 14.8. In Figure 14.8(a) the IS curve is relatively steep, reflecting the Keynesian position. The monetarist position of a vertical LM curve is depicted in Figure 14.8(b).

FIGURE 14.8: THE KEYNESIAN AND MONETARIST DEBATE

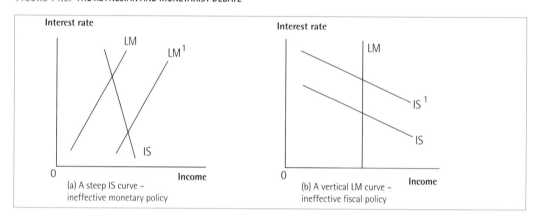

Both the liquidity trap and crowding out are extreme cases and are unlikely to exist in reality. Notwithstanding this fact, the above analysis is worthwhile in that it provides us with a brief account of some of the differences between two of the main schools of economic thought. It is also important to acknowledge that both these alternatives, as represented above, ignore supply-side considerations and changes in the price level. These must be included in a more comprehensive discussion of the Keynesian/ monetarist controversy.

SUMMARY

1. The IS/LM model is a static, short-run model which integrates the goods market with the money market. It is similar to the Keynesian model of income determination in that prices are fixed and demand determines output and employment. It is a model for a closed economy. It differs to the extent that interest rates are endogenous and the money market matters.
2. The IS curve illustrates the combinations of interest rates and income levels for which the goods market is in equilibrium. It is negatively sloped. Lower interest rates increase the level of investment which, in turn, increases national income. Its position is determined by the level of autonomous spending. The interest rate elasticity of investment and the multiplier determine its slope.

3. The LM curve shows the combinations of interest rates and income levels where the demand for and supply of money are equal. It is positively sloped. Higher income levels increase the demand for money which, in turn, increases interest rates. The stock of money determines the position of the LM curve. Its slope is determined by the interest rate and income elasticities of money demand.

4. The goods market and the money market do not operate independently. The intersection of the IS curve and the LM curve is the equilibrium point. Both markets are in equilibrium simultaneously at this point. A change in fiscal policy shifts the IS curve whereas a change in monetary policy shifts the LM curve. Changes in equilibrium interest rates and income levels will result.

5. Expansionary fiscal policy results in higher interest rates and higher income levels. Crowding out limits the increase in national income. Expansionary monetary policy results in lower interest rates and higher income levels. An example of a policy mix is a monetary accommodation of a fiscal expansion.

6. The IS/LM framework is very useful in explaining the divergent views of Keynesians and monetarists. The liquidity trap is the extreme Keynesian case. The classical case of full crowding out is supported by the monetarists.

KEY TERMS

IS curve
Interest rate elasticity of investment
LM curve
Income elasticity of money demand
Interest rate elasticity of money demand
Fiscal policy
Monetary policy
Transmission mechanism
Monetarists
Policy mix
Liquidity trap
Crowding out

REVIEW QUESTIONS

1. What are the differences between the Keynesian model of income determination and the IS/LM model? What are the limitations to the IS/LM model?
2. Explain why the IS curve slopes down from left to right. What factors determine the position and the slope of the IS curve?
3. Why is the money market equilibrium curve upward sloping? What factors determine its slope?
4. Explain what effect a contractionary monetary policy would have on the equilibrium level of interest rates and national income.
5. What effect would a contractionary fiscal policy have on (a) the IS curve; (b) equilibrium income; and finally (c) equilibrium interest rates?
6. Explain 'crowding out'. What action can the Central Bank take to avoid the rise in interest

rates which is usually associated with crowding out?

WORKING PROBLEMS

1. The following equations describe an economy:
    $C = .85Y$
    $I = 700 - 25i$
    $\bar{G} = 540$
    $L = .5Y - 70i$
    $$\frac{\bar{M}}{P} = 400$$

    (a) Derive the IS equation.
    (b) Derive the LM equation.
    (c) Calculate the equilibrium levels of interest rates and income.
    (d) Sketch the equilibrium position.

    [Calculations to two decimal places]

2. If investment is insensitive to changes in the interest rate, is monetary or fiscal policy more effective? Explain your answer.

MULTI-CHOICE QUESTIONS

1. The IS/LM model is an extension of the Keynesian income determination model with an adjustment for:
    (a) wages;
    (b) income levels;
    (c) exchange rates;
    (d) interest rates;
    (e) none of the above.

2. The IS curve:
    (a) is derived from the goods market;
    (b) shows combinations of interest rates and income such that expenditure equals income;
    (c) is the goods market equilibrium curve;
    (d) is drawn for a given level of autonomous spending;
    (e) all of the above.

3. The slope of the LM curve:
    (a) is determined by the interest rate elasticity of investment;
    (b) is relatively flat given a small income elasticity of money demand;
    (c) is relatively steep given a high interest rate elasticity of money demand;
    (d) both (a) and (b) above;
    (e) both (a) and (c) above.

4. Suppose investment becomes less responsive to changes in interest rates. As a result the:
   (a) IS curve will shift to the left;
   (b) IS curve will shift to the right;
   (c) IS curve will become flatter;
   (d) IS curve will become steeper;
   (e) none of the above.

5. Suppose the government decreases public expenditure. All other things equal, the likely result will be:
   (a) an increase in interest rates;
   (b) a decrease in national income;
   (c) a decrease in interest rates;
   (d) both (a) and (b) above;
   (e) both (b) and (c) above.

6. The extreme case of crowding out:
   (a) occurs when the LM curve is horizontal;
   (b) is caused by a large interest rate elasticity of money demand;
   (c) leads to ineffective fiscal policy;
   (d) is supported by Keynesians;
   (e) none of the above.

TRUE OR FALSE (SUPPORT YOUR ANSWER)

1. The IS/LM model is a demand-side model.

2. Equilibrium prices and income can be determined by the IS/LM model.

3. The position of the IS curve is determined by the size of the multiplier and the interest rate sensitivity of investment.

4. The real money supply is constant along any given money market equilibrium curve.

5. A cut in taxes is an example of contractionary fiscal policy and is likely to result in lower income and interest rate levels.

6. In the case of full crowding out, fiscal policy is ineffective.

CASE STUDY

Extract from the *New York Times*
How much of the world is in a liquidity trap?
by Paul Krugman

As I've written many times in various contexts since the crisis began, being in a liquidity trap reverses many of the usual rules of economic policy. Virtue becomes vice: attempts to save more actually make us poorer, in both the short and the long run. Prudence becomes folly: a stern determination to balance budgets and avoid any risk of inflation is the road to disaster. Mercantilism works: countries that subsidize exports and restrict imports actually do gain at their trading partners' expense. For the moment – or more likely for the next several years – we're living in a world in which none of what you learned in Econ 101 applies.

But what's the definition of a liquidity trap? How much of the world is in one? There's a lot of confusion on that point; here's how I see it. In my analysis, you're in a liquidity trap when conventional open-market operations – purchases of short-term government debt by the central bank – have lost traction, because short-term rates are close to zero. Now, you may object that there are other things central banks can do, and that they actually do these things to some extent: they can purchase longer-term government securities or other assets, they can try to raise their inflation targets in a credible way. And I very much want the Fed to do more of these things. But the reality is that unconventional monetary policy is difficult, perceived as risky, and never pursued with the vigor of conventional monetary policy.

Consider the Fed, which under Bernanke is more adventurous than it would have been under anyone else. Even so, it has gone nowhere near engaging in enough unconventional expansion to offset the limitations created by the zero lower bound. A while back Goldman estimated that if it weren't for the lower bound, the current Fed

funds rate would be minus 5 percent, and that to achieve the same effect as a further 5 points of Fed funds cuts the Fed would have to expand its balance sheet to $10 trillion; I wouldn't stake my life on those estimates, but they seem in the right ballpark. Obviously, the Fed isn't doing that.

Or put it a different way: suppose the real economic outlook were the same as it is – with all indications being that unemployment will stay very high for years to come – but that the current Fed funds rate were, say, 4 percent. Clearly the Fed would feel obliged to engage in a lot more expansion, cutting rates sharply and rapidly. But with short-term rates at zero, the Fed is instead merely on hold – it is *not* expanding its quantitative easing, and is in fact in the process of pulling back. The point is that while you can think of things the Fed can do even at the zero lower bound, that lower bound is in practice a major constraint on policy. By all means let's yell at the Fed to do more, but when you're considering other issues – like the effects of fiscal policy or the effects of renminbi undervaluation – you have to assess them in terms of the central bank you have, not the central bank you wish you had.

And by that criterion, how much of the world is currently in a liquidity trap? Almost all advanced countries. The US, obviously; Japan, even more obviously; the eurozone, because the ECB probably couldn't engage in Fed-style quantitative easing even if it wanted to, given the lack of a single backing government; Britain. Not Australia, I guess. But still: essentially the whole advanced world, accounting for 70 percent of world GDP at market prices, is in a liquidity trap.

Source: The New York Times, 17 March 2010.

Questions

1. What are the implications for conventional monetary policy if an economy is in a liquidity trap? What are the policy alternatives for the monetary authorities?
2. How will the LM curve slope if the economy is in a liquidity trap? What are the policy implications? Show using the relevant IS/LM diagram.
3. What is quantitative easing? How does it work? Why have central banks engaged in quantitative easing since the start of the credit crunch and the global recession of the late 2000s?

APPENDIX 14.1: ALGEBRAIC DERIVATION OF THE IS AND LM CURVES

To derive the equation for the IS curve we begin with the aggregate expenditure function:

$$AE \equiv C + I + G \qquad \text{[14.2]}$$

In the Keynesian aggregate expenditure model, investment was autonomous. In the IS/LM model, it depends on the interest rate. Therefore, we will define the components of aggregate expenditure in the following way:

$$C = \overline{C} + bY \qquad \text{[14.3]}$$

$$I = \overline{I} - di \qquad \text{[14.1]}$$

$$G = \overline{G} \qquad \text{[12.14]}$$

Substitute these equations into Equation 14.2:

$$AE = \overline{C} + bY + \overline{I} - di + \overline{G} \qquad \text{[14.4]}$$

Let $\overline{A} = \overline{C} + \overline{I} + \overline{G}$ the autonomous components of aggregate expenditure.

Substitute $\overline{A}$ into Equation 14.4:

$$AE = \overline{A} - di + bY \qquad \text{[14.5]}$$

Equilibrium in the goods market is where:

$$Y = AE \qquad \text{[12.9]}$$

Substitute Y for AE in Equation 14.5 and solve for Y:

$$Y = \frac{1}{1-b}(\overline{A} - di) \qquad \text{[14.6]}$$

Let $k = \dfrac{1}{1-b}$ as in Chapter 12. Substituting this expression into Equation 14.6 yields:

$$Y = k\,(\overline{A} - di) \qquad [14.7]$$

Equation 14.7 shows that the relationship between the interest rate and income in the goods market is negative. Therefore, the IS curve is downward sloping. The strength of the relationship will be reflected in the slope of the line. This is determined by the expenditure multiplier, k and the interest rate elasticity of investment, d.

To derive the equation for the LM curve, we begin with the money market. The demand for money equation is:

$$L = jY - hi \qquad [14.8]$$

where j is the sensitivity of money demand to changes in income and h is the sensitivity of money demand to changes in the interest rate.

In equilibrium in the money market, money demand equals real money supply ($\frac{\overline{M}}{P}$). Hence,

$$jY - hi = \frac{\overline{M}}{P} \qquad [14.9]$$

Solve for Y:

$$Y = \frac{1}{J}\left(hi + \frac{\overline{M}}{P}\right) \qquad [14.10]$$

In terms of i:

$$i = \frac{1}{h}\left(jY - \frac{\overline{M}}{P}\right) \qquad [14.11]$$

We can see that the relationship between the interest rate and income in the money market is positive. The LM curve is upward sloping. The strength of the relationship is reflected in the slope of the line. The variables which affect the slope of the LM curve are the two elasticity measures, j and h.

CHAPTER 15

Open Economy Macroeconomics

'There is no way in which one can buck the market.'[1]

MARGARET THATCHER

'In short, there is no meaningful economic argument for a single currency in Europe – now or ever.'[2]

BERNARD CONNOLLY

CHAPTER OBJECTIVES

Upon completing this chapter, the student should understand:

- the balance of payments;
- exchange rate determination;
- devaluation and exchange rate systems;
- Ireland's record within the ERM;
- Economic and Monetary Union and the single currency.

OUTLINE

15.1 **Balance of payments**
15.2 **Exchange rate determination**
15.3 **Exchange rate regimes and the balance of payments**
15.4 **The European Monetary System (EMS)**
15.5 **Economic and Monetary Union**
15.6 **The Irish experience**

INTRODUCTION

I n Chapter 10 we examined the circular flow of economic activity. We began by studying the exchange between households and firms. We then adjusted this model to include the government and the foreign sector. A similar method of analysis was used for the income determination model. Variables such as prices, wages and interest rates were assumed to be fixed. Moreover, the government and the foreign sector were initially excluded before they were eventually incorporated into the model.

Even with these adjustments for the foreign sector, our examination of macroeconomics until now has largely ignored the value of the domestic currency vis-à-vis foreign currencies and its role in the economy. Foreign interest rates, exchange rate volatility, foreign markets and external trade (of goods, services and capital) were only briefly mentioned. In reality, these variables are very important and play a vital role in any modern economy. We now examine these variables in detail.

15.1 BALANCE OF PAYMENTS

We begin our investigation of the foreign sector by discussing the balance of payments.

> **Definition**
>
> *The balance of payments is a set of accounts showing all economic transactions between residents of the home country and the rest of the world in any one year.*

It is a 'flow' concept rather than a 'stock' concept. We are not measuring the assets and liabilities at a point in time. Rather, we are looking at outflows and inflows over a period of time, usually a year.

Receipts of foreign exchange from the rest of the world (e.g. arising from exports, sale of government bonds, etc.) are treated as a credit item and are denoted by a positive (+) sign in the balance of payments. Payments of foreign exchange to the rest of the world (e.g. arising from imports, purchase of French works of art, etc.) are treated as a debit item and are denoted by a negative (−) sign.

At the end of the calendar year this statement must balance, i.e. receipts or inflows equals payments or outflows. It does so by following the principles of double-entry book-keeping.

The balance of payments consists of two subsections: the current account and the capital and financial account. These are explained below.

Current account balance

> **Definition**
>
> *The current account in the balance of payments records all visible and invisible trade.*

Merchandise trade is an example of visible trade. Invisible trade includes services such as tourism and travel.

This section of the Irish balance of payments is subdivided into four categories, including:

- merchandise trade, as explained below;
- services such as tourism and travel, communications and financial services;
- net income. This includes investment income arising from Irish investors' investment abroad and foreign investors' investments in Ireland;
- current transfers such as Irish aid to developing countries and monies from EU funds.

The addition of all these plus a number of miscellaneous items is defined as the current account balance. If the value of receipts is greater than the value of payments, a surplus is recorded. If the value of receipts is less than the value of payments, a deficit is recorded. In 2009 there was a current account deficit of €4,853m.

Merchandise trade balance

The merchandise trade balance is the most publicly discussed component of the current account.[3]

> **Definition**
> *The merchandise trade balance, or the balance of trade as it is sometimes called, is a record of transactions of merchandise exports (X) and imports (M) during a year.*

If the value of exports exceeds the value of imports (X > M) a trade surplus results. A trade deficit results when the value of imports exceeds the value of exports (M > X). If the value of exports and imports is equal (X = M) we have a trade balance.

Figure 15.1 shows the record of the Irish external trade balance between 1980 and 2010.

FIGURE 15.1 TRADE BALANCE IN IRELAND, 1980–2010

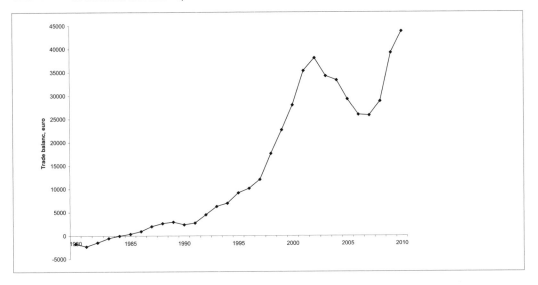

It is evident from the figure above that Ireland's first trade surplus in modern economic times was recorded in 1985. This 'favourable' trend has been repeated in each year. It is widely believed that this improvement in the trade surplus is due, in no small part, to the activities of multinationals operating in Ireland.

The composition of trade by commodity and geographical location is shown in Tables 15.1 and 15.2 respectively.

TABLE 15.1: TRADE BY COMMODITY, 2009

Category	Exports (%)	Imports (%)
Food and live animals	7.5	9.8
Beverages and tobacco	1.3	1.7
Crude materials (except fuels)	1.2	1.3
Mineral fuels, lubricants and related materials	0.7	9.9
Chemicals and related products	56.6	16.4
Manufactured goods	1.5	7.6
Machinery and transport equipment	16.5	31.8
Miscellaneous manufactured	10.9	13.5
Others	3.8	8.0

Source: Central Statistics Office, 2010.

TABLE 15.2: TRADE BY GEOGRAPHICAL AREA, 2009

Destination	Exports (%)	Imports (%)
UK	16.2	30.3
Rest of EU	44.9	28.7
(of which eurozone)	(41.7)	(24.1)
USA	21.1	17.5
Others	17.6	21.1
Unclassified/unknown	0.2	2.4

Source: Central Statistics Office, 2010.

Capital and financial account balance

Definition

The capital and financial account in the balance of payments is a record of a country's inflows and outflows of capital or assets.

More specifically, the capital account records all transfers intended for capital purposes whereas the financial account reports foreign financial assets and liabilities, that is, claims on and obligations to non-residents. In the financial account, there are four categories of investment, namely direct investment, portfolio investment, other investment and reserve assets. A full description of each category can be found in the CSO *Statistical Bulletin*.

Purchases of Irish financial stocks and loans to Irish residents by foreigners are capital inflows. Capital outflows include purchase of foreign financial securities and loans to foreigners by Irish residents. In 2009, the balance on the capital account was −€1,252m. The balance on the financial account was −€3,315m.

The Irish balance of payments for the year 2009 is reprinted in Table 15.3.

TABLE 15.3: THE IRISH BALANCE OF INTERNATIONAL PAYMENTS 2009

Current Account	€m
Merchandise	32,367
Services	−8,416
Net factor income	−27,901
Current transfers	−901
Balance on current account	**−4,853**
Balance on capital account	**−1,252**
Financial Account	
Direct investment	476
Portfolio investment	18,760
Other investment	−22,631
Reserve Assets	79
Balance on financial account	**−3,315**
Net errors and omissions	*9,419*

Source: Central Statistics Office, 2010.

In principle, the sum of the debit entries should equal the sum of the credit entries in the balance of payments. Differences in coverage, timing and valuation in the three accounts mean that, in practice, this does not occur. The entry called 'net errors and omissions' as shown above in the balance of payments is a balancing item. This entry ensures that there is an overall balance in the account. In 2009, net errors and omissions was €9,419m.

15.2 EXCHANGE RATE DETERMINATION

We will continue our discussion of the foreign sector by considering exchange rates.

> **Definition**
>
> *The exchange rate between two currencies is the price of one currency in terms of another.*

Similar to interest rate determination, the equilibrium price can be explained in terms of demand and supply analysis. It is the equilibrium price that we call the exchange rate. The market in this case is the foreign exchange market.

There are many similarities between a market for a product and the foreign exchange market. However, there are a few important differences. We consider the market of a single good, like tea. When we discuss the foreign exchange market, we are considering two currencies, e.g. the US dollar (US$) and the euro. For example, in the market for €/US$, a demand for euros implies a supply of US$ and a supply of euros implies a demand for US$. This is evident in our analysis of the €/US$ market below.

Another important difference which we will explain shortly is that the demand for and the supply of foreign exchange is derived. In spite of these differences, we will see that the foreign exchange market looks, and in many ways behaves, like a product market.

The state often intervenes in the foreign exchange market and we will discuss that in the next section. However, we will begin our discussion of exchange rate determination by considering a foreign exchange market where the state does not intervene. We will see that the exchange rate is determined by the forces of demand and supply.

We will explain how the exchange rate is determined using a simplified example.

Assume there are only two countries, Europe and the USA, with respective currencies, the euro, €, and the American dollar, US$. In this case the price will be expressed as the number of dollars per one euro.[4] We must examine both the demand for and the supply of euros in order to derive the market exchange rate.

The demand for euros

The demand for euros on the foreign exchange market is a derived demand. Holders of American dollars purchase euros in order to pay for:

- European goods and services;
- European assets including shares, government bonds and property.

When Americans buy European goods and assets, they supply dollars in exchange for euros. For example, if the rate of exchange is €1 = $1, €1m of European goods costs an American importer $1m.

Suppose the value of the euro increases or appreciates relative to the dollar. The new rate of exchange is €1 = $2. The same €1m of European goods now costs the American importer $2m. In other words, European goods are more expensive in the American market after the euro appreciates. At this exchange rate, the demand for goods, and therefore the demand for euros will be less than at the previous rate.

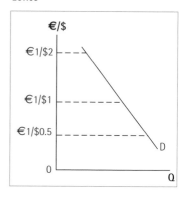

FIGURE 15.2: THE DEMAND CURVE FOR EUROS

Alternatively, the euro could decrease in value or depreciate relative to the dollar. Suppose the new exchange rate is €1 = $0.5. The delighted importer can now purchase €1m of European goods for only $500,000. At this exchange rate, the demand for European goods will be higher and so will the demand for the euro.

In summary, the higher the exchange rate of dollars for euros, the lower the demand for euros. As the euro depreciates, the demand for the euro increases. Therefore, the demand curve (or line) for the euro is downward sloping as drawn in Figure 15.2.

The supply of euros

The supply of euros on the foreign exchange market is also derived. Holders of euros wish to purchase dollars to pay for:

· American goods and services;
· American assets including shares, US government bonds and real estate.

When European residents buy American goods and assets, they supply euros in exchange for dollars. For example, if the rate of exchange is €1 = $1, $1m of goods from the USA costs a European importer €1m.

Suppose the value of the euro appreciates. At the new rate of €1 = $2, the same $1m of merchandise will cost the European importer only €500,000. In other words, US goods are cheaper at this exchange rate. European importers may now be willing to supply more euros in exchange for US dollars.

Alternatively, the euro could depreciate relative to the dollar. Consider another exchange rate of €1 = $0.5. The European importer will have to exchange €2m in order to purchase the goods valued at $1m. At this exchange rate, US goods are more expensive in the European market. The demand for US goods will be less and so will the quantity of euros supplied on the foreign exchange market.

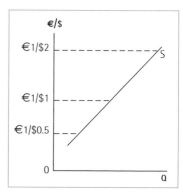

FIGURE 15.3: THE SUPPLY CURVE FOR EUROS

In summary, the higher the exchange rate of dollars for euros, the higher the supply of euros. As the euro depreciates, the supply of the euro decreases. Therefore, the supply curve (or line) is upward sloping as drawn in Figure 15.3.[5]

Equilibrium in the foreign exchange market

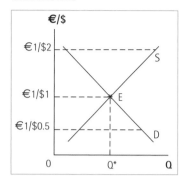

The demand for euros, represented by D, and the supply of euros, represented by S, determine the equilibrium rate of exchange in the €/US$ market. This is illustrated in Figure 15.4.

The demand curve for euros and the supply curve for euros intersect at point E, the equilibrium exchange rate. As in other markets there is an automatic process which moves the market towards equilibrium.

If the exchange rate is above equilibrium, the supply of euros exceeds the demand. At the exchange rate indicated by €1/$2 in Figure 15.4, American products to the European market are relatively cheap and European importers are willing to trade euros for dollars in order to buy them. However, European exports to the American market are relatively expensive. At this exchange rate, the American importer of European goods does not demand as many goods and therefore does not need euros to pay for them. In a market without restrictions, the exchange rate will fall. Equilibrium is restored when quantity demanded equals quantity supplied.

Similarly, if the exchange rate is below the equilibrium, at the rate indicated by €1/$0.5 in Figure 15.4, demand for euros exceeds the supply. American products are relatively expensive and European importers are not willing to trade euros for dollars in order to purchase them for the European market. However, European exports to the American market are relatively cheap and the American importers are willing to purchase euros in order to buy them for the American market. The shortage of euros will lead to an appreciation of the exchange rate. Equilibrium is restored when quantity demanded equals quantity supplied.

Factors which shift the demand curve or the supply curve

The foreign exchange market considers the relationship between the exchange rate and the quantity of euros demanded and supplied, *ceteris paribus*. Other variables which influence the exchange rate between the two currencies are held constant. These include, among others, interest rate differentials, inflation differentials, income differentials and speculation. A change in any of these factors will cause the demand curve and/or the supply curve to shift. We will examine each of these factors briefly.

1.   *Interest rate differentials*   Suppose European interest rates rise above US interest rates. American investors, seeking the highest rate of return, respond to this interest rate differential by investing in European assets. The change in demand for capital assets, caused by the interest rate differential, leads to a change in demand for the euro. The demand curve for the euro shifts out and to the right, as shown in Figure 15.5.

We can see that at every exchange rate, the demand for euros has increased.

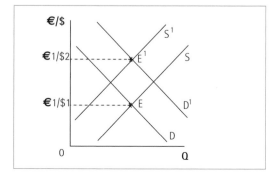

In this situation, the supply curve may also shift. European investors are unwilling to purchase American assets since the return on European assets is higher. Fewer euros are supplied to the market. This change in the underlying variable causes the supply curve to shift to the left as shown in Figure 15.5. At each exchange rate, the supply of euros has decreased.

We can now compare the old equilibrium E with the new equilibrium E^1. The combination of increased demand and decreased supply results in an increase in the €/US$ exchange rate. Hence, the higher interest rate in Europe vis-à-vis the United States causes an increase in the value of the euro against the dollar. Alternatively, lower interest rates in Europe will cause a decrease in the exchange rate, all other things being equal.

2. *Inflation differentials* Suppose the European inflation rate increases, resulting in an inflation differential with the United States. European goods are now relatively more expensive. This may lead to a decrease in demand for euros in the USA, depending on the elasticity of demand for European exports. This change in an underlying variable means that the demand curve for euros shifts to the left.

The supply curve for euros also changes because the relatively low inflation rate in the USA causes the demand for US goods, which are relatively cheaper, to increase. These goods must be paid for by exchanging euros for US dollars. As the demand for US dollars increases, the supply of euros increases. The supply curve for euros shifts to the right.

As a result, the higher inflation rate in Europe vis-à-vis the United States leads to a decline in the value of the euro against the dollar. The relationship between exchange rates and inflation rates is expressed in terms of Purchasing Power Parity. For more on this subject, see Appendix 15.1 and Section 15.6 on the Irish experience.

3. *Income differentials* Suppose European GDP increases at a rate that is higher than its trading partners. As national income increases, domestic consumption increases. Part of this increase in consumption is met by purchasing more imports. As demand for imports (and, with that, US dollars) increases, the supply of euros increases. As a result, the exchange rate falls. Hence, the higher income level in Europe causes a decline in the value of the euro against the US dollar, all other things being equal.

4. *Speculation* This is a curious but powerful factor in the determination of the exchange rate. Suppose the demand for the euro is expected to be weak. Expectations are for a fall in the value of the euro. Market participants, in anticipation of making a capital gain, sell their euro holdings.[6] As a result, the supply of euros in the foreign exchange market increases. This is represented by a rightward shift of the supply curve. If enough market participants act on this expectation, the value of the euro will fall. The actions of speculators, as described in this example, caused the fall in the value of the euro. Although it is difficult to assess the level of speculation on the foreign exchange markets, it is estimated that less than one-fifth of daily foreign exchange transactions in London is trade/investment-related, with speculation accounting for the remainder.

We now examine the relationship between the balance of payments and the exchange rate. Also, the different exchange rate regimes are explained.

15.3 EXCHANGE RATE REGIMES AND THE BALANCE OF PAYMENTS

The composition of the balance of payments and how it actually balances depends on the ability of the domestic currency to adjust in value to other currencies. There are different types of exchange rate systems. The flexible and fixed exchange rate systems are polar opposites and do not reflect the exchange rate systems which operate in practice. However, we will begin by discussing the extremes (and the arguments in favour of each) and then explain the semi-fixed and managed exchange rate systems which we often observe. Figure 15.6 illustrates the range of exchange rate regimes.

FIGURE 15.6: EXCHANGE RATE SYSTEMS

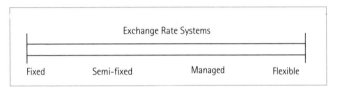

Flexible exchange rate systems

Under this regime, the value of the domestic currency is allowed to change, vis-à-vis other currencies.

> **Definition**
>
> *A flexible exchange rate system operates on the basis of market forces whereby the exchange rate between two currencies is determined by demand and supply.*

The central banks are not required to intervene on the foreign exchange market.

Under a flexible exchange rate regime there is an automatic adjustment process in operation. For example, a current account deficit is financed by an equal capital account surplus. How does this work?

If a country records a current account deficit, it means that it is importing more goods and services than it is exporting. The foreign exchange needed to pay for these imports must come from some source. It comes from either borrowing from foreigners or from the sale of domestic assets. When a country sells more assets than it buys, it runs a capital account surplus. This net inflow of foreign exchange is the source used to finance the deficit in the current account.[7] Likewise, a current account surplus is matched by an increase in the ownership of foreign assets.

A current account deficit may result in a change of the exchange rate. All other things being equal, a current account deficit causes the home country's currency to depreciate. This is because at the old exchange rate, there exists an excess supply of the home country's currency. With flexible exchange rates, the excess supply leads to a depreciation. As a result, exports become cheaper whereas imports become more expensive. Likewise, a current account surplus is eliminated by an appreciation of the exchange rate.

In theory, flexible exchange rates will eliminate a current account surplus or deficit. Like any market system, it is the price mechanism that will eliminate any disequilibrium. If the foreign exchange market is at equilibrium, the balance of payments should balance. In practice there may be a discrepancy caused by book-keeping errors and omissions.

The arguments in favour of a flexible exchange rate system are listed below.

1. Adherence to a flexible exchange rate system does not involve any costly interventions by the monetary authorities. Imbalances will be corrected automatically if there are any shocks to

the economy. The costs which are normally associated with the depletion of a country's external reserves are eliminated.

2. There is no loss of autonomy with a flexible exchange rate system. There is no balance of payments constraint on domestic policy. Hence, the government is free to pursue whatever policy suits domestic conditions.

3. In times of severe recession the government may allow the currency to depreciate. This would increase the volume of exports and in doing so boost demand. Also, during inflationary times the government may allow the currency to appreciate. In doing so, it may stem the inflationary pressures from abroad. Also, flexible exchange rates can insulate the domestic economy from external shocks.

4. The exchange rate at any given time is the 'true' exchange rate; true in the sense that it is determined by the forces of demand and supply. There is no Central Bank intervention. Currencies are not under- or over-valued or misaligned.

5. Under a flexible exchange rate system, monetary policy is effective.

Fixed exchange rate systems

Alternatively, governments often attempt to maintain the value of their currency vis-à-vis other currencies.

Definition

Currencies that belong to a fixed exchange rate system are pegged to each other at rates which are usually agreed by their respective central banks.

In order to maintain the currencies at the fixed rates, intervention by the central banks is required.[8]

Under a fixed exchange rate regime, the balance of payments will balance with the external reserves playing a central role.

Definition

The external reserves are the stock of foreign currency held by the central bank for the purpose of intervention in the foreign exchange market.

To illustrate the operation of external reserves, we will consider the balance of payments for a fictitious state for the year 2012, as outlined in Table 15.4.

TABLE 15.4: BALANCE OF PAYMENTS, 2012

Current account	2,500	Change in external reserves	800
Capital account	−1,700		
	800		800

In Table 15.4, we observe a current account surplus of 2,500 units which is partially offset by a capital account deficit of 1,700 units. Under these circumstances, there is excess demand for the domestic currency which should lead to a rise in its value. However, under a fixed exchange rate system, the central bank is obliged to intervene to maintain the value of the domestic currency vis-à-vis other currencies. To eliminate the shortage, the central bank purchases external reserves. In other words, foreign currencies are exchanged for the domestic currency. The stock of external reserves increases and with it, the foreign currency reserves of the central bank. In this example, the external reserves increase by 800 units.

On the other hand, a negative balance in the current and capital accounts means that there is an excess supply of the domestic currency. In this situation, the Central Bank sells external reserves and purchases the domestic currency to eliminate the surplus. The balance of payments statement at the end of the year would show a decrease in the external reserves.

The arguments in favour of a fixed exchange rate are as follows:

1. It creates a more stable trading environment. It facilitates international trade with importers and exporters assured of fixed payments in terms of their domestic currency. Governments need not fear the damage caused by market uncertainty or volatile exchange rate movements. International institutions operate more effectively under a fixed exchange rate system.
2. Adherence to a fixed exchange rate system can result in favourable economic conditions at home. For example, low inflation, stable interest rates and a favourable trade balance can all result from a fixed exchange rate policy.
3. The transition to a single currency is easier from a fixed exchange rate system than it is from a flexible exchange rate system. Fewer adjustments and fewer sacrifices are necessary.
4. Fiscal policy is effective under a fixed exchange rate system.
5. By imposing increased discipline on internal economic policy, it can sometimes prevent national governments from adopting irresponsible economic policies for short-term political gain.

It was within the context of fixed exchange rates that the concept of Optimum Currency Areas (OCA) was developed. This is discussed in Information Box 15.1.

INFORMATION BOX 15.1

EMU and Optimum Currency Areas

The Palgrave *Dictionary of Economics* defines an OCA as 'the "optimum" geographical domain having as a general means of payment either a single common currency or several currencies whose exchange rates are immutably pegged to one another with unlimited convertibility for both current and capital transactions, but whose exchange rates fluctuate in unison against the rest of the world.'[9] By the end of the 1990s, Optimum Currency Areas (OCA) had re-emerged to become one of the most recognised theories in the economics profession. This coincided with the launch of the single currency in 1999 and, in the same year, the awarding of the Nobel Prize in Economics to Robert Mundell, the person most responsible for the advancement of OCA theory. It is within the context of the viability of European Economic and Monetary Union and the suitability of its participating member states that we briefly review the theory of Optimum Currency Areas.

The benefits of monetary union, namely lower transaction costs, policy credibility and elimination of exchange rate variability need to be assessed against the costs of monetary union, namely loss of monetary policy autonomy associated with the exchange rate instrument. For a monetary union to work, participating regions or countries should be closely integrated. Integration of factor and product markets is considered necessary. More specifically, the theory outlines a number of criteria for assessing the degree of economic integration. The criteria are as follows:

- factor mobility;
- wage and price flexibility;
- similarity of economic structures;
- diversity of production.

Regions with a high degree of labour and capital mobility and where wages and prices are flexible are considered suitable for a currency area. In addition, regions that have similar economic structures and high industrial diversification tend to be suited to a single currency area. It is argued that highly diversified countries are better candidates as the diversification provides some insulation against shocks.

Essentially, the theory of OCA depends on the type and size of disturbances and the speed with which the economy or region can adjust to these disturbances. In the case of a currency area, it is asymmetric or country-specific shocks (i.e. shocks that affect different countries differently) that matter. As for the speed of adjustment, this depends on the adjustment mechanisms that are available. In the absence of exchange rate autonomy, the remaining adjustment mechanisms are factor mobility, flexibility of prices and fiscal stabilisers. If, for whatever reason, these are absent, output and employment levels will adjust, resulting in higher emigration and unemployment.

These adjustment mechanisms weaken the case for a European monetary union, it is argued. Within the EU, labour mobility is low, more due to cultural and linguistic differences and rigidities in housing markets than to border controls. There is evidence of wage rigidities across the EU member states. As for fiscal federalism, the absence of a centralised budget and any meaningful fiscal redistribution in the EU means that a region adversely affected by an asymmetric shock will not be compensated with lower taxes and higher transfers. The EU budget is small and lacks any automatic mechanism that would transfer funds to adversely affected regions. Taking these into account, it would appear to be the case that the European Union is less of an optimum currency area than, say, the United States. There is considerable evidence to support this claim. However, supporters of European EMU point to the endogeneity of OCA, that is, the suitability of regions or countries participating in a currency area may increase as membership of the currency area becomes more likely. In the context of EMU, the euro itself may encourage closer economic integration. For example, the European Commission has argued that greater economic integration in the EU will reduce the probability that countries will be hit by asymmetric shocks. This claim is still subject to debate.

Managed floating exchange rate systems

The managed floating exchange rate system closely resembles the flexible exchange rate system.

Definition

The managed floating exchange rate system is characterised by an exchange rate which changes with the market forces of demand and supply. However, the Central Bank intervenes periodically, particularly when the currency is very weak or very strong.

The danger of a weak currency is that inflationary pressures may arise. A strong currency may have a negative effect on the volume of exports. To avoid both of these threats to the domestic economy, the central bank may intervene.[10]

Semi-fixed exchange rate systems

The semi-fixed exchange rate system closely resembles the fixed exchange rate system but it is more 'flexible'.

Definition

Member states of a semi-fixed exchange rate system set the value of their currencies in relation to other participating currencies. However, currencies are permitted to fluctuate above and below these rates.

The 'fluctuation bands' are normally one or two percentage points above and below the established rate. If the domestic currency fluctuates within the band, the central bank does not normally intervene. If the domestic currency approaches the limit of the band, the central bank intervenes in the market to stabilise the exchange rate within the band.

Countries that participate in a semi-fixed exchange rate system must offset their interventions using external reserves.

One example of a semi-fixed exchange rate system was the European Monetary System (EMS), the precursor of the single currency. Since Ireland was a member of this system, we will discuss it here.

15.4 THE EUROPEAN MONETARY SYSTEM

The EMS came into operation on 13 March 1979. Its aim was the 'creation of closer monetary co-operation leading to a zone of monetary stability in Europe'.[11] How did the EMS operate?

There were three separate components to the EMS. The first was the ECU, the European Currency Unit. It was a weighted basket of EU currencies, with the weightings changed every five years or when a new currency joined the system. The weights were based on a country's GNP and level of intra-EU trade.

The second component was the EMCF, the European Monetary Co-operation Fund. On joining the system member states were obliged to submit 20% of their holdings of gold and foreign exchange reserves in return for ECUs. These funds were used for settling accounts after foreign exchange intervention.

The third and most important part of the EMS was the Exchange Rate Mechanism (ERM). This was a semi-fixed system where members' currencies were allowed to fluctuate against each other's currencies within an agreed band.[12]

All currencies of the ERM were assigned a central rate against the ECU. Each member's currency was also committed to a central rate against other currencies, with bands of fluctuation.

When the ERM was first established, it was decided to operate two bands of fluctuation: a narrow band of 2.25% and a wide band of 6%. The wider band was perceived to be a temporary measure and was assigned to member states with volatile currencies. It was hoped that as their economies converged towards the European average their currencies would become more stable and they would eventually enter the narrow band.[13]

There were three options available to any central bank involved in maintaining the value of its currency within the ERM fluctuation bands. A short-term measure was foreign exchange intervention which altered the external reserves. Central banks could intervene on a daily basis. Domestic currency was bought and sold in exchange for foreign currency. According to the rules of the ERM, intervention was a joint responsibility, i.e. it involved the respective central banks of the strongest and weakest currencies. For example, if the IR£/DM rate was close to its intervention limits both the Central Bank of Ireland and the Bundesbank were required to act. Of course, there is a finite stock of external reserves. Hence, this was only used as a short-term measure.

A medium-term measure was an interest rate change. If a currency was continually weak and central bank intervention was unsuccessful, the monetary authorities could decide to increase domestic interest rates. We have already seen from Section 15.2 that there is a positive relationship between interest rates and the exchange rate. Frequent changes in interest rates have a destabilising effect on the economy. In theory, this was not a long-term option. However, it became a long-term practice for many countries.

The long-term measure was a realignment of a currency within the ERM. Both devaluation and revaluation involved a change in the central rate between two currencies.

> **Definition**
>
> *Devaluation is a reduction in the value of a currency vis-à-vis other currencies. In terms of the ERM, the central rate is lowered by a certain percentage.*

In a market without restrictions, the currency may depreciate due to the forces of demand and supply. Within the ERM the devaluation of a currency had to be negotiated with other participating members. However, the reason for the devaluation was generally a disequilibrium in the market for the currency.

For example, suppose that the demand for the Irish pound was continually weak, indicating that Irish goods were not competitive on the international market. Foreign exchange intervention and interest rate changes failed to strengthen the pound. The only option left for the Central Bank was to negotiate a devaluation of the Irish pound. Alternatively, increased demand for Irish goods and for the Irish pound could lead to a revaluation.

> **Definition**
>
> *Revaluation is an increase in the value of one currency vis-à-vis other currencies. In terms of the ERM, the central rate is raised by a certain percentage.*

We now examine devaluation as a possible policy option within a semi-fixed exchange rate system.

Devaluation as a policy option

The end of the 1993 currency crisis was the last major realignment of the European currencies.

On 30 January 1993 the Irish pound was devalued by 10%. For several months prior to this, the Irish pound weakened against the core currencies of the ERM (German mark, Dutch guilder and Belgian franc). This problem was aggravated by a weak US dollar and an even weaker pound sterling.

The Irish and the British currencies were linked in the foreign exchange markets. This is because of the strong trade links that persist between the two countries. Therefore, if the Irish pound gained in strength relative to the pound sterling, Irish exports became dearer in their main market. Under those conditions, the foreign exchange markets often anticipated a devaluation of the Irish pound.

Between the months of July and September 1992, the IR£/UK£ exchange rate increased from IR£1 = UK£.93 to parity and then to IR£1 = UK£1.09. Irish firms exporting to the UK faced severe difficulties. Margins were squeezed. In addition, interbank interest rates were extremely high, with the one month lending rate close to 50%. As speculators continued their domination of the foreign exchanges, the situation became unsustainable. The result, months later, was a devaluation of the Irish pound.

Arguments favouring devaluation

A devaluation improves a country's competitiveness by increasing the domestic price of imports and reducing the foreign price of the country's exports. In the Irish context (pre-euro days) such a devaluation would probably return the IR£/UK£ exchange rate to its former trading rate. Prior to the 1993 currency crisis the IR£/UK£ exchange rate had traded at approximately IR£1 = UK£.93 for a period of over two years.

A weaker Irish exchange rate was particularly important for indigenous firms who rely, often exclusively, on the British market. Because the firms are often small, many cannot afford to 'hedge' against exchange risk.[14] This contrasts sharply with their Irish-based multinational competitors who either hedge or simply invoice their Irish exports in US dollars. Either way, their exchange risk is lessened. Also, indigenous companies do not have the resources to maintain operations until the exchange rate becomes more favourable. Because the Irish firms are more labour intensive than foreign multinationals, the likely closure of indigenous firms added to an already serious unemployment problem.

Also, a devaluation would allow the Central Bank to lower interest rates as it would no longer have to defend the currency. High and rising interest rates were particularly devastating to mortgage holders, whose monthly payments increased. They had less income to spend which negatively affected consumer spending. Firms were unable to borrow money at the penalising rates of interest. The consequences of this lack of investment were felt in the medium term and the long term.

Arguments opposing devaluation

A devaluation is inflationary, particularly for a country that imports as much as Ireland. A devaluation has the effect of increasing the price of imports. If there are domestic substitutes, they become more competitive and so a devaluation can have a positive impact on indigenous industry. However, because the Irish economy is small, many goods are not produced here and many raw materials are not found here. Therefore, consumers and firms are forced to pay for higher priced imports which leads to inflation.

Devaluations can also lead to a vicious circle of inflation and devaluation which, once established, is difficult to break. For example (again, pre-EMU), suppose a number of Irish firms lobby the government for a devaluation. The government subsequently devalues the currency. Irish firms gain a short-term competitive advantage over their trading partners. However, as import prices begin to rise, the Irish inflation rate increases. Consequently, the inflation rate differential with the UK worsens. Irish firms become even less competitive. As a short-term solution to the problem, Irish industry requests another devaluation. The government, facing a general election in the near future, devalues again. The inflation rate in Ireland increases, again. Another cycle begins. This is the devaluation-price inflation spiral which is sometimes used as an argument against devaluation.

Also, as we mentioned in Chapter 10, part of the government debt is denominated in foreign currency. If the domestic currency is devalued relative to these foreign currencies, the size of the foreign debt increases along with the debt service repayments. Therefore, the decision to devalue undermines a government's commitment to contain sovereign debt.

Short-term interest rates usually decline following a devaluation. However, the devaluation itself could lead investors to believe that the Irish pound is volatile and that investments denominated in Irish pounds are risky. Investors would demand a premium on Irish interest rates relative to, for example, German interest rates to compensate for the risk. Therefore, the benefit of lower interest rates might only last for a short time. Long-term interest rates may be higher as a result of the decision to devalue.

To summarise, those who oppose devaluation argue that the decision to devalue places too much emphasis on the short-term goal of preserving employment. The long-term goals of the economy include maintaining low inflation rates, low interest rates and a stable exchange rate regime. Attaining these goals would encourage long-term growth and promote increased employment. The devaluation is a political expedient at the expense of the long-term national interest, it is argued.

In conclusion, it can be seen from the above analysis that the decision to devalue is a difficult one to make. There are many who favour devaluation as a credible policy option; others are not so supportive. For one, Harold Wilson, the former UK Prime Minister who, in 1963, said 'Devaluation, whether of sterling, or the dollar, or both, would be a lunatic, self-destroying operation.' Incidentally, four years later he had this to say: 'From now on the pound abroad is worth 14% or so less in terms of other currencies. It does not mean, of course, that the pound here in Britain in your pocket or purse, or in your bank has been devalued.' Not surprisingly, this statement followed the decision to devalue sterling, in 1967. It is left to the readers to decide for themselves the reason behind the change of opinion!

Membership of the ERM was a precondition for participation in Economic and Monetary Union. This is the subject of the next section.

15.5 ECONOMIC AND MONETARY UNION

The origins of Economic and Monetary Union, or EMU, date back to 1957, the year that the European Economic Community (EEC) was established.

The main features of an economic union are:

- the free mobility of capital, labour, goods and services;
- a community-wide competition policy;
- co-ordination of macroeconomic policy;
- economic and social cohesion and regional development.[15]

The main features of a monetary union are as follows:

- the abolition of all exchange controls culminating in the complete liberalisation of all capital transactions;
- the irrevocable fixing of exchange rates culminating in a single currency;
- a European Central Bank and a common monetary policy.

The Delors Report, published in 1989, established a three-stage process and a timetable to achieve these goals. These were slightly modified at the Intergovernmental Conference in 1991. They were published in the Treaty on European Union, more commonly known as the Maastricht Treaty, in December 1991. Because of problems in achieving the objectives set out in the Delors Report, the timetable was amended by the European Council at a meeting in Madrid during December 1995. The three stages for achieving EMU and the amended timetable are outlined below.

Stage 1: Laying the foundation

This stage began in July 1990 and ended in December 1993. One of the goals of the stage was to complete the Internal Market, made possible by the passage of the Single European Act in 1987. Theoretically, within the Single European Market there is free movement of people, goods, services and capital. All barriers to entry between European Union member states were to be eliminated. In other words, it was to be a Europe without national frontiers. Although much has been achieved, work continues to harmonise tax systems, to standardise technical specifications across member states and to reduce national incentives to industries.

Another goal of this phase was to co-ordinate macroeconomic policies between member states. It was hoped that the exchange rates of member states could be maintained within their 'narrow bands'. Exchange rate stability and the discipline that it imposes on national governments was to pave the way to the single currency.

In order to reduce disparities in the living conditions between member states, structural funds were awarded, particularly to countries whose GDP per capita was significantly below the EU average.

Stage 2: Moving towards union

Stage 2 was designed as a transitional phase. The European Monetary Institute (EMI) was established in Frankfurt to begin the transition from independent national monetary policies to a common European monetary policy. The EMI itself was a 'transitional' institution and it was to be replaced by a European Central Bank. This happened in June 1998.

Under the terms of the Maastricht Treaty, the EMI and the Commission were to report to the EU Council at the end of 1996 on the progress made by member states in fulfilling the convergence criteria. At the summit in Madrid, the Council extended this deadline. In May 1998 eleven countries were deemed eligible to participate in EMU. Of the remaining four, Greece was the only country deemed ineligible. The UK, Sweden and Denmark decided not to participate. The irrevocable conversion rates for the euro, based on the ERM bilateral central rates were announced.

Stage 3: Completing the union

Under the terms of the Maastricht Treaty, Stage 3 was to begin between 1997 and 1999, at the latest. The Council in Madrid confirmed the starting date for the irrevocable fixing of the exchange rates for 1 January 1999. With the launch of the single currency in January 1999, the euro became a currency in its own right, with the national currencies (including the Irish pound) becoming, in effect, units of the euro. Euro notes and coins came into circulation on 1 January 2002, with national currencies going out of circulation shortly afterwards.[16] The new European Central Bank and the national central banks of the EU countries constitute the European System of Central Banks (ESCB). These institutions are responsible for the formulation and implementation of a common, EU monetary policy.

The road to EMU is highlighted in Figure 15.7.

FIGURE 15.7: THE ROAD TO EMU

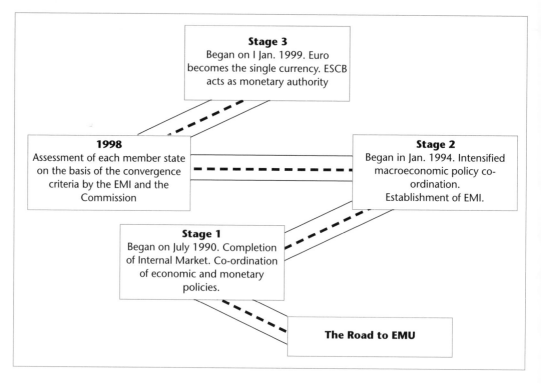

Convergence criteria to join the single currency

To prepare for the transition to a single currency, the Maastricht Treaty established a set of targets called the convergence criteria. The treaty did not specify policies. It was up to the national governments of each member state to determine how to achieve each criterion. The convergence criteria are listed below (with the direct quotes from the treaty in quotation marks).[17]

- Inflation rates: 'an average rate of inflation . . . that does not exceed by more than 1.5 percentage points that of, at most, the three best performing Member States in terms of price stability';
- Interest rates: 'a Member State has had an average nominal long-term interest rate that does not exceed by more than two percentage points that of, at most, the three best performing Member States in terms of price stability';
- Exchange rates: 'the observance of the normal fluctuation margins provided for by the exchange-rate mechanism of the European Monetary System, for at least two years, without devaluing against the currency of any other Member State';
- 'the sustainability of the government financial position', as judged by the following two measures:

Government deficit: 'the ratio of the planned or actual government deficit to gross domestic product at market prices' should not exceed '3%'.
Government debt: 'the ratio of government debt to gross domestic product at market prices' should not exceed '60%'.

If the deficit is above the reference value, it would still be deemed suitable if either the ratio has declined substantially or, alternatively, the excess is only exceptional and temporary. Likewise, if the debt is above the reference value, it would be deemed suitable if the ratio is sufficiently diminishing and approaching the reference value at a satisfactory pace.

These conditions, known as the Excessive Deficit Procedure (EDP), were written in the knowledge that it would be at least six years before any assessment would take place. Hence, the wording had to allow for a certain amount of leeway. Given the difficult economic conditions that prevailed after the Maastricht Treaty was adopted, a loose interpretation of the convergence criteria was indeed required.

As stated earlier, the decision on eligibility was taken in May 1998. It was based on data for the fiscal year 1997. Table 15.5 reports the outcome of the fiscal criteria for member states of the EU, as these proved the more difficult to satisfy. It would appear that all three non-participating countries (UK, Sweden, Denmark) were 'suitable' whereas both Belgium and Italy were 'ineligible'. For obvious political reasons, Belgium and Italy were deemed suitable. Other EU countries were later to join the euro, namely Greece (2001), Slovenia (2007), Malta and Cyprus (2008), Slovakia (2009) and Estonia (2011).

TABLE 15.5: FISCAL CONVERGENCE, 1997

Country	Deficit/GDP[1]	Debt/GDP[2]
Austria	−1.9	64.3
Belgium	−1.9	123.4
Denmark	+0.4	63.6
Finland	−1.2	54.9
France	−3.0	58.1
Germany	−2.7	61.5
Greece	−3.9	109.4
Ireland	+1.1	61.3
Italy	−2.7	122.4
Luxembourg	+2.9	6.4
Netherlands	−0.9	71.2
Portugal	−2.5	61.7
Spain	−2.6	67.5
Sweden	−0.7	76.7
UK	−1.9	52.1

Source: ECB *Annual Report 1998, 1999.*
Notes: 1. General Government Deficit (−)/Surplus (+).
      2. General government, consistent with the Maastricht Treaty definition.

Economic policy in EMU

'In short, most domestic macroeconomic policy instruments will, for good or ill, be removed.'[18] (Honohan, 1999). For national authorities, the loss of policy autonomy is one of the most significant implications of EMU membership. As participants in the euro area, no independent exchange rate instrument is available. The objective of exchange rate policy is to maintain price stability. According to the Maastricht Treaty, responsibility for the formulation of exchange rate policy is shared between the Council of Economics and Finance Ministers (ECOFIN) and the ECB. Ireland's reliance in the past on exchange rate realignments is no longer a policy option.

The same applies to monetary policy. Interest rate adjustments, either to dampen down inflation or to boost spending, are no longer available to the national authorities. A single monetary policy, aimed at achieving price stability in the euro area, is unlikely to reflect economic conditions in the Irish economy, or for that matter, in other small countries in the euro area. Economic conditions in the large European economies are more likely to influence the monetary decision-making authority, namely the European Central Bank.

With independent exchange rate and monetary policy constrained, the national authorities will be more reliant than ever before on fiscal policy. However, since the launch of the euro in 1999, independent fiscal policy has been constrained by the Stability and Growth Pact (SGP). The objective of the Pact was to constrain fiscal policy in EMU and, in doing so, reconcile the apparent conflict between, on the one hand, a centralised monetary policy and a single currency and, on the other hand, independent fiscal policies and decentralised fiscal structures in the eurozone member states. Some member states (particularly Germany) were concerned about profligate governments and the fiscal indiscipline of some countries leading up to EMU and, more particularly, once monetary union was in place. Concerns over potential spillovers (such as higher interest rates, capital outflows and bailouts) arising from excessive deficits, unsustainable debts and the so-called deficit bias led to calls for some type of a preventive procedure, later to become the SGP.[19] Although the Maastricht Treaty forbid the monetary financing of budget deficits by the ECB and contain a no-bailout clause preventing other member states from rescuing a distressed government (i.e. one likely to default), it also included the EDP. The details of the EDP were left to the 1996 European Council summit in Dublin and the result was the Pact which, in essence, codifies and formalises the EDP.

According to the Pact, a fiscal deficit at over 3% of GDP is considered excessive. In addition, it stipulates that the eurozone governments should balance their budgets over the cycle. It did, however, allow for two let-out clauses. In the case of exceptional (when a country experiences a severe economic downturn, deemed to be a decline of 2% or more) and temporary (in the sense that the deficit is forecast to fall below 3% in the near future) circumstances, there is an automatic exemption. In the case where GDP falls by between 0.75% and 2%, fines are discretionary as the recalcitrant government can apply for a suspension of the EDP. In all other cases – that is, when the GDP growth rate is above the discretionary limit of minus 0.75%, and when the fiscal deficit reaches the 3% limit – the recalcitrant country is subject to penalties or fines. Once found to have violated the conditions of the Pact, the European Commission submits its report to ECOFIN, which in turn makes the final decision. If the Council finds against a country, it issues recommendations with a deadline, and following this, the member state must take corrective action. If the country fails to do so, ECOFIN can then impose fines, in the form of a non-remunerated deposit. There is a fixed deposit of 0.2% of GDP and a variable deposit equal to 0.1% of GDP (for each percentage point above the 3% threshold) up to a maximum of 0.5%. In subsequent years, it is the variable deposit only that applies and it continues to be imposed until the excessive deficit is corrected. However, only after two years does the deposit, in the case where the deficit has not been corrected, become a fine. If sanctioned, these fines can translate into significant amounts of money.[20]

Despite the severity of the rules and the detailed procedure outlined, the Pact has not been very successful in its implementation or in its attempt to constrain eurozone member states. The decision to impose sanctions is highly politicised as the final decision is with ECOFIN. Second, in the early years, it was predominately the bigger member states of Germany, France and Italy that found themselves in deficit and subject to warnings. If large member states can avoid sanctions, all others are likely to follow and thus undermine the credibility of the Pact. Critics of the Pact point to various problems, both with the idea in principle and with its original design. For one, it is argued that the Pact places a deflationary bias on member states. With exchange rate policy and monetary policy no longer available, fiscal policy assumes greater importance. Yet, the constrained use of fiscal policy through the imposition of the Pact greatly limits the use of stabilisation policy. Adherence to the Pact limits the scope for discretionary counter-cyclical fiscal policy. It may even result in pro-cyclical fiscal policy, resulting in an intensification of recessions and an aggravation of the business cycle. Others point to various weaknesses in the design of the Pact. Aside from the obvious lack of credibility, Lane (2004) points to the use of the fiscal deficit measure rather than the more appropriate public debt measure, the purpose of the debt finance (difference between productive capital spending versus consumption or transfers), and the omission of implicit liabilities owed by governments. Others point to the absence of fiscal federalism in the European EMU and the subsequent lack of EU automatic stabilisers (that would allow the EU to adopt a counter-cyclical fiscal policy), the appropriateness of the cyclically-adjusted budget deficit rather than the actual budget deficit and the asymmetric nature of the Pact as it binds member states in bad times only. The latter point was particularly relevant in the boom years of the early and mid-2000s, when budgets, although often in surplus, were inefficiently large (as in the Irish case).

The failure of some member states to maintain fiscal discipline and the reluctance of the Council to sanction those responsible led to a credibility crisis for the Pact. As member states chose to ignore the Pact, reforms were called for, ranging from outright abolition, to an overhaul of its design, to minor changes in its rules. In March 2005, an agreement was reached under which the rules of the Pact were redefined, allowing for a number of extra exceptions and special arrangements. Changes included refinements in the definition of, and adjustment path to, the medium-term budgetary objectives, the introduction of differentiation between countries and the special treatment of expenditure categories. Supporters of the Pact were dismayed with the changes, arguing that the loosening of the rules endangers commitment to fiscal discipline and undermines sound fiscal policy in the eurozone. Much worse was to follow in the run-up to the eurozone and sovereign debt crisis (see end of section 15.6).

The implication for economic policy arising from this loss of economic independence is that the national authorities will have to rely on, to a much greater extent than in the past, wage bargaining and price flexibility to ensure competitiveness in the face of economic shocks. This will apply to all EMU member states, including Ireland.

15.6 THE IRISH EXPERIENCE

In this section, we will examine Ireland's participation in the fixed or semi-fixed exchange rate systems in the context of exchange rate policy. Price stability, characterised by a low and stable inflation rate, has been the primary objective of Irish exchange rate policy, both before and after the introduction of the single currency. We begin with Ireland's decision to join the EMS.

Ireland and the EMS

Ireland joined the EMS in 1979. It was a difficult decision to make for the Irish authorities. We will begin by discussing the arguments advanced by those who favoured membership in the EMS and then consider the arguments of the opponents.

Arguments favouring entry to the EMS

The main argument in favour of membership was the prospect of lower inflation. Until 1979, the pound was linked with sterling and its inflation rate mirrored the British rate. At the end of the 1960s and throughout the 1970s, both countries experienced persistently high inflation rates, peaking at almost 25% in the mid-1970s. The Irish monetary authorities believed that a link with a 'hard currency' which appreciates over time, like the German mark, was preferable to the British link with its inflationary tendency. They hoped that the link with the German mark would result in a convergence of the Irish inflation rate to the German inflation rate which fluctuated between 3% and 4% per annum.

Also, the policy-makers believed that membership of the EMS would facilitate stronger trading links with other member states. This would diminish the reliance of indigenous industries on Britain as a destination for their products.

Finally, Irish authorities expected financial aid from the European Economic Community to assist Ireland to adjust to the new system.

Arguments opposing entry to the EMS

The main argument advanced by those who opposed EMS membership was that the UK decided not to enter. The British authorities were opposed to membership on the basis that it would result in a loss of autonomy, particularly in the area of monetary policy. They believed that Britain, as an exporter of oil, was subject to different, oil-related shocks than the other European countries. They wanted to maintain control over their monetary policy to respond to these shocks.

Hence, the attraction to joining a fixed exchange rate system was dampened by the absence of Ireland's largest trading partner, the UK. Although Irish exporters were promised a more favourable trading environment as members of the ERM, the prospect of a flexible, not to mention a volatile IR£/UK£ exchange rate, was chilling. In the end, the Irish authorities were attracted more by the fixed exchange rate with the German mark than by the old link with sterling. So, after much deliberation, Ireland decided in favour of the ERM. In 1979, the 153-year, one for one, no margins link with sterling was broken.

Next, we will attempt to evaluate Ireland's performance within the ERM.

Ireland's experience within the ERM

An assessment of Ireland's experience within the ERM is normally divided into two distinct periods, 1979–86 and 1987–92.[21] The first period was, in general, disappointing. Ireland's inflation rate remained high, as did Irish interest rates. Trade with member states of the ERM increased but not by a significant amount.

There are a number of reasons for the poor performance during these early years of membership. Possibly the most significant reason was the 'sterling' problem. Sterling was not a member of the ERM and subsequently the IR£/UK£ exchange rate was not subject to any fluctuation bands. Nonetheless, Irish authorities shadowed sterling and at the same time attempted to maintain the formal links with the member states of the ERM. The authorities were literally caught between a rock and a hard place because sterling and the German mark often moved in opposite directions.

The financial markets, both at home and abroad, were aware of this dual policy. It caused the markets to question Ireland's commitment to the ERM. The market scepticism led to speculation whenever the Irish pound appreciated relative to sterling. The tendency for the Irish authorities to devalue in the face of uncertainty reinforced the market view of Ireland's relaxed attitude towards ERM membership.

The belief that Ireland's inflation rate would fall towards the German level on membership of the ERM was based on the theory of PPP. PPP is a theory of exchange rate determination. It states that changes in the exchange rate are accounted for by inflation differentials. In the context of Ireland's membership of the ERM, PPP implies that Ireland's inflation rate will be equal to the core member's (Germany) inflation rate, if the exchange rate between the Irish pound and the German mark is fixed. In this context, PPP is a theory of inflation. See Appendix 15.1 for more on the theory of PPP.

For PPP to hold, a sizeable amount of trade must exist between the two countries. A country cannot benefit from having a fixed exchange rate with another unless a sufficient amount of foreign trade is evident between the two states. Unfortunately, trade between Ireland and other ERM member states did not increase sufficiently during the early years of membership.

Finally, a precondition of entry to a semi-fixed exchange rate system is the agreement to sacrifice national autonomy over certain macroeconomic policies and to co-ordinate policies with other member states. A single member state cannot expect the benefits of a fixed exchange rate system unless its mix of demand-management policies is broadly in line with other member states. This did not happen in the early years of the ERM. Some member states, including Ireland, adopted short-term demand policies which sharply contrasted with the policies adopted by the core member states of the ERM. This is another reason for Ireland's poor performance from 1979 to 1986 (see Appendix 15.2 for a discussion on fiscal and monetary policy in the context of alternate exchange rate regimes).

The performance generally improved during the second period between 1987 and 1992. Unexpectedly, the Irish inflation rate fell below the EU average and the German rate. Interest rates also declined. The differential between Irish and German interest rates narrowed from 9% in 1986 to 3% in 1988. The trade account recorded a surplus, as did the current account. The IR£/DM exchange rate stabilised with the Irish pound reaching the top of the ERM band on a number of occasions.

The improvement in performance came from two sources, domestic and international. The domestic source was the fiscal restraint exercised by the government beginning in 1987. The improvement in industrial relations and the moderate wage increases arising from the Programme for National Recovery also contributed to an Irish environment characterised by low inflation. The international economy, so important to the Irish domestic economy, was buoyant, contributing to the combination of low inflation rates and strong demand for Irish products. The combination of internal discipline and external demand helped Irish policy-makers to maintain the value of the pound within the ERM while experiencing strong rates of economic growth.

Exchange rate policy 1993–98

After the currency crisis the Irish authorities operated exchange rate policy under wide bands within an ERM that was no longer a semi-fixed exchange rate system. With the British pound and the German mark going in opposite directions, the Irish authorities tried to straddle the Irish pound between the two currencies. Although no explicit policy announcement was made, the effective or exchange rate index for the Irish pound remained remarkably stable in this period.

> **Definition**
>
> *The effective or trade-weighted exchange rate index for a currency is the weighted average of the value of the currency against its largest trading partners.*

By assigning trade weights for each country which reflect the importance of various foreign currencies in Ireland's international trade, we can calculate an index of the average value of the Irish pound vis-à-vis currencies of our largest trading partners. For example, the largest weight is assigned to the UK as it is Ireland's largest trading partner. Using bilateral exchange rates, the trade-weighted exchange rate index is calculated by multiplying each bilateral exchange rate, expressed as an index, by the respective trade weights. Summing for all of Ireland's major trading partners, we find the effective exchange rate index.

The effective exchange rate index for the Irish pound for the period 1994–97 is shown in Figure 15.8.

In view of the fall in the value of the Irish pound against the German mark in late 1997 and the subsequent fear of inflation ahead of the 1999 launch of the single currency, a decision to revalue the Irish pound was taken. In March 1998, the authorities announced a 3% revaluation of the Irish pound, resulting in a new central rate of DM2.4833. This was the last realignment before the changeover to the single currency in January 1999.

FIGURE 15.8: THE EFFECTIVE EXCHANGE RATE INDEX, 1994–97

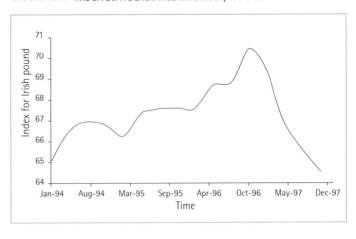

At the same time that this was happening, it was recognised that Irish interest rates would have to fall in order to converge with German levels. Given the level of domestic demand, the Irish authorities delayed the interest rate reductions for as long as possible. In late 1998, the Central Bank of Ireland reduced interest rates on three separate occasions, by over 3% in total. By December 1998, Irish interest rates were in line with interest rates in other EMU countries.

Ireland and the single currency

From an Irish perspective there are arguments in favour of and against the adoption of a single currency.[22] We begin by examining the arguments favouring a single currency.

Arguments supporting Irish participation in the single currency

A transformation to a single currency should result in lower transaction costs. One important transaction cost which will be eliminated is the cost of converting the domestic currency to foreign currencies when goods are imported and exported. Since most of Irish trade is conducted with other EU countries, this saving should be significant. It was estimated that the elimination of transaction costs alone would increase Ireland's GDP by an additional 1%.

Also, exchange rate risk will be eliminated. Exchange rate risk occurs because exchange rates may change between the time when a sale is negotiated and when the goods and services are actually delivered. Large firms can eliminate this risk by purchasing foreign currencies in the forward exchange market to ensure that they pay in the future the price that they agree today. However, this is costly and requires a level of expertise, often lacking in small exporting/importing firms.

Many believe that a single currency will lead to increased competition and trade within the single currency area. Price discrepancies will be more obvious to firms. A higher price, charged in a market of a member state, should signal firms from other countries that opportunities exist in that market. Increased competition should lead to lower prices for consumers. Additionally, heightened competition should strengthen European firms and prepare them to compete in other markets like North America and the Far East.

Another argument in favour of the move to a single currency area is the positive effects which have resulted from the convergence criteria. These requirements have acted as a constraint on the Irish authorities when dealing with the public finances. Given the events of the late 1970s and the early 1980s when public expenditure was out of control, restrictions on the public finances are a welcome feature of Irish budgetary policy.

Finally, a European Central bank is independent from national governments and political favouritism. This is likely to enhance the credibility of the monetary institution, it is argued. A country such as Ireland which relies heavily on foreign trade is likely to benefit from such an institutional change.

All of these changes are likely to impact favourably on Irish economic growth, as measured by GDP.

Arguments opposing Irish participation in the single currency

By far the most important economic argument against participation is the future consequences for the Irish economy if Britain continues to 'opt out'. Although the level of trade with Britain has fallen in the past thirty years, it is still Ireland's most important trading partner and the outlet for most indigenous exports. Opponents of EMU are particularly concerned that the exchange rate links between EU countries inside the single currency area and those outside will not be strong enough. A weak sterling hurts Irish exporters. A strong sterling causes inflationary worries in Ireland. Either way, Britain's refusal to participate makes EMU an unattractive proposition for Ireland.

Another significant issue is the problem of peripherality and whether EMU can lead to economic convergence. A brief look at history would indicate that economic activity tends towards the centre, where the benefits of economies of scale are most evident. Although labour costs tend to be much lower in the peripheral regions compared to the more central regions, further economic integration may result only in a widening of the wealth gap between the core nations and the weaker nations of the EU.[23]

Another drawback is the absence of a fiscal union, which exists in other monetary unions like Australia and the USA. Member states of the EU do not share common tax and welfare systems. If there is a localised demand or supply shock in the USA, the tax burden is reduced and social welfare payments increase, acting as 'automatic stabilisers' for the local economy. An adverse shock to an EU state is not followed by an automatic transfer of funds from the EU or a reduction of tax payments to the EU. Because of the stability pact, the national government is limited in its response to negative shocks. Given the UK's fierce resistance to a fiscal union, it is unlikely that it will be adopted by the EU in the near future.

Finally, devaluation as a policy option will no longer be available in a single currency market. In the past, public authorities have tackled unemployment by devaluing the domestic currency in order to boost foreign demand for Irish products. This will no longer be possible. Related to this is the issue of policy sovereignty. Membership in the EMU is likely to result in a loss of autonomy, and in particular control over monetary policy. This is an important issue in the UK where an independent monetary policy is a central part of its overall economic strategy. In Ireland, it was not such an important issue because monetary policy was largely outside the control of the Irish authorities.

The single currency since its launch in January 1999

The euro was launched in January 1999. The prediction was for a strong currency, with early gains against the US dollar and sterling expected. The outcome was very different, as Figure 15.9 shows.

In the first month of its launch, the average exchange rate was 1.161 US dollars to one euro. The average €/UK£ exchange rate for the same month was 0.703 (UK£ per one €). Eleven months later, the €/US$ had fallen in value

FIGURE 15.9: EURO EXCHANGE RATES, JANUARY 1999–OCTOBER 2000

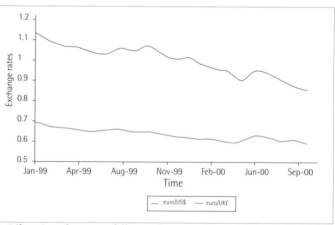

to 1.011, a decline of almost 13%. Likewise, the euro fell in value against the UK£, to 0.627 in December 1999. The euro continued to fall in value for most of the following year. Eventually, the ECB intervened to support the currency. At first, it increased interest rates. Numerous ECB interest rate hikes followed. Later in the year and with the support of other central banks, it intervened in the foreign exchange market. Despite this support, the euro's perception as a weak currency persisted. Let us consider some possible explanations for this fall in the value of the euro.

On economic grounds, the initial fall in the value of the euro can be explained partly by the growth differential between the USA economy and the euro area economies. Whereas the US economy was booming throughout 1999, economic growth in the big euro area countries such as Germany and Italy was sluggish. In addition, better returns on assets in the form of higher interest rates attracted capital flows to the USA and UK in preference to Euroland.

Aside from these economic reasons, there were institutional and political reasons for the weak currency. The ECB is the sole monetary institution responsible for exchange rate policy within the euro area. Although the Maastricht Treaty conferred unprecedented powers of independence on the ECB, the euro was subject to political pressure within weeks of its launch. It would take some time before the ECB could gain the same anti-inflation reputation that the Bundesbank had earned. Aside from political interference, the credibility of the ECB was not helped by a number of events in its first two years. A perceived lack of accountability and openness, unhelpful comments by ECB personnel (including its president) and indecisive action by its governing council contributed to the euro's weakness on foreign exchange markets.

The fall in the value of the euro continued until the end of 2000. By then, it had lost over 25 per cent of its value against the US dollar, almost 30 per cent against the Japanese yen and over 16 per cent against the pound sterling. Despite this decline (and concerns over the viability of the euro and the greater European project), the euro started to recover in 2001.

As is evident from Figure 15.10, the €/US$ exchange rate recovered and by late 2002 had reached parity and by May 2003 was at 1.16, the rate in January 1999 when the euro was launched. Further weakness in the dollar caused by a number of factors (the twin deficits and the fear of more fundamental problems in the US economy have been cited) were to result in the €/US$ exchange rate rising to a high of just over 1.30 in spring 2005 before it stabilised in a 1.20–1.25

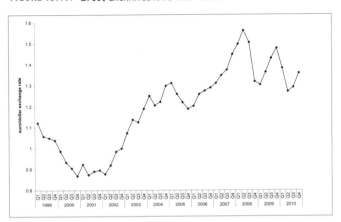

FIGURE 15.10: €/US$ EXCHANGE RATE 1999–2010

range in the summer of 2005. The euro weakness may have given an initial boost to Irish exporters, but this was short-lived. The rise in the value of the euro was cited as one of the reasons for the continued sluggishness of some eurozone economies. For others, including Ireland, this was a period of rapid economic growth. However, by the late 2000s, circumstances were to change, particularly for the peripheral member states of the eurozone.

The 2010/11 Eurozone Crisis

From a European perspective, 2010/11 will long be remembered for the Greek, Irish and Portuguese fiscal crises and subsequent bailouts, the eurozone countries' public debt problems and contagion affects, concerns over sovereign default (Ireland included) and the fear of a partial or complete break-up of the single currency project. We begin, however, by outlining the underlying causes of the 2010/11 eurozone crisis.

Underlying causes

The eurozone crisis was not simply a crisis of the single currency project and its design, dating back to the Maastricht Treaty and the Stability and Growth Pact, as it is often depicted. Nor can speculation by profit-seeking 'amoral' market participants, as cited by some populist governments and politicians, be blamed.[24] The reasons behind the eurozone debacle and the related sovereign debt crisis were more fundamental and relate to the post-euro growth model that pertained in many of the eurozone countries. The underlying causes were threefold, namely:

- growing imbalances and excesses in the form of current account deficits, asset bubbles and consumption booms (mainly in Southern Europe, but also in Ireland and the UK);
- a weak financial system with under-regulated and overleveraged European banks;
- high fiscal deficits and public debts (but again, in *only* some eurozone countries), but also rising private indebtedness of households, (some) businesses and financial institutions.

These problems, together, were reflected in a deterioration in competitiveness and in a crisis of governance, resulting from an overall interconnectedness of government debt, bank crises and policy mistakes (Baldwin, Gros and Laeven 2010; De Grauwe 2010). Reminiscent of the fear of asymmetric shocks in a common currency area, the result has been a significant divergence of economic conditions and outcomes between eurozone countries, most especially between Germany and the Southern European member states.

This interconnectedness of debt between eurozone governments and banks, and between public and private debt, was of a systemic nature. The eurozone countries at the centre of the sovereign debt crisis, infamously termed PIIGS (Portugal, Ireland, Italy, Greece and Spain), were heavily indebted to each other, and to the bigger and richer member states of France and Germany. This is a depiction of the eurozone's public debt crisis. As for private indebtedness, many of the largest commercial banks in the eurozone countries were overleveraged and over-exposed to a residential and commercial property bubble that burst in the late 2000s. Financial institutions and the households (and commercial entities, especially property developers) that they had lent to were heavily indebted. Other European banks were heavily exposed to either USA-originated toxic assets or to Eastern European countries that had gambled on a fixed exchange rate and early euro membership, resulting in, for these EU accession countries, excessive flows of speculative short-term capital and an overheated economy. This depicts the private debt crisis in the eurozone. On the relationship between private and public debt, Reinhart and Rogoff's (2009) timely study of eight centuries of financial crises and folly highlights the frequency of severe banking crises followed by sovereign debt crises, similar in many ways to the sequence of events culminating in the Second Great Contraction of 2008/9, when private debt (in the USA, UK and some smaller eurozone countries) and the banking (and global economic) crisis that followed, eventually resulting in a public (sovereign) debt crisis – or a real and substantial fear of one – among some eurozone countries, including Ireland. What followed then was the great austerity versus stimulus debate of 2010/11 and the fear, at that time, of a double-dip recession.

The crisis began with the Greek bailout of May 2010 and it is to this sovereign debt crisis and rescue that we now turn.

A Greek tragedy

The Greek debt crisis was brought to the fore by the election of a new Greek government in October 2009 and the subsequent disclosure of a misreporting of fiscal deficits for previous years.[25] The actual Greek budget deficit for 2009 was in excess of 13.5 per cent of GDP, with its public debt at 115 per cent of GDP.[26] In early 2010, markets responded to the Greek crisis and the country's creditworthiness by demanding higher interest rates on government debt. As rates continued to rise, the Greek authorities found it more difficult to access funds on international markets. Fears mounted as concerns rose that the Greek 'solvency' crisis would spread, with a contagion extending to other eurozone states such as Spain, Portugal and Ireland. The credit ratings of the most profligate eurozone countries (not to mention eurozone banks) were all downgraded. In April 2010 the Greek credit rating was downgraded to junk bond status by

Standard & Poor's – themselves, and other credit agencies, subject to much criticism for their role in the financial crisis – amidst fears of a default by the Athens government. Yields on Greek government bonds soared with the Greek/German bond yield spread rising to over 1,000 basis points (or 10 percentage points), as international investors effectively abandoned Greece. Under pressure from partners in the eurozone to reassure its commitment to fiscal correction, the Greek government introduced an austerity package, comprising tax changes (aimed at increasing taxes, reducing tax evasion and widening the tax net), welfare cuts (raising the retirement age, pension reforms, etc.) and reductions in government spending (public sector pay cuts and public expenditure reductions). Greece was hit with industrial strikes and nationwide protests, further exacerbating its reputation and credibility abroad.[27]

In May 2010 the eurozone countries and the IMF agreed with the Athens government to provide a €110bn (€80bn from euro area countries plus €30bn from the IMF) loan agreement – effectively a rescue package, or bailout – conditional on implementation of accelerated fiscal austerity measures agreed by the European Commission and the IMF. Later that month, at an emergency meeting of EU economics and finance ministers the member states of the EU agreed a new European stabilisation fund, the European Financial Stability Fund, the EFSF (with ECB and IMF funds), amounting to €750bn. The aim of the EFSF is to preserve financial stability in Europe by providing assistance to distressed and indebted eurozone countries. Also, the ECB, reluctantly it must be said, announced its willingness to buy eurozone bonds to improve liquidity and alleviate funding problems of deficit-stricken eurozone nations. The ECB sovereign bond purchase programme was seen by many commentators as contrary to the Maastricht Treaty's provisions on ensuring fiscal discipline. In designing EMU, and cognisant of member states' inability to devalue, but with a fear of moral hazard with respect to recalcitrant countries, the Maastricht Treaty contained three safeguards against fiscal profligacy. These were the no-bailout clause, the prohibition of public debt purchases (that is, the non-monetising of public debt) by the ECB, and the EDP of the SGP.[28] By summer 2010, all three provisions had been breached, as Greece was rescued by an EU/IMF bailout, the ECB conceded to buy government bonds and the SGP had been violated for years by many eurozone countries, including the larger member states.

An Irish bailout

In autumn 2010, the focus turned to Ireland. Ireland's membership of the eurozone meant that it could not devalue, at least in an external sense (that is, a currency devaluation was not an option). Given conditions at home and within the eurozone, Ireland was faced with the need for an internal devaluation, in the form of reductions in costs, wages and prices in order to restore the country's competitiveness. Although its fiscal deficit was large, at, in 2009, almost 12% of GDP (excluding the €4bn transfer to Anglo Irish Bank), it was not insurmountable. The bigger problem was the private bank debt that the government had guaranteed in the blanket guarantee of September 2008. As the estimated cost of the bank bailout rose throughout 2010, the international debt markets responded by demanding higher interest rates on Irish government bonds. In late September 2010, in an announcement made in an attempt to appease markets, the Irish government announced that the total cost of the bank bailout would be in the region of €45bn–€50bn. On the same day it was announced that a four-year plan would be published in advance of the 2011 budget and that the government would not proceed with bond auctions for the remainder of the year. Market sentiment remained negative throughout the following two months, with the spread on German bonds rising, albeit in the secondary market, to punitive levels. Fears of a sovereign Irish default spread throughout Europe, with European banks and peripheral eurozone countries fearing contagion. Moreover, concerns mounted over the future of the euro. As Ireland's woes continued, other highly indebted eurozone countries, including Portugal and Spain, but also Belgium and Italy, feared a similar fate. With the ECB providing emergency funding for the Irish banks, pressure mounted on the Irish authorities to end months of speculation about a possible bailout or rescue. At end November 2010, the second eurozone country in the space of six months capitulated, with Ireland accepting financial support in the form of an EU–IMF programme. In terms of the euro, discussions moved on to other troubled eurozone countries and the need to agree on a European stability mechanism to replace the temporary stability facility that expires in 2013. The position of various types and categories of bondholders and the likelihood of debt restructuring will occupy the minds of the authorities in Brussels and other European capital cities for some time to come as they muddle through the eurozone's biggest crisis since its launch in 1999.

Medium-term issues, reforms and lessons

The 2010/11 eurozone and sovereign debt crisis has raised a number of fundamental issues concerning EMU and the single currency project. Posed in this textbook as questions, these include (in no particular order) the following related issues.

- Can a monetary union that lacks a fiscal and political union – where, according to EMU critics, politics trumps economics – be sustainable? Without the (unlikely) federal arrangements in place, how can EMU, described by its supporters as 'politically feasible and economically adequate', succeed?
- With respect to the (incomplete, at the time of writing) design of the euro and the defects that were well recognised at its inception over a decade ago, how can these structural flaws and institutional deficiencies be addressed? (See below.)
- How can fiscal discipline be strengthened, or is it a case of weak enforcement of existing provisions?[29] Assuming discretion is not enough, what fiscal rules are required? Should it be done at a national level, where fiscal sovereignty lies, or at the supranational level, but where centralised resources are limited? More specifically, how can the design and architecture of the euro and eurozone institutions and governance, and, in particular, the much discredited Stability and Growth Pact, be reconstituted? If alternative fiscal rules and mechanisms (such as the peer review of national budgets agreed by EU economics and finance ministers in June 2010) are required, what sanctions are needed to ensure compliance?
- Continuing from above, how can pro-cyclical policy be avoided, or at least curbed? At the national level, should independent fiscal councils be a requirement for all member states of the eurozone? Or is a eurozone fiscal council necessary? What about other institutional arrangements, such as balanced budgets as constitutional requirements, as in Germany? Is a one-size-fits-all arrangement suitable, given the diverse budgetary and fiscal culture of the eurozone member states? At the supranational level, how can the system of EU fiscal accounts, and budgetary monitoring and surveillance, be improved? Likewise, how can private debt levels be monitored and, if necessary, curtailed?
- In terms of crisis management, as opposed to crisis prevention dealt with above, is there a need, in the absence of federal arrangements and a centralised EU budget, for a European Monetary Fund, and within that a medium-term financial assistance facility as per the IMF, to provide financial assistance in times of crisis? If so, how can the associated problem of moral hazard be averted?
- Is membership of the eurozone irreversible or, putting it another way, is the no-exit strategy

from the euro credible? Alternately, as critics like to point out, is the euro doomed, for either economic and/or political reasons? Would a eurozone break-up (into, for example, a smaller core group) be advantageous (for countries exiting and/or those remaining), or, in the words of one expert, be the 'the mother of all financial crises' (Eichengreen 2007)?

· Beyond a remedy for the euro and the required fiscal consolidation, will the EU push through the necessary structural reforms to avoid a repetition of the eurozone crisis, and, in the medium to long run, ensure a more competitive, balanced trading bloc while at the same time protecting the social solidarity for which the European project is renowned?

Students are encouraged to consider the questions raised above, and to inform themselves of the related issues surrounding economic and monetary integration, common currency areas and the eurozone, fiscal discipline and rules versus discretion, and finally, financial crises, contagion affects, bailouts and defaults. We refer the reader to the relevant list of sources and references at the end of the textbook.

CASE STUDY

Extract from *The Irish Independent*
Euro falls again as doubts grow about Greece bailout

The euro fell for a third day against the dollar as Greece tried to end speculation that it may be having doubts about a plan that provides European Union and International Monetary Fund support in refinancing its debt. Europe's common currency slid the most versus the yen in almost six weeks after a report that Greece wants to bypass IMF involvement if it needs assistance because the conditions would be too stringent. The nation's finance minister denied the story ... 'There are a lot of questions about a bailout that haven't been answered yet,' said Aroop Chatterjee, a currency strategist at Barclays Plc in New York. 'We don't expect the situation to spiral out of control. It will be slow-burning, and there will be greater downside pressure on the euro until clarity comes.'

The currency tumbled 1.5 percent, the most on an intraday basis in almost two months. It was down 0.88 percent against the dollar at $1.3364, after hitting a session low of $1.3357, the lowest in more than a week. It also fell 3 percent against the yen to 125.55 yen. The dollar remained stronger than the euro and weaker than the yen after minutes released

yesterday of the US Federal Reserve's 16 March meeting showed policy makers saw signs of a growing economic recovery that could be hobbled by unemployment and tight credit.

Greece's borrowing costs shot up following a report, later denied, that Athens was seeking to revise a deal hammered out last month which would provide a European and International Monetary Fund rescue to prevent a default. Markets have so far appeared unconvinced that the bailout plan, which would provide Greece with bilateral loans, would be sufficient to contain the country's debt crisis.

The interest rate gap, or spread, between Greek 10-year bonds and equivalent German issues surging to 406 basis points, or 4.06 percentage points, yesterday afternoon. 'Today was a very bad day for Greek bonds,' Finance Minister Mr Papaconstantinou said. '(But) Greece is not seeking to borrow today.' 'The country has covered all its borrowing needs for April and now ... has more than a month before it is forced to borrow again,' he said on TV, adding that Greece would seek to raise more than €10 billion in May. But Mr

Papaconstantinou added that Greece 'cannot continue for long' paying high interest rates for its borrowing. However, markets have remained jittery. 'Today's 60 basis points surge in Greek government bond yields underlines yet again the continued precariousness of the troubled economy's position,' said Jonathan Loynes of Capital Economics.

Today, inspectors from the IMF are due in Athens to review progress in government austerity cuts. Greece has promised draconian fiscal reforms to reduce debt but remains under pressure from high borrowing costs.

Source: The Irish Independent, 7 April 2010.

Questions

1. Explain the nature of the connection between the Greek debt crisis and the fall in the value of the euro.
2. Using the ECB Monthly Bulletin (www.ecb.int), report the monthly euro exchange rate against both the dollar and sterling for the first six months of 2010. Briefly outline the main economic events occurring at that time, relating to the Greek crisis.
3. How does a weakened currency affect an economy? With no possibility of devaluation, what is the normal adjustment mechanism in an economy?

Answers on website

SUMMARY

1. The balance of payments is an accounting record of all transactions between economic agents of one country and the rest of the world. It comprises a current and a capital account. The current account records the movement of all goods and services whereas the capital account is a statement of all capital transactions into and out of a country. The way in which the balance of payments actually balances depends largely on the exchange rate regime.
2. An exchange rate is the price of one currency in terms of another. Factors which influence the exchange rate include the level of foreign trade, interest rate differentials, inflation differentials, speculation and income differentials. There are a number of different exchange rate regimes. Under a fixed exchange rate system the Central Banks are obliged to maintain currencies at predetermined rates in terms of gold or of a 'hard' currency. Under a flexible exchange rate system, the exchange rate is determined by the forces of demand and supply. Semi-fixed exchange rate systems and managed floating systems are other examples of exchange rate regimes.
3. The European Monetary System, the precursor to the eurozone, is an example of a semi-fixed exchange rate system. Its aim was to create a zone of monetary stability. Central to the EMS is its exchange rate mechanism wherein member states are committed to a central rate and a band of fluctuation. Central banks, in attempting to support the value of a currency, can intervene using external reserves or by changing interest rates or realigning the currency within the ERM.
4. A devaluation (revaluation) is a reduction (increase) in the value of a currency vis-à-vis other currencies. With a devaluation the level of exports is likely to increase, jobs in the exposed sector may be saved and the pressure on interest rates may be reduced. The drawbacks include higher

import prices, the possibility of higher interest rates in the long term, an increase in the size of the foreign debt and larger debt service repayments. Devaluation is no longer a policy option for the euro area countries.

5.   Economic and Monetary Union has been an aim of the EU since its foundation. Central to the economic union is the creation of a single market where the flow of goods, services, labour and capital is unrestricted. Monetary union involves the creation of a single currency and one Central Bank. Co-ordination of economic policies is another feature of EMU, resulting in a loss of macroeconomic policy autonomy. The three stages towards EMU were laid out in the Maastricht Treaty. The convergence criteria related to inflation rates, interest rates, exchange rates and a country's fiscal position.

6.   The aim of Irish exchange rate policy is price stability. Within the ERM, this was best achieved, according to the monetary authorities, by fixing the Irish pound to other member states' currencies. Ireland's experience within the ERM was mixed. Sterling's absence from the exchange rate mechanism of the EMS caused policy problems for the Irish authorities, and trading problems for Irish businesses. Sterling's absence from the single currency causes similar problems for Ireland, despite the lower transaction costs that accrue from EMU participation. Other problems for the single currency include its design, the profligacy of certain member states and the lack of political and fiscal union.

KEY TERMS

Balance of payments	Realignment
Current account	Devaluation
Merchandise trade balance	Revaluation
Capital account	Economic and monetary union
Exchange rate	The Maastricht Treaty
Flexible exchange rate system	Internal market
Fixed exchange rate system	European Monetary Institute
External reserves	Euro
Optimum currency areas	Convergence criteria
Managed floating	Excessive Deficit Procedure
Semi-fixed exchange rate system	Stability and Growth Pact
European Monetary System	Purchasing power parity
European currency unit	Effective exchange rate index
Exchange rate mechanism	Economic and social cohesion
Fluctuation bands	Peripherality
Foreign exchange intervention	Fiscal union

REVIEW QUESTIONS

1.   Explain the term 'balance of payments'. Distinguish between the trade balance, the current account balance and the capital account balance.
2.   Imagine that the only two currencies traded on the foreign exchange market are the UK pound sterling and the Japanese yen. Explain how the UK£/yen exchange rate is determined. What factors influence this exchange rate? Explain.
3.   Explain the link between the balance of payments and the different exchange rate systems.

4. What is the objective of exchange rate policy? In the Irish context, explain how it was to be achieved (a) pre-1979; (b) in the ERM; (c) in EMU.
5. (a) Outline the three stages to EMU as laid down in the Maastricht Treaty.
   (b) What are the benefits and drawbacks to EMU as they relate specifically to Ireland?
6. How has the euro performed against the US dollar since the launch of the single currency in 1999? What factors might bring about a collapse of the single currency project?

WORKING PROBLEMS

1. Items normally found in a balance of payments statement are randomly listed in Table 15.6. You are a Central Bank employee and it is your job to set up the balance of payments statement in its new format. You are also required to insert headings where appropriate.

TABLE 15.6: THE BALANCE OF PAYMENTS, €M

Reserve assets	−2,280	Other investment	7,459
Balance on current account	706	Merchandise	17,771
Direct investment	4,422	Balance on capital account	840
Net income	−9,382	Portfolio investment	−8,466
Balance on financial account	1,135	Net errors and omissions	−2,681
Services	−9,002	Current transfers	1,319

2. Using monthly data, tabulate the value of the euro against both the UK pound and the US dollar in the twelve-month period January 1999 to December 1999.
   [Note: The European Central Bank *Annual Report* or *Monthly Bulletin* is a good source. The ECB's website is www.ecb.int.]

MULTI-CHOICE QUESTIONS

1. In the case of the UK£/US$ exchange rate, an increase in UK imports will:
   (a) push the supply curve of UK pounds to the left, leading to an increase in the UK£/US$ exchange rate;
   (b) push the demand curve for UK pounds to the right, leading to an increase in the UK£/US$ exchange rate;
   (c) push the demand curve for UK pounds to the left, leading to a reduction in the UK£/US$ exchange rate;
   (d) push the supply curve of UK pounds to the right, leading to a reduction in the UK£/US$ exchange rate;
   (e) none of the above.

2. Suppose US national income increases. All other things being equal, the euro/US$ exchange rate:
   (a) increases on account of a rise in US imports;
   (b) decreases on account of a rise in US imports;
   (c) increases on account of a rise in US exports;
   (d) decreases on account of a rise in US exports;
   (e) none of the above.

3. There is a surplus in the current account of the balance of payments. Under a fixed exchange rate system this is reflected in:
   (a) a rise in external reserves;
   (b) a fall in the exchange rate;
   (c) a fall in external reserves;
   (d) both (a) and (b) above;
   (e) both (b) and (c) above.

4. The central rate of the DM/Frf before August 1993 was DM1 = 3.3539Frf, with a 2.25% band of fluctuation. The upper limit (rounded off to two decimal points) was:
   (a) 3.56;
   (b) 3.41;
   (c) 3.28;
   (d) 3.43;
   (e) none of the above.

5. The Treaty on European Union:
   (a) is an amendment to the Treaty of Rome;
   (b) arose out of the Intergovernmental Conference of 1991;
   (c) sets out the path to EMU;
   (d) is commonly known as the Maastricht Treaty;
   (e) all of the above.

6. The Stability and Growth Pact restricts the use of:
   (a) exchange rate policy;
   (b) competition policy;
   (c) fiscal policy;
   (d) monetary policy;
   (e) none of the above.

TRUE OR FALSE (SUPPORT YOUR ANSWER)

1. The balance of payments statement always balances.

2. If the euro is the base currency and the US dollar is the counter currency, then the exchange rate is expressed as the number of US dollars per one euro.

3. Ireland and Britain joined the EMS on its inception in 1979.

4. Devaluation is simply another term for depreciation.

5. The ultimate aim of Irish exchange rate policy is parity with sterling.

6. EMU involves a monetary and fiscal union.

CASE STUDY

Extract from *The Economist*
Euro follies: The European Union's plans to repair its single currency risk missing the main point

At least the panic of the spring, when Greece was on the edge of default, has receded a bit. The most vulnerable euro-zone members, Greece and Ireland, still pay more for their money, but austerity measures are in place. This week the huge euro-zone bail-out fund won a much-coveted AAA rating. So this is a good time to repair the euro's rules. Next week the European Commission will present some ideas that a task force under the European Council's president, Herman Van Rompuy, will discuss. Unfortunately, the likelihood is that they will take potshots at the wrong targets and ignore deeper problems.

Europe's single currency has by no means been a disaster. It has met its main goal of price stability. Had it not existed, the European Union would in the past two years have been convulsed by a more extreme version of the currency instability that rocked it in the early 1990s. The single market would have been under serious threat. In the currency markets the euro is less disliked than the dollar. Yet it is clear from the troubles of Greece, Ireland and others that changes must be made if the euro is to survive in the long run.

Fervent federalists (and a few Eurosceptics) have rushed to claim that the euro's long-term survival requires a United States of Europe, with a big central budget. This is a pointless debate. The logic is dubious: plenty of previous examples of a shared currency, from the Latin Monetary Union to the currency union between Britain and Ireland, managed without a shared government. More important, a United States of Europe is not going to happen, because neither EU governments nor voters want it. So it is an excuse for European politicians to ignore the right answer, which is a mixture of three things: a dose of transparency, a bit more intrusion by outsiders

– and a lot of liberalising reforms by national governments. Greece is an advertisement for the first two changes. Its sudden revelation that its finances were in worse shape than it had previously admitted was proof that all euro-countries need properly independent statistical offices. It was also an argument for greater intrusion – especially by the International Monetary Fund (previously kept out of the euro zone), which can impose and monitor strict conditions for a bail-out.

The case for other forms of intrusion by Brussels is more problematic. There is talk of near-automatic sanctions on countries that break the euro's rules, such as cancelling offenders' voting rights, withholding EU funds or even suspending euro membership. But are these credible? The stability and growth pact was designed to limit budget deficits, but nobody believed its sanctions would be enforced. France and Germany flouted the pact, ignoring threats of swingeing fines. Even after the crisis, governments will not – and, being democratically elected, should not – become flunkies meekly accepting Brussels diktats. (Another intrusive idea, for euro-zone countries to guarantee a 'safe' portion of each other's debts, runs into similar problems of efficacy and sovereignty.)

Might the markets be the answer to keeping discipline in the euro zone? That investors have belatedly woken up to sovereign risk in the euro zone is to be welcomed. Pressure to trammel the markets (banning trading in credit-default swaps, setting up a more pliable European rating agency) should be dismissed as an attempt to shoot the messenger. But the markets may one day go back to sleep. One way to keep them awake would be to retain the possibility of sovereign default, and work out an orderly procedure for restructuring a euro member's debts if they become insupportable – as may still happen for Greece or even Ireland. If a euro-zone member can default, the chances are good that investors will impose tougher discipline on any country with excessive debts.

Yet neither the European Commission nor the markets can fix the euro's deeper problem, which does not lie in fiscal profligacy. Ireland and Spain did not flout the fiscal rules in the boom years, yet both are in trouble now. The bigger failing is that several (mostly Mediterranean) members have suffered a huge loss of competitiveness against Germany and other northern countries. This shows up in yawning imbalances inside the zone. Too many governments believed that, once in the euro, they could worry less about competitiveness. Actually, they should have worried more, because they have lost for ever the let-out of devaluation.

This suggests three conclusions. First, the Mediterranean countries must carry through reforms to boost productivity and curb unit labour costs (Brussels can play its part by pushing to complete the single market in services). But second, it would be folly to put the burden of adjustment solely on them, for that would create a huge deflationary bias. Germany and other surplus countries must do more to sustain growth, if need be by borrowing more when, as now, demand is weak. Third, new countries must not be let into the euro, as Greece was, before they are sufficiently flexible to cope. If the commission and Mr Van Rompuy fail to press these points, they will be dancing around the heart of the matter.

Source: The Economist, 23 September 2010.

Questions

1. What are the arguments made in favour of a single currency? In Ireland's case, what were the arguments made against membership of the single currency? In terms of the latter, are these arguments still relevant today?
2. In the design of the single currency for the euro area countries, what were the main rules to enforce fiscal discipline and prevent fiscal profligacy? Outline some problems in the specific design of these safeguards as it relates to the euro.
3. The theory behind the single currency is Robert Mundell's Optimum Currency Area. What criteria does the theory identify as important in assessing the degree of economic integration? Generally, how does the euro area do, in terms of meeting these criteria?

APPENDIX 15.1: PURCHASING POWER PARITY

PPP or the law of one price explains changes in exchange rates in terms of inflation differentials. PPP can be expressed in many different ways.

In its simplest form, the law of one price states that the price of a commodity in different countries, but expressed in a common currency, should be equal. It can be written as follows:

$$P_{\text{€}} \times E = P_{\text{US}} \qquad [1]$$

where $P_{\text{€}}$ is the price of the good in the eurozone, E is the exchange rate (expressed as the number of dollars per one euro) and P_{US} is the price of the same good, sold in the USA and expressed in US dollars. This is called the strong version of PPP.[30]

For example, we can compare the price of a McDonald's Big Mac in the eurozone with a Big Mac in New York by adjusting for the exchange rate.[31] In 2010, a Big Mac cost €3.38 on average in the eurozone and US$3.73 in the USA. The actual exchange rate in 2010 was €1 = $1.28. We can compare the two prices by converting into a common currency. Consider converting euros into dollars, as follows,

$$€3.38 \times 1.28 = US\$4.33$$

By converting into a common currency, in this case US$, we can compare the price of a Big Mac in the USA with the price in the eurozone. If these prices are equal we can say that the law of one price holds. In this case they are not equal. In the USA, a Big Mac costs US$3.73 whereas according to the law of one price a Big Mac in the USA should cost US$4.33. This begs the question – why, in theory at least, should they be equal and why, it seems in practice, are they not equal? In theory, prices should equate across frontiers because of price competition and arbitrage where arbitrage is the buying and selling of goods in different markets in order to exploit price differentials and to make a riskless profit. Suppose, for example, that a personal computer is relatively cheap in the USA compared to the eurozone. By buying them in the USA and selling them in the eurozone, a profit can be made. As a result, US exports will increase. Holding all other things equal, this will give rise to a balance of payments surplus in the USA.

Two possible results may emerge. First, the balance of payments surplus will cause an increase in the exchange rate (explained in Section 15.3). Second, the increase in demand for computers will push up the domestic price level. Either way, the differential between the domestic price level and the foreign price level diminishes. Over time, the price differential between the personal computer sold in the USA and that sold in the eurozone disappears.

In the real world, however, factors exist which allow price differentials to persist. These factors include transport costs, tariffs, quotas and indirect taxes. These drive a wedge between prices.

APPENDIX 15.2: THE MUNDELL-FLEMING MODEL

We use the Mundell-Fleming model, which was first developed in the early 1960s, to assess the effectiveness of fiscal and monetary policy within an open economy framework. We examine both policies under fixed and flexible exchange rate systems with the assumption that capital flows are perfectly mobile.

Monetary policy under a fixed exchange rate regime

Consider an increase in the money supply by the Central Bank. As the money supply increases, interest rates fall and national income increases. Because domestic interest rates are lower than world interest rates, an outflow of capital results. A deficit in the current account also emerges as a result of the higher income levels and the subsequent higher import levels. We know from our analysis of the exchange rate market that an overall balance of payments deficit causes a depreciation of the domestic currency against other currencies. Because of its membership in the exchange rate system, the Central Bank is obliged to maintain the value of its currency. Hence, the Central Bank intervenes by selling the stock of foreign currency in exchange for domestic currency. By taking this domestic currency out of circulation the domestic money supply decreases. In doing so, the economy reverts to its original level of national income. Hence, an independent monetary policy is ineffective.

Fiscal policy under a fixed exchange rate regime

Consider an increase in spending by the government. As government expenditure increases, interest rates and national income levels rise. Because domestic interest rates are now higher than world interest rates, an inflow of capital results, leading to a capital account surplus. This surplus is only partly offset by a deficit in the current account which arises because the higher income level means that more goods are imported. The overall surplus results in an increase in the exchange rate. The Central Bank intervenes in order to maintain the value of the domestic currency. It buys foreign currency and sells domestic currency. By injecting more currency into circulation, the Central Bank increases the domestic money supply. In doing so, it increases income levels further. Hence, fiscal policy is effective.

Monetary policy under a flexible exchange rate regime

Consider an increase in the money supply by the Central Bank. As the money supply increases, interest rates fall. With domestic interest rates now lower than world interest rates, an outflow of capital results. A capital outflow results in a lowering of the domestic currency against other currencies. As the domestic currency depreciates, imports become more expensive and exports become cheaper. We know from the Keynesian income determination model that an increase in exports will increase the level of national income. Under this flexible exchange rate system national income increases, initially out of the increase in the money supply and subsequently from an increase in exports. Hence, monetary policy is effective.

Fiscal policy under a flexible exchange rate regime

Consider an increase in spending by the government. As government expenditure increases, interest rates and income levels rise. The increase in interest rates leads to an inflow of capital, resulting in a capital account surplus. This surplus is partly offset by a deficit in the current account which arises from the higher income levels and the higher import levels. This overall balance of payments surplus results in an increase in the exchange rate. As the exchange rate appreciates, exports become more expensive whereas imports become cheaper. The subsequent decline in exports reduces the income level which in turn reverts to its original position. Hence, fiscal policy is ineffective.

In summary, under a fixed exchange rate system fiscal policy is more effective than monetary policy whereas under a flexible exchange rate system monetary policy is more effective than fiscal policy.

CHAPTER 16

Explaining the Macroeconomy – The AD/AS Model

> 'Although economists can tell the government much about how to influence aggregate demand, they can tell it precious little about how to influence aggregate supply.'[1]
>
> ALAN S. BLINDER

> 'To many economists this [supply-side economics] has the potential to be the greatest single breakthrough in economic thinking since the Keynesian revolution.'[2]
>
> MARK BROWNRIGG

CHAPTER OBJECTIVES

Upon completing this chapter, the student should understand:

- aggregate demand;
- aggregate supply and potential output;
- short-run and long-run aggregate supply;
- macroeconomic equilibrium;
- demand-management policies;
- supply-side policies.

OUTLINE

16.1   Aggregate demand
16.2   Aggregate supply
16.3   The policy debate
16.4   The Irish experience

INTRODUCTION

Until now our analysis of macroeconomics has been limited. Our model of the economy is incomplete. For one, the focus has been exclusively on the demand side of the economy. We considered planned expenditure or spending. We assumed that the supply side of the economy was passive, reacting largely to changes in aggregate demand. Policy considerations were limited to demand-side policies, i.e. fiscal or monetary policy. In addition, prices were fixed throughout the short-run model. Therefore, we could not explore inflation, a possible side-effect of government demand-side policies.

A complete model of the economy is inherently complex with many different variables. In this chapter, we discuss a model called the aggregate demand/aggregate supply (AD/AS) model. Both the demand and the supply sides of the economy are considered. Price is a variable. The purpose of the AD/AS model is to provide the student with a more complete framework which can be used to analyse macroeconomic principles and policy options.

16.1 AGGREGATE DEMAND

In the Keynesian model of income determination we defined aggregate expenditure as the total spending in the economy by all economic agents. It is comprised of consumer expenditure, investment expenditure, government expenditure and net exports. With the help of the income determination model, we examined the level of expenditure at each level of income. We now examine the level of expenditure at each price level.

Definition

Aggregate demand is the total output which is demanded at each price level holding all other variables constant.

The curve (or line) which shows the relationship between the level of demand and the aggregate price level is called the aggregate demand curve, or simply the AD curve.

The AD curve is normally downward sloping, showing that the lower the price level, the greater will be the aggregate quantity of goods and services demanded in the economy. The demand for national output is inversely related to the price level.

This negative relationship between price and the aggregate quantity of goods and services demanded exists for a number of reasons. First, as the price level falls, the purchasing power of money balances increases. This results in an increase in people's wealth. This so-called real balance or wealth effect leads to a rise in consumption.[3] As consumption increases, aggregate demand increases. This effect may be small on account of the weak link between prices, wealth and consumption.

Second, the increase in purchasing power arising out of lower prices may induce a separate effect. Lower prices translate into higher real money supply. This, in turn, forces interest rates downwards. The lower cost of borrowing induces greater investment expenditure by firms and possibly greater spending by households. As investment increases, aggregate demand increases. This is called the interest rate effect and it may also be weak.

A third reason why the AD curve slopes downwards is called the international trade effect. As the price level falls (or, to be more accurate, as the domestic price level falls relative to the foreign price level) domestic firms become more competitive. Accordingly, the level of domestically produced goods sold in foreign markets increases, i.e. exports increase. As exports increase, aggregate demand increases.

Derivation of the AD curve

In order to derive the AD curve we return to the income determination model. The top panel of Figure 16.1 is similar to Figure 14.2, but now with variable prices. Aggregate expenditure is measured on the vertical axis and income is measured on the horizontal axis. The AE curve shows total spending for each level of income at a particular price level.

We now examine the relationship between aggregate expenditure and price. The AE curve is drawn for a price level, P^0. The equilibrium level of income is Y^0. Suppose prices fall. We know from our previous discussion that as prices fall aggregate expenditure rises. This is reflected in the higher AE curve, AE (P^1). The higher AE level results in a higher level of equilibrium income, in this case, Y^1. As price continues to fall, to P^2, AE rises further leading to, yet again, a higher level of income, Y^2. The result in (P,Y) space is a locus of points which form a downward sloping AD curve.

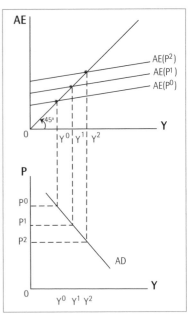

FIGURE 16.1: DERIVING THE AD CURVE

Definition

The aggregate demand (AD) curve shows the level of national output demanded at different price levels.

As the aggregate price level rises, the quantity of output demanded falls. An alternative way of deriving the AD curve is depicted in Appendix 16.1.

We have already stated that the real balance and interest rate effects may be quite small. Hence, the increase in aggregate expenditure arising out of the fall in prices is small. In graphic terms, the upward shift of the AE curve is quite modest. As a result, the subsequent AD curve is likely to be relatively inelastic or steep.

The AD curve depicts the relationship between price and total output demanded, *ceteris paribus*. The variables which we are holding constant include government spending, taxes and the money supply. A change in any of these factors will cause a shift of the aggregate demand curve. We will examine changes in the underlying variables in greater detail in Section 16.3.

16.2 AGGREGATE SUPPLY

The term 'aggregate supply' is a macroeconomic concept.

Definition

Aggregate supply describes the total quantity of national output supplied by all producers at each level of price.

It is closely associated with the capacity of the economy to produce. This is often referred to as potential output.

Definition

Potential output represents the maximum level of output that can be produced given a country's productive capacity.

It is determined by the amount of natural, capital and human resources available and the efficiency with which these resources can be put to use.

The aggregate supply curve or simply the AS curve is to macroeconomics what the supply curve (of Chapter 2) is to microeconomics. It is, however, much more complex than the individual or market supply curve.

> **Definition**
>
> *The aggregate supply (AS) curve shows the output of GDP produced at different price levels.*

There is a distinction between the short-run AS curve and the long-run AS curve. This distinction is largely based on the speed at which factor inputs, particularly labour, react to a change in economic conditions.

In the short run, the costs of factors of production are assumed to be constant or at least to respond slowly to changes in the demand for the factor input. For example, wage rates may be constant in the short run because of contracts between employers and employees. In the long run, wages and prices are assumed to be fully flexible, with output levels independent of price changes.

A positive relationship between output and prices is depicted in an upward sloping AS curve. It is drawn in Figure 16.2.

The AS curve, as drawn in Figure 16.2, becomes steeper as the level of national income increases. Why?

Initially, the AS curve is elastic. At low levels of output, there is excess capacity in the economy. Thus, a small increase in the price level, from P^0 to P^1, elicits a large increase in output, from Y^0 to Y^1.

The next portion of the AS curve is steeper. From our discussion in Chapter 5, we know that in the short run, some inputs are fixed and others are variable. As production levels increase, some firms reach full capacity. Further, as all firms demand more labour and other variable inputs, the cost of those inputs may increase. If prices continue to rise, output increases, but only by small increments. An increase in the price level from P^1 to P^2, similar in magnitude to the last price increase, leads to a much smaller increase in output, from Y^1 to Y^2.

FIGURE 16.2: THE CONVENTIONAL UPWARD SLOPING AS CURVE

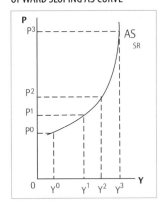

The final section of this AS curve is inelastic. We can think of Y^3 as the limit of what this economy can produce if all of its factors of production are fully employed. Even if the price level increases above P^3, the level of national output will not expand.

The AS curve is drawn to show the relationship between national output and price, *ceteris paribus*. The variables which are held constant include technology, the capital stock and the skills of the labour force. Any change in these determinants will alter the position of the AS curve. We will examine changes that shift the AS curve in greater detail in the next section.

This version of the AS curve combines the extreme classical and Keynesian views which are based on different assumptions about the labour market (see Section 11.3 for a more complete discussion on the differences between the classical and Keynesian interpretations of the labour market). We will look briefly at the two perspectives.

The classical view

According to classical economists, the output of the economy is based on the labour market. As long as wages and prices are flexible, the labour market returns to full-employment equilibrium.

Labour is combined with the economy's other inputs to produce goods and services. Therefore, in the classical view, the real output of the economy is the same as the potential output because all factors of production are fully employed. The classical AS curve is vertical at the full-employment output level, as shown in panel (a) of Figure 16.3.

FIGURE 16.3: THE EXTREME CLASSICAL AND KEYNESIAN AS CURVES

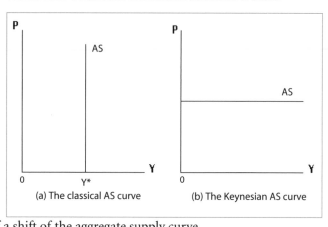

(a) The classical AS curve   (b) The Keynesian AS curve

The inelastic AS curve means that output is unresponsive to changes in the price level. Any change in output occurs because of a shift of the aggregate supply curve.

The Keynesian view

Recall from our discussion in Chapter 11 that, from the Keynesian perspective, demand for labour depends on the demand for output. In other words, causation is reversed. In the classical model, national output is determined by the number of people employed when the labour market is at equilibrium. From the Keynesian perspective, the number of people employed is derived from the demand for goods.

Also, recall that Keynes believed that there are institutional factors which cause wages to be rigid in the short run. In other words, firms can hire additional workers at the same wage that they are paying their current labour force. If firms are producing at less than full capacity, they can increase their variable inputs and increase production at a constant cost per unit.

This means that as demand increases, the level of output will increase, even though the price level has not changed. In other words, the short-run AS curve is perfectly elastic as shown in panel (b) of Figure 16.3.

As stated previously, the upward sloping AS curve is an intermediate position between the extreme views of the classicals and the Keynesians.

The elastic portion of the AS curve as shown in Figure 16.2 is Keynesian. At low levels of output, where there is excess capacity, changes in output can occur without increasing the price level. This means that over a range of production, the cost of variable inputs, particularly labour, is not changing. The upward sloping portion of the AS curve means that, as the price level rises, the level of production increases. The vertical section of the AS curve reflects the classical view that the maximum output of an economy is constrained at the level where all factors of production are fully employed.

FIGURE 16.4: THE LONG-RUN AS CURVE

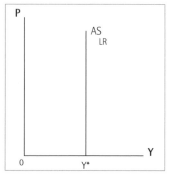

In the long run, changes to factor prices and, in particular, wages are incorporated into the model. Input prices adjust fully to changes in the price level in the long run. There is no dispute between Keynesians and classical economists concerning the aggregate supply curve in the long run. The vertical long-run AS curve is drawn in Figure 16.4, at the potential level of national output, Y*. It shows the maximum output that the economy is able to produce at different price levels, assuming that input prices fully adjust to changing economic conditions.

16.3 THE POLICY DEBATE

The AD/AS model is the centrepiece of modern macroeconomics. Both the demand and supply aspects of the economy are considered. Price changes are also incorporated in the analysis. Short-run equilibrium in the AD/AS model is shown in Figure 16.5, using the more conventional (as opposed to the horizontal) upward sloping AS curve.

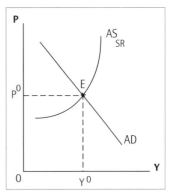

FIGURE 16.5: EQUILIBRIUM IN (P,Y) SPACE

The downward sloping AD curve depicts the relationship between total spending and different price levels. The upward sloping, short-run AS curve shows the level of output which the economy produces at different price levels. Macroeconomic equilibrium occurs at (P^0, Y^0), the intersection of the AD and the AS curves. At this point the output which households and firms demand is equal to the output which firms are willing to supply. Hence, equilibrium price and output are simultaneously determined by the interaction of aggregate demand and supply.

If the price level is above equilibrium, aggregate supply exceeds aggregate demand. For equilibrium to be restored, price must adjust downwards. Similarly, if the price level is below equilibrium, aggregate demand exceeds aggregate supply resulting in an excess demand of goods and services. In order for equilibrium to be restored, price adjusts upwards. At P^0, aggregate demand equals aggregate supply.

With a more complete model of the economy than before, we can analyse the full effects of both demand-management policies and supply-side policies. The analysis is divided into short-run and long-run effects.

We begin, however, with a brief explanation of both types of policy. We previously defined demand-management policies as the collective term used to explain various government policies which target the level of aggregate demand in the economy.

Examples of demand-management policies include changes in government spending, the tax rate, the money supply or the interest rate. Any of these policies will shift the AD curve.

Definition

Supply-side policies are targeted at increasing the productive capacity of the economy.

Measures include improving the infrastructure, adopting training programmes to reduce the costs of production and developing new technologies.

Any of these policies will shift the AS curve.

Short-run analysis

Demand-management policies

We will use the AD/AS model to assess the effect of discretionary fiscal policy on the aggregate price level and national income.

> **Definition**
>
> *Discretionary fiscal policy refers to deliberate, as opposed to automatic, changes in government expenditure or tax rates in order to influence national income.*

Expansionary fiscal policy involves increasing government spending or cutting the tax rate in an effort to increase national income. Contractionary fiscal policy is initiated by decreasing government spending or raising the tax rate.

The AD curve is initially drawn for one set of fiscal policy variables, i.e. a particular level of government spending and a particular tax rate. Any change in a fiscal policy variable causes the AD curve to shift. Figure 16.6 illustrates the effect that an increase in government spending has on the aggregate demand curve.

In effect, the increase in government expenditure shifts the original AD curve to the right. Along AD^1, there is a higher level of output demanded for each given price level. Alternatively, contractionary fiscal policy, initiated by a decrease in government spending, shifts the AD curve to the left.

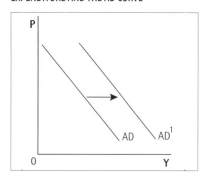

FIGURE 16.6: AN INCREASE IN GOVERNMENT EXPENDITURE AND THE AD CURVE

The analysis is incomplete without the supply side of the economy. The overall effect in the short run is illustrated in Figure 16.7 (assuming factor prices are not completely flexible).

The more conventional upward sloping short-run AS curve is depicted in Figure 16.7. The economy is initially in equilibrium at the intersection of the AD curve and the AS curve: at the point (P^0,Y^0). We know from our previous analysis that an increase in government expenditure shifts the AD curve to the right, from AD to AD^1. At the original price level, P^0, there is excess demand caused by the increase in government expenditure. In order to re-establish equilibrium, the price level must rise. At the new equilibrium (P^1,Y^1), both price and output have increased. The extent of the output increase and the price rise will depend on the potential output of the economy and in particular the sensitivity of output changes to price changes. This is reflected in the slope of the AS curve.

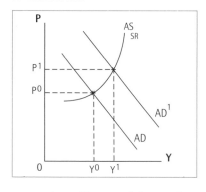

FIGURE 16.7: EXPANSIONARY FISCAL POLICY IN THE SHORT RUN

In this model, the increase in aggregate demand causes the price level to rise, which partly offsets any subsequent change in output. The final result is a combination of higher prices and higher output but with a smaller change in output than in the Keynesian model of income determination (see below).

We have illustrated demand management using the example of an increase in government spending. However, a tax cut or an increase in the money supply would result in a similar rightward shift of the AD curve. Contractionary monetary or fiscal policy results in a leftward shift of the AD curve.

Keynes and the classicals

The increase in output from Y^0 to Y^1 in Figure 16.7 is less than the increase which arose out of the simple Keynesian model. The difference is accounted for by the price change. In the short-run Keynesian income model, prices are fixed. We assume that firms expand their output without increasing the price. In terms of the economy, production can expand without increasing the price level. Hence, any change in autonomous spending results, via the multiplier process, in a change in equilibrium output.

The Keynesian AS curve is depicted in panel (a) of Figure 16.8. We can see that a change in demand, caused by an increase in government spending, has a different result than what emerged from the conventional short-run AS curve.

Because the aggregate supply curve is perfectly elastic, an increase in government expenditure leads to a change in national income without changing the price level. For Keynes, excess capacity meant that idle factors of production could be put to work without fuelling inflationary pressures. If the AS curve is horizontal, the expansionary fiscal policies which Keynes advocated are rational and advisable.

FIGURE 16.8: EXPANSIONARY FISCAL POLICY: THE KEYNESIAN AND CLASSICAL CASES

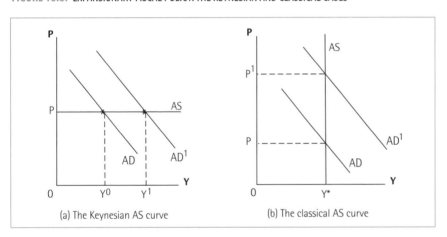

(a) The Keynesian AS curve

(b) The classical AS curve

The classical aggregate supply curve is depicted in panel (b) of Figure 16.8. From the classical perspective, expansionary fiscal policy is indefensible. With a vertical AS curve, an increase in government expenditure results only in higher prices. There is no change in the level of national output. Again, this reflects the classical assumption that output is determined by real factors such as, among others, technology and the training of human capital. From the classical perspective, demand-management measures can only lead to changes in price.

Supply-side policies

Aggregate supply is determined by a number of factors, including technology, population size and capital accumulation. Supply-side policies generally promote private enterprise within the market system by cutting costs or increasing incentives in order to stimulate output.[4] These policies found favour with both the US President Ronald Reagan and the UK Prime Minister Margaret Thatcher during their time in office (see Information Box 16.1). Examples of supply-side policies are included below.

The functioning of the market is enhanced by:

- reducing government controls;
- promoting competition;
- privatisation and deregulation;
- legislating against monopolies.

Costs are reduced by:

- cutting tax on labour (reductions in marginal tax rates and social insurance rates);
- cutting benefits and reforming the welfare state.

The incentive system is improved by:

- lowering capital gains tax and corporation tax;
- encouraging profit-related pay and wider share ownership.

Many commentators regard the incentive effects of tax cuts as the central plank of supply-side economics. Whereas Keynesians emphasise the demand-side effects of a tax cut, supply siders focus in on the supply-side effect. They argue that lower taxes increase incentives and, in turn, stimulate work, savings, risk-taking and investment. For Keynesians, a tax cut shifts the aggregate demand curve to the right, while for supply siders, a tax cut shifts the aggregate supply curve to the right. Although this seems to be a relatively minor point, the implications are not. For the Keynesians, government action is leading to an increase in output. For the supply siders, the reduction of government involvement is improving the incentive system which promotes expansion in the private sector. The key to long-term growth for supply siders is to unleash the productive capacity of the private sector.

The AS curve describes the relationship between price and national output, *ceteris paribus*. Among the variables which are held constant are the level of technology, the skills of the labour force and the availability of natural resources. Any change in these factors causes a shift of the AS curve. An example is illustrated in Figure 16.9.

Equilibrium is initially at the point (P^0, Y^0). Let us suppose that the discovery of a new national source of oil allows for an expansion of the productive base of the economy, in the short run. As production costs are lowered, the AS curve shifts rightwards; firms are willing to produce more output at any given price level. The lower costs increase the likelihood of profits which, in turn, induces greater production. A new equilibrium is reached at a higher output level and a lower price level. This new equilibrium is at point (P^1, Y^1). The extent of these changes will depend on the shape of the AD curve.

FIGURE 16.9: A RIGHTWARD SHIFT OF THE AS CURVE

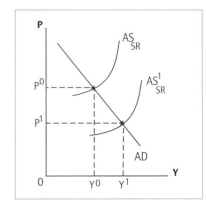

INFORMATION BOX 16.1

The supply-side policies of the 1980s

The disillusionment with Keynesian economics set in well before Reagan became the President of the United States in January 1981. The emergence of stagflation in the early 1970s left the economics profession asking many questions about the usefulness of Keynesian policies. A decade earlier, Milton Friedman criticised the active demand-management policies of previous administrations and advocated non-interventionist policies. With the 1980 election of Ronald Reagan, this economic philosophy found a political advocate. The emergence of supply-side economics is associated with the Reagan administration between 1981 and 1982.

The background to 'Reaganomics' reportedly dates back to a December evening in 1974. In the Two Continents restaurant in Washington DC, three individuals were discussing the state of the US economy: Arthur Laffer, a young economist; Richard Cheney, a White House aide under President Ford; and Jude Wanniski, an editorial writer for the *Wall Street Journal*. Laffer convinced his colleagues that the fundamental problem with the economy was the high marginal tax rates. This is the rate paid on each additional dollar earned. Laffer was discussing the relationship between the tax rate and the total tax revenue collected by the government. At low tax rates, he claimed, when tax rates rise, tax revenue increases. There was nothing sensational about this assertion.

It was his additional proposition that beyond a certain point, a cut in taxes may also increase tax revenue, which surprised his colleagues. In support of his proposition, he argued that high taxes act as a disincentive. Work, savings and investment are discouraged. By cutting taxes, the supply side of the economy is stimulated. Lower taxes increase the attractiveness of work relative to leisure. Tax avoidance declines. In addition, investment and production increase. Encouraged by lower tax rates, new workers and firms broaden the tax base. Theoretically, these new sources of tax revenue meant that the total tax revenue collected by the state would increase.

The relationship, which is known as the Laffer curve, is illustrated in Figure 16.10.

FIGURE 16.10: THE LAFFER CURVE

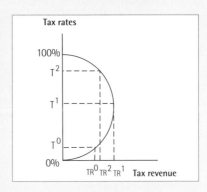

The tax rate is measured on the vertical axis and tax revenue is measured on the horizontal axis. If taxes are zero, total revenue amounts to zero. As tax rates increase, first from 0 to T^0 and then from T^0 to T^1, tax revenue increases from 0 to TR^0 and then to TR^1. Tax revenue is maximised when the tax rate is T^1. Any subsequent increase in the tax rate, from T^1 to T^2 for example, will only reduce tax revenue, in this instance from TR^1 to TR^2. Finally, if taxes are raised to 100%, nobody will work, resulting in zero tax revenue.

This diagram illustrates the essence of Laffer's argument. According to Laffer, marginal tax rates in the USA had risen during the 1970s to levels beyond T^1. A tax cut would increase the incentive to work and to invest and possibly lead to an increase in tax revenue. On that basis, cuts in personal and business taxes were justified, even though there was a national debt which the state was trying to reduce.

While many people were sceptical of these proposals, they had the support of Ronald Reagan, the Republican candidate in the 1980 presidential election. Reagan was influenced heavily by Jack Kemp, the New York Congressman who three years earlier, together with Senator William Roth of Delaware, had introduced a bill to Congress proposing a 30% cut in personal income tax over a three-year period.

On taking office, Reagan appointed Murray Weidenbaum as his first chairman of the Council of Economic Advisers. Their economic plan centred around 'the four pillars of wisdom' which were:

- steady growth of the money supply;
- regulatory reform;
- cutting personal and business taxes;
- reducing federal spending.

The Kemp-Roth tax cuts (1981–83), enacted by the Economic Recovery Tax Act of 1981, were the centrepiece of Reaganomics – cited by President Reagan as a 'second American Revolution'. The proposal was designed to cut marginal tax rates by 10% per year over a three-year period.

Supply-side economists were criticised by their peers within the neoclassical school and by Keynesian economists. Their critics included J. K. Galbraith, Walter Heller (President Kennedy's chief economist) and Herbert Stein (President Nixon's chief economic adviser). All of these economists questioned the wisdom of the supply-side policies of the Reagan administration. In the words of Heller, 'Only an ostrich could have missed the contradictions in Reaganomics.' In criticising supply siders, they highlight the record of supply-side policies – a large and rising federal debt, a failure to curtail government spending and sluggish output. They also assert that the so-called 'supply-side' Reagan recovery of the mid-1980s was largely attributable to the demand-side expansionary effects of the Reagan tax cuts rather than the supply-side effects.

Even Reagan's successor and fellow Republican George Bush was not convinced, once describing his predecessor's policies as 'voodoo economics'. Although the influence of the supply siders subsided after the early 1980s, there was a reluctance to return to the interventionist policies of previous governments. While supply-side policies may have been discredited they did manage to raise some 'justifiable' doubts about the effectiveness of demand-management policies. That is their legacy.

At the same time that Reagan was espousing the virtues of supply-side policies, Margaret Thatcher and others in the UK were embracing free-market economics. Like Reagan, Thatcher was sceptical of discretionary monetary and fiscal policies. During her three periods in office, she adopted many of the policies advocated by supply siders. Lower taxes, reforming the welfare state, reducing the power of trade unions and the privatisation programme were all examples of policies aimed at increasing competition, reducing costs and increasing productivity. Similar to the US experience, the record is one of many disappointments combined with limited successes.

Like all the other theories that went before it, supply-side policies have their shortcomings. For one, supply siders failed to produce a coherent and rigorous model of the economy. Also, the assertion that a tax cut could possibly increase tax revenue was proven incorrect by the significant increase in the US budget deficit in the early 1980s. More critically, the evidence asserting a link between tax cuts and work incentive is conflicting. Moreover, a cut in the rate of personal taxation may have demand-side as well as supply-side implications. In the long run, the output of the economy might increase. However, in the short run, if income increases in excess of output, excess demand can lead to inflationary pressures.

On a broader level, welfare 'reform', even if it is combined with lower taxes, can often lead to greater hardship for the poor in society. The removal of statutory restrictions can often lead to a return of the abuses, to the environment and banking for example, which were responsible for the imposition of the regulations in the first place. Many of these side-effects are the 'unacceptable face of capitalism', as described by former UK Prime Minister Ted Heath.

We leave the last few words on supply-side economics to Martin Feldstein. 'Experience has shown that the notion "supply-side economics" is a malleable one, easily misused by its supporters, maligned by its opponents, and misinterpreted by the public at large.'[1]

1. Feldstein, 'Supply Side Economics: Old Truths and New Chains'. *American Economic Review*, 76, May 1986.

A supply-side shock

> **Definition**
>
> *A supply-side shock or a supply disturbance refers to sudden changes in the conditions of productivity or costs which in turn impacts on aggregate supply.*

Supply-side shocks were uncommon prior to the 1970s. In 1973, and again in 1979, the world economy suffered a sudden supply-side shock in the form of higher oil prices. A more recent example was in the 1990s, when, embarking on a transition to a market economy, the former socialist countries of Central and Eastern Europe (including Russia) suffered a supply-side shock resulting in a severe recession.

The effects of the supply-side shock caused by higher oil prices in the short run are illustrated in Figure 16.11.

The economy is initially in equilibrium at (P^0, Y^0), the intersection of the AD curve and the AS curve. The increase in costs arising out of the rise in the price of oil causes a leftward shift of the AS curve. In the short run, the excess demand gives rise to an increase in the price level. Equilibrium in the short run is restored at the intersection of AD and the new AS curve, AS^1 at the point (P^1, Y^1), at E^1. This rather unusual combination of higher prices and sluggish output became known as stagflation. Another period of stagflation occurred at the end of the 1970s.

FIGURE 16.11: A SUPPLY-SIDE SHOCK

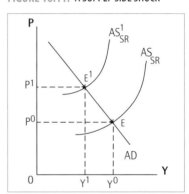

Long-run analysis

In the long run, factor costs adjust to changing economic conditions. In particular, wages will respond to changes in prices.

We know from our discussion in Section 16.2 that the long-run AS curve is vertical at the full-employment level of output. We now examine the effectiveness of demand-management policies and supply-side policies in the context of a vertical AS curve.

Demand-management policies

Consider an increase in government expenditure. We have already discovered that an increase in government expenditure shifts the AD curve to the right. In the short run, output and prices adjust upwards. In the long run, the only effect is an increase in prices: there is no change in output. This is illustrated in Figure 16.12.

We begin at the full-employment equilibrium in the short run with the AD curve intersecting the short-run AS curve, AS_{SR} at point E. Y^*, the potential output of the economy, equals the actual output. The increase in government expenditure shifts the AD curve out to the right, from AD to AD^1. The new point of intersection occurs at E^1, with prices at P^1 and output temporarily raised beyond the potential level, to Y. As a result many firms begin to experience supply bottlenecks; they want to increase production but limited resources do not permit such an increase.

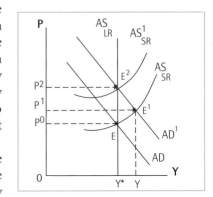

FIGURE 16.12: EXPANSIONARY FISCAL POLICY IN THE LONG RUN

The higher price level induces wage increases. The rising costs of production shift the short-run AS curve leftwards, to AS^1. The long-run equilibrium is shown by the intersection of AD^1 and AS_{LR} which is point E^2 and combination (Y^*, P^2). We can see that demand-management policies led to an increase in price from P^0 to P^2, but that output does not increase beyond the full-employment level in the long run.

To summarise, in the long run, this model predicts that a change in aggregate demand cannot affect output. The only change is a change in the level of prices.

Supply-side policies

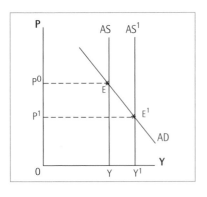

FIGURE 16.13: SUPPLY-SIDE POLICIES IN THE LONG RUN

Consider a supply-side policy directed at increasing potential output in the long run.[5] It is illustrated in Figure 16.13.

The long-run AS curve is vertical. A supply-side policy intended to increase potential output results in a rightward shift of the AS curve, from AS to AS^1. The net effect is an increase in output combined with a lower price level. This occurs because the quantity of the factor inputs increases or because existing resources are employed more efficiently. An example that will shift the supply curve is an improvement in the education or training of the labour force.

Keynes and the classicals

Keynesians and classical economists disagree about the effectiveness of supply-side policies. Essentially, the classical case is depicted above. The economy is always moving towards full-employment equilibrium. Technology and the magnitude and quality of capital and labour constrain the level of output in the economy. An economy may be able to move beyond the full-employment level of output in the short run by working overtime, but ultimately, technology or the factors of production must change to expand national output in the long run. Therefore, if the state wishes to facilitate an increase in output, policies which shift the AS curve are the only ones which will achieve this goal.

Keynes did not agree that the economy moved toward full-employment equilibrium in the short run. If people are unemployed, labour is available for employment at the market wage. It is only if the short-run equilibrium of the AD curve and AS curve is at full employment, that demand-side polices put pressure on wages and ultimately on prices. Otherwise, demand management can be used to move the economy to full employment.

Supply-side policies, on the other hand, are completely ineffective. When Keynes wrote during the Great Depression, there was excess capacity and labour was idle. Supply-side policies have the effect of increasing capacity. This scenario is illustrated in Figure 16.14.

In Figure 16.14 the AS curve is drawn with a 'kink' at a point where the factors of production are fully utilised. An increase in the aggregate supply, in this case from AS to AS¹, will have no effect on the actual output level, according to Keynesians. Output can only be increased by boosting aggregate demand.

In terms of the long run, it is not clear what Keynes thought. In effect, he saw the economy moving from short run to short run. So the question of whether an economy ever reached its long-run capacity was not an issue.

FIGURE 16.14: THE KEYNESIAN VIEW OF SUPPLY-SIDE POLICIES

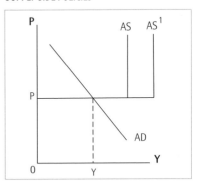

A summary of policy effectiveness

At this stage, there is a need to sum up the policy conclusions. In the short run where there are unemployed resources, there appears to be a role for demand management. Wage and price rigidities allow output to respond to changes in aggregate demand over a short period of time. In the long run, however, fiscal and monetary policies have no effect on output. Output can only be expanded in the long run by supply-side policies.

Finally, one way of explaining the differences between demand-management policies and supply-side policies is by focusing on the business cycle. Figure 16.15 illustrates the business cycle.

The actual output line depicts the annual increase in national output, as measured by changes in GDP. The potential output line depicts the rate at which the economy would grow if all resources were fully utilised. The purpose of demand-side policies is to stabilise actual output close to its potential. In terms of Figure 16.15 this involves the convergence of the actual output and the potential output lines. This entails short-term fine-tuning of the economy through frequent changes in tax rates, money supply, interest rates and expenditure levels.

In contrast, the purpose of supply-side policies is to increase potential output beyond its present levels. In terms of Figure 16.15 an upward shift of the potential output line is sought. This involves a long-term strategy, enhancing the efficiencies of the market system and lowering production costs wherever possible.

FIGURE 16.15: THE BUSINESS CYCLE

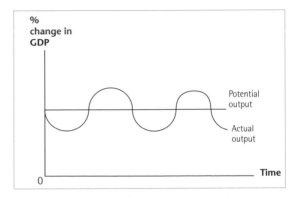

We will end this section with a note by A. Protopapadakis which summarises the value of both demand-management and supply-side policies:

> 'supply-side policies should not be looked at to replace counter-cyclical demand-management policies. Demand management may be the appropriate policy response to recessions that periodically are brought about by special sequences of economic events. But these policies are ill-suited to improving long-term growth in productivity and output, because they don't necessarily increase incentives to produce, save and invest. Supply-side policies do precisely that, but they are likely to work slowly and therefore can't be used to combat recessions'.[6]

16.4 THE IRISH EXPERIENCE

Ireland's experience of demand-management policies has been well documented. Extensive use of fiscal policy was the norm during the 1970s and 1980s. At different times, this was combined with a mix of monetary, exchange rate and incomes policies.

Supply-side policies were not as prevalent in Ireland in the 1980s as they were in the UK or the USA. This was due to a number of factors.

First, in other countries there was a deeper divide between the left and right political parties. This focused the economic debate between those who favoured state intervention and those who preferred a limited role for the state. The 'right', who initiated the supply-side policies, were represented by the Republicans in the USA and by the Tories in the UK. Until the formation of the Progressive Democrats in 1985, the economic policies of the 'right' were not coherently presented by any political party in Ireland. This partly explains why Irish policy-makers were slow to adopt supply-side policies.

Second, given the state of the public finances in the early 1980s, the Irish authorities were concerned less with ideology and more with restoring order and confidence to the financial markets at home and abroad.

By the late 1980s there was some evidence of a change in policy. Two semi-state companies, Irish Life and Irish Sugar (Greencore), were privatised. Other state bodies such as B&I and Irish Steel were sold to foreign companies. A plan to restructure Aer Lingus was agreed and implemented. The remaining semi-state companies were encouraged to cut costs with a view to competitiveness, commercialisation and future competition from foreign companies.

Taxes on labour were cut in order to increase the incentives for both employers and employees. Controls on public expenditure were also implemented. Pump-priming the economy was frowned upon. The business sector was also targeted via a lowering of corporate taxes, an expansion of the Business Expansion Scheme (BES), an increase in profit-sharing schemes and tax reliefs relating to capital acquisition.

During the 1990s, the Culliton report became the blueprint for job creation in Ireland.[7] Among its many recommendations were a fundamental reform of the tax system, greater competition in air services, telecommunications and energy supply and an improvement in training in Ireland. These and many of the other sixty-plus recommendations are 'essentially supply-side in tone'.[8]

By the late 1990s, government policy was certainly supply-side in tone. Greater competition, deregulation, privatisation and tax cuts were introduced by successive governments to increase the productive capacity of an already booming economy. Paul Tansey (1998) goes further and claims that Ireland had witnessed a supply-side revolution, albeit by stealth.[9] The combination of foreign direct investment, low taxes, EU funding and an improvement in human capital had raised Ireland's productive capacity. Yet, this supply-side revolution was different from the UK and US experience. It relied much more on social partnership, government spending and public consensus than the ideological, class-based, private sector revolution associated with Reagan and Thatcher.

In conclusion, in contrast to the late 1970s and the early 1980s, by the early 1990s Irish policy-makers appeared to be concentrating on the supply side of the economy. Economic policies were aimed at the private sector. This is obvious in the privatisation of semi-state companies, including eircom and Aer Lingus. A sustained effort to improve the incentive system through tax and welfare reform had broad support across the political spectrum. Irish industrial policy encouraged technological change and constant upgrading of the factors of production. All of these policies were aimed at increasing the potential national output. In short, they were designed to shift the aggregate supply curve. Furthermore, Ireland's membership of the eurozone constrained its use of demand management instruments. This increased Ireland's reliance on supply-side measures.

CASE STUDY

Extract from *The Financial Times*
Growth raises real spectre of over-heating Ireland
by John Murray-Brown

Ireland's economy continues to grow at record levels, outpacing the rest of Europe. With the republic now part of the eurozone, interest rates are close to historic lows. Consumer demand looks set to continue to grow, with the government promising tax cuts to sweeten the unions. At first glance, it would seem a recipe for over-heating. Add to that a housing market which is booming for the fifth straight year, and it is little wonder international commentators such as the Organisation for Economic Co-operation and Development are starting to get the jitters about the sustainability of the Irish miracle.

The OECD, in its twice-yearly *Economic Outlook*, says the risks of over-heating are rising, pointing out that unemployment is set to fall, wages are picking up steadily and house prices continuing to soar. Ireland, it says, has 'no choice' but to limit domestic demand through a contractionary budget policy. It also warns the government should not accede to wages

demands from the unions in the latest negotiations on a new pay agreement which would put Irish industry at a competitive disadvantage to its continental partners.

. . .

Part of the problem is the government is tied into a bargaining process on pay in which moderate wages are bought in exchange for tax cuts and a say in economic policy. The unions believe, with some justification, the last three-year deal did not adequately reflect the strong performance of the economy. Corporate profits are currently rising in excess of 20 per cent, while the unions are restricted by the agreement to annual wage increases of just over 2 per cent, with some local bargaining flexibility. Pressure on wages is being fuelled by considerable labour supply problems in construction and the increasingly important information technology sectors. Eunan King, senior economist with NCB stockbrokers, says labour shortages will increase unless immigration rises as

→

employment opportunities are rising faster than current growth in the labour supply. According to official figures, employment rose by 97,000 in the year to May while the numbers in the labour market only grew by 67,000. As a result unemployment has fallen. Mr King says the government needs to consider policy changes to stimulate more immigration flows, whether through a liberalisation of non-EU immigration or a policy which targets UK labour by lowering taxes, which still act as a disincentive to workers coming to Ireland from the UK.

The other pressure on prices comes from the threat posed by increased competition and privatisation. The recent arrival of Bank of Scotland in the mortgage market and Northern Rock undercutting local banks in the deposit market has underlined that banking in Ireland is due for a further shake out. Telecom and other utility prices have further to fall if Irish services are going to come down in line with the UK and other continental European economies – all of which will put downward pressure on inflation. A more

long-term challenge for the authorities is the strain Ireland's recent growth rate is putting on the country's infrastructure, with bottlenecks appearing. The strains on the system were underlined on one Friday last month, when telephone and mobile systems in the whole of the south Dublin area went down for more than two hours after an overload at one of the main telephone companies.

The government's response to this crisis is pure Keynes, increasing the capacity of the economy through a major programme of public works. In mid-November, Charlie McCreevy, the finance minister, announced a £40bn national development plan aimed at boosting the infrastructural capacity of the economy, with major spending in transport, education and energy. Bernard Feeney, director with Goodbody stockbrokers, says that while the ambitious spending programme is welcome, 'its success depends on the government's commitment to speed up the planning and procurement processes and take action to address the labour supply shortages'.

Source: *The Financial Times*, 3 December 1999.

Questions

1. Show, using the AD/AS model, how each of the following demand policies affect prices and output:
   (a) a Keynesian-style public works programme;
   (b) a contractionary budget policy.
2. Comment on the statement that the 'government's response to this crisis is pure Keynes, increasing the capacity of the economy through a major programme of public works.'
3. What supply-side measures are referred to in the article?

Answers on website

SUMMARY

1. Aggregate demand refers to the total quantity of output demanded at different price levels. There is a negative relationship between aggregate demand and price and this is represented by a downward sloping AD curve. The wealth effect, the interest rate effect and the international trade effect are the reasons for the negative relationship. The AD curve is drawn for given levels of autonomous spending. Any change in autonomous spending or monetary variables results in a shift of the AD curve.

2. Aggregate supply is the total output supplied at different price levels. Potential output refers to the maximum output that a country can produce given the resources available and the efficiency with which they are put to use. The AS curve relates output levels to price levels. Factors such as technology, the level of human capital and capital accumulation determine the position of the AS curve.

3. There is a distinction between the AS curve in the short run and the long-run AS curve. The assumption underlying the short-run AS curve is that factor costs are constant. Hence, the AS curve is horizontal at the aggregate price level. In the long run factor costs can vary; they adjust fully to price changes. With complete adjustments in the long run possible, the AS curve is vertical at the full-employment level of output. It is unresponsive to changes in the price level. An intermediate case is the upward sloping AS curve.

4. Demand-side policies include both fiscal and monetary policy. They are designed to influence the level of expenditure in the economy and, in turn, the level of output. In the short run, expansionary demand-side policies result in higher output levels and higher prices. Contractionary demand-side policies reduce both output levels and prices. In the long run a change in aggregate demand cannot affect output. The only change is in the level of prices.

5. Supply-side economics is concerned with changing the aggregate supply. Supply-side policies seek to influence production directly, by lowering production costs or by increasing incentives. A supply-side shock refers to changes in the conditions of productivity or costs which in turn affect aggregate supply. The adverse effects of a negative supply-side shock are twofold: higher prices and lower output.

6. The Irish authorities were slow to adopt demand-management policies. Active use of short-term fiscal policy only became the norm in the mid-1970s. Once tried, demand-side policies were extensively used thereafter. Supply-side policies were largely absent until the late 1980s. Possible reasons include the absence of a right-left political divide and the concern over the state of the public finances. There was some evidence of supply-side influences in economic policy by the 1990s.

KEY TERMS

Aggregate demand
Real balance effect
AD curve
Aggregate supply
Potential output
Short-run AS curve
Long-run AS curve
Full-employment output level
Macroeconomic equilibrium

Demand-management policies
Supply-side policies
Discretionary fiscal policy
Reaganomics
Laffer curve
Supply-side shock
Business cycle

REVIEW QUESTIONS

1. Outline the reasons why the AD curve is downward sloping. What causes a shift of the AD curve?
2. Explain why the AS curve might slope upwards. What accounts for the difference between the short-run and the long-run AS curves?
3. Using a short-run AD/AS model, explain what effect a contractionary fiscal policy would have on the equilibrium price and output.
4. What is a supply-side shock? Use the AD/AS model to illustrate the effect of an adverse supply-side shock on the equilibrium price and output.
5. Assess the use of supply-side policies both in the USA and the UK since the early 1980s.
6. Comment on Ireland's use of both demand-management and supply-side policies.

WORKING PROBLEMS

1. Data (expressed in billions of euros) for aggregate demand and aggregate supply curves are presented in Table 16.1. The price level is presented as an index number.

TABLE 16.1

Price level	100	110	120	130	140	150	160	170	180
Aggregate demand	7.0	6.7	6.4	6.1	5.8	5.5	5.2	4.9	4.6
Aggregate supply	1.4	2.4	3.4	4.3	5.0	5.5	5.8	5.8	5.8

    (a) Plot the aggregate demand and aggregate supply curves.
    (b) What do the portions of the AS curve reflect?

2. Sketch appropriate AD/AS diagrams (as they relate to Ireland) for the following:
    (a) the expansionary phase of fiscal policy during the 1970s;
    (b) the fall in oil prices in the early 1980s.

MULTI-CHOICE QUESTIONS

1. The AD curve slopes down from left to right because of:
    (a) the international trade effect, the income effect and the substitution effect;
    (b) the price effect, the real balance effect and the substitution effect;
    (c) the income effect, the price effect and the interest rate effect;

    (d) the interest rate effect, the real balance effect and the international trade effect;
    (e) none of the above.

2. If the AD curve is relatively steep, which of the following is a likely source?
    (a) This is because the changes in AE arising out of price changes are relatively small.
    (b) A weak international trade effect.
    (c) The real balance effect is weak.
    (d) A weak interest rate effect.
    (e) All of the above.

3. Assuming spare capacity, constant input costs and a demand-constrained economy, the AS curve is:
    (a) vertical;
    (b) horizontal;
    (c) perfectly inelastic;
    (d) upward sloping;
    (e) both (b) and (c) above.

4. Under short-run conditions, contractionary demand-side policies are likely to:
    (a) reduce output and prices;
    (b) increase output, reduce prices;
    (c) increase prices, reduce output;
    (d) increase output and prices;
    (e) none of the above.

5. According to supply siders:
    (a) more government intervention is necessary;
    (b) high taxes are necessary to finance the welfare system;
    (c) higher government spending is always desirable;
    (d) tax rate cuts can cause total tax revenue to increase;
    (e) both (c) and (d) above.

6. In the long run, a change in which of the following is likely to cause a shift of the AS curve?
    (a) welfare expenditure;
    (b) money supply;
    (c) interest rates;
    (d) technology;
    (e) none of the above.

TRUE OR FALSE (SUPPORT YOUR ANSWER)

1. The AD curve shows total spending for each level of income at a fixed price level.

2. Underlying the short-run AS curve is the assumption that all prices are flexible.

3. The classical AS curve reflects supply constraints.

4. Both Keynesians and classical economists agree that the AD curve is downward sloping.

5. Supply siders perceive tax cuts as, among other things, disinflationary.

6. An adverse supply-side shock can lead to higher prices and lower output.

CASE STUDY

Extract from *OECD Economic Surveys: Ireland*
Effectiveness of policy mix of fiscal and incomes policies

Since the start of EMU in January 1999, fiscal and incomes policies have become the only demand management tools available. One of the objectives of the Stability and Growth Pact is to make budgetary room for manoeuvre. But the effectiveness of fiscal policy is perceived to be quite limited in the first place because of the openness of the Irish economy. Although joining EMU may in theory strengthen the effectiveness of fiscal policy in the short run because of the disappearance of crowding-out effects as domestic interest and exchange rates become virtually exogenous, in practice the effectiveness of fiscal policy is likely to be rather small and will be eroded further by greater regional integration in the long run. Thus, the effect of fiscal policy on output seems limited; indeed, how sensible it is for a 'regional' government to adopt active demand management is unclear.

. . .

It is not easy to assess the impact of a discretionary fiscal action on the economy when its supply-side effect is significant. Suppose, for example, that the announced future cuts in income tax rates by 4 percentage points were to be postponed as a way of restraining aggregate demand. If the postponement is perceived to be temporary, thereby leaving aggregate demand almost unchanged, inflation might even pick up as labour supply decreases (compared with the baseline of no postponement) in response to this announcement. The elasticity of labour supply in Ireland is likely to remain higher than those of other countries because another source of labour supply, migration, is available in addition to intertemporal substitution. Hence, only if the postponement is perceived to be permanent will the effect on demand be important. However, because people understand that the partnership approach ensures low nominal pre-tax wage growth and competitiveness in exchange for tax cuts, the permanence of any postponement might not be credible. Thus, taking account of the effects on the supply side, the effectiveness of discretionary fiscal policy seems even more limited.

The authorities' inclination to use the budget as a policy instrument to improve the supply side, rather than to manage aggregate demand, makes sense. Given the current low tax rate compared to other countries, however, tax tools should be used selectively. In this sense, tax measures to reinforce work incentives incorporated in the 1999 Budget can be considered as a step in the right direction.

Source: OECD Economic Surveys: Ireland, 1999.

Questions

1. Using the AD/AS model, show how active demand-management policies can affect prices and output.
2. Outline, using the AD/AS framework, the favourable supply-side effects arising from the type of discretionary fiscal policy outlined in the extract.
3. Identify some of the reasons given for why expansionary fiscal policy is inappropriate for Ireland, particularly in response to the economic crisis of the late 2000s.

APPENDIX 16.1: USING THE IS/LM MODEL TO DERIVE THE AD CURVE

FIGURE 16.16: DERIVING THE AD CURVE

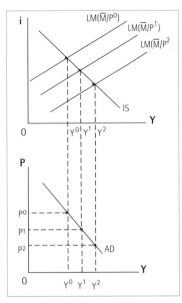

An alternative way to derive the AD curve is by using the IS/LM model. The IS curve is drawn for a given level of autonomous spending. The LM curve is drawn for a given real money supply. At a given price level P^0 the IS and LM curves intersect, giving us our first equilibrium level of national income, Y^0. In turn, we have our first point in (P,Y) space.

Suppose the price level falls. As price falls from P^0 to P^1, the real money supply increases from $\dfrac{\overline{M}}{P^0}$ to $\dfrac{\overline{M}}{P^1}$.

The LM curve shifts rightwards, from $LM\left(\dfrac{\overline{M}}{P^0}\right)$ to $LM\left(\dfrac{\overline{M}}{P^1}\right)$.

This results in a new and higher level of equilibrium income, Y^1 and our second point in (P, Y) space.

Assume the price level falls further. The fall in price from P^1 to P^2 results in a further increase in the real money supply, causing another rightward shift of the LM curve. This new equilibrium point results in another and yet again higher equilibrium level of income, Y^2. This is our third point in (P,Y) space.

A similar exercise can be carried out for all possible price levels. The subsequent income levels provide us with a relationship between the aggregate price level and national income. The relationship is depicted by a downward sloping AD curve. The goods market and the money market are both in equilibrium at every point on the AD curve.

CHAPTER 17

Macroeconomic Issues

'*Inflation occurs when too much money is chasing too few goods.*'

ANONYMOUS

'*We believe that if men have the talent to invent new machines that put men out of work, they have the talent to put those men back to work.*'[1]

JOHN F. KENNEDY

'*No nation was ever ruined by trade.*'[2]

BENJAMIN FRANKLIN

CHAPTER OBJECTIVES

Upon completing this chapter, the student should understand:

- the meaning of inflation;
- the causes, consequences and remedies;
- problems of defining and measuring unemployment;
- the costs and theories of unemployment;
- traditional trade theory, comparative advantage and trade barriers;
- new trade theory and economies of scale.

OUTLINE

17.1 **Inflation**
17.2 **Unemployment**
17.3 **International trade**

INTRODUCTION

There are many important and controversial issues in macroeconomics. Throughout the centuries, economists, sociologists and philosophers together with taxi drivers, domestic workers and shopkeepers have argued over the costs of inflation, the evils of unemployment and the merits of free trade. The debate remains lively because problems relating to these issues remain unresolved.

In this chapter, we will begin by discussing the issue of inflation and then continue with the topics of unemployment and international trade.

17.1 INFLATION

17.1.1 Defining and measuring inflation

We will begin by defining the relevant terms.

> **Definition**
>
> *Inflation refers to a rise in the general or aggregate price level.*

Alternatively, inflation can be defined as a fall in the value of money because it erodes the purchasing power of money. In any discussion on inflation, we generally refer to changes in the inflation rate.

> **Definition**
>
> *The inflation rate is the percentage change in the price level from one period to the next period.*

Since inflation refers to an increase in the price level, the percentage change is positive.

> **Definition**
>
> *Deflation is a fall in the general level of prices.*

In this situation, the percentage change in the price level is negative; the price level is falling from one period to the next. Often, this term is used loosely, to refer to policies or events which will lead to a slowdown in economic activity. Contractionary monetary and fiscal policies are sometimes labelled as 'deflationary'. A more accurate description is 'disinflationary'.

> **Definition**
>
> *Disinflation is defined as a reduction in the rate of inflation.*

In this case, the rate of inflation is positive but decreasing from one period to the next. Contractionary policies normally reduce, rather than reverse inflation.

There are different categories of inflation including creeping inflation, hyper-inflation and stagflation. Creeping inflation exists when the rise in the price level is both relatively modest and stable. Hyper-inflation refers to a situation where inflation is escalating and the value of money diminishes so quickly that it ceases to perform its main functions. Table 17.1 shows the unfortunate state of the Hungarian currency between 1938 and 1946. Finally, stagflation refers to the simultaneous existence of both high rates of inflation and stagnant or negative economic growth. Unemployment is often a problem during periods of hyper-inflation or stagflation.

TABLE 17.1: THE HUNGARIAN HYPER-INFLATION 1945–46

	Mid-1938 = 100	% increase at an annual rate
Mid-1939	100	–
Mid-1941	139	18
Mid-1943	217	25
15 July 1945	9,200	527
31 Aug.	17,300	15,000
30 Sept.	38,900	1,700,000
31 Oct.	250,300	5.0×10^{11}
30 Nov.	1,545,700	3.1×10^{11}
31 Dec.	3,778,000	4.5×10^{6}
31 Jan. 1946	7,089,000	1.9×10^{5}
28 Feb.	45,845,300	5.4×10^{11}
31 Mar.	205,060,000	6.4×10^{9}
30 Apr.	3,575,600,000	7.9×10^{16}
31 May	1,076,400,000,000	5.5×10^{31}
30 June	470,300,000,000,000	4.8×10^{33}
31 July	12,572,000,000,000,000,000	1.3×10^{55}

Source: Falush, P. 'The Hungarian Hyper-Inflation of 1945–46' *NatWest Quarterly Review,* August 1976.

Inflation is measured using a price index.

Definition
A price index measures the level of prices in one period as a percentage of the level in another period called the base period.

The price index most frequently discussed by the media in Ireland is the Consumer Price Index.

Definition
The Consumer Price Index (CPI) is designed to measure the average change in the level of the prices paid (inclusive of all indirect taxes) for consumer goods and services by all private households in the country.

A price index is composed of a number of goods and services, each with its own weighting. For the CPI, these weights express the proportion of the household's budget which is spent on each category of good and service. The weights are updated every seven years following the publication of the *Household Budget Survey.*[3] The 'basket of goods' used for the Irish CPI and the respective weightings of each category are shown in Table 17.2.

TABLE 17.2: WEIGHTS USED FOR THE CPI FROM 2006 BASE

Food and non-alcoholic beverages	11.7
Alcoholic beverages and tobacco	6.1
Clothing and footwear	5.4
Housing, water, electricity, gas, and other fuels	16.5
Furnishings, household equitment and routine household maintenance	4.4
Health	3.2
Transport	13.3
Communications	3.4
Recreation and culture	10.1
Education	2.0
Restaurants and hotels	15.4
Miscellaneous goods and services	8.4

Source: Central Statistics Office.

As an example, we will calculate the Irish rate of inflation for the year 2004 using the CPI. Suppose the base is December 2001. The CPI was 106.3 in 2003 and 108.6 in 2004. To find the annual inflation rate for 2004 we use the following formula:

$$\textbf{2004 Inflation rate} = \frac{\textbf{CPI 2004} - \textbf{CPI 2003}}{\textbf{CPI 2003}} \times \textbf{100} \qquad [17.1]$$

Insert values for CPI 2003 and for CPI 2004 to get:

$$\frac{108.6 - 106.3}{106.3} \times 100 = \frac{2.3}{106.3} \times 100 = 2.2\%$$

Using the CPI as an index, the inflation rate for 2004 was approximately 2.2%. In other words, the general price level in Ireland rose by 2.2% in 2004.

In Ireland the inflation rate is measured by the Central Statistics Office (CSO) on a monthly and yearly basis.

Although used in both the USA and Ireland, the CPI has a number of weaknesses. Its shortcomings include the use of a constant market basket despite frequent changes in consumption patterns, the difficulty in capturing changes in quality and the omission of asset, including housing, prices. Despite this, the CPI is considered to be the best measure of Irish inflation.

However, the Harmonised Index of Consumer Prices (HICP) is also an important measure. The HICP was introduced in 1997 as an international measure of comparison for EU member states. It was used to determine if countries met the convergence criterion on inflation for participation in the single currency. The HICP expenditure includes about 90% of the CPI total expenditure. One notable item that is missing from the HICP is mortgage interest repayments.

Finally, the GDP deflator (alluded to in Chapter 10) is a price index which measures changes in the entire range of goods and services produced in the economy. It is the most comprehensive measure of inflation. We can calculate the GDP deflator by using the following formula:

$$\boxed{\text{GDP deflator} = \frac{\text{Nominal GDP}}{\text{Real GDP}} \times 100}$$ [17.2]

For example, in 2004, nominal GDP (GDP at current prices) was €148.6bn. Real GDP or GDP at constant prices was €145.3bn. With a base year of 2003, the GDP price index or deflator is 1.02 approximately. This indicates that prices increased by just over 2% in 2004.

17.1.2 Consequences of inflation

The consequences of inflation are many and varied. Before we discuss them, we will define some relevant terms.

Definition

The nominal rate of interest is the actual rate of interest which is charged when money is borrowed.

Definition

The real rate of interest is the nominal rate of interest adjusted for the inflation rate.

It is calculated by subtracting the inflation rate from the nominal rate of interest. For example, if the nominal interest rate is 12% and the inflation rate is 5%, the real rate of interest is 7%.

Definition

People are on fixed incomes if their income is set at a particular nominal amount which is not adjusted for inflation.

Definition

Menu costs refer to the costs which result when prices are adjusted.

For example, wholesalers must publish and mail new catalogues if prices increase. At the retail level, vending machines must be reprogrammed and merchandise must be physically reticketed when prices change. These costs are explicit and are fairly easy to monitor. What is more difficult to calculate is the loss of goodwill which firms encounter if they constantly increase their prices. Also, retailing firms may be slower to reorder if all of their current stock must be repriced.

The following is a comprehensive, although not exhaustive list of the possible effects of inflation.

- Depending on the level of real interest rates, inflation can involve a redistribution of income from lenders to borrowers. For example, suppose Helen borrows €2,000 from her local bank manager at a fixed rate of interest of 6% for one year. Unexpectedly, the annual inflation rate increases to 10%. The real rate of interest paid by Helen is negative, at minus 4%. When repaying the loan, Helen will return euros to the bank which are worth less in purchasing power terms than the euros lent to her by the bank. As a result of inflation, the borrower gains at the expense of the lender. In general, borrowers welcome unanticipated inflation.

Interestingly, the biggest borrower of all can often be the government.

- Savings are adversely affected by inflation. Since inflation reduces the value of money, any stock of savings over time will lose its purchasing power. The inflation-adjusted interest rate, i.e. the real rate of interest, may be low or even negative. Hence, during inflationary times savings are discouraged and consumption is encouraged.

- Those sections of society that are on fixed incomes lose. Moreover, it is usually the more vulnerable sections of society, pensioners for example, who are on fixed incomes. In this instance inflation is a form of 'tax' on money holdings. The adjustment of incomes in line with price changes, called indexation, allows for some protection against inflation.

- Inflation often changes the pattern of investment. Capital moves out of assets like government bonds or gilts because the real rate of interest is low or negative. Investment in 'real' assets like property, fine art or gold increases because, in general, they appreciate over time. These assets are safe but unproductive. In a period characterised by growing inflation, productive investments, which lead to national economic growth, may be avoided because firms are unable to evaluate the potential for profit. Inflation breeds uncertainty which is generally unfavourable to investment decisions.

- Inflation can also affect the level of government expenditure and revenue. For example, if there is no indexation built into the tax system, tax revenues automatically increase as inflation forces more taxpayers into higher tax brackets. This is commonly known as fiscal drag. In effect, it is a transfer of resources from the taxpayer to the government.

- Inflation has serious implications for international competitiveness. For example, if Ireland's inflation rate is low relative to its trading partners' inflation rate within a fixed exchange rate system, a competitive advantage is gained. Exports increase and contribute to an increase in Irish GDP. In the absence of a fixed exchange rate system, inflation differentials can cause movements in exchange rates.

- Inflation can lead to money illusion. Money illusion exists when economic agents confuse changes in money variables with changes in real variables. In times of inflation, workers who receive higher wages might be fooled into thinking that they are better off. In reality, however, the wage increase is offset by the higher prices. These workers are said to be suffering from money illusion.

- Inflation prevents money from fulfilling its functions effectively. The primary function of money is as a medium of exchange. During periods of hyper-inflation, the domestic currency is shunned because of its rapid loss of value. If possible, exchanges are transacted in a reliable, foreign currency. Bartering, which is both time-consuming and inefficient, is often a feature of an economy experiencing hyper-inflation.

Finally, the effects of inflation are often different depending on whether inflation is anticipated or unanticipated. In general, anticipated inflation imposes fewer costs on society than unanticipated inflation. The normal costs to anticipated inflation are changes in menu costs and the extra time spent managing the finances. In turn, this may involve more frequent visits to the bank. The cost of these extra trips is called the 'shoe leather' effect.

Unanticipated inflation is not built into wage contracts or tax brackets/bands. The additional costs associated with unexpected inflation include misallocation of resources, income redistribution, tax distortions and the adverse impact on the incentive to save.

17.1.3 Explanations of inflation

Many explanations of inflation have been advanced over the years. In this section, we will look at four: demand pull, the Quantity Theory of Money, cost push and imported inflation. We will also briefly discuss the role of expectations. Although we will discuss each case separately, in reality they may occur simultaneously.

Demand pull inflation

We will begin by defining the concept of demand pull inflation and then we will explain it within the context of the model of income determination.

> **Definition**
>
> *Demand pull inflation occurs when the total demand for goods and services is greater than the total supply of goods and services.*

There is unsatisfied demand at the existing price level. The excess demand 'pulls up' the price level.

Demand pull inflation is generally but not exclusively associated with the Keynesian school. Although Keynes was primarily concerned with the issue of unemployment, he did consider the implications of inflation in an essay that was published in 1940 entitled *How to Pay for the War*. In this essay, Keynes looked at the problem of an increase in government spending caused by a war, particularly if the economy is at full-employment equilibrium at the outbreak.

We can illustrate demand pull inflation by using the AD/AS model, and examine an increase in aggregate demand, similar to what was represented in Figure 16.7.

The increase in aggregate demand causes the AD curve to shift rightwards, from AD to AD^1. As a result of the increase in aggregate demand, the price level rises from P^0 to P^1. There is also an increase in output, from Y^0 to Y^1. The extent of the increase in price will depend on the steepness of the AS curve, and, in turn, the timeframe (short-run versus long-run) involved. If, at the time of the increase in aggregate demand, the economy is operating along the flat part of the AS curve, the result will be an increase in output. If, as in Figure 17.1, the economy is operating on the upward sloping part of the AS curve, much of the increase in aggregate demand will result in a price increase. How much firms increase prices will depend

FIGURE 17.1: DEMAND PULL INFLATION

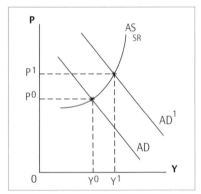

on how much their costs rise as a result of increasing output and, in turn, how close actual output is to potential output. When actual output exceeds potential output, there is an inflationary gap.

> **Definition**
>
> *An inflationary gap exists when the equilibrium of the economy is greater than the full-employment level of output.*

With the economy above its potential output level, wage costs rise, resulting in a leftward shift of the AS curve. Aggregate supply will continue to fall until equilibrium is restored, at the full-employment equilibrium level of output but at a higher aggregate price level. In this case of a general increase in the price level, the inflation is caused by the initial increase in aggregate demand. Demand pull inflation is usually associated with a booming (overheated) economy.

This model demonstrates the essential features of demand pull inflation. Inflation is caused by excess demand which causes the price level to increase. In the first instance, the excess demand may be caused by greater spending or tax cuts or some combination of these factors.

The Quantity Theory of Money

The Quantity Theory of Money (QTM) is the oldest theory of inflation. It is attributed to the classical economists, but it was popularised by Irving Fisher at the beginning of this century (see Information Box 17.1). In the years following World War II, inflation was not a pressing issue and the QTM was considered to be an appropriate topic for a course on the history of economic thought. However, the monetarist Milton Friedman revived the QTM in 1956 with the essay 'The Quantity Theory of Money – A Restatement'.[4] The powerful policy conclusions of this model concerning the ineffectiveness of monetary policy continue to influence the thinking of monetarists in particular and neoclassical economists in general.

The classical view

In its simplest form the QTM states that there is a relationship between the money supply and the price level. It predicts that the price level will change with changes in the money supply. The more rapid the rate of increase in the money supply, the higher the inflation rate.

The following equation describes the income version of the QTM.

$$\mathbf{M\bar{V} = P\bar{Y}}$$ [17.3]

where: M = money supply; V = velocity of money; P = the price level; Y = real income or output or GDP.

Notice that there is a bar over V and Y. This means that these variables are held constant. This is not an arbitrary decision, but reflects the assumptions of the classical economists. We can think of the velocity of money as the number of times a sum of money changes hands in a year. Advocates of this model believe that velocity is determined by institutional factors which change slowly over time. Holding real output as constant reflects the classical belief that the economy is always close to its full-employment output level.

If we hold velocity and output constant, any change in the money supply is reflected by a proportional change in the price level. Continuous increases in the money supply cause inflation. This model implies that monetary policy is ineffective. It causes deflation or inflation, but does not lead to changes in 'real' variables like output or employment.

INFORMATION BOX 17.1

The Quantity Theory of Money

Irving Fisher, the great American economist of the early twentieth century, is credited with popularising the Quantity Theory of Money.[1] In his book *The Purchasing Power of Money* (1911) he began with the simple equation of exchange MV = PT where M is the quantity of money, V is the rate of turnover of money or the velocity of money, P is the price level and T is the number of transactions. Since T is difficult to measure it can be replaced by output, Y.

As it stands, this equation is simply an identity or truism – something which is true by definition. It states that for the aggregate economy, the value of transactions, PT, is equal to the value of receipts, MV. A number of assumptions have to be made about the level of transactions and the velocity of money in order for this identity to be converted into a theory of inflation.

Fisher assumed that the level of transactions was fixed because it bore a close relationship with income which in the classical model was fixed at a level consistent with full employment. In addition Fisher argued that the velocity of money was determined by institutional factors which had a stabilising effect in the short term. If velocity and transactions are fixed, these assumptions transform the equation of exchange into a theory of inflation where changes in the money supply determine the price level.

Although the Cambridge version of the Quantity theory is similar, there are some important differences. Whereas Fisher focused solely on the transactions demand for money, the approach developed by Marshall and Pigou extended the functions of money to include the store of value function. This cash-balance approach also allowed for some flexibility in terms of how much money was held, with individual choice playing an important role. In the Fisher model, institutional constraints prevented any freedom in terms of the amount of money held. Finally, interest rates were not ruled out of the Cambridge version as a possible factor explaining changes in money demand. It was left to others, however, including Keynes, to investigate the possible relationship between interest rates and money demand.

---

1   Fisher was not the first to develop the theory. It is believed that the first attempts at formulating the Quantity Theory of Money were independently made by David Hume in 1752 and Simon Newcomb in 1885.

The monetarist view

The monetarist view can be easily understood if we return to the AD/AS model developed in Chapter 16. Recall the downward sloping AD curve which depicts the relationship between the price level and national output, *ceteris paribus*. One variable which was held constant was the money supply.

The AS curve also depicts the relationship between the price level and national output, holding the characteristics of the labour force, technology and capital accumulation constant. The conventional aggregate supply curve is depicted as upward sloping in the short run as shown in Figure 17.2.[5]

The AS curve is upward sloping, which reflects the assumption that as price rises, the output level also rises. The monetarists agree with the classical economists that the economy returns to full-employment equilibrium, represented by point E in Figure 17.2.

During the period when interest in the QTM resurged, monetarists believed in adaptive expectations (see Appendix 17.2 on expectations). Briefly, adaptive expectations refers to a phenomenon where neither management nor labour accurately interpret the meaning of a change in the price level. In the short run, they may be temporarily fooled into

FIGURE 17.2: THE AD/AS MODEL

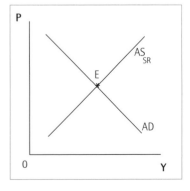

producing at a level of output which is higher than full employment. In the long run, the economy will return to full employment, at a higher price level.

We will demonstrate the model by illustrating an increase in the money supply which shifts the AD curve to AD[1], shown in Figure 17.3.

The change in the money supply has caused the price level to increase.

Firms interpret upward pressure on price as a signal to increase production. To do this, they hire more labour. Since the labour supply curve is upward sloping, they must pay a higher nominal wage. A new equilibrium is reached in (P,Y) space at E[1].

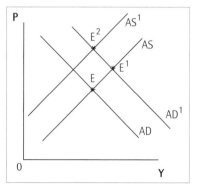

FIGURE 17.3: AD/AS MODEL FEATURING ADAPTIVE EXPECTATIONS

Recall that we began at full employment. The wage has increased, but so has the price level. Labour has not correctly understood that the change in the price level is eroding their purchasing power. In other words, although their nominal wage is increasing, their real wage has not increased.[6] When labour 'cops on', they will cut back the amount of labour that they are willing to supply at the new price level. This causes the AS curve to shift to AS[1] as shown in Figure 17.3. At the new equilibrium, E[2], the price level is higher, but the level of output returns to the full-employment level.

This led the monetarists to conclude that changes in the money supply have short-term effects on output, but in the long run, they are inflationary. According to Friedman, 'Inflation is always and everywhere a monetary phenomenon in the sense that it is and can be produced only by a more rapid increase in the quantity of money than in output.'[7] Essentially, he revived the QTM. For more information on Milton Friedman and monetarism, see Information Box 17.2.

INFORMATION BOX 17.2

Monetarism

Monetarism is the economic school of thought which lays special emphasis on the role of money in the economy. It does not, however, confine itself to the topic of money. Monetarists have a view on the role of government, the role of the market, fiscal policy, unemployment, inflation and many other issues.

Just as the classical economists succeeded the physiocrats, the monetarists are the modern bearers of the classical tradition. Like the classicals, monetarists believe in the efficacy and the efficiency of the market. They are suspicious of government intervention in the economy. Gaining insights from extended periods of demand management, they cast a jaundiced eye on the efforts of government to change the level of output and employment by altering government expenditure.

It is their view of money, however, which distinguishes monetarism from other economic doctrines. According to monetarists, the rate of money growth is paramount in the determination of short-run output and long-run inflation. In order to combat inflation, money growth must not exceed output growth. A steady rate of money growth ensures low levels of inflation and facilitates long-term economic prosperity.

The emergence of monetarism in the 1970s in the USA was largely due to the Nobel Laureate Milton Friedman. His most famous works include *A Monetary History of the United States* and the best-seller *Free to Choose* in which he makes a strong defence of free enterprise and the market.

Although he wrote widely on many different issues in economics he will be remembered for restoring many of the tenets of the classical doctrine of economics.

The most famous proponent of monetarism was the British Prime Minister, Mrs Thatcher. With the support of Keith Joseph and Professor Alan Walters, Mrs Thatcher strongly advocated the principles of monetarism. Combating inflation became the ultimate priority for the Tory government. The economic instrument used to achieve this objective was the money supply. Monitoring the money supply growth rate was central to the Medium Term Financial Strategy (MTFS). Fiscal spending was no longer used to increase aggregate demand. Mrs Thatcher was more concerned with how spending was to be financed.

By the late 1980s, the star of monetarism began to fall. Fiscal rectitude and scrupulous adherence to monetary targets did not ensure employment creation. While these goals have not been abandoned, some governments believe that some intervention is necessary to combat the high rates of unemployment that persist across western Europe. This belief was to extend to the USA and elsewhere in the late 2000s with the onslaught of the financial crisis and the 2008/9 Great Recession. Monetarism and concerns over inflation were replaced by Keynesians and unemployment concerns.

Cost push inflation

During the post-war years inflation continued even in times when there was little or no evidence of excess demand in the economy. This prompted economists to examine other explanations and, in particular, possible causes arising from the supply side of the economy.

We begin by defining cost push inflation and then we will explain its application using the AD/AS model.

Definition

Cost push inflation occurs when the source of upward pressure on prices is the rising costs of the factors of production in the absence of any corresponding increase in productivity.

The most important factor cost is labour. Consider a situation where an important labour union signs an agreement for a significant wage increase which sets off a round of wage increases throughout the economy. This causes the AS curve to shift to the left as shown in Figure 17.4.

The original equilibrium, E, represents a level of output where all factors of production are fully employed. At the associated price level P^0, aggregate supply is now less than aggregate demand. In response to the wage increase, firms are unwilling to supply the original level of output to the market at that price. Eventually, the economy reaches a new equilibrium at E^1, at a higher price level and a lower level of output. Higher taxes or the imposition of more extensive legislation would result in a similar outcome.

This particular pattern of inflation can lead to a wage-price spiral. Labour unions force a wage increase. To return the economy to full employment the state responds by adopting expansionary monetary and/or fiscal policies. This shifts the AD curve to the right resulting in another increase

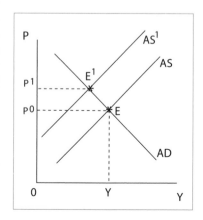

FIGURE 17.4: COST PUSH INFLATION

in the price level. Labour unions look for another wage increase to compensate for higher inflation. The AS curve shifts leftwards. Once started, the spiral is difficult to end.

Imported inflation

This type of inflation is another form of cost push inflation which is particularly relevant to countries, like Ireland, with open economies. Suppose the domestic currency falls in value. Many raw materials and inputs for industry are imported. As a result of the fall in the value of the domestic currency, Irish-based firms are faced with higher import costs which, in turn, are reflected in higher prices for their finished good. This leads to inflation in the domestic market, which again leads to problems with competitiveness in foreign markets.

Expectations

In an economy where people become accustomed to high rates of inflation, they expect it to persist into the future. Workers incorporate the inflation rate into their contract demands. To compensate for the higher prices, higher wages are sought. This, in turn, causes the price level to increase further. We can see from this that the expectation of inflation is validated by actual increases in the inflation rate. Even after the initial causes of inflation have been removed, people's expectations may cause the inflationary process to continue.

The importance of expectations in explaining the actual rate of inflation (and other related topics) has become increasingly recognised by economists in recent years. As you might expect, there is considerable disagreement, and it is one of the most controversial topics in economics today (see Appendix 17.2).

17.1.4 Counter-inflationary policies

Policies aimed at combating inflation are usually categorised as either demand-side policies or supply-side policies. Although the solutions to inflation should redress the specific source of the rise in the price level, it may be difficult in reality to correctly assess the actual cause. If there is more than one source, a package of measures may be required. It may also be difficult to completely eradicate inflation. In fact it has been argued that a little inflation is not necessarily a bad thing as it may be conducive to economic growth.

Demand-side policies

In the last section, we discussed inflationary pressures placed on an economy due to a country's entry into a war. Theoretically, that increase in autonomous expenditure could be offset by either contractionary monetary or fiscal policy. Contractionary monetary policy causes an increase in the interest rate and leads to a fall in the level of private investment. Contractionary fiscal policy can take the form of a tax increase which would cut disposable income and therefore income-induced consumption.

Supply-side policies

There are two objectives of supply-side policies. One is to moderate inflation by increasing the rate of growth of output. The other objective is to reduce the rate of increase of the costs of production. Achieving either of these objectives shifts the AS curve to the right and is therefore deflationary as we can see from Figure 17.5.

Supply-side policies generally focus on promoting competition, containing labour costs and increasing work incentives. Examples of policies which promote competition include restricting the number of mergers and takeovers. Monopoly powers are curbed to limit the control over price and profits.

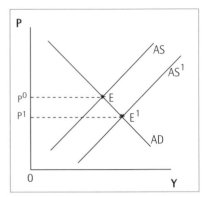

Supply-side economists recommend lowering the corporate and personal tax rates which they believe will have beneficial effects on the competitiveness of firms (see Section 16.3). Although Keynes argued that the tax changes work by altering the demand side of the economy, this group of economists believe that this particular type of fiscal policy affects the supply side. The primary focus of these policies is to increase national output supplied.

Containing labour costs can take two forms. Traditionally, supply-side economists advocate restricting the power of labour unions and avoiding legislation which guarantees a minimum wage. In neoclassical models, the economy moves towards full employment if – and only if – wages are flexible. Unionised labour, it is believed, can negotiate a wage rate above the equilibrium wage rate, causing unemployment. They argue that minimum wage legislation has the same effect. Many feel that if labour is unorganised and if contract arrangements are decentralised, wage demands will be lower and more flexible.

A different model has been used in Ireland since 1987 (see Chapter 7). The social partners negotiated successive national wage and social partnership agreements beginning with the Programme for National Recovery (1987). This was replaced by the Programme for Economic and Social Progress (1991), the Programme for Competitiveness and Work (1994), Partnership 2000 for Inclusion, Employment and Competitiveness, the Programme for Prosperity and Fairness (2000), Sustaining Progress (2003) and Towards 2016 (2006). This process allows the economic interests of different sections of society to be considered in an organised way. The wage increases negotiated under the earlier programmes were modest, influenced by the high rates of unemployment in the early 1990s. While many have argued that these agreements promote price stability, some commentators have argued that returning to decentralised agreements would increase labour market flexibility and lower the wage bill.

Finally, a strong currency is anti-inflationary because it ensures stable import prices from the country's main trading partners. In the context of EMU, Irish authorities have lost control over exchange rate policy. The policy of a 'strong' euro must be implemented by the European Central Bank.

The success of all anti-inflationary policies depends on the credibility of government. Trade unions, firms and consumers form their expectations based on government actions, rather than government statements. Policies must be both reasonable and consistently applied.

17.1.5 The Irish experience

Ireland is a small open economy (SOE). On account of its size, it has little or no control over the international price of goods and services. In other words, it is a price taker in an international environment.

In 2009, exports were valued at €144.8 billion, which is over 90% of Irish GDP. Imports were valued at over €120 billion, which represents approximately 75% of GDP. Both of these figures attest to the extreme openness of the Irish economy.

As Ireland is an SOE, Irish policy-makers must take the issue of inflation seriously. A high domestic inflation rate erodes the competitiveness of Irish goods and services on foreign markets. High foreign inflation rates, particularly from Ireland's main trading partners, can be quickly imported to the Irish economy. It is widely accepted that inflation in Ireland is largely determined by exchange rate movements and inflation in its major trading partners.

Until 1979 when the fixed exchange rate between Ireland and Britain was finally broken, the Irish inflation rate was largely determined by the UK inflation rate, and the Irish authorities had little control over Irish inflation. The level of trade with the UK, UK interest rates, UK monetary policy and sterling's value on the foreign exchange markets were the primary factors in determining the Irish inflation rate.

Ireland joined the exchange rate mechanism of the EMS in 1979. Although the 'sterling factor' did not disappear, the IR£/DM exchange rate and the inflation rates of EU countries, particularly Germany, participating in the ERM became determining factors of Irish inflation.

The Irish inflation rate for the period 1970–2010 is illustrated in Figure 17.6.

FIGURE 17.6: IRISH INFLATION RATE 1970–2010

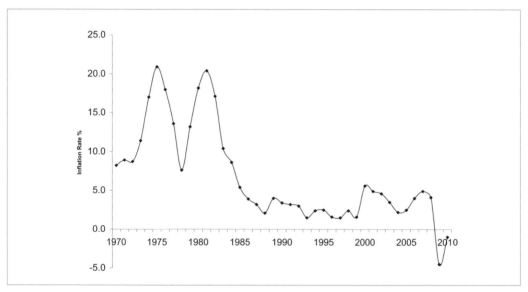

It is evident from Figure 17.6 that inflation in Ireland was high from 1973 to 1982. From the early 1980s the inflation rate began to decline. By the early 1990s the Irish inflation rate was close to, and often below, the EU average. Ireland had become a low inflation economy. However, by 2000, there was evidence of a pick-up in Irish inflation, partly associated with the booming economy.

The inflationary period 1973 to 1980 coincided with an increase in inflationary pressures throughout western Europe. The main sources of Irish inflation were the volatility of sterling and the supply-side shocks of 1973 and 1979 arising from the increase in the price of oil. As a small open economy, Ireland is likely to record similar rates of inflation to its main trading partners. Expansionary fiscal policy practised by Irish governments after 1973 also contributed to the high inflation rates.

Likewise, the decline in the inflation rate experienced by most EU countries in the mid- to late 1980s was also evident in Ireland. Although the international experience of low and stable inflation was a contributory factor in reducing the Irish inflation rate, it was not the only factor.

Domestic policy was largely deflationary in the late 1980s. The combination of tight fiscal policy and moderate pay increases reinforced the international anti-inflationary experience of the time.

The firm exchange rate policy followed by the Irish authorities may also have contributed to the reduction of Irish inflation. Price stability had become the sole objective of domestic exchange rate and monetary policy. Interest rate levels were set in order to attain low and stable inflation. By the mid-1990s, the Irish inflation rate was one of the lowest in the EU. In addition, by achieving a low inflation rate, Ireland met the inflation criterion as set down in the Maastricht Treaty. Given the Irish authorities' determination to participate in the single currency, Ireland's commitment to achieving a low and stable inflation rate was both desirable and necessary.

A number of factors may account for the relatively high inflation rate in late 1999 and into the first couple of years of the new millennium. External factors, proven in the past to be the main determinant of Irish inflation, include, in this period, the fall in the value of the euro and the rise in the price of oil. Although external factors are more prevalent in explaining the inflation rate of a small and open economy, domestic factors may also have played a role during this period. Discretionary tax changes and the fall in Irish interest rates arising from the convergence of interest rates across EMU-participating states gave a boost to an already booming economy. Claims of extensive labour shortages and evidence of rising wage inflation in certain sectors of the economy fuelled, if not reinforced, inflationary expectations. In addition, rising equity and house prices gave rise to rapid asset price inflation and the fear of a collapse of an asset price bubble.

This pessimistic view was disputed by many in the economics profession and elsewhere. It was argued that the rise in house prices in Ireland was not driven by an inflow of speculative capital, as happened in many of the real estate booms elsewhere, but was due to changes in economic fundamentals, namely, demographics factors, the economic boom, fall in mortgage rates, shortages of supply and so on.

As a member of the euro area, the Irish economy could be viewed as a region within a low-inflation trading area. Despite a single monetary policy, price differentials may still exist. With the fastest growing economy or region within the euro area (up to the mid-2000s), Irish inflation may, at times, be higher than the average inflation rate across participating states. This was the case in the first few years of the new millennium when the Irish inflation rate was the highest in the euro area. By mid-decade, Ireland's inflation rate had fallen (as had growth rates), and the gap between it and the inflation rate in the eurozone had narrowed.

All this was to change in the late 2000s with the financial crisis, the international credit crunch and the global recession. Concerns over inflation turned to fears over deflation. As spending by firms and consumers fell, on the back of much uncertainty, prices began to fall. Countries, for the first time in half a century, witnessed deflation. Ireland was no exception. In 2009, prices fell, on average by 4.5% in Ireland. Although a fall in prices (with falling costs) was welcomed, there were fears of a deflationary spiral and a double-dip recesion. By late 2010, deflation had replaced inflation as the number one topic of the day.

CASE STUDY

Extract from *The Irish Independent*
Inflation at lowest rate in 11 years

Ireland's inflation rate fell in January to the lowest rate in 11 years on tumbling commodity prices and waning demand.

Inflation, based on a European Union measure, dropped to 1.1 percent from 1.3 percent in December, the Central Statistics

Office said today. That's the lowest since February 1998, when the rate was 1 percent. Prices fell 0.8 percent in January from the previous month. The EU measure excludes mortgage interest payments. Based on an Irish gauge, annual inflation was minus 0.1 percent, the first negative reading since May 1960. The European Central Bank cut its benchmark rate by 0.5 percent to 2 percent in January.

Crude oil has dropped around 75 percent since reaching a record close to $150 a barrel in July, cutting petrol and heating oil costs and cooling inflation across Europe. Inflation may continue to ease in the coming months as lower raw material costs and falling consumer spending undermine companies' scope to raise prices. 'It is clear that prices are on an accelerated downward trend, which is likely to persist for the current year and on into 2010,' Deirdre Ryan, an economist at Goodbody Stockbrokers in Dublin, said in an e-mailed note. 'From the point of view of restoring competitiveness to the Irish economy, this can be seen as a positive development.'

Prices for fuels such as home heating oil fell 5.2 percent in January from the previous month, according to the statistics office. Petrol fell 4.3 percent in the month, while clothes and footwear prices dropped 13 percent. The ECB's 2 percent interest rate already matches a record low for the euro area and President Jean-Claude Trichet has indicated the bank may lower the rate again next month.

Source: The Irish Independent, 12 February 2009.

Questions

1. Identify and explain the two main measures of consumer price inflation in Ireland. Using both measures, report (using www.cso.ie) the annual inflation rate for Ireland for the three-year period 2007–2009.
2. What does the fall in the inflation rate reflect, in general economic terms, in Ireland at the end of the 2000s? Explain your answer.
3. Explain the relationship between the inflation rate and the interest rate as set by the ECB. Report and analyse the eurozone inflation rate and the ECB main interest rate (from www.ecb.int) data for 2007–2009.

Answers on website

17.2 UNEMPLOYMENT

Undoubtedly, the most serious economic problem facing society is unemployment. A section discussing this topic is an exercise in humility for any economist. We have trouble defining it. The number of unemployed depends on the statistic that we use. We cannot come close to measuring the opportunity cost of unemployment. Many of the theories that we cling to may have never been appropriate. The persistently high rates of unemployment observed in western Europe offer no consolation that our policies are effective.

Unfortunately, we cannot offer a solution to the unemployment problem in this section. Hopefully we can explain the issues in such a way that the policy discussions which you hear and read about will make more sense. You are already familiar with many of the definitions and the models.

17.2.1 Defining unemployment

Unemployment is surprisingly difficult to define and to measure. We will begin by looking at the Quarterly National Household Survey (QNHS) and the Live Register (LR), two measures of Irish unemployment. The two measures have one thing in common. In both, unemployment is a stock concept; they look at the number of unemployed at a point in time.[8] However, each measure defines unemployment differently and, as a result, the number of people they count as unemployed differs widely.

Quarterly National Household Survey

The QNHS replaced the annual Labour Force Survey (LFS) in 1997. The survey was changed in order to harmonise the collection of labour market statistics throughout the EU. About 39,000 households are surveyed four times per year. For QNHS results, the primary classification used is the International Labour Organisation (ILO) labour force classification. According to the classification, the population includes everyone who is 15 years or older. It is divided between those who are in the labour force and those who are not in the labour force. Those who are not in the labour force are classified as students, on home duties, retired or 'other'.

> **Definition**
>
> *The labour force includes those who are employed and those who are unemployed.*

> **Definition**
>
> *The unemployed include those who are not working and who are available for, and are actively seeking work.*

People are unemployed because they lost or gave up their previous job. Also included are school-leavers and people who are looking for their first regular job.

> **Definition**
>
> *The unemployment rate is the number of people unemployed divided by the labour force.*

The QNHS allows people to classify their own employment status.

Live Register

The LR figures are released on the last Friday of each month and published by the CSO in the *Statistical Bulletin*. The LR defines unemployment in the following way.

> **Definition**
>
> *The Live Register counts as unemployed the people who are registered at local offices of the Department of Social Protection for either jobseeker's benefit or jobseeker's allowance.*

As the LR is a count of claimants eligible for jobseeker's benefit (JB) or assistance (JA), it is not really designed to measure unemployment. For example, the LR includes part-time workers and seasonal and casual workers entitled to JB or JA.

    The LR excludes the following categories of people who receive jobseeker's benefit or assistance: smallholders/farm assists, persons on systematic short-time and self-employed individuals. Individuals who are involved in industrial disputes are also excluded.

The difference between the two measures

The difference between the two measures is a matter of some interest in the media. There is a large gap between the two measures which is shown in Table 17.3.

TABLE 17.3: DIFFERENCE BETWEEN THOSE CLASSIFIED AS UNEMPLOYED ON THE QNHS AND THE LR

Year	LR (April) (thousands)	QNHS[1] (thousands)
2000	164.7	79.6
2001	139.5	69.4
2002	157.5	82.3
2003	170.3	86.7
2004	167.1	87.8
2005	152.7	95.8
2006	158.1	97.9
2007	156.0	103.1
2008	196.4	126.7
2009	381.9	264.6
2010	432.7	293.6

Source: Central Statistics Office.

1 April–June.

Other than the inclusion of part-time, casual and seasonal workers in the LR, what accounts for the gap? Recall that for the QNHS, people classify themselves. Women particularly classify themselves as 'on home duties' if they are not employed. In the QNHS, this classifies them as 'not in the labour force'. However, since the equality legislation of the mid-1980s, they may also be entitled to social welfare payments and therefore appear on the Live Register. Therefore, on the LR, they are classified as both in the labour force and unemployed. Each measure is defining 'unemployment' differently.

Social welfare fraud appears to be another reason why the two statistics differ. A survey commissioned by the government to compare the LR with the LFS found that for a sample of 2,600 cases, 16% of the people claiming jobseeker's benefits were working and not entitled to those benefits. Promises made by the government to prosecute cases of social welfare fraud led to an immediate drop in the Live Register. In October 1996, for example, over 11,000 'signed off' the dole. Other possible reasons for the difference include arrangements for splitting entitlements between spouses and the introduction of signing on as an eligibility requirement for subsequent participation in training and/or employment schemes.

Unravelling the differences between the two statistics is difficult. Parties in power tend to focus on the lower unemployment rates derived from the QNHS. These are also the figures which are used for international comparisons. Opposition parties concentrate on the higher LR figures.

The 'best measure' probably depends on the policy issue. One thing is certain. Each measure should be fully understood prior to the policy discussion.

Unemployment can be classified into a number of different types. These include frictional, seasonal, structural, demand deficient and classical. These classifications correspond broadly with the causes of unemployment.

Frictional This arises when workers who are 'between jobs' find themselves unemployed for a short period of time although work is available. A job vacancy may remain unfilled for a period of time because of imperfect information in the labour market or because of an immobile work force. This is also called search unemployment. Economists and policy-makers are not overly concerned with frictional unemployment, which they see as inevitable in any dynamic economy. Measures that will shorten the job search time are likely to reduce frictional unemployment.

Seasonal Employment in certain industries is seasonal in nature, requiring a work force for only a particular time of year (e.g. summer). Employees are then laid off when the season ends. This is also called 'casual' unemployment. Industries which hire seasonally include tourism, construction and farming.

Structural Economies sometimes face fundamental or structural changes which lead to unemployment. Technological change and the invention of new products may make old products and even whole industries obsolete. If that industry is important to a region or to a national economy, unemployment may persist until new firms and new industries are developed or until labour can be retrained to work in different industries. Classic examples include the mining industry in the UK and the linen industry in Northern Ireland.

Demand deficient This type of unemployment arises from a deficiency in aggregate demand in the economy. It occurs during the downturn of the business cycle. It is often caused by too much savings and an insufficient amount of spending.

Classical This is the explanation of unemployment associated with the classical school. It arises from a combination of uncompetitive forces at work in the labour market. Powerful trade unions, costly labour legislation and monopoly influences are all sources of wage inflexibility which are thought to cause unemployment. This is also called 'real wage' unemployment.

17.2.2 The costs

So far, we have stated that unemployment is difficult to define and to measure. We will begin this section by admitting that the costs of unemployment are impossible to calculate. Some of the costs, like the total of social welfare payments, can be determined. Many costs, including the loss of production, of tax revenue and of self-esteem, are difficult to quantify. They are felt by all sections of society, but disproportionately by the unemployed and their dependants.

The unemployed do not earn an income. This is only partially offset by the state in the form of unemployment allowances, rental allowances and medical cards. Although a person on the dole may not be literally dying of hunger, their relative standard of living is below that of people who are working. In a world where success is measured by our accumulation of material goods, there is a stigma attached to those who cannot participate in that accumulation. Higher security costs, both public and private, are incurred by societies as the size of the gap between the social classes widens. Length of life can be affected along with the quality of life. The poverty associated with unemployment leads to increased physical and mental breakdowns.

The unemployed tend to be 'ghettoised'. They live in areas where the rates of unemployment are substantially higher than the national average. These neighbourhoods face high levels of crime and substance abuse. Few students finish with second-level qualifications. Fewer still participate at third level. Not only are their surroundings bleak, their exits are blocked by a lack of access to education.

Society loses if people are unemployed. The unemployed are a resource which is not being utilised. If all of the unemployed were working, an economy would produce more and the national income would increase. If everyone was working, the tax base would be broader; there would be more sources of tax revenue. More public goods could be provided.

The money transferred to the unemployed is taken from the taxpayer. This constitutes a redistribution of resources from one section of society to another. This is not considered to be a cost to society in an economic sense. However, if the unemployment rate is high, the tax base is relatively narrow and individuals who are working must pay high rates of taxes to finance government spending. Some economists suggest that high tax rates act as a disincentive to employment, so the productive capacity of the economy may again be affected.

This brief discussion shows the difficulty of 'counting the costs'. The costs that we can count are huge. The magnitude of the opportunity cost of unemployment is painful to contemplate. We will now discuss some of the theories developed to explain unemployment.

17.2.3 The theories and policies

There are a number of different theories of unemployment. Some of them are conventional, others are radical; some are modern whereas others are centuries old; some blame government and the state while others apportion blame to the market. The one feature common to the different theories is the recognition of the social and economic costs associated with unemployment. We begin with the classical explanation.

The classical theory

The classical model of the labour market was explained in detail in Section 7.1. The downward sloping demand curve for labour is based on the diminishing marginal productivity of labour. In order for firms to hire more labour, the real wage must fall. The upward sloping supply curve of labour is based on the idea that workers trade off the disutility associated with work with the utility associated with consuming goods and services. In order for labour to work additional hours or for more people to enter the labour market, the real wage rate must increase.

Figure 17.7 shows the classical labour market.

Full employment is shown at point E. The level of output of goods and services is determined by the number of people working. The classicals believed that the labour market moves automatically toward full employment, if wages are flexible. At point E, there is no involuntary unemployment. The supply curve above point E represents people who are voluntarily unemployed. Their utility-maximising decision is to withhold their services, preferring leisure to labour.

If unemployment persisted in the economy, the classicals believed that the source of the unemployment must be in the labour market itself. Since full employment depended on wage flexibility, unemployment meant that wages were not flexible. Rigidities were caused by labour unions, minimum wage legislation or other anti-competitive practices.

FIGURE 17.7: THE CLASSICAL LABOUR MARKET

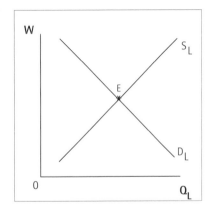

The solution to classical unemployment follows directly from their model; the sources of wage rigidity must be eliminated. The labour market will then return to full employment.

The Keynesian theory

The Keynesian theory of unemployment can be explained within the context of the model of income determination. Keynes did not think that the source of unemployment was to be found in the labour market. Instead, he believed that the source of unemployment was in the goods market. Labour demand was derived from the demand for goods. There was nothing automatic about full employment. Deficient demand led to persistent unemployment.

Suppose we begin at a point where the level of output corresponds coincidentally with full employment in the labour market. Panel (a) of Figure 17.8 shows the model of income determination. The equilibrium level of output is determined by adding together the different sources of aggregate expenditure including personal consumption, investment, government spending and net exports. The economy is at equilibrium indicated by point E, which corresponds to full employment in the labour market shown in panel (b).

FIGURE 17.8: INVOLUNTARY UNEMPLOYMENT EXPLAINED USING THE KEYNESIAN MODEL

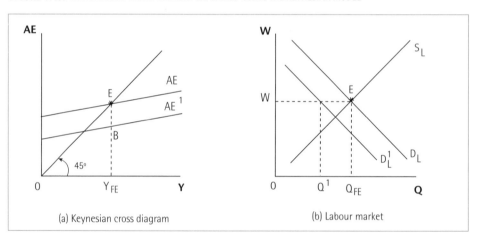

(a) Keynesian cross diagram   (b) Labour market

Now, suppose that there is a world recession, in which global output, and demand for goods and services, falls. Investment falls, causing the AE curve to shift downwards to AE^1.

Because labour demand is determined by the demand in the goods market, the decrease in investment means that the demand for labour falls. This is shown by a shift of the demand curve for labour to $D_L{}^1$. An additional feature to the Keynesian model is the assumption that wages are rigid for institutional reasons such as the existence of labour contracts. Therefore, the wage rate does not fall, but remains at W. The gap between Q^1 and Q_{FE} represents involuntary unemployment.

Keynes did not argue in favour of flexible wages. He believed that the source of unemployment was demand-determined. A fall in wages would lead to a fall in consumption, another component of aggregate expenditure. Government intervention in the form of expansionary monetary or fiscal policy is the preferred solution. Only government controls a sufficient level of resources to overcome the deficiency in demand.

The monetarist theory

The monetarist theory essentially agrees with the classical conception of the economy and of the appropriate role of government. Additions to the theory resulted from their observation of what they considered to be inappropriate demand-management policies enacted by the Keynesian economists who influenced policy-makers in the 1960s and the 1970s.

Monetarists believe that the existence of unemployment in the labour market is due to imperfections in the market system and misguided demand-management policies. A flexible labour market without excessive government interference should return to the 'natural rate' of unemployment.[9] Examples of market imperfections include the existence of monopolies, powerful labour unions and minimum wage legislation.

The source of employment creation, according to monetarists, is in the private sector. Demand-management policies are not only ineffective in increasing the level of employment, but are also inflationary. Inflation interferes with the price mechanism, the most important source of information between households and firms. Inflationary policies short-circuit the price mechanism and counteract the ability of the private sector to create jobs.

The supply-side theory

Supply-side economists also begin with the classical conception of the economy. Total output depends on factors such as the level of technology, the training of the labour force and the accumulation of capital. One source of unemployment in the economy is 'supply-side' shocks. The most memorable example of a supply-side shock is the oil crisis. Figure 17.9 shows how a negative supply-side shock moves an economy to a level of output which is less than full employment.

The supply siders also agree with the monetarists that government spending/tax policy impedes the natural progress of the economy to full employment. Some of the supply-side economists believe in the validity of the Laffer curve relationship (see Information Box 16.1). Briefly, this economist suggested that tax rates act as a disincentive to work. The more heavily work is taxed, the greater the disincentive. Onerous tax rates limit the productive output of the economy. For this reason, supply siders advocate a revision of the tax system to limit this disincentive.

FIGURE 17.9: A SUPPLY-SIDE SHOCK

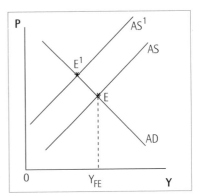

The supply-side economists differ from the Keynesians because they believe that tax reform will affect the supply side, rather than the demand side, of the economy. Tax reform pushes the aggregate supply curve to the right, increasing the economy's output. Supply siders differ from the monetarists because they focus primarily on fiscal policy rather than monetary policy.

The Marxian theory

Marxian unemployment theory is based on the conflicting relationship between labour and the capitalist. Marx believed that labour is productive and the source of all surplus. This surplus is divided between labour and the capitalist, depending on who is the most powerful. If labour is more powerful, wages rise above the subsistence level. If the capitalist is more powerful a larger share of the surplus goes to the capitalist in the form of profit.

Marxians agreed with Keynes that the capitalist system is prone to periodic expansions and contractions.[10] Involuntary unemployment of labour is a feature of both models in recessions and depressions. In the Keynesian model, involuntary unemployment is caused by the failure of private investment which occurs because of the 'animal spirits' of investors. In the Keynesian model, the failure of investment is a consequence of instability; in the Marxian model, it is a tactic designed to create instability.

In the Marxian model, high levels of unemployment serve a regulatory purpose. During periods when workers are powerful, profits decline. If profits are falling, capitalists reduce investment. This leads to a recession, which reduces labour power. When unemployment is high, workers are in a weaker bargaining position. The capitalist can force workers to increase productivity and to work for less. Workers realise that there is a 'reserve army of unemployed' waiting to take their place.

We have already observed that differences in modelling the unemployment problem lead to different policy prescriptions. The Marxian model is no exception. Marx believed that government, in protecting the private property rights of the capitalist, was an active participant in the problem of unemployment. Profits, extracted from the workers who produced the surplus, were protected by the police and the legal system. The source of unemployment in the Marxian model is the link between profits and investment. The solution is to break that link. It was in this sense that Marx advocated the abolition of private property. To end the exploitation of labour and to eradicate unemployment, the capitalist system had to be destroyed. For more on the life of Marx, see Information Box 17.3.

INFORMATION BOX 17.3

Karl Marx (1818–83)

Karl Marx was born in Germany and educated at the University of Bonn where he studied law. He furthered his education at the University of Berlin where he began to take a keen interest in philosophy. His teacher was the radical philosopher Georg Hegel. Marx was influenced by Hegel and began work on a thesis with a view to getting a university lectureship. He received his doctorate in 1841.

Marx's radical views, however, were a major obstacle in his search for an academic position. Instead he worked as a freelance journalist. After marrying his childhood sweetheart, Marx moved to Paris, the centre of radical reformers, where he met Friedrich Engels, the revolutionary socialist. They became lifetime friends and collaborators.

Marx and his family were expelled from France in 1845, and subsequently moved to Brussels where he organised a Communist Correspondence Committee. Three years later, the outline to Marx's theory *The Communist Manifesto* was complete. According to Engels it was 'to do for history what Darwin's theory has done for biology'. It concluded with the famous lines 'The workers have nothing to lose in this but their chains. They have the world to gain. Workers of the world, unite!'

After being expelled from a number of European cities, Marx moved to London where he lived for the rest of his life. Although he contributed regularly to the *New York Tribune*, he and his family spent many years in poverty. It was during this time that he wrote his most famous work *Das Kapital* wherein he prophesied that capitalism would collapse and would be replaced by an alternative economic system – socialism. Socialism in turn would be replaced by the utopian state of communism.

While his personal finances improved considerably in the later years of his life, due to inheritances, his personal life was shattered by the early deaths of his four children and his grandchildren. This was followed by the death of his wife in 1881 and his eldest daughter shortly afterwards. He died of bronchitis at the age of 65 in March 1883.

In recent times, explanations of unemployment focus on specific features of the economic system in general and the labour market in particular. These include the time and effort involved in searching for employment, the insider-outsider composition of the labour market and the effects of long-term wage contracts.[11]

17.2.4 The Irish experience

One of the most unforgettable comments by a senior political figure in Ireland was made in 1978. The Taoiseach and leader of Fianna Fáil, Jack Lynch, was interviewed by RTÉ's *This Week* programme. In response to a question on unemployment and whether the electorate should put the government out of office if the figures rose to 100,000, Mr Lynch replied, '. . . if we don't deliver then the electorate are entitled to put us out of office.'[12]

Since then governments from different political parties have come and gone. Yet the unemployment figure increased steadily until it was over 300,000 by January 1993. It had become the second highest rate in the EU (second to Spain) and the third highest in the OECD (behind Spain and Finland). One in five of the labour force was unemployed.

High unemployment is not a recent phenomenon in Ireland. In the past there have been periods of high and rising unemployment. Our analysis of unemployment is limited to the period since the early 1970s.

The unemployment rate in Ireland during the period 1970–2010 is shown in Figure 17.10. We will separate the discussion of unemployment during this forty-year period into three sections.

FIGURE 17.10: UNEMPLOYMENT RATE IN IRELAND 1970–2010

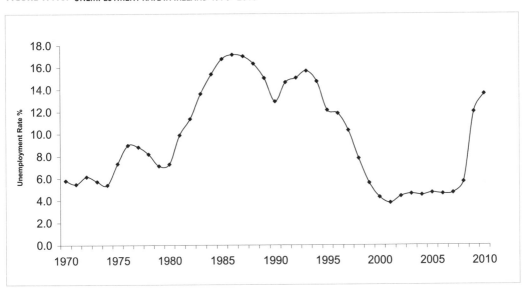

We will begin with the 1970s and 1980s. During this period, the numbers unemployed increased and then remained persistently high. We will then look at the 1990s (a period of falling unemployment) and the 2000s (a period of low unemployment). The last section covers the late 2000s, when unemployment in Ireland was to soar once again.

The rise and persistence of Irish unemployment

The causes of the high Irish unemployment rate of the 1980s were many and diverse. Factors such as the lack of natural resources, peripherality and the absence of entrepreneurial spirit are some of the causes which often got a mention. In reality, their contribution to the high unemployment rate is questionable.

The unemployment problem is complex. In order to gain some understanding of the nature of the problem, we will begin by attempting to group possible causes into four classifications: demographic factors, external factors (incorporating UK unemployment), inappropriate demand-management policies and other domestic factors.

The demographic factor

There is considerable disagreement over the relationship between population changes, changes in the labour force and changes in unemployment in Ireland. As a result of the increase in birth rates and the reversal of the emigration pattern from the 1960s onwards, the Irish labour force began to record significant increases in new entrants. Although many new jobs were created during this period, unemployment numbers also rose. Many experts, however, do not view these demographic changes as a significant factor contributing to the increase in Irish unemployment. In support of their argument, they highlight the following points: Irish birth rates peaked in the early 1980s (21.9 per 1,000), falling close to EU levels thereafter; and other countries, including the USA and Japan, recorded similar increases in population without any matching increase in unemployment levels.

External

A number of shocks external to the economy contributed to the poor performance of the Irish labour market. These include the two oil crises, the break-up of the Bretton Woods system, the liberalisation of financial markets and high real interest rates, the world recessions of 1980–82 and 1990–91 and the poor performance of the UK economy. The supply-side shocks of the 1970s were price inflationary and demand deflationary. This caused problems for policy-makers throughout the western world, including Ireland. Higher oil prices added to the production costs of many Irish and Irish-based firms. The break-up of the fixed exchange rate system created uncertainty in financial markets both at home and abroad. Exchange rate volatility and greater interest rate fluctuations caused problems for both exporters and importers. World recession, and in particular the sluggish growth recorded in the UK, contributed to the already weak domestic demand. In fact, the trend in Irish unemployment during this period was similar to the trend in UK unemployment; this suggests, unsurprisingly, the existence of a strong link between the Irish and UK labour markets. Conditions in the UK labour market impact on Irish unemployment, via inward and outward migration. The combination of all these events had an adverse effect on Irish economic growth and, likewise, Irish unemployment.

Inappropriate demand-management policies

The fiscal, monetary, incomes and exchange rate policies adopted by different governments may have contributed in different ways to the high unemployment rates of the 1970s and 1980s. In terms of fiscal policy, a number of mistakes were made. First, the authorities responded to the supply-side shocks of the 1970s with orthodox demand-management policies.[13] Second, the borrowing which subsequent governments undertook was partly to finance day-to-day spending.[14] Third, fiscal policy from the mid-1970s until the mid-1980s was largely pro-cyclical.[15] Fourth, although the Fine Gael/Labour Coalition government of the 1980s was forced by the burgeoning debt to enact contractionary fiscal policy, their policy mix was flawed.[16] Hence, we arrive at the assessment of some commentators that the legacy of Irish fiscal policy of the 1970s and early 1980s was one of high unemployment and massive debt.

Fiscal policy was not the only culprit during this period. Job creation was hindered by the combination, at different times, of high interest rates arising from tight monetary policy, a real exchange rate appreciation arising from Ireland's participation in the EMS exchange rate mechanism and excessive increases in wage levels arising from pay agreements between the government and the social partners.[17]

Other domestic factors

There were a large number of other domestic factors which contributed to high unemployment in Ireland during this period; most of these affected the supply side. Production was adversely affected because of factors which contributed to high costs. We deal with two: taxation and labour market rigidities.

Taxation

There were many aspects of the tax system which hindered job creation and contributed to the high unemployment rates. A number of these are considered below:

- The Irish tax system treats labour and capital differently. Since the early 1960s the cost of capital has been subsidised by the state in order to attract foreign investment. Allowances against corporate tax for capital expenditure in addition to flexible depreciation allowances were offered to multinationals as part of the incentive package. Tax on labour, on the other hand, was considered, by many, as excessive. Labour was the main source of tax revenue, with the PAYE sector carrying the burden. In particular, marginal tax rates on labour were high and were applicable at low income levels. With a large excess supply of labour, it was surprising to see labour treated in this fashion.
- The lack of integration between the tax and welfare systems in Ireland was highlighted as a possible contributing factor to the unemployment crisis in Ireland. The non-integration of the tax and welfare systems resulted in many anomalies. One such anomaly is referred to as the unemployment trap. This occurs when an unemployed person finds that s/he is financially worse off if s/he accepts a job offer. One measure of the unemployment trap is the replacement ratio (RR), described in [17.4] below.

$$\text{Replacement ratio} = \frac{\text{unemployment benefits}}{\text{after-tax income}} \times 100 \qquad [17.4]$$

This is the proportion of a worker's after-tax income that is replaced by unemployment benefits. As the replacement ratio approaches 100, the gap narrows between working and remaining unemployed. The higher the ratio, the less financial incentive there is to work.

High replacement ratios were not uncommon in the 1980s and early 1990s in Ireland. For example, for a single person earning IR£6,000 or less a year, the welfare system might have replaced over 75% of take-home pay. The disincentive to work was more striking for larger families. Welfare payments could have been up to 1.5 times higher than the after-tax income of a married couple with two children. For families earning close to the average industrial wage, the replacement ratio could have been close to 70%.

Replacement ratios increased in Ireland during the period 1977–94. There is both international and domestic evidence to indicate a correlation between rising replacement ratios and the persistence and duration of unemployment.[18]

- Another anomaly within the tax system is the occurrence of a poverty trap. A poverty trap exists when there is no financial incentive for an employed person to take up a better job offer. Given the nature of the tax and welfare systems in Ireland, a poverty trap existed for low-paid workers who were supporting large families. Before the tax reductions that were initiated in the mid- to late 1990s, many low-paid workers had little or no financial incentive to accept higher (gross) paid jobs. This is because the increase in their income resulted in a decrease in their social welfare benefits and a larger tax liability to the state. The worker in this position was caught in a poverty trap. An increase in gross pay led to a decrease in net income.

- For there to be low unemployment, employees must have an incentive to accept employment in addition to the employers having an incentive to hire additional workers. Central to this issue is the level of labour costs and the tax applied to wages. The tax wedge, as it is commonly referred to, is the difference between the after-tax earnings of the employee and the gross cost incurred by the employer. A significant tax wedge acts as a dual disincentive. Considering the supply curve for labour, a low take-home pay does not overcome the disutility of labour. The tax-inflated marginal cost of hiring another worker is a disincentive on the demand side of the labour market.

In 1980/81 the tax wedge for a single person earning the average industrial wage amounted to IR£1,835.93. Ten years later, the tax wedge was IR£5,004.57. This 173% increase far exceeds the rise in prices over the same period.[19] Arthur Andersen & Co. (1991) estimated that the marginal tax wedge for a single person in Ireland was 61%, the second highest of the countries surveyed.[20] An OECD study in 1991 calculated that the economy-wide tax wedge in Ireland was the fourth highest in the OECD, behind the wealthier nations of Denmark, Holland and Sweden.[21]

Labour market rigidities

Neoclassical labour market models predict that in a market without rigidities, the wage rate should fall, eliminating involuntary unemployment. Similar to other national labour markets, the Irish labour market is characterised by a number of rigidities.

Obviously, we cannot talk about the elimination of rigidities without acknowledging that this will lead to an erosion of the institutional arrangements, developed over the years to protect labour. It is not easy to strike a balance. In this section, we will describe some of the economic problems which arise because of the rigidities. However, we acknowledge that the resolution of these issues must take place within the context of a wider social debate.

- The wage bargaining process in Ireland has been characterised as an example of the insider-outsider model. Those employed are 'insiders' who negotiate for their own income and job security to the detriment of the 'outsiders' who are the unemployed. The insiders' demands impose a floor on wages which is above the market clearing wage.

Since 1987, centralised wage agreements have been the norm. Until 1996 the negotiations between the government and the social partners excluded the unemployed. Between 1987 and 1993 real earnings in Ireland, as measured by the average hourly earnings index, rose by over 30%. Over the same period unemployment increased by 47,000. In the words of Dermot McAleese, 'The insiders did what came naturally – put themselves first, while protesting concern for the unemployed – and the outsiders stayed outside.'[22] Not everyone accepts the validity of Professor McAleese's claim.

- In terms of trade union membership, Ireland is quite similar to many continental European countries. Trade union membership in Ireland was about 31% in 2009. This union density, although declining, is much higher than the union densities for either the UK or the USA, the two countries whose labour markets are most relevant to Ireland. The USA has traditionally been a low-union membership country whereas in the UK the trade union movement was badly damaged by Thatcherite policies. Trade unions seek to improve the working conditions of their members. In addition, they negotiate wage increases for workers.
- In the past forty years Irish workers have benefited from protective labour legislation. Notwithstanding the importance of protecting workers' rights, the drawback of such extensive legislation is the added cost to the employer. The net effect for many indigenous firms is higher costs, a loss of business and subsequent job losses. When confronted with extensive labour legislation in Ireland, multinationals may be enticed abroad to countries where labour costs are lower (e.g. Eastern Europe) or to countries where legislation is not as extensive (UK). A study by Emerson in 1988 concluded that workers in Ireland were no worse off in terms of protection than their counterparts in other EU countries.[23]

We now turn our attention to the fall in unemployment that took place in Ireland in the mid- to late 1990s.

The fall in Irish unemployment

It appears that the significant fall in unemployment that took place in the mid- to late 1990s was due largely to the rapid growth in the Irish economy. In the six years from 1993 onwards, the economy grew, as measured by changes in GNP, by 57% in real terms. In the same period, the unemployment rate fell by 10 percentage points, from 15.7% of the labour force in 1993 to 5.7% of the labour force in 1999. This can be explained by Okun's Law.

Definition

Okun's Law depicts the inverse relationship between output growth and unemployment.

It is named after the American economist, Arthur Okun, who studied the relationship between changes in real GDP and fluctuations in unemployment in the USA. In his study, for every one percentage point decrease in the unemployment rate, output increased by about three percentage points.

It is recognised that the relationship between changes in the unemployment rate and output growth may not be as strong in Ireland as it is in the USA. On account of the close link between the Irish and the UK labour market, the trend in the Irish unemployment rate has been remarkably similar to the UK trend in unemployment. This similarity in the historical behaviour of Irish and British unemployment rates is well documented in the unemployment literature. With migration flows sensitive to labour market conditions in both countries, the *a priori* relationship between unemployment and output in Ireland might prove weak. Despite this, the association between changes in unemployment rates and output growth in Ireland appears quite strong. In Figure 17.11 we plot the change in the unemployment rate (as measured by labour force data) on the horizontal axis and the percentage change in real GDP on the vertical axis. We can see from the scatterplot that there is a negative relationship between the two variables. Although we show the relationship for the thirty-year period 1975–2004, we are particularly interested in the seven-year period beginning in 1994, when unemployment began to fall. These points, marked 1994 to 2000, are all clustered in the top left-hand corner of the graph. The rapid fall in unemployment appears closely associated with the remarkable growth in the Irish economy during the same period. According to one expert, output (i.e. GNP) growth in Ireland in excess of 3.5% per annum leads to falling unemployment.[24] Although simplified, this provides a reasonable explanation for the fall in Irish unemployment.

FIGURE 17.11: UNEMPLOYMENT AND ECONOMIC GROWTH, 1975–2004

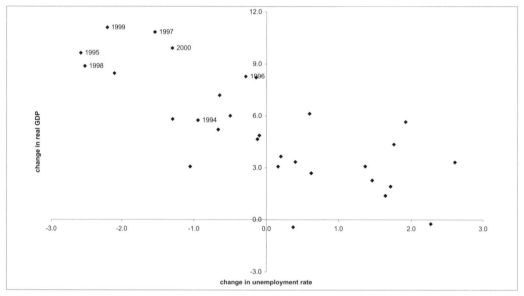

This raises another question, that is, an explanation for Ireland's remarkable growth rates throughout most of the 1990s and into the early part of the new millennium. Ireland's long-term growth performance is explained in the next chapter. A brief outline follows.

In simple terms, we can account for economic growth by increases in the quantity of factor inputs, that is capital and labour, and by increases in productivity, that is output per unit of input. As ever, it is difficult to assess the contribution of capital due to the paucity of data on physical capital stock. What we can say is that the capital stock has been upgraded and modernised by the inflow of foreign direct investment. Nonetheless, there is no doubt that the most significant input contribution comes from labour. In the Irish case, an elastic supply of labour, arising from a combination of factors including rising female labour force participation, favourable demographics and a drawdown of a large stock of unemployed, resulted in a rapid rate of growth in employment in the 1990s. The remarkable increase in employment numbers for the period 1994–2004 is shown in Table 17.4.

TABLE 17.4: EMPLOYMENT NUMBERS 1994–2004

	1994	1995	1996	1997	1998	1999	2000	2001	2002	2003	2004
Employment ('000s)[*]	1221	1282	1329	1380	1494	1589	1671	1722	1764	1793	1836
Annual change (%)	3.2	5.0	3.7	3.8	n.a.	6.4	5.2	3.1	2.4	1.6	2.4

Source: Central Statistics Office.
• For the QNHS, we report the results from the 2nd quarter (March–May) surveys.

These employment growth rates are unusual for a developed country. They are more associated with high-growth developing countries whose agricultural sector supplies a large stock of labour. Interestingly, given its history of immigration, another developed country that has recorded, in its recent past, rapid increases in employment contributing to economic growth is the United States.

In addition to the increased labour supply, real productivity gains have contributed to the growth performance. Advances in technology allow for a more efficient use of available inputs.

Definition

Total factor productivity (TFP) growth is the change in output that arises from technological progress.

Several different studies indicate that total factor productivity growth increased by between 4% and 4.5% per annum in Ireland in the period 1987–97.[25] This compares favourably to productivity growth in Ireland in the late 1970s and 1980s and also, surprisingly, to the productivity growth achieved by the East Asian countries during their period of rapid economic growth. It is somewhat similar to the total factor productivity growth attained by the big western European economies during the post-war Golden Age era. The conclusion of the OECD report into Ireland's economic boom is that '. . . it is clear that while factor input increases have played an important part in fuelling the growth process, total factor productivity gains have played at least as large a role . . .' (OECD, 1999).

As for these productivity gains, it is yet again a combination of factors that has been responsible. Among others, they include investment in human capital, an industrial policy that opened up trade and allowed for an inflow of foreign direct investment (FDI), a shift from traditional, low-productivity sectors to high-technology sectors, corporatism or centralised wage agreements and improvements in demand management that involved tax reform and fiscal prudence. Of course, many of these factors were in place before 1994 and, in some cases, were initiated before the 1987 regime change. This suggests that the remarkable achievement that has happened, namely the transformation of one of western Europe's poorest countries (the 'poorest of the rich' as *The Economist* described it in 1988) to one of its richest ('Europe's shining light' as *The Economist* described it ten years later), required the right mix of mutually reinforcing factors and policies.[26]

The return of high unemployment

In 2007, the unemployment rate in Ireland was 4.7% of the labour force. This was one of the lowest rates in the EU and indeed throughout seventy years of modern Irish economic history. Unemployment remained low for a decade, not rising above 6%. Employment numbers had grown from 1.3 million in 1995 to over 2.1 million in 2007, an increase of over 800,000 persons. A lot of the increase was related to the boom in the Irish economy, and particularly in construction, retail, financial services and the public sector. All of this was to change in 2008 with the global crisis and Ireland's recession. The end of the property boom saw thousands of construction workers – and those in other related sectors/professions such as surveyors, engineers, architects, auctioneers, the legal profession, etc. – laid off. As national output fell, businesses laid off workers, with many firms going under. As consumer spending was cut back, retail sales and jobs in the retail sector collapsed. Unemployment numbers soared, from, using the ILO definition, 103,000 in 2007 to over 290,000 in 2010. Unemployment numbers, using the QNHS data, between spring 2008 and winter 2010 are reported in Table 17.5.

TABLE 17.5: UNEMPLOYMENT IN IRELAND, 2008–2010

	2008			2009				2010			
	Q2	Q3	Q4	Q1	Q2	Q3	Q4	Q1	Q2	Q3	Q4
Numbers (000s)	126.7	159.4	169.7	222.8	264.6	279.8	267.4	275.0	293.6	299.0	299.0
Percentage	5.7	7.0	7.6	10.2	12.0	12.7	12.4	12.9	13.6	13.9	14.1

Source: Central Statistics Office.
Note: Q1 = January–March; Q2 = April–June; Q3 = July–September; Q4 = October–December.

By late 2010, the unemployment rate was 14% of the labour force, with significantly higher rates for the young (aged under 25 years) and, in particular, young men (with a third of all young men in the labour force unemployed). At the same time, more than four out of every ten unemployed were long-term unemployed. The unemployment crisis of the past had returned. At the time of writing (early 2011), the unemployment rate had risen to over 14.5%.

The authorities, faced with trying to simultaneously tackle the banking crisis and the gap in the public finances, were confronted with an ever-growing jobs crisis. A jobs strategy was called for. Some criticised government's budgetary policy which, they argued, only worsened the labour market. Either way, policies to tackle the unemployment crisis were called for and to some extent introduced. These included training for the unemployed; restrictions on social welfare payments (to induce the unemployed to take up any available offers of work); an Employment Subsidy Scheme aimed at retaining workers under threat of redundancy; a Employer Job Incentive Scheme, whereby employers are given a PRSI tax contribution holiday on the employment of a jobseeker from the Live Register; green and renewable energy-related initiatives; and a focus on jobs in the innovation, knowledge and smart economy, etc. A similar jobs initiative programme was launched in 2011 by the new coalition government. A sense of the unemployment crisis in Ireland in 2009/10 is given in the following case study.

CASE STUDY

Extract from *The Irish Examiner*
Record set as 427,000 on Live Register last month
by Seán McCárthaigh

There are fresh fears that the worst of the economic recession may not be over as figures show the number of people on the Live Register reached its highest-ever level in December. Data from the Central Statistics Office show that the seasonally adjusted Live Register rose by 3,300 last month to reach 426,700. The unadjusted December figure, which does not take seasonal factors into account, was up by 10,090. Overall, the number of people on the Live Register, which is not a strict measure of unemployment as it includes some casual and part-time workers, has risen by more than 46% in the past 12 months. The official unemployment rate also rose slightly to 12.5%, although many economists believe it will rise to as much as 14%.

Commenting on yesterday's figures, most analysts stressed that the rate at which people were losing their jobs was slowing down and stabilising. Separate figures from the Department of Enterprise, Trade and Employment show that there were 77,000 notified redundancies during 2009 – an annual increase of almost 90%. A total of 4,121 were officially laid off last month, a 28% increase on December 2008, although last month's figures were less that those recorded earlier in the year.

Labour leader Eamon Gilmore said the latest CSO figures cast serious doubts about claims made by the Taoiseach, Brian Cowen, and other ministers that the recession had bottomed out. 'These are by far the worst December Live Register figures ever recorded. There are now 142,000 more out of work than in December 2008, and 269,000 more than at the time of the general election in 2007,' he said. Mr Gilmore predicted that more people would join dole queues over the coming months despite an increase in emigration for the first time since the 1980s.

Fine Gael employment spokesman, Leo Varadkar, said the record number meant Ireland was a long way from turning the corner. He criticised the Government for failing to introduce measures to help create and retain jobs. 'The Government has become obsessed with balancing the books and the banks, and has done nothing about the collapse of the real economy and the ongoing haemorrhage of jobs.'

Meanwhile, EU figures show that the overall unemployment rate across the 27 member states has reached its highest level in more than a decade. The jobless rate rose to 9.5% in November – up 2% since the same month in 2008, and the highest level since it was first calculated in 2000. Unemployment rates in individual states ranged from 3.9% in the Netherlands up to 22.3% in Latvia. Unemployment in Ireland was measured at 12.9% – the sixth highest rate in the EU. All EU countries recorded a rising number of people out of work over the past year with the Baltic states – Latvia, Lithuania and Estonia – experiencing the most rapid increase in rates. The unemployment rate among people under 25 rose to 21.4% last November compared to 16.6% in the same month in 2008. In Ireland, the rate was 28.7%, the fourth highest in the EU. The general EU unemployment rate of 9.5% compares to 10% in the US and 5.2% in Japan.

Source: The Irish Examiner, 9 January 2010.

Questions

1. Identify and describe the two measures of unemployment in Ireland. Which is a better measure of unemployment, and why? Using the preferred measure, report the unemployment rates for all 27 member states of the EU for 2009. Comment on the cross-country differences.
2. Using the Live Register data for December 2009, profile the unemployed using gender and age data. Using the QNHS (ILO classification) data for 2009, profile the unemployed using duration, education and regional data. Use percentages where possible.
3. The article refers to redundancies, jobs and emigration. Using CSO (www.cso.ie) and Department of Enterprise, Trade and Innovation (www.deti.ie) data, report the yearly numbers, for the three-year period 2007–2009, for total redundancies, employment and net migration. Why does unemployment generally continue to rise after the trough in the economy, as measured by GDP levels?

Answers on website

17.3 INTERNATIONAL TRADE
BY EITHNE MURPHY

17.3.1 *Traditional trade theory*

Mercantilism

Mercantilism was the principal economic doctrine of the seventeenth and eighteenth centuries. As a doctrine it probably reflected as well as influenced the prevailing commercial practices of the period. According to mercantilists, countries get wealthy through the accumulation of precious metals; in that instance, gold and silver. Since gold and silver were the means of payment for goods and services, a country could accumulate such wealth if it ran continuous balance of payments surpluses; that is to say, if it exported more than it imported. Hence policies designed to achieve this end were those that limited imports (especially imports of high value-added products) and encouraged exports.

This philosophy, although subsequently discredited intellectually, has continued to influence international trade practice. The few exceptions were the UK in the nineteenth century and contemporary Hong Kong. Most policy-makers consider a balance of payments surplus to be a positive economic sign. Most policy-makers consider the removal of trade barriers in their national markets to be a concession on their part and one that has to be paid for by reciprocal trade barrier dismantlement on the part of other countries. This is simply mercantilist philosophy in modern guise.

Absolute advantage

Adam Smith is generally considered to be the founding father of economics.[27] For the purposes of the history of international trade theory, two aspects of his philosophy will be highlighted. First, he considered that the objective of all economic activities was consumption. Here we have the first blow against mercantilism. Gold and silver do not contribute directly to our individual welfare; the consumption of goods and services do. Metals are only useful to the extent that they aid consumption. A country that runs a continuous balance of payments surplus is akin to the miser who will not spend his money.

Second, individual self-sufficiency is never efficient, in the sense of representing an optimum use of an individual's energies and talents. Most individuals specialise in their choice of work, which still allows them to consume a wide variety of goods and services if they trade with one another.

Laissez-faire, which is a policy of non-interference in the economic affairs of individuals, will ensure that the goods produced in the economy will be those that consumers want, while competition will ensure that the consumer gets these goods at the cheapest possible price. What holds for the individual also holds for the nation state. If self-sufficiency is inefficient for an individual, it must also be inefficient for a country. A country should specialise in production, producing what it does best, and import other products; this will ensure global efficiency, and it will also allow a country to enjoy a higher overall level of consumption.

TABLE 17.6: PRODUCTION PER PERSON PER WORKING DAY

	Ireland	Britain
Beef	20 kg	5 kg
Grain	2 kg	10 kg

If one person fewer engages in grain production in Ireland and instead devotes his energies to beef production, then grain output will fall by 2 kilos per day and beef output will increase by 20 kilos per day. Do the opposite in Britain and beef output will fall by 5 kilos while grain production will rise by 10 kilos. The net effect is that overall beef production rises by 15 kilos per day and overall grain production rises by 8 kilos per day. If both countries trade with each other, both can enjoy the benefits of higher overall production.

Comparative advantage

The problem with the theory of absolute advantage is that it assumes that countries and the world can gain from specialisation and trade if they are absolutely more efficient than other countries in some line of production. David Ricardo, however, showed that a country and the world can gain from specialisation and trade even if one country is better at producing all goods. He called this the theory of comparative advantage.[28]

TABLE 17.7: PRODUCTION PER PERSON PER WORKING DAY

	Ireland	Britain
Beef	6 kg	10 kg
Grain	2 kg	10 kg

Workers in Britain are more productive in both beef and grain production. How then can Ireland and Britain gainfully trade? According to David Ricardo, if each country specialises in what it does 'relatively' best, both can gain from trade. We can see that in grain production, Britain is five times more productive than Ireland, whereas in beef production it is less than twice as productive. Accordingly, Ireland should specialise where its absolute disadvantage is least, i.e. in beef production, and Britain should specialise where its absolute advantage is greatest, i.e. in grain production.

In Ireland the true cost of a kilo of grain is 3 kilos of beef. Taking a person away from beef production and employing them in the grain sector means sacrificing 3 kilos of beef daily in order to have 1 kilo of grain. In Britain the cost of a kilo of grain is 1 kilo of beef. True cost is opportunity cost. Alternatively the cost of 1 kilo of beef in Britain is 1 kilo of grain. If Britain can import beef and pay less than 1 kilo of grain for it then Britain is better off than it was before. If Ireland can import grain and pay less than 3 kilos of beef for 1 kilo of grain then Ireland is better off than it was before.

So an exchange of beef for grain at a price somewhere between 1:1 and 1:3 will benefit both countries. In other words, if international terms of trade (the cost of a unit of imported goods in terms of the amount of exports required to purchase them) are different from a country's opportunity cost of production, then the country can gain from specialising and trading. If, for example, the international terms of trade were 2 kilos of beef for 1 kilo of grain, then the gains to Ireland and Britain from specialising in beef and grain respectively would be the following:

Ireland

Take a person away from grain production and put them working in the beef sector. Output of beef would rise by 6 kilos a day while output of grain would fall by 2 kilos a day. But 6 kilos of beef buys 3 kilos of grain on the international market. So Ireland can actually enjoy a higher level of grain consumption than before.

Britain

As an exercise, see how Britain can also gain and enjoy a higher level of beef consumption than it did before, by specialising out of beef and into grain.

We can represent graphically the production and consumption possibilities of both countries both before and after trade. The only additional information that we need are the number of workers in an economy. For simplicity let us assume that both countries have 1 million workers.

FIGURE 17.12: PRODUCTION POSSIBILITIES FOR IRELAND AND BRITAIN

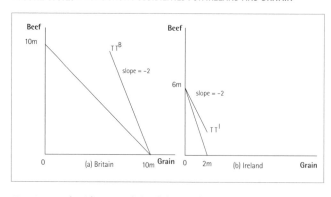

Figure 17.12 shows both countries' production possibilities for a day. If all workers are fully employed in Britain in the beef sector only, it can produce 10 million kilos of beef daily. Alternatively, if all workers are employed in the grain sector, it can produce 10 million kilos of grain daily. Or if some workers are employed in the beef sector and others in the grain sector it can produce less than 10 million kilos of both goods daily. For example, if 70% of the labour force were employed in the beef sector and 30% in the grain sector, it could produce 7 million kilos of beef and 3 million kilos of grain daily. The production possibility frontier (PPF) shows all the different combinations of beef and grain that are feasible, given the resource base and given the productivity of the resource base in both sectors (see Chapter 1). The slope of the PPF shows the cost of a kilo of grain in terms of beef which is −1. Before trade, Britain is forced to consume exactly what it produces.

Similarly Ireland can produce either 6 million kilos of beef daily or 2 million kilos of grain daily or some combination thereof. The slope of the PPF is –3 indicating the cost of a kilo of grain. Again before trade Ireland can only consume what it produces.

With trade Ireland produces only beef and Britain only grain. The international terms of trade are 2 kilos of beef for 1 kilo of grain. Both countries are now no longer obliged to consume exactly what they produce: they are merely obliged to ensure that the value of domestic production equals the value of domestic consumption, where prices are determined internationally. The line TT^I for Ireland shows us Ireland's potential consumption. We can see that potential consumption with trade is greater than it was without trade. Similarly for Britain, the line TT^B shows us Britain's potential consumption post-trade and we can see that it dominates pre-trade consumption possibilities. The rate at which goods exchange internationally is determined by international demand and supply.

What we can conclude from David Ricardo's analysis of trade is that all countries, even the most inefficient, can gain from trade, provided that they specialise in what they do relatively best and provided that the international terms of trade differ from the domestic opportunity cost of production.

Revealed comparative advantage and competitiveness

How do we know where a country's comparative advantage lies? One way is to look at the unit cost of producing different goods; another is to look at the prices of these goods before trade, assuming, of course, that prices equal unit costs. If the only factor of production is labour and all labour gets paid the same wage, then the price of grain in Ireland will be three times the price of beef since workers in the grain sector are only one-third as productive as workers in the beef sector. In Britain the price of a kilo of grain will be the same as the price of a kilo of beef since workers are equally productive in both sectors and get paid the same amount.

	Ireland	Britain
$\dfrac{P\text{ beef}}{P\text{ grain}}$	$\dfrac{1}{3}$	$\dfrac{1}{1}$

Since one-third is less than 1, indicating that Ireland's relative price of beef is less than that of Britain, it follows that Ireland has a comparative advantage in beef production.

	Ireland	Britain
$\dfrac{P\text{ beef}}{P\text{ grain}}$	$\dfrac{3}{1}$	$\dfrac{1}{1}$

Since 1 is less than 3, indicating that Britain's relative price of grain is less than that of Ireland, it follows that Britain has a comparative advantage in grain production. It is interesting and important to note that in our stylised two-good, two-country world, as long as the domestic opportunity cost of production is different in both countries, then it is impossible for one country to have a comparative advantage in the production of both goods.

Many individuals still find the theory of comparative advantage counter-intuitive. It is all very well to say that what matters for trade purposes is domestic opportunity, cost of production or domestic relative prices, but in the real world what matters are absolute prices. How then in the real world can an Ireland of the above example compete with Britain if it is less productive in all lines of production?

The answer to this puzzle is to realise that prices are determined by two elements, the productivity of factors of production and the cost of employing factors of production. Since workers in Ireland are less productive than workers in Britain, they will earn less, even after trade. For example, if Irish workers were paid €10 a day and British workers UK£6 a day and the euro–sterling exchange rate was €1 = £0.6, then we can see the Irish and British workers get the same return. In this situation Ireland would not be able to export anything to Britain; it would be uncompetitive as its prices would be too high.

If on the other hand, Irish wages were €4 a day to Britain's UK£6 and the exchange rate was still €1 = £0.6, then Ireland would be able to successfully export beef at a lower price than the British. This is because although the Irish worker in the beef sector has a productivity of only 60% of his British counterpart, his wages are only 40% of British wages. They would still, however, not be able to export grain as the price of grain in Ireland would still be higher than in Britain. This is because an Irish worker has a productivity in the grain sector which is only 20% of that of a British worker in grain production but his wages are 40% of British wages.

So lower wages in the less productive country allow it to compete successfully against the more productive country. This does not mean that the less productive country does not gain from trade. If the imported good costs less than it did before trade, then the country has gained.

Another means by which a less productive country pays its workers less than the more productive country is through a depreciation of its currency. Let us return to the example where Irish workers were paid €10 a day to Britain's UK£6. At the €1 = £0.6 exchange rate, Ireland would want to import both grain and beef from Britain, and Britain would not want to import anything from Ireland. The excess demand for sterling and the excess supply of euros would cause a depreciation of the euro against sterling. This depreciation would continue until such time as the excess demand for sterling and the corresponding excess supply of euros had been eliminated. If the exchange rates were for example €1 to £0.3 then Ireland would be able to successfully export beef at that exchange rate.

It should be noted that an exchange rate depreciation is analogous to a reduction in the return to domestic factors of production. In this example, the exchange rate depreciation is the same as a cut in the domestic wage rate.

The sources of comparative advantage

In the previous section we saw that all countries can engage in mutually beneficial trade, provided that the relative prices of their goods prior to trade differ. This naturally begs the question, what determines pre-trade relative prices? The answer is straightforward. Prices of goods in a country are determined by the interaction of supply and demand. If pre-trade relative prices differ among countries, this is indicative of inter-country differences in domestic conditions of supply and demand. All other things being equal (*ceteris paribus*), the greater the supply of a good, the lower its price; and the greater the demand for a good, the higher its price. There are two principal theories as to why supply conditions differ among countries. These are, first, technological and climatic differences and second, resource differences.

David Ricardo's explanation of international trade, which was based on differences in the levels of productivity per person per day in various industries, could be an example of technological or climatic differences among countries. In the example of Britain and Ireland, the British worker has a higher productivity in all sectors compared to the Irish worker. This could be due to a climate that is more conducive to higher yields or, alternatively, it could be due to superior British technology.

Ricardo's model is essentially based on a labour theory of value, since labour is the only factor of production that he considers and it is the productivity of labour that determines the domestic opportunity cost of production. There are no distribution effects in Ricardo's model because labour is considered to be the only factor of production. Hence, if free trade benefits a country, then it must be benefiting all of its workers, since all income earned accrues to workers.

At the beginning of the last century two Swedish economists, Eli Heckscher and Bertil Ohlin, offered a new explanation as to why supply conditions and hence relative prices differ among countries; countries differ in terms of natural endowments.[29] These endowments (for example land, labour and capital) are inputs that are used in the production of goods and services. So differences in endowments get reflected in differences in the cost of producing various goods. For example, one would expect that a country with an abundance of good farmland would be an efficient producer of agricultural products. The reasoning is simple: an abundance of good farmland means low rental values for land and hence low prices for agricultural products, since agricultural products are intensive users of land.

The Heckscher–Ohlin model of trade (as it is popularly known) differs from the Ricardian model in another respect: the distribution consequences of free trade. In this model, notwithstanding the fact that the country as a whole gains from trade, there are income redistribution effects within a country. Putting it more starkly, there are winners and losers when a country opens its borders and engages in free trade. This is a consequence of the fact that there is more than one factor of production. Free trade will not only change the production structure of a country (more specialisation), it will also change the demand for factors of production.

Take the example of a country that, as a result of free trade, now specialises in the production of land-intensive agricultural products, whereas before free trade, it was also producing capital-intensive industrial products. The change in the country's production structure would have increased the demand for land and reduced the demand for capital. This would have resulted in increased returns for landowners and decreased returns for the owners of capital. Landowners gain and capitalists lose as a result of free trade.

These two principal theories of comparative advantage are similar, to the extent that they conclude that a country will have a comparative advantage in products which they produce in relative abundance, regardless of whether that abundance is determined by climate, technology or resource availability.

Demand conditions can also help determine a country's comparative advantage. If, for example, two countries had identical supply conditions but different tastes, pre-trade relative prices would differ. If the Irish consumer displayed a relatively stronger preference for grain than her British counterpart, this would lead to higher pre-trade prices for grain in Ireland compared to Britain (assuming identical supply conditions) thus indicating comparative disadvantage in Ireland in grain production. So in trade between Ireland and Britain, we would expect Ireland to be an importer of grain.

Although demand differences across countries can help explain comparative advantage, it is little more than a theoretical curiosity since it is unlikely that it is the principal determinant of comparative advantage.

Policy implications of traditional trade theory

The common feature of traditional trade theories (be they of the Ricardian or Heckscher–Ohlin variety) is that economic agents are assumed to be operating in perfectly competitive markets. In other words increasing returns to scale or spillover effects do not exist and no individual or firm can influence prices. Countries trade because they are different and the greater the differences between countries the greater the gains from trade. We also expect trade between countries to be of an 'inter-industry' variety. In other words countries will not have two-way trade in the same product: they will either be an exporter or importer of that product.

In an earlier section we saw how a country can enjoy a higher level of consumption in the aggregate if it removes its trade barriers. If all countries remove barriers to trade, all countries will enjoy a higher level of aggregate consumption and income. But even if some countries continue to pursue protectionist policies, the countries that unilaterally remove their trade barriers increase their level of national income. This is an incredibly strong result: it implies that all policy-makers can increase real national income simply by removing trade barriers. Moreover, it also means that policy-makers can increase national welfare through trade barrier dismantlement and a proper redistribution of the gains from trade.

Of course in practice, liberalisation will hurt some sections of society, but if the national cake has grown, a taxation and transfer policy that taxes the beneficiaries of trade liberalisation and transfers the proceeds of this tax to those whom trade liberalisation has made worse off could ensure that everybody gains. This does of course presuppose that there are no inefficiencies associated with a tax and transfer policy. If we ignore the possibility of a tax and transfer system, then we can assert that the principal beneficiary of free trade is the consumer, who is now able to enjoy cheaper imported goods than was previously the case.

If trade liberalisation is so beneficial we must ask why the world is not characterised by free trade? What causes governments to interfere with trade? A whole literature has developed to answer this question and we will address it in a later section. For the moment the most important thing to remember is that the gains from trade outlined so far all depend on the assumption that markets are perfectly competitive. Remove this assumption (as we will do later) and the whole edifice of unilaterally realisable gains from trade becomes much more fragile.

Trade barriers

Governments interfere with the international movement of goods and services for a variety of economic, political and fiscal reasons. In this section we will identify the principal instruments that governments use which impede free trade. A good overview of the effects of trade policy is provided by Corden (1971).[30]

Tariffs

A tariff is a tax on imports and is usually *ad valorem*; a percentage of the price of the imported goods. It is inherently discriminatory, since it does not apply to domestic goods that compete with imports. It results in a redistribution of income away from consumers in favour of domestic producers and the government. Governments have a new source of revenue while domestic producers can now charge a higher price thanks to the protective effect of the tariff. The real income of consumers is reduced as they must now pay more for those goods that are subject to tariffs.

Quotas

Tariffs operate by taxing imports and allowing demand and supply to adjust to the new domestic price. Quotas operate by restricting the volume of imports and allowing the domestic price to adjust in such a way that the domestic market clears, i.e. domestic demand equals domestic and foreign supply. If a quota is to be effective in restricting imports it will inevitably result in higher domestic prices for the product subject to such a restriction. This is because the restriction of foreign supply will result in excess demand for the product, which will increase its price.

Again, as with the tariff, the consumer will suffer a loss in real income due to higher domestic prices for the good subject to quantitative import restrictions. Domestic producers of competing products will gain due to higher prices for their output but there will be no fiscal gain for the government. Those fortunate enough to hold import licences (or quotas) will gain as they now hold a valuable asset: the right to import good(s) at world prices and sell them at inflated domestic prices.

Voluntary restraint on exports

This is very similar to a quota except in this instance it is the exporting country that agrees to limit the quantity of its exports to the importing country, thus increasing the price of such goods in the countries that import them. The only difference in the income redistribution effect of this measure compared to quotas is that it is the foreign exporter, as opposed to the holder of import quotas, who enjoys the rent (the difference between the domestic price of the good in the importing countries and its world price) associated with this form of trade restriction. It is also a very popular means of restricting trade, as it is not very visible and it allows countries to contravene international trade laws in a way that would be impossible with tariffs or import quotas.

Administrative barriers

The governments of many countries make it difficult for foreign exporters to penetrate their domestic markets by putting in place a whole series of rules and regulations with which the foreign exporter must comply, at some cost. These rules often come in the guise of health and safety standards or measures designed to give consumers protection.

Frontier delays and the paperwork associated with crossing national borders add to the cost of trying to penetrate certain markets and hence is akin to a tax on imports.

Governments are important players in an economy, not just as the overseer who determines the rules of the game, but also as a player in the market. In a free international market, governments would purchase goods from the supplier who offers the product(s) that they desire at the best price, regardless of the nationality of the supplier. In reality, public procurement tends to have a decidedly nationalistic bent; in other words public contracts often go to domestic firms.

Export subsidies and export taxes

Giving domestic producers a subsidy when they export encourages them to produce more for foreign markets at the expense of the domestic market. The cost of this policy is borne by the taxpayer and the domestic consumer, since the diversion of supply away from the domestic market raises domestic prices. Export taxes have the opposite effect of penalising producers who serve foreign markets, with positive fiscal consequences for the government and lower prices for the domestic consumer.

All the above measures, be they designed to protect producers who serve the domestic market or aid producers who serve foreign markets, are an interference with free trade. In a perfectly competitive world, such measures reduce national and global income through their interference with the market mechanism. They distort the allocation of resources between different sectors of the economy, promoting some sectors at the expense of others.

Justifying trade restrictions

Non-economic reasons

The government of a country may restrict the importation of certain goods in order to be self-sufficient in those products. Self-sufficiency, although it entails an economic cost, may be desired to achieve some political goal. This goal could be national security, it could form part of a country's international strategic objectives or merely be designed to protect a country from foreign influences that are considered dangerous and pernicious. For example, self-sufficiency in agriculture and armaments could be justified as a precautionary measure in case imports of these products are cut off in times of war. One means of settling scores, when countries' governments disagree politically with one another, is to impose a trade embargo. The importation of animals into rabies-free countries is restricted for obvious national health reasons; the same goes for drugs. All these restrictions are costly, but that is not to say that the realisation of such objectives does not merit such a cost.

Economic reasons

A good survey of economic arguments for and against protectionism is provided by Corden (1974).[31]

The principal economic reasons given for interfering with free trade are the protection of infant industries and the maintenance of employment. The infant industry argument is associated with the German economist Friedrich List (1789–1846), who advocated the protection of industries from foreign competition in order to allow them to develop. Without such protectionism, such industries would not be able to withstand foreign competition. Once these industries had developed sufficiently so as to be in a position to compete with foreign producers, such protection could be removed.

There are two principal criticisms of this theory: the first criticism questions the *a priori* assumption that there are market factors which prevent the spontaneous emergence of these industries in an unrestricted market, and the second criticism asserts that overprotected infants never mature.

Recall that traditional trade theory operates within the neoclassical framework of perfect competition. Perfect competition implies, *inter alia*, perfect knowledge, no barriers to entry and no spillover effects or externalities. In such a world, if there are potentially profitable industries that are as yet undeveloped, then entrepreneurs, driven by a desire to make profit, will enter these industries. If those industries are potentially profitable, even if that profit is not immediately realisable, then there is no need for government-inspired protection to help them develop. The second criticism makes the point that protectionism, instead of aiding the development of industries, can often inhibit their development by shielding them from the forces of international competition.

Protectionism allows workers in protected industries to retain jobs that would otherwise have been lost. However, in a perfectly competitive world, removing trade restrictions would cause the import competing sector to shrink but the export sector would expand, so workers and resources would move from the import competing sector to the export sector. Unemployment should only be a temporary phenomenon, lasting as long as it takes displaced workers to find new jobs. If it persists, then according to economists there must be some reason (other than the removal of trade barriers) that is causing its persistence, such as inflexible labour markets and minimum wages. Removal of these institutionally imposed rigidities will solve the problem of unemployment. Protectionism is a more costly way of achieving the same objective.

Distributional reasons

As mentioned earlier, the removal of trade barriers, like any other form of structural adjustment, involves winners and losers. Losers are those who witness a reduction in their real income as a result of trade liberalisation. Governments are very susceptible to political pressure and those sections of society that are threatened with a reduction in income, as a result of trade liberalisation, have every incentive to organise in order to lobby the government against such measures.

Many political economists argue that the protectionist bias of most governments reflects the political power of interest groups associated with protected industries. But just as some sections of society are adversely affected by free trade, others are adversely affected by protectionism; namely consumers. If commercial policy has a protectionist bias, it must mean that the political power of pro-protectionist groups is greater than the political power of free trade groups.

How can this be? Olson (1965) discusses the logic of collective action and the impact of interest groups on the political process.[32] Consumers, who are the main beneficiaries of free trade policies, are a large dispersed group. So the benefits of free trade are spread over a large body of people. Hence, even though in the aggregate the gains to consumers outweigh the losses to those associated with protected sectors, their *per capita* gains must be much less than the *per capita* losses of the losers.

Moreover, these gains, since they come in the form of lower prices, are not very visible whereas the losses (which usually take the form of a fall in earnings) are highly visible. Thus there exists an asymmetry in the incentive to organise and lobby among consumers and protectionist interests; the latter having a much greater incentive than the former to defend their position. It is also much easier to organise a lobby group when the number is smaller and geographically and sectorally concentrated, which is usually the case with protected industries.

Concluding remarks on traditional trade theory

All of the preceding analysis takes as its starting point the assumption of perfectly competitive markets. As a consequence, we see that protectionism unambiguously reduces national income and that there is no economic or even distributional justification for its existence. In the next section we will look at new theories of trade and specialisation that assume that markets are imperfect. We will see that in the context of imperfect markets, trade restrictions may not necessarily be welfare reducing. However, we will also see that trade restrictions are a second-best means of achieving certain economic and distributional objectives. In other words, free trade combined with other policies can realise the same objectives at a lower social cost.

17.3.2 New trade theory

Traditional trade theory dominated intellectual thinking for more than a hundred years. However, increasingly, academics, students and general observers began to notice the disparity between theory and reality. Most world trade in the post-war period was not trade between very different nations but trade between developed countries with similar resource bases, similar technology and similar tastes. Moreover, most trade between these nations was not of an inter-industry variety but rather of an intra-industry type; that is the simultaneous import and export of similar products.

In the 1980s, economists put forward new theories to explain this phenomenon. Foremost among them was Paul Krugman; in fact his name has become almost synonymous with new trade theory.[33] First, they claimed that consumers desire diversity. Some Germans drive BMWs and some drive Peugeots: likewise in France. If diverse consumer tastes cannot be satisfied by domestic supply, we will witness a two-way flow of trade in similar products, in this instance a two-way flow in car trade.

What makes intra-industry trade in identifiable branded products more probable and profitable is the existence of economies of scale. When technology exhibits economies of scale, it tends to result in high levels of output, since the more a firm produces the lower the unit cost of production. So it does not make sense for French or German manufacturers of cars to try and produce all varieties themselves, since this would lead to much shorter production runs, and much higher costs and prices as a result. Therefore, the combination of diverse consumer tastes and economies of scale are sufficient to ensure trade of an intra-industry variety.

It should also be noted that the market structure in which such trade takes place is necessarily imperfect, since goods are distinguishable by brand (which is never the case under perfect competition) and economies of scale tend to promote large firms who dominate an industry. The industrial structure may be monopolistic or oligopolistic, depending on the degree of competition that exists in an industry.

According to traditional trade theory, if two countries had identical demand and supply conditions and hence identical pre-trade prices, there would be no basis for mutually beneficial trade. When, however, economies of scale exist, two identical countries can engage in mutually beneficial trade by specialising and realising the lower unit cost that specialisation brings. Unlike trade based on comparative advantage, trade based on increasing returns to scale is hard to predict in advance of its occurrence. We cannot with confidence predict what country is likely to produce what product. All we know is that the country with the largest domestic market is probably more likely to be competitive in industries exhibiting increasing returns to scale.

Other forms of market imperfections that have important implications for trade policy are externalities or spillover effects. In many instances the private and social cost of an action differs. An individual entrepreneur thinking about setting up a plant in a certain region will weigh up the private costs and benefits of such a decision. He will reject the option if, *ex ante*, it appears to be unprofitable. Yet if many firms take this decision, what appeared initially as a non-viable option could become viable due to positive spillover effects. Without being exhaustive, these spillover effects (or externalities) could be: the availability of cheaper and more varied services (which are greater, the greater the concentration of industry); greater access to skilled labour (which tends to be attracted to regions with a high firm density); and easier access to vital information, which is so crucial to the success of business in a competitive environment.

The policy implications of new trade theory or the policy implications of imperfect markets

When markets exhibit imperfections there is always a justification for government intervention to correct the market imperfection; this does not mean that intervention always improves upon the market outcome. Efficiency-improving intervention requires appropriate information in order to know where market imperfections exist and their extent. It also requires the choice of the correct instrument of intervention.

All the aforementioned is relevant to new trade theory, since the latter is firmly rooted within an imperfect market context. For example, in a world characterised by diverse industries, some of which exhibit increasing returns to scale, while others exhibit decreasing or constant returns to scale, the effect of trade liberalisation is much less clear. The beauty of traditional trade theory was that it showed that trade liberalisation benefited all countries, even the most technologically backward. New trade theory, on the other hand, can make a case for free trade based on global efficiency or even the need for good international relations between countries, but it cannot unambiguously claim to benefit all countries.

Free trade brings about a restructuring of an economy. If a country witnesses a decline in its increasing returns industries and growth in its decreasing or constant returns industries, due to trade liberalisation, then the average productivity of resources will have declined. This does not mean that the country is necessarily worse off as a result, since this loss in terms of the productivity of its resources has to be weighed against the gain to consumers from cheaper imports.

The situation is no longer clear-cut. Such a result is not as startling as it may first appear, since we are all familiar with the phenomena of declining or economically backward regions within what is often a prosperous country. Since free trade exists between regions within a country, it is not obvious all have benefited from free inter-regional trade.[34]

The policy implication of new trade theory is that it creates a 'case' (that is to say a necessary but not sufficient condition) for intervention. Intervention could take the form of import barriers or export subsidies or even production subsidies in those industries where economies of scale exist. The objective is clear: to try and ensure that a country has a high percentage of increasing returns or high value-added industries. The decline of the traditionally high wage manufacturing sector in the UK and its replacement by low-wage services should not be a matter of policy indifference. Of course the negative side of the intervention argument is that it is a zero sum game. Not all countries can have a monopoly on increasing returns industries. If all try, then all will suffer as a consequence. Also, certain kinds of intervention such as export subsidies only serve to antagonise international competitors and can easily degenerate into a trade war from which no one emerges as victor.

Externalities are in essence the core of the infant industry argument. Social and private benefits and costs differ, so governments protect certain industries, where they consider that the social benefits of that industry's existence outweigh the private benefits to the industry's proprietors. Often, however, there are more effective and direct means of tackling market imperfections. If, for example, private entrepreneurs are unable to exploit a sector where a country may have a potential comparative or competitive advantage, due to lack of availability of finance, the correct response by policy-makers is to improve the nature of financial institutions, to overcome this imperfection. Barring this strategy, capital or loan subsidies may be appropriate. Protectionism, according to economists, is down this list of appropriate policy measures to combat market imperfections.

Even though theoretically there is a strong case to be made against unlimited free trade, very few of the new trade theorists actually advocate protectionism or other forms of interference with the market mechanism. Their failure to breach the gap between theory and policy could be due to an innate conservatism or to their fear of what can be broadly termed political failures. The market is not the only social system riddled with imperfections. The informational requirements necessary to intervene correctly are enormous and, at a more serious level, there is always the fear that governments will become hostages to vested interests if they make it standard politics to intervene in trade policy.

For these reasons, notwithstanding the less rosy picture presented by new trade theory (especially for poorer and smaller countries), new trade theorists still advocate free trade as the best option in an imperfect world.

17.3.3 The Irish experience

Irish trade policy

It is difficult to find real-world examples of the polar extremes of trade policy as defined in theory; that is to say self-sufficiency and complete free trade. The reality is that nearly all countries engage to some extent in the international exchange of goods and services and nearly all countries have rules and regulations in place, that interfere to some extent with the volume and direction of international trade. However, along the spectrum from self-sufficiency to free trade, we can judge the bias of a country's trade policy over time and also make comparisons between countries.

It is in this context that we can say that Ireland's trade policy was relatively liberal (free-trade oriented) in the 1920s, highly protectionist from the 1930s to the end of the 1950s, and progressively liberal ever since. The global environment during the period of protectionism varied considerably. The 1930s witnessed a worldwide global depression, followed by a world war, followed by a period of reconstruction and very rapid growth in the post-war period.

Despite the varying fortunes of the world economy in this period, the contemporaneous Irish economic experience singularly failed to live up to expectations. The disillusionment with protectionism as a strategy for economic development led to a reversal in the direction of commercial policy. This shift in policy direction was reflected in a unilateral cut in tariffs in 1963 and 1964, followed by the Anglo-Irish Free Trade Agreement in 1965 and culminating in our admission to what was then the European Economic Community (EEC) in 1973.

The principal aim of the EEC, which was set up by the Treaty of Rome in 1957, was to foster free trade among its member states and to pursue a common trade policy with regard to non-member states. Hence since 1973, Ireland has essentially waived its right to an autonomous trade policy, by agreeing to abide by the rules and regulations of the EEC. The European Economic Community has itself evolved since its original inception. It now has many more member states (and potential applicants knocking on the door) and has renewed itself and its commitment to freer internal trade through the Single European Act, which came into force in July 1987, the Treaty on European Union (which was finalised at Maastricht in December 1991), the Amsterdam Treaty 1997, the Nice Treaty 2001 and the 2007 Lisbon Treaty.

The European Union (as it is now known) has also participated in international agreements and signed treaties designed to foster freer trade at a more global level. Some of these arrangements are bilateral, such as its free trade agreement with EFTA (European Free Trade Association), while others are more global and non-discriminatory such as its participation in the GATT (General Agreement on Tariffs and Trade), which was itself replaced by the WTO (World Trade Organisation) in 1995.

GATT/WTO has been the most important organisation governing world trade in the post-war period. It has been committed to global free trade as enshrined in its principles of National Treatment and Non-Discrimination. 'National Treatment' is a commitment to give equal treatment to national and international transactions, while 'Non-Discrimination' is a commitment to not distinguish between countries on the grounds of origin. It has also overseen successive rounds of multilateral trade barrier reductions, whereby all member countries agreed to reduce trade barriers by some agreed amount. The last round of multilateral trade negotiations, the Doha Development Round, started in 2001 and is still, at the time of writing, incomplete. Notwithstanding the suspension of talks, the WTO is still making progress on further liberalisation, particularly in the areas of services and agriculture.

What should be clear is that Ireland's trade policy has to be looked at within the international institutional framework, first as a member of the EU and second within the context of the EU's membership of the WTO. The fact that Ireland and all the other member countries of the EU and WTO have agreed to bind themselves to rules that increasingly curtail these countries' rights to interfere with international trade is testament to the general faith that global prosperity requires the unfettered movement of goods and services between countries.

SUMMARY

1. Inflation is a rise in the general price level. There are many different causes of inflation. The Quantity Theory of Money is the earliest model of inflation. It suggests that the price level increases with the money supply and that monetary policy is ineffective in changing an economy's level of output. Demand pull inflation is caused by increases in aggregate demand. Cost push inflation results from a rise in costs in general, and of wages in particular. A depreciating currency, unless checked, results in imported inflation. Expectations also play an important role. During inflationary periods, debtors gain at the expense of creditors, individuals on fixed incomes lose, consumption is encouraged, and fixed-income assets become less attractive.

2. Policies to combat inflation concentrate on either the demand side or the supply side of the economy. Tighter control over the money supply, increases in tax rates and reductions in public expenditure are all examples of demand-side measures. Increasing competition and cutting labour costs are examples of supply-side measures.

3. Unemployment is a stock concept: it measures the number of people who are out of work at a particular point in time. There are different types of unemployment. They include frictional, seasonal, structural, demand deficient and classical. The costs of unemployment are both private and social. They accrue to the unemployed, to the taxpayer and to society at large. Whereas it is possible to measure the economic costs arising from unemployment, it is very difficult to estimate the social costs.

4. There are many different explanations of unemployment. With the assumption of freely flexible wages, unemployment in the classical world is temporary and voluntary. For Keynes, unemployment could be long-term and involuntary. It is caused by insufficient aggregate demand and requires government action. Fiscal policy is the preferred option. The monetarist and the supply-side theories of unemployment are similar to the classical explanation. Government intervention is seen as part of the problem rather than the solution. A large number of unemployed is a cyclical characteristic of the capitalist system, according to Marx: unemployment is the result of the inevitable class struggle between capitalists and workers.

5. Trade theories attempt to explain the causes and consequences of the international exchange of goods and services. The multiplicity of theories can be broadly categorised into two schools of thought: traditional trade theory and new trade theory. The essential difference between the two approaches is that traditional trade theory assumes that markets are perfectly competitive, while new trade theory assumes that markets are imperfectly competitive to a greater or lesser extent.

6. The key concept in traditional trade theory is 'comparative advantage'. It says that all countries can engage in mutually beneficial trade by specialising in what they do 'relatively' best. Countries trade because they are different and this difference reflects itself in their domestic relative costs. The greater the differences between countries, the greater the gains from trade. Such trade will be inter-industry in type. The optimal trade strategy in a perfectly competitive environment is unilateral trade barrier dismantlement. The bases for new trade theory are

economies of scale and consumer demand for product diversity. Such trade tends to be intra-industry in type and to take place between relatively similar countries. It results in global production efficiency but all countries may not necessarily gain from such trade. The optimal trade strategy in this context may be interventionist in order to maximise a country's share of the gains from trade.

KEY TERMS

Inflation
Inflation
Inflation rate
Deflation
Disinflation
Creeping inflation
Hyper-inflation
Stagflation
Price index
Consumer Price
    Index
Harmonised Index of
    Consumer Prices
GDP deflator
Nominal interest rate
Real interest rate
Menu costs
Indexation
Fiscal drag
Money Illusion
Shoe leather effect
Unanticipated inflation
Anticipated inflation
Demand pull inflation
Inflationary gap
Quantity Theory of Money
Money velocity
Monetarism
Adaptive expectations
Cost push inflation
Imported inflation
Rational expectations

Unemployment
Quarterly National
    Household Survey
Live Register
Labour force
Unemployment rate
Frictional unemployment
Seasonal unemployment
Structural unemployment
Demand-deficient
    unemployment
Classical unemployment
Voluntary unemployment
Involuntary unemployment
Deflationary gap
Natural rate of
    unemployment
Reserve army of
    unemployed
Unemployment trap
Replacement ratio
Poverty trap
Tax wedge
Labour market rigidities
Wage bargaining process
Insider-outsider model
Labour legislation
Okun's Law
Total factor productivity growth

International trade
Mercantilism
Absolute advantage
Comparative advantage
International terms of trade
Opportunity cost of
    production
Production possibility frontier
Pre-trade relative prices
Revealed comparative
    advantage
Factor endowments
Inter-industry trade
Tariffs
Quotas
Voluntary export
restraints
Export subsidies/taxes
Infant industries
Imperfect markets
Economies of scale
Externalities
Intra-industry trade

REVIEW QUESTIONS

1. Explain the term 'inflation'. Why is inflation undesirable? Who benefits from inflation?
2. Explain the causes of inflation. Suggest how each cause can be tackled.
3. What are the costs of unemployment?

4. Explain the theories of unemployment. How do they relate to the Irish experience of unemployment?
5. Explain the theory of comparative advantage. How does it differ from absolute advantage? According to the theory of comparative advantage, what countries are most likely to engage in mutually beneficial trade?
6. By what mechanism is comparative advantage translated into absolute competitiveness?

WORKING PROBLEMS

1. The figures in Table 17.8 were taken from the annual Income and Expenditure report for a country called Hibernia. It shows GDP at current market prices and GDP at constant market prices.

TABLE 17.8: GDP AT CONSTANT AND CURRENT MARKET PRICES (2003–2011)

Year	Current GDP (€ million)	Constant GDP (€ million)
2003	28,598	32,986
2004	29,675	33,622
2005	31,529	34,746
2006	34,054	35,682
2007	36,624	37,736
2008	41,409	41,409
2009	45,634	44,594
2010	52,760	49,382
2011	60,582	53,609

(a) What is the base year? Explain your answer.
(b) Calculate the GDP deflator for each year. What is the general trend?
(c) Calculate the inflation rate for 2011.

2. The working population of the home country is two million. The working population of the foreign country is ten million. Both countries can only produce two goods: beer and grain. The average productivity of labour in the production of both goods is shown in Table 17.9.

TABLE 17.9

	Home	Foreign
Beer (litre per person per day)	4	16
Grain (kg per person per day)	8	8

Describe and explain the pattern of trade between the home country and the foreign country.

MULTI-CHOICE QUESTIONS

1. The inflation rate for 2010 was 1.6%. The CPI for 2009 was 119.6. What was the CPI for 2010?
    (a) 115.1;
    (b) 124.6;
    (c) 121.5;
    (d) 118.2;
    (e) none of the above.

2. Anticipated inflation:
    (a) imposes no costs on society;
    (b) can result in menu costs and the shoe leather effect;
    (c) imposes more costs on society than unanticipated inflation;
    (d) both (b) and (c) above;
    (e) none of the above.

3. For monetarists, unemployment:
    (a) is largely involuntary;
    (b) is caused by a deficiency in demand;
    (c) often results from inappropriate demand-management policies;
    (d) can be cured by active demand-management policies;
    (e) both (b) and (d) above.

4. Involuntary unemployment:
    (a) is caused by a deficient demand for goods;
    (b) is closely associated with Keynesian unemployment;
    (c) is difficult to measure accurately;
    (d) is a measure of those who are willing to work but who cannot find a job at the market wage rate;
    (e) all of the above.

5. In working problem 2, what is the domestic opportunity cost of grain production in the home country?
    (a) 2 litres of beer per 1 kg of grain;
    (b) 1 litre of beer per 1 kg of grain;
    (c) 5 litres of beer per 1 kg of grain;
    (d) $\frac{1}{2}$ litre of beer per 1 kg of grain;
    (e) there is no opportunity cost.

6. Refer again to working problem 2. If wages are identical in both countries then the 'competitive' position of home and foreign will be as follows:
    (a) Home is competitive in grain only and foreign in beer only.
    (b) Home is competitive in beer only and foreign in grain only.
    (c) Home is competitive in grain and foreign is competitive in both grain and beer.
    (d) Home is not competitive in either grain or beer and foreign is competitive in both grain and beer.
    (e) None of the above.

TRUE OR FALSE (SUPPORT YOUR ANSWER)

1. Disinflation is defined as a continuous decline in the price level.

2. In combating inflation, monetarists advocate a steady rate of growth of the money supply.

3. The total cost of unemployment can be measured by summing the amount of money spent on social welfare benefits.

4. The poverty trap is the estimated number of citizens below the poverty line.

5. A country can have a 'comparative advantage' in the production of 'all goods' if it is more efficient at producing all goods than its competitors.

6. The infant industry argument for protection is only valid if some market imperfection has prevented thus far the emergence of that industry.

CASE STUDY A: INFLATION

Extract from *The Irish Times*
Irish deflation rate eases in April
by Ciara O'Brien

The rate at which annual consumer prices are falling continued to moderate in April, with prices 2.1 per cent lower compared to a year earlier, the Central Statistics Office said today. The latest figures follow a decrease in annual prices of 3.1 per cent in March and 3.2 per cent in February. Deflation peaked at 6.6 per cent in October 2009, and since then the rate of decline has fallen. Services prices fell by 1.4 per cent in the year to April, while the price of goods fell by 2.9 per cent.

Clothing and footwear fell 10.9 per cent over the year. Prices for food and non-alcoholic beverages were down 7.1 per cent, while furnishings, household equipment and routine household maintenance saw a 4.7 per cent decline in prices. Education prices rose 8.9 per cent, and increases in the cost of petrol and diesel pushed transport costs up 4.4 per cent over the year.

On a monthly basis, prices rose 0.2 per cent in April compared to March, compared to a decrease of 0.8 per cent recorded in April of last year. The cost of housing, water, electricity, gas and other fuels rose 1.5 per cent as the price of home heating oil rose and mortgage interest repayments were higher. Transport costs were up 0.6 per cent on the month. Sales brought down the cost of clothing and footwear by 0.5 per cent over the month, while the lower cost of food and non-alcoholic beverages reduced prices by 0.3 per cent.

'The domestic economy is experiencing no price inflation whatsoever bar energy prices (determined overseas) and mortgages (where banks are raising rates),' Davy analyst Rossa White wrote in a note. 'If the euro weakens further against sterling, as we expect, it will eventually raise Irish import prices. One-third of Irish consumer goods imports come from the UK, but the lag before it hits the CPI is about a year.'

There was no change over the month in the EU Harmonised Index of Consumer Prices (HICP), and annual prices were down an average of 2.5 per cent compared with April 2009. The Irish trend for deflation is in contrast to European prices, where the HICP is increasing by 1.5 per cent in the euro area. 'As such progress in addressing the price gap versus Europe continues to be made, and we estimate that the differential has been narrowed by 6 per cent thus far,' said Goodbody analyst Deirdre Ryan. National Irish Bank said Ireland was showing the way for Mediterranean countries, but said the negative inflation was likely to change in the future.

The Irish Small & Medium Enterprises Association (Isme) called on the Government to reduce State-controlled business costs, including energy, transport and local charges. 'A prime example is the recent decision to allow a carbon tax on gas, which will result in a 6 per cent cost increase to the business sector,' said Isme head of research Jim Curran. 'These types of irrational decisions undermine business, leading to further company closures and job losses.'

Source: The Irish Times, 13 May 2010.

Questions

1. Explain the term 'deflation'. Using the CSO consumer price index data (www.cso.ie), report the monthly change in prices for the twelve-month periods both before and after the deflation peak of October 2009. Interpret the data with respect to the trend in consumer prices.

2. Explain the relationship between the exchange rate (the value of euro against sterling in this instance) and the inflation rate, as implied by the article.

3. The article refers to a general inflation trend, although moderate, in the other euro area member states. Using Eurostat (eu.europa.eu/eurostat), report the 2009 inflation rates for both eurozone countries and non-eurozone EU countries. Comment on the data, and, in particular, the different inflation rates across the member states.

CASE STUDY B: UNEMPLOYMENT

Extract from *The Daily Telegraph*
Ireland fears recession as unemployment rises

Irish unemployment jumped to a nine-year high of 5.7pc last month, the Central Statistics Office reported, in the latest sign that Ireland is heading towards a recession. The rise follows confirmation earlier this week that Ireland's economy shrank by 1.5pc in the first quarter of 2008 – the first retreat in more than two decades. Ireland's budget deficit nearly quadrupled in the first half of the year to €5.6bn (£4.4bn) and Finance Minister Brian Lenihan said on Wednesday he expected the economy to stall this year after growing 6pc in 2007.

The common factor is a sudden reversal in the construction sector, a key plank in the Celtic Tiger economic boom that began in 1994 and finally petered out last year. Property prices have dropped by about 10pc in recent months, driven by weakening consumer confidence and tightening credit following the US sub-prime crisis. More than a decade of price rises spurred Ireland to build upwards of 70,000 new homes a year, but economists expect less than half that figure to be built this year. Several developments have been suspended and developers have filed for bankruptcy.

The European Central Bank's decision to raise benchmark interest rates to 4.25pc on Thursday did not help, as Ireland's construction boom has left it vulnerable to higher lending costs – its housing industries account for about 10pc of its economy, twice the EU average. Unemployment last rose this high in 1999, when 5.8pc of the workforce was jobless. But Ireland's jobs market has grown rapidly since the so-called Celtic Tiger economy delivered double-digit growth, putting Ireland among the richest nations in Europe.

During the boom times the country attracted more than 200,000 foreign workers who now fill the bulk of new jobs, particularly in shops, restaurants and pubs. The threat of a recession will be a headache for Irish Prime Minister Brian Cowen, who has faced a baptism of fire since he took office in May. Irish voters rejected the EU's Lisbon Treaty in June, plunging the 27- member bloc into institutional uncertainty.

Source: The Daily Telegraph, 5 July 2008.

Questions

1. The article refers to an unemployment rate at a nine-year high of 5.7% in mid-2008. Using CSO data (www.cso.ie), report the yearly unemployment rates (using ILO classification), for the period 2000–2008. Comment on the numbers. How do they compare with the unemployment rates since mid-2008? What do the numbers at the end of the 2000s reflect?
2. Explain the relationship between the economic growth rate, the unemployment rate, the budget deficit and the interest rate, as implied by the article.
3. In terms of jobs, report, using CSO data, numbers employed in the construction industry during the later years of the Celtic Tiger boom, 2004–2007. Express as a percentage of the total employment numbers. How do these numbers compare with the trend since 2007?

CASE STUDY C: INTERNATIONAL TRADE

Extract from the *Guardian Weekly*
Putting Trade in its Proper Place
by Larry Elliot

Fauchon's, in the Place de la Madelaine in Paris, is a gastronomic paradise. In the section devoted to fruit and veg. there are dainties to whet the appetite of Parisian foodies – mangoes from Mali, maracujas from Colombia and kiwanos from Portugal. This is the way supporters of global liberalisation would have us believe it could be everywhere from Kuala Lumpur to Knightsbridge. It is taking as read that the meshing of free trade and unfettered capital flows lead to rising world prosperity and a way out of poverty for the developing world.

Last week the Organisation for Economic Co-operation and Development summed up current thinking when it said globalisation 'gives all countries the possibility of participating in world development and all consumers the assurance of benefit from increasingly vigorous competition between producers'.

The theory is that liberalisation and deregulated capital flows allow countries to specialise in what they are good (or least bad) at, and this international division of labour raises global income.

. . . the developing countries that do best are those with the least state intervention and the freest trade and those new 'tiger economies' pose a massive competitive threat to living standards in the developed world.

Source: Guardian Weekly, 2 June 1996.

Questions

1. Why does the OECD think that freer trade can be beneficial to all countries?
2. If workers in developing countries are not as productive as workers in developed countries (due to the superior technology that is to be found in developed countries), how will such countries be able to compete in an era of globalisation?
3. Who gains and who could possibly lose in the so-called developed countries from freer world trade?

APPENDIX 17.1: THE PHILLIPS CURVE

The Phillips curve was named after A. W. Phillips, a professor at the London School of Economics. In 1958, he published a paper based on an empirical study. He stated that in the UK, during the period between 1861 and 1957, there was a stable, inverse relationship between the rate of change in money wages and the unemployment rate.[35] In other words, a high rate of money wage inflation was associated with a low rate of unemployment.

In 1960, Samuelson and Solow redefined the variables to look at the relationship between the inflation rate and the unemployment rate. This adaptation, shown in Figure 17.13, is called the Phillips curve.

Keynesian economists accepted the Phillips curve relationship into their theoretical framework. The omission of a price variable was one of the main weaknesses of the Keynesian model.

The Phillips curve appeared to offer a 'menu of choice'. Economists could choose between different rates of inflation and unemployment. Unfortunately, when the relationship was exploited, it broke down. To combat the high rate of unemployment in the 1970s, many western governments followed policies which were inflationary. Unfortunately, the unemployment rates did not fall.

FIGURE 17.13: THE PHILLIPS CURVE

Friedman (1968) and Phelps (1967) tried to explain the breakdown of the Phillips curve relationship in terms of price expectations. Friedman argued that there is a natural rate of unemployment associated with variables like the skills of the labour force, the size of the capital stock and the level of technology. Figure 17.14 depicts the natural rate of unemployment (U^*), at 5%.

Initially, the economy is at equilibrium at point A. The inflation rate is stable at 3% and unemployment is at the natural rate. Suppose the government decides to reduce the unemployment rate by adopting expansionary policies. On the initial short-run Phillips curve PC_{SR}, the economy moves from point A to point B. The inflation rate rises from 3% to 6% and the unemployment rate falls below the natural rate, U^*, to 3%.

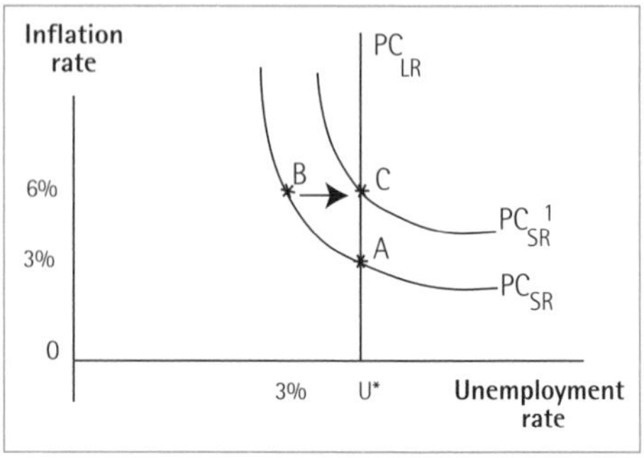

According to Friedman, workers do not realise that increasing inflation means that the real wage is falling. However, they are not fooled for long. A change in expectations shifts the Phillips curve upwards, from PC_{SR} to PC_{SR}^1. The economy returns to equilibrium at point C. Unemployment is again at the natural rate, but the inflation rate is higher.

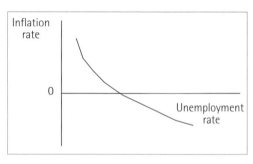

FIGURE 17.14: THE PHILLIPS CURVE

The inverse relationship between inflation and unemployment is temporary, according to Friedman. Unemployment returns to the natural rate as soon as expectations adjust. A continuation of expansionary policies leads inevitably to accelerating inflation.

In the long run, Friedman argued that the Phillips curve is vertical, at the natural rate of unemployment, U*. For Friedman, inflation has no long-run effect on the unemployment rate. The long-run expectations-augmented Phillips curve is labelled PC_{LR} in Figure 17.14.

The policy implications differ from the simple case. In attempting to reduce unemployment below its natural rate, the government only succeeds in accelerating domestic inflation. In the long term the natural rate of unemployment can only be reduced by supply-side measures. These changes result in a shift of the aggregate supply curve.

Incidentally, the Phillips curve is simply another way of depicting the AS curve. Consider the different types of AS curves. The conventional AS curve depicts a positive relationship between prices and output levels. Unemployment fluctuates inversely with output. Hence, the rate of change in the price level and unemployment are inversely related. This is depicted in the downward sloping Phillips curve.

The classical AS curve is vertical. Output is independent of the price level; a price rise has no effect on the level of output. Unemployment remains constant. This is depicted by the vertical Phillips curve where the inflation rate and the unemployment rate are unrelated.

From this brief analysis we can see that the Phillips curve is another way of expressing and explaining aggregate supply.

APPENDIX 17.2 EXPECTATIONS

Because of Keynes, expectations are an important feature of all modern macroeconomic models. Recall that Keynes believed that investors' expectations about the future were the main cause of instability in the national economy. He discussed the 'animal spirits' of investors, which is very different from the careful, cost-benefit analysis which many believe underlie any profit-maximising investment decision.

The volatility of expectations, so colourfully described by Keynes, was very difficult to model and too unpredictable to be accepted by the neoclassical economists. Until the 1970s, the neoclassicals believed that adaptive expectations could be used to explain the behaviour of economic agents. According to this theory, expectations for the current period are based on what actually happened in the past. If we use this concept in a model, the success of that model depends on how accurately the past explains the present and can be extrapolated into the future.

For example, we can develop a model incorporating adaptive expectations to predict the inflation rate. The most basic model is described by Equation [1]

$$\Pi^*_t = \Pi_{t-1}$$

[1]

which states that the predicted inflation rate (Π^*t) for period t is the same as the actual inflation rate for the previous period (Π_{t-1}).

We can expand this model to take account of errors which we made in our previous prediction. In other words, we are adapting our predictions based on our previous mistakes. One such model is described by Equation [2]

$$\Pi^*_t = \Pi^*_{t-1} + \emptyset \, (\Pi_{t-1} - \Pi^*_{t-1}) \text{ where } 0 < \emptyset < 1$$

[2]

where:

$\prod^*_t$ = inflation forecast for the present period.

$\prod^*_{t-1}$ = inflation forecast for the previous period.

ø = weight attached to last period's forecasting error.

$\prod_{t-1}$ = actual inflation rate for the previous period.

The expression inside the parentheses represents the forecasting error. It shows the discrepancy between the actual inflation rate in period t – 1 and the predicted inflation rate. ø represents the importance which we attach to that discrepancy. If we think that the discrepancy will persist into the future, ø will have a value close to one. Then our new inflation rate will equal our old inflation rate plus last period's mistake. If we think that the discrepancy will not persist, we will assign to ø a number which is close to zero. This means that we expect the inflation rate in period t to equal the predicted inflation rate in the previous period.

The importance of this model is that it allows us to incorporate our previous errors into our predictions. Our predictions for the future are based on the mistakes that we made in the past. Unfortunately, if we made consistent errors in the past, they will persist into the future. The adaptive expectations models were criticised for this and also because they limit the information which economic agents utilise.

The concept of adaptive expectations was replaced by rational expectations. Rational expectations assumes that economic agents will use all relevant past and current information when making decisions. In the inflation example, agents consider the past inflation rate but also changes in government monetary and fiscal policy, pressures in the labour market and international problems. Models based on rational expectations assume that all agents have 'perfect information'. They are fully informed of all relevant information which they need to make their forecast.

This simple concept has surprising implications for the effectiveness of economic policy and, in the broader sense, of government intervention in the economy. An important assumption of this model is that wages are fully flexible and that labour, as rational economic agents, will increase their wage demands in line with any inflationary pressures. Under these circumstances, the aggregate supply curve is vertical in the short run.

Under the rational expectations hypothesis, governments cannot 'fool' the people. People will anticipate the government's behaviour and act accordingly. Hence, any demand-management policies of the state will lead only to a change in the price level. Fiscal and monetary policies are ineffective in the short run and in the long run. Proponents of the rational expectations hypothesis were also concerned with policy issues of credibility and sustainability.

The leading proponents of rational expectations were Robert Lucas of Chicago, Thomas Sargent of Stanford and Robert Barro of Harvard.[36]

The new Keynesians responded to this with another modification to the expectations story. While acknowledging the possibility of rational expectations in the long run, new Keynesians were primarily concerned with the short run; a period of time when full adjustments in the labour market were unlikely. This allowed for the existence of high unemployment and as a policy response, active demand-management policies. As for the long run, '. . . we are all dead'.[37]

Regardless of which doctrine you support, expectations are considered to be a crucial feature of modern macroeconomics.

CHAPTER 18

Economic Growth and the Irish Economy

BY MATTHEW COFFEY AND GERARD TURLEY

'People are the common denominator of progress. So . . . no improvement is possible with unimproved people, and advance is certain when people are liberated and educated. It would be wrong to dismiss the importance of roads, railroads, power plants, mills, and the other familiar furniture of economic development. . . . But we are coming to realise . . . that there is a certain sterility in economic monuments that stand alone in a sea of illiteracy. Conquest of illiteracy comes first.'[1]

JOHN KENNETH GALBRAITH

'I had one fundamental question about economics: Why do some places prosper and thrive while others just suck?'[2]

P. J. O'ROURKE

CHAPTER OBJECTIVES

Upon completing this chapter, the student should understand:

- the basic theory of economic growth and the Solow growth model;
- the influence of population and capital stock on economic growth;
- the factors which have led to economic growth in different countries around the world;
- the factors which have led to economic growth and decline in Ireland.

OUTLINE

18.1 Economic growth: the basic theory
18.2 Economic growth around the world
18.3 The Irish experience

INTRODUCTION

This chapter explains how a nation can increase the size of its macroeconomy. In Chapter 10 we discussed the measurement of economic activity, but how does a country increase that activity? This chapter focuses on long-run changes in economic activity and the living standards of a nation. The first step is to provide a simple model to explain this growth, namely the Solow growth model. However, this model, while instructive, omits many factors which are important for an economy's growth.

These factors are best illustrated and explained by telling the stories of economic growth from around the world. These stories give us a wide range of examples with which to illustrate the importance of factors such as government and education. The chapter ends by presenting the story of economic growth of the Irish economy and provides a number of possible explanations for the 'Celtic Tiger' and its subsequent demise.

18.1 ECONOMIC GROWTH: THE BASIC THEORY

The wealth of a nation and the living standards of its citizens are typically measured using gross national product (GNP) and gross national product per person. But once wealth and living standards are measured, the next basic questions facing students of economics are the following: How can that wealth be increased over time? What can a nation's government and citizens do to increase their own living standards? These are the questions and problems of economic growth.

GNP measures the amount that is produced by a nation within a given year. As such it is a measurement of the nation's income in that year because everything produced is sold and becomes income for someone. GNP also gives us a measure of a nation's wealth; not one based on gold, silver and money, but one determined by the production potential of a country. That is, the ability of a nation to produce food, health care, cars and other goods is the real measure of its wealth and living standards. Increasing this production potential so that the wealth and living standards of a nation increase can be studied in two different ways.

One approach focuses on the short-run effects on national income. This approach notes that **GNP = Consumption + Investment + Government Spending + Net Exports**. It focuses on the short run and the actions taken by consumers, businesses and the government to change GNP over a few months or years. The main focus of this approach to measuring national income is on its components. GNP is divided into its components of consumption, investment, net exports and government spending. Each of these components is studied individually with a view to how they change. National wealth and living standards are constructed from their basic components.

Alternatively, the second approach takes a larger, long-run view of a nation's wealth. Over longer periods of time, trends in population, capital, geography, technology and other factors will lead to changes in GNP and living standards. These changes occur over the course of years and even decades. It is this long-run view that is discussed in this chapter. This chapter presents the story of economic growth over a long period of time, both in Ireland and in the rest of the world.

There are of course a number of different ways to tell the story of economic growth.[3] We could start with the most common model of economic growth and work with that model to derive predictions and descriptions of how economies grow. Or we could examine a wide range of countries and look at which countries have done well and which have not. Then we could derive the lessons of growth from those countries that have thrived. Or we could look at one particular country, examine its history and evaluate its actions and policies. Each of these three approaches will give us a different part of the growth story and all three will be presented here.

First, however, let me add a word of caution. When studying the economic growth of nations, it is tempting to develop an economic model, present some economic statistics, or tell the story of one nation's growth and then proclaim that the problem of economic growth has been solved. To be sure, every economic growth model or story of national economic growth from around the world offers lessons to be learned for students and for other nations. However, the question of how to increase living standards and national wealth remains too complex to have any single answer.

Therefore, this chapter will not present a single answer to the question of how to increase living standards and economic growth. Rather it will provide some theory from a model of economic growth, some evidence of economic growth from economies throughout the world, and some of the recent economic history of Ireland in an attempt to provide an understanding of some of the factors that may help or hinder growth.

To begin with, let us look at the growth in the Irish economy over a fifty-five-year period beginning in 1950. Table 18.1 shows GDP per capita, population and the investment share from 1950 to 2005. GDP per capita is simply national income divided by the population, which is also listed in the table. The investment share is investment as a percentage of (per capita) GDP.[4]

TABLE 18.1: THE IRISH ECONOMY, 1950–2005

Year	GDP per capita, PPP (2005 US$)	5-year change	Population (thousands)	Investment share
1950	5,597	..	2,963	22.0
1955	6,243	13.3	2,916	24.9
1960	6,666	5.1	2,832	21.5
1965	8,218	23.3	2,876	30.6
1970	10,064	22.5	2,950	33.6
1975	11,367	12.9	3,177	29.3
1980	13,699	20.5	3,401	33.8
1995	13,859	1.2	3,540	30.2
1990	17,257	24.5	3,508	32.7
1995	20,617	19.5	3,614	28.9
2000	31,389	52.2	3,792	34.8
2005	38,659	23.2	4,016	34.0

Source: Alan Heston, Robert Summers and Bettina Aten, Penn-World tables version 6.3, Centre for International Comparisons of Production, Income and Prices at the University of Pennsylvania, August 2009.[5]

Looking at Table 18.1, we can make a number of observations. First, despite all the recent doom and gloom, Ireland's economy has actually grown significantly and steadily since the 1950s. The exceptions are the periods 1955–60 and 1980–85, both exhibiting quite low growth; in some of the intervening years the economy actually shrank. However, the most notable change has been that the GDP per person grew almost sevenfold between 1950 and 2005.

The second notable fact is the following: along with a steady increase in the gross domestic product per person, there have also been increases in the population and the investment share of GDP. The population increased only slightly for the first haf of the period, but witnessed big increases thereafter. For much of this period emigration was still the norm in the Irish economy. During the 1950s and the late 1980s the population decreased as a result of a net outflow of migrants. However, coupled with the threefold increase in GDP per capita, there has been an increase in the share of GDP accounted for by investment. In the simplest terms, over this time period there has been a dramatic increase in the amount of capital goods (e.g. factories and machines, as well as buildings) at the disposal of workers. This increase is largely the result of a change in Irish economic policy away from protectionism and toward an outward-oriented economic growth strategy. This included an active pursuit of foreign investment, encouragement of exports and an era of more openness toward international trade, including joining the European Union and the eurozone.[6]

Solow growth model

Table 18.1 focuses on three factors: national income per person, population and the capital stock per worker. These factors are the main ingredients of one basic explanation for economic growth known as the Solow growth model[7] which was developed by Robert Solow, a Nobel Prize-winning economist from the Massachusetts Institute of Technology.[8] This model provides a picture of the economy and how it produces goods and services for its residents to consume. Its use of the relationship between labour and capital is similar to a firm's production function. National income, which we denote as Y, is the amount of goods and services produced in a nation's economy. To produce a certain level of output, labour, factories and machinery are required. We summarise this relationship by writing:

$$Y = F(K,L)$$ [18.1]

In this equation, Y is national income or GDP, K is the capital stock, that is, the amount of machines and factories that can be used to produce goods, and L is the labour supply, or more simply, the population. The function $F(K,L)$ tells us that capital stock is combined with the population in (ideally) an efficient way to produce goods. While it is simple enough to write this function, specifying the actual relationship between K and L is quite difficult, as we will see shortly.

In microeconomics, we studied a firm and saw that its output depended on the capital and labour that it used. It also depended on the particular production function. The Solow growth model uses the same idea, but for the whole economy. So the amount that can be produced by a country at any given time depends on its available population and its capital stock. Table 18.1 shows an increase in GDP per person as well as an increase in population and capital stock. So one simple theory of economic growth which we can state immediately is that just increasing a country's population L or amount of capital K will increase its income.

Let's look first at population growth, which introduces a number of interesting issues. Population can be increased by allowing increased immigration or through more traditional methods. But despite the theoretical prospect that the economy grows when the population grows, most countries take actions to limit their own population growth. These limitations range from quotas on immigrants in the United States to China's one child policy.

Another contradiction is that some of the best economic growth in the world has taken place in countries with little or no population growth. Consider Ireland, and compare the population and growth rate in Table 18.1 between 1950 and 1970. Over the twenty-year period, the population fell while the income per capita increased by 80%. At the same time, some of the countries with the lowest economic growth have had very high increases in population. For example, China and India are the two most populous nations and yet they are ranked 85th and 113th in the world in terms of GNP per capita.[9] However, it is too simple to blame only a low or high population growth rate for the state of a country's economy. Remember it is the combination of labour and capital that is important. Population increase alone may not yield very high growth, because the interaction between labour and capital is an important factor. So in addition to population, we must study capital stock. But where do these machines and factories come from?

A closed economy, one that is isolated from the rest of the world, must produce any capital stock independently. That is, the amount of capital stock, K used to produce output, Y in any one year must have been produced in the previous years. If your country needs a factory to produce goods in the year 2011, you must build that factory sometime in the years before then. So part of today's output is used in future years. The only other possible use of this output is to consume it.

So, a major determinant of future K is today's consumption, or more specifically, the amount of today's output that is not consumed and is saved for use as tomorrow's capital stock. An equivalent way of thinking about the accumulation of capital is to consider investment. The only use for output is savings or consumption and the only use of savings is for it to be invested in the economy. For example, you place your money in a savings account and the bank loans the money to businesses to build machines and factories. If your economy is isolated from the rest of the world, the only source of investment is domestic savings and the only use of savings is investment. The amount of savings equals the amount of investment. Isolated economies therefore limit themselves to using only capital stock produced domestically. (Removing this limitation has benefited many countries, as we will see in Sections 18.2 and 18.3.)

We can now outline a process by which national output and national income grow. If more is saved and invested, more capital stock is available for future production of output. A country that saves more of its output to invest will accumulate capital stock and increase its production of Y. However, this process of capital accumulation has a limit. When a country has more machines and factories, it must invest more money in their repair and upkeep. If a country has a certain level of savings, its capital stock K and output will grow until its entire savings is being used to repair and replace the old machines and factories. If savings increases, the amount of capital will increase at first, but then the additional machines will need to be repaired also. Just because a country is saving and investing more does not imply that its capital stock is increasing without limit.

The process by which machines and factories break down, become obsolete, and must be replaced is called depreciation. A country can grow only if its savings and investment outweigh the amount of depreciation. When the level of savings equals the amount of depreciation, the capital stock K and output Y remain the same. This final stable point is known as the steady state level of capital.

> Definition
>
> *The steady state consists of a level of capital and a savings rate such that the level of savings and investment equal the capital that is lost due to depreciation.*

At first glance then, countries with higher savings rates will grow faster since they accumulate capital more quickly. But it is possible to go a bit further and say that poor countries with low levels of capital tend to grow more quickly than wealthier countries that have abundant capital. The extra savings and investment in a country with very few machines and factories has a larger impact whereas wealthier countries already have a lot of capital and find it harder to increase their level of K by as much. This point can be illustrated numerically.

Suppose, in the imaginary country of Aslan, K=100. Savings and investment add 10 units of capital. Therefore, its growth in capital is 10%. In the poorer imaginary country of Beowulf, K=50. The same addition of 10 units of capital represents a much higher increase of 20%. Assuming each country's population remains the same, the output of Beowulf will grow faster than Aslan's. Therefore savings, along with the existing level of capital stock, affects the growth rate of output. A major question and problem for a nation's government is the following: what level of capital and savings is best for an economy?

This question is not as straightforward as it might seem. One might be tempted to conclude that a country should save and invest as much as possible because higher levels of K are better. And while a country that saves more will boost its capital, it may not need that extra capital. It may also fail to recognise the opportunity cost of that savings. Remember that in order to save, people have to consume less. If we consider that it is consumption that makes people happy, then the best level of savings and capital will maximise the amount of people's consumption.

For example, a country saving 0% of its output will not have any capital stock in the future. Eventually all its K will depreciate away and it will not be able to produce anything. On the other hand, a country saving 100% of its output will have nothing available for its people to consume. The workforce starves and nothing is produced. Between these two extremes lies an optimal savings rate. This optimal savings rate allows for investment to accumulate and maintain the optimal level of K. This optimal level of capital allows a country's citizens to have the highest possible consumption from year to year. The goal for a government is to find the Golden Rule level of capital.[10]

Definition

The Golden Rule level of capital is the steady state with the highest level of consumption.

Consumption is maximised not just today but for all future generations, hence treating future generations as you wish past generations had treated you. If the economy currently has too little capital, savings should be increased and capital accumulated. If the economy has too much capital, savings and investment should be decreased until the capital stock falls to the Golden Rule level.

In conclusion, a higher level of savings will in turn lead to more capital stock with which to produce a larger output. Further, there is a level of K which leads to the maximum consumption per capita. However, once the savings rate equals the rate of depreciation, there will be no further changes in K. With no changes in capital there will be no further changes in output. Growth stops. The simplified Solow model describes economies growing to a certain level depending on their savings rates and then staying at that level of national income for ever after that. This leads to the following predictions.

1. Countries that save more of their national output will grow faster. These countries will invest more and will accumulate a larger amount of capital. The higher level of capital will allow them to produce more in future years. But, there is a limit to the amount of savings and investment that can occur. Any time the capital stock is increased, depreciation, the cost of maintaining that capital, increases as well. Eventually savings will just cover the replacement value of depreciated capital. There are a few notable exceptions to this prediction. For example, the United States has had strong growth in its history despite having a lower savings rate than many other countries.

2. Poor countries tend to grow more quickly than rich countries. There is convergence between economies around the world. This does not mean that the poorest countries in the world are quickly approaching the richest; the opposite is actually occurring. It means that among countries with similar characteristics, savings rates and technology, the poorer countries within a given group are approaching the richer ones within the same group. For example, Japan started out as a poor industrialised country and grew very quickly to become one of the richest. Ireland's living standards have surpassed the UK's level as measured by GDP per capita. This is due to the faster growth evident in the Irish economy over the last forty years.

However, the gap between countries such as the United States and Ethiopia is actually increasing. Convergence tends to occur within similar groups, not between them.

3. Capital and labour are paid their marginal products. This is not really a prediction, but rather the result of using a production function. When studying the firm in microeconomics, we found that the theory of the firm predicts that labour is paid a wage equal to its marginal product. Also, capital receives a wage or rent equal to its marginal product. The same is true if we consider a national economy with its production function. Now, the returns to capital and labour must be paid from total output, so capital and labour receive shares of GNP. Depending on the production function that we apply to a country's economy, the theory predicts a percentage of GNP paid to capital and a percentage paid to labour in a country. These can be compared to the actual economic statistics.

The Solow growth model, while simple, yields all of these predictions and results. In this regard, the model does a fairly good job of explaining some facts of economic growth. However like many economic models, there are limitations. The equation offered for an economy $Y=F(K, L)$ contains a relationship between output, labour and the capital stock. This relationship can be examined using the statistics of a country; it is possible to add up the L and K and see how much output was produced. But the main limitation of the Solow growth model is that it offers no explanation of how labour and capital interact to produce Y. With the Solow growth model, we have a form of growth accounting and the measurement of some key factors, but the model only explains so much.

In fact, the Solow growth model is interesting partly because of what it cannot explain and the factors for economic growth that it does not include. When the equation is given for a country, no matter what the savings rate is, the Solow growth model predicts that growth will eventually stop unless other factors are 'added in'. For example, technology can be added to the Solow growth model, but only in a way that leaves the exact role of technology unexplained. Technology is this special extra 'something' which creates growth. Because growth stops unless we add technology and other factors to the model, the Solow growth model points to the importance of such factors.

The bottom line: There is more to the story of economic growth than is contained in this one model, and we only have to look at economic growth in different countries to see this.

18.2 ECONOMIC GROWTH AROUND THE WORLD

The main limitation of the Solow growth model is its simplicity. While on the one hand this gives us some nice explanations about economic growth, it neglects some key factors that we would expect to be important to a country's economy. While these factors may not be included easily in our growth model from the previous section, it does not mean that they cannot be discussed. The principal aim of this section is to categorise and explain other factors that influence a country's prospects for growth. To do so, we will make some broad comparisons between different economies.

Cross-country comparisons are quite common in the study of economic (pre-crisis) growth. Typically these take the form of 'horse races' where most of the attention is paid to the winners. In recent times, the best example of this was the 'Celtic Tiger' economy of Ireland, and past examples include the Asian tigers in the early 1990s and the German and Japanese economies of the 1970s and 1980s. Usually when these winners are identified, economists and politicians comment on the lessons that these winners have to teach the rest of the world.

Let us take Table 18.2, listing fifteen countries, their GDP per capita and their growth rates since 1970/1. What lessons can be learned from the experiences of these countries? Why have some of them languished while others have thrived? And finally, what lessons do the 'winners' provide for the Irish economy and other economies overall?

TABLE 18.2: ECONOMIC GROWTH AROUND THE WORLD[11]

Country	GDP per capita, PPP 2005 (US$)	Annual Growth 2005	Average Annual Growth 1971–2005
China	6,483	9.3%	6.2%
Denmark	32,162	3.4%	2.0%
Egypt	5,230	4.6%	3.2%
Ethiopia	963	8.1%	0.4%
France	28,779	1.3%	1.9%
Germany	29,548	0.8%	1.9%
India	3,365	7.0%	2.9%
Ireland	38,659	5.2%	4.0%
Italy	27,795	−0.3%	2.1%
Japan	29,780	2.0%	2.2%
Poland	12,666	3.5%	2.4%
South Korea	22,048	3.4%	5.9%
United Kingdom	30,276	1.3%	2.3%
United States	41,870	2.4%	2.2%
Venezuela	10,973	7.3%	−0.1%

Source: Penn-World tables version 6.3 and author's calculations.

From this table, looking at the average annual growth in the economy from 1971 to 2005, we can see that the 'winners' in this economic growth race are China and South Korea followed by Ireland, Egypt and India. This is a story of delayed convergence (in some cases) with, in all cases, a large degree of catching up. South Korea and China are examples of countries with low levels of income which grew quickly because they were starting from a relatively low base. Any increase in the economy will seem like a larger percentage simply because the starting level of output is lower. We will leave the case of Ireland until Section 18.3. The unique (or otherwise) case of China is discussed in Chapter 19.

The rest of the countries all have an average growth rate of less than 2.5% with the lowest growth occurring in Ethiopia and Venezuela. Compared to most of the rest of the world, these countries have become relatively poorer. Our theory of economic growth must not only account for high growth, but must also be able to explain these low growth cases. Poland, with its moderate growth, is an exception because that country was operating under a communist system for the first half of the time studied. It has recently been growing much faster as it makes the transition to a market economy and it provides an illustration of the impact that the political system can have on an economy. The other unusual case is Japan, with very high growth rates in the first half of the period, but followed by a lost decade (or more) after 1990.

This leaves the countries where economic growth has not been exceptional but where initial levels of income (in 1970) were already relatively high. The USA and the Western European countries of Denmark, Italy, France, Germany and the United Kingdom have all had growth rates around 2%. While this is low compared to Ireland and South Korea, it still leads to a substantial change in living standards over time. In fact, even with a growth rate of 'only' 2%, the living standards of a country as measured by GDP per capita will double in about thirty-five years. The implication is that over thirty-five years, the average citizen realises such large gains in material living standards that they are twice as wealthy. So, even a low growth rate will, over time, imply more national wealth. Of course, GDP per capita will double much more quickly in India and South Korea. However, the most recent evidence points to slower growth in these countries as they approach the levels of the USA and Europe. For the low growth countries, the economy can take up to seventy years to double in size, so they fall further behind in terms of poverty relative to the rest of the world.[12]

As Table 18.2 shows, there is a wide disparity in living standards among different countries, and a wide disparity in growth rates. What are the reasons for these differences in growth rates? Why have some countries done remarkably well, while others have stagnated or even fallen behind? While economists do not have the answers for every country, it is possible to identify some key characteristics and properties that provide a good environment for economic growth. Although not an exhaustive and complete list, the growth of a nation is influenced by:

1. the political system and government, including institutions;
2. openness to the world economy;
3. human capital and education; and
4. technology.

We begin with the political system and the quality of governance.

Political system and government

A quick comparison of economies may lead one to conclude that democracy and capitalism are best for economic growth. In Table 18.2, the richest eight countries, namely Denmark, France, Germany, Ireland, Italy, Japan, the UK and the USA are all advanced democracies whose markets have a large degree of freedom. Now some economists may argue that they are stable, free market democracies because they are rich, while others would argue that they are rich because they are stable, free market democracies. In any case, all of these countries have a number of helpful characteristics with regards to the political and economic systems. These characteristics, otherwise known as institutions (see Information Box 1.1), include a stable, independent judicial system which can enforce contracts and settle disputes, clearly defined property rights which allow entrepreneurs to profit from industry, and a government which does not intervene unnecessarily in the daily actions of the economy.

It does not mean that all economies must have these factors in order to grow, but the government of a country can hinder the growth of its economy through actions that make the business environment unstable and uncertain. It is also quite probable that heavy government interference in the market can divert resources away from their most productive use.

For example, for decades industries in the economies of Central and Eastern Europe relied on a captive market dictated by the Soviet Union. This allowed businesses to remain in existence even though they were not competitive, because they were guaranteed a closed market in which to sell their goods. Once the Soviet Union dissolved and these markets were no longer guaranteed, many firms in Central and Eastern Europe found themselves uncompetitive when compared to firms from the western industrialised countries. The heavy government interference of the communist system allowed inefficient firms to stay in business and reduced the incentives to innovate and grow. Hence the poor growth exhibited in Poland over the years 1970–92.

Openness to the world economy

This concept could also be called a country's degree of globalisation. A country opening its economy to the world economy faces some benefits and drawbacks. The benefits of openness include the ability to buy cheaper imports, to export and sell goods to the world market and the ability to attract foreign businesses to invest in your country. If a country is open to the world economy, it has the possibility of importing the latest technology. The drawbacks include competition from cheap imports harming domestic firms and the exposure to foreign capital flight. That is, foreigners that invest money into your country can just as quickly pull their money out, often with dire effects.[13]

As for the effect of openness on growth, it is almost universally agreed that countries with a larger degree of openness will grow faster than those countries that try to shut themselves off from the rest of the world. Again, there is a debate among economists over causation – are they open economies because they have grown or vice versa – but there is agreement that the two main facets of globalisation that benefit growth are export-led growth and the attraction of foreign direct investment.

One strategy available to an economy is to try to increase its level of exports. If successful, this country engages in export-led growth. An economy would specialise in a number of goods for exports. Examples include textiles or electronic goods. Exports provide more money for a nation to use for its development. Some countries may attempt to climb an export ladder. They start by exporting cheap low-technology goods such as clothing and simple manufactures. After gaining success there, they invest their profits in technology and more capital to begin exporting more expensive high-technology goods such as cars and electronics. Japan grew in this fashion. It started producing cheap goods like toys and simple consumer goods before moving on to advanced technology products such as computer chips and televisions.

An alternative strategy for an economy opening to the world economy is to actively attract foreign direct investment. This investment usually takes the form of a foreign multinational building a factory locally and producing goods for export. To attract this investment, a country may offer low tax rates or subsidies to foreign firms. The benefit of this type of investment is that it provides capital and technology to a home country when they may not have been able to afford the investment. The foreign multinational provides the capital and the technology, while the host nation usually provides tax incentives and relatively cheap labour.

Education and human capital

While capital stock K consists of factories, machines and technology, human capital refers to human knowledge and know-how. It can be accumulated like regular capital, and countries can invest and increase their level of human capital by spending on training and education. One of the stories told about the Irish economic growth experience is that it results from the exceptional educational system, though there is some debate about this (see Case Study below). If, however, we look at Table 18.3, we can see some statistics on human capital and education for our fifteen countries.

From the data we can see the large expenditure on education made by many countries. Like investment in machines and factories, we can consider the money spent on education to be an

TABLE 18.3: MEASURES OF EDUCATION

Country	Public expenditure on education % of GDP 2007	Expected years of schooling (of children) 2007
China	..	11.2
Denmark†	7.9%	16.9
Egypt	3.7%	11.0
Ethiopia	5.5%	8.0
France†	5.6%	16.2
Germany†	4.4%	15.6
India†	3.2%	10.3
Ireland	4.9%	17.9
Italy	4.3%	16.3
Japan	3.4%	15.1
Poland	4.9%	15.2
South Korea	4.2%	16.7
United Kingdom	5.6%	15.9
United States	5.5%	15.7
Venezuela	3.7%	13.6

Source: World Bank, *World Development Report* 2009.

† = 2006 data for public spending percentages.

investment in the human capital of a nation. We would expect that the larger amount of human capital accumulated would translate into higher growth. Also, all the countries that can be considered middle to high income have high figures for expected number of years of schooling obtained by their citizens.

While all economists and the available economic data would agree that education and investment in human capital are important factors in a nation's growth, it is useful to clarify what kind of education. The type of education required to promote growth in an economy depends in part on the stage of a country's development. A nation that is just transforming itself from an agricultural economy to a manufacturing economy does not necessarily need to teach all of its citizens philosophy, physics, or even economics. Rather, if a country is newly industrialising, a basic level of literacy and technical training is necessary. On the other hand, if a country is an advanced industrial economy, it needs people trained in innovation and invention. We expect this country to invest more money and time training scientists and entrepreneurs. In short, the level and type of human capital accumulated depends on the level and type of technology being used in an economy. Technology is considered by many economists to be the main determinant of economic growth.[14]

Technology

For economists, the simplest definition of technology is that it is the interaction of labour and capital. Technology is embedded in machines and factories but it also exists in the ways workers use machines and processes of production. Better technology typically translates into more efficient methods of production and therefore more national output. For a country, the goal is to increase its own level of technology and potential for economic growth. There are essentially three ways to obtain higher levels of technology and the ability to implement any of these three will have a large effect on the economic growth of a country.

The first is for the citizens of a country to invent new technology. This approach requires a substantial level of existing technology and human capital. There are prerequisites necessary for certain innovations. A country needs telephones in order to invent answering machines and computers to write software. Among the countries listed in Table 18.2, Denmark, France, Germany, Ireland, Italy, Japan, South Korea, the UK and the USA are all countries doing a significant amount of technological innovation. The standard measurement of innovation is the number of patents filed in the United States.[15] Unsurprisingly, these are the rich countries that have shown a large degree of growth already. They are poised, given their existing technology, to augment their technological lead through invention and innovation. It is a virtuous cycle where their past innovation has made them rich enough to afford the R&D that will make future innovations more likely.

For example, as measured by US patents granted in 1997, the top five countries represent 10.4% of the world's population, yet they filed 87.2% of the total patents throughout the world in that year. These same top five countries accounted for 41% of the world's GNP that year. Innovation and invention pay.[16]

The second approach for accumulating new technology is to adopt already existing technology that has been developed elsewhere. This, however, requires not only a certain degree of technical expertise, but also an ability to purchase the technology. Such countries would be considered technological adopters and include Poland and certain regions of China and India. These technology adopters have certain advantages, namely location and education. For example, as can be seen in Table 18.3, Poland has a well-educated population, and its location on the border of the European Union gives it access to high-technology goods. Adopting new technology is easier. Some regions of China and India, most notably the coastal regions, also benefit from their proximity to Hong Kong, Singapore and other East Asian markets.

Finally, the third approach to increase a nation's level of technology is to encourage foreign investment in factories and businesses. Foreign firms bring their technology and their processes to a host nation. Domestic workers learn new techniques and other local firms benefit from the example set by the foreign multinational. If there is a large degree of 'spill over' of knowledge between foreign multinationals and domestic firms, the amount of new technology can be significant. This has been the approach of countries like Ireland and China as discussed earlier under globalisation and foreign direct investment.

If a country cannot use one of these three approaches to accumulate new technology, then it is excluded, for the most part, from using any new techniques and machines. These countries may not be rich enough to afford top scientific research to innovate themselves, and they may also be too poor to buy and adopt existing technology. Furthermore, if the country is not an attractive place for foreign investment, then the rate of technology acquisition may be quite slow or even non-existent. Among the countries listed in Table 18.2, Egypt, Ethiopia, Venezuela and the inland regions of India and China are excluded through poverty and isolation from accumulating technology. These areas are caught in a vicious cycle of being too poor to acquire new technology and hence remaining poor because of the lack of new technology.[17]

These four factors or characteristics illustrate that economic growth across countries may differ, not just because of savings rates, the capital stock and labour as predicted by the Solow growth model, but also because of institutional or structural aspects of an economy. The main implication is that even countries with similar technology or human capital may face quite different futures if other aspects of their economies such as their degree of openness or their political systems differ.

In real terms, the lessons that the 'winners' of the economic growth race can teach are quite varied. The lessons for growth are not that countries such as Egypt, Ethiopia and India should suddenly start innovating or importing technology. That is not feasible given their current national income and level of human capital. Rather, they should start by opening their economies to more foreign direct investment and work on establishing a healthy relationship between their governments and the economy. We now turn to Ireland and its record in terms of economic growth and performance.

18.3 THE IRISH EXPERIENCE

Having discussed the theory of economic growth and compared the growth experience of a number of different countries around the world, what are the lessons about economic growth that we can learn from the experience of Ireland?

If we were to tell the conventional story about how a country develops and grows it might sound like the following: A country starts out with an economy dependent largely on agriculture. The agricultural sector becomes more mechanised with tractors and other farm machinery and this leads to fewer people employed on farms. The large number of people displaced from farms provides a ready and cheap labour force for industries, which have started to appear. These new industries, in the early stages of a country's growth, are largely in light manufactured goods, like textiles and simple goods.

Eventually, as the country's economy grows, the goods that it manufactures become more complex and more highly valued, like steel, ships and cars. As the country develops further and acquires more technology and knowledge, it may begin to manufacture electronics, computers and software. At this stage the country has a small agricultural sector relative to the whole economy and its manufacturing sector is heavily weighted in favour of high-tech and high-value products. Then, in the advanced stages of economic growth, a process of de-industrialisation occurs.[18] With less actual manufacturing taking place, the economy of an advanced industrial state sees an increase in the size of its service sector, providing goods like design, research, business and financial services, tourism and entertainment.

This story of development is similar to that which occurred in the United Kingdom, Japan, France, Germany and the United States, just to name a few countries. The countries of China, Egypt, Ethiopia, India, South Korea and Venezuela are at different stages of this process. As for Ireland, the story is a little bit different, although it starts out the same.

Ireland has historically had a large agricultural sector, and that sector has been subject to the same stresses of mechanisation as elsewhere in the world. In practical terms, it means that fewer workers can do more work. Hence each farm supports fewer people. Now, in other countries the surplus labour that is displaced from farms would be welcome in growing industries, and those industries would be attracted by the abundant and therefore cheap labour.

However, because of Ireland's proximity to the UK and the ease with which people could emigrate there and to the USA, Canada, Australia, New Zealand and elsewhere, Ireland did not have the large amount of cheap labour that would attract industry and help it develop. The wage in Ireland was kept high by large emigration. One could almost consider Ireland a regional economy within Europe.[19] Certainly with its mobile labour force and its proximity to the UK, when jobs were scarce in Ireland, workers left. This left fewer people behind and a smaller supply of workers. This relative scarcity of workers kept the wage higher than expected in a developing country. Hence, manufacturing of simple goods with low technology never truly developed in Ireland to the same extent as in other countries.

The second way in which Ireland's economic growth differs from the conventional story is that Ireland moved almost directly from an agriculture-based economy to a high-tech manufacturing and services economy. There was a jump in development, and Ireland did not develop much of the heavy manufacturing that characterises other newly industrialised countries.

A brief history of the twentieth-century Irish economy would read as follows. Though the economy was largely agricultural, the industry that did exist tended to locate in the north-east, close to Belfast. As industries started to locate there, it became an attractive place for other industries to locate as well. This is known as clustering. After independence and partition, the fledgling Irish republic was left with few indigenous industries. Its agriculture sector was then faced with an increasing mechanisation in which farming supported fewer people. Many farm workers were displaced and left without work.

Starting in the 1930s and continuing until the 1960s, the government introduced protectionist policies aimed at increasing economic activity domestically. These included tariffs on imported goods and subsidies to some industries. And while some industries were helped, the main result of this protectionism and inward focus of economic policy was that the industries that did develop tended to be inefficient because they were not subject to international competition. These industries also tended to focus on producing goods mainly for domestic consumption, and given the relatively small size of the Irish home market, their growth was limited.

The major change in economic policy in the 1960s was a shift toward encouraging a more outward-oriented economy. This shift did not mean simply the abolishment of tariffs. Rather, the government actively sought to grow through exports and the attraction of foreign direct investment. It was, in short, an opening of the Irish economy to the global economy. As seen in Table 18.1, this largely worked. GDP per capita grew at a much higher rate after 1965, growing by over 12% in every five-year period except 1980–85.

All of this historical explanation and storytelling just tells us about the foundation of the 'Celtic Tiger' and its economic growth. In short, Ireland industrialised very rapidly by increasing exports and attracting more foreign businesses. The growth was so quick because Ireland had been catching up to the rest of Europe and the other industrialised countries. Growth from 1960 to 2005 was good compared to richer, more developed countries, but this is what the Solow growth model would predict. As such, it was good news for the Irish economy, but not necessarily earth-shattering news to the rest of the world.

But what astonished many economists and brought Irish economic growth to the attention of the world was its performance in the 1990s and early 2000s. By some economic measures, Ireland was not just catching up to the level of Europe, but surpassing it. This fact caused much debate among Irish economists and questioning by economists everywhere. All of them were looking for the lessons for economic growth that could be learned from Ireland.

First, let us look at the actual growth in the Irish economy during the Celtic Tiger period, 1994–2007, in PPP terms.

TABLE 18.4: IRISH ECONOMIC GROWTH, 1994–2007

	1994	1995	1996	1997	1998	1999	2000	2001	2002	2003	2004	2005	2006	2007
GDP, in US$ 2005 prices (€m)	70,878	77,706	83,779	93,382	101,254	112,286	123,191	130,214	138,739	144,859	151,520	160,636	169,185	178,704
GDP, growth rate	5.8	9.6	7.8	11.5	8.4	10.9	9.7	5.7	6.5	4.4	4.6	6	5.3	5.6
GDP per capita, in US$ 2005 prices	19,850	21,577	23,104	25,510	27,261	29,906	32,383	33,701	35,286	36,242	37,253	38,614	39,704	40,936
GDP per capita, growth rate	5.5	8.7	7.1	10.4	6.9	9.7	8.3	4.1	4.7	2.7	2.8	3.7	2.8	3.1

Source: UNECE Statistical Division database.

The most notable aspect is the high growth in the period. Up to this point economic growth had certainly been respectable, but growth rates of 6% and higher are exceptional. And while the process of economic growth started in the 1960s with the introduction of globally oriented economic policies, it was not until the late 1980s that Ireland's economic prospects really took off.

In the late 1980s, the government introduced cuts in its spending to reign in its deficits and debts. Government spending had grown so much that the level of the national debt was larger than the size of the economy. At that level, a substantial portion of government spending is on interest payments alone. Part of the pressure for reducing government debt and hence spending was international, coming from such bodies as the International Monetary Fund and the European Union. Around the same time, a national wage agreement was signed in 1987 that brought about wage restraint in exchange for reductions in income taxes. These two factors set the stage for the high growth in the 1990s.

So from the statistics in Table 18.4, we can see that the Irish economy was growing strongly, but the magnitude of the change in the Irish economy can be illustrated in other, more tangible ways. For example, unemployment fell from 11% in 1997 to as low as 5% in the summer of 2000. Instead of one in ten people being out of work, only one in twenty people were still without jobs. A second visible sign that the economy was doing well was the change in migration. More people moved to Ireland than left: contrast this with the fact that half of the people who left school in the 1950s had also left the country by 1961. The number of automobiles bought in 1999 was 25% higher than the number bought in 1998.[20] Strong economic growth exhibits itself in a variety of ways.

As for explanations of this growth, there are a number of possibilities. The most common are the high level of foreign investment, the well-educated workforce, the level of European Union funding and social partnership. Of course, there is also the theory that current Irish economic growth, no matter how robust, is nothing more than the continuation of growth that has been occurring since the 1960s. Let us look at a number of these explanations for Ireland's growth.

Foreign investment

The clearest sign that Ireland has benefited greatly from foreign direct investment is the large difference between gross national product and gross domestic product. Currently in Ireland, GDP is much larger than GNP. The discrepancy is largely due to foreign firms repatriating profits to their home countries. The ability to attract foreign investment has made it possible for Ireland to acquire technology and human capital. So, Ireland, instead of moving from light manufacturing to heavy manufacturing and then to high-tech products, has actually skipped a few steps. The recent foreign investment has been in software, electronics and medical equipment, to name just a few sectors. For example, by 1994, investment from the USA alone totalled almost $3,000 per person. This compared to $2,000 per person in Britain and $500 per person in France and Germany.[21]

Ireland's ability to attract foreign investment is due to a number of factors. These include, but are not limited to, the following:

- Ireland is an English-speaking nation within the euro area.
- Ireland's workforce is relatively young and a high percentage of the labour force have a third-level degree.[22]
- The cluster effect: a number of firms have already invested in Ireland and that makes it more likely that other, similar firms will invest in Ireland. For example, investments by Medtronic mean that Boston Scientific is more likely to invest because of the existence of trained workers and secondary markets geared for the pharmaceutical industry.
- Social partnership has brought industrial peace over the years.
- Tax on manufacturing industry is one of the lowest in the EU.

The educated workforce

This point is more debated than foreign investment, partly because of the problems involved in trying to tie educational spending and attainment to specific trends in growth. Suffice to say that currently Ireland is enjoying a demographic boom. Its workforce is among the youngest in Europe, and as can be seen in Table 18.3, it spends a larger percentage of its GDP on education than many other rich nations. Perhaps a more important factor for economic growth is not the education of a workforce or its cost but rather its flexibility. Many economists argue that Ireland's reduction in unemployment during the boom period was due, in part, to the flexibility of its labour market. On the one hand, this flexibility leads to large migration in and out of Ireland. On the other hand, it did allow Ireland to reduce its unemployment rate to below 5% during the Celtic Tiger years while many areas in the rest of Europe were still wrestling with double-digit unemployment rates.

The European Union

Critics of Irish economic growth typically say that all of the growth is due to European Union subsidies. In fact, the level of subsidies stayed at roughly the same level while the growth rate continued to climb. If the growth was due solely to EU aid, then continued growth would necessitate larger and larger subsidies from the EU. So while Ireland has benefited from transfers from the EU, it is not the only reason for growth. Rather, membership in and of itself has probably done more for Irish economic growth than direct monetary aid. When joining the EU in 1973, Ireland was committing itself to a process of opening itself to the European and global economies. This openness increased competition and hence forced Irish companies to be more efficient. Furthermore, the process of deregulating industries such as airlines and telecommunications lowered the costs for consumers and other businesses.

Social partnership

Irish economic growth is sometimes portrayed as a shining example of the benefits of partnership between firms, unions and the government. Certainly, the benefit of partnership agreements in the early years of the Celtic Tiger was a very stable wage environment in which wage increases were restrained and industrial actions were curtailed. However, this is not a characteristic unique to the Irish economy. Other countries such as Germany and Austria have also exhibited a large degree of co-operation between unions, businesses and the government. The major benefit of having a national wage agreement is its attraction to foreign businesses looking to invest. However, maintaining the social partnership may not be easy (or desirable) and could pose one of many problems for economic growth.

CASE STUDY

Extract from *The Irish Times*
Economic miracle long time coming
State's growth has merely been in line with figures laid down in 1950
by Cormac Ó Gráda and Kevin O'Rourke

As the 21st century dawns, official Ireland is feeling smug. Between 1994 and 1999, per capita income (GNP) grew at an astonishing 7.9 per cent. Between 1987 and 1998, per capita output (GDP) grew at 6.7 per cent in Ireland, but at only 1.7 per cent in the US and 1.8 per cent in the rest of western Europe. Some commentators seem to think this headlong growth will last, while some politicians seem to think it ought to. Meanwhile, the Economist magazine, which once referred to Ireland as 'The Poorest of the Rich' now muses about 'what Ireland can teach the rest'. However, an historical and comparative view of the Irish boom yields a more sobering perspective.

One of the most robust facts about European growth over the past 50 years has been that poorer countries tend to grow faster than richer countries: thus, the fastest growing economies have been Greece and Portugal, while the slowest growing economies have been Switzerland and Britain (which has, in turn, grown slightly faster than the US). This 'convergence' tendency reflects the ability of laggards to catch up on economic leaders by importing both capital and best practice technology.

Between 1950 and 1987, the outstanding exception to this general rule was Ireland, which only managed to grow at 2.8 per cent per annum (the same rate as affluent Belgium), while its peripheral peers were clocking up growth rates in excess of 4 per cent.

. . .

Viewed in this light, the interesting question is not why Ireland has done so well in the last decade, but why it took so long to catch up. A useful comparison is provided by Italy, another traditionally agricultural economy whose per capita output was roughly the same as Ireland's in 1950. By 1998, its per capita output (if not its income) was 8.8 per cent lower, but it would be wrong to view this as a case of Irish success and Italian failure. By 1973, GDP per capita was almost 60 per cent higher in Italy than in Ireland, a gap which persisted as late as 1990. The net present value of Irish income, discounted back to 1950, would have been 28.9 per cent higher had it grown at the same pace as Italy throughout, rather than making up for lost ground in the 1990s. The moral is that if you are going to converge on richer countries, then the sooner you do so

→

the better. If Ireland's long-run performance has not been exceptional, then neither have the mechanisms by which we achieved our belated success. Indeed, Ireland's 'Golden Age' bears a striking resemblance to the Golden Age the rest of western Europe enjoyed four decades earlier, and which lasted from 1950 to 1973.

Then as now, growth was largely due to convergence; then as now, the economies concerned received substantial external funding, giving governments a little extra room for manoeuvre; then as now, this led to a more structured approach towards economic and infrastructural planning; then as now, the bestowers of this largesse (the US government in the earlier episode, Brussels in the later) insisted that market-friendly reforms be adopted by recipient governments.

. . .

The argument that recent Irish success is due to our educational system has been oversold. For one thing, the timing is wrong: trends in educational spending cannot account for the sharp improvement in our fortunes which occurred from 1987 on. Second, it is not enough to educate the young, . . . Job creation has played a crucial role during this boom . . . This suggests that social partnership was critically important, just as it was in Europe in the 1950s and 1960s.

An historical perspective makes it clear why current growth rates cannot last: rapid growth is only possible while economies converge on the frontier economy (in practice, the US). Once all possible convergence has been achieved, further growth will only be at the rate at which the frontier itself expands, or, historically, 2 per cent. Even boosters of the 'new economy' and the Nasdaq only claim that long-run frontier growth has increased from 2 per cent to 3 per cent. It would be folly to expect that Ireland could do much better than this in the long run. Indeed, US technology firms have played such a crucial role in Irish growth that it is tempting to conclude that our boom has been largely a product of the Greenspan boom. On this view, the possible implications of an American crash are worrying.

History also emphasises the political nature of the Irish boom. Labour's share of national income has declined steadily during the 1990s, but workers have until now been bought off with tax cuts (rather than the improved welfare benefits which mollified an older generation of European workers). Europe's Golden Age ended when the oil crises heightened distributional tensions to the point where they became unmanageable. We look forward to speculating about why Ireland's social partnership experiment finally collapsed – was it the political scandals? the McCreevy budgets? or EMU entry and the consequent housing crisis? – when we have an adequate historical perspective on the question. Say 50 years from now.

Source: The Irish Times, 9 June 2000.

Questions

1. How unique has Ireland's economic growth been?
2. What is the problem of citing education as a reason for economic growth in Ireland?
3. Among the EU countries, it was the peripheral countries of Greece, Ireland and Portugal that were worst hit by the eurozone crisis of 2010/11. Explain why.

Answers on website

By the middle of this century's first decade, the Republic of Ireland had become one of the most affluent countries in the world. According to the World Bank 2006 *World Development Report*, Gross National Income in 2004 was $137.8bn; GNI per capita was $34,280 (ranked seventh highest). In PPP terms, Ireland's 2004 gross national income of $133bn, or GNI per capita of $33,170, was the fifth highest in the world, behind Luxembourg, the USA, Norway and Switzerland. Using national income as the economic indicator of wellbeing, Ireland surpassed the UK and both the EU and OECD averages. Even though the position is not as favourable if alternative measures are employed, such as consumption per capita or the HDI, Ireland still ranked in the top ten richest countries of the world. This is far removed from the early 1980s, when Ireland was one of the poorest countries in the EU. The Celtic Tiger is the term often used to capture this recent surge in output and prosperity. The Tiger analogy is used as a similar boom in economic activity was witnessed by the newly industrialised countries (NICs) or, as they are commonly referred to, the Tiger countries of South East Asia.[23]

Given Ireland's economic record in the 1980s of sluggish economic growth, job losses and rising unemployment, the 1990s brought a welcome surprise. The period 1994–2000 witnessed 8% annual growth rates on average, rising employment and falling unemployment rates. The growth spurt during the Celtic Tiger era led to a situation where the economy was effectively at full employment. This increase in employment numbers was probably the most remarkable feature of the economic boom. In 2005, the total number employed stood at 1.93m: in 1995, the number employed was only 1.28m. However, it is generally recognised that the economic growth rates of the 1990s were unlikely to be repeated as the demographic dividend (exemplified by a rising share of adults in the working population) and the growth rate in the labour supply would not be matched again. As we now know, the source of the boom in the 2000s was different.

The growth performance of this small open European economy attracted considerable international attention. Much of the focus was on accounting for Ireland's growth spurt and the lessons that might be learned as other countries (whether the new EU accession states and/or developing countries) attempt to replicate Ireland's Celtic Tiger story. Aside from some radical interpretations of Ireland's success, the mainstream view attaches importance to a number of explanatory factors (see next section).

Most studies conclude with an admission that no 'smoking gun' or 'silver bullet' was evident in Ireland's success: it was a multi-dimensional story with some factors contributing more than others. However, even with the benefit of hindsight it is not clear how important each of these factors was in contributing to the economic boom, in what can only be described as a virtuous circle (up to a point) of policies, reforms, institutions and events. Moreover, some of these factors predated the Celtic Tiger period and thus are more consistent with prerequisites of growth rather than factors that explain the exact timing of the economic boom. It is probably fair to say that a combination of wise policy-making, favourable external factors and a measure of good luck contributed largely to the arrival of the Celtic Tiger (in the same way that policy errors, adverse external conditions and some bad luck were largely responsible for the poor performance in the 1980s and the subsequent delay in the convergence). In a more general sense, Ireland did not opt for either the market, neoliberal approach or the developmental state approach in its adoption of economic policy but, like many other small European states, carved out a path between liberalism and statism, as successive governments have been pragmatic rather than driven by any one ideology (Bradley 2000).

Before we rush to the conclusion that what was witnessed was an 'economic miracle', consider the following two observations on the early years of the Celtic Tiger era. First, some economists and, particularly, economic historians, are quick to inform us that what we witnessed was a (delayed) convergence in living standards with the rich advanced countries of the world, including the EU: it was a story of a belated catch-up (with something a little extra, depending on which measures of prosperity are employed). What might be regarded as more remarkable than the growth rates of the 1990s/2000s was the dismal performance of the 1980s (and, indeed, the 1950s), and over a longer period of time, Ireland's poor economic record before the early 1990s, and the length of time for the convergence process to materialise (Lee 1985; Mjøset 1992; Ó'Gráda and O'Rourke 2000). Second, was the increase in prosperity and wealth, much of it debt financed in the 2000s, well managed? There is a view (which unfortunately has been confirmed over time) that the economic wealth created in the 1990s and early 2000s could have been managed better (particularly in terms of improvements in public services and better health provision and public infrastructure) and that the benefits of economic growth could have been shared more equally (in preventing unacceptable levels of poverty, inequality and highly concentrated income/wealth distributions).

The story of the Celtic Tiger

Although there are different accounts of and explanations for the Celtic Tiger (both in the mainstream literature and from alternative perspectives) and with no consensus on contributing factors, what is clear is that there is no single factor that accounts for Ireland's remarkable economic growth at the turn of the century. Much of the mainstream literature on the Celtic Tiger distinguishes between long-term factors and proximate-type factors and it is this type of narrative that we now briefly present.

We begin, however, with some numbers. From 1988 to 2007, real GDP growth was, on average, 6.5% per annum, a record far superior to any other Western European country over the same time period. Employment numbers doubled, from 1.1 million in the mid- and late 1980s to over 2.1 million in 2007/08. Unemployment, which stood at 17% of the labour force in 1986, was as low as 3.9% in 2001 before it increased, albeit marginally, to 4.6% by 2007; effectively an economy at full employment. With respect to migration numbers, whereas net migration was estimated to be almost −42,000 (with over 60,000 emigrants) in 1988, it stood at over 67,000 (with over 110,000 immigrants) in 2007. Another indication of the extraordinary turnaround in the Irish economy during that period was the state of the public finances. Whereas the 1980s was dominated by high and rising budget deficits, at between 12% and 15.5% of national income in the early 1980s (and an ever-increasing government debt, at over 95% of GDP in 1991), the period from 1997 onward witnessed budget surpluses (with the general government surplus peaking at 4.8% in 2000) and a falling debt/GDP ratio, to as low as 25% by 2006. As one distinguished commentator remarked, 'With Ireland at the frontier of economic prosperity, this economic miracle was widely admired and emulated' (Honohan 2010).[24]

The long-term (or long-tailed impact as they are sometimes described) factors that created the conditions for the economic growth of the 1990s are usually identified as the consistent government actions, dating as far back as the 1960s, with respect to industrial policy and human capital/education.[25] These progressive policies, combined with good-quality, long-established institutions such as the rule of law, protection of property rights and private business contracts, and the quality (more or less) of public administration were in place decades before the Irish economy took off in the early 1990s. However, it was a confluence of a fortunate set of circumstances and policies in the late 1980s that triggered Ireland's take-off. These proximate causes (or enabling factors as described in the literature) include fiscal stabilisation initiated by a correction – albeit painful – to the public finances, a favourable US and worldwide economic environment, a social partnership model leading to wage moderation and industrial peace, and a flow of EU funds which were, on the whole, well managed.

An analysis of the prosperous Celtic Tiger era is best divided into two distinct periods with the turning point coinciding, coincidentallly, with the new millennium. Before 2000, economy growth was export-led, the economy was cost competitive and domestic demand was strong. According to one analysis of the Celtic Tiger period, 'The boom was exceptional, not just by historical Irish standards but also in an international perspective. Apart from the "Asian Tigers" between 1960 and 1990, and China since 1978, no other countries have sustained such rapid growth for a comparable length of time' (Clinch *et al.* 2002).

If we view this period as a story of a belated structural transformation resulting in delayed convergence (as per the Solow growth model depicted earlier) and catch-up to Western European living standards – whilst acknowledging that there is nothing guaranteed or automatic about convergence, and that even with catch-up there is an inevitable slowdown as it cannot be sustained – the policy mistakes of the 1950s and 1970s meant that there was a lot of ground to be made up.[26] That does not explain why it happened when it did and what set it off, so to speak. The timing and speed of the catch-up is due to a number of factors (listed below and as identified in the third edition of this textbook, including a measure of sheer good luck) which, fortunately for Ireland, came together in the late 1980s/early 1990s and set off a virtuous circle leading to output and employment growth. These factors are:

- openness and Ireland's embrace of internationalisation, economic integration and shifting global technology (incorporating accession to the EU and the Single European Market, membership of the eurozone, attraction of export-oriented foreign direct investment (FDI) and US manufacturing/high-tech MNCs);[27]
- the social partnership approach built on consensus (incorporating a broad-based social pact, national partnership agreements, collective pay bargaining and wage moderation, a tax-based incomes policy and industrial peace);
- a favourable demographic profile arising from the baby boom of the 1960s/70s and manifesting itself in an improving dependency ratio, inward migration and an exceptionally elastic supply of labour;
- EU structural and cohesion funds that were generally well spent on much-needed infrastructural investment;
- fiscal stabilisation, tax reform and sound macroeconomic management;[28]
- a favourable international economic environment, particularly in the USA.

Employing an accounting for growth framework, economic growth in this period came more from employment growth than productivity growth. Indeed, the really exceptional feature of the Celtic Tiger era was the increase in employment numbers, as indicated earlier. Nevertheless, this remarkable and unprecedented growth in employment, achieved through an increase in female labour force participation, a reduction in unemployment numbers and a reversal in migration patterns (that is, net immigration, both of returning emigrants and new immigrants), was a one off.[29] This reflected a very elastic (and, generally, skilled) supply of labour in what was regarded as a highly flexible and open labour market, characterised by high labour mobility. Indeed, the labour market (of the 1980s) characterised by high unemployment, job losses and emigration was transformed in the early 2000s to one of full employment, labour shortages and inward migration. Unfortunately, the late 2000s witnessed a reversal to the labour market of earlier, with labour surpluses returning again, as has unfortunately been the case in Ireland for most of the time since independence.

As for the second period and into the new millennium (satirically dubbed by some as the Celtic Tiger II: The Sequel), continued and accelerated – but clearly unsustainable – growth was fuelled by a construction boom and property bubble, cheap money and easy credit, and large increases in government spending.[30] This pursuit of continued rapid growth, described by NESC (2008) as a '. . . profound shift in what was driving the Irish economy . . .' was partly triggered by the sharp decline in nominal and real – turning negative in some years – interest rates that Ireland witnessed on entry into the eurozone (indeed, for a couple of years both preceding 1999 and thereafter). The expansionary effects of EMU membership were followed by years that witnessed significant increases in wage earnings, take-home pay and ultimately costs, leading to a decline in competitiveness. For example, average earnings per hour for all industries increased from €8.81 in 1996 to €10.66 in 2000. However, by 2006, earnings had increased to €15 per hour (CSO 2010). In doing so Ireland had '. . . moved from being the 6th cheapest EU-15 country in which to live and carry on business in 1996, to being the 4th most expensive in 2001 and the second most expensive in 2007' (NESC 2008).

The change in the nature of economic growth before and after the new millennium is also reflected in the composition of growth due to factor accumulation and to increases in productivity. Whereas the period before 2000/1 witnessed increases in both factor inputs and productivity (as measured by growth in TFP), the period after 2000/1 saw increases in factor accumulation but no real change in total factor productivity.[31]

The change that took place after the start of the new millennium is reflected in a number of trends. Investment as a share of GNP rose from 20% in 1995 to over 30% by the mid-2000s. Much of the investment increase was in building and construction as opposed to machinery and equipment. During the 2000–2006 period, employment numbers increased not only in construction (29%) but also in health (20%), financial and other business services (18%), and wholesale and retail trade (13%). In contrast to the pre-2001 period when industrial and manufacturing employment rose substantially, numbers employed in manufacturing in 2000–2006 fell by over 8% or, on an annual basis, by 1.6%. Moreover, in respect of other economic indicators, the difference between the two expansions (pre- and post-2001) is clearly shown in Table 18.5.

TABLE 18.5: ECONOMIC PERFORMANCE IN THE MOST RECENT EXPANSIONS (AVERAGE ANNUAL GROWTH RATE, PER CENT)

	1995–2000	2002–2007
GNP per capita	7.9	3.2
Labour utilisation	3.9	2.8
Capital services	8.9	6.5
Output per hour worked	5.5	2.6
Real wage	1.6	2.8
Export volume	17.7	5.1

Source: OECD 2009.

In sum, by 2006/07 there were clear signs of an overheated economy, further fuelled by misguided and inappropriate pro-cyclical fiscal policy. Whelan (2010) argues that it was 'endemic' and 'unwarranted' over-optimism that was the fundamental source of the misguided policy mistakes of the 2000s. Many, including ourselves, would argue that this is a rather benign view of the times and culture that we lived in. Indeed, the 'prudence, realism, and restraint' that Honohan and

Walsh (2002) claimed policy-makers and social partners showed (in an era of 'heightened expectations') in the 1990s was well and truly gone by the 2000s, to be replaced by recklessness, falsity and abandonment (not just by policy-makers but also by private sector actors, including credit institutions and property developers).

Having discussed Ireland's two distinctive booms we now turn to the post-Celtic Tiger period.

The post-Celtic Tiger era[32]

Given Ireland's embrace of globalisation and economic integration, exposure to an international downturn was always a danger. Events since 2007, both domestic and global, have often been described in the media (and elsewhere) as the perfect storm. A financial and banking crisis led to an economic (and fiscal, not to mention social) crisis that surpasses anything since the Great Depression of the 1930s. As we move into the next decade, the years 2008–2009 will be remembered as the Great Recession. The economic collapse in Ireland, culminating (of sorts) in the 2010 EU–IMF financial assistance programme, has been one of the worst in the developed world. The background to this crisis is presented below, under three headings, namely the global financial crisis and worldwide recession, the Irish property bubble, and the domestic banking crisis. We begin externally, with the international recession.

Financial crisis, international credit crunch and global recession

Autumn 2008 will be long remembered as some of the most uncertain times in our modern economic history. Although still a source of debate, there is some agreement that the financial crisis that accelerated the world recession of 2008/09 was a bank-led crisis, similar in many ways to previous post-World War II banking and financial crises, but in this case triggered by subprime residential mortgage defaults (see Information Box 18.1). We begin by briefly outlining the series of events that culminated in the Great Recession of 2008/09 (elsewhere in the literature referred to as the Great Contraction or the Great Credit Crisis).

INFORMATION BOX 18.1

Financial instruments: what do they all mean?

Much of the earlier discussion and analysis of the financial crisis centred on the role of exotic and highly complex and sophisticated financial products and derivatives. Appearing as acronyms, the most important of which were CDOs, MBS and CDS, these financial instruments played an important role in unintentionally bringing about the near collapse of the financial system in the USA, and banking systems elsewhere. So what exactly were these products?

Collaterised Debt Obligations (CDOs) are securities backed by a pool of bonds, loans or other assets, and are used by financial institutions for offloading risk. If the assets or loans are mortgages, they are called mortgage-backed securities (MBS). More formally, MBS, or securitisation, is where mortgages and other debt obligations are pooled and then repackaged to be sold on, as securities of different risks, to investors. Taking loans off-balance sheet, securitisation allows banks to spread (and, by doing so, reduce their own) risk – but, as we know from recent events, actually increased it – while at the same time increasing lending.

A credit default swap (CDS) is a financial instrument that contracts both parties to the transaction to swap the risk of debt default. From the buyer's perspective, a CDS is a way of insuring against a debt default; i.e. in the event of a default, the seller pays out to the buyer.

How are these instruments or products, which were originally intended to reduce risk but in effect increased it, with devastating consequences, connected? The risk associated with MBS can be reduced by taking out insurance. The contracts on these insurance policies are the CDS, which are in turn traded on secondary markets. In this context, a Special Purpose Vehicle (SPV) is a legal entity that banks create to hold the mortgage-backed securities, and in doing so, separate them from the other obligations of the bank.

Finally, a subprime mortgage is a type of mortgage made out to borrowers with low credit ratings, but where higher rates of interest apply.

In March 2008 the US investment bank Bear Sterns collapsed and was sold to JP Morgan Chase at a huge discount.[33] Bear Sterns was the company that pioneered securitisation in the US mortgage market and was one of the leading underwriters of mortgage-backed securities in the USA. Another of America's old investment banks, Merrill Lynch & Co., was bought by Bank of America on 15 September 2008. Much worse was to follow that same week when Lehman Brothers investment bank – considered by many as 'too big to fail' – was declared bankrupt, making it (at that time) the largest bankruptcy in US history. Lehman Brothers had run up enormous losses due to its exposure in the subprime mortgage market.[34] At the same time, AIG (American International Group), the world's largest insurance company, was kept afloat by US government support, resulting in a majority public ownership of AIG. This bailout followed the earlier US Treasury's decision to take over the quasi-government mortgage finance companies Fannie Mae and Freddie Mac, government-sponsored enterprises that accounted for over half the US mortgage market. In response to the financial panic, and fearful of a collapse on Wall Street (and the knock-on effects on Main Street), the US government announced a $700bn bailout package, TARP (Troubled Asset Relief Program), established under the 2008 US Emergency Economic Stabilisation Act (EESA).[35]

Despite this enormous bailout, by the following month the crisis had spread, making it a global phenomenon. Due to the bundling of obligations and the non-transparency of it all, it was unclear which financial institutions were awash with so-called toxic assets. International capital markets froze. Interbank rates soared, as did the default risk spreads. In the real economy, international trade plummeted as economic activity worldwide collapsed, resulting in the severest post-World War II global recession (with only China, India and some smaller Asian countries managing to record growth rates of any significant size). At its trough, global industrial production was 13% below its previous peak. The equivalent figure for international trade was about 20 per cent. Comparisons with the Great Depression of the 1930s became popular and not unrealistic (see Eichengreen and O'Rourke 2009).

In the EU, sovereign debt ratings for some of the weaker eurozone countries were downgraded, as the cost of borrowing for many countries, reflected in the yield spread vis-à-vis Germany, rose significantly (for Ireland, matters were to deteriorate significantly in autumn 2010 when Irish bond yields – that is, the cost of borrowing on international markets for the Irish state – rose to over 6.5% in the fear of a sovereign debt default). Outside the EU, the biggest victim of the global financial crisis was Iceland, when in October 2008, Iceland's banking system collapsed, with devastating consequences for the Icelandic economy and its people. Eventually Iceland had to turn to the IMF for support, as did some Eastern European countries, most especially Hungary, Latvia, and Romania, three EU accession nations that had become vulnerable to a financial crisis as many European banks had lent these – and others – large amounts during the boom years. With loans in euros (as some of the newly joined EU countries were anticipating early membership of the eurozone) and a domestic currency in decline, the cost of repayments soared.

The difference between this crisis and previous crises (especially the Great Depression) was the policy response of the authorities.[36] Monetary authorities in the USA, Europe and elsewhere aggressively slashed interest rates (often in a co-ordinated move) and massively injected liquidity by quantitative easing (i.e. when interest rates are zero or close to zero central banks can ease monetary policy further by buying securities through open market operations).[37] Fiscal policy was highly expansionary in those countries that could afford it (that is, those that had the 'fiscal space' to do so), with tax cuts and large increases in public spending. Indeed, the extraordinary fiscal stimuli that were implemented (and, indeed, required in the face of the global crisis), left many countries with very large fiscal deficits and sovereign debt, at a time when private indebtedness was also very high.

With hindsight, the world recession of the late 2000s was a problem waiting to happen. From the 1990s onward, the global economy was characterised by high growth, low inflation and falling interest rates arising from, it was argued, globalisation and technological progress, and improved macroeconomic policies (a period known as the Great Moderation, when macroeconomic volatility had substantially declined). Economic growth of later years was, however, fuelled by lax regulation, cheap and abundant credit, a decline in lending standards by credit institutions (in many but not all advanced economies) and an alarming rise in indebtedness, most particularly private debt in the USA and UK.[38] The problems that first emerged in the USA spread to the rest of the world, further exacerbating the already sizeable global imbalances. The collapse of the subprime market and the spread of the banking crisis to Europe and elsewhere resulted in a virtual breakdown of the financial system. Credit dried up as many banks went to the wall. Ireland's position was made worse by economic imbalances or excesses at home, and, in particular, a property bubble that burst and a banking system that virtually collapsed. We now turn to these two domestic developments.

Property bubble

Unlike the financial crisis in the USA, which was triggered by banking developments from the early 1990s onward, pertaining to financial deregulation, the subprime market, mortgage-backed securities and other off-balance sheet vehicles, the Irish property bubble more resembled a classic or old-fashioned credit-fuelled asset bubble, but with some significant – in terms of their contribution to the bubble – Irish characteristics (such as the Irish preference for property, poor long-term urban planning and close connections between bankers, property developers and politicians).

Figure 18.1 shows the rise in house prices in Ireland during the boom. Nationwide, the average price (in nominal terms) of a new house in 1987 was €48,151. For second-hand houses, it was €46,330. Twenty years later, when prices were at their peak, the average price for new and second-hand houses was €322,634 and €377,850 respectively. The increase in house prices in the Dublin region was even larger, rising, for new (second-hand) houses, from €50,864 (€49,139) in 1987 to €416,225 (€495,576) in 2007. Simply put, taking 1994 as a start date, average real house prices trebled between 1994 and 2007. Prices peaked in early 2007 and have fallen significantly since then, wiping out much of the gains of previous years.[39] The increase in house prices was due, it

FIGURE 18.1: AVERAGE HOUSE PRICES IN IRELAND 1987–2007

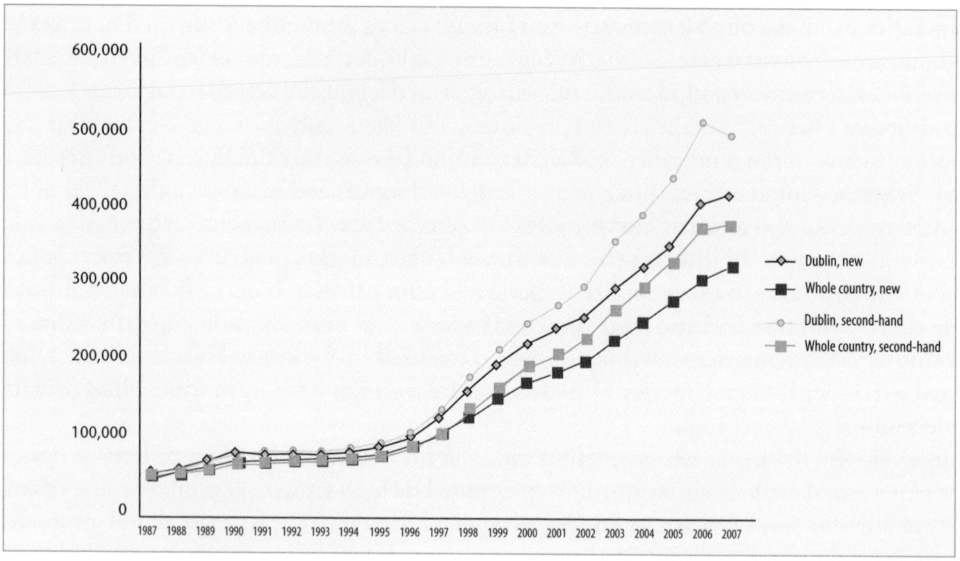

was argued, to a number of 'fundamental' factors, including demographic changes (with the rise in the key house-buying population cohort), the growth in national output and employment, rising disposable incomes, falling interest rates and – exceptional – credit expansion.[40] Of course, while some of this was true, much of the increase in house prices was due to speculation (of future price increases) in what can only be described, with hindsight, as a housing frenzy on the back of a credit binge and exuberant property markets.[41] Whatever about the precise causes of the price increases in the property bubble, there was no doubt about the 'positive' short-term effects it was having on the economy. As house prices continued to soar, so did all types of house building, home improvements and DIY, and general consumption as house-buying consumers spent – and borrowed – on the back of rising property prices. The construction industry, real estate agents, property surveyors and the legal profession were not the only beneficiaries. Central government also gained through higher tax revenues in the form of stamp duty, capital gains tax and VAT receipts. Local authorities also benefited through the development levies incurred, but not always paid, by property developers.

As property prices accelerated, a larger share of resources were diverted from elsewhere in the economy to the non-traded building and construction sector which, by its very nature, is a labour-intensive and low-productivity industry. In 2006, when building residential properties was at a peak, over 93,000 units were completed, raising the stock of dwellings to over 1.8 million as compared with a figure of 1.2 million fifteen years earlier.[42] At the zenith of the boom, Ireland was building 21 units per 1,000 population, which was four to five times higher than the equivalent figures across the EU and, with hindsight, well beyond the needs of the population. Indeed, by the mid-2000s, housing and residential construction accounted for over 13% of the economy's national output, double the equivalent figure just a decade earlier and what is considered typical for a developed country. Over 275,000 persons were employed in construction by 2007, equal to almost 13.5% of total employment (making it the highest share in the OECD countries), or put another way, almost equal to the total number employed in manufacturing.

An indication of the property bubble and excessive building is the stock of unsold properties and vacant houses. The 2006 population census published in 2007 reported that over 266,000 housing units (or 15% of the housing stock) were vacant on census night. Whilst acknowledging the difficulties in cross-country comparisons of house prices, studies have shown that prices in Ireland (and Dublin) were extraordinarily high. For example, in a comparison of average sale prices in 2004 across a dozen of European cities, the price per square metre was higher in Dublin than everywhere else.

Another indication of a property market driven way beyond fundamentals is the difference in trends between rents and house prices that emerged during the 2000s boom. In theory, consider house buying as the opportunity cost of not renting. In the long run, real house prices should approximate to the present discounted value of future rents.[43] If the rise in house prices is due to fundamentals, we might expect real rents and real house prices to track each other. Although this was true during much of the first, export-led boom in the early to mid-1990s (as reflected in a relatively constant price–rent ratio), the second, construction-led boom of the 2000s witnessed a dramatic increase in the price–rent ratio, almost doubling by the mid-2000s (Shiller 2006; Kelly 2007).

An even bigger problem in the property market was the overvaluation of commercial property and the exposure of Irish credit institutions to commercial real estate and property developers. Internationally, it is exposure to commercial (as opposed to residential) property that generally causes the biggest losses for the banking sector due, *inter alia*, to greater cyclical volatility and a larger incidence of defaults on commercial property-related loans. Although data on commercial property can be somewhat unreliable, it was clear that by 2006/7 there was mounting concern about the unsustainability of commercial investments. For example, in late 2001 property-related lending was 38% of total private sector lending. By 2006, it had increased to 62%. Specifically in terms of commercial lending, commercial property loans as a percentage of outstanding private sector credit increased from 8% in 1999 to almost 27% in 2007. With respect to commercial property values, the cumulative increase in capital values over the period 2003–2006 was approximately 46% (Woods 2007). Of course, by 2007, even if remedial action had been taken, it was too late. The small number of large, highly leveraged clients that dominated the Irish commercial property market faced large losses on deteriorating asset quality and were unable to make their repayments to credit institutions (see below).

Claims of overshooting, bubbles and hard landings were offset by counterclaims that the market was sound, driven by strong fundamentals and that somehow Ireland's experience was different, despite the fact that, internationally and historically, construction building and residential investment tends to be highly cyclical and characterised by pronounced boom–bust cycles. In particular, it was argued (by many, including some economists, and especially many working for financial institutions and stockbroking firms) that the Irish demographics and its labour market – a young population with an elastic supply of labour – would ensure an orderly correction, i.e. a soft landing. Yet, by the mid-2000s, the OECD and others (including the IMF and the European Commission) were noting that 'Ireland stands out by its extraordinary strong increase in house prices over the past decade' (Rae and van den Noord 2006).[44] Indeed, the same report acknowledged that soft landings were 'not especially common'. In the 49 residential construction booms in 23 countries between 1960 and 2004 (for which data were available) that they examined, and with a soft landing defined as both *mild* and *gradual*, the report concluded that 'there has not been a single case out of the 49 boom–bust cycles'.

Eventually, prices did fall as the economy was hit by a perfect storm – a worldwide recession combined with a banking crisis and a property collapse, with one feeding off the other. As prices fell and expectations suddenly reversed, the immediate effect on the real economy was devastating.

Thousands of construction workers were laid off (with the negative effect on government revenues and welfare spending, household income and consumer spending), many households found themselves in negative equity (with the knock-on effect of rising levels of indebtedness and lower consumer spending), businesses cut production, reduced their workforce and in many cases closed, developers and builders went to the wall, with the banks that did the lending turning to the state for support while at the same time curtailing their lending to the rest of the economy. In the longer run, the landscape of Ireland is peppered with a large oversupply of houses, vacant units, ghost estates, unfinished buildings (both residential and commercial) and a legacy that will take years, if not decades, to correct. Central to the property boom was the banks and other financial institutions operating in Ireland. We now turn to the Irish banking crisis.

The banking crisis

As with the (related) property bubble, the underlying cause of the Irish banking crisis was domestic, with Irish-controlled credit institutions engaged in excessive risk-taking and reckless property-related lending, overextended Irish borrowers (namely residential mortgage holders, developers, builders) who borrowed too much, and Irish policy-makers (i.e. Government, Department of Finance, Central Bank, Financial Regulator) that failed to act decisively and responsibly in the long-term national interest.

Throughout the Celtic Tiger era, banks in Ireland published large annual profits at a time when bank lending skyrocketed to over 200% of national income. Moreover, the banks were heavily exposed to the property boom, both at home and abroad. In some cases, up to 70% of the loan books of Irish banks and building societies were property-, land- or construction-related, making for a financial sector that was heavily exposed to commercial property and thus vulnerable to its collapse. Throughout the 2000s, financial institutions continued to lend – with hindsight, excessively large amounts – to builders and developers, while, at the same time, extending mortgage loans (bigger in size, as measured by the euro amount borrowed, and longer in duration, as measured by the period of the mortgage) to buyers of increasingly expensive houses and apartments. With house buyers and investors, developers and builders, banks and building societies (not to mention the exchequer, with ever-increasing tax returns) all willingly participating, the ingredients for a classic asset bubble and a domestic financial crisis were at hand.

With very little regulatory oversight (and what there was, with arguably insufficient resources and expertise, tended to be timid and accommodating vis-à-vis financial institutions), the directors and senior management of the Irish credit institutions, once renowned for their traditional and conservative outlook and behaviour, relaxed their lending conditions (and, in many cases, engaged in excessive risk-taking and unsound management practices with breaches of internal guidelines, policies and procedures common among some of the worst offenders) as they sought ever larger profits and market share in what had become a highly competitive market.[45] For example, the assets of the major credit institutions in Ireland increased dramatically in the 2000s, from €355bn in 2000 to over €1,410bn in 2008 (Central Bank 2009). Aside from the exceptional amounts lent and the small number of large clients involved, concerns emanating from the commercial lending side were the inadequacy of loan appraisals, securing of (and the value of that) collateral (with personal guarantees in some cases), and a lack of proper loan documentation. With respect to residential mortgages, some disquiet was raised over a number of new and risky practices such as 100% loan-to-value (LTV) mortgages, long maturity (of 35 or 40 years) mortgages, interest-only mortgages, loans five or six times the applicant's income (as opposed to earlier multiples of two or three), etc. One such concern was the trend in the LTV ratios. For example, the percentage of house buyers on a LTV of 100% trebled in just two years, from 5% in 2004 to 15% in 2006. The increase for first time buyers was even greater, from 6% in 2004 to an alarming 34% (it was 39% for second-hand houses) in 2006 (Department of Environment, Heritage and Local Government 2010).

Dependent on deposits in the past, Irish banks turned increasingly – as indeed did other banks worldwide – to foreign borrowing and inter-bank markets for funding. Although not exposed to US-originated assets that caused much of the financial panic initially, borrowing short-term on international money markets in order to lend long-term for property-related transactions was a very risky, not to mention costly, business, as was the aggressive growth strategy employed by some of the new entrants to the more integrated European financial markets. When the global financial crisis hit, certain Irish banks could not roll over their borrowing as capital markets had either dried up or viewed certain institutions as being too risky or too big, or both. Ireland Inc.'s international reputation took a battering. This was reflected in falling share prices of Irish-controlled banks (to levels of 5% or lower of their peak values), higher premia on Irish government bonds and a downgrading of sovereign debt. The end result was a systemic failure of the Irish banking and financial system, making it 'in relative terms . . . the largest banking collapse of any Eurozone member' (McCarthy 2009).

In late September 2008, with the banking sector in crisis and a fear of contagion from an imminent collapse of Anglo Irish Bank (subsequently nationalised) as its access to wholesale funding dried up, the government decided to give a blanket state guarantee, for two years, of all deposits and liabilities of the main Irish-controlled banks.[46] The sums involved in the contingent liability of the state were €436bn (that is, €351bn under this new guarantee scheme plus the €85bn under the existing Deposit Protection Scheme), amounting to over two times annual GDP, making it very large compared to other government guarantees introduced elsewhere, for this or previous crises. Other options at that time such as a limited and temporary nationalisation (of, for example, one or two financial institutions) or a shorter or more selective guarantee (of, for example, new borrowings only, or a smaller number of banks, or a limited classification of creditors) might have been less costly options. In general, although state guarantees are often considered necessary (in times of great difficulty) their introduction can lead to very considerable problems, notably that once introduced they are difficult to withdraw, and, as with other insurance schemes, the likelihood of increased moral hazard.

In 2009, the government announced the establishment of National Asset Management Agency (NAMA), an asset management company to deal with the problem assets of the Irish banks. Land and development loans were transferred to NAMA, at a heavy discount, with the stream of income from the assets and the proceeds from the sale of any underlying assets accruing to NAMA. In turn, the government-guaranteed NAMA bonds transferred to the banks were to be used as collateral in order to access loans from the ECB and the markets. In the event of NAMA making a loss over its expected lifespan of seven to ten years, a levy or surcharge would be imposed on the participants – many of which, ironically, will be majority state-owned – to make up the shortfall. As of the time of writing, NAMA is expected to acquire about €80bn of loans, at a discount of over 50%, from the participating credit institutions. NAMA sparked much controversy, with many commentators objecting to it on numerous operational (not to mention more fundamental) grounds, including the price and the valuation process, based on their 'long-term economic value', at which the impaired loans were to be transferred to NAMA (and the subsequent distribution of the losses between the parties involved, namely the state – that is, the taxpayer – and the remaining creditors of the banks, that is, shareholders and bondholders), the treatment of the NAMA bonds in the national accounts and the lack of reliable information coming from the distressed banks whose impaired loans NAMA bought.[47]

In more general terms, in previous banking crises (of which there were many) the solvency problems – as opposed to the liquidity crisis which many in financial circles claimed Ireland was only suffering from in 2008 – of undercapitalised banks have been usually addressed using a combination of bank restructuring (both containment and resolution) policies including guaranteeing liabilities, recapitalising the banks affected, and separating out the bad assets (Furceri and Mourougane 2009). These policies, aimed at preventing or, at the very least, limiting the extent of 'zombie' banks, are not meant to be mutually exclusive, but complementary. As with many other troubled countries, Ireland opted for a combination of all three policies (albeit introduced at different times and at different speeds), with the first and last of these (the state guarantee and NAMA) attracting most controversy, most especially in terms of the sharing and distribution of the burden, with the taxpayer absorbing very large losses.[48]

Ireland's sovereign debt crisis and the 2010 EU–IMF Deal

The economic and financial crisis had, as expected, a dramatic effect on the Irish economy. It is fair to say, however, that the financial crisis only exacerbated an already weakened economy, with significant domestic vulnerabilities, including extraordinary house price appreciation, excessive bank credit growth, historically high household indebtedness and a growing current account deficit.

According to official data, the Irish economy's decline between 2008 and 2010 surpassed all previous post-World War II Irish downturns.[49] Indeed, the collapse of the Irish economy amounts to one of the most severe contractions suffered by a developed country since the Great Depression of the 1930s. Measured by changes in prices, the deflation figures from 2008/09 indicate the first sustained period of deflation that Ireland witnessed in well over half a century. As with prices, wages have also seen a considerable adjustment downward.

After 2008, consumer spending, retail sales and investment fell significantly. Business closures escalated, and despite the recapitalisation of the banks by the state, credit to the business sector continued to contract. Over two years after the start of the financial crisis, private sector credit to the (non-property) business sector was 17.8% lower in the quarter ending Q3 2010 than in the third quarter of 2009. The year-on-year fall was even greater for certain sectors, with a 21% decline for manufacturing. For hotels and restaurants, the fall in lending since the peak of Q2 2008 was 23.1% (Central Bank 2010). Employment numbers fell from over 2.1 million in 2007 to 1.85 million in late 2010, with a decline of over 8% alone recorded in 2009. Unemployment, as a percentage of the labour force, rose from 4.4% in 2006 to over 13.5%, or over 450,000 persons using Live Register figures, in 2010. Youth unemployment was much higher (in fact, double), with more than one in every four of those aged under 25 without a job. For young males, the unemployment rate was one in every three (with big regional differences), making it one of the highest rates in the EU. By early 2011, at the time of writing, the unemployment rate has risen to over 14.5%. All in all, as the OECD (2009) noted, Ireland's adjustment since 2008 was 'without precedent in recent times among industrialised countries'.

One consequence of the global recession and crisis in Ireland was the very rapid deterioration in the public finances.[50] Fortunately, Ireland entered recession with public finances that were relatively favourable, with (although, now with hindsight, insufficiently large) fiscal surpluses and a relatively low debt/GDP ratio. However, it was noticeable during the boom years that tax revenue as a share of national income did not rise over the period 1996–2006 despite all the wealth and income that was generated. As public expenditure continued to rise from 2001 onward – much, but certainly not all, of it (despite persistent claims of a bloated public service) spent on many worthwhile and under-resourced public services and still below levels in many EU countries – it was evident that the public finances were vulnerable to a downturn in economic activity, global or domestic. With respect to revenues, successive reductions in income tax rates and increases in tax expenditures (of which there were already a large number), resulted in a tax base that was simply too narrow and, moreover, tax revenues that had become dependent less on traditional taxes (income tax, excise and VAT) and more on transient, asset-related or transaction taxes (stamp duty and capital gains tax) and corporation tax. With government revenue highly dependent on the housing boom and asset transactions, and with large public expenditure increases throughout the 2000s, the downturn in the economy led to a collapse in tax revenues – one of the most pronounced falls in all of the OECD countries – and a dramatic turnabout in the state's finances, from a surplus of 3% in 2006 to a deficit of almost 12% in 2010. In 2009 for example, whereas tax revenue amounted to €33bn (down from a peak of €47bn just two years earlier), (voted) expenditure totalled over €47bn, with an exchequer deficit of almost €25bn and a general government deficit of over €19bn, the latter amounting to 11.8% of GDP, or when including the €4bn transfer to Anglo Irish Bank, over €23bn and 14.6% of GDP.

Government debt as a percentage of GDP, which had fallen to 25% in the mid 2000s, rose to 44% by 2008, and doubled by 2010, raising concerns about the sustainability of budgetary policy.[51] A large fiscal adjustment, through tax increases and expenditure reductions, was called for (given, *inter alia*, the government funding crisis on international financial markets, the fear of a sovereign default and the not unrelated size of the structural deficit) despite the fact that fiscal contraction would, in the short run, further dampen economic activity. The government's fiscal austerity package was, at least initially, praised internationally, with, for example, the IMF claiming that it 'was achieved in a remarkably socially-cohesive manner . . ', representing '. . . a balance of economic and social considerations.' (IMF 2010). Remedial action in the form of reductions in public expenditure (including cuts in the public sector wage bill) combined with increases in taxation (much in the form of 'short-term' levies) in four budgets stretching from late 2008 to end 2010 appeared to restore some order to the public finances and partially rehabilitated Ireland's international reputation.

As for the global position, according to official IMF data, the world economy, which contracted by 0.6% in 2009, emerged from recession in the second quarter of 2009, much quicker than many commentators had forecast. Aside from strong economic activity in China and elsewhere in Asia, the global rebound was no doubt helped by the performance of the USA, which came out of recession in late 2009, with moderate quarterly growth rates thereafter (at least up to the time of writing). From an Irish perspective, one of the few positives to emerge during this time was the resilience of Irish exports. Whereas eurozone exports declined by over 13% in 2009, the decline in Irish exports was just 2.3% (following a 1% decline in 2008). Although this is due to the composition of Irish exports and the dominance of certain multinationals, and as great care needs to be taken with the interpretation of numbers, especially for a small open economy, it was one of the few positives that emerged during the 'doom and gloom' years that followed the 'boom and bloom' era of the Celtic Tiger.[52]

As alluded to earlier, events escalated in autumn 2010 when the huge scale of the bank bailout became more apparent. As the yield spread with Germany widened, international debt markets demanded significantly higher interest rates on Irish government bonds. Fears of a sovereign debt default and the prospects of an IMF rescue loomed as market concerns over the sustainability of Ireland's budgetary position, arising from the *one-off* bank bailout and the *annual* fiscal deficits, increased. Unfortunately, given the 2008 blanket guarantee, international investors had reason to view the private bank debt and the public state debt as inextricably tied. Taking the two of them together, Ireland was considered by many to be close to insolvent. Even though the government was no longer seeking funding in the market (as it had enough cash reserves until the middle of 2011), the interest rate on government debt in secondary markets rose to above 9%. The Irish banks, unable to fund themselves and with deposits leaving the country, had to seek emergency funding from the ECB, which had already provided massive support to the markets by injecting billions of euro since the financial crisis began back in 2008. Fear of contagion spread to other peripheral eurozone countries, including Portugal and Spain. As European banks and eurozone sovereign countries faced mounting uncertainty, fears over the sustainability of the euro soared. In late November 2010, the Irish government conceded, beginning negotiations with the IMF and the EU on a programme for financial assistance.

The final deal involved a three-year €85bn package, of which €22.5bn is IMF funding, €22.5bn from the European Commission's European Financial Stability Mechanism, €17.7bn from the European Financial Stability Fund, €4.8bn of bilateral loans and €17.5bn of an Irish contribution, in the form of €5bn of cash reserves and €12.5bn from the National Pension Reserve Fund. The average interest rate was estimated to be 5.8%, regarded by many as punitive. A memorandum of understanding between Ireland and the EU–IMF was signed in December 2010, with future disbursement of financial assistance subject to quarterly reviews of conditionality, resulting in what many viewed as a dark day for Irish economic sovereignty. Others were more sanguine, arguing that Ireland's economic sovereignty had been lost (or 'pooled') some time ago, while some others viewed the arrival of technocrats from Washington and Brussels as a relief given the mismanagement by the Irish authorities (while, in sharp contrast, others were in equal measure very critical of our European partners in the Commission and the ECB for the 'deal imposed' on Ireland). Either way, it was a bailout or rescue that Ireland, in modern times, had managed to avoid even during the difficult decades of the 1950s and 1980s. At the time of writing, there was no consensus on the future likelihood of burden-sharing by bondholders, a permanent crisis mechanism at the EU level to replace the temporary €750bn stability fund, the possibility of a sovereign default (debt restructuring) by Ireland and the future prospects for the euro.

So, to end, who is to blame and what can we learn? With respect to the former, is it the banks? The government? The Central Bank or Financial Regulator? The Department of Finance, or independent economic advisors? Our partner institutions in Europe, both in Brussels and Frankfurt? Ourselves, i.e. the general public? The economic system, i.e. capitalism, or a particular brand of capitalism, such as global capitalism, Anglo-Saxon capitalism or Irish-style crony capitalism? Ireland's political and electoral system? Does it depend on one's view of the world? As one might expect from a social scientist analysing a complex phenomenon, there is no simple answer. The philosophy and ruling ideology of the time in this part of the world was self regulation (or, at best, light-touch regulation), (over) reliance on market mechanisms, and consumption financed by debt. This culture, combined, in Ireland, with a 'strong and pervasive' preference for property as an asset, a deference to banks and senior management, in conjunction with a political system that has elements of cronyism, opportunism and corruption and with a tradition of clientelism (exemplified by a fixation on local issues at the expense of addressing national issues) together resulted in a crisis that once again, but this time for all the wrong reasons, thrust Ireland into the attention of the world's international media.[53]

Tentative lessons from the global and Irish experience

As for general observations and lessons, there are some that are common to both the Irish and global experience of the past decade, while others apply primarily to the Irish experience. We will simply list them here – in the form of questions – but we encourage the student reader to investigate further. One way, for example, would be to read some of the relevant references and sources listed at the back of this textbook.

International

- In the light of financial deregulation and regulatory capture, how much more rules-based and intrusive should the system of regulation and prudential supervision of banks and the financial system be? How can the regulatory structures keep pace with the evolution of financial markets and, in particular, financial innovation? Is the international financial architecture capable of dealing with the global and cross-border nature of financial transactions and activities?
- How should financial markets deal with risk, as there was a massive underpricing (and offloading) of risk on the eve of the crisis? How do we deal with the danger of leveraging-up?
- Should the Anglo-Saxon model of corporate governance, with its focus on short-term profits, shareholder value, and bonus package incentive schemes (the 'bonus culture') be radically reformed, or replaced?
- How can we improve the role and behaviour of hedge funds, accountants and auditors, stockbroking and banking economists, mortgage brokers and ratings agencies so that there is not a recurrence of events?
- Is it now time to consider a tax on speculation and financial transactions, e.g. a Tobin-type tax?[54]
- Was the recovery from the global crisis due to policy, both macro and otherwise (that is, monetary and fiscal policies, and bank bailouts) or some other factors and engines of growth? In particular, how effective is fiscal policy? In general, how can we achieve a better balance between the market and the state?
- How can the monetary authorities prevent a repeat of the inappropriately low interest rates that fuelled the excessive and reckless lending (and borrowing)? How can the authorities prevent a repeat of the levels of indebtedness, both public and private?
- How can we ensure that macro-prudential measures are given the prominence they deserve? In respect of the monetary authorities, how can they reconcile price stability, financial stability and prudential supervision? Should asset prices (including house purchases) be included in the standard measure of inflation – the Consumer Price Index – pursued by Central Banks?

Ireland

- How can the authorities better deal with the pro-cyclical nature of the financial system (where credit is easy in good times, but difficult to access in tough times) and the pro-cyclical experience of Irish fiscal policy? More specifically, what changes to institutions and governance structures of national and supranational (EU) bodies are required to ensure that the aforementioned events are not repeated?

- What is the developmental model that can underpin Ireland's next stage of development? Does it require electoral and political reform, as well as economic and financial reform?
- How can Ireland's obsession with property be better managed? Why did policymakers persist with long-established tax breaks for house purchases and a tax bias towards construction?
- How can financial institutions remodel their lending strategies to SMEs, innovative projects and new business formation?
- Is there a need to re-visit our decision to opt for low-density housing, as against high-density city centre living, with the consequences of urban sprawl in Dublin and other urban centres?
- Why is it that during a financial and economic crisis, the consequences (in terms of job losses and the need for a jobs strategy, to include, *inter alia*, active labour market strategies) do not get the attention they deserve? Is 'getting the right environment' sufficient for job creation? Or, how can jobless growth be avoided?

SUMMARY

1. This chapter examined economic growth and the performance of an economy over a long period of time. Factors that influence economic growth in the long run include changes in population, capital and technology.
2. The Solow growth model details a relationship between labour L, capital stock K and national income Y. Part of this relationship is savings. A country must save part of its output to use as capital stock in future years; the remainder of its output is consumption.
3. The Solow growth model predicts that countries with similar characteristics tend to grow together and converge in terms of income per capita. Dissimilar countries may actually grow apart with wealthy countries growing much faster than poorer ones.
4. Based on experiences from countries around the world, factors such as political systems and institutions, education, degree of openness to the world economy and levels of technology play significant roles in the economic growth of a country.
5. Ireland's economic growth has taken its own unique path. Strong economic growth can be considered a continuation of growth that started in the 1960s.
6. Factors that contributed to Ireland's economic growth during the Celtic Tiger era include the amount of foreign investment, membership in the European Union, an educated workforce and social partnership. After 2000, accelerated and unsustainable growth was fuelled by cheap money and easy credit, and a domestic construction boom and property bubble. The decline in the Irish economy that followed was dramatic.

KEY TERMS

Solow growth model	Foreign direct investment
Capital stock	Human capital
Labour	Celtic Tiger
Production function	Clustering
Depreciation	Social partnership
Steady state level of capital	Financial crisis
Golden Rule level of capital	Great Recession
Export-led growth	Property bubble

REVIEW QUESTIONS

1. What is the main equation for the Solow growth model and what does it tell us about economic growth in a country?
2. What is foreign direct investment and how can it help a country's economy grow?
3. List four factors that can influence a country's economic growth.
4. Explain why a poorer country is likely to grow faster than a wealthier one.
5. List four factors that influenced Ireland's economic growth during the early years of the Celtic Tiger.
6. In the context of the Irish economy, explain the background to its collapse in the late 2000s.

MULTI-CHOICE QUESTIONS

1. The Golden Rule level of capital refers to the:
   (a) level of capital at which a country grows most quickly over time;
   (b) level of capital with the largest amount of savings over time;
   (c) level of capital with the largest amount of consumption over time;
   (d) level of capital with the largest amount of gold in an economy;
   (e) level of capital with the most technology.

2. In the simple Solow growth model, if savings is larger than the depreciation of the capital stock:
   (a) the country will lose capital;
   (b) the country will accumulate capital;
   (c) consumption will increase;
   (d) growth will slow down;
   (e) capital will depend on the level of technology.

3. All of the following are factors that influence the long-term economic growth of a country, except:
   (a) level of technology;
   (b) the political system;
   (c) the level of education;
   (d) interest rates;
   (e) the degree of openness to the world economy.

4. Invention and innovation are more likely to occur in wealthier, highly developed countries because:
   (a) wealthier countries exploit their workers more efficiently;
   (b) wealthier countries have the resources to spend on R&D;
   (c) wealthier countries already have existing technology and knowledge;
   (d) wealthier countries are able to exploit poorer countries;
   (e) both (b) and (c).

5. Which of the following is not a reason for Ireland's economic success during the Celtic Tiger era?
   (a) the economic policies of the 1960s;
   (b) membership in the European Union;

(c) the level of foreign direct investment;

(d) tough government policies on immigration and asylum seekers;

(e) a well-educated workforce.

6. Ireland's crisis in the late 2000s was caused by:
    (a) poor regulation of the financial system;
    (b) the international credit crunch;
    (c) the global recession;
    (d) inappropriate government policy;
    (e) all of the above.

TRUE OR FALSE (SUPPORT YOUR ANSWER)

1. A country is poor because it chooses to be poor.

2. A country will grow quickly only if it is wealthy.

3. Poorer countries tend to catch up to wealthier countries in terms of economic growth.

4. The Golden Rule level of capital entails the highest consumption for people in a country over time.

5. A country can acquire technology through foreign direct investment.

6. The only reason Ireland's economy grew in the 1990s was because of money from the European Union.

CASE STUDY

Extract from *The New York Times*
Irish Miracle – or Mirage?
by Peter Boone and Simon Johnson

With the European Central Bank announcing that it has bought more than $20 billion of mostly high-risk euro-zone government debt in one week, its new strategy is crystal clear: We will take the risk from bank balance sheets and give it to the central bank, and we expect Portugal-Ireland-Italy-Greece-Spain to cut fiscal spending sharply and pull themselves out of this mess through austerity. But the bank's head, Jean-Claude Trichet, faces a potential major issue: the task assigned to the profligate nations could be impossible. Some of these nations may be stuck in a downward debt spiral that makes greater economic decline ever more likely. Prime Minister George Papandreou said this week that Greece needs to see strong investment in order for the austerity program to work. While the government cuts fiscal spending, he said, it needs new private business to employ the dismissed workers so that they are productive, can pay taxes and do not need unemployment benefits.

The problems are strikingly reminiscent of Latin America in the 1980s. Those nations borrowed too heavily in the 1970s (also, by the way, from big international banks) and then – in the face of tougher macroeconomic conditions in the United States – lost access to capital markets. For 10 years they were stuck with debt overhangs, just like the weak euro-zone countries, which made it virtually impossible to grow. Debt overhangs hurt growth for many reasons: business is nervous that taxes will go up in the near future, the cost of credit is high throughout society, and social turmoil looms because continued austere policies are needed to reduce the debt. Some Latin America countries lingered in limbo for a decade or more.

Mr Trichet and Mr Papandreou can look more closely at home to see what might soon be going wrong. Ireland was one of the first nations to introduce tough fiscal austerity in this cycle – in spring 2009 the government slashed public-sector spending and raised taxes. Despite the cuts, the European Commission forecasts that Ireland will have one of the highest budget deficits in the world at 11.7 percent of gross domestic product in 2010. The problem is clear: when you cut spending you also lose tax revenues from people who earned incomes from that money. Further, the newly unemployed seek benefits, so Ireland's spending cuts in one category are partly offset by more spending in another. Without growth, the budget deficit still looms large.

Ireland's problems are, sadly, far deeper than the need for simple fiscal austerity. The Celtic Tiger's impressive reported growth over the past decades was in part based on its aggressive attempts to help major corporations in the United States reduce their tax bills. The Irish government set corporate taxes at just 12.5 percent of profits, thus attracting all sorts of businesses – from computer services like Google and Yahoo, to drug companies like Forest Labs – that set up corporate bases and washed profits through Ireland to keep them out of the hands of the Internal Revenue Service. The remarkable success of this tax haven means that roughly 20 percent of Irish gross domestic product is actually 'profit transfers' that raise little tax for Ireland and are owned by foreign companies. Since most of these profits are subject to the tax code, they are accounted for in Ireland where they are lightly taxed; they should not be counted as part of Ireland's potential tax base. A more robust cross-country comparison would be to examine Ireland's financial condition ignoring these transfers. This is easy to do: a nation's gross national product excludes the profits of foreign residents. For most nations, gross national product and G.D.P. are nearly identical, but in Ireland they are not.

When we adjust Ireland's figures accordingly, the situation is dire. The budget deficit was about 17.9 percent of G.N.P. in 2009, and based on European Commission projections (and assuming the G.N.P.–G.D.P. gap remains the same) it will be roughly 14.6 percent in 2010 and 15.1 percent in 2011, while the debt-to-G.N.P. ratio at the end of this year is expected – by our calculation – to be 97 percent, and 109 percent at the end of 2011. These numbers make Ireland look similarly troubled to Greece, with a much higher budget deficit but lower levels of public debt.

Ireland's politicians, rather than facing up to their problems, are making things ever worse. Simply put, the Irish miracle was a mirage driven by clever use of tax-haven rules and a huge credit boom that permitted real estate prices and construction to grow quickly before declining ever more rapidly. The biggest banks grew to have assets twice the size of official G.D.P. when they essentially failed in 2008. The government has now made a fateful choice:

rather than make creditors pay some part of the losses, it is taking the bank debt onto the national balance sheet, effectively ballooning its already large sovereign debt. Irish taxpayers are set to be left with the risk of very large payments to make on someone else's real estate deals gone bad.

There is no simple escape, but if the government hopes to avoid a sovereign default, the one overriding priority should be to stop bailing out the banks. Instead, the government should wind down existing banks in a 'bad bank', while moving their deposit base and profitable businesses into new, well-capitalized banks that can function without a taxpayer burden. This will be messy, but it is far better than a sovereign default. Second, the Irish must take the tough fiscal steps that will be required under any circumstances. The International Monetary Fund and the European Union have made clear that funding is available to Ireland – so the government should use this to bridge the tough journey of fiscal cuts ahead. Finally,

the Irish need to consider seriously whether being in the euro zone is worth the cost. The adjustment to this awful situation would be far easier outside the euro zone – even though leaving the zone might have adverse repercussions for other nations. Once again, a comprehensive program with European Union and I.M.F. support might make this the least worse option.

Given the depths of Ireland's problems, it is no wonder the markets are looking with skepticism at the announced bailout package for the entire euro zone provided by the European Union and the International Monetary Fund. Policy makers are still not dealing with the core problems of each nation in the euro zone. With the debt hangovers remaining, who will want to invest in Europe's periphery, and so how can Greece, let alone Ireland, grow? One thing we can be sure of: Europe's political leaders are doomed to be spending much more time at emergency meetings in Brussels over the coming months and years.

Source: The New York Times, 20 May 2010.

Questions

1. Other than the low corporation tax, identify factors underlying the Celtic Tiger phenomenon that would counter the argument that the Irish economic boom was simply a mirage. In your opinion, was it miracle or mirage? Support your answer.
2. Explain how the 'huge credit boom' evolved in Ireland and what the monetary authorities could have done to prevent the excesses of the credit boom.
3. Whatever about GNP or GDP growth rates, it is widely acknowledged that it was the increase in employment that constituted the real economic miracle in Ireland. Using CSO Quarterly National Household Survey data (www.cso.ie), report the yearly employment numbers for the period 1995–2007. For the same period, report the numbers, per annum, of unemployed and the total labour force. Comment on the numbers. As a contrast, report the same data for the three-year period 2008–2010.

CHAPTER 19

Development and Transition

'There is no wisdom on economic development, and there are no wise men. There is only economic theory, imperfect as it is, and empirical evidence; we should try to use them.'[1]

PAUL KRUGMAN

'The shift from planned to market economies is a social and economic transformation of unprecedented scale. History offers no time-tested blueprints.'[2]

THE WORLD BANK

CHAPTER OBJECTIVES

Upon completing this chapter, the student should understand:

- the meaning of development and transition;
- the different theories of development and transition;
- obstacles in developing and transition countries;
- reform policies in developing and transition economies;
- economic performance and lessons.

OUTLINE

19.1 Development
19.2 Transition

INTRODUCTION

In terms of economic events, the first half of the twentieth century was dominated by the Great Depression (in the First World) and the socialist revolution in the Soviet Union (the Second World). In contrast, the second half of the last century, when the developed nations of the world continued to prosper, was overshadowed by the destitution of many developing countries (in the Third World) and by the collapse of the socialist system and the subsequent transition from planned economy to market economy.[3] The emergence of issues and problems pertinent to developing and transition countries coincided with two new branches of economics, namely development economics and transition economics. The economics of development is concerned with the societies and economies of developing countries in Africa, Asia and Latin America. The economics of transition relates to the former socialist economies of Central and Eastern Europe, the former Soviet Union and parts of East Asia, particularly China and Vietnam. This chapter outlines the most important economic concepts, issues, problems and policies related to development and transition.

19.1 DEVELOPMENT

> 'Development is the most important challenge facing the human race. Despite the vast opportunities created by the technological revolutions of the twentieth century, more than 1 billion people, one fifth of the world's population, live on less than one dollar a day.'

WORLD DEVELOPMENT REPORT 1991

In 2005, less than fifteen years after the publication of the World Bank's 1991 *World Development Report: The Challenge of Development*, it is estimated that 2.8 billion people – more than half the people in developing countries – live on less than $700 a year and, of that figure, 1.2 billion earn less than $1 a day. According to World Bank estimates, 51% and 40% of the population in sub-Saharan Africa and South Asia respectively live on less than $1.25 a day (at 2005 international prices). Development, or the lack thereof, obviously remains the greatest challenge confronting the human race. In this chapter we outline some of the most important aspects of development, including the obstacles to economic development, the different development paradigms, the main development strategies and policies and the major development issues of our time.[4]

We need to begin by defining development. As economists, we can distinguish between an old and a new view of development. The old version views development as synonymous with economic growth. Progress in economic development was measured by the growth rate of GDP or some other variant of national income. In broader terms, this traditional perspective on development was primarily an economic view. Development was seen as essentially a matter of economics – a problem of resource allocation. In contrast, the new view of development treats it as a complex, multifaceted process in which national income is only one factor contributing to development. In addition to economic growth, improvements in poverty levels, inequalities and unemployment are viewed as necessary in order for development to occur. In this context, Michael Todaro (1977) defines development as focusing primarily on the economic, social, political and institutional mechanisms needed to bring about rapid and large-scale improvements in levels of living for the masses of poor people in the developing nations.

We now turn our attention to the countries of the developing world. Both the United Nations and the World Bank employ classification systems to categorise countries. The United Nations classifies areas as developing regions (and within that classification there is a sub-category of least developed countries), transition countries and developed regions. The UN notes that there is no established convention for the designation of 'developed' or 'developing' countries in the UN classification system. The World Bank, using per capita gross national income (GNI) as its main criterion, classifies countries (as at 2009) as low-income ($995 or less), lower middle-income ($996–$3,945), upper middle-income ($3,946–$12,195) or high-income ($12,196 or more).[5] Notwithstanding the difficulty in precisely defining what is meant by a developing country and at the same time acknowledging that classification by income does not necessarily reflect development status, the World Bank's low-income and middle-income countries are often referred to as the 'developing' countries. Accordingly, Table 19.1 reports a listing of developing countries from the World Bank classification system.

TABLE 19.1: CLASSIFICATION OF COUNTRIES BY INCOME[6]

Low-Income Countries	Afghanistan	Congo, Dem. Republic of	Korea, Dem. People's Republic	Mozambique	Togo	
	Bangladesh	Eritrea	Kyrgyz Rep.	Nepal	Uganda	
	Benin	Ethiopia	Lao PDR	Niger	Uzbekistan	
	Burkina Faso	Gambia, The	Liberia	Rwanda	Vanuatu	
	Burundi	Ghana	Madagascar	Senegal	Yemen, Republic of	
	Cambodia	Guinea	Malawi	Sierra Leone	Zambia	
	Central African Republic	Guinea-Bissau	Mali	Somalia	Zimbabwe	
	Chad	Haiti	Mauritania	Tajikistan		
	Comoros	Kenya	Mongolia	Tanzania		
Lower Middle-Income Countries	Albania	China	Guyana	Lesotho	Palau	Swaziland
	Angola	Congo, Rep. of	Honduras	Maldives	Papua New Guinea	Syrian Arab Rep.
	Armenia	Côte d'Ivoire	India	Marshall Islands	Paraguay	Thailand
	Azerbaijan	Djibouti	Indonesia	Micronesia, Federated States of	Philippines	Timor-Leste
	Belize	Ecuador	Iran, Islamic Rep. of	Moldova	Samoa	Tonga
	Bhutan	Egypt, Arab Rep. of	Iraq	Morocco	São Tomé and Principe	Tunisia
	Bolivia	El Salvador	Jordan	Nicaragua	Solomon Islands	Turkmenistan
	Cameroon	Georgia	Kiribati	Nigeria	Sri Lanka	Ukraine
	Cape Verde	Guatemala	Kosovo	Pakistan	Sudan	West Bank and Gaza
Upper Middle-Income Countries	Algeria	Chile	Grenada	Malaysia	Peru	St Lucia
	American Samoa	Columbia	Jamaica	Mauritius	Poland	St Vincent and the Grenadines
	Argentina	Costa Rica	Kazakhstan	Mayotte	Romania	Suriname
	Belarus	Cuba	Latvia	Mexico	Russian Federation	Turkey
	Bosnia and Herzegovina	Dominica	Lebanon	Montenegro	Serbia	Uruguay
	Botswana	Dominican Republic	Libya	Myanmar	Seychelles	Venezuela
	Brazil	Fiji	Lithuania	Namibia	South Africa	
	Bulgaria	Gabon	Macedonia, FYR	Panama	St Kitts and Nevis	

Source: World Bank.

Although developing countries are not all the same (e.g. different continents, different traditions and customs engaged in different economic activities with different trading partners), it is apparent that there are certain characteristics common to countries in the developing world. Although there is some disagreement on the nature of these common features, we set out below the most recognised common characteristics of developing countries.

TABLE 19.2: GNI PER CAPITA AND HDI, 2010

Country	GNI per capita (PPP US$)	GPNI per capita Rank	HDI	HDI Rank
Fiji	4,315	107	0.669	86
Sri Lanka	4,886	101	0.658	91
Mongolia	3,619	112	0.622	100
Honduras	3,750	111	0.604	106
Morocco	4,628	104	0.567	114
Cambodia	1,868	136	0.494	124
Bangladesh	1,587	141	0.469	129
Madagascar	953	157	0.435	135
Senegal	1,816	137	0.411	144
Zambia	1,359	145	0.395	150
Mali	1,171	153	0.309	160
Zimbabwe	176	169	0.140	169

Source: UNDP *Human Development Report 2010.*

Note: GNI per capita was formerly GNP per capita.

19.1.1 *Common characteristics of developing countries*

Low levels of living standards and welfare

Table 19.2 reports two measures of a country's wellbeing, for a selection of developing countries. The first is the conventional measure of economic activity, namely national output or gross national income (GNI). The second is the UN Human Development Index (see Chapter 10), a socio-economic indicator based on standard of living (measured by national income per capita in PPP US$), a long and healthy life (measured by life expectancy at birth) and education, attainment and knowledge (measured by adult literacy rates and enrolment ratios). It is a more comprehensive measure of a nation's welfare. As shown in the table, income per capita for the developing countries is very low. It ranged from a low of $176 per head (Zimbabwe) to a high of $4,886 per head (Sri Lanka). This compares to $33,078 per capita for Ireland (ranked twenty-fifth). Equally, the HDI values for the developing countries are low, ranging from 0.140 to 0.669. In contrast, Ireland's HDI in 2010, ranked fifth, was 0.895. The GDP per capita rank and HDI rank, from a list of 169 countries, are also reported.

High rates of population growth

It is well known that the vast majority (estimated at over 80%) of the world's population currently lives in developing countries. Moreover, this will remain a feature for decades and perhaps even centuries to come. The UN predicts that, by the year 2200, 90% of the world's population will live in developing countries. High birth rates, often over double the rate common in developed countries, combined with falling death rates (due to improvements in health systems and control of most major diseases) have contributed to a population growth rate far in excess of the average growth rate in the developed world. In contrast to the past, when large-scale international migration acted as a safety valve for countries experiencing rapid natural increases in population, the current levels of international migration are not large enough to slow the rate of population increase in developing countries. Other negative features of the demographic trap in developing countries include high infant mortality rates, low life expectancy rates and very high dependency ratios, i.e. the numbers of young (< 15 years) and old (> 64 years) as a proportion of the labour force (15–64 years).

Population data for a selection of developing (and developed) countries are reported in Table 19.3.

TABLE 19.3: POPULATION AND POPULATION GROWTH

Country	Population 2008 (m)	Annual population growth rate (%) 2000–2008	Fertility rate 2008
Albania	3	0.3	2
Kazakhstan	16	0.6	3
Ireland	4	2.0	2
US	304	0.9	2
India	1140	1.4	3
Panama	3	1.8	3
Mozambique	22	2.2	5
Bolivia	10	1.9	3
Philippines	90	1.9	3
Iran	72	1.5	2
Angola	18	2.9	6
Congo, Dem. Rep.	64	3.0	6
Uganda	32	3.2	6
UK	61	0.5	2
Germany	82	0.0	1

Source: World Bank, World Development Report 2010.

The differences between the demographics of developing and developed countries are striking. Are the rapid rates of population growth experienced in developing countries a hindrance to development? This and other obstacles to development are examined later.

High agriculture share of GDP

The dominance of the agricultural sector over industry (and services) and the importance of rural living as opposed to urban centres are central features of developing countries. Moreover, it is the type and productivity of the agricultural activities that matter. Small-scale, traditional agriculture as practised in most developing countries generates low yields and returns as compared to the higher productivity levels common in the commercialised agriculture sector of the developed world. Peasant subsistence farming, the use of primitive techniques, small farms and traditional land ownership arrangements often contribute to low productivity levels in agriculture and other primary production activities. The agriculture share of national output is high, as is the percentage of the labour force engaged in agriculture. Whereas agriculture normally contributes 2–5% of GDP in the developed world, it is not uncommon for the agriculture share of GDP in developing countries to exceed 35–40%. As for the numbers engaged in agriculture, 3–7% of the labour force is the norm for most developed countries, in contrast to shares often in excess of 50% for developing countries. The urban/rural divide contrasts sharply between developing and developed countries. Whereas the urban/rural ratio in developed countries is usually close to 3:1, the ratio in developing countries is reversed, with the rural population often twice the size of the urban population.

Dependence on primary exports

Whereas developed countries engage in the domestic production and foreign trade of manufacturing and service activities, most developing countries are highly dependent on the production and export of primary products. According to the World Bank, developed countries account for over 80% of manufactured exports. Developing countries, in contrast, account for in excess of 70% of the world's primary exports. Although there are exceptions, the primary commodities traditionally exported by developing countries include basic foodstuffs, cash crops (non-food) and some raw materials. Moreover, it is often the case that a developing country will be dependent on a small number of export commodities rather than on a diverse range of exports. In any one year, price fluctuations or poor harvests may threaten the foreign exchange earnings and, ultimately, the livelihood of the export trade and farmers in developing countries. In the longer term, developing countries are vulnerable to the long-run decline in the real price of primary commodities. Related to this is the observation that, unlike developed countries that have other sources of tax revenue, many developing countries reply heavily on foreign trade taxes as a reliable and easily collectable source of revenue.

Colonial heritage

Most of the developing countries share some common historical features. They were colonies of Western powers, whether it was France, Spain, Britain, Portugal, Belgium, the Netherlands or even the USA or Japan. Although there were differences between colonisers, we can identify a common colonial burden or experience. Notwithstanding some benefits of colonisation, there were undoubted drawbacks of imperial domination, including widespread economic neglect, repression, exploitation and a legacy of inferiority and dependency. Africa, in particular, was harshly served by its colonial past.

High levels of poverty and inequality

Developing countries tend to be poor with high levels of poverty and income inequality. As in the developed world, neither defining nor measuring poverty and inequality are simple tasks to undertake. Although there are well-established techniques to measure both, there are often problems with the data coverage and comparability across countries. For example, one such difficulty across developing countries is the differences in the relative importance of consumption of non-market goods.

The World Development Report publishes a range of indicators that measure poverty and income distribution. These include poverty lines, the Gini coefficient and the percentage share of income or consumption that accrues to subgroups of the population, usually indicated by deciles or quintiles. Although there are sizeable cross-country differences among developing countries (as, indeed, there are among developed countries), the evidence supports the claim that levels of poverty and inequality are especially high in developing countries. For example, whereas Gini coefficients rarely exceed 0.40 in the developed world, values in excess of 0.50 are not uncommon in developing countries. In terms of income (or consumption) distribution, the gap between rich and poor in developing countries is generally greater than the gap in developed countries. In some developing countries the richest 10% of the population receives over 40% of income/consumption. By contrast, in a developed country like Ireland, the richest 10% receives 28% of income/consumption (UNDP 2005). Despite some cross-country differences, income distribution in developing countries tends to be highly skewed, with income, assets and wealth highly concentrated. The economics literature has identified reasons, beyond those of equity, why economists should be concerned with poverty and inequality. Rising poverty and widening inequalities are, among other things, likely to increase economic inefficiencies, facilitate bribery and corruption and undermine social stability and security.

19.1.2 Theories of development

Here is a brief explanation of the main 'classic' theories of development.

Rostow's (1960) five stages of growth model of development was based on the assertion that, in the (linear) progression from underdeveloped to developed, all countries pass through the same sequence of steps or stages of economic growth. The five historical stages are: the traditional society; the pre-conditions for take-off; the take-off into self-sustaining growth; the drive to maturity; and the age of high mass consumption. Developing countries, identified by their traditional society or pre-condition stages, were expected to complete all the stages of development. The key was the take-off stage, which was characterised by an increase in the growth rate of investment and a significant contribution by primary or leading sectors.

The link between investment and economic growth is outlined in the Harrod-Domar (AK) growth model. The AK growth model, in its attempt to apply Keynesian economics to growth theory, states that the rate of economic growth is dependent on the level of saving and (the productivity of) investment, i.e. the so-called capital-output ratio. The growth rate of output is equal to the ratio of the propensity to save and the capital-output ratio. As developing countries have an abundant supply of labour, it is the lack of physical capital that impedes growth and development. As with Keynesian theory, the model concludes that an economy does not find stable rates of economic growth naturally.

The two models outlined above are examples of linear stages of growth models of development. In contrast, the following two models, emphasising the structural transformation from traditional agricultural economies to modern industrial economies, are examples of structural change models of development.

Lewis' (1954) theoretical labour-surplus model has an underdeveloped economy consisting of two sectors. There is a traditional, overpopulated, rural, subsistence sector where surplus labour exists. There is also a modern, urban, industrial, capitalist sector that attracts the surplus labour. With an elastic or unlimited supply of labour, the modern sector can earn a surplus. As the capitalist's surplus is reinvested, the share of saving and investment in national income rises, thereby expanding output. In the context of a two-sector model, development is defined as the process by which the traditional sector declines as the modern sector expands. Developing countries are associated with small capitalist sectors and a subsistence sector characterised by rural underdevelopment.

Chenery's (1975) work on structural change and patterns of development were empirical studies on developing countries in the post-war period. The findings helped to identify several characteristics of the development process, including the transformation of the structure of production from agriculture to industry, the shift from rural to urban centres and changes in consumer demands from basic (food)stuffs to manufactured goods and services. There is an identifiable process of growth and change and certain well-defined patterns of development are experienced by all developing countries (notwithstanding inevitable variations across nations).

Dependency theories

International dependency theories arose from disenchantment with previous models and a rejection of neoclassical resource allocation models of development. The assertion here is that, due to international power imbalances, developing 'peripheral' nations are dependent on, exploited and dominated by others, whether former colonial powers or, more recently, international financial institutions (IFIs) and MNCs. The causes of underdevelopment are external forces and the problems of developing countries are perpetuated by the unequal relationship between rich and poor countries. Hence, there is a need for radical and fundamental change in social, political and economic systems, both domestic and international. Three such variants of this approach include the neocolonial dependency theory, the false-paradigm model and the dualistic development theory.[7]

Neoclassical paradigm

Underdevelopment, according to the neoclassical counter-revolution, is due to poor resource allocation, market distortions, and inefficiencies arising from inappropriate state intervention. What are required are free markets and sound money, less government interference and laissez-faire-type policies emphasising privatisation, deregulation and liberalisation. Modern views of development, as espoused by followers of neoclassical economics who focus on government failure as opposed to market failure, deny the need for a special case for developing countries and reject the need for the separate branch of economics traditionally called development economics.

Since the evolution of development economics in the 1940s there have been many approaches and debates aside from the list above. Among others these include the following:

Structuralist school and the contribution of the Argentinean economist Raoul Prebisch (and others, including Hans Singer and Celso Furtado) and the Latin American ECLA (Economic Commission for Latin America). In contrast to those in support of the neoclassical tradition and conventional trade theory, advocates of the structuralist school emphasised the bottlenecks, rigidities and weak price responses, shortages and surpluses, lags and other structural characteristics of developing countries. These were often caused by the international economic system and the developed nations (hence the similarity with the dependency theorists). The policy recommendations centred on the structural transformation of underdeveloped economies away from the traditional reliance on primary exports, of which it had a highly pessimistic view, in favour of the development, through government intervention, of a diversified domestic industrial sector.

The balanced versus unbalanced growth debate. On one side, there was Paul Rosenstein-Rodan and his 'Big Push' (1943) strategy of investment in different industries simultaneously in order to capture complementarities and externalities, and Ragnar Nurkse's Balanced Growth (1953) idea of the need for synchronised application of capital to a number of different industries. Opposing this was Albert Hirschman and his Unbalanced Growth (1958) strategy whereby investment is concentrated in industries or sectors with forward or backward linkages (i.e. supplying inputs and/or purchasing output), with government deliberately creating imbalances to stimulate the investment.

Contemporary models of growth and development include new growth theory, as represented by the Romer endogenous growth model in which technological change is endogenously determined (as opposed to exogenous as in the Solow growth model), and other theories that focus on co-ordination failures, increasing returns to scale, imperfect competition and information problems.

19.1.3 Obstacles to development

Why are developing countries poor? What are the main restraints to economic development? The economics literature has identified a number of obstacles to development. As the list below indicates, some are of a domestic nature while others have an international dimension. Although some are viewed as more important than others (in restraining economic development), they are listed here in no particular order.

Physical and human resource endowment

Although many developing countries have few natural resources, the link between natural resource endowment and economic development is not clear cut. *A priori*, we might expect that the absence of natural resources may hinder development. However, the evidence is somewhat mixed. In some cases, countries with little or no natural resources have still managed to develop and foster economic activity. Examples include Singapore and Japan. Likewise, the presence of natural resources does not guarantee economic development. Examples include Russia (oil and gas) and Nigeria (oil). This may be due to a number of factors including the so-called Dutch disease,[8] conflict resources (such as diamonds, where high-valued commodities attract disputes and conflicts), the high cost of exploration, rent-seeking attached to government regulation of the resource, and delays in reform. In this knowledge-based modern age, the supply of human resources is evidently important. Both the quantity and the quality are, in turn, affected by education and health systems, diseases (TB, malaria and most recently HIV/Aids in sub-Saharan Africa[9]) and malnutrition. It is more often the case that developing countries have inadequate systems of public health and education, are crippled by diseases (which affect the workforce and productivity levels) and suffer from high levels of malnutrition and illiteracy. This vicious circle is compounded by the brain drain, whereby many of the developing countries' brightest and most educated citizens emigrate in order to find more suitable, well-paid jobs. The number of returning migrants, and the inevitable benefits that follow, will depend on other domestic factors, including governance and corruption, customs and cultures, conflicts and war. Often, these factors, combined with the pull factors of the host country, work against the likelihood of these migrants ever returning home.

Population growth

Are rapid rates of population growth a constraint on development? The relationship between population growth and development is not straightforward. There are many opinions on how population growth impacts on development, ranging from the view that population growth is a cause of underdevelopment (and has negative consequences for income per capita, poverty and inequality) to the view that population growth per se is not the problem (but, for example, population distribution is) to the view that population growth is beneficial (given certain conditions). What we can be more certain of, arising from advances in technological progress and empirical evidence on the microeconomic determinants of family fertility, is that the doomsday scenario painted centuries ago by Malthus and others, concerning the prevalence of a low-level equilibrium trap due to the growth in population exceeding the growth in food supplies, is not applicable to modern-day developing countries. Recognising the complex relationship between population growth and development, there is a view forming that, on balance, rapid population growth, although not the primary cause of low standards of living, intensifies the problems of underdevelopment and that slower growth rates would be beneficial for most developing countries. Then the issue is the design of suitable measures and effective policies to reduce population growth.

Conflicts and war

It is difficult to foster economic development if a country is waging war with another country or if there is internal strife and conflict. It is no coincidence that most of the tribal and ethnic conflicts that are currently being waged are in the developing countries of sub-Saharan Africa. Aside from the loss of life and economic activity, destruction of infrastructure, and damage to international goodwill and borrowing capacity, armed conflicts are generally financed from central exchequer funds. Large defence budgets mean funds are diverted away from critical areas of public spending such as physical infrastructure, education, health and the environment. Ceasefires and peace agreements are considered to be a necessary condition for economic development to take place.

Weak institutions

Economists emphasise the importance of institutions in explaining cross-country variations in long-run economic growth. Institutions are the rules of the game that determine social, economic and political interaction. Although many developing countries resemble market economies within a modern capitalist system (with market prices and private ownership), the institutions that underpin the successful market economies of the developed world are often absent or function poorly in the developing world. Important examples include secure property rights, rule of law, well-established enforcement mechanisms and good state governance.

TABLE 19.4: CORRUPTION PERCEPTIONS INDEX 2010

Country	CPI 2010	Country Rank	Country	CPI 2010	Country Rank
Denmark	9.3	1†	China	3.5	78
Australia	8.7	8	Guatemala	3.2	91
Ireland	8.0	14	Argentina	2.9	105
USA	7.1	22	Indonesia	2.8	110
UAE	6.3	28	Eritrea	2.6	123
Botswana	5.8	33	Philippines	2.4	134
Korea	5.4	39	Iran	2.2	146
Poland	5.3	41	Tajikistan	2.1	154
South Africa	4.5	54	Venezuela	2.0	164
Turkey	4.4	56	Burundi	1.8	170
Italy	3.9	67	Somalia	1.1	178

Source: Transparency International, 2010.
† = joint first

Domestic political structure and distribution of power

Developing countries are known for their high levels of corruption, bribery and poor governance. Often, the ruling elite governs at the expense of the masses. Bribes replace the tax revenues that normally finance infrastructure and public services. Variations in corruption are measured annually by Transparency International, using its Corruption Perceptions Index (CPI). The Berlin-based organisation ranks countries, on the basis of surveys, in terms of the degree to which corruption is *perceived* to exist among public officials and politicians. The CPI score ranges from 0 (highly corrupt) to 10 (highly clean). Table 19.4 reports the CPI for 2010 (and the respective country rank, out of a total of 178 nations) for a range of countries, including developing countries from Asia, Latin America and Africa, transition countries from Eastern Europe and the former Soviet Union and developed countries belonging to the OECD.

Other obstacles to development often cited in the literature include the unequal distribution of world income and power, cultural barriers inherent in the customs and traditions of some developing countries, climatic conditions and physical geography and, more important from an economic perspective, the lack of capital accumulation, arising from inadequate domestic savings and foreign capital.[10] Moreover, in respect of the latter, many developing countries experience high levels of capital flight, due to different reasons including economic and political uncertainty, a predatory and corrupt state, insecure property rights, lack of investment opportunities, a confiscatory tax system and underdeveloped capital markets.

19.1.4 Development policies and strategies

Since the 1950s dramatic changes have taken place in the policies and trade strategies regarded as most suitable for industrialisation, growth and, ultimately, development. We begin with the policy of import substitution.

Import substitution

The dominant view in the 1950s and 1960s was an inward-looking, protectionist strategy that advocated active state intervention, government subsidies and import substitution on the basis of, it was argued, a deterioration in the terms of trade in the traditional primary commodity exports of developing countries.

> **Definition**
>
> *Import substitution replaces imports with domestic production under the protection of tariffs and/or quotas.*

This self-reliant philosophy was supported by so-called trade pessimists who believed that 'free' trade hurts developing countries. Its purpose was to foster infant industries, often state-owned and protected by trade barriers, that would eventually be able to compete internationally without any protection. In terms of results, the view among many economists is that the import-substitution strategy was ineffective, and, moreover, resulted in inefficient, non-competitive firms at the enterprise level and sluggish growth and high inflation at the macro level.

Export promotion

From the 1970s onwards, a policy targeted at export promotion dominated. The emergence of this outward-looking, export-led growth strategy was influenced by world events, including the perceived failure of import substitution policies in many developing countries, the collapse of central planning in socialist countries, the success of NICs in South East Asia and the domination of MNCs and the importance of FDI. On the grounds of the benefits accruing from free trade and competition, advocates of the export promotion strategy called for a new model, based on trade liberalisation, less state intervention and FDI promotion. Those in favour of the strategy were later to become advocates of the Washington Consensus. Strictly speaking, the Washington Consensus refers to a set of policy guidelines for most Latin American countries in the late 1980s for which, it was argued, a consensus was reached among Washington-based international agencies, the US government and mainstream economists. John Williamson of the Institute for International Economics, the person who coined the phrase, viewed these policy reforms as the lowest common denominator of policy advice by 'Washington' to Latin American countries as of 1989. The ten economic reforms focused primarily on structural adjustment policies of price and trade liberalisation, macroeconomic stabilisation and fiscal discipline, deregulation of entry barriers and privatisation of state-owned enterprises. Table 19.5 lists the ten policy reforms identified by the Washington Consensus.

TABLE 19.5: THE WASHINGTON CONSENSUS

Policy Reform Item	Policy Reform Detail
Fiscal Discipline	(Operational) budget deficit of no more than about 2% of GDP
Public Expenditure Priorities	Redirection from politically sensitive projects to expenditures in education, health and infrastructure
Tax Reform	Broadening the tax base, moderate marginal tax rates and improving tax administration
Financial Liberalisation	Interest rate liberalisation — market-determined (moderately positive real) interest rates and abolition of preferential rates for privileged borrowers
Exchange Rates	Unified and set at a competitive level
Trade Liberalisation	Quantitative restrictions to be replaced by low and uniform tariffs
Foreign Direct Investment	Abolish barriers to entry of foreign firms
Privatisation	State-owned enterprises to be privatised
Deregulation	Easing barriers to entry and exit; regulations only to ensure safety, environmental protection and prudential supervision of financial institutions
Property Rights	Secure property rights and made available to the informal sector

Source: Williamson, 1990.

The influence of the Washington Consensus stretched beyond developing countries and emerging markets to affect the policy debate in the former socialist countries of the Soviet bloc. This will be dealt with in the transition section of the chapter.

Both the import substitution and export promotion strategies were employed, at different stages, by many developing countries. In the 1950s and 1960s, many Latin American countries adopted the import-substitution trade policy; many African states followed. In contrast, the South East Asian countries – Korea, Taiwan and Singapore – advocated and implemented an export-promotion trade policy (having earlier adopted protectionist policies in certain sectors to support infant industries).

Stabilisation and structural adjustment

Similar in principle to the outward-looking, export-led growth policies were the so-called IMF stabilisation policies and the World Bank Structural Adjustment Programmes (SAPs). IMF stabilisation programmes are meant as short-run, demand-side policies to correct macroeconomic problems of high inflation, rising balance of payments deficits and large budget imbalances. A typical stabilisation package would involve such orthodox policies as reductions in government deficits (through cuts in spending and/or improved tax collections) and financing of budget deficits through non-monetary means as ways of reducing inflation. More trade-promotion policies would include reductions in import controls, liberalisation and devaluation of the exchange rate and opening up of the economy to foreign investment. These 'conditions' had to be adopted before countries could qualify for new loans from the IMF. IMF conditionality became hugely unpopular in developing countries as it was seen as draconian and 'imperial', while some of the Fund's policies were seen as inappropriate, excessively austere and, at worst, counterproductive.

The World Bank SAPs are more long-term in nature. They provide financial and technical assistance for purposes of structural adjustment and microeconomic reform. The aim of structural adjustment lending is to increase the economy's supply capacity by eliminating structural imbalances and rigidities. Advocates of the SAPs argued that they increase economic efficiency and improve long-term economic performance. Critics of the IFIs noted the growing similarity between the Fund's stabilisation policies and the Bank's structural adjustment policies (despite the distinct roles given to the two organisations at the end of World War II).[11] Criticisms of the stabilisation policies and structural adjustment programmes, despite some changes in their implementation in recent years, by other international agencies, NGOs and governments and citizens alike of developing countries, continue.[12] For more on SAPs, and Africa, see Information Box 19.1.

Development planning

As economic planning was generally regarded as successful in wartime Britain, it became popular in some developing countries, and in particular in India in the early 1950s with the first Five Year Plan.

> **Definition**
>
> *Economic planning is when governments attempt to target and co-ordinate economic decision-making in order to influence economic outcomes.*

Of course, much of the inspiration for economic planning came from the Soviet Union. In the West, development planning was advocated by many leading development economists, including Arthur Lewis and Jan Tinbergen. Modern advances in economic theory, computers and statistics allowed for greater sophistication in the planning techniques used, including linear programming, input-output models and cost-benefit analysis. However, the demise of the Soviet Union accelerated the already evident decline in the popularity of development planning. Despite this, the bigger issue here, and still as relevant today, is one of government failure versus market failure and the respective roles of state and market.

INFORMATION BOX 19.1

Economic Performance in Africa
United Nations Conference on Trade and Development (UNCTAD)
From the 2001 *Economic Development in Africa* Report

Africa as a whole experienced moderate growth from the mid-1960s until the end of the 1970s. While the average growth rate was well below the rate achieved by a handful of East Asian economies, it equalled or exceeded the growth rates attained by many developing countries in other regions. In particular there was a notable acceleration of growth in sub-Saharan Africa (SSA) during the 1970s (see table), supported by a boom in commodity prices and foreign aid. Investment in many countries in the region exceeded 25 per cent of GDP, and the savings gap remained relatively moderate.

Economic performance deteriorated rapidly in SSA in the late 1970s and early 1980s, whereas the slowdown of growth was relatively moderate in North Africa. Unlike many countries in other developing regions which managed to restore growth after the lost decade of the 1980s, stagnation and decline continued in SSA during the first half of the 1990s due to a combination of adverse external developments, structural and institutional bottlenecks and policy errors, examined in some detail in earlier work undertaken by the UNCTAD secretariat. As socio-economic conditions deteriorated and spilled over into political and civil unrest, the international community launched various initiatives including UN-NADAF, to address the problems faced by the countries in the region. At the same time, more and more African countries came to adopt structural adjustment programmes supported by the Bretton Woods institutions, encompassing rapid and extensive liberalisation, deregulation and privatisation of economic activity in search for a solution to economic stagnation and decline. However, while structural adjustment programmes have been applied more intensely and frequently in Africa than in any other developing region, barely any African country has exited from such programmes with success, establishing conditions for rapid, sustained economic growth. This is true not only for countries which are said to have slipped in the implementation of stabilisation and adjustment programmes (the so-called non-adjusters or bad-adjusters), but also most of the core- and good-adjusters.

TABLE 19.6: AVERAGE ANNUAL GDP GROWTH IN AFRICA, 1965–99 (%)

	1965–69	1970–79	1980–89	1990–99	1990–94	1995–99
Africa	4.5	4.2	2.5	2.3	0.9	3.5
North Africa	5.3	6.7	4.2	3.1	2.1	4.2
Sub-Saharan Africa	2.4	4.0	2.1	2.4	0.8	3.9
Including South Africa	4.2	3.3	1.7	2.0	0.4	3.2
Excluding Nigeria	3.5	3.9	2.5	2.3	0.3	4.2

The widespread pessimism about African prospects was somewhat dispelled by a fairly broad-based economic upturn that started in the mid-1990s and allowed the average income growth rate to exceed the population growth rate for four consecutive years, thereby resulting in gains in per capita income across the continent for the first time for many years. The performance of SSA was even stronger without Nigeria, where growth remained below the average of the other countries in the region. Similarly the Republic of South Africa (RSA) had a relatively poor performance, particularly towards the end of the decade. Growth in RSA and Nigeria together, which account for about 50% of the total GDP of the continent excluding North Africa, was about 2.2% per annum during 1995–99, while the remaining countries in SSA had a moderate growth rate of 4.2% per annum over the same period.

Overall, per capita income in SSA at the turn of the new century was 10% below the level reached in 1980, and the gap is even larger compared to the level attained three decades earlier. Economic growth remains well below the UN-NADAF target of 6% per annum. For the region as a whole, only two countries, Mozambique and Uganda, met this target during the 1990s. Growth rates needed to attain the target of reducing African poverty by half by 2015 are estimated to be even higher than the UN-NADAF target of 6%. On the basis of these trends, these targets are unlikely to be reached.

19.1.5 Development issues

Three of the most important issues in development are foreign aid, debt (and debt relief) and trade. Although dealt with separately here, these issues are related and the search for solutions must take into account the inter-relationships between aid, debt relief and trade.[13]

Foreign aid

Like many other issues related to economic development, the relationship between foreign aid (defined as public official development assistance (ODA) and private assistance provided by NGOs) and development is not as simple as it might first appear. The foreign aid debate flows back and forth between those who argue that foreign aid benefits the developing world and those who believe that foreign aid has no beneficial effects and may even be detrimental to its recipients. Aside from the moral, humanitarian and political motivations, the main economic arguments advanced in support of foreign aid are of two types: donor interest; and recipient need. Either way, self-interest plays an important role in determining aid allocation. For example, much of foreign aid is tied aid, tied to the trade interests of the donor. Those critical of foreign aid point to the insignificant relationship, at the macro level, between aid and development. They argue that, among other things, foreign aid may simply substitute for domestic savings and investment, prevent recipient governments from collecting taxes, be appropriated by corrupt governments in their attempts to remain in power, spent on large and often unproductive but favoured projects or accentuate the dependency culture in the developing world. Despite the large empirical work on the economic effects of aid, the foreign aid debate continues. What is more certain is that foreign aid can be made more effective by reducing ties to donor exports (the purchase of arms and missiles, for example), improving co-ordination between the donors, and by making aid to developing countries conditional on the recipients' record on governance, corruption, poverty alleviation and improving the general welfare of their citizens.

Debt and debt relief

An equally controversial aspect of development is debt and debt relief. The debt crisis emerged in the 1980s and, despite various attempts to resolve the crisis, the problem of the debt overhang still remains. The origins of the debt crisis are well documented: it began with an unprecedented rise in borrowing during the 1970s when oil prices soared, inflation rates rose and real interest rates were low or negative. By the turn of the decade, however, the international climate had deteriorated with further rises in oil prices combined with rising interest rates. Debt service repayments skyrocketed. As debt service repayments are made in foreign exchange, highly indebted nations were forced either to curtail imports (as increasing export earnings were unlikely in the short run) or increase external borrowing. As we know, external borrowing rose significantly. Subsequently, IMF stabilisation policies were viewed by many as necessary if the indebted nations were ever to return to pre-crisis debt levels. Others viewed those attempts at alleviation as unnecessary and, in some cases, given the severity of the stabilisation policies, harmful. Either way, debt relief initiatives came to the fore from the 1980s onward. Various initiatives for debt restructuring, reduction or forgiveness were advanced. What remains imperative is how the burden should be shared between borrowers (developing countries in this case) and lenders (developed countries, international agencies, commercial banks) so that a repeat of the crisis is prevented, developing countries' capacity to borrow on international markets for productive investment projects is not jeopardised and, more important from a developmental stance, the welfare of citizens in indebted countries is not further harmed by their own irresponsible governments and the seemingly harsh prescriptions of the IFIs.

Trade

Is foreign trade beneficial to development? The orthodox view, espoused by mainstream economists educated in the classical and neoclassical tradition, is that international trade has a positive effect on economic growth. With the benefits of trade outweighing the costs, foreign trade is seen as an engine of growth. Critics of this traditional view of trade include neo-Marxists, dependency theorists, structuralists and some conventional economists who are sceptical of the universal benefits of 'free trade'. Critics of the free trade proponents have questioned whether access to international trade and adoption of free trade policies is indeed favourable to the welfare of developing countries and their citizens. Arguments range from the exploitative imperialism that determines trade relations between the developed, former colonial powers of the West and the developing, former colonies of the underdeveloped world to the 'economic geography' proponents who counsel caution on the basis of external economies resulting from the interaction of firms' locational decisions and increasing returns at the level of the firm. An alternative view is that many developing countries are indeed supportive of free trade; but the trade barriers that continue to exist prevent developing countries from benefiting fully from international trade while at the same time they are often pressurised to liberalise and open (sometimes prematurely) their markets to the high-income countries of (fortress) Europe and (protectionist) America. For a start, the lifting of these trade barriers and the elimination of trade-distorting subsidies by developed countries allows developing nations to increase exports to the high-income countries of the world. Future WTO rounds must also ensure that developing countries gain from future trade reforms. Recognising that responsibility for change must also lie, if not predominantly, with developing countries themselves, it is important that internal restraints and barriers to trade be reduced. More generally, as with the foreign aid and debt relief issues, arguments for and against free trade for developing countries continue unabated.

This part of the chapter has outlined the main characteristics, problems, policies and issues confronting developing countries and the branch of economics commonly referred to as development economics. The next part examines similar issues for a different subset of countries, namely the former socialist countries (the transition countries, as they have been known since the collapse of the socialist system), and the sub-discipline of economics referred to as transition economics.

19.2 TRANSITION

The transition from plan to market and from socialism to capitalism has been described as one of the most important economic, social and political experiments of modern times. At the peak of the socialist system, in excess of 1.65 billion people lived in socialist countries. However, within a short space of time (beginning for the most part in 1989–1991), these countries had abandoned state socialism or communism, as it was often referred to, and embraced the capitalism system and the market economy. Although the transformation was remarkably peaceful, it has proved to be both costly and arduous for many citizens. For others, it has been a time of extraordinary opportunities, in both political and financial terms. In this part of the chapter we will outline the important aspects of economic transition, including the paradigms of transition, the main policies and economic reforms, the performance of transition countries and lessons of transition. We begin, however, by briefly outlining certain aspects of the socialist system.

19.2.1 The socialist system

Although the year 1917 is usually associated with the start of the Soviet socialist system, it was in 1928, with the launch of the first Five Year Plan, when the administrative command economy (or the centrally planned economy (CPE), as it was commonly known), based on Marxist-Leninist ideology, began to take shape. The main co-ordination mechanism for resource allocation in the CPE was the central plan, as opposed to the decentralised market arrangements common in the West. Although changes took place throughout the next sixty years (and, particularly, in the late 1980s during the Gorbachev 'perestroika' era), the central tenets of the economic system remained. Those central features included state ownership, central planning, bureaucratic hierarchical structures, collectivised agriculture, rapid industrialisation and extensive economic growth.

> **Definition**
> *Extensive economic growth is greater output through a larger quantity of inputs used.*
> *Intensive economic growth is greater output through more productivity from existing inputs.*

The basic questions in economics (what to produce? how to produce? for whom to produce?) were to be resolved by the central plan, administratively set by the planners, and to be fulfilled largely by the state-owned enterprises (SOEs). Although orders were passed down, in a vertical hierarchy rather than the horizontal relations common in the market system, information flowed both down and up (although not always accurately as there were incentives for SOEs both to underestimate productive capacity and to overestimate input requirements) with all parties engaged in bargaining.

The rapid and extensive structural transformation that resulted from the nationalisation, collectivisation and planning changes of the 1930s, and thereafter, was evident in the rising share of industry (and investment) in GDP. Acknowledging the significant growth rates achieved in the earlier years (helping the USSR to begin the process of 'catch up' with the West), the 1960s onwards brought an economic slowdown or stagnation as it was referred to in the Soviet Union. Declining Soviet rates of economic growth forced those in power to make many changes in the system throughout the 1960s and 1970s. However, by the 1980s, it was evident that the Soviet socialist system was in serious decline. Even the perestroika reforms of the late 1980s were not able to prevent the collapse of the system (and may even have accelerated the timing of the break-up) and the demise of the Soviet Union. In December 1991, the USSR was disbanded. In accounting for the demise of the socialist system, scholars of comparative economic systems point to the informational and incentive problems inherent in state socialism. Two common incentive problems in the socialist system were the ratchet effect and the soft budget constraint.

> **Definition**
>
> *The ratchet effect is where output targets are ratcheted up if managers over-fulfill their plans.*

This provided an incentive for managers of enterprises to exert lesss effort. Knowing that output targets for future years would be increased if current production plans were over-fulfilled, managers of SOEs had an incentive to underperform.

> **Definition**
>
> *The soft budget constraint is the persistent or recurring expectation of a refinancing or bailout of loss-making enterprises. Firms that are in financial trouble are consistently bailed out by the state.*

This provided an incentive for managers to look to the state for external support. As firms were not held responsible for losses (or profits) and where their survival was secure, their behaviour was adversely affected. Firms' incentives to cut costs, generate revenue or innovate were dampened.

Similar features of the socialist system were prevalent in China from 1949 to 1978, when reforms first began to be introduced. However, the more interesting issue is the differences that existed between pre-1978 Communist China and the Soviet system. The communist system in China was in place for a much shorter duration, was less centralised, had fewer gigantic SOEs and there was less concentration of state employees in the workforce. It is also true that China had a longer history of private enterprise pre-1949 than Russia had in feudal Tsarist pre-1917 times. In terms of economic structure, China and the Soviet Union (and its most important successor state, Russia) were very different. Whereas Russia was a middle-income, urbanised, over-industrialised country on the eve of transition, China in 1978 was a low-income, agrarian country with a huge surplus of labour. It was argued that market reforms in agriculture would allow for a flow of workers from rural, agricultural inland China to urban, industrialised coastal China. Indeed, this is what happened with the introduction of the household responsibility system in China after 1978. At the start of the reforms (1978 in China and 1992 in Russia), macroeconomic conditions were very different. Whereas the CCP in China retained control and macro conditions were reasonably stable, the situation in the Soviet Union in late 1991 was much worse. The CPSU had lost control of the Union, output was stagnating and macroeconomic conditions were deteriorating, with both inflation and the budget deficit soaring. Although China did not have the same level of distortions as were evident in the former Soviet bloc countries, it did, however, have to face the dual problem of development and transition which many of the Soviet satellite states did not have to confront.

Conditions at the outset of transition throughout the socialist bloc of countries, and not just between China and Russia, varied significantly, as we will now outline.

19.2.2 Initial conditions

Despite the common legacy of one-party rule, public ownership and central planning, the former socialist countries of the Soviet bloc and China were not all the same (despite claims to the contrary by some) at the outset of transition. Initial conditions varied greatly, not just between the countries of Central and Eastern Europe (CEE) and the republics of the former Soviet Union (FSU) but even within these two groups of countries. Understanding these cross-country variations in circumstances is also useful when addressing, at a later stage, the issue of the large differences in economic performance and the outcomes that emerged between countries once transition began. Differences in initial conditions may also partly explain the different reform policies adopted by the various transition economies (TEs), acknowledging that other factors (political constraints, electoral support, institutions, ideologies, pressure or support from the West) also played a part. The economics literature on transition indicates that the role of the inherited economic conditions was an important factor in the complex transition process. Not surprisingly, TEs, to varying degrees, are burdened with the legacy of the past. We now provide some detail on these initial conditions.

TEs differed in many respects at the beginning of transition. Aside from political, cultural and historical factors, there was a range of economic factors that indicated differences between these countries. Cross-country differences in levels of human capital, income distribution, demographics, the extent of pre-transition reform and the size of government existed at the outset of transition. The problem with these and many other factors is the difficulty of acquiring accurate and comparable cross-country data. Several studies on transition have identified a list of factors that are both quantifiable and provide a reasonable account of the differences in circumstances. In particular, a 1997 World Bank study classifies a large number of variables into three categories, namely development and structure, economic distortions and institutional characteristics. Nine variables, for former socialist countries, are reproduced in Table 19.7.[14]

The variables that proxy for the level of development, resources and growth include income (measured as income per capita at PPP), and changes in income, urbanisation, the sectoral share of GDP, natural resource endowment and location or proximity to well-established market economies. Economic distortions and macroeconomic imbalances are measured by the extent of repressed or hidden inflation, the exchange rate premium and the share of Council for Mutual Economic Assistance (CMEA) trade.[15] Variables reflecting the institutional characteristics of transition countries include the number of years under central planning (capturing what is commonly known as 'market memory') and nationhood prior to transition (as many of the transition countries were not independent states prior to 1989–92, thus making the transition process longer and more arduous).

The message from Table 19.7 is clear: at the outset of transition not all TEs were the same. Sizeable differences existed between countries, and even, in the case of large or federal states, between regions within countries (for example, Western and Eastern Poland, West and East Ukraine, European Russia and Asian Russia). Similar studies have identified other indicators that reflect cross-country differences. These include secondary school enrolment, foreign debt and even culture. Whatever variables are chosen, differences in initial conditions raise the question

TABLE 19.7: THE INITIAL CONDITIONS*†

Country	Per capita income at PPP US$ 1989	Average % growth 1985-89	Urban-isation 1990	Industry share of GDP	Natural resource	Repressed inflation	Black market premium 1990%	CMEA trade 1990%	Years under central planning
CEE									
Albania	1400	3.6	37	0.37	Poor	4.3	434	6.6	47
Bulgaria	5000	2.7	68	0.59	Poor	18	921	16.1	43
Croatia	6171	0.2	62	0.35	Poor	12	276.0	46	
Czech Republic	8600	1.6	65	0.58	Poor	-7.1	185	6.0	42
Hungary	6810	1.6	62	0.36	Poor	-7.7	46.7	13.7	42
FYR Macedonia	3394	0.2	59	0.43	Poor	12	276.0	47	
Poland	5150	2.8	62	0.52	Moderate	13.6	277	8.4	41
Romania	3470	-0.8	53	0.59	Moderate	16.8	728	3.7	42
Slovakia	7600	1.6	57	0.59	Poor	-7.1	185	6.0	42
Slovenia	9200	-0.4	62	0.44	Poor	12	274.0	46	
Yugoslavia	n.a.	0.2	..	0.45	Poor	12	276.0	..	
Czechoslovakia	n.a.	1.6	..	0.59	Poor	-7.1	185	6.0	..
FSU									
Armenia	5530	2.7	68	0.55	Poor	25.7	1828	25.6	71
Azerbaijan	4620	0.8	54	0.44	Rich	25.7	1828	29.8	70
Belarus	7010	5.2	66	0.49	Poor	25.7	1828	41.0	72
Estonia	8900	2.7	72	0.44	Poor	25.7	1828	30.2	51
Georgia	5590	2.4	56	0.43	Moderate	25.7	1828	24.8	70
Kazakhstan	5130	4.3	57	0.34	Rich	25.7	1828	20.8	71
Kyrgyz Republic	3180	5.2	38	0.40	Poor	25.7	1828	27.7	71
Latvia	8590	3.5	71	0.45	Poor	25.7	1828	36.7	51
Lithuania	6430	2.9	68	0.45	Poor	25.7	1828	40.9	51
Moldova	4670	5.7	47	0.37	Poor	25.7	1828	28.9	51
Russia	7720	3.2	74	0.48	Rich	25.7	1828	11.1	74
Tajikistan	3010	1.9	32	0.34	Poor	25.7	1828	31.0	71
Turkmenistan	4230	5.0	45	0.34	Rich	25.7	1828	33.0	71
Ukraine	5680	2.4	67	0.44	Moderate	25.7	1828	23.8	74
Uzbekistan	2740	3.9	41	0.33	Moderate	25.7	1828	25.5	71
USSR	n.a.	3.8	..	0.44	Rich	25.7	1828	..	..
East Asia									
Mongolia	2100	5.4	60	0.41	Moderate	7.6	1400	31.0	70
China¶	800	9.0	18	0.49	Moderate	2.3	208	1.0	46
Vietnam¶	1100	5.0	19	0.23	Moderate	15.0	464	7.2	21

Notes

*   The location variable is not reported in the table. It is a dummy variable (1,0) with '1' = geographical proximity (i.e. a neighbour) to a thriving market economy, and '0' = otherwise. The countries with a '1' are Albania, China, Croatia, Czech Republic, Hungary, Poland, Slovak Republic, Slovenia, Russia, Vietnam, and the three Baltic countries. All others are '0'.

†   The nationhood variable is not reported in the table. It is a categorical variable with '2' = independent state prior to 1989; '1' = member of decentralised state or core country of centralised federal state; '0' = new nation state. The countries with a '2' are Albania, Bulgaria, China, Hungary, Mongolia, Poland, Romania and Vietnam. The countries with a '1' are Croatia, Czech Republic, FYR Macedonia, Slovenia and Russia. All others are '0'.

¶   The data for China and Vietnam are for the years 1978 (and before) and 1986 (and before) respectively.

Source: de Melo *et al.*, 2001.

of the likelihood of conformity, or not, in the reform process, the adoption of similar or diverse policy reforms and the extent of the variation in the performance of transition countries. In sum, it is evident that initial conditions mattered (as we will see later, so do policies and institutions). The evidence of path dependency, country-specific efforts and the inherited legacy of the socialist system and central planning is an important element in the transition experience.

We now outline the two broad theoretical approaches to economic transition.

19.2.3 Theories of transition

Strictly speaking, there is no 'theory' of transition from a centrally planned system to a market system. What evolved over time, since transition began, are two different approaches, or paradigms, to understanding the transformation from plan to market. The standard paradigm of economic transition that dominated in the early years of the 1990s and had the support of the IFIs (the World Bank and, more notably, the International Monetary Fund) is often referred to as the Washington Consensus. This orthodox or mainstream approach, especially popular in the Anglo-Saxon world – seen by many as an expression of the neoclassical tradition – views the transition from a centrally planned to a market economy as a reform process emphasising the universality of the laws of the market and the undoubted economy-wide efficiency gains accruing from the standard policy prescriptions of the trinity of liberalisation ('getting prices right'), stabilisation and privatisation. This blueprint for transition, based on the spontaneity of markets and private enterprise, traditional neoclassical price theory and general equilibrium theory, promotes the primacy of policy reforms and economic fundamentals and the replication or transplantation of international best-practice institutions (with the emphasis on laws, property rights and the legal and regulatory framework) of the West to the ex-socialist countries of the former Soviet bloc (a kind of utopia based on 'societal engineering').

Although the Washington Consensus emerged from a different set of conditions, it argues that these one-size-fits-all market-oriented reforms are appropriate to any setting, including the post-socialist CEE and FSU countries. A knowledge or experience of the state socialist system and the centrally planned economy is not required. Liberal economic reform strategies are implemented along a scorched-earth approach, with textbook reforms being designed by technocrats and introduced as rapidly and comprehensively as possible in view of the reform complementarities that exist. Not surprisingly, in terms of the speed of the radical reforms, this approach is often referred to as the 'big bang' or 'shock therapy' view of transition. This also applies to the economic role of the state where what is required is a depoliticisation of the economy, a break of the nexus between government and business, and a dismantling of the state, or, according to critics of the Washington Consensus approach, in the extreme case of neoliberal market fundamentalism, state desertion.

The institutional-evolutionary paradigm, more popular within academic circles, views transition as a large-scale institutional transformation in which the focus is on the institutional underpinnings of capitalism appropriate to the specific conditions of each country and in accordance with the initial conditions at the outset of transition. This approach is critical of the revolutionary vision of transition and, instead, views transition as an evolutionary process involving systemic change in the face of great uncertainty and complexity, unlike the competitive neoclassical model and its notion of equilibrium, which arguably is inherently static. As opposed to equilibrium processes, the emphasis of the institutional-evolutionary approach is on the dynamics of institutional change within an evolutionary perspective, based on contracting and nonco-operative games in modern microeconomic theory. Here, the focus is on the gradual development of the institutional supports or arrangements for a market economy, accepting the dangers of institutional voids and that not all existing or inherited institutions, organisational forms or social capital are redundant. Transitional second-best institutions and the preservation of social capital can be both worthwhile and necessary in order to prevent further economic disruption.

Whereas the Washington Consensus view of transition is a top-down approach, the institutional-evolutionary perspective is a bottom-up view focusing on the institutional design of market economies, the importance of social norms and the organic development of the private sector. Markets and economic agents do not exist in a vacuum but in an institutional framework – 'the rules of the game' – that facilitates exchange and interaction. Institution building and the provision of a framework for well-functioning market structures and organisations is the focus of this approach and it argues for the gradual or incremental implementation of sequenced reforms (often through experimentation and learning by doing) in order to ensure growing support for policies. In the institutional-evolutionary approach, although there is recognition for the need to reduce the role of the state, the emphasis is on a reconstituted state and improving state capacity (so as to, among other things, enhance the market environment) as opposed to a weakened state. It also stresses the path dependency of system development and is mindful of the historical continuity and the communist legacy, unlike the ahistorical, tabula rasa Washington Consensus approach.

Many observers feel that the debate between the two schools of thought and, in particular, the controversy between 'shock therapy' and gradualism and the tendency to label countries as either one or the other, has not been very helpful and has unintentionally diverted attention away from some of the more important aspects of economic transition. We now turn to the economic policy reforms adopted during transition.

19.2.4 Transition reforms and policies

One of the main problems in respect of devising policies suitable for transition was the absence of any historical precedence or theoretical framework. Although there were several examples of countries in the twentieth century that had adopted reforms in the face of systemic change and great upheaval – developing countries of Latin America; Germany and Japan after World War II; the NICs of South East Asia – the transition from a centrally planned economy to a market economy was unprecedented (and a reversal of the socialist revolution of 1917). Although both the starting point (a dysfunctional centrally planned economy) and the end point (a well-functioning market economy) were known, the path or process from beginning to end was unclear. Despite the lack of a blueprint for reforms in the context of transition, the first decade was dominated by the trinity of stabilisation, liberalisation and privatisation. It was argued that the distortions and inefficiencies of the old system would be corrected by (rapid) price and trade liberalisation combined with (austere) macroeconomic stabilisation. The other (which later proved to be the most controversial) part of the trinity was the transfer of ownership from state to private hands by a process of privatisation. These three policies formed the basis of the reform package advocated by mainstream economists and the international financial organisations. Figure 19.1 outlines the list of policies and the timeframe involved. Although some policies, by their very nature, were to be implemented throughout the entire time period, it was argued that the success of the reform agenda hinged on the immediate and simultaneous introduction of liberalisation, stabilisation and privatisation policies. We deal briefly with each of these reforms.

FIGURE 19.1: REFORM POLICIES IN TRANSITION

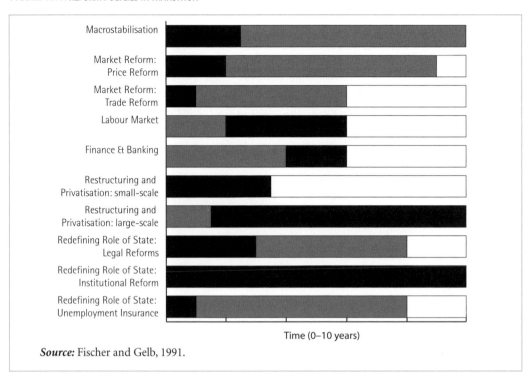

Source: Fischer and Gelb, 1991.

Liberalisation

Price and trade liberalisation was an essential component of the package of reforms associated with the Washington Consensus. In the socialist system, prices reflected the preferences and decisions of planners. Taxes, subsidies and monopolies were all part of the pricing system. Queues, infamous in Soviet times, were the main rationing mechanism. By comparison, in a market economy, prices reflect costs and scarcity, and steer resource allocation. For domestic trade, the intention of price liberalisation was to bring about a change in relative prices and to lift the price controls, thus allowing prices to be 'freely' determined by market forces of demand and supply. Once price controls were lifted, the combination of (pre-transition) low fixed price levels, government subsidies and the monetary overhang (i.e. the excess of cash over goods and services) was likely to result in an increase in the aggregate price level. However, it was also predicted that a rapid response in supply, based on the belief in the spontaneity of markets, would increase the quantity of goods and services available, thus damping down the general price increase. Unlike many other reforms, the implementation of price liberalisation was straightforward as it could be done with a 'stroke of the pen'. Indeed, this is what happened in most transition economies as price controls were lifted and subsidies were reduced. There were some exceptions, including energy prices, housing, public transport and basic foodstuffs. In respect of subsidies, most TEs witnessed large declines in budgetary subsidies: in some countries to levels similar to those found in mature market economies where subsidies are tied to the provision of public services.

Although the intention of foreign trade liberalisation was similar – bringing prices of goods and services in the traded sector in line with international prices – the changes involved greater and more difficult choices. Among others, this involved the abolition of licences and the state monopoly on foreign trade, the unification of the exchange rate (as multiple exchange rates were common), current account convertibility (where exporters and importers can freely buy or sell foreign exchange for trade purposes), lifting quantitative restrictions, membership of the IFIs and relaxing laws (and, in other cases, introducing new laws) on FDI flows. Tariffs were expected to remain, often for revenue-generating purposes but also as part of a country's industrial policy in its attempt to support infant industries, as were capital controls as premature liberalisation of capital can lead to large and damaging capital flows. Again, as these policies were advocated by the international financial organisations, most of the transition countries implemented the reforms, with some differences across countries. The issue of a regional trading association had already been resolved with the abolition of the CMEA in 1991.

China, in contrast, followed a more unconventional approach. It implemented a dual-track or two-tier liberalisation strategy. The dual-track pricing system is where the planned output remains, and, at the same time, at the margin, any residual output can be traded at market prices. The planned track was, in an incremental fashion, eventually phased out by the early 1990s, and replaced by the market mechanism.

Stabilisation

Macroeconomic stabilisation is the second part of the trinity. Macroeconomic policy, as understood in the market system, was absent in socialist economies, as controls were prevalent at the micro unit level. However, by the late 1980s, some of the (pre-transition) reform policies that had been adopted by the socialist countries had unintentionally led to rising fiscal problems. As central authorities had ceded control to SOEs, wage concessions increased and tax collections declined. In some cases, transition exacerbated the problem with further falls in tax revenue, the emergence of inter-enterprise arrears, an increase in barter transactions and rising pressures on public expenditures. 'Orthodox' macroeconomic stabilisation, involving a combination of tight fiscal and monetary policies, was aimed at cutting the rate of credit expansion, reducing budget deficits and lowering inflation rates. This involved reducing (and, in other cases, redirecting) government expenditures, tax reforms targeted at introducing new taxes (VAT and corporate tax systems, for example), cutting marginal tax rates combined with improving tax collections, non-monetary financing of budget deficits and positive real interest rates. In many cases, an incomes policy (based on a wage bill tax on excessive wage increases) was also used. The choice of exchange rate policy varied from the extreme of a flexible exchange rate to a currency board where the national authorities cede monetary autonomy.

Privatisation

State ownership was a central feature of the socialist system. Privatisation was necessary to transfer ownership from public to private hands. It was argued that privatisation would, *inter alia*, eliminate the tendency for SOEs to fulfill political (as opposed to profit-maximising) objectives, improve the quality of managers and encourage greater financial discipline (via, for example, the fear of bankruptcy). As the 1980s saw a worldwide increase in privatisation, it was inevitable that the transition countries would follow the privatisation route. Aside from differences in the number of enterprises undertaking privatisation (hundreds in the case of non-transition countries as against thousands in TEs), the form of privatisation often differed. With inadequate savings, poorly functioning capital markets, 'fuzzy' property rights, underdeveloped legal systems, a plethora of unviable SOEs, public opposition to privatisation and reluctant foreign investors (if even allowed to participate as in some cases foreign investors were excluded from competing), the normal forms of privatisation, including individual sell-offs of publicly owned firms, were inadequate and, in some cases, inappropriate.

A new form of privatisation, called mass privatisation schemes, was initiated, whereby enterprises were sold for free (subject sometimes to a nominal fee) to a country's citizens, via vouchers or certificates. Many TEs, particularly most of the FSU countries, adopted the mass privatisation schemes. Although supporters of mass privatisation cited the usual economic arguments for doing so (see above), often the politics of privatisation was invoked. Rapid privatisation would ensure a depoliticisation of economic activity – that is, break the nexus between government and business – and, in turn, prevent a return to the old state-dominated socialist system. However, it became evident in the mid- to late 1990s that all was not well with privatisation. In particular, there were problems with the process and outcomes of privatisation in many transition countries, including the high-profile schemes in the Czech Republic and Russia. Later, it became clear that, among other things, the form that privatisation takes (direct sales, voucher schemes, management buyouts) matters. Well-functioning legal systems and capital markets also matter. Equally important are the related issues of corporate governance mechanisms, enterprise restructuring, hardening the budget constraint and the development of a new private sector (comprising *de novo* SMEs). Different results emerged from privatisation depending on whether the process favoured insiders (managers, workers) or outsiders (banks, enterprises, investment funds), dispersed or concentrated ownership, domestic or foreign investors, the absence or presence of enterprise restructuring and the hardening or softening of the budget constraint.

One particularly interesting finding from the empirical literature on the determinants of enterprise restructuring and performance is the better performance of new private firms as opposed to all others (state or privatised). This indicates the importance of the emerging new private sector and the development of a vibrant and strong SME sector. To foster new firms and entrepreneurship, governments in the transition countries were encouraged to demonopolise existing SOEs, reduce barriers to entry, implement competition policy and provide supports (financial and otherwise) to SMEs. The leading TEs in terms of SMEs and new firms were, among others, Poland and Hungary, whereas in many of the FSU republics, including Russia and Ukraine, SME development was sluggish (due to a range of factors including corruption and bribery, bureaucracy and red tape, poor financial intermediation and low levels of domestic demand). In China, it was the township-and-village enterprises (TVEs) that generated jobs and economic growth. Although (local) government-owned, TVEs were, crucially, and unlike the traditional SOEs, subject to competition, but not subject to budget softness. A list of these policies (including the provision of a social safety net), relating to what is often called 'initial phase reforms', for a sample of countries, is outlined in Table 19.8.

Aside from these 'first generational' policies, structural and institutional reforms were equally necessary. Enterprise restructuring, banking and financial sector reforms, labour market and fiscal reforms, social security and pension reforms tended to take longer and often required a strong state and increasing administrative capacity (as opposed to the earlier reforms, which called for a smaller state). Reform of government (everything from civil service reform to new arrangements for intergovernmental fiscal relations) was also required. Table 19.9 outlines country-specific detail on these so-called second phase reforms, for a selected sample of countries.

TABLE 19.8 INITIAL PHASE REFORMS

	Transition Economy								
Reform Policies	*Czech Republic*	*Latvia*	*Poland*	*Croatia*	*Romania*	*Georgia*	*Russia*	*Kyrgyzstan*	*China*
Macroeconomic stabilisation	Starts Jan 1991	Starts 1992	Starts Jan 1990	Starts late 1993	Starts 1990 but stalled until relaunch in 1997	Starts late at end 1994	Starts Jan 1992 and relaunch from 1995 onward	One of the first CIS countries to start, in May 1993	Moderate inflation controlled periodically by administrative means
Exchange rate	Fixed until 1997 currency crisis, managed float adopted thereafter	New currency (lat) in 1993; initially floating and then fixed rate after 1994	Crawling peg followed by managed float with fluctuation bands	New currency (kuna) in 1994; managed float thereafter	Regulation until 1997 when exchange rate unified and float adopted	New currency (lari) in 1995; managed float changed to free float in 1998	New currency (rouble) in 1993; initially floating, then currency crisis in 1994 followed by crawling peg/currency corridor	New currency (som) in 1993; managed float thereafter	Unified since 1994; managed float thereafter; controls on capital flows
Incomes policy	Excess wage bill tax	None except for minimum wage	Excess wage tax (popiwek)	Heterodox, with a strict incomes policy and wage restraint via administrative control of wages	Excess wage bill tax	–	Excess wage tax	Excess wage bill tax	–
Liberalisation	Most prices liberalised by end 1991; same with foreign trade controls	Almost full liberalisation; some controls on energy prices	Most prices liberalised in Jan 1990; same with foreign trade controls	A relatively late (after 1993) liberaliser	Delay with only most prices liberalised in 1995	Majority of prices liberalised in 1992; as with foreign trade controls	Starts Jan 1992 with most prices liberalised; energy (and some other) price controls remain	Most prices liberalised in 1992	Dual-track price liberalisation from 1978, beginning in agriculture and extending to industry
Privatisation	Mass/voucher privatisation begins in 1992; investment funds; direct cash sales	Direct sales and voucher privatisation from 1992 onward	Delayed with a mix of cash sales and MEBOs; National Investment Funds (NIFs)	MEBOs and voucher privatisation from 1992 onward	Slow start with MEBOs and direct sales methods	Slow start with mass/voucher privatisation and direct sales	Voucher privatisation in 1992–4. 'Shares for loans' auctions in 1995/6	Delayed voucher auctions and MEBOs from 1996	Very slow to privatise, particularly large SOEs; focus on new TVEs and foreign joint ventures
Social safety net	Unemployment benefit; minimum wage; partial wages indexation	Minimum wage	Unemployment benefit; minimum wage; wages indexation	Unemployment benefit; minimum wage	Unemployment benefit, minimum wage	Minimum social transfers; low unemployment benefits; arrears	Low unemployment benefits; minimum wage; arrears	Unemployment Compensation Scheme (UCS) in place; minimum pension	Unemployment insurance scheme administered by provinces, benefits are low and only to urban workers; minimum wage

Sources: Turley and Luke 2010; various EBRD Transition Reports; IMF Country Reports.

TABLE 19.9: SECOND PHASE REFORMS

	Transition Economy								
Reform policies	**Hungary**	**Estonia**	**Slovak Republic**	**Bulgaria**	**Albania**	**Moldova**	**Ukraine**	**Uzbekistan**	**Vietnam**
Enterprise restructuring competition policy	State Property Agency established 1990/ competition law adopted 1991 (amended 1997, 2000)	Estonian Privatisation Agency established 1993/ competition law adopted 1993 (amended 1998, new Act 2001)	National Property Fund established 1991/ competition law adopted 1991 (amended 1995)	Privatisation Agency established 1992, restructuring programme 1996/competition law adopted 1991 (amended 1998)	Enterprise Restructuring Agency established 1993/ competition law enacted 1995	Enterprise Restructuring Agency established 1995/ competition law adopted 1991	State Property Fund established 1992/ competition law adopted 1991 (amended 1998)	State Property Committee established 1992 (amended 1996)/ competition law adopted 1992 (amended 1996)	Some enterprise reforms in the form of equitisation (non-strategic SOEs), mergers, liquidations and joint ventures; reductions in budgetary subsidies
Financial sector reform	Banking law adopted 1990 (new 1997)/Stock Exchange established 1990/SEC established 1995	Banking law adopted 1993 (amended 1994, 1999)/Stock Exchange established 1996/SEC established 1993	Banking law adopted 1992 (new 1994)/Stock Exchange established 1993	Banking law adopted 1992 (new 1997)/Stock Exchange established 1991/SEC established 1995	Banking law amended 1998/ Stock Exchange established 1996/SEC established 1996	Stock Exchange established 1995/SEC established 1994	Stock Exchange established 1992/SEC established 1995	Banking law adopted 1996/Stock Exchange established 1994	Incomplete reforms. 2-tier banking system dominated by state-owned commercial banks/banking law adopted 1998
Social protection reform	Pension reform adopted 1997	Pension reform law adopted 1998	Reform of health and pension system initiated 2003	Pension reform 1999	Poverty Reduction and Growth Strategy adopted 2001	Pension reform adopted 1998	Laws on pension reform 2003	Pension reform 2001	Informal support mechanisms and private contributions have replaced state system
Fiscal reform	T-bills market initiated 1992/all three PIT, CIT and VAT systems by 1989	T-bills market initiated 1993/all three PIT, CIT, VAT systems by 1993	T-bills market initiated 1992/all PIT, CIT, VAT systems by 1993	T-bills market initiated 1991/all PIT, CIT, VAT by 1994	T-bills market initiated 1994/PIT, CIT, VAT by 1996	T-bills market initiated 1995/PIT, CIT, VAT by 1992	T-bills market initiated 1995/PIT, CIT, VAT by 1992	T-bills market initiated 1996/PIT, CIT, VAT by 1992	T-bills market initiated 1995/low-yield PIT from 1990, CIT (was profit tax) and VAT (was turnover tax) from 1999
Legal and regulatory reform	Bankruptcy law adopted 1991 (amended 1993); Central Bank law enacted 1991/electricity regulator 1994; telecomm. regulator 1993	Bankruptcy law enacted 1992; Central Bank law enacted 1993/both electricity and telecomm. regulator 1998	Bankruptcy law adopted 1991 (amended 1993, 1998; new 2000); Central Bank law enacted 1992/electricity regulator 2001; telecomm. regulator 2000	Bankruptcy law adopted 1994 (amended 1996); Central Bank law enacted 1991/electricity regulator 1999; telecomm. regulator 2002	Bankruptcy law enacted 1995 (amended 2002); Central Bank law enacted 1992 (amended 1996)/electricity regulator 1996; telecomm. regulator 1998	Bankruptcy law adopted 1992 (amended 1997); Central Bank law enacted 1991 (new 1996)/ electricity regulator 1998; telecomm. regulator 2000	Bankruptcy law adopted 1992 (new 2000); Central Bank law enacted 1991 (new 1999) /electricity regulator 2000	Bankruptcy law adopted 1994 (amended 1996); Central Bank law enacted 1992 (amended 1995)/ electricity regulator 2000	Bankruptcy law adopted 1994 (new 2004)/Central Bank law adopted 1998/ electricity law 2005

Sources: Turley and Luke 2010; various EBRD Transition Reports; IMF Country Reports.

If we view transition as large-scale institutional change, the role of institutions and institutional reforms becomes paramount (see Chapter 1).

> **Definition**
>
> *Institutions are humanly devised mechanisms or constraints that structure economic behaviour and interaction. They are the 'rules of the game' that facilitate exchange.*

Accordingly, market reforms can only succeed in establishing a well-functioning market economy if suitable institutions are in place. The socialist system had its own institutional and organisational capital. For transition to succeed, a new institutional order with market-based institutions was required. However, by their very nature, the institutional arrangements required for a market economy take time to evolve. They also depend on the norms and patterns of social behaviour. The protection of property rights and the rule of law are generally regarded as two of market economies' most important institutions. As transition progressed (and the problems of transition became more evident), the role and importance of institutions became more apparent. Well before the second decade, institutional reform had become a – if not *the* – key constituent of the reform agenda. This was in contrast to the first decade of transition, which was dominated by the big bang vs. gradualism debate. Those in favour of the big bang, shock therapy approach argued in favour of simultaneous reforms in order, among other things, to avail of the reform complementaries and avoid a return to the old system. Most of the CEE and FSU countries adopted a reform agenda similar to the radical big bang approach (notwithstanding some differences in reform priorities). Those in favour of the gradual, incremental approach argued, in the context of evolutionary change, the need for sequenced reforms, in order, *inter alia*, to minimise disruptions and aggregate uncertainty and build a constituency for reform. This school of thought gave more prominence to the role of institutions, both formal (laws and regulations, for example) and informal (for example customs and norms). China, it is often argued, more closely followed this approach.

Debate continued over the most appropriate sequence of reforms, and, in particular, the order of enterprise restructuring vs. privatisation, institutional reform vs. market reforms, enterprise reform vs. financial/banking reform, liberalisation vs. demonopolisation and competition. Inevitably, those reforms that were easiest to implement, attracted less opposition from powerful vested interests and were popular in policy circles (including the IFIs of the Fund and the Bank) were advocated and implemented first. These reforms included price liberalisation and macroeconomic stabilisation. Those reforms that took longer to implement, attracted most opposition from interest groups and were less frequently championed in policy circles were slower to emerge. These included changes to governance (both at national and corporate levels) and financial sector reform.

Acknowledging that reforms may partly explain cross-country variations in economic performance, progress in economic reform is useful to measure but difficult to quantify. However, since the early 1990s, both the World Bank, using its liberalisation index (defined as a weighted average of policy reforms in three areas, namely internal markets, external markets, and privatisation and private sector entry), and the European Bank for Reconstruction and Development (EBRD), using its transition indicators, have developed methodologies for assessing, quantitatively, the progress in economic reform. Table 19.10 shows a summary of the cross-country progress in transition reforms, based on the EBRD's transition indicators. We report a simple average of eight transition indicators for 25 countries for the years 1990, 1995, 2000, 2005 and 2010.

The EBRD transition indicators purport to measure, as judged by the EBRD's Office of the Chief Economist, progress in reform in a number of different policy areas, including markets and trade, enterprise restructuring and privatisation, and financial institutions reform.[16] A score of 1 indicates little progress in market reforms, whereas a score of 4+ indicates full market reforms (i.e. standards and performances typical of advanced industrial economies). Despite the cross-country and cross-dimension variation, clearly-identified trends are evident (as seen in Table 19.10 and Figure 19.2).

TABLE 19.10: EBRD TRANSITION INDICATORS 1990–2010

Country	EBRD Transition Indicator 1990	EBRD Transition Indicator 1995	EBRD Transition Indicator 2000	EBRD Transition Indicator 2005	EBRD Transition Indicator 2010
CEE countries and the Baltic States					
Albania	1.0	2.4	2.6	3.0	3.2
Bulgaria	1.0	2.5	3.0	3.5	3.6
Croatia	1.7	2.8	3.2	3.5	3.6
Czech Republic‡	1.0	3.5	3.5	3.9	–
Estonia	1.0	3.2	3.5	3.8	4.0
FYR Macedonia	1.7	2.5	2.9	3.1	3.3
Hungary	2.0	3.5	3.7	4.0	4.0
Latvia	1.0	2.8	3.1	3.6	3.7
Lithuania	1.0	2.9	3.2	3.7	3.8
Poland	2.0	3.3	3.5	3.8	3.9
Romania	1.0	2.5	2.8	3.2	3.5
Slovak Republic	1.0	3.3	3.4	3.8	3.8
Slovenia	1.7	3.2	3.3	3.4	3.5
Commonwealth of Independent States (CIS)					
Armenia	1.0	2.1	2.6	3.2	3.3
Azerbaijan	1.0	1.6	2.4	2.8	2.7
Belarus	1.0	2.1	1.5	1.9	2.2
Georgia	1.0	2.0	2.9	3.1	3.2
Kazakhstan	1.0	2.1	2.7	3.0	3.0
Kyrgyz Republic	1.0	2.9	2.8	3.1	3.1
Moldova	1.0	2.6	2.7	2.9	3.1
Russia	1.0	2.6	2.5	3.0	3.1
Tajikistan	1.0	1.6	2.2	2.5	2.6
Turkmenistan	1.0	1.1	1.3	1.3	1.5
Ukraine	1.0	2.2	2.5	3.0	3.2
Uzbekistan	1.0	2.4	2.0	2.2	2.2

Source: various EBRD Transition Reports.

‡ There is no transition indicator for the Czech Republic, as it 'graduated' from the EBRD at end 2007.

FIGURE 19.2: PROGRESS IN TRANSITION REFORMS, 2010

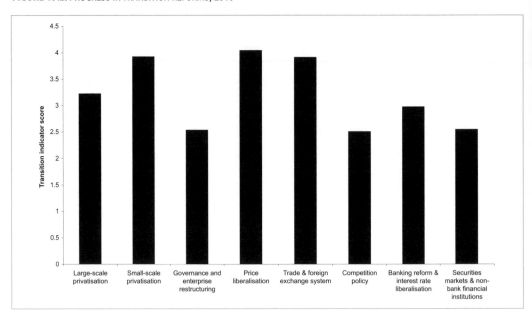

In terms of the dimension of reforms, most reform has been made in the area of liberalisation and privatisation. The least progress in reform has been made in areas of financial sector reform, competition policy and corporate governance. It is evident that initial phase reforms were easier to implement and were completed, for most reforming countries, within the first decade of transition. The second phase reforms were more complex and required a much longer period to implement. In terms of countries closer to Western Europe (historically and geographically, with the lure of EU membership playing a positive role) have made most progress in reform. This includes Hungary, Czech and Slovak Republics, Poland and the Baltic States. Countries further afield such as the Caucasus states (Georgia, Armenia, Azerbaijan) and some of the five Central Asian Republics (Tajikistan, Kazakhstan and Uzbekistan) have made the least progress. Belarus and Turkmenistan have made little or no change to the old economic system, due to the presence of old-style authoritarian leaders. A number of other countries, including the partial reform countries of Ukraine, Bulgaria and Romania, have made uneven progress (and, in some cases, policy reversals).

The next question is: what impact did these reforms have on the economic performance of transition countries? Were the outcomes in terms of output, inflation, unemployment, poverty and income distribution related to reforms? Were the rapid reformers most likely to perform better, in terms of economic growth? What was the impact of delayed reforms on economic outcomes? We now turn to the issue of the economic record of the TEs, and, in particular, the cross-country variation in performance.

19.2.5 Performance and outcomes in transition countries

There are a number of issues relating to the performance and outcomes in TEs. First, there are data problems, particularly in the first few years of transition when the capacity of national statistical offices to produce reliable, regular and comparable data was limited. This problem has more or less been resolved with the passage of time. Second, there is a wide range of indicators that can be used to measure the performance of transition countries. The most appropriate indicators include economic growth and income per capita, inflation and unemployment rates, consumption and investment patterns, poverty and income distribution levels, population changes and life expectancy rates. We will report a selection of these for the TEs. Third, one of transition's stylised (and surprising) facts is the decline in output that was recorded in CEE and FSU countries (but not China or Vietnam) for much of the first half of the 1990s. Various theories have been given to explain the collapse in GDP, ranging from systemic reasons to statistical illusions. A brief explanation of the most important theories will be given here. Fourth, irrespective of what indicator is used to measure performance during transition, significant cross-country differences have emerged; some expected (the relatively good performance of Hungary and Slovenia and the relatively bad performance of Ukraine and Tajikistan), some unexpected (the relatively good performance of the three Baltic States and the relatively bad performance of Bulgaria and Romania). Explanations for these variations in output growth are briefly outlined. Finally, despite the hardship and poor performance of many countries during transition, there is a need to

TABLE 19.11: PERFORMANCE AND OUTCOMES IN TRANSITION ECONOMIES

Country	GDP per capita (US$)		Inflation (CPI, av. %)		Unemployment (%)		Population (m)		Life expectancy (yrs)	
	1990	2009	1990	2009	1990	2009	1990	2009	1990	2009
CEE and Baltics										
Albania	639	3,750	..	3.4	9.5	13.7	3.3	3.2	72	77
Bulgaria	2,377	6,210	26.3	2.8	1.6	6.8	8.7	7.6	72	73
Croatia	5,185	14,222	610	2.4	9.3	9.2	4.8	4.4	72	76
Czech Republic	3,366	18,139	9.7	1.0	0.7	6.7	10.4	10.5	71	77
Estonia	3,193	14,238	23.1	-0.1	0.6	13.8	1.6	1.3	69	74
FYR Macedonia	2,342	4,515	608	-0.8	..	32.2	1.9	2.0	71	74
Hungary	3,186	12,868	28.9	4.2	1.4	10.5	10.4	10.0	69	74
Latvia	2,788	11,616	10.5	3.5	0.5	17.3	2.7	2.3	69	72
Lithuania	2,841	11,141	8.4	4.2	..	13.7	3.7	3.3	71	72
Poland	1,547	11,273	586	3.8	6.5	8.5	38.1	38.1	71	76
Romania	1,650	7,500	5.1	5.6	..	7.8	23.2	21.5	70	73
Slovak Republic	2,218	16,176	10.8	1.6	1.2	12.1	5.3	5.4	71	75
Slovenia	8,699	23,726	552	0.9	4.7	6.0	2.0	2.0	73	79
CIS										
Armenia	637	2,826	10.3	3.4	..	6.8	3.5	3.1	68	74
Azerbaijan	1,237	4,899	7.8	1.5	..	6.0	7.2	8.8	65	70
Belarus	1,705	5,069	4.7	12.8	..	0.9	10.2	9.7	71	70
Georgia	1,492	2,447	3.3	1.7	..	16.9	5.5	4.3	70	72
Kazakhstan	1,647	6,870	..	7.3	..	6.6	16.3	15.9	68	66
Kyrgyz Republic	605	860	..	6.8	..	8.5	4.4	5.3	68	67
Moldova	973	1,516	..	-0.1	..	6.4	4.4	3.6	67	68
Russia	3,485	8,676	5.6	11.7	..	8.2	148.3	141.9	69	68
Tajikistan	496	716	5.6	6.4	..	2.1	5.3	7.0	63	67
Turkmenistan	881	3,904	4.6	-2.7	..	..	3.7	5.1	63	65
Ukraine	1,570	2,468	4.2	15.9	..	8.1	51.9	46.0	70	68
Uzbekistan	651	1,182	4.0	14.1	..	0.4	20.5	27.8	67	68

Source: WB, EBRD.

recognise and acknowledge the fundamental changes that have taken place since transition began. These economies, once characterised by the trinity of collectivisation, nationalisation and industrialisation, are now, more or less, characterised by market-based private sector activities, market-determined prices, a sizeable and growing services and SME sector, foreign trade and integration with the rest of the world. This is a considerable achievement in such a short space of time. However, despite these changes in the economic system, and the recovery in economic growth that followed, there is also a need to accept that in many CIS countries the standard of living and wellbeing of many of its citizens did not improve in the first decade or so of transition. Accordingly, one 2004 UN *Economic Survey of Europe* report concluded, '. . . in many cases the ultimate objective of transition – improving the lives of ordinary people – appears to have taken second place to the imperative of economic growth.'[17]

Table 19.11 reports the performance of 25 CEE/FSU countries for the first two decades of transition.

Across most of the measures, the early 1990s was a difficult time, with huge upheaval. Output collapsed, prices soared, unemployment rose, demographics deteriorated, poverty levels increased and inequalities widened.[18] However, by the mid-1990s in the CEE countries and the late 1990s in the FSU countries there was evidence of a recovery, although uneven and erratic.[19] Output levels recovered, inflation rates fell and unemployment levels stabilised.[20] By the beginning of the second decade, the vast majority of TEs were performing well. This was particularly true of the 2004 EU accession states, namely Poland, Hungary, Slovenia, Czech Republic, Slovak Republic, Estonia, Lithuania and Latvia. For these countries, some commentators viewed their transition as over. For others, mainly the CIS countries, the majority of which experienced a boom in the early and mid-2000s, the data indicate that they still have a long way to go. For example, the former socialist Central and East Asian states resemble, in many respects, less developed countries in other parts of the world. More recently, the financial crisis and global recession of the late 2000s hit many transition countries, especially in Eastern Europe, badly. Financial and economic integration combined with a growth strategy based on excessive borrowing and cheap credit resulted in many TEs, notably Hungary, Latvia, Ukraine and Romania, overly exposed, culminating in an IMF rescue and austerity programmes.

The output collapse

At the outset of transition, many economists (particularly those unfamiliar with the socialist system) predicted a closing of the gap between East and West. Recognising the distortions and inefficiencies of the old socialist system, it was argued that implementation of the reform package and improved resource allocation would result in an increase in output levels and higher economic growth rates. Others were more pessimistic and predicted a difficult transformation. The initial decline in output that occurred in all of the CEE and FSU countries appears to vindicate the latter's position.

Table 19.12 reports the fall in output during the period 1990–2000. Notwithstanding the difficulties in measuring GDP at the outset of transition (as mentioned earlier) and acknowledging the under-reporting of economic activity due to the significant size, and growing in the first few years of transition, of the underground or unofficial economy (estimated to be in excess of 40% of GDP in some of the TEs, particularly the CIS countries), the collapse in output in the early years of transition was unprecedented in modern economic times and for some countries even exceeded the economic decline recorded during the Great Depression years of the 1930s. As is evident from Table 19.12, Poland experienced the shortest and mildest

TABLE 19.12: OUTPUT DECLINE IN TRANSITION COUNTRIES

Country	Consecutive years of output decline	Cumulative output decline (%)	Real GDP, 2000 (1990 = 100)
Central and Southern Europe and the Baltic States	3.8	22.6	106.5
Albania	3	33	110
Bulgaria	4	16	81
Croatia	4	36	87
Czech Republic	3	12	99
Estonia	5	35	85
Hungary	4	15	109
Latvia	6	51	61
Lithuania	5	44	67
Poland	2	6	112
Romania	3	21	82
Slovak Republic	4	23	82
Slovenia	3	14	105
Commonwealth of Independent States	6.5	50.5	62.7
Armenia	4	63	67
Azerbaijan	6	60	55
Belarus	6	35	88
Georgia	5	78	29
Kazakhstan	6	41	90
Kyrgyz Republic	6	50	66
Moldova	7	63	35
Russia	7	40	64
Tajikistan	7	50	48
Turkmenistan	8	48	76
Ukraine	10	59	43
Uzbekistan	6	18	95
Output decline during the Great Depression 1930–34			
France	3	11	n.a.
Germany	3	16	n.a.
United Kingdom	2	6	n.a.
United States	4	27	n.a.

Source: World Bank, 2002.

recession. Although other CEE countries witnessed longer and deeper recessions, it was the FSU republics that experienced the steepest declines. Ukraine witnessed ten consecutive years of economic decline while Georgia experienced the largest fall in output, estimated at almost 80%. It is important to note here that for many of these countries, the fall in output, although often associated with the start of liberalisation, had started before the collapse of the Soviet system. The surprise for many analysts was that this decline in output was not halted by the economic reforms as part of the transition to the market system, and, indeed, for some countries, the output decline accelerated in the initial years of transition before a recovery was evident.

The economics literature identifies several explanations for the output collapse.[21] Kornai (1994) identifies the transformational recession as caused by the systemic change from a planned, supply-constrained, shortage economy to a decentralised, demand-constrained economy. The decline in output in the state sector was not sufficiently compensated for by the nascent private sector activity. Blanchard and Kremer's (1997) disorganisation theory identifies problems in the supply chain between producers. As transition began with price liberalisation, the taut plans resulted in disruption of links in existing production chains with the inevitable decline in output to follow. Calvo and Coricelli's (1993) credit crunch explanation blames the early recession on high interest rates and tight monetary policy leading to a decline in credit and resulting falls in output levels. In contrast, Amsden *et al.* (1994) blame the austere macroeconomic stabilisation policies, leading to a slump in aggregate demand. Rodrik (1994) identifies the collapse in foreign trade arising from the Soviet trade shock and the abandonment of the discredited CMEA as a significant factor in explaining the output decline. It is difficult to establish the relative importance of these and other theories. However, it is likely that the decline in output was due not to one factor alone (whether the slow response in supply, the decline in aggregate demand, systemic reasons, policy errors or trade implosions) but to some combination of these factors.

The other interesting feature in the performance of TEs is accounting for differences in economic outcomes. Various studies in transition have identified and empirically tested the significance of explanatory factors, such as the initial conditions and the legacy of the socialist system,[22] political change and constraints, institutions, external factors (war and civil strife, state collapse, trade flows, financial crises and contagion), and, most notably, the impact of market reforms. A priori, it is argued that the more rapid and more comprehensive the reforms, the fewer the number of years in decline and the quicker and greater the recovery. Here, there are issues over the endogeneity of reforms (i.e. reforms may not be exogenous but in fact determined by such factors as inherited conditions, political constraints or performance), the extent to which reforms can be measured accurately, and the nature of reforms (the distinction between macro reforms, structural reforms and institutional reforms). In sum, the evidence would appear to indicate that, as outlined in the early years of transition, market reforms matter, but so do the initial conditions (although their significance dissipates over time) and institutions also matter. Debate continues over a number of issues including which institutions are most important, the design of a package of practical and implementable institutional reforms, the timing of market reforms versus institutional reforms, best practice vs. transitional institutions, balance between winners and losers (from the reforms) and how best to deal with the political constraints.

For obvious geopolitical reasons, the economic record of Russia versus China has been analysed, with respect to the initial conditions, political changes and reform paths. In many respects, although the two leading socialist countries of the last century, Russia and China are very different. At the outset of transition (1978 in China; 1992 in Russia) initial conditions were different. China was a largely agrarian, rural, low-income country whereas Russia was an urban, (over)industrialised middle-income country. In terms of policy reforms, Russia (unsuccessfully) tried to follow the radical big bang approach. Market liberalisation and privatisation were fundamental to the Russian reforms. In China, government reforms (through decentralisation), agricultural reforms and SME development (vis-à-vis the township and village enterprises, TVEs), were more central. In terms of performance, there is a clear difference. China has managed to grow at an annual rate in excess of 8% over the past thirty years. Income per capita has increased and millions of its citizens have been taken out of poverty, although with alarming rates of inequality evident. Russia, in contrast, witnessed a dramatic decline in economic activity (of Great Depression proportions), a rise in poverty levels and widening inequalities in the first decade of transition. Its record in the 2000s was better, with increased output and consumption, improvements in poverty rates and, in general, a more stable society. Economists and other social scientists continue to probe the lessons that can be learnt from this two-country comparison. If we widen the coverage to include the other transition countries of Central and Eastern Europe and Asia, there are a number of general lessons that can be identified. This is the subject matter of the final section. Before this, we present a case study on Russia.[23]

CASE STUDY

Extract from *The Economist*
Putin's Choice
by Edward Lucas

Is Russia under President Putin heading for regeneration, stagnation or decay? Probably all three at once.

From the outside, it looks pretty good. For more than a decade, Russia has been, more or less, a democracy and a market economy, and on civilised terms with its neighbours. Against the dismal standards of Russian history, that is a big achievement. But so far the fruits have been meagre, bringing little comfort to most Russians. All they can see around them is physical, cultural and moral decay. The paradox is underpinned by three con-tradictory trends at work in today's Russia. The first is revival. This started under Mikhail Gorbachev, as the Communist monopoly of power and the planned economy collapsed together. That allowed the beginnings of independent life in many spheres. Freed from totalitarian controls, the energy and brains of millions have brought countless changes for the better. There are plenty of new businesses, and such old ones as have survived are better run than they used to be . . .

The second trend, though, is stagnation. The collapse of communism, it turns out, was superficial and partial. Well-connected people and organisations – especially the security services – started clawing back power straight away, and many became rich as well as powerful. Changes for the better are often stopped in their tracks by greedy bureaucrats, and by the peculiar difficulties and perversities of life in Russia. The state, at all levels, dislikes criticism and opposition. Many Russians, for their part, still hanker for the certainties, real or imagined, of the past: tradition, authority and unity, rather than experiment, competition and pluralism.

The third trend is accelerating decline. Nobody in Russia's political or economic elite has seriously tried to halt the downward slide that underlay the Soviet Union's defeat in the cold war. Most of what the Soviet Union built was shoddy to start with, but modern Russia lacks the money and willpower to sustain even that unimpressive standard. As a result, the country is falling apart. Things built during the Soviet era are crumbling, leaking, rusting and rotting. Spills, collapses, and fires that in other countries would cause a huge public outcry are shrugged off as everyday events.

The education system is being corroded by low salaries and corruption. Worst of all, Russians are simply dying out: smoke-ridden, drink-soused lifestyles, together with unchecked infectious diseases, have created a demographic abyss. According to one gloomy prediction, the population could fall from 145m now to 55m by 2075 . . .

On the economic front, the early 1990s brought hyperinflation and food panics. But there were also high hopes, fuelled by the thought of vast quantities of underused brainpower and raw materials that were now joining the world economy. Some talked of a coming boom that might take Russia's income per head above Spain by 2010. Such wishful thinking led to the financial bubble of 1997–98, when hot money from abroad piled into flimsy stocks and bonds, culminating in the default, devaluation and banking collapse

of August 1998. This was followed a year later by a big money-laundering scandal. Russia turned from darling to pariah . . .

If the present seems just about tolerable, there are big question marks about the future. Is the recent political and economic solidity just a temporary lull, after which Russia's unsolved problems will crowd forward again, bringing new disasters in their wake? Or will Russia muddle along like this for years – economically stagnant, politically not as democratic as many might wish, a pretty miserable place to live for most of its people, but at least a menace neither to itself nor its neighbours? Or might this new stability – just possibly – serve as the base for the profound changes needed if Russia is to become a full member of the developed and democratic world, as its size, its culture and its past achievements suggest it should?

Source: *The Economist*, 21 July 2001.

Questions

1. The article mentions that the early 1990s brought hyperinflation and food panics. What happened to Russian output and economic growth in the early 1990s? (See the section on 'Performance and outcomes in transition countries', above.) How can the hyperinflation and the transformational recession be explained?
2. Identify, from the article, the traditional factors that account for economic growth. How do these factors compare to the market reforms advocated during transition?
3. What economic factors might explain the 'demographic abyss' in Russia as highlighted by the rapid decline in population?

Answers on website

19.2.6 Lessons from transition

After two decades of economic transformation in transition countries, what lessons can be learnt from transition? What can the economics profession learn from the experience of transition countries? Can other countries undertaking similar changes in economic systems, rules and behaviour learn from the transition experience? Transition, however it is defined, is extraordinarily complex, involving wholesale systemic and large-scale institutional change. Economic transition, combined with the political and social transition of the 1990s, was unprecedented. One consequence of this systemic change is that the discipline of economics now has a greater understanding of capitalism and its institutional foundations, the interplay of politics and economics, and the importance (and unpredictability) of dynamic change. We now appreciate more the difficulties involved in creating a market economy (and all its institutional underpinnings) since that is what transition (to market, from plan) entailed.

In transition countries policy-makers were confronted with the dual problems of transition and development, of emerging markets and destatisation, of market reform and institutional reform, of structural adjustment and reconstruction, of political change and economic change, resulting in outcomes that included, for the majority of transition countries, a large fall in output, rapid inflation, social disruption, and, for many CIS countries, disturbing demographic trends. From an economic theory perspective, the lesson here is the inadequacy of any one school of economic thought (neoclassical or institutional) to fully explain transition or to adequately inform policymakers of the complexities of the transition process. Over two decades on, institutions are now considered mainstream, and institutional reform is considered as important (if not more important, according to its supporters) as the market reforms that were advocated by the IFIs, policymakers and the majority of influential Western academic economists at the outset of transition. This is a lesson that has relevance beyond transition and transition countries, to topics such as the determinants of economic growth, governance of developing and emerging markets, the role of IFIs and the suitability (and conditionality) of market reforms, etc.

If there was ever an event in the twentieth century that required a political economy perspective, it was the transition from socialism to capitalism and from plan to market. The interplay between politics and economics is crucial in helping to understand the policy reforms, performance and outcomes in transition countries. The experience of TEs clearly illustrates the importance of political constraints. Politics matters and the political economy of reform is central to an understanding of transition. In reforms, political considerations dominate as much as, if not more than, economic deliberations. More generally, the events and outcomes during transition simply reinforce the need for the economics profession today, as was the case in earlier times when the discipline was known as political economy, to emphasise and reiterate the link between economics and politics, as Adam Smith and Karl Marx did centuries ago.

In terms of market reforms, although a crucial element of transition, it is now clear from the transition experience, from what worked and what did not work, that there are no one-size-fits-all reforms. In general, policy reforms need to be tailored to the reforming country, with its history, culture and local conditions. That is not to say that there are no economic fundamentals (what one might call 'good economics') that can apply regardless of location, custom or tradition. The evidence from transition countries, and elsewhere, indicates that economic growth is associated with macro stability and a conducive business environment (where entry and competition is free and unrestricted), well-defined property rights and suitable enforcement mechanisms, openness to foreign trade and participation in world markets, and a sound, well-functioning banking and financial system. Transition countries that have failed to correct macro imbalances, to secure and enforce property rights, to reap the gains from international trade and to support and regulate the financial sector are preventing improvements in economic growth.

With respect to reform in general, speed may not be as important an issue as was originally argued (in the early 1990s), but the phasing or sequencing is probably of significant importance. Of course, some reforms, by their very nature, can and should be implemented early and rapidly. A good example is macroeconomic stabilisation. In contrast, other reforms require more time: these reforms can be staged, and done slowly. An example is enterprise restructuring and corporate governance changes. A corollary of this is the importance of phased or sequenced reforms. It is generally agreed that, at the outset of transition for those countries with a macro crisis or serious imbalance, macroeconomic stabilisation is a priority: it must be done quickly and is required in advance of other reforms. Liberalisation is also required at an early stage, although there is some debate over how quickly and comprehensive it need be and whether a single track (as was adopted in the CEE/FSU countries) or a dual track (as adopted in China and Vietnam) is preferable. Legal and regulatory reform is also required at an early stage, although it is likely that such reform will be continuous throughout transition. With other reforms, from ownership structure to infrastructural reforms, initial change may be minimal and will only accelerate as transition progresses, and beyond. Overall, with respect to transition and market reforms, the evidence from transition (and non-transition) countries is that there is no panacea – no single reform that will ensure a resumption of sustainable economic growth. Although reforms are complementary, it is not an exact science. It is difficult to predict the precise effect of one reform change relative to another policy change. Benefits from one reform may be contingent on implementation of other reforms.

Although market reforms have a significant role to play in increasing a country's level of economic activity and ultimately improving the standard of living for a country's citizens, it is evident from the transition experience, and elsewhere, that the institutional arrangements that support market transactions matter a great deal. Market reforms without institutional reform will not improve economic prosperity: given the circumstances of each country, market reforms in the absence of institution building may undermine future economic development. Again, depending on a country's historical, cultural and social circumstances, the evidence from some transition countries indicates that the transplantation of best practice institutions may be inferior to the adoption of transitional institutions. Rules of the game need to be credible and have the support of the electorate.

Another lesson from the transition experience is the role of the state in the modern capitalist system. It was inevitable that transition from a centrally planned to a market economy would involve a change in the role of the state. Many commentators argued in favour of a significant reduction in state involvement. Some even argued for the dismantling of the state. In cases where this occurred (deliberately or otherwise), state collapse and the problem of a weakened state emerged. No doubt, reform of government was necessary. A reconstituted state was required. However, as learnt from elsewhere (particularly in the post-World War II era and in the NICs of South East Asia), markets and governments complement each other. Lessons from individual countries, both positive and negative (whether decentralisation in China, enterprise restructuring in Poland or state collapse in Georgia and Russia) indicate the important role of the state (and government reforms) in the capitalist system. Despite the tendency during transition to dismantle the state, it became clear that, in many respects, a strong (though limited) state was required, albeit playing a much more different role than before.

With respect to the enterprise sector, two lessons are worth noting. One, when addressing the issue of enterprise performance and privatisation, the evidence from many transition countries indicates that although ownership is important (with new private firms outperforming all others), there are other important factors. Proper corporate governance mechanisms, the hardening of the budget constraint, enterprise restructuring and competition are also important determinants of enterprise performance. As for privatisation itself, and contrary to most expectations (where some claimed that any privatisation is better than none), privatisation outcomes were partly determined by the form of privatisation and whether the privatisation process favoured insiders or outsiders, and/or dispersed or concentrated ownership and/or domestic or foreign investors. A related issue is the role of the SME sector. Again, at the outset of transition, the importance of a (*de novo*) SME sector was outweighed by (claims of) the importance of closing down SOEs, enterprise restructuring, changes in ownership and privatisation. Evidence indicates that a vibrant and growing enterprise sector is more likely to come from new SMEs rather than the privatisation and break-up of existing SOEs. The public policy lesson is that attention to the business environment and, in particular, addressing barriers to entry, competition policy and supports to entrepreneurship and SME development is more likely to generate a dynamic business sector than policies solely designed to restructure and privatise SOEs. Unfortunately, it was the latter policy than dominated the enterprise reform agenda in CEE and FSU countries. Of course, the optimal policy reform at the enterprise level is a combination, depending on country circumstances, of both encouragement (of new firms) and discipline (of older enterprises).

The final lesson here is the importance and the general applicability (to non-transition countries) of a concept that was most prevalent in the socialist system. János Kornai's soft budget constraint refers to the persistent or recurring expectation of a bailout of loss-making enterprises. This incentive problem was inherent in the socialist system when the state would consistently bail out troubled firms. Given that a paternalistic state and public ownership of firms were viewed as reasons for the budget softness in the socialist system (and, thus, less common in the market system where the state is less paternalistic and public ownership is not as prevalent), the expectation was that privatisation, in conjunction with other reforms, including new bankruptcy laws, would harden the budget constraint. Unfortunately, during the early years of transition, the soft budget constraint persisted, often in new and different guises, including the unusual (in a market economy) phenomenon of tax and wage arrears. The lesson learnt from this costly experience is that political will and reductions in budgetary subsidies alone will not harden the budget constraint. It requires institutional changes in order for the commitment to a no-bailout policy to be credible. Moreover, the soft budget constraint has relevance much beyond transition and loss-making enterprises. Seemingly diverse economic issues such as state bailouts (and the debate on EU state aids to industry), fiscal federalism (intergovernmental fiscal relations and sub-national borrowing), devising bankruptcy laws and the design of fiscal discipline in monetary unions can be framed in the context of the soft budget constraint syndrome. The broad lesson here is that the general incentive problem first identified in the socialist system over three decades ago has relevance to various different economic relationships, whether they are between superiors and subordinates, funding organisations and recipients, or government and business (whatever the setting, transition or otherwise).

SUMMARY

1. The old traditional view of development focused primarily on economics and changes in economic growth. The new view of development is multi-dimensional, with improvements in economic growth and standard of living, poverty levels and inequalities, job creation and unemployment all viewed as necessary in order for development to occur.

2. Developing countries are characterised by low levels of living standards and high levels of poverty and income inequality, a dependency on primary exports, a high agricultural share of output and rapid population growth. Common obstacles to development include insufficient resource endowment and lack of capital accumulation, weak institutions, conflicts, corruption and poor governance.

3. Development policies include economic planning, import substitution, export promotion and structural adjustment. Despite these various strategies, serious development issues remain unresolved, including the benefits accruing from foreign aid, the usefulness of debt relief and the gains from free trade.

4. Transition is the social, political and economic transformation from a centrally planned system (characterised by state ownership, collective action and central planning) to a market

system (characterised by decentralised economic decision-making, voluntary exchange and private sector market transactions). In transition, initial conditions varied, as did reforms and economic performance.

5. The two paradigms of transition are the Washington Consensus approach and the institutional-evolutionary approach. Although the debate between shock therapy versus gradualism dominated the early years of transition, second-generation reforms proved more difficult. Transition required, at different stages, macro, structural and institutional reforms. The trinity of stabilisation, liberalisation and privatisation were necessary but not sufficient conditions to guarantee a return to growth and an improvement in living standards.

6. Regional patterns of performance and outcomes emerged during transition. The most successful were the Central European countries and the Baltic states, now members of the EU. Transition proved arduous for most of the republics of the former Soviet Union countries and the Balkans. The legacy of the Soviet system, the nature of reforms and political constraints, conflicts, corruption and poor governance contributed to the poor performance and, most notably, the severe economic recession of transition's first ten years. Outcomes were much better in the second decade, particularly for many CIS countries.

KEY TERMS

Development
Developing countries
Dependence
Linear stages of growth
Structural change
Structuralist school
Balanced growth
Unbalanced growth
Institutions
Corruption Perceptions Index
Import substitution
Export promotion
Washington Consensus
Structural adjustment programme
Planning
Foreign aid
Debt relief
Free trade

Transition
Transition economies
Socialist system
Extensive economic growth
Ratchet effect
Soft budget constraint
Institutional-evolutionary paradigm
Shock therapy
Gradualism
Liberalisation
Stabilisation
Privatisation
Enterprise restructuring
Corporate governance
Liberalisation index
Transition indicators
Transformational recession
Disorganisation

REVIEW QUESTIONS

1. What characterises developing countries as distinct from developed countries?
2. Outline the range of policies required for a successful transition from plan to market.
3. What are the lessons from the policy reforms adopted in the developing and transition countries?

CASE STUDY

Extract from the *Financial Times*
Continent still a cause for concern
by David White

This year has been billed by development organisations as the Year of Africa but, even before it started, the Asian tsunami monopolised the world's attention. None the less, sufficient impetus has built up to ensure Africa's problems remain near the top of the international agenda.

In September, a United Nations summit will assess progress on the Millennium Development Goals set in 2000. Africa is the one region falling seriously behind. At the Group of Eight leading industrialised countries of which the UK is currently chairman, Gordon Brown, UK chancellor, dubbed this a 'once in a generation opportunity' to forge coherent policies on a new deal for the continent. He has proposed doubling the rate at which aid flows into developing countries by using financial markets.

The UN's Africa regional arm reckons there is a $20bn–$25bn shortfall in the amount needed to achieve high enough growth in the next 10 years to meet the first of the UN targets: halving the number living in absolute poverty compared with 1990. The shortfall is equivalent to the current total of foreign aid to the continent.

For the HIV/Aids epidemic alone – affecting an estimated 25m people in Africa, 60 per cent of the world's total, and fuelling poverty in many countries – Stephen Lewis, special UN envoy, has pointed to a gap of several billion dollars a year. While a broad consensus exists on the main elements of a more favourable deal for Africa – summarised by Hilary Benn, UK international development secretary, as 'more aid and better

aid, less debt and more trade' – the difficulty has been creating the momentum to back these policies.

Attempts to recast the rich world's relationship with Africa and tackle the nexus of poverty, disease, conflict and corruption coincide with new dynamics within the continent – the bold ambitions of the reformed African Union, the higher profile of regional organisations and the spreading influence of South Africa, by far the continent's richest and most advanced country. Strategies to promote better governance range from the explicit leverage the US is seeking in its selective aid programme to the lead-by-example approach of the Partnership for Africa's Development, which has a scheme for voluntary reviews.

Linah Mohohlo, governor of Botswana's central bank, told a London conference last month that the international community could not be blamed for all Africa's failures. She said: 'The problems of Africa are mainly problems that Africans themselves have created.'

Economic performance has improved, but still lags behind the rest of the developing world. According to World Bank estimates, sub-Saharan Africa grew last year by 3 per cent, much faster than in the 1990s but slower than almost anywhere else. Per capita income rose by little more than 1 per cent.

South Africa's growth has been dampened by the rand since 2002, while many less developed countries remain dependent on a few commodities with volatile prices. Africa's share of world exports is well below that of the 1980s. This month's report by the UN's

Millennium Development Project concluded that sub-Saharan Africa was not on course to meet any of the goals set in 2000, covering poverty, health, education, and environmental standards. On present trends, the number of Africans in absolute poverty would rise from 345m today to 432m in 2015.

Source: Financial Times, 26 January 2005

Questions

1. Identify the obstacles to economic growth and development that are mentioned in the article.
2. What are the most serious economic implications of the HIV/Aids epidemic?
3. What are the Millennium Development Goals? Is the 3% growth rate for sub-Saharan Africa sufficient to achieve these goals? Explain your answer.

[Useful sources include the UN www.un.org and World Bank www.worldbank.org websites]

Sources and Readings for Students of Economics

Putting together a list of sources for students of economics is not a straightforward task as there is an enormous amount of material available both in hard copy format and online. The following is a list of sources that the authors of this textbook are familiar with, believe are relevant and strongly feel students of economics should be aware of, read, engage with and use. We have limited the list to a few pages (with separate limits for each category). The list of entries is in alphabetical order with the exception of the classics, which are listed in chronological order.

BOOKS/PAPERS

Principles of economics

Begg, David, Rudiger Dornbusch and Stanley Fischer *Economics*, McGraw Hill
Case, Karl E. and Ray C. Fair *Principles of Economics*, Pearson
Frank, Robert, Ben Bernanke, Rodney Thom and Moore McDowell *Principles of Economics*, McGraw Hill
Lipsey, Richard and Alec Chrystal *Economics*, Oxford University Press
Mankiw, Gregory N. and Mark P. Taylor *Economics*, Cengage
McAleese, Dermot *Economics for Business: Competition, Macro-stability and Globalisation*, FT Prentice Hall
McConnell, Campbell and Stanley Brue, *Economics*, McGraw Hill
Parkin, Michael, Melanie Powell and Kent Matthews *Economics*, Addison Wesley
Samuelson, Paul and William D. Nordhaus *Economics*, McGraw Hill
Sloman, John *Economics*, Pearson

General

Bagwati, Jagdish N. *In Defence of Globalisation*, Oxford University Press
Galbraith, John Kenneth *The Affluent Society*, Mariner Books
Harford, Tim *The Undercover Economist*, Random House
Kay, John *The Truth about Markets: Why Some Countries are Rich and Others Remain Poor*, Penguin
Krugman, Paul *The Return of Depression Economics*, W.W. Norton & Company
Landsburg Steven E. *The Armchair Economist: Economics and Everyday Life*, Pocket Books
Levitt, Steven D. and Stephen J. Dubner *Freakonomics; A Rogue Economist Explores the Hidden Side of Everything*, Penguin
O'Rourke, P.J. *Eat the Rich; A Treatise on Economics*, Atlantic Monthly Press
Sachs, Jeffrey *The End of Poverty: Economic Possibilities for our Time*, Penguin
Stiglitz, Joseph *Making Globalisation Work*, W.W. Norton & Company
Wiseman, Richard *Quirkology: How We Discover the Big Truth in Small Things*, Basic Books

Classics

Smith, Adam *An Inquiry into the Nature and Causes of the Wealth of Nations*, W. Strahan and T. Cadell, 1776

Ricardo, David *On the Principles of Political Economy and Taxation*, John Murray, 1821

Marx, Karl *Das Kapital*, Dent, 1867

Marshall, Alfred *Principles of Economics*, Macmillan, 1890

Keynes, John Maynard *The General Theory of Employment, Interest and Money*, Macmillan, 1936

Schumpeter, Joseph A. *Capitalism, Socialism and Democracy*, Allen and Unwin, 1942

Polanyi, Karl *The Great Transformation*, Farrar & Reinhart, 1944

Von Hayek, Frederick *The Road to Serfdom*, Routledge, 1944

Samuelson, Paul *Foundations of Economic Analysis*, Harvard University Press, 1947

Friedman, Milton *Capitalism and Freedom*, University of Chicago Press, 1962

Ireland and the Irish economy

Honohan Report, *The Irish Banking Crisis: Regulatory and Financial Stability Policy 2003–2008: A Report to the Minister for Finance by the Governor of the Central Bank*, 31 May 2010

Kennedy, Kieran, Thomas Giblin and Deirdre McHugh *The Economic Development of Ireland in the Twentieth Century*, Routledge

Ó Gráda, Cormac *The Rocky Road: The Irish Economy since the 1920s*, Manchester University Press

O' Hagan, John W. and Carol Newman (eds) *The Economy of Ireland: National and Sectoral Policy Issues*, Gill & Macmillan

O' Sullivan, Michael and Rory Miller (eds) *What Did We Do Right? Global Perspectives on Ireland's Miracle*, Blackhall Publishing

Walsh, Brendan and Anthony Leddin *The Macroeconomy of the Eurozone: an Irish Perspective*, Gill & Macmillan

The 2008/09 Great Recession and financial crisis

Global

Bootle, Roger *The Trouble with Markets: Saving Capitalism from Itself*, Nicholas Brealey Publishing

Cassidy, John *How Markets Fail: The Logic of Economic Calamities*, Farrar, Straus and Giroux

Davies, Howard *The Financial Crisis: Who is to Blame?*, Polity

Johnson, Simon and James Kwak *13 Bankers: The Wall Street Takeover and the Next Financial Meltdown*, Pantheon

Pozen, Robert *Too Big to Save? How to Fix the US Financial System*, Wiley

Rajan, Raghuram G. *Fault Lines: How Hidden Fractures Still Threaten the World Economy*, Princeton University Press

Reinhart, Carmen M. and Kenneth S. Rogoff *This Time is Different: Eight Centuries of Financial Folly*, Princeton University Press

Roubini, Nouriel and Stephen Mihm *Crisis Economics: A Crash Course in the Future of Finance*, Penguin

Stiglitz, Joseph *Freefall: Free Markets and the Sinking of the Global Economy*, Penguin

Tett, Gillian *Fool's Gold: How Unrestrained Greed Corrupted a Dream, Shattered Global Markets and Unleashed a Catastrophe*, Little, Brown

Eurozone

Baldwin, Richard and Daniel Gros *Completing the Eurozone Rescue: What More Needs to be Done?*
    Ebook, voxEU.org
Buti, Macro, Servaas Deroose, Vitor Gaspar and João Nogueira Martins (eds) *The Euro: The First*
    Decade, Cambridge University Press
De Grauwe, Paul *Fighting the Wrong Enemy* voxEU.org
Eichengreen, Barry 'The Breakup of the Euro Area' NBER Paper No. 13393.
Wyplosz, Charles 'High Deficits and Debts: What to do about them?' European Parliament:
    Economic and Monetary Affairs

Ireland

Cooper, Matt *Who Really Runs Ireland? The Story of the Elite that Led Ireland from Bust to Boom*
    . . . and Back Again, Penguin
Kinsella, Stephen and Anthony Leddin (eds) *Understanding Ireland's Economic Crisis: Prospects*
    for Recovery, Blackhall Publishing
Mulholland, Joe and Finbarr Bradley (eds) *Ireland's Economic Crisis: Time to Act*, Carysfort Press
Murphy, David and Martina Devlin *Banksters: How a Powerful Elite Squandered Ireland's Wealth*,
    Hodder Headline
Power, Jim *Picking Up the Pieces: Economic Crisis and Hope in Ireland*, Blackhall Publishing

JOURNALS

Economic Policy
Economic and Social Review
The Economists' Voice
Journal of Economic Literature
Journal of Economic Perspectives

WEBSITES

Econlinks – http://econlinks.com
Economic and Social Research Institute – www.esri.ie
The Economist – www.economist.com
History of Economic Thought (hosted by the Department of Economics at the New School for
    Social Research, New York) – www.cepa.newschool.edu/het
Intute: Economics – www.intute.ac.uk/economics
Irish Economy Blog – www.theirisheconomy.ie
National Economic and Social Council – www.nesc.ie
Resources for Economists on the Internet – www.rfe.org
New Palgrave Dictionary of Economics Online – www.dictionaryofeconomics.com
Vox (website established by the Centre for Economic Policy Research (CEPR), London) –
    www.voxEU.org

ONLINE DATA AND STATISTICAL SOURCES

Bank for International Settlements – www.bis.org
Central Bank of Ireland – www.centralbank.ie
Central Statistics Office – www.cso.ie
Department of Finance – www.finance.gov.ie
European Bank for Reconstruction and Development – www.ebrd.org
European Central Bank – www.ecb.int
European Union statistics – http://ec.europa.eu/eurostat
International Labour Organisation – www.ilo.org
International Monetary Fund – www.imf.org
Organisation for Economic Co-operation and Development – www.oecd.org
Penn World Tables – http://pwt.econ.upenn.edu
United Nations Economic Commission for Europe – www.unece.org
United Nations Statistics Division – www.unstats.un.org
World Bank Development Indicators – data.worldbank.org
World Trade Organisation – www.wto.org

Endnotes

CHAPTER 1

1 Barbara Wootton, *Lament for Economics*, Allen, 1938.
2 George Bernard Shaw, attributed.
3 Milton Friedman, quoted in interview in William Breit and Roger W. Spencer (eds), *Lives of the Laureates*, MIT Press, 1986.
4 Milton Friedman, *Capitalism and Freedom*, University of Chicago Press, 1982.
5 Ibid. He states, 'Every extension of the range of issues for which explicit agreement is sought further strains the delicate threads that hold society together . . . The wider the range of activities covered by the market, the fewer the issues on which explicit political decisions are required and hence on which it is necessary to achieve agreement.'
6 Ibid.
7 This discussion is based on the work of Ingrid Rima, *Development of Economic Analysis*, 4th edition Irwin Press, 1986.
8 Thorstein Veblen, *The Theory of the Leisure Class*, New American Library, a division of Penguin Books, 1953 (originally published by Macmillan, 1899).
9 Ibid.
10 Rima, *op.cit.*
11 To find out more about Marx and Engels, read Robert C. Tucker, editor, *The Marx–Engels Reader*, 2nd edition, W. W. Norton & Company, 1978. For a contemporary treatment of Marxian economics, read E. K. Hunt and Howard J. Sherman, *Economics: An Introduction to Traditional and Radical Views*, 6th edition, HarperCollins Publishers, 1990.
12 Pope Leo XIII, 15 May 1891, *On the Conditions of Workers Rerum Novarum*, Office of Publishing and Promotion Services, United States Catholic Conference. For a more current discussion of the Catholic Church's view of the labour market see Pope John Paul II, 1 May 1991, *On the Hundredth Anniversary of Rerum Novarum Centesimus Annus*, Office of Publishing and Promotion Services, United States Catholic Conference.
13 R. D. Dickenson, *A Dictionary of Philosophy*, Ballantyne Press, 1887.
14 Paul W. Humphreys, 'Induction' in *The New Palgrave: A Dictionary of Economics*, edited by J. Eatwell, M. Milgate, P. Newman, 3, Macmillan, 1987.
15 Rima, *op.cit.*

CHAPTER 2

1 George Bernard Shaw, 'Socialism and Superior Brains', *The Fortnightly Review*, April 1894.
2 Alfred Marshall, *Principles of Economics*, 8th edition, Macmillan, 1920.
3 It is possible that Giffen did not make this observation. It was Alfred Marshall who attributed it to Giffen. See Marshall, *Principles of Economics*.
4 J. FitzGerald and D. O'Connor, 'Economic Consequences of CAP Reform' in J. Bradley, J. FitzGerald and D. McCoy, *Medium-Term Review: 1991–96*, ESRI, 1991.

CHAPTER 3

1 Denis Healey was the UK Chancellor of the Exchequer from 1974 to 1979.
2 W. Stanley Jevons, *The Theory of Political Economy*, 5th edition, A. M. Kelley, 1957.

CHAPTER 4

1 See Bonar's Preface to *Letters of Ricardo to Malthus*, Clarendon Press, 1887.
2 Jevons, *The Theory of Political Economy*.
3 He went on to say 'Nothing is more useful than water: but it will purchase scarce any thing; . . . A diamond, on the contrary, has scarce any value in use; but a very great quantity of other goods may frequently be had in exchange for it.' Adam Smith, *An Inquiry into the Nature and Causes of The Wealth of Nations*, edited by Edwin Cannon, reprinted, Methuen and Co. Ltd, 1961. (Originally printed in 1776.)
4 Researchers now believe that Giffen never made this claim. It appears that Paul Samuelson was responsible for accrediting Giffen with this observation. In addition, there is no evidence to suggest that the consumption of potatoes increased during the famine years. Indeed, with the potato blight damaging the crop, it is hard to imagine how the consumption of potatoes could have increased. This adds credence to the argument made in Chapter 2 that a Giffen good, although theoretically possible, is seldom observed in reality.
5 Marshall, *Principles of Economics*.

CHAPTER 5

1 Augustin Cournot, *Researches into the Mathematical Principles of the Theory of Wealth*, trans. Nathan T. Bacon, Macmillan, 1897. (Originally published in 1838.)
2 Joan Robinson, 'What is Perfect Competition?', *Quarterly Journal of Economics*, November 1934.
3 Smith, *An Enquiry into the Nature and Causes of the Wealth of Nations*.
4 John Stuart Mill, *Principles of Political Economy*, edited by Sir W. J. Ashley, A. M. Kelley, 1961. (Originally published in 1848.)
5 The economist who first developed the envelope curve was Jacob Viner in 1931. In the drafting of the envelope curve he and his draftsman, a mathematician at the University of Chicago, made what has become a famous error. He drew the LAC curve from the minimum points of the SATC curves. He acknowledged his mistake in a supplementary note written in 1950, in which he wrote 'future teachers and students may share the pleasure of many of their predecessors of pointing out that if I had known what an "envelope" was, I would not have given my excellent draftsman the technically impossible and economically inappropriate assignment of drawing an AC curve which would pass through the lowest cost points of all the ac curves and yet not rise above any ac curve at any point.' However, this error does not, in any way, take from Viner's contribution to the theory of costs. The name of the article, regarded as a classic, is 'Cost Curves and Supply Curves', *Zeitschrift für Nationalökonomie*, 3, 1931. Finally, it should be noted that the explanation of the envelope curve which is to be found in the text is rather brief. A fuller explanation is left to authors of intermediate textbooks.
6 The average revenue received is simply the price of the product. This can be confirmed as follows:
$$TR = P \times Q$$
Divide both sides by Q:
$$\frac{TR}{Q} = \frac{P.Q}{Q}$$
The left-hand side is equal to AR. The right-hand side simplifies to P with the cancellation of Q above and below the line. Thus AR = P.

CHAPTER 6

1 Joan Robinson, 'What is Perfect Competition?' *Quarterly Journal of Economics*, Vol. 49, No. 1, November 1934.
2 Smith, *An Enquiry into the Nature and Causes of the Wealth of Nations*.
3 We noted in Chapter 3 that the elasticity of demand for a product is determined by the number of available substitutes. The greater the number of readily available and close substitutes, the more elastic

is demand. Under conditions of perfect competition, there are many close substitutes for the firm's product. The result is an elastic demand curve. It is important to recognise that this feature does not apply to the market demand curve. The market as an entity can only sell a greater amount of products if it lowers its price. There still exists a negatively sloped market demand curve.

4 Edward Chamberlin, *The Theory of Monopolistic Competition*, 1933; Joan Robinson, *The Economics of Imperfect Competition*, 1933; Piero Sraffa, *The Law of Return under Competitive Conditions*, 1926.

5 See P. M. Sweezy, 'Demand under Conditions of Oligopoly,' *Journal of Political Economy*, 47, August 1939 and R. L. Hall and C. J. Hitch, 'Price Theory and Business Behaviour', *Oxford Economic Papers*, No. 2, May 1939. Sweezy was interested in the downward stickiness of prices which was evident during the Great Depression.

6 J. von Neumann and O. Morgenstern, *The Theory of Games and Economic Behaviour*, Princeton University Press, 1944.

CHAPTER 7

1 Karl Marx, 'First Manuscript' in *Early Writings, (of) Karl Marx*, trans. Rodney Livingstone and Gregor Bentan, introduced by Lucio Colletti, Penguin, 1975.

2 Frederick B. Hawley, *Enterprise and the Productive Process*, G. P. Putnam and Sons, 1907.

3 The American economist J. Bates Clark is credited with writing the most comprehensive book on marginal productivity theory. The book entitled *The Distribution of Wealth: A Theory of Wages, Interest and Profits* (1899) became the basis for the theory of income distribution. The idea for the book came from issues raised by his fellow American Henry George (see endnote 10). The marginal productivity theory has a number of shortcomings. First, it is extremely difficult to calculate the marginal productivity of labour. Second, it assumes that all other factor inputs are constant. This is unlikely in reality. Third, it fails to account for wage differentials. Fourth, it ignores imperfections in the market. Fifth, it is difficult to separate out the marginal products of the various factor inputs. Notwithstanding these limitations, the marginal productivity theory makes a significant contribution to factor markets and the theory of income distribution.

4 For arguments by economists who favour the imposition of the minimum wage, see David Card and Alan B. Kruger, *Myth and Measurement: The New Economics of the Minimum Wage*, Princeton University Press, 1995.

5 Inter-Departmental Group on Implementation of a National Minimum Wage, *Interim Report of the Inter-Departmental Group on Implementation of a National Minimum Wage*, October 1998, Stationery Office.

6 Barry O'Keefe, 'Minimum wage would hurt business, says SFA survey', *The Irish Times*, December 1997.

7 Rent was defined by Ricardo as '. . . that portion of the produce of the earth which is paid to the landlord for the use of the original and indestructible powers of the soil'. See Ricardo, *The Principles of Political Economy and Taxation*.

8 Economic rent is to factor markets what consumer surplus is to product markets. In Chapter 4 we defined consumer surplus as the difference between the price the consumer pays for the product and the maximum price s/he is willing to pay for the product. Economic rent can be defined in the same terms: it is the difference between the actual factor price that the owner receives and the minimum factor price at which the owner is willing to supply the factor input.

9 In reality, the supply of land is not necessarily fixed and there are alternative uses. Apart from the rezoning of land, irrigation, other forms of reclamation and fertilisers allow for the existing parcels of land to be extended or improved. For the sake of simplicity, however, we assume a fixed supply of land with no alternative uses.

10 As land is in fixed supply and has zero supply cost, all its earnings are economic rent. Any change in demand, small or large, will have no effect on the supply. It is unearned income and it is for this reason that a tax on land is often proposed. Rent could be subject to tax in the knowledge that the supply of land will remain unchanged. Those who argue against a land tax maintain that with all the alternative uses, land is not fixed in reality. In addition, they argue that there are many other factors which earn economic rent and are viable sources of tax, e.g. income tax levied on the salaries of movie actors or

professional sports stars. For a definitive analysis on the reasons why landowners should be subject to tax, read Henry George's (of the single tax movement) classic *Progress and Poverty* (1879).

11   Classical economic theory divided factor income into three rather than four categories – wages (the return on labour), rents (the return on land) and profits (the return on capital). For classical economists, profit and interest were indistinguishable. This reflected the structure of the corporate sector in the nineteenth century when the role of the capitalist and the entrepreneur were combined.

12   F. Knight, *Risk, Uncertainty and Profit*, Houghton Mifflin Co., 1921.

13   David Ricardo, *The Principles of Political Economy and Taxation*.

CHAPTER 8

1   Adam Smith, *An Inquiry into the Nature and Causes of the Wealth of Nations*.

2   Arthur Okun, *Equality and Efficiency: The Big Trade-Off*, Brookings Institution, 1975.

3   Adam Smith, *op. cit.*

4   For the original case study, see J. E. Meade, 'External Economies and Diseconomies in a Competitive Situation', *Economic Journal*, Vol. 62, 245, 1952.

5   See G. Akerlof, 'The Market for Lemons: Quality Uncertainty and the Market Mechanism', *Quarterly Journal of Economics*, Vol. 84, 1970. George Akerlof, along with Michael Spence and Joseph Stiglitz, were awarded the 2001 Nobel Prize in Economics for their work in the economics of asymmetric information.

6   The Rawlsian social welfare function is associated with the work of the moral philosopher John Rawls. For example, see *A Theory of Justice*, Belknap Press of Harvard University Press, 1971.

7   See R. Coase, 'The Problem of Social Costs', *Journal of Law and Economics*, Vol. 3, Oct. 1960.

8   See, for example, C. Pitelis, 'Market Failure and the Existence of the State: a Restatement and Critique', *International Review of Applied Economics*, Vol. 5, No. 3, 1991.

9   Arthur Okun, *op. cit.*

10   See J. Farrell, 'Information and the Coase Theorem', *Journal of Economic Perspectives*, Vol. 1, No. 2, Fall 1987.

CHAPTER 9

1   The individual profit-maximising firm, whether in perfect competition or monopoly, produces a level of output at which marginal revenue is equal to marginal cost, i.e. MR = MC. From the individual firm's perspective in perfect competition, however, marginal revenue is equal to price, i.e. MR = P. Therefore, in perfect competition, the individual firm produces a level of output at which price is equal to marginal cost, i.e. P = MC.

2   However, a high own-price elasticity of demand (in absolute terms) does not necessarily imply the absence of substantial market power. Such a result would show that the firm is not able to profitably increase price beyond the present price – it does not, in itself, show that the firm has not, in the past, increased price substantially above the cost of production.

3   Profits would decrease if the price increase resulted in a large fall in volume demanded. The reduction in demand caused by these increased prices comes from two sources – demand substitution by consumers and supply substitution by new competitors. Demand substitution represents the reduction in consumer demand caused by the increased prices and supply substitution by new competitors represents the response of new competitors in terms of producing new (relatively close substitute) products in response to the increased prices.

4   G. Stigler, *The Organisation of Industry*, Irwin, 1968.

5   J. Bain, *Barriers to New Competition*, Harvard University Press, 1956.

6   The breadth (or scope) of a natural monopoly may be determined by the existence of, and degree of, so-called economies of scope. Technically, economies of scope arise if $C(Q_A, Q_B) < C(Q_A,0) + C(0,Q_B)$, where A and B represent different products. Economies of scope arise where it is cheaper for one firm to produce two different products than it is for two firms to each produce one of the two products; wool and mutton offers an obvious example. The provision of a national electricity grid

and the provision of a national natural gas grid represent a possible example in the context of natural monopolies.

7 The term 'X-inefficiency' is used to denote a situation in which the costs of a monopolist are higher than the costs of a perfectly competitive firm.

8 *Why do some Countries Innovate more than Others?*, CEPS Paper No. 5, Centre for European Policy Studies, 1984.

9 Ibid.

10 Ibid.

CHAPTER 10

1 Simon Kuznets, *Economic Growth and Structure: Selected Essays*, Heinemann, 1966.

2 Paul Ormerod, *The Death of Economics*, Faber and Faber, 1995.

3 Quesnay was one of the leading physiocrats (see Chapter 11 for an explanation of the physiocrats) of the eighteenth century. His main work *Tableau Économique (Economic Table)* was published in 1758. This table analysed the circulation of wealth in the economy and it is believed that it was one of the first models to describe the macroeconomy in a circular flow fashion.

4 Kuznets' contribution to macroeconomics was recognised by the profession in 1971 when he was awarded the Nobel Prize in economics for his work on accounting and measurement techniques. At the same time, work was being carried out in the UK on the construction of the national accounts by Richard Stone and James Meade. In recognition of his work Stone received the 1984 Nobel Prize in economics.

5 Irish GDP is artificially inflated because of 'transfer pricing'. Transfer pricing refers to a practice of transferring tax liabilities abroad. This is where multinational corporations use their foreign subsidiaries that operate in a low tax jurisdiction (e.g. Ireland) to reduce their overall tax burden. Partially manufactured inputs, manufactured by a subsidiary in another country, are imported into Ireland. Some processing occurs in this country and the intermediate or final good is exported. The 'value added' by the manufacturing process which takes place in Ireland is inflated to take advantage of the low Irish corporate tax rate. In doing so, the multinationals minimise their tax bill. The Irish measure of GDP is overvalued as a result of this practice.

6 E. Friedman, S. Johnson, D. Kaufmann, P. Zoido-Lobaton, *Dodging the Grabbing Hand; The Determinants of Unofficial Activity in 69 Countries*, 2000. A more recent publication by Schneider (2006), using a multi-causal approach, returned a higher estimate for Ireland.

7 In more recent times, national statistics offices have tried to incorporate an evasion adjustment into their calculation of GDP in order to capture activity in the hidden economy.

8 Economists and sociologists have attempted to develop satisfactory measures of economic and social well-being. A review of the international research is included in S. Scott, B. Nolan and T. Fahey, *Formulating Environmental and Social Indicators for Sustainable Development*, Economic and Social Research Institute, 1996.

9 T. Callan, R. Layte, B. Nolan, D. Watson, C. T. Whelan, J. Williams and B. Maître, *Monitoring Poverty Trends*, June 1999; H. Russell, B Maître and B. Nolan, *Montoring Poverty Trends in Ireland 2004–2007*, September 2010, ESRI, Dublin.

10 A. B. Atkinson, L. Rainwater, and T. M. Smeeding, *Income Distribution in OECD Countries: Evidence from the Luxembourg Income Study*, OECD, 1995; V. J. Verma, *Robustness and Comparability in Income Distribution Statistics*, Stockholm, 1998.

11 Brian Nolan and Bertrand Maître, 'Economic Growth and Income Inequality: Setting the Context', in T. Fahey, H. Russell and C. T. Whelan (eds), *Best of Times? The Social Impact of the Celtic Tiger*, IPA, 2007.

12 World Bank, *World Development Report*, 2010.

13 James Tobin was a member of President Kennedy's Council of Economic Advisers and a winner of the Nobel Prize in Economics in 1981. William Nordhaus served as a member of President Carter's Council of Economic Advisers from 1977 to 1979.

CHAPTER 11

1   J. R. Hicks, 'Mr. Keynes and the "Classics"; A Suggested Interpretation', *Econometrica*, 5, April 1937.

2   Quoted by Benjamin Higgins, *What do Economists Know?*, Melbourne University Press, 1951.

3   It is generally believed that Keynes got his inspiration for the title of *The General Theory* from Einstein's general theory of relativity. The classical doctrine was a special case in economics that held under specific conditions with Keynes' analysis being described as the general case just as Sir Isaac Newton's (also a Professor at Cambridge University) classical Newtonian mechanics was a special case of Einstein's General Theory. This general/special case relationship and his criticism of the special case are evident from the opening words of *The General Theory*: 'I shall argue that the postulates of the classical theory are applicable to a special case only and not to the general case, the situation which it assumes being a limited point of the possible positions of equilibrium. Moreover, the characteristics of the special case assumed by the classical theory happen not to be those of the economic society in which we actually live, with the result that its teaching is misleading and disastrous if we attempt to apply it to the facts of experience.' *The General Theory of Employment, Interest and Money*, Macmillan, 1936.

4   Quoted in R. F. Harrod, *The Life of John Maynard Keynes*, Macmillan, 1951.

5   J. M. Keynes, *The General Theory of Employment, Interest and Money*.

6   Letter to George Bernard Shaw, 1 January 1935.

7   The 1944 UK White Paper on *Employment Policy* was also heavily influenced by the Beveridge Report of 1942. The welfare state as we know it today has its origins in the writings of Lord Beveridge.

8   A similar crash occurred on Monday, 19 October 1987 when the Dow Jones Industrial average on Wall Street fell 508 points and in the process wiped over 22% off share values. This collapse on Black Monday was almost double the drop on the worst day of the 1929 crash. In London £50 billion, or 10%, was wiped off the value of publicly quoted companies. The major difference between the 1929 crash and the 1987 crash was not the extent of the collapse on any one day but the economic decline that followed. The first crash was followed by the Great Depression whereas a similar downturn in economic activity was avoided after the second crash of 1987. This was due to the deliberate actions taken by the authorities after October 1987.

9   'The Past', *Business Week*, 3, September 1979.

10   The actual responses from the US and the UK administrations varied. In Washington President Hoover requested extra funds from Congress for a federal programme to create jobs. Yet in the depths of the depression, he also increased taxes, justifying it by the need to balance the federal budget. In fact, Hoover was criticised by his opponent, Franklin Roosevelt, in the election of 1932 for not cutting government expenditure and for failing to balance the budget (Roosevelt himself was to oversee some 'Keynesian-style' policies in the second period of the New Deal). In London the Labour government announced a public works programme. Opposition parties were critical of the government's response and called for urgent action on the jobs front. In particular the Liberals, led by Lloyd George, proposed an increase in the amount of public works programmes. He was advised by a young radical economist by the name of John Maynard Keynes. The advice given was based on the model of income determination (see Section 12.1).

11   J. M. Keynes, *The General Theory of Employment, Interest and Money*.

12   Ibid.

13   J. M. Keynes, *A Tract on Monetary Reform*, Macmillan, 1923.

CHAPTER 12

1   L. Tarshis, 'Keynesian Revolution' in *The New Palgrave: A Dictionary of Economics* edited by J. Eatwell, M. Milgate, P. Newman, 3, Macmillan, 1987.

2   J. M.Keynes, 'National Self-Sufficiency', *Studies*, 22, 1933.

3   J. M. Keynes, *The General Theory of Employment, Interest and Money*.

4   The terms 'aggregate demand' and 'total expenditure' are also used to describe the aggregate expenditure function. We use aggregate expenditure rather than aggregate demand in order to avoid confusion with the aggregate demand curve which is derived and explained in Chapter 16.

5   In order to keep our model simple we assume that taxes are zero ($T = 0$). A more complex analysis would incorporate taxes as autonomous ($T = \bar{T}$) or as a function of income ($T = tY$). Normally government spending is financed from taxes. In our simplified model, government spending is financed from other sources (e.g. foreign aid). This is only for illustrative purposes.

6   J. M. Keynes, *The General Theory of Employment, Interest and Money.*

7   The equation

$$€1,000 + €750 + €562.50 + €421.875 + €316.40625 + \ldots$$

can be written as

$$€1,000 + (€1,000 \times .75) + (€1,000 \times <.75^2>) + (€1,000 \times <.75^3>) + (€1,000 \times <.75^4>) + \ldots$$
$$= €1,000 \,(1 + <.75> + <.75^2> + <.75^3> + <.75^4> + \ldots)$$

8   Infinite geometric progressions can be summed if the absolute value of the multiplying coefficient is less than 1. In this case the sum of the infinite series $1 + b + b^2 + b^3 + b^4 \ldots$ is equal to $\frac{1}{1-b}$. From our description of the MPC we know it to be less than 1.

Our series can be summed and in this particular case it adds to 4. Appendix 12.3 contains the formal derivation of the Keynesian multiplier.

9   The new equilibrium level of income can be calculated by using the formula as derived in the text. In this case:

$$\bar{A} = \bar{C} + \bar{I} + \bar{G} = 50 + 100 + 90 = €240$$
$$b = .75$$

Thus,

$$Y = \bar{A} \times \frac{1}{1-b} = 240 \times \frac{1}{1-.75} = 240 \times 4 = €960.$$

10   This contrasts sharply with those economists who argue that inappropriate monetary policy by the Fed was the significant factor in explaining the Great Depression of the 1930s. A good account of this view is given by Milton and Rose Friedman in *Free to Choose*, Penguin, 1980.

11   If consumer expenditure is determined by disposable income (gross income minus taxation), the multiplier is equal to $\dfrac{1}{MPS + MPM + bMPT}$.

12   These values are taken from Walsh and Leddin's *The Macroeconomy of the Eurozone: An Irish Perspective*. Norton's estimates are slightly different. For more, read B. Walsh and A. Leddin, *The Macroeconomy of the Eurozone: An Irish Perspective*, Gill & Macmillan, 2003; and D. Norton, *Economics for an Open Economy: Ireland*, Oak Tree Press in association with Graduate School of Business UCD, 1994.

13   The relatively small size of the Keynesian multiplier for small open economies was noted as far back as 1956 by T. K. Whitaker when he wrote 'In the real world, however, there are few, if any, completely isolated economies and the effects of the creation of new incomes are, therefore, not wholly retained within the system', 'Capital Formation, Saving and Economic Progress', reprinted in *Interests*, Institute of Public Administration, 1983. O. Katsiaouni came to the same conclusion in his paper 'Planning in a Small Economy: The Republic of Ireland' read to the Statistical and Social Inquiry Society of Ireland in May 1978. He explicitly referred to the Irish situation when he wrote 'demand management, thus is rendered ineffectual . . .' Des Norton emphasises the point in his open economy textbook *Economics for an Open Economy: Ireland*. He writes 'The tax leakage aside, Ireland's high marginal propensity to import explains why national income multipliers for the small open economy of Ireland are quite low.' Finally, on account of a high MPM, a domestic fiscal boost may only succeed in aggravating the trade balance between Ireland and the rest of the world (see Chapter 15).

14   Budgets are to be distinguished from plans or programmes. In Ireland the relationship between the annual budget and government plans has been, at times, rather loose and ambiguous.

15   The first capital budget was introduced by Patrick McGilligan, the Finance Minister, in 1950. Some economic commentators view this as the first evidence of Keynes' influence on the Irish budgetary process. In terms of personalities, Patrick Lynch (Professor of Political Economy at UCD) was one of the first Irish academics to espouse Keynesian economics. On a political level, it was Sean Lemass (former Taoiseach) who enthusiastically embraced the economics of Keynes. T. K. Whitaker, the person primarily responsible for the First Programme for Economic Expansion, devoted a section to the Keynesian multiplier in his seminal paper 'Capital Formation, Saving and Economic Progress' of 1956. Interestingly, two of the people who were involved in a debate on 'full-employment' back in April 1945 at the Statistical and Social Inquiry Society of Ireland were Patrick Lynch and T. K. Whitaker. It is also far from coincidental that the public speech given by the then Taoiseach, John A. Costello, in 1949 on the need for a sufficient level of demand in the economy was drafted by Patrick Lynch, his adviser.

16   The responsibility for managing the National Debt has changed hands from the Department of Finance to the National Treasury Management Agency (NTMA).

17   The 'business cycle' is the term used to explain fluctuations in the level of national income. Terms such as troughs, peaks, booms, slumps, recession, depression and recovery relate to different phases of the business cycle. The business cycle is a well-established economic phenomenon, observed since the industrial revolution. However, there is little consensus among economists and academics on the causes of such fluctuations. The one economic factor, however, which is constantly referred to in the literature on business cycles is investment expenditure and its inherent volatility. This suggests a role for government policy, which is aimed at stabilising the economy close to its potential output level. This is referred to as stabilisation policy. This is simply a collective term to describe various short-term demand-side policies such as fiscal, monetary and exchange rate policy which attempt to smooth out fluctuations in output and keep the actual level of output close to its potential level, i.e. the output level that results in the full employment of resources.

18   This does not suggest that Keynes, a former member of the Apostles and the Bloomsbury group, which advocated personal freedom and liberty, approved of Hitler's authoritarian methods. Solving unemployment at the expense of freedom was not to be tolerated, according to Keynes.

19   The Phillips curve depicts the relationship between the unemployment rate and wage inflation. Supporters of Keynesian economics who were disenchanted with the simple fixed-price Keynesian model used this concept to develop a more sophisticated theory of inflation and explain how price changes were related to the changes in demand, output and unemployment. The Phillips curve is explained in Appendix 17.1.

20   Whereas the Labour party in Ireland was constrained in its use of fiscal policy by the Maastricht criteria, President Clinton disappointed many of his supporters by adopting more 'conservative-style' policies.

21   A good example of this was the advice given by Keynes at the first Finlay lecture in UCD in 1933. In his address 'National Self-Sufficiency' he congratulated the de Valera government in its commitment to maintaining protectionism in order to support indigenous industry. Eighty years later, the same advice would be rejected by the vast majority of the economics profession, even if given by Keynes. This article can be found in *Studies*, 22, 1933.

22   This is not to suggest that Keynesian ideas lacked support in Ireland before the 1970s. In fact, Keynes had many followers in Ireland, including Sean Lemass, Taoiseach from 1959 to 1966. Lemass had a keen interest in economics. Before he ever entered politics he had read many books on Keynes and his policies. However, Lemass was more interested in adopting Keynesian policies to enhance the long-term development of the country. It was not until the early 1970s that short-term Keynesian policies were adopted in Ireland. To find out more about Lemass and his interest in economics in general and Keynes in particular read M. O'Sullivan, *Sean Lemass: A Biography*, Blackwater Press, 1995.

23   *Budget 1972*, Government Publications Office, 1972.

24   *Budget 1976*, Government Publications Office, 1976.

25   The Tallaght Strategy, of supporting the government's austere fiscal measures, receives its name because it began with a speech given by the then leader of the main opposition party, Mr Alan Dukes, in Tallaght, Dublin.

26   The phrase 'Expansionary Fiscal Contraction' originated from work done by F. Giavazzi and M. Pagano at the University of Bologna in 1990.

CHAPTER 13

1 George Bernard Shaw, *John Bull's Other Island: and Major Barbara, Also How He Lied to Her Husband*, Constable, 1911.

2 J. R. Hicks, *Critical Essays in Monetary Theory*, Clarendon Press, 1967.

3 This system dates back to the Middle Ages when people deposited gold with goldsmiths. Over time, goldsmiths noticed that it was unlikely that all depositors would withdraw their gold all at once. On recognising this, they kept some gold in reserve to meet the immediate demands of their depositors. The remainder was lent out to new clients. This is the way in which the early banking system developed.

4 This assumption is rather restrictive. In reality, a portion of the loan may not find its way back into the banking system but instead end up in the form of cash. This implies that the subsequent increase in the money supply will not be as large as originally suggested. This curtailment in the money creation process may also happen if the bank decides to keep reserves over and above the minimum amount that is required by law. See Appendix 13.1 on the money multiplier.

5 Required reserve ratios are common features in any modern banking system. Pre-1999, credit institutions in Ireland were required to maintain a reserve ratio, called the 'liquidity' ratio. The primary liquidity ratio is the ratio of required holdings of primary liquid assets to relevant resources. Its purpose when introduced in 1972 was to avoid a 'run' on the banking system and also to control the amount of lending. Although they are an essential part of monetary policy, they should also be seen as prudential protection for depositors. Since the launch of the euro, credit institutions across the participating member states are subject to reserve requirements, imposed by the Eurosystem.

   Credit institutions are continually faced with the conflict between profitability and liquidity where liquidity is the ease with which an asset can be converted into cash without financial loss. In order for financial institutions to make a profit, they must engage in the act of lending. On the other hand, credit institutions must always be ready to meet the daily demands of their clients, both personal and corporate. Maintenance of a reserve ratio helps to resolve this conflict and in doing so, contributes to a relatively secure banking system.

6 Its derivation is similar to the derivation of the expenditure multiplier. The sum of the created deposits forms a geometric series. It can be proven that this sum is equal to the reciprocal of the reserve ratio. This is called the deposit multiplier. With 10% kept in reserves, reserves increase by €1,000. Hence, bank deposits increase by €10,000. In practice, the multiplier will be much smaller than the above example suggests. This is because the public is likely to hold some of their borrowings in the form of cash. Also, some banks may decide to hold a greater amount of their deposits on reserve than is generally required.

7 Firms can also finance capital goods from retained earnings. However, their decision will still be determined by the interest rate. We can think of the interest rate as the opportunity cost. The opportunity cost of purchasing capital goods is the best opportunity forgone. If the interest rate is high, the firm could earn the market rate of interest. If the firm earns more by lending than investing, we must assume that at higher rates of interest, their demand for capital goods is low.

8 This assertion depends on the relative strengths of substitution and income effects arising from changes in interest rates. See Chapter 7 for a similar discussion.

9 A bond or a fixed-interest security is a government IOU. It is an instrument in which one party (the debtor/borrower) promises to repay the other party (lender/investor) the amount borrowed plus interest. They can be bought or sold on the equity (capital) market.

10 J. M. Keynes, *The General Theory of Employment, Interest and Money*.

11 The negative relationship that exists between the price of a bond and the interest rate can be explained by defining the price of a bond as the present value of a set of future cash flows. The lower the interest rate that is earned on any sum invested today, the greater is the amount that needs to be invested (today) in order to realise a specified value (in the future). Hence, for a given future value at some specified time in the future, the lower the interest rate, the higher the present value. By now applying the definition as above, we observe the negative relationship that exists between interest rates and the price of a bond.

12   The Swedish Central Bank is the oldest, dating back to 1668. The Bank of England was established shortly afterwards in 1694. In contrast, the US Federal Reserve System ('Fed' for short) was set up in 1913. The Central Bank of Ireland was established as recently as 1943. In 1998, the European Central Bank was formally established.

13   The Irish pound had a chequered history. We begin in 1689 when an exchange rate of 13:12 was set for the Irish pound/British pound. In 1826 the two currencies were amalgamated. Over a century later, the Banking Commission of 1927 established the Saorstat pound, which was set at parity with sterling. Parity was maintained until 1979 when the Irish pound became a member, unlike the British pound, of the Exchange Rate Mechanism (ERM) in the European Monetary System. With this the 153-year, one-for-one, fixed link with sterling ended. In January 1999, the Irish pound became irrevocably fixed to the euro, effectively bringing about the demise of the Irish pound. In 2002, Irish notes and coins were replaced by euro notes and coins.

14   We know from the discussion on money creation that the amount of money which the banking system can create is a multiple of the amount of reserves that they hold. Hence, if the monetary authorities can control the amount of reserves which the banks hold, they can then regulate the amount of money which they can create. For example, by simply creating more reserves, it provides the banks with the opportunity to make more loans and consequently more deposits. As a result, money supply increases. The three tools of monetary policy which are described in the chapter are, in effect, ways of controlling the supply of reserves rather than the supply of money, *per se.*

15   The Keynesian cross diagram which we used in the previous chapter was based on the assumption that investment is exogenous. In this analysis investment is dependent on the rate of interest. Panel (b) depicts this relationship between interest rates and investment. Consequently, there is an adjustment to the AE function. There is more material on this in Chapter 14.

16   D. Romer, 'Comment on Bosworth', *The Brookings Papers on Economic Activity*, no. 1, 1989.

17   Some of the material used to describe the ineffectiveness of monetary policy for an SOE is unfamiliar. A more detailed explanation of this and other material is contained in Chapter 15.

18   One party to the contract agrees to the spot purchase (sale) of one currency for another. This is one part of the swap. The other part of the swap is the forward sale (purchase).

19   Paul Tansey, 'Money Matters', *Magill*, August 1989.

20   Maurice Doyle, 'Monetary Policy – The Hidden Stabiliser', *Central Bank Annual Report 1988*, Spring 1989.

21   The objective of monetary policy in Ireland was price stability. There was no commitment to other goals. In other countries, the USA for example, central banks are committed to achieving a number of objectives, including low inflation, low unemployment and high growth rates.

22   'Monetary Policy Statement 1992', *Central Bank Report*, Spring 1992.

23   Officially, the currencies of the EU member states that do not participate in the single currency are linked to the euro by means of the new Exchange Rate Mechanism (ERM II), membership of which is voluntary.

24   The reference value of 4.5% per annum was derived from the quantity theory of money relationship. $MV = PY$, which is explained in Chapter 17. Using the definition of price stability as defined by the ECB and the assumptions for trend GDP growth and M3 income velocity, a value for M3 growth of 4.5% results. See the ECB *Monthly Bulletin* November 2000 for a detailed explanation.

25   It has been said that many central banks, in their implementation of a monetary policy strategy that pursues an inflation target, appear to be following the so-called Taylor rule, named after the Stanford University economist John Taylor. The formula says that the Central Bank will raise (reduce) interest rates if inflation is forecast to rise above (fall below) its target rate. The emphasis here is on the forecast rather than the current inflation rate. This might explain changes in interest rates by a central bank even when current (but, assumingly, not forecast) inflation rates are close to the target rate. Of course, there is a bigger issue here than simply following a rule, Taylor or otherwise. The broader issue is one of monetary policy rules versus discretion. The so-called rules versus discretion debate in monetary policy sets the proponents of monetary policy rules against the advocates of discretionary monetary policy.

26   Two useful references for monetary policy in the context of European monetary union are Paul De Grauwe,

The Economics of Monetary Union, Oxford University Press, 2007; and Richard Baldwin and Charles Wyplosz, *The Economics of European Intergration*, McGraw-Hill, 2009.

CHAPTER 14

1   Christopher Bliss, 'John R. Hicks' in *The New Palgrave: A Dictionary of Economics*.

2   Jordi Gali, 'How Well Does the IS-LM Model Fit Postwar U.S. Data?', *Quarterly Journal of Economics*, 67, May 1992.

3   Hicks has received most of the credit for the development of the IS/LM framework and, as a result, for spreading the Keynesian doctrine among his contemporaries and to the general public. Although Alvin Hansen did not receive the same acknowledgments his contribution was of no lesser importance. His book succeeded in spreading Keynes' ideas to countless academic institutions and universities throughout the USA. See A. Hansen, *A Guide to Keynes*, McGraw-Hill, 1953.

4   Prices are incorporated into the macro model in Chapter 16, and again in Chapter 17.

5   We know from Chapter 12 that equilibrium in the goods market (without the government sector) can be expressed in terms of investment and savings. It is this view of equilibrium (investment, I = savings, S) which gives us the name the IS curve. This simple injections-leakages approach is useful in explaining the negative relationship that exists between interest rates and income levels in the goods market. A lower interest rate level induces lower savings and higher investment. This increase in investment causes a multiplier effect which will result in higher income levels. Hence, with an initial reduction in interest rates, equilibrium is maintained in the goods market (I = S) through a subsequent increase in national income.

6   With interest rates as an explanatory variable, the resulting AE function is different from that presented in Chapter 12. In Chapter 12, the AE function was of the form $AE = \bar{A} + bY$. In this chapter the AE function is of the form $AE = \bar{A} - di + bY$ (see Figure 14.2). The algebraic derivation of this function is contained in Appendix 14.1.

7   In the analysis of the money market, we are concerned with the supply of real balances $\left(\frac{\bar{M}}{\bar{P}}\right)$. Hence, our discussion is limited to the real money stock (and not nominal money supply, M_s) and the real money supply curve.

8   This can be explained by reference to the upper panel (the Keynesian cross diagram) of Figure 14.2. Point A would coincide with a point corresponding to income level Y^0 and interest rate level i^1. This point lies on a higher aggregate expenditure curve than AE^0. This means that the demand for goods exceeds the level of output, i.e. there is an excess demand for goods.

9   This can be explained by reference to the right-hand panel (the money market diagram) of Figure 14.3. Point A would coincide with a point corresponding to interest rate, i^1 and an income level, Y^0. This point lies on a lower money demand curve than $L(Y^1)$. With the demand for money less than the supply of money, an excess supply of money will result.

10   An important aspect of expansionary fiscal policy is the method of financing. Two methods exist. First, the government can finance the additional spending through an expansion of the money supply. This method is called monetary financing. Second, additional spending can be financed by issuing government bonds or gilts to the non-bank public. This method is commonly known as bond financing. The effectiveness of expansionary fiscal policy may depend on whether the additional spending is monetary or bond financed. For example, additional spending financed from monetary sources tends to be accompanied by increases in the money supply. With no subsequent rise in interest rates, the risk of crowding out is reduced. Alternatively, additional spending financed by the sale of bonds to the non-bank public may push interest rates higher.

11   The presentation of expansionary fiscal policy in this format is helpful. For example, the effectiveness of fiscal policy depends largely on the strength of each link in the chain and, in particular, between [increases Y → increases L] and [increases i → reduces I]. As an exercise the student should change the slope of the LM curve to see the impact on interest rates and national income.

12   In Chapter 16 we will see that fiscal expansion can lead to higher inflation. This possibility is not considered here because the IS/LM is a fixed-price model.

CHAPTER 15

1   Margaret Thatcher, *The Downing Street Years*, HarperCollins Publishers, 1993.

2   Bernard Connolly, *The Rotten Heart Of Europe*, Faber and Faber, 1995.

3   The trade balance must be distinguished from the terms of trade which is simply the ratio of export prices to import prices, i.e. it reflects relative prices Px/Py. An improvement in the terms of trade implies that the prices of exports have risen relative to the prices of imports. In other words, we need to export less in order to secure a given quantity of imports.

4   With two currencies involved, there are two ways to express the exchange rate. We can express it as the number of euros per one dollar or as the number of dollars per one euro. On this side of the Atlantic it is customary to express the €/US$ exchange rate as the number of dollars per one euro. The euro is called the base currency and the US dollar is called the counter currency.

5   In particular, we make no explicit reference in the text to the role that the price elasticity of demand for imports plays in determining the supply of the base currency. The supply curve will only appear as a 'normal' upward sloping curve if the demand for imports is elastic, i.e. a lower exchange rate (higher import prices) leads to less imports and hence a lower quantity of euros supplied. This assumption is implicit in the text when we discuss the supply of euros. In the case of inelastic demand, the supply curve will have a negative slope. Norton in his book *Economics for an Open Economy: Ireland* (1994) points out that this possibility could arise if the 'Home' country were ' . . . a large country relative to the rest of the world'. A discussion on the price elasticity of demand for imports (and exports) usually leads to some debate on the related topics of the J-curve effect and the Marshall-Lerner condition.

6   Market participants, in the belief that the value of the euro will be lower, sell the euro today (known as selling short) with the intention of buying it back some time in the future at a lower rate. If this happens, the traders are left with a tidy profit from this euro trade.

7   The deficits and surpluses recorded in the balance of payments are an indicator of whether a country is a net borrower from or a lender to the rest of the world. For example, under a flexible exchange rate system a current account deficit is matched by a surplus in the capital account. The deficit in the current account is financed by either running down its assets or borrowing from abroad. The latter is done by the sale of bonds and other financial assets, recorded in the capital account as a surplus. This signals that the country is a net borrower from the rest of the world. A country is defined as a net debtor when it owes more to the rest of the world than it is owed; a net creditor is owed more from the rest of the world than it owes.

8   The two great fixed exchange rate systems were the Gold Standard (1815–1914) and the Bretton Woods system (1945–71). The Gold Standard fixed the value of each participating currency in terms of gold. The Bretton Woods system, set up at the end of World War II, fixed all currencies in terms of the dollar. Not surprisingly, it was also called the Dollar Exchange Standard. An interesting feature of the Bretton Woods system was the adjustable peg, i.e. although currencies were pegged to each other, adjustments were permitted in the event of persistent imbalances.

9   *The New Palgrave: A Dictionary of Economics.*

10 The US dollar is an example of a managed float. The value of the dollar was the main topic for consideration at both the Plaza Accord (1985) and the Louvre Agreement (1987). The former acknowledged that the dollar was overvalued and set as its aim a reduction in the value of the US dollar. The Louvre Agreement, although less concerned with the dollar's value, acknowledged the danger of volatile foreign exchange markets and called for greater co-ordination of monetary policy in order to provide a more stable economic environment.

11 'The Exchange-Rate Mechanism of the European Monetary System', *Central Bank Annual Report 1978*, Spring 1979. This article includes a detailed discussion on how the ERM operated.

12 From 1979 to 1987 the ERM operated as an adjustable peg system. Realignments were quite common in those early years. The convergence of many economic indicators such as interest rates, government borrowing and inflation rates among member states was partly responsible for the change in the system to a semi-fixed exchange rate system by the late 1980s. Until the autumn of 1992, member states were reluctant to realign their currencies. By August 1993, the bands of fluctuation were widened to 15% either way for all but two member states. In reality, the ERM had become more of a managed floating system rather than a semi-fixed exchange rate system.

13 We will explain how the ERM operated by discussing an example. Consider the relationship between the Irish pound and the German mark. Before January 1993, the central rate for the IR£/DM was IR£1 = 2.6789DM. This means that one Irish pound was worth approximately 2.68 German marks. At that time, both the Irish pound and the German mark operated within the narrow band. The Irish pound could move between a lower band of 2.6190DM and an upper band of 2.7400DM. These figures are 2.25% below and 2.25% above the central rate. In other words, if the value of the Irish pound fell below 2.6190DM or rose above 2.74DM, the Central Bank was obliged to intervene. In a 'normal' day's trading, the IR£/DM would trade within these limits.

14 'Hedging' is practised by importers and exporters in order to reduce possible losses arising from fluctuations in the exchange rate. For example, suppose the Galway dealership for Toyota contracts for 10 billion yen of automobiles and has to pay for them in 30 days. If the euro depreciates against the Japanese yen during these 30 days, the cost of the automobiles in euros will increase. To ensure against an exchange rate loss the automobile dealer contracts to buy 10 billion yen at the forward exchange rate. This protects the dealer against loss due to depreciation. As he is locked into an agreement at a specified rate, the automobile dealer will not benefit from an appreciation of the euro *vis-à-vis* the Japanese yen. The practice of hedging involves a transaction cost.

15 Economic and social cohesion is an essential component of monetary union and the single currency. In practice, this involves the transfer of funds from the wealthy nations to the weaker nations. Ireland has benefited substantially from these EU funds. For years, Ireland was the largest net beneficiary per head of EU funding. These funds have been used in the areas of human resources, agriculture, industry and physical infrastructure. Many worthwhile projects, beyond the means of the Irish state and the private sector, were co-financed from the EU exchequer. The EU accession states are now the primary recipients of these funds.

16 It was decided that there could be a dual circulation period of up to six months at most. As this period could be shortened by national law, the Euro Changeover Board of Ireland recommended that this period should end on 9 February 2002.

17 The Council and Commission of the European Communities, *The Treaty on European Union*, Office for Official Publications of the European Communities, 1992.

18 Honohan, Patrick, 'Fiscal Adjustment and Disinflation in Ireland: Setting the Macro Basis of Economic Recovery and Expansion', in F. Barry, editor, *Understanding Ireland's Economic Growth*, Macmillan, 1999.

19 The deficit bias is the tendency for governments to continue running budget deficits, resulting in large public debts.

20 As part of the EC peer-monitoring arrangements and multilateral surveillance, there are the Broad Economic Policy Guidelines (BEPG) and the stability programmes aimed at enhancing co-operation between member states and ensuring economic policy co-ordination. See endnote 28.

21 This division, incidentally, is similar to the split in the fortunes of the ERM itself. In the first few years realignments were quite common, exchange rates were volatile and little or no convergence between the member states took place. By the late 1980s things had changed. Realignments were fewer, exchange rates were stable and greater convergence was evident between member states. In fact, many commentators viewed the ERM by the turn of the decade as a *de facto* fixed exchange rate system. We take 1992 as an end point because of the currency crisis and its effect on the ERM.

22 A comprehensive analysis of the costs and benefits to Ireland of membership in the EMU was carried out by the Economic and Social Research Institute. For more, read *Economic Implications for Ireland of EMU*, edited by T. Baker, J. FitzGerald and P. Honohan, Economic and Social Research Institute, no. 28, July 1996. For alternative conclusions, see P. Neary and R. Thom, *Punts, Pounds and Euros*, Centre for Economic Research UCD; and F. Barry, 'The Dangers for Ireland of an EMU without the UK: some Calibration Results', *Economic and Social Review*, 1997.

23 The existence of a gap between the richest nations and the poorest member states of the EU has always been a lively issue. The structural funds and the EU commitment to 'economic and social cohesion' arose out of the debate on the 'wealth gap'. The progress of the peripheral countries, as a group, has been patchy. Ireland has achieved most of the four (the others being Spain, Portugal and Greece) in the past forty years. In 1975 Ireland's GDP per capita was 64.1% of the EU average. In the first decade of the new millennium it was in excess of 100% according to the European Commission.

24   Notwithstanding the underlying economic and fiscal causes, some market players or speculators, as in other previous crises, did respond to – indeed, accentuate – the market uncertainty and financial panic by betting on certain events, such as a currency – the euro – depreciation or a government – Greek or Irish – default. Indeed, given the levels (both in absolute terms, and in relative terms when compared with debt levels elsewhere, as in the UK or USA, for example) of government debt in the eurozone countries, there is a case to be made that financial markets over-reacted to the Greek crisis in the contagion that followed to other less debt-laden countries, such as Spain or Ireland, both of which, it can be argued, were not fiscally reckless in the sense that they had, albeit insufficiently large, budget surpluses and relatively low debt/GDP ratios on the eve of the 2008 global crisis. Equally, one can argue that the 2010/11 sovereign debt crisis, as with the global financial crisis that preceded it (where financial markets systematically underestimated and mispriced risk), illustrates that market discipline does not always work, or, in all cases, work well.

25   Eurostat reported that Greece's budgetary numbers were unreliable and had been falsified to hide deficits above the eurozone limits. Later it emerged that Goldman Sachs, JP Morgan Chase and other banks had been paid large sums of money by successive Greek governments for transactions that hid the real amount of borrowing incurred by the Greek authorities. Although not unimportant, this should not hide the fact that successive Greek governments, and its citizens, have lived beyond their means for many years, by indulging 'in blatant fiscal indiscipline for more than three decades' (Wyplosz 2009).

26   Although large and of concern, the figures for the deficit and debt in Greece were not incomparable to figures for some other advanced countries during the 2007–2009 financial crisis. For example, fiscal deficits of similar magnitude were recorded in both Ireland and the UK in 2009, whereas government debt in Belgium, Italy and most notably Japan exceeded 100% of GDP in 2009/10 (with the UK and USA close to, if not exceeding, the 100% level at the time of this book's publication, in 2011). As for its external imbalances, Greece, in amassing a large current account deficit, was again not unlike many other peripheral eurozone countries during the 2000s. It is also worth noting here that, despite the focus on the sovereign debt crisis in the eurozone, the US government debt/GDP ratio in 2009–2010 was actually higher than the eurozone government debt/GDP ratio (and much higher than the debt ratio for many individual eurozone member states, including the bigger countries of France and Germany). In the case of both the USA and the eurozone, the debt ratio increased from pre-global crisis levels of about 65% of GDP to levels close to 100% of GDP by the end of the crisis.

27   As Greek national output accounts for less than 3% of eurozone GDP, it is too small on its own to cause a regional or global crisis. However, the concern was that the interconnectedness between the eurozone governments and banks – as most of the Greek debt is external, held by financial institutions from other euro area countries, many of which themselves are in difficulty – might result in contagion spreading to the other debt-laden eurozone countries and to the survival of the euro itself. Although the authorities decided in May 2010 to rescue Greece, alternatives did exist, including, among others, an orderly rescheduling of its debt with its creditors, under the auspices of the IMF. An earlier and well-managed default, not uncommon worldwide, might have proved to be, in the long run, the least costly option. Of course, the May and November 2010 bailouts may well only postpone an eventual rescheduling of Greek and Irish debt. By spring 2011 contagion had spread to Portugal, resulting in the third eurozone country to be 'bailed' out.

28   The eurozone rules contain a preventive and a corrective arm. Aimed at averting excessive deficits, the preventive arm, in the form of an EC Regulation (adopted in 1997, amended in 2005) is concerned with surveillance of budgetary positions and requires Stability Programmes submitted by member states. The dissuasive arm, in contrast, again in the form of an EC Regulation (same dates as above), lays down the procedure to be followed in the case of a member state's deficit exceeding the 3% of GDP limit, i.e the Excessive Deficit Procedure. With economic policy across the member states regarded as a matter of common concern and to ensure economic policy co-ordination, the Broad Economic Policy Guidelines (BEPG) contains policy recommendations. For an outline of the surveillance of budgetary policy by the EU including the so-called 2001 Brussels–Dublin controversy when the Council issued (the first, and only, one in the first ten years of the euro) a recommendation – effectively a formal censure of budgetary policy – against a member state, which happened to be Ireland (see O'Leary 2009).

29 Despite some eurozone countries breaching the terms of the SGP, no country has ever been fined. From an economics perspective, countries often incur large budget deficits because of downturns in the economy (and not because of irresponsible fiscal policy). Imposing fines in the face of a depressed economy might just exacerbate the difficulties and end up being counterproductive. Politically, of course, imposing fines on other member states, irrespective of the underlying cause of the fiscal deficit, is a difficult task.

30 A weaker version of PPP is written as follows:

$$\Delta E = \Delta P_{US} - \Delta P_{\text{€}}$$

where

$$\Delta E = \text{the change in the exchange rate}$$
$$\Delta P_{US} = \text{change in the US price level, i.e. US inflation rate}$$
$$\Delta P_{\text{€}} = \text{change in the euro price level, i.e. eurozone inflation rate.}$$

This weaker version states that changes in the exchange rate arise out of inflation rate differentials.

31 'When the Chips are Down', *The Economist*, 22 July 2010. $3.73 is actually the average price of a Big Mac in four American cities. Ideally, an internationally traded good should be used in any discussion of PPP. Incidentally, the results from the 2010 Big Mac Index suggest that the euro is overvalued against the dollar, by 16%.

CHAPTER 16

1 Alan S. Blinder, 'Hard Heads, Soft Hearts', *Tough-Minded Economics for a Just Society*, Addison-Wesley.

2 Mark Brownrigg, *Understanding the Economy*, Addison-Wesley. A good description of supply-side economics is given in Chapter 10 of this textbook.

3 The real balance effect owes its prominence in the economics literature to A. C. Pigou and Donald Patinkin who independently worked on the existence of such an effect.

4 We generally discuss the negative aspects of government policy when we discuss the 'supply side'. For example, according to economists who focus on the supply side, demand-management policy is ineffective and inflationary. However, there are some government policies which are advocated by these economists. 'Positive' supply-side policies promote the research and adoption of new technologies and programmes to provide relevant training opportunities for labour. These measures actually push the AS curve out and to the right, increasing the potential output of the economy.

5 At full employment, the economy is at a point on its production possibility frontier (see Chapter 1). Supply-side policies attempt to push out the boundaries of the nation's production possibility frontier. In other words, a rightward shift of the long-run AS curve is equivalent to an outward shift of the production possibility frontier.

6 A. Protopapadakis, 'Supply-Side Economics: What Chance for Success?' in *The Supply-Side Solution* edited by B. Bartlett and T. P. Roth, Macmillan, 1983.

7 In response to the lacklustre performance of Irish industry during the 1980s, the then Minister for Industry and Commerce, Des O'Malley, established the Industrial Policy Review Group. Its role was to assess the performance of Irish industry and, in particular, Irish-owned companies and to recommend appropriate policy changes. The report entitled *A Time for Change: Industrial Policy for the 1990s* was published in January 1992 (Government Publications Office). It is commonly referred to as the *Culliton report*.

8 D. Ó Cearbhaill, 'The same, and more', *Fortnight*, February 1992.

9 Paul Tansey, *Ireland at Work; Economic Growth and the Labour Market 1987–1997*, Oak Tree Press, 1998.

CHAPTER 17

1 John F. Kennedy. Speech, 1962.

2 Benjamin Franklin, *Thoughts on Commercial Subjects*.

3   The Household Budget Survey is conducted periodically by the CSO. Between 6,800 and 8,000 rural and urban households complete the survey which is designed to provide details concerning household income and expenditure.

4   M. Friedman, 'The Quantity Theory of Money – A Restatement', in *Studies in the Quantity Theory of Money*, Chicago University Press, 1956.

5   In this chapter, we draw the AS curve as a straight line. Our basic assumptions still hold.

6   Remember that the supply curve of labour is based on the assumption that work causes disutility. An increase in the real wage compensates for the disutility caused by work. For this reason, the relationship between the number of hours worked or the number of people working and the real wage is positive. Workers should be interested in their real wage, rather than their nominal wage because they are concerned about the quantity of goods and services which they can purchase.

7   Wincott Memorial lecture, London, 16 September 1970.

8   If the number of unemployed decreases by 5,000 between 2010 and 2011, the number of people counted at the end of 2011 is 5,000 fewer than the number of people counted at the end of 2010. However, 15,000 new people may have become unemployed because they lost their jobs, finished school or returned home from abroad and could not find employment. On the other hand, 20,000 people must have found jobs, retired from the labour force or emigrated. In other words, a small change in the stock of the unemployed may mask larger flows of people into and out of unemployment.

9   The natural rate of unemployment is a term used by monetarists and new classical economists. When the economy is at full employment, frictional unemployment is inevitable. The rate of unemployment associated with full employment is called the natural rate of unemployment. It is also the unemployment rate which is consistent with a stable rate of inflation, hence the name 'the non-accelerating inflation rate of unemployment' or simply NAIRU.

10   Marx and Keynes had very different views on the long-term prospects for the capitalist system. Whereas Keynes was largely optimistic about the future, Marx predicted a total collapse of the capitalist system. To date, Marx is wrong.

11   The insider-outsider theory is a relatively new way of looking at the behaviour of participants in the labour market. The insiders are those who already have jobs whereas the outsiders are those who are unemployed. Given the conservative nature of the labour market, which confers advantages on the insiders at the expense of the outsiders, this model predicts no great change in the unemployment structure.

12   *The Jobs Crisis*, edited by Colm Keane, Mercier Press, 1993.

13   The increase in the price of oil was both price inflationary and demand deflationary for oil-importing countries, including Ireland. Expansionary fiscal policy only fuels inflation whereas contractionary fiscal policy slows down economic activity further. Policy-makers were faced with a dilemma. The Irish authorities opted for an expansion of fiscal policy. Yet unemployment numbers increased, inflation rose, the budget deficit soared and the balance of payments deteriorated.

14   Although there are valid economic arguments in favour of borrowing to finance productive investment, there is less justification for borrowing to finance current spending. Current spending is usually financed out of tax revenue.

15   It is argued that for fiscal policy to be effective, it must be counter-cyclical. During the mid-1970s the Irish economy was experiencing strong growth. The domestic economy was benefiting from an increase in world trade. Hence, restrictive fiscal policy was required. The government, however, opted for an expansionary phase. In the early 1980s economic activity was sluggish. The international background was unfavourable. Yet, driven by the urgent need to restore order to the public finances, a highly contractionary fiscal policy was implemented. In both these periods Irish fiscal policy was pro-cyclical. Although the contractionary policy of the early 1980s was inappropriate on theoretical grounds, the Irish authorities were forced to practise fiscal rectitude because of the poor state of the public finances. In retrospect, the decision taken seems to have been the correct one. The same cannot be said for the experience of the mid-1970s. With the economy growing at a satisfactory rate, there was little or no need for a fiscal stimulus by the state. The long-term costs of such a policy outweighed the short-term gains. This was a feature of Irish fiscal policy in more recent times. Although there were budget surpluses in the boom years of the 2000s, they were insufficiently large. Tax breaks and spending

increases provided an unnecessary fiscal stimulus. When recession hit in the late 2000s, fiscal policy was constrained by the rapid deterioration in the public finances.

16 The coalition government of the early 1980s began to tackle the problem of the public finances. Both capital spending and taxation were targeted. Increases in capital spending were to be curtailed while at the same time tax rates were increased in order to boost revenue. Current spending was left largely intact. This policy mix, however, was flawed. Capital expenditure, assuming it is productive, is essential for the long-term prosperity of the economy. Moreover, capital expenditure was not the problem. The primary source of the high budget deficits was the growth in current expenditure. Yet the increases in current spending went largely unchecked. The increase in the tax rates was also considered as unhelpful. Tax rates were already penal. The revenue raised from the hike in the tax rates was not enough to compensate for the damage done to both the demand side and the supply side of the labour market.

17 There is considerable debate over each of these issues and their contribution to Irish unemployment. For example, the Irish authorities had little control over the level of interest rates. Hence, should blame be apportioned to our counterparts in Europe rather than to the monetary authorities in Ireland? The same argument applies to the value of the Irish pound. Membership of the ERM and the link with the German mark were helpful in achieving price stability. Was this achieved, however, at the cost of thousands of job losses? Finally, did the employed benefit, in terms of pay increases, at the expense of the unemployed? Were the centralised pay agreements successful or was there a need for local wage bargaining given the high unemployment numbers?

18 The evidence of a link between replacement ratios and unemployment rates is not conclusive. For a synopsis of the international and Irish studies, read 'Implications of Incentives for Employment. A review of the Economic Evidence', in *Expert Working Group Report on the Integration of the Tax and Social Welfare Systems*, Government Publications Office, June 1996.

19 Paul Tansey, *Making the Irish Labour Market Work*, Gill & Macmillan, 1991.

20 Arthur Andersen & Co., 'Reform of the Irish Tax System from an Industrial Point of View', a report to the Industrial Policy Review Group. A table of the tax wedge for the different countries is reprinted in NESC No. 96, *A Strategy for Competitiveness, Growth and Employment*, National Economic and Social Council, November 1993.

21 *OECD Economic Surveys: Ireland, 1990/91*, Organisation for Economic Co-operation and Development, 1991.

22 Dermot McAleese, 'Solutions and Political Implications' in *The Dark Shadow of Unemployment in the Republic and Northern Ireland*, Studies, 82, no. 325, Spring 1993.

23 See M. Emerson, 'Regulation or Deregulation of the Labour Market', *European Economic Review*, 32, no. 4, 1988. In contrast, Goodhart claimed that Ireland, along with the UK and Denmark, were the 'three most *laissez-faire* countries when it comes to closures and sackings'. See D. Goodhart, 'Ground Rules for the Firing Squad', *Financial Times*, 15 February 1993. This view was endorsed by the OECD in their 1994 *Jobs Study* report.

24 Brendan Walsh has written extensively on this topic. Among his works are the following: *The Macroeconomy of the Eurozone. An Irish Perspective* (2003) with Anthony Leddin; 'What's in Store for the Celtic Tiger?' (1999) in the *Irish Banking Review*; and 'Cyclical and Structural Influences on Irish Unemployment' (2000) in *Oxford Economic Papers*.

25 Studies include G. Kenny, 'Economic Growth in Ireland: Sources, Potential and Inflation', *CBI Bulletin*, Autumn 1996; J. Nugent, 'Corporate Profitability in Ireland: Overview and Determinants', *CBI Bulletin*, Winter 1998; OECD *Economic Surveys: Ireland*, 1999. An interesting account of Ireland's growth is given by F. Barry and N. Crafts in 'Some Comparative Aspects of Transformation', *Irish Banking Review*, 1999. More recent studies, including B. Walsh and P. Honohan, 'Catching up with the Leaders: The Irish Hare', *Brookings Papers on Economic Activity*, 2002, question the claim of a productivity miracle, pointing instead to changes in demographics and in the labour market.

26 'Poorest of the Rich: A Survey of the Republic of Ireland', *The Economist*, 16 January 1988 and 'Europe's Shining Light', *The Economist*, 17 May 1997.

27 Adam Smith, *An Inquiry into the Nature and Causes of the Wealth of Nations*.

28 David Ricardo, *The Principles of Political Economy and Taxation*.

29 Eli Heckscher, *The Effect of Foreign Trade on the Distribution of Income*, Ekonomisk Tidskrift, 21, 1919. Bertil Ohlin, *Interregional and International Trade*, Harvard University Press, 1933.

30   W. M. Corden, *The Theory of Protection*, Clarendon Press, 1971.
31   W. M. Corden, *Trade Policy and Economic Welfare*, Clarendon Press, 1974.
32   Mancur Olson, *The Logic of Collective Action*, Harvard University Press, 1965.
33   Paul Krugman, 'Increasing Returns, Monopolistic Competition and International Trade', *Journal of International Economics*, 9, 1979. Also, 'Scale Economies, Product Differentiation and the Pattern of Trade', *American Economic Review*, 1980.
34   Of course it could be argued that these regions would have remained poor even if they were not engaged in free inter-regional trade. But if this were true, it merely serves to highlight that free trade will not necessarily bring great economic advancement to a region with poor resources.
35   A. W. Phillips, 'The Relation between Unemployment and the Rate of Change of Money Wages in the United Kingdom 1861–1957', *Economica*, 25, November 1958.
36   The theory of rational expectations dates from the early 1960s and to a seminal paper, written by John Muth and entitled 'Rational Expectations and the Theory of Price Movements', *Econometrica*, 29, 1960.
37   J. M. Keynes, *A Tract on Monetary Reform*, Macmillan, 1923.

CHAPTER 18

1   J. K. Galbraith, *The Affluent Society*, Hamish Hamilton, 1958.
2   P. J. O'Rourke, *Eat the Rich*, Picador, 1998.
3   The concept of using stories to explain economic growth rather than relying solely on a formal model is advocated by David Colander in 'Telling Better Stories in Introductory Macro', *AEA Papers and Proceedings*, May 2000.
4   GDP per capita is used for most international comparisons rather than GNP per capita. For a full explanation of the difference between GNP and GDP see Chapter 10. For Ireland, GNP is the more accurate measurement because it measures the output of Irish firms and workers and it does not include some of the distorting effects of foreign companies using Ireland as an export base.
5   The table is derived from the Penn-World tables, 6.3. The tables are available online at the following website: http://pwt.econ.upenn.edu.
6   Frank Barry, 'Irish Growth in Historical and Theoretical Perspective', Chapter 2 in Frank Barry, editor, *Understanding Ireland's Economic Growth*, Macmillan, 1999. This idea will be discussed further in Section 18.3.
7   Robert Solow, 'A Contribution to the Theory of Economic Growth', *Quarterly Journal of Economics*, 70, February 1956.
8   For a brief synopsis of Robert M. Solow's life and contribution to economics, read P. Samuelson, 'Paul Robert Solow: An Affectionate Portrait', *Journal of Economic Perspectives*, Volume 3(3), Summer 1989.
9   *Human Development Report 2010*, United Nations Development Programme.
10   Edward Phelps, 'The Golden Rule of Accumulation: A Fable for Growthmen', *American Economic Review*, 51, September 1961.
11   The columns containing GDP per capita for 2005 and annual growth 2005 are from the Penn-World tables version 6.3: the last column is the author's calculations.
12   The relationship between growth rates and doubling in GDP per capita illustrates the 'rule of 72'. Divide 72 by your annual growth rate and this yields the number of years it takes for GDP per capita to double. For example, an economy growing at 4% per year will double in size in $72 \div 4 = 18$ years.
13   The Asian crisis of 1997 and the crisis in Mexico in 1994 were caused in part because international investors tried to pull their investments out of these countries very quickly. This mass exit of money caused the currencies to fall drastically in value.
14   In fact, technology is so important that one major variation of the Solow growth model includes technology and the rate of growth in national income per capita equals the rate of technological growth.
15   Jeffrey Sachs, 'A New Map of the World', *The Economist*, 24 June 2000.
16   Ibid.
17   Ibid.

18 De-industrialisation does not mean economic decline. On the contrary, there is evidence to suggest that it is an important step in a rich economy's development.

19 This point is made by Frank Barry, 'Irish Growth in Historical and Theoretical Perspective', Chapter 2 in Frank Barry, editor, *Understanding Ireland's Economic Growth*, Macmillan Press, 1999 and by Paul Krugman, 'Good News from Ireland: A Geographical Perspective', in Alan Gray, editor, *International Perspectives on the Irish Economy*, Indecon, 1997.

20 'Europe's Tiger Economy', *The Economist*, 17 May 1997 and 'Hot and Sticky in Ireland', *The Economist*, 29 July 2000. A note about automobiles: the introduction of the National Car Test for older cars probably hastened many automobile purchases. Nevertheless, by July 2000, County Galway had registered over 10,000 autos for the first time ever.

21 'Europe's Tiger Economy', *The Economist*, 17 May 1997.

22 Ibid.

23 Kirby (2002) and others categorise Ireland (and its development trajectory) as a NIC, having similar characteristics to the late developers in Asia and Latin America. Whereas it is true that Ireland's Celtic Tiger era has some similarities with the experience of the Asian Tigers (particularly in terms of the export-led strategy), Ireland's economic boom of the 1990s, unlike those of the Tiger countries of South East Asia, was not built on a surge in investment rates and large capital expenditures.

24 Of course, not all commentaries were positive. Outside the mainstream, both in economics and sociology, there were many who criticised various aspects of the Celtic Tiger, from the type of model underpinning Irish development (see Kirby 2002) to the limitations and beneficiaries of the Celtic Tigerhood (see O'Hearn 1998) to its impact on workers and society (see Allen 2000).

25 A notable feature of Irish government policy has been the consensus-based approach to policy formulation, based, from the 1960s onward, on a developmental model or strategy centred on export-led growth and EU integration, (US) FDI promotion and a low corporation tax regime, social partnership and a relatively flexible and open labour market. Notwithstanding its contribution to Ireland's success (at least up to the 2000s), it is also true that an overly consensual approach often prevents difficult and unpopular decisions being taken. A further criticism of the conventional wisdom is that investment in human capital is always the preferred investment. The cost (in terms of the opportunity forgone of more investment in physical capital and infrastructure such as roads, rail and telecommunications) and the quality and standards (relative to education systems in other OECD countries) of investment in human capital is raised by Ó Gráda (2002) and others.

26 The delayed convergence hypothesis is given by Honohan and Walsh (2002), Ó Gráda (2002) and Fitzgerald (2006). An alternate explanation is the regional boom hypothesis espoused by others including Krugman (1997) and Barry (1999, 2002), and depicts Ireland as a peripheral regional (initially UK, possibly even US) EU economy.

27 Crafts (2008), and others, emphasis the importance of ICT (information, communications and technology) and the ICT sector to Ireland's success during the Celtic Tiger period. This was an industry that worldwide experienced 'phenomenal technological progress and productivity growth at this time' (Crafts 2008). Ireland certainly benefited from the growth in this sector. In the wider context of globalisation, Ireland was often depicted as the exemplar and poster child for global capitalism and liberalisation. In practice, Ireland followed neither the 'liberal' Boston nor the 'corporatist' Berlin model, as it often straddled the two 'alternative' economic strategies.

28 Ireland's fiscal austerity of the late 1980s attracted much international attention and, in academic circles, partly formed the basis for the theoretical (and later, empirical) work on the Expansionary Fiscal Contraction (EFC) theory, i.e. credible fiscal contraction, through expenditure reductions rather than tax increases, can be expansionary, because of signalling effects and improved confidence and expectations – in both private consumption and investment – about the future. Debate over the validity of this hypothesis is still ongoing, particularly in the light of the 2007–2009 financial and global crisis, and the subsequent fiscal retrenchment implemented by many indebted countries, including Ireland.

29 In recognising the poor performance of the Irish economy before the emergence of the Celtic Tiger, Kennedy (2001) notes that, for total employment, 'the 1993 level was still 7 per cent *below* that of 1926' (emphasis added).

30   The construction boom was fuelled by a number of property-related tax reliefs and benefits. Certain types of construction investment were eligible for tax concessions, including rural and urban renewal, hotels, student accommodation, multi-storey car parks, nursing homes and private hospitals. Some of these may have been justified when first introduced, but not at the height of the boom. The extension of expiry dates for such property incentive schemes contributed to prolonging the unsustainable boom and, inevitably, the severity of the property collapse thereafter.

31   A separate issue from the sources of the income generated is the use or management of it. Many of the critics of the Celtic Tiger, economists and sociologists alike, have claimed that, in terms of infrastructure (notwithstanding the improvement in the road network), poverty and inequality, health and social services, Ireland's wealth was poorly spent and distributed. A surprising – in the sense that it comes from a stockbroking firm, considered by many as the bastions of free markets and capitalism – contribution to this literature is White (2010), who claims that the high income of 2000–2008 was 'largely wasted'. Much of the support for this claim is taken from CSO data on Ireland's stock of wealth and capital allocation, available from the CSO publication entitled *Capital Stock of Fixed Assets.*

32   NESC (2009), in providing an account of Ireland in crisis, describes it as a crisis of five dimensions: banking crisis, fiscal crisis, economic crisis, social crisis and reputational crisis, brought on by three factors, namely: declining competitiveness as a consequence of Ireland's prolonged boom; a property bubble which Irish financial institutions, a regulatory system and a system of land management did not prevent; and an international credit crisis and world recession caused by structural weaknesses in the current global process. Although we do not disagree with much of this analysis, our review is centred on three key elements, namely: the financial crisis and world recession; the property bubble and subsequent crash; and the banking crisis and policy response.

33   The sale, initially for $2 per share (later increased to $10 per share) was brokered by the Federal Reserve Bank of New York in an attempt, it was argued, to minimise counterparty credit risk due to the importance and interconnectedness of Bear Sterns. The New York Fed also agreed to grant a $30bn loan to the buyers. In September 2008 JP Morgan Chase was to acquire, for $1.9bn, the banking subsidiaries of Washington Mutual (WaMu), a savings and loan institution that before been placed into receivership was the seventh largest bank in the USA. That same month Wachovia announced a sale of its banking operations. On the other side of the Atlantic, the UK was experiencing similar collapses and subsequent bailouts. In February 2008, Northern Rock had been nationalised after the UK witnessed its first run on a British bank for over 100 years, and over six months later Bradford & Bingley was rescued with its branch network sold to Spanish bank Santander, while troubled HBOS was sold to Lloyds TSB. One month later, the UK government effectively nationalised the merged TSB/HBOS bank, and RBS, when it announced a huge state injection of funds, amounting to £37bn, into three of the UK's largest banks. Mainland Europe did not escape the financial turmoil. Many large financial institutions, including Belgium's Fortis, Germany's Hypo Real Estate, Switzerland's UBS and the Dutch ING were rescued by their respective governments. However, the first signs of trouble date as far back as summer 2007 when certain financial institutions on both sides of the Atlantic showed signs of distress. For a timeline of events leading up to autumn 2008, see Brunnermeier (2009) and, from an Irish perspective, Honohan (2010).

34   With Goldman Sachs and Morgan Stanley becoming commercial banks, effectively what we were witnessing in the USA was an end of the model of traditional investment banks (OECD 2009).

35   This was followed in 2009 by the American Recovery and Reinvestment Act (ARRA), commonly referred to as the Recovery Act, which provided $787bn of spending increases and tax cuts, amounting to a fiscal stimulus of roughly 2% of annual GDP.

36   How different was this financial crisis to previous ones? Using data from the major post-war banking crises in the developed world, Reinhart and Rogoff (2008) find 'stunning quantitative and qualitative parallels across a number of standard financial crisis indicators', with financial crises sharing 'striking similarities in the run-up of asset prices, in debt accumulation, in growth patterns and in current account deficits' (see also Laeven and Valencia 2008, 2010). Although financial innovation and engineering made the 2007–2009 financial crisis look different – where highly leveraged banks were making risky investments on the back of new and complicated financial instruments – the academic research would indicate that financial crises and history have a habit of recurring. Of course, this is an ex post analysis and must be seen in the context of a profession, with some notable exceptions

(including, internationally, staff at the Bank for International Settlements, Nouriel Roubini of New York University and Robert Shiller of Yale University and at home, Alan Ahearne of NUI, Galway and Morgan Kelly of UCD) that did not predict the hard landing and the 2007–2009 crisis (nor, for that matter, the era of the Celtic Tiger!).

37   An indication of how worried the US Fed was in early 2008 was the decision on January 22, only a week ahead of its scheduled meeting, to cut the federal funds rate by 0.75 percentage points to 3.5%, the first emergency cut by the Fed in over a quarter of a century. At its regular meeting on 30 January, the Federal Open Market Committee – the committee of the US Fed that is responsible for interest rate decisions – announced a further cut of 0.5 percentage points. The target Fed funds rate was lowered again two months later (just shortly after the collapse, and subsequent sale, of Bear Sterns), first by 0.75 percentage points and then by a further 0.25 percentage points, to stand at only 2% by March 2008. In acknowledging the aggressive and necessary easing of monetary policy by policy-makers in the USA and elsewhere, it must be also remembered that it was excessively loose monetary policy that initially triggered, along with other well-documented factors, the global crisis (see next endnote). This problem was summed up very well by George Soros when he wrote, in 2010, 'the authorities had to do in the short term the exact opposite of what was needed in the long term: they had to pump in a lot of credit, to replace the credit that had disappeared, and thereby reinforce the excess credit and leverage that had caused the crisis in the first place. Only in the longer term, when the crisis had subsided, could they drain the credit and reestablish macroeconomic balance' (Soros 2010).

38   Monetary policy, often cited as a reason for why macroeconomic volatility had declined during the Great Moderation, was too lax for much of the 2000s, contributing to the economic and financial crisis of 2007–2009. Yet again, as with many of the modern macro models that underpinned much of the policy recommendations, this is an example of where policy-makers and an economics profession should show less hubris and more humility. For more on this, see Willem Buiter's blog at http://blogs.ft.com/maverecon/2009/03/the-unfortunate-uselessness-of-most-state-of-the-art-academic-monetary-economics/.

39   For an explanation of house price increases, and for a more complete account of housing in Ireland, see Drudy (2007).

40   Private sector credit increased from 128% of annual GNP in 2002 to 215% in 2007. This amounts to an annual increase of over 20%.

41   Robert Shiller's *Irrational Exuberance* comes to mind when explaining speculative bubbles (not just the Irish property market but property markets elsewhere in the 2000s, and, of course, stock markets worldwide pre-2007). Incidentally, the term 'irrational exuberance' was based on comments made in a speech in 1996 by the then US Fed Governor Alan Greenspan. In analysing the housing boom in the USA, Shiller (2006) noted that 'the magnitude of the current boom is practically unique in history . . .' given that '. . . until the recent explosion in home prices, real home prices in the United States were virtually unchanged from 1890 to the late 1990s.' Returning to equity markets, the collapse in 2008 of world stock markets was far greater in magnitude than anything else witnessed at that time (including the fall in house prices) or even the stock market crash of 1929. The difference between now and then is that equity markets recovered, although only partially, in 2009/10, whereas stock prices continued to fall for years after the 1929 crash (Almunia *et al.* 2010).

42   This compares with a figure at that time of fewer than 200,000 completions in the UK, a country that also experienced a housing boom but with a population almost 15 times the size of Ireland and only a little over twice the number of new units built.

43   White (2006), as part of Davy Research on the Irish economy, wrote an article in 2006 with the alarming heading 'Dublin house prices heading for 100 times rent earned'. Calculating 2006 estimated yields in Dublin using advertised house prices based on AMV (Advised Minimum Value) plus stamp duty and legal/surveyor fees, and annual rents based on 11 months' rent (from the Daft.ie website), the results have 'yields well below the rate of consumer price inflation in many areas . . .' with certain properties '. . . trading on a price to earnings (rents) ratio of 65+.' The headline number of 100 is calculated on the basis of further increases in house prices of 20% per annum for three years as against increases in rents of an optimistic, given that they were unchanged in the previous five-year period, 5% per annum. Although written in early 2006, the last line of the article is worth repeating. It read, 'the fundamentals suggest that it will be an adjustment in prices, rather than rents, that will eventually

bring valuations down to more realistic levels.' Contrast this with the tone of a similar, in the sense that it comes from the financial markets, report by Bank of Ireland Private Banking. In its 2007 report entitled *The Wealth of the Nation*, it reported that Ireland, in terms of 2005 data for household wealth per capita (measured using net wealth, that is, household assets minus household debt) ranked second in a survey of eight leading OECD countries, ahead of the UK, the USA, Germany and France. It did acknowledge that these high levels for Ireland were 'largely underpinned by the value of the domestic housing stock'. As we now know, things were to change dramatically shortly after the publication of this report. As we also know, the seeds of Ireland's downfall were sown long before the period covered in the report.

44   The much respected economist and Central Bank Governor Patrick Honohan described Ireland's 'world-beating property bubble' as 'the steepest and longest of the several national property bubbles of the late 1990s and early 2000s around the world' (Honohan 2009, 2010). While expressing concern about the overheated economy and the need for a correction, many of the international organisations (such as the IMF, OECD, EU) also claimed, at the same time, that a soft landing was possible for Ireland. This raises the issue over the quality of external surveillance which, with hindsight, was deficient. In contrast, Kelly (2007), on the basis of comparisons with similar house booms in OECD countries since 1970 where the size of the initial boom is a strong indicator of the size and duration of the subsequent bust – typically, real house prices give up 70% of what they gained – raised the possibility of a 40–60% fall in Irish house prices (unlike other studies of that time that estimated price reductions in the region of 20%) over a period of eight to nine years, which by international standards would not be 'unprecedented.' *The Economist*, in their cover study of 18 June 2005 where they describe the global housing boom – unprecedented in terms of both the number of countries involved and the size of house price gains – as the biggest financial bubble in history, wrote about the 'dizzy heights' of property prices in Ireland, and elsewhere. *The Economist* reported a 192% increase in the house price index in Ireland over the period 1997 to 2005, as against a 154% increase in Britain, a 145% increase in Spain and a 73% increase in the USA.

45   Yet, despite all these unsound and reckless practices in what was supposed to be a well-functioning (though lightly regulated) financial sector based on trust and proper corporate governance, there were no sanctions or penalties ever imposed on a credit institution for breaches of prudential regulations during the boom years preceding the banking collapse. From reading the two reports on the Irish banking crisis published in June 2010, it appears that the authorities (that is, the Central Bank and the Financial Regulator) were more concerned about consumer protection, competition and promoting the Irish financial services industry than ensuring prudential regulation, supervision and overall financial stability. The lack of enforcement reflects the dominant culture and philosophy of the time, with a reluctance by the authorities to intervene (more often described as 'interfere') or distort the actions of private sector agents supposedly behaving rationally in the marketplace.

46   The comprehensive government guarantee included all deposits (including corporate and interbank) and debts (holders of senior debt, subordinated debt and covered bonds), for a two-year period. The subsequent Eligible Liabilities Guarantee (ELG) scheme aimed at guaranteeing new issues out to maturity was passed in December 2009. Much of the controversy relating to the decision to provide a state guarantee, described by Karl Whelan, Professor of Economics at UCD, in an *Irish Times* article (accessed 21 June 2010) as 'perhaps the most momentous economic policy decision in the history of the State', was in relation to its blanket coverage and, in particular, its extension to all existing debt holders, including subordinated debt. There have also been arguments over what constitutes a bank of systemic importance and, in particular, whether Anglo Irish Bank was of systemic importance to the Irish banking system. As for a precedence, state deposit guarantees have been used in previous banking crises, but Ireland's version was more comprehensive, guaranteeing all deposits and liabilities. Unfortunately, but like some other European countries, Ireland in 2008 did not have the appropriate legal framework or statutory powers in place, in the form of a Special Resolution Regime scheme, to deal with failing banks in an orderly and swift fashion, as has happened with hundreds of small banks in the USA since the crisis first began in 2007/08.

47   For an outsider's opinion, read Buiter (2008), who argues that, in terms of risk-sharing, the 'worst of all possible worlds would be the Irish (and now the Danish) approach where all the creditors of the

banks are guaranteed by the government (for a fee that undoubtedly will not cover the government's opportunity cost) and the taxpayer is left without any upside.' The *Financial Times* described the Irish response to the banking crisis as the slowest and most complex banking solution adopted around the world. Others, including the IMF, have been more favourable.

48 As for the third element, namely the recapitalisation of the major banks, Bank of Ireland and AIB were in receipt of €3.5bn each in 2009. Since then, Ireland's two largest banks have taken different paths on the way to recapitalisation. The better of the two, Bank of Ireland, in attempting to fill its capital shortfall from private sources, went to the market in April 2010 to raise over €3bn. As for AIB, although it managed to offload its profitable assets in both Poland, selling its 70% stake in Bank Zachodni WBK to Spanish giant Bank Santander for €3.1bn, and in the USA, selling its 22% stake in US bank M&T, the Irish government announced on 30 September 2010 (on what became known as Black Thursday when the bank bailout figures were released, amounting to a state bailout costing an *estimated* €45–€50bn, of which €29–34bn was for Anglo Irish Bank) a further €3bn in funding for AIB. By end 2010, the total requirement for Ireland's biggest bank was €10bn, with the result that AIB was close to 100% state owned. The smaller, but hugely damaged, Irish Nationwide, also nationalised, was to receive, in total, €5.4bn in capital to cover losses incurred by the building society. The result of this extra capital support, subject to EC approval under the state aid rules, was a headline government deficit for 2010 of 32% of GDP, and a (gross) general government debt of close to 100% of GDP. As it transpired, the €50bn estimate was not sufficient, as a figure of €70bn was announced in March 2011 after months of stress tests on bank capital and funding.

49 Honohan (2010) reports that for (quarterly) GNP, the fall from peak to trough was estimated at 17%, as compared with a fall, from peak of trough, of about 12% when GDP is used, due to the relatively better performance of MNCs based in Ireland as against activity in the Irish indigenous sector. In terms of the actual numbers, GNP fell by 3.5% in 2008 and 10.7% in 2009 as against a fall of 3.5% in 2008 and 7.6% in 2009 for GDP. Regarding the components of GDP, the fall in investment was, not surprisingly, the largest, at 14.3% in 2008 and 31% in 2009.

50 It was at this time (April 2009) that Nobel Prize-winning economist Paul Krugman penned his controversial *New York Times* article 'Erin Go Broke', wherein he painted a very pessimistic picture of the Irish economic and fiscal position. As with the era of the Celtic Tiger when there was a large interest in Ireland in the international community (both from well-known economists – a good example is *The International Perspective on the Irish Economy*, edited by Alan Gray with contributions from leading economists including Paul Krugman, Jeffrey Sachs, Kenneth Arrow, John Vickers, Tony Atkinson and others – and the international media), Ireland's crisis (and the policy response of the authorities) has been closely watched by the international press and governments worldwide, with articles (many critical of the extravagance during the boom years but generally, at least initially, appreciative of the government's post-crisis response) in the *New York Times*, *Wall Street Journal*, *Financial Times*, *Guardian*, *Economist*, etc.

51 Although a concern, these debt levels are not unmanageable. However, the decision by the state (and ultimately the taxpayer) to absorb the losses of the banking system was, in the view of the authors of this book, unnecessary and regrettable. As for the banking system itself, the decline in the supply of credit (after years of plenty) is understandable, as banks attempt to rebuild balance sheets (and reputation) and are cautious (unlike in the boom times) in lending in an environment of uncertainty, business failures and indebtedness. Likewise, lending decisions by banks, fully nationalised or partly state controlled, should avoid been heavily politicised. At end 2010, the government introduced the controversial 2010 Credit Institutions (Stabilisation) Bill, granting exceptional powers, at least up to the end of 2012, to the Minister for Finance in dealing with banking and financial matters.

52 It was the distinguished macroeconomist Olivier Blanchard who, when commenting on the Honohan and Walsh 2002 Irish Hare paper, noted, 'beware of numbers – especially in a small economy with a large export–import sector, low taxation of profit, and transfer pricing' (Blanchard 2002). This very neatly describes the Irish economy. Despite this caveat, Blanchard (2002) goes on to write, 'even after correction, both the Irish productivity and employment performance since the mid 1980s are very impressive. I don't know the rules by which miracles are officially defined, but this seems to come close.' How times have changed!

53   The 'strong and pervasive' reference is taken from Regling and Watson (2010) whereas the reference to deference to banks is taken from Honohan (2010). On the financial and economic crisis worldwide, Furceri and Mourougane (2009) conclude that it was the interactions – as opposed to one or even a small number of factors – of several market, regulatory and macroeconomic policy failures that caused the financial and banking crisis. For more detail, see Table 2 in Furceri and Mourougane (2009).

54   The initial idea, at least in modern times, for a financial transactions tax came from the late Nobel laureate economist James Tobin in 1972, who proposed a (small) tax on foreign exchange transactions to, among other things, deter currency speculation that often destabilises and harms the real economy. The global crisis of 2007–2009 has seen a renewal of calls for a Tobin-type tax. Modern-day proponents include two other Nobel Prize-winning economists, namely Joseph Stiglitz and Paul Krugman. Opposition to the tax comes from many different quarters, including the financial services industry and conservative groups.

CHAPTER 19

1   Paul Krugman, 'Cycles of Conventional Wisdom on Economic Development', *International Affairs*, 72, 1996.

2   World Bank, *Transition – The First Ten Years: Analysis and Lessons for Eastern Europe and the Former Soviet Union*, 2002.

3   The Third World is the term sometimes used, although now outdated, to distinguish countries in the rest of the world from the advanced industrialised nations (the First World) and the former Eastern Bloc socialist countries (the Second World). Our use of the words 'first', 'second' and 'third' is simply to reflect the historical sequence of industrialisation and has no other connotation.

4   This chapter draws upon material from a number of sources, including: Nicholas Stern, 'The Economics of Development: A Survey', *Economic Journal*, 99, 1989; Michael Todaro and Stephen Smith, *Economic Development*, Pearson; Diana Hunt, *Economic Theories of Development: An Analysis of Competing Paradigms*, Harvester Wheatsheaf; Barbara Ingham, *Economics and Development*, McGraw-Hill; Paul Krugman, 'Cycles of Conventional Wisdom on Economic Development', *International Affairs*, 72, 1996; Gerald Meier and James Rauch, *Leading Issues in Economic Development*, Oxford University Press. Data sources include the World Bank's *World Development Report* and the UNDP's *Human Development Report*.

5   Gross national income, formerly gross national product, is equal to GDP plus net flows of factor income from abroad (as defined in Chapter 10). The World Bank Atlas method is used. In order to reduce the impact of exchange rate fluctuations, the Atlas method uses a three-year moving average, price-adjusted conversion factor.

6   The countries are listed as per the World Bank regional classification (East Asia and the Pacific; Europe and Central Asia; Latin America and the Caribbean; Middle East and North Africa; South Asia; sub-Saharan Africa). More recently, the IMF, in its *World Economic Outlook*, divides countries into advanced economies, and emerging and developing countries, with the latter group of interest to us. The emerging and developing group of countries comprises, more or less, the same group of countries classified by the World Bank as low-income or middle-income countries.

7   The neocolonial dependency theory focuses on the historical evolution of rich and poor countries with unequal power relations allowing for exploitation by the developed world. The false-paradigm model centres on the bad advice from the West, and the dualistic development theory focuses on the theme of dualism (a common theme in development) characterised by superior vs. inferior elements.

8   The Dutch disease, named after the effects of natural gas discoveries in the Netherlands, refers to the adverse effect on a country's manufacturing industry when rising natural resource exports cause a real appreciation of the exchange rate (making manufactured goods less competitive).

9   The scale of the HIV/Aids epidemic in developing countries and sub-Saharan Africa in particular is terrifying. With its detrimental impact on the labour force (especially women), households, businesses and school enrolment, it is having a chilling effect on life expectancy, economic growth and, ultimately, development. According to theWorld Bank Development Indicators the HIV prevalence (% ages 15–49) for 2007 was 5% for countries in sub-Saharan Africa as compared to 0.6% for Europe and Central Asia.

10   For two informative accounts of poverty and the problems of developing countries, read Paul Harrison, *Inside the Third World: An Anatomy of Poverty*, Penguin, 1982; and, almost a quarter of a century later, Jeffrey Sachs, *The End of Poverty: Economic Possibilities for Our Time*, Penguin, 2005.

11   As outlined in its Articles of Agreement, the purpose of the IMF is to promote international monetary co-operation, exchange stability, and orderly exchange arrangements; to foster economic growth and high levels of employment; and to provide temporary financial assistance to countries to help ease balance of payments adjustment. According to the World Bank Group, its mission is to fight poverty and improve the living standards of people in the developing world. The main criticism currently faced by the IFIs is the impact of their policies on poverty reduction.

12   A good example of the criticism is contained in the UNCTAD's *Economic Development in Africa* 2001 report. It says that '. . . subsequent experiments with structural adjustment programmes have not been successful in establishing the conditions for sustained growth. These programmes have sought to leave accumulation and growth to free market forces without paying adequate attention to shortcomings of domestic markets and enterprise, physical and human infrastructure, and institutions. Again, pragmatism has been trumped by ideology, this time by a bias against state intervention *per se*. Adjustment programmes have dismantled the state-mediated mechanisms of capital accumulation, but have not succeeded in putting viable alternative mechanisms in their place. Unleashing market forces through liberalisation and deregulation has often led to greater instability and failed to generate appropriate incentives, while institutional weaknesses and structural constraints have prevented incentives from being translated into a vigorous supply response through new investment for the expansion and rationalization of production capacity.'

13   According to the *Our Common Interest: An Argument*, 2005 Report of the Commission for Africa, 'What Africa requires is clear. It needs better governance and the building of the capacity of African states to deliver. It needs peace. It needs political and economic stability to create a climate for growth – and a growth in which poor people can participate. It needs investment in infrastructure and in the health and education systems which will produce a healthy and skilled workforce as well as a happy and fulfilled people. It needs to trade more, and on fairer terms than the rich world has allowed to date. It needs more debt relief. It needs aid of a better quality than at present. And it needs a doubling of aid to pay for this.'

14   The 2001 published paper originated from a 1997 working paper by De Melo, Denizer and Gelb, based on a presentation to the First Dubrovnik Conference on Transition in 1995.

15   Repressed inflation, in the form of the monetary overhang, is measured as the percentage change in the real wage less the percentage change in real GDP over 1987–90. The exchange rate premium is the difference between the official exchange rate and the black market exchange rate. CMEA trade dependency is measured as the ratio of the average of CMEA exports and imports to GDP.

16   Markets and trade include price liberalisation, trade and foreign exchange system and competition policy. Enterprise reform includes governance and enterprise restructuring and privatisation (small-scale and large-scale). Financial institutions reform includes banking reform and interest rate liberalisation, and securities market and non-bank financial institutions. Infrastructure (including electric power, railways, roads, telecommunications, water and waste water) and legal reform indicators were added later.

17   United Nations Economic Commission for Europe, *Economic Survey of Europe*, 2004, No.1.

18   The increase in inequality has even been acknowledged by the IMF, the international organisation most associated with, and supportive of, market reforms in transition. In its 2000 *World Economic Outlook*, it admits, '. . . there is little doubt that inequality has risen substantially and the economic situation for a substantial number of people, particularly those at the lower end of the income scale or whose savings were wiped out by high inflation at the start of transition, has worsened . . .' (IMF 2000).

19   The pattern or evolution of output is often described as the J-shaped recovery in the CEE countries and the U-shaped (or, in some cases, V-shaped) recovery in the FSU countries. Others refer to the inverse J-shaped recovery in the worst-affected transition countries that suffered a deep and protracted recession.

20　In many FSU countries the registered unemployment rate remained low despite the severe economic decline. Several factors may account for this, including the observation that, unlike CEE countries where the main adjustment to the output decline was in significantly fewer numbers employed, the adjustment in many FSU countries was primarily in lower wages; the reluctance of many enterprises to lay off workers (continuing the practice of labour hoarding); the reluctance of workers (despite wage arrears) to detach themselves completely from their (former) employer (as some enterprises continued to provide social benefits); and, finally, derisory unemployment benefits.

21　A small number of commentators view the output decline as largely a statistical illusion. For more on this rather unconventional and controversial perspective, read Anders Åslund, *Building Capitalism: The Transformation of the Former Soviet Bloc*, Cambridge University Press, 2002. As already stated, the explanations given in the text focus primarily on economic phenomena. If we broaden our discussion to include the political and institutional dimensions of transition, it is argued that the output decline was caused by the political and institutional structures that existed at the start of transition. In particular, countries with a longer tradition of sovereignty had, on average, more developed public sector institutions, a greater history of civil societies and a stronger tradition of collective action influencing the political process. These countries suffered less from the venal state capture that was rampant in many of the newly established successor states of the former Soviet Union. These new states, while adopting market reforms and, at the same time, building the institutions of a modern state, were weakened by the actions of powerful vested interests, comprising both the old nomenklatura and new private business groups. Moreover, the symbiosis of politics and economics that was a central feature of the socialist system resulted, at a great social cost, in a lack of separation between government and business, and a blurring of the distinction between public and private interests. It is these historical legacies of politics and institutions in conjunction with insufficient economic and political contestability that determine the policy choices, and in turn, explain the (variation in) performances and outcomes in transition countries (World Bank 2000).

22　It is important to recognise that the legacy of the socialist system is not entirely negative. Compared with countries of similar levels of income per capita and development, the former socialist countries of the Soviet bloc began transition with favourable levels of education and human capital, a more even distribution of income and a much respected social safety net.

23　For two contrasting views of Russia's transition, see Andrei Shleifer and Daniel Treisman, 'A Normal Country', *Foreign Affairs*, 83, 2004 and Steven Rosefielde, 'Russia: An Abnormal Country', *European Journal of Comparative Economics*, 2, 2005.

Glossary of Terms

Absolute advantage A country has an absolute advantage if it can produce more of a commodity than any other country with the same amount of resources.

Adverse selection characterises the situation where hidden information leads to incomplete or missing markets.

Aggregate demand is the total output which is demanded at each price level holding all other variables constant.

Aggregate demand curve This shows the level of national output demanded at different price levels.

Aggregate expenditure is the amount that households and firms plan to spend on goods and services.

Aggregate supply describes the total quantity of national output supplied by all producers at each level of price.

Aggregate supply curve It shows the output of GDP produced at different price levels.

Arbitrage refers to the buying and selling of products in different markets in order to exploit price differentials and to make a riskless profit.

Arc elasticity measures the elasticity of demand over a price range using the midpoint or average price as the base.

Average product is the total output divided by the number of units of the variable input utilised.

Average revenue is a firm's total revenue divided by the quantity sold.

Average total cost (or average cost) is total cost divided by the number of units produced.

Balance of payments It is a set of accounts showing all economic transactions between residents of the home country and the rest of the world in any one year.

Balance of payments capital and financial account This is a record of a country's inflows and outflows of capital or assets.

Balance of payments current account This records all visible and invisible trade.

Broad money supply is defined as M1 plus deposit account balances.

Budget line It illustrates the maximum combination of two products that the consumer can purchase, given the consumer's level of income and prices.

Capital goods are durable assets used during the production process.

Capital stock is all of the capital goods controlled by a firm.

Cartel A group of firms in a particular market who collude on price and output decisions in an effort to earn monopoly profits.

Ceteris paribus means that all other variables are held constant.

Comparative advantage A country has a comparative advantage in producing a commodity if it can produce that commodity at a lower opportunity cost than any other country.

Complements are products that are bought and consumed together. This implies that if the price of either product falls (rises), demand for the other product increases (decreases).

Concentration ratio measures the total market share of a given number of the largest firms.

Constant returns to scale exist when a change in inputs results in an equal change in output.

Consumer price index This index is designed to measure the average change in the level of the prices paid for consumer goods and services by all private households in the country.

Consumer surplus is the excess of what a person is willing to pay for a product over what the person actually pays.

Consumption function It shows consumer expenditure at different levels of income.

Cost push inflation occurs when the source of upward pressure on prices is the rising costs of the factors of production in the absence of any corresponding increase in productivity.

Cross-price elasticity measures the sensitivity (in terms of percentages) of quantity demanded of one product to a change in the price of another product.

Deflation is a fall in the general level of prices.

Demand is the quantity of a product that consumers are willing to purchase at each conceivable price during a particular time period.

Demand, principle of refers to the inverse or negative relationship between price and quantity demanded, *ceteris paribus.*

Demand management is the collective term used to explain various government policies which influence the level of aggregate expenditure in the economy.

Demand pull inflation occurs when the total demand for goods and services is greater than the total supply of goods and services.

Demand schedule A table which indicates the quantity of a particular product which consumers are willing to purchase at various prices during a specified time period.

Deposit multiplier The multiple by which deposits will increase for every unit increase in reserves.

Depreciation is the value of capital which has been used up over a certain period of time during the production process.

Derived demand for an input means that it is not demanded for its own sake but for its use in the production of products.

Devaluation refers to a reduction in the value of a currency *vis-à-vis* other currencies in a fixed or semi-fixed exchange rate regime.

Diminishing marginal utility, principle of It states that the more of a product a consumer consumes, the less extra (or marginal) satisfaction the consumer receives.

Diminishing returns, law of means that if at least one factor is fixed, a point is reached when an additional unit of a variable factor adds less to total product than the previous unit.

Discount rate The rate which the Central Bank charges financial institutions that borrow from it for purposes of maintaining the reserve requirement.

Discounting is the process of reducing the future value of a sum of money or a flow of revenues to the present value.

Discretionary fiscal policy refers to deliberate, as opposed to automatic, changes in government expenditure or tax rates in order to influence national income.

Diseconomies of scale exist where an increase in the scale of production leads to higher costs per unit produced.

Disinflation is a reduction in the rate of inflation.

Double counting occurs if the expenditure on intermediate goods is included in the calculation of national output.

Economic planning is when governments attempt to target and co-ordinate economic decision-making in order to influence economic outcomes.

Economic profit is the difference between revenue and economic costs (including normal profits).

Economic rent is a payment to a factor of production in excess of its opportunity cost.

Economies of scale exist where an increase in the scale of production leads to lower costs per unit produced.

Effective exchange rate index for a currency is the weighted average of the value of the currency against its largest trading partners.

Elasticity measures the percentage change in one variable in response to a percentage change in another variable.

Equi-marginal principle This states that utility is maximised when the utility for the last euro spent on each product is the same.

Equilibrium implies a state of balance, a position from which there is no tendency to change.

Exchange rate The exchange rate between two currencies is the price of one currency in terms of another.

Exchequer Borrowing Requirement This is the total amount of money that the central government borrows in any one fiscal year if current and capital expenditure exceeds current and capital revenue.

Excise duties are imposed to (i) discourage consumption and production of goods and services which have detrimental effects on individuals other than direct consumers or producers; and/or (ii) collect taxation revenue.

Expenditure multiplier It is the ratio of the change in income to the change in autonomous spending.

Extensive economic growth is greater output through a larger quantity of inputs used.

External reserves refer to the stock of foreign currency held by the Central Bank for the purpose of intervention in the foreign exchange market.

Externalities are positive or negative non-priced by-products of production or consumption decisions.

Factors of production are the resources of an economy. They include land, labour, capital and enterprise.

First degree price discrimination occurs when every consumer is charged the maximum price that each is willing to pay.

Fiscal policy refers to the use of government expenditure and taxation in order to influence aggregate expenditure and, in turn, national output.

Fixed exchange rate system A system where member states' currencies are pegged to each other at rates which are usually agreed by their respective central banks.

Fixed incomes People are on fixed incomes if their income is set at a particular nominal amount which is not adjusted for inflation.

Flexible exchange rate system This operates on the basis of market forces whereby the exchange rate between two currencies is determined by demand and supply.

GDP at constant prices measures economic activity in the prices of a fixed or base year.

GDP at current prices is a measure of economic activity based on the current prices of the goods and services produced.

GDP deflator This is the ratio of nominal GDP to real GDP expressed as an index.

General Government Deficit is calculated by adding the EBR to the balance of local authorities and non-commercial state-sponsored bodies.

Giffen good A Giffen good has an upward sloping demand curve over a range of prices. A Giffen good is a very inferior good.

Golden Rule level of capital is the steady state with the highest level of consumption.

Gross domestic product is the value of all goods and services produced domestically in the economy, regardless of the nationality of the owners of the factors of production.

Gross national product is the value of all goods and services produced by a country's productive factors regardless of their geographical location.

Herfindahl-Hirschman index is the sum of the squared percentage share of all firms of the relevant variable in the market.

High-powered money is equal to currency plus reserves held by the central bank.

Import substitution replaces imports with domestic production under the protection of tariffs and/or quotas.

Income effect It is the change in demand that is caused by a change in real income (i.e. purchasing power).

Income elasticity of demand measures the responsiveness (in terms of percentages) of the quantity demanded for a product to a change in income.

Increasing marginal returns means that an additional unit of a variable factor adds more to total product than the previous unit.

Indifference curve It shows all the bundles or combinations of two products that give the same level of utility to the consumer.

Inferior good A good is classified as inferior if demand for that good falls when income increases and vice versa.

Inflation A rise in the general or aggregate price level.

Inflation rate The percentage change in the price level from one period to the next period.

Inflationary gap An inflationary gap exists when the equilibrium of the economy is greater than the full-employment level of output.

Institutions are humanly devised mechanisms or constraints that structure economic behaviour and interaction. They are the 'rules of the game' that facilitate exchange.

Intensive economic growth is greater output through more productivity from existing inputs.

Interest is the amount that is paid on a loan or the amount that is received on a deposit.

Interest rate This is the interest amount expressed as a percentage of the sum borrowed or lent.

Investment expenditure is the corporate or business expenditure on machinery, fixtures and fittings, vehicles and buildings. It also includes inventory build-ups of raw materials, semi-finished and finished goods.

IS curve It depicts the combination of interest rates and income levels that is consistent with equilibrium in the goods market.

Isocost line It shows all the combinations of two inputs that can be employed for a certain amount of money.

Isoquant It is a locus of points, showing the various combinations of two inputs that can be used to produce a given level of output.

Labour force includes those who are employed and those who are unemployed.

Liquidity preference is the desire by households to hold assets in liquid form.

LM curve It depicts the combination of interest rates and income levels that is consistent with equilibrium in the money market.

Long run This is a period of time when all the factors of production can be varied in quantity.

Macroeconomics is concerned with the operation of the economy as a whole.

Main refinancing operations are reverse transactions using tenders and are normally executed weekly, with a maturity of one week.

Managed floating exchange rate system A system characterised by an exchange rate which changes with the market forces of demand and supply. However, the Central Bank intervenes periodically, particularly when the currency is very weak or very strong.

Marginal cost is the extra cost incurred from producing an additional unit of output.

Marginal product is the change in total output obtained from using an additional unit of a variable input, holding other inputs constant.

Marginal propensity to consume is the fraction of each additional unit of disposable income that is spent on consumer goods and services.

Marginal propensity to import is the fraction of an increase in income that is spent on imports.

Marginal propensity to save is the proportion of a change in disposable income that is saved.

Marginal propensity to tax is the proportion of any increment in income paid in taxes.

Marginal rate of substitution indicates the willingness of the consumer to give up a certain number of units of one product in order to obtain one more unit of the other product without changing utility.

Marginal rate of technical substitution is the amount of an input that can be replaced by one unit of another input without changing the level of output.

Marginal revenue is the change in total revenue resulting from a one unit change in output.

Marginal revenue product is the addition to revenue from the employment of an extra unit of an input.

Marginal social cost is the total cost to society from producing an additional unit of output.

Marginal utility is the extra or additional satisfaction that the consumer gains from consuming one extra unit of a product.

Market It is any institutional arrangement that facilitates the buying and selling of a product.

Menu costs refer to costs which are associated with adjustments in prices. Examples include the printing of price lists and the reticketing of merchandise.

Merchandise trade balance This is a record of transactions of merchandise exports and imports during a year.

Microeconomics studies individual decision-making units.

Monetary policy refers to the use of money supply, credit and interest rates to achieve economic objectives.

Monetary transmission mechanism is the process where a change in monetary policy affects aggregate expenditure and national output.

Moral hazard characterises the situation where hidden action leads to incomplete or missing markets.

Narrow money supply is defined as the notes and coins in circulation plus current account balances at credit institutions.

Natural monopoly exists if total output can be produced more cheaply by a single firm than by two or more firms.

Net factor income from the rest of the world is the outflows of income earned by foreigners operating in Ireland minus the inflows of income earned by foreign subsidiaries of Irish companies.

Nominal rate of interest The actual rate of interest which is charged when money is borrowed.

Normal good There is a positive relationship between income and demand. Demand for a normal good increases with income. If income falls, demand for the normal good falls.

Normal profit is the amount or percentage of profit which the entrepreneur requires to supply his or her entrepreneurship.

Okun's Law depicts the inverse relationship between output growth and unemployment.
Open market operations involves the buying and selling of government securities or bonds.
Opportunity cost The opportunity cost of an activity is measured in terms of the highest valued alternative forgone.

Pareto efficiency means that there is no allocation of resources that leaves anyone better off without leaving at least one individual worse off.
Potential output represents the maximum level of output that can be produced given a country's productive capacity.
Present value is the estimate of what the revenue stream of a capital asset is worth today.
Price can be defined as that which is given in exchange for a good or service.
Price ceiling is a form of price control generally designed to help consumers. No selling price can exceed this maximum price.
Price controls are government regulations which limit the ability of the market to determine price.
Price discriminating monopolist is a monopolist who charges different prices to different customers for the same product for reasons other than differences in costs.
Price discrimination occurs when a firm charges different prices to different customers for the same product for reasons other than differences in costs.
Price elastic The demand for a product is price elastic if the percentage change in quantity demanded is greater than the percentage change in price.
Price elasticity of demand measures the responsiveness (in terms of percentages) of quantity demanded to changes in the price of the same product.
Price elasticity of supply measures the responsiveness (in terms of percentages) of quantity supplied to changes in price.
Price floor is a form of price control generally designed to help producers. No selling can fall below this minimum price.
Price index A price index measures the level of prices in one period as a percentage of the level in another period called the base period.
Price inelastic The demand for a product is price inelastic if the percentage change in quantity demanded is less than the percentage change in price.
Principle of demand refers to the inverse or negative relationship between price and quantity demanded, *ceteris paribus.*
Producer surplus is the excess in revenue that a producer receives for a product over the minimum revenue that the producer would have accepted for the product.
Product differentiation means that the product produced by one firm is different from the products produced by the firm's competitors.
Production function This shows the relationship between the amounts of inputs used and the maximum amount of output generated.
Production possibility frontier shows all possible combinations of two products that can be produced using available technology and all available resources.
Public goods are consumed by all consumers to the same extent (non-rivalry) and no one can be excluded from consumption (non-excludable).

Ratchet effect is where output targets are ratcheted up if managers over-fulfill their plans.

Rate of return on capital is a measure of the productivity of a particular capital asset.

Real rate of interest is the nominal rate of interest adjusted for the inflation rate.

Reserve requirement This is the percentage of deposits which banks are legally obligated to lodge at the Central Bank.

Returns to scale refers to the long-run relationship between changes in inputs and subsequent changes in output.

Revaluation is an increase in the value of one currency *vis-à-vis* other currencies in a fixed or semi-fixed exchange rate regime.

Savings function It shows the relationship between savings and disposable income.

Semi-fixed exchange rate system is a system where member states set the value of their currencies in relation to other participating currencies. However, currencies are permitted to fluctuate above and below these rates.

Short run This is a period of time where there is at least one factor of production which cannot change.

Shutdown price is any price less than the short-run average variable cost of producing a unit of output.

Small open economy refers to an economy that is so small relative to the world economy that domestic economic events have no effect on the rest of the world. The domestic economy is a price taker: it accepts world prices. Also, external trade (exports and imports) represents a high proportion of the country's GDP.

Soft budget constraint is the persistent or recurring expectation of a bailout of loss-making enterprises. Firms that are in financial trouble are consistently bailed out by the state.

Steady state level of capital consists of a level of capital and a savings rate such that the level of savings and investment equal the capital that is lost due to depreciation.

Substitutes Two products are substitutes if consumers consider each product a suitable alternative for the other product. If the price of one product changes, demand for the other product changes in the same direction.

Substitution effect It is the change in consumption that is caused by the change in the relative prices of the two products.

Supply is the quantity of the product that sellers are willing to offer at each conceivable price during a particular period of time.

Supply schedule A table which indicates the quantity of a particular product which producers are willing to supply at various prices, over a particular period of time.

Supply-side policies are targeted at increasing the productive capacity of the economy.

Supply-side shock This refers to changes in the conditions of productivity or costs which in turn impacts on aggregate supply.

Tariffs A tariff is a tax on imports and is usually *ad valorem* which means that a percentage of the price is added to the price of the imported good.

Third degree price discrimination occurs when a firm separates consumers into a small number of classes and establishes a different price for each class.

Total utility is the total satisfaction that a consumer gains from the consumption of a given quantity of a product.

Total factor productivity growth is the change in output that arises from technological progress.

Transfer earnings are what a factor of production could earn in its best alternative use.

Transfer payments redistribute wealth. They include pensions, unemployment benefits, disability allowances and other payments.

Unemployed The unemployed include those who are not working and who are available for, and are actively seeking, work.

Unemployment rate The number of people unemployed divided by the labour force.

Unit elastic The demand for a product is unit elastic if the percentage change in quantity demanded is equal to the percentage change in price.

Utility is the satisfaction or pleasure that is derived from consuming a product (i.e. a good or service).

Value Added Tax is an integrated sales tax levied (on a percentage basis) at each stage of production and distribution.

Yield curve This shows the way in which the yield on a security varies according to its maturity or expiry date.

Index